ECDL4

The Complete Coursebook for Microsoft® Office XP

Brendan Munnelly
and Paul Holden
Ed. Patrick Scully

ECDL® International Computer Driving Licence®
Approved Courseware Syllabus Version 4.0

PEARSON Prentice Hall

Harlow, England • London • New York • Boston • San Francisco • Toronto • Sydney • Singapore • Hong Kong
Tokyo • Seoul • Taipei • New Delhi • Cape Town • Madrid • Mexico City • Amsterdam • Munich • Paris • Milan

PEARSON EDUCATION LIMITED
Head Office:
Edinburgh Gate
Harlow CM20 2JE
Tel: +44 (0)1279 623623
Fax: +44 (0)1279 431059

and Associated Companies throughout the world

Visit us on the World Wide Web at:
www.pearsoned.co.uk

First published 2004

ISBN 0 13 129397 4

British Library Cataloguing-in-Publication Data
A catalogue record for this book is available from the British Library

Rédacteurs Limited is at www.redact.ie
Brendan Munnelly is at www.munnelly.com
Consultant Editors: Sadhbh O'Dwyer, Judith Cuppage

10 9 8 7 6 5 4 3 2
08 07 06 05 04

Typeset by Rédacteurs Ltd, 165 Howth Road, Dublin 3, Ireland.
Printed by Ashford Colour Press Ltd, Gosport.

The publisher's policy is to use paper manufactured from sustainable forests.

Contents

17: Mail merge and templates 244

18: File formats and importing spreadsheet data 268

21: Functions, formatting and printing 319

45: Finding information and shopping on the web *711*

46: Taking control of the web *724*

47: E-mail with Outlook 740

1 Basic Concepts of Information Technology

Learning about computers for the first time is rather like learning about a foreign country. A land where words like 'megabyte' and 'peripheral' are part of the everyday conversation. The only crop grown and harvested is something called 'data'. And it is important to be not only faster than your neighbour but smaller too!

But you need to learn about this country. It was once an out-of-the-way place that attracted only a handful of scientists to its shores. Now no other destination is more popular.

Like all good tourist guides, this module introduces you gently to the more commonly spoken words of the computer dialect. It points out the major landmarks (the hard disk, memory and processor are all places you need to take in). And it steers you away from the pitfalls that most offend native computer speakers – such as confusing an 'operating system' with an 'application program'.

Have a pleasant trip. And good luck!

Chapter 1: A short history of computing

In this chapter

This chapter gives you a brief overview of the history of commercial computing and paints a picture of the role of computers in the world today.

New skills

At the end of this chapter, you should know that computers:

- Have been developed relatively recently.
- Become faster, more reliable, and cheaper every year.
- Are being used widely in business and education.

A long line of machines

From earliest times, people have counted things, measured things, kept records of things, and told other people about things. The 'things' could have been the number of sheep in a flock, the weight of a child, the size of a field, the length of time since the last drought or the intensity of an earthquake.

From earliest times, people used tools and techniques to help them count more reliably, measure more accurately, record more indelibly, transmit more clearly – they used, for example, measuring tapes, slide rules, sextants, weighing scales and clocks.

The computer is simply the latest in this long line of calculating and recording machines. That's all it is. Everything we see computers doing today – and we see them doing a lot – they are doing because they can calculate and they can store the results of their calculations.

However, this principle is masked by one outstanding fact: what computers do may be simple, but they do an incredible amount of work, quickly and reliably. The speed of computers today is measured in millions of operations per second. The operations may be simple, but they can be combined in all sorts of ways to yield a vast array of useful functions.

This has almost all come about within the last thirty or forty years, which is the entire history of commercial computers.

In the 1960s, a commercial computer occupied a large air-conditioned room; it needed a team of specialists to operate it; it consumed vast amounts of electricity; and it frequently broke down.

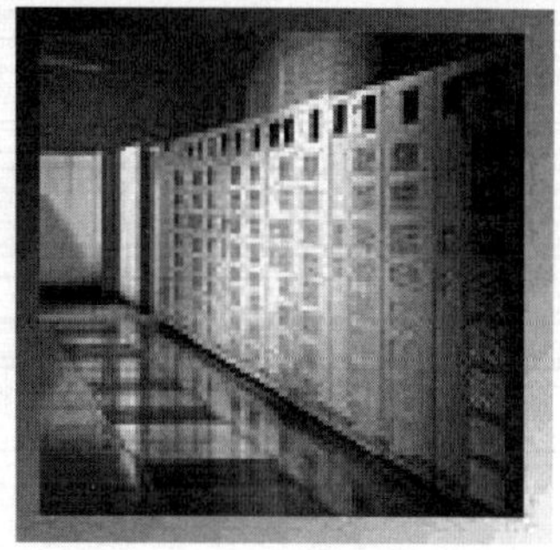

Today's computers are typically much smaller and faster: what previously took up a full room fits into a small box. They can store more information; they consume less power; and they have become far easier to operate.

To give you some idea of the speed of advance, the first personal computers (PCs) were launched in 1979, with a clock speed (don't worry about it – it's just how we measure the speed of computers) of about five megahertz (MHz). Today, if you go out to buy a new PC, it is unlikely that you will be offered anything less than one gigahertz (GHz) – two hundred times as fast. Similar progress has been made in the other main measure of computer power – storage capacity.

You don't need to understand how this has been achieved, and you don't need to know all the details. However, you should be aware of the speed of progress and the main ways in which it is measured. So, if you go out to buy a computer, you will at least know what questions to ask and understand the answers.

Every year, computers are becoming smaller, faster, cheaper, more reliable, and easier to use. They are being used in all sorts of situations where it would previously have been impossible to use them: not only in business and government, but also in education, entertainment, health care, sport, art and design. You see computers in homes, clubs and restaurants; you don't see them (but they are there) in car engines, bank automatic teller machines, supermarket checkouts, washing machines, telephone systems and video recorders. You are probably wearing one at this moment, on your wrist, buried inside your watch.

You're surrounded.

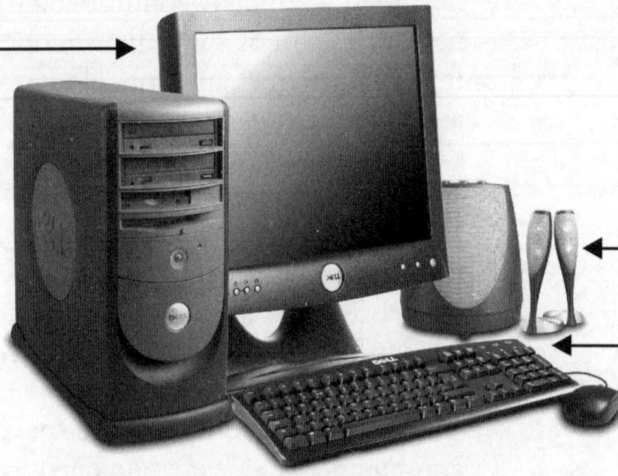

But you're *not* under threat: computers are machines, tools. They are designed by people to meet people's needs; they are operated by people. People turn them on. People turn them off.

People like you.

The ECDL is designed to take the fear out of computing, to give you the knowledge and the skills you need to use this technology. With this book, you will learn about the most common PC applications. You won't learn everything: it is not necessary to know everything – it's not even possible. What this book aims to do is to teach you *enough* – enough to perform most of the tasks that most people do most of the time, to give you enough confidence to tackle the unknown, and to learn from experience.

Chapter summary: so now you know

The computer is the latest in a long line of tools used to perform calculations and store the results. As they have developed, they have become faster, more reliable, and capable of storing more information. These developments have enabled them to be applied in many areas of commercial life, administration, education and entertainment.

Quick quiz: a short history of computing

Circle the correct answer to each of the following multiple-choice questions about the history of computing.

Q1	Today's PCs are approximately how much faster than the first PCs?
A.	Five times as fast.
B.	Ten times as fast.
C.	Two hundred times as fast.
D.	A thousand times as fast.

Q2	Which of the following devices may incorporate a computer? (Pick as many as you think, and for each say what the computer might do.)
A.	A car engine.
B.	A video recorder.
C.	A bank cash machine.
D.	A bicycle.

Q3	Computers built by hand in the 1960s are more reliable than today's computers.
A.	True.
B.	False.

Q4	Because of the tiny size of modern computers, they are very hard to make, virtually impossible to repair, and, as a result, very expensive.
A.	True.
B.	False.

Answers

1: C, **2:** A, B, C, **3:** B, **4:** B.

Chapter 2: What exactly is a computer?

In this chapter

In this chapter you will learn what distinguishes a computer from other machines. You will also learn about the different types of computer in use today.

New skills

At the end of this chapter you should know:

- What a computer is.
- The difference between hardware and software.
- The various categories of computers.

New words

At the end of this chapter you should be able to explain the following terms:

- Hardware
- Software
- PC
- Mainframe
- Dumb terminal
- Intelligent terminal

The trouble with definitions

It is relatively easy to define a washing machine, a motor car, or a telephone: these devices may be complicated and technologically advanced, but we can talk about them in terms of what they do. They wash clothes, transport people from A to B, enable people to hold conversations with one another over a distance.

As we saw in the previous chapter, a computer can be used for almost anything – including controlling the different washing cycles in a washing machine.

In fact, the first part of our definition of a computer recognizes this fact: computers are *general-purpose* machines. The same computer can operate over a few hours as a typewriter, desktop publishing studio, sound editor, video editor, accounts tracker, e-mail sender, Internet browser, and so on.

When you flick the light switch, the light comes on: you could say that the light has obeyed your instruction. Well, computers respond in the same way to instructions: these instructions are called *programs*. And programs are written to make computers behave in specific ways: to act as word processors or to control electricity generating stations. Computers are *programmable*.

Different programs enable the same computer to operate under different guises. We could leave our definition at that, but it will help to add two other ideas: computers can *calculate*, and they can *store* the results of their calculations.

Computer
A computer is a general-purpose, programmable device that is capable of calculating and storing results.

One way of thinking about a computer is as a 'black box' that accepts input on one side, processes it in some way, and then produces output on the other side.

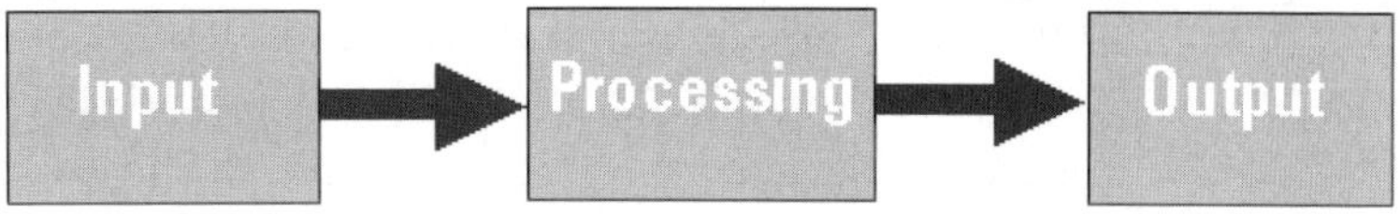

The input might be a mathematical problem, the supplier invoices for the month, a search for a good restaurant in Sydney, or the temperature of a furnace. The output might be the answer to the mathematical problem, the cheques to pay the invoices, the name and address of the restaurant, or the instructions to shut the control valves on the fuel supply.

What goes on inside the black box is called *processing*: the manipulation of the input necessary to produce the output.

However, the black box is not magic: everything – *everything* – going into a computer is first converted into numbers, and all forms of output – including text on the page, graphics on the screen, music, even telephone conversations – have to be converted into their final form from numbers. In the middle – inside the black box – the numbers are added together in various ways and combinations, under a set of rules called a program. The only magic is the fact that these calculations take place at a rate of millions per second – and, of course, the human ingenuity in the design and the programming.

Computer systems consist of two very different types of elements: *hardware* and *software*:

- Hardware includes all the physical things that you can touch, feel, weigh, and, on rare occasions, kick.
- Software is the intangible information component – the instructions, or programs, that tell the hardware how to behave.

Hardware
Hardware is the term used to describe the physical parts of a computer system.

Software
Software is the term used to describe the instructions that cause the computer system to behave in a given way.

Types of computer

Computers fall into a number of different categories, although the dividing line between the categories is not always clear. At one end of the spectrum are *mainframes*. These are big, expensive machines, typically used by large corporations, governmental organizations and scientific research establishments. They are expected to run continuously, 24 hours a day, 365 days a year. They are capable of processing huge numbers of transactions and performing extremely complex calculations.

At the other end of the spectrum are the computers most of us are familiar with – the PC (*personal computer*), formerly known as the *microcomputer*. Today, PCs can be bought for less than £1000. PCs come in various shapes and sizes. *Desktop* computers are the most common: they generally include a system unit, a screen and a keyboard, as separate components. *Laptop* or *notebook* computers are more portable: the screen is a flat *liquid crystal display* (LCD), which forms a lid hinged to cover the keyboard and system unit. Laptops are somewhat more expensive than desktop PCs. *Personal digital assistants* (*PDAs*) or palmtop computers bring together many of the functions of a PC in addition to organizer, calendar, diary, calculator, and mail and contacts programs – all within a convenient pocket-sized package.

In between these two ends of the computer spectrum lie *minicomputers*, which are typically used by medium-sized enterprises, or by departments within larger organizations. Like mainframes, they offer greater processing power, storage capacity and reliability than PCs.

Network computers (*network servers*) are computers that administer, support and protect the security of a computer network. Users on a network are able to use the resources (data, software, hardware) on the network server. In the past, such users mainly used *dumb terminals* – devices that simply accepted input from the user and displayed results. All the processing and storage was done by the server. Nowadays, most users have *intelligent terminals* – PCs that have their own 'local' processing and storage capacity.

Chapter summary: so now you know

Computers are general-purpose machines. What distinguishes a computer calculating a payroll from one forecasting the weather is the *program* it is running. And in fact the same computer could be programmed to do both tasks.

Computers accept information from the outside (*input*), do something to it (*processing*), and display or print out the results (*output*). The two main elements in a computer system are *hardware*, which is the term used for the physical parts, and *software*, which describes the instructions or programs that cause the computer to behave in a given way.

The most familiar computers are called PCs or microcomputers. The biggest and most expensive – used by large organizations – are called mainframes. In between are minicomputers.

A computer network is controlled by a network computer, or *network server*. The devices connected to the server are called terminals. These may be *dumb terminals* – with no processing or storage power of their own – or *intelligent terminals* – with their own processing and storage capability.

Quick quiz: what exactly is a computer?

Circle the correct answer to each of the following multiple-choice questions about computers.

Q1	What is the difference between a computer and a pocket calculator?
A.	A calculator is purpose-built and is therefore more accurate.
B.	There is no difference, as a calculator contains a computer.
C.	A computer includes a word processor; the calculator doesn't.
D.	A computer has a bigger screen.

Q2	Which of the following statements is/are true?
A.	Cables and other flexible parts of a computer are called software; all the solid parts are called hardware.
B.	Hardware is the term used to describe the physical parts of a computer system.
C.	Floppy disks and CDs are software; the screen and keyboard are hardware.
D.	Software is another word for programs.

Q3	Which of the following statements is/are true?
A.	A mainframe is a large computer built in the 1960s or 1970s that is now obsolete.
B.	A mainframe is a large computer typically used by a big company or governmental organization.
C.	A mainframe is a metal framework inside the plastic casing of a computer.
D.	Mainframe is another word for hardware.

Q4	A microcomputer is often called a PC. The abbreviation 'PC' stands for:
A.	Personal computer.
B.	Portable computer.
C.	Politically correct.
D.	Personal calculator.
E.	Professional capacity.

Q5	Which of the following is/are portable computer(s)?
A.	Minicomputer.
B.	Microcomputer.
C.	Laptop.
D.	Notebook.

Q6	Which of the following statements is/are true?
A.	A network server is another name for a dumb terminal.
B.	A dumb terminal is useless without a network server.
C.	A network server is useless without a dumb terminal.
D.	A dumb terminal is a computer without any loudspeakers.
E.	An intelligent terminal is a computer used for military or industrial espionage.
F.	An intelligent terminal is another name for a bank cash machine.

Answers

1: C and D, **2:** B and D, **3:** B, **4:** A, **5:** C and D, **6:** B.

Chapter 3: Computer hardware

In this chapter

When you go out to buy a computer, you are immediately faced with a range of options that even experienced computer people find bewildering. To make a sensible choice, you need to know the function of the main components in a computer system, and the criteria upon which you should base your decision.

A PC system is made up of a number of components. Some of these are essential, and some are optional. In some cases, a number of options are available, from which you have to choose.

This chapter takes you on a tour of the typical computer system, and identifies all the hardware components. We look first at the components that are normally inside the main *system unit* ('in the box'), and then at the other components in a typical system ('outside the box').

New skills

At the end of this chapter you should be able to:

- Name the hardware components in a computer system.
- Say what each component is for.
- Describe some of the optional extras.
- Describe how to look after your computer.

New words

At the end of this chapter you should be able to explain the following terms:

- Processor
- Hard disk
- Keyboard
- Mouse
- Modem
- CD-ROM
- Memory
- Floppy disk
- Screen
- Printer
- Multimedia
- DVD

Unfortunately, when talking about computer hardware, a certain amount of jargon is unavoidable. Other new terms in this chapter are in *italics* and explained in their context.

In the box

The system unit – usually a beige or dark grey box – is the most essential part of the computer. It houses the processor (the 'brain'), the various kinds of memory (described below), and the electronics to control all the other components. It also usually includes a fan, designed to keep the whole unit cool. The fan is responsible for the hum from the computer when you turn it on. The system unit may stand vertically on the floor (a *tower*), or horizontally on the desk, usually with the screen on top (a *desktop* unit). In a *laptop* or *notebook* computer, the system unit is usually built underneath the keyboard.

Processor

The processor chip and the electronics that support it are known as the *central processing unit* (CPU). The CPU is at the heart of the computer – it performs calculations, controls logic flow, and communicates with and controls the operation of the other parts of the system, including memory and input and output devices.

The length of time it takes a computer to perform a task depends on a number of factors. The first of these is the speed of the processor chip. This is measured in megahertz (MHz) or gigahertz (GHz), and the bigger the number, the faster the processor (the more calculations it can perform per second). This measure of the computer's performance is so critical that it is usually included in the name of the computer. So the Dell Dimension R450, for example, includes the Intel Pentium II 450 MHz processor.

The CPU comes with a *cache* that can help to speed up the performance of some applications. Like memory and disk capacity, cache is measured in bytes, typically ranging between 128 kB and 512 kB.

Memory

The definition of a computer includes the idea of storage: the computer has to be able to store the results of its calculations. In practice, a computer has to store a huge amount of information. It has a number of different kinds of memory, two of which are regularly cited in the advertisements for computers: RAM and disk space.

Random access memory

Random access memory (RAM) is used by the computer as a sort of working area while it is carrying out a given task. (It is often called *working storage*.) Here it holds the list of instructions that it is currently working on, the data on which it is working, and the interim results of its calculations. The 'R' in RAM is its main advantage. It can be accessed randomly, which means that the computer can get at any piece of data directly – it does not have to look through the storage area from the start until it finds the piece of interest. This makes it fast. In general, the more RAM the better, and a certain minimum is required for many programs. RAM is often called *main memory*.

Memory capacity is measured in *bytes*. One byte consists of eight *bits*. You can think of a bit in electrical terms as a switch – on or off – or in mathematical terms as a single binary number – 0 or 1. Eight of these – a byte – can represent a letter of the alphabet or a single number.

A thousand bytes (actually, 1024 bytes) is known as a *kilobyte* (KB), a thousand kilobytes is known as a *megabyte* (MB), and a thousand megabytes is known as a *terabyte* (TB).

You are likely to be offered a new computer with 128 megabytes or possibly 512 MB of RAM. (This is twice as much as you would have been offered for the same price last year, and probably half as much as you will be offered this time next year.)

Random access memory (RAM)
RAM is the computer's working memory, an important factor in determining a computer's speed. RAM is volatile. As soon as the power is turned off, whatever was in RAM is lost.

It is relatively easy to upgrade the memory on your computer by buying additional memory chips. They are inexpensive and easy to install. Depending on what you are using your computer for, additional memory can make a huge difference to its performance – for example, you can have more applications open at the same time. Remember that having lots of applications running at the same time can have a significant impact on the performance of the computer. (Don't, however, attempt to install additional memory without expert guidance.)

Read-only memory

Don't confuse RAM with another kind of memory that you may occasionally hear of: ROM (read-only memory). This is where the computer stores its low-level programs – the ones that tell it how to behave, how to check its own circuitry, how to treat various kinds of input devices, and so on. ROM differs from RAM in two ways: first, it is not changed after the computer is assembled (you can read it, but you can't write to it), and second, its contents remain unchanged even when the power is turned off. (RAM is *volatile* – its contents are erased if the power supply is cut off.)

Read-only memory (ROM)
Computers typically contain a small amount of ROM that holds small programs for starting up the computer. Unlike RAM, ROM cannot be written to.

Disk space

After processor speed and amount of RAM, the next major determinant of computer power is the amount of disk space. A disk is a device for storing information. It is very different from RAM, for a number of reasons:

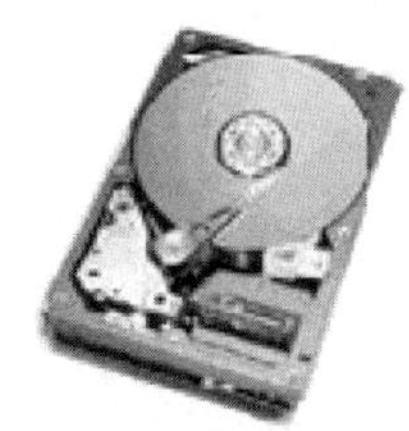

- Disks record information magnetically, in much the same way as music tapes or video tapes. They are not volatile: once the information is recorded, it remains on the disk until it is changed or deleted.
- The process of getting information on to a disk or retrieving information from a disk involves mechanical movement. The disk revolves at a constant high speed, and a *read/write head* moves in and out just above the surface of the disk. The read/write head can change the polarization of tiny magnetic particles on the surface of the disk, and can detect the polarization of particles. Moving parts wear out eventually, and as a result disks are more likely to malfunction than non-moving RAM. The moving parts also introduce delays into the processes of reading and writing, whereas reading from RAM is almost instantaneous.

Like memory capacity, disk capacity is measured in *bytes*. Disk capacity is bigger by several orders of magnitude: a new computer today will typically come with a 12-gigabyte (12 GB – 12 billion bytes) disk, rising to 60 gigabytes.

Let's consider this slowly: 12,000,000,000 bytes. The 32 volumes of *Encyclopaedia Britannica* contain approximately 44,000,000 words, or approximately 220,000,000 characters (bytes). A 12-GB disk could hold that text almost 56 times, yet it weighs only about one kilogram and takes up less space than one of the encyclopaedia's volumes. The amount of information that a disk can hold is the third performance measure that you should consider when buying a computer.

Hard disk
A spinning magnetic disk on which computer data can be stored. Typical storage capacities range from a few to a few tens of gigabytes.

Floppy disks, CD-ROMs, DVDs, Zip disks, tapes

The disks described above are generally built in to the computer and are not moved from one computer to another (although you can also buy external hard disks, which are connected to your computer by a cable). There is, however, a wide range of removable storage devices that can be transferred easily from one computer to another, or used as security backups in case of loss, damage or theft of the computer.

Floppy disks

Another kind of disk is the so-called *floppy disk* or *diskette*. (Early removable disks were housed in flexible envelopes, which earned them the name 'floppy'. The more recent design, with which you are probably familiar, uses a hard plastic shell with a sliding metal cover.)

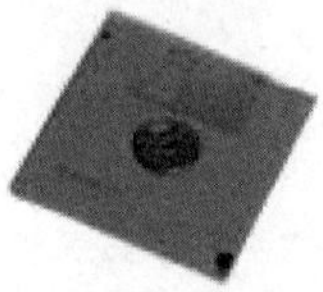

The most common type of floppy disk holds 1.4 MB. This is enough to hold many typical word processing documents, so that they can easily be passed from one person to another. You can use a floppy disk to transfer a document from your office computer to your home computer – simply copy the document to the floppy disk, and bring it home in your pocket. The entire text (but not the graphics) of this book fits on a single floppy disk, with room to spare!

Just as RAM is often referred to as 'working storage' or 'main memory', disks and floppy disks are often called 'backing storage' or 'secondary storage'.

The magnetic surface of a floppy disk needs to be divided into tracks and sectors before it can be used. This preparation is known as *formatting*, and most floppy disks sold today are pre-formatted.

Floppy disk
A small magnetic disk that can be removed from the computer. A floppy disk typically holds 1.4 MB of information.

CD-ROMs and DVDs

Until a number of years ago, floppy disks were also the principal way of loading programs on to a computer. Nowadays, however, software is most often supplied on CD-ROM (compact disk read-only memory). Physically, a CD-ROM is indistinguishable from a music CD, and in fact CD readers in computers are almost all capable of playing music CDs.

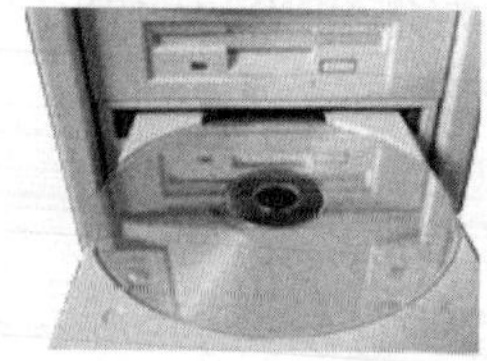

The move from floppy disk to CD-ROM as the favoured medium for distributing software has taken place mainly because of the size of modern software systems: they need more storage space. (More space is required because the programs have added functionality, because they are more graphic in design, and because they may include other multimedia elements.) A single CD-ROM can hold as much information as 460 floppy disks – about 650 MB.

CD-ROM drives (the part of the computer that reads CD-ROMs) are now offered as standard on all new computers. The only performance measure to watch out for is the speed of the drive, always quoted as a multiple of the normal music CD-player speed: nowadays, 40x or 48x speed CD-ROM drives are normal.

A limitation of standard CD-ROMs is that although they can be read as often as necessary, they can be written to only once. A newer type of CD-ROM is the rewritable CD or CD-RW. You can work with CD-RWs just as you would with floppy disks or hard disks by writing data to them more than once.

CD-ROM
A disk that typically stores about 650 MB of data. Standard CD-ROMs can be written to only once. CD-RW disks can be written to more than once.

CD-ROMs are now being overtaken by DVDs (digital versatile disks), which look similar but have a great deal more storage capacity – up to 5.2 GB.

To record or copy information on a CD, you need a CD writer (or 'burner'). Information is encoded on the surface of CDs as tiny holes, which are detected by a laser beam.

Magnetic tape

Magnetic tape – usually in cassettes not unlike music cassettes – is used for distributing software and for keeping backup copies of large volumes of data. It is less useful in normal everyday use, because it cannot be accessed randomly: the computer has to read it through from the beginning to find the part of interest.

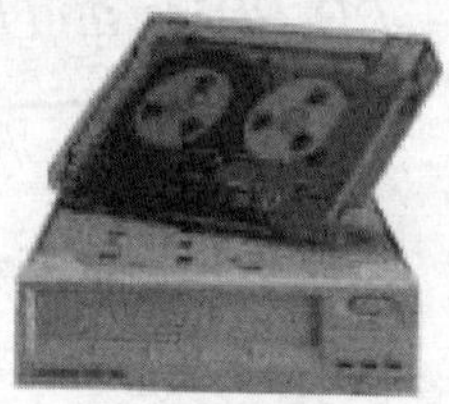

Zip disks, etc.

High-capacity removable floppy disks are gaining favour for keeping backups and for transferring large files between computers. Some use magnetic technology, some laser technology. Among the most popular of such devices is the *Zip drive*, which attaches to any computer's parallel port (printer connection) and provides storage on 100-MB or 250-MB removable disks.

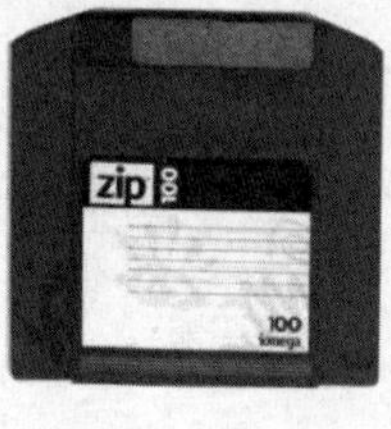

Storage media summary

This table summarizes the typical capacity and cost of the various storage media.

Medium	Typical capacity	Typical cost of medium (March 2003)
Hard disk (fixed)	20–50 gigabytes	£60–£250
Floppy disk	1.4 megabytes	Less than £1
CD	650 megabytes	Less than £1
DVD	5.2 gigabytes	£20–£30
Zip	100–250 megabytes	Less than £10
Tape	4–100 gigabytes	£20–£70

Out of the box: the essentials

Everything outside the dark grey box is peripheral, which is why all the other objects are called *peripherals*. (Here we're cheating a little: technically, all secondary storage, such as disks, CD-ROMs, etc., can be considered to be peripheral as well.) In most computer systems, the three *essential* peripherals are the keyboard and the mouse (used for input) and the screen (used for output).

Keyboard

A keyboard is a set of typewriter-like keys that enables you, the user, to enter information and instructions into a computer. Keys on a computer keyboard are of three types:

- **Alphanumeric keys:** Letters and numbers.
- **Punctuation keys:** Comma, full stop, semicolon, and so on.
- **Special keys:** Function keys, control keys, arrow keys, Caps Lock key, and so on.

Screen

The screen looks somewhat like a television. It is also called the *monitor* (because you use it to monitor what is going on in the computer) or the *visual display unit* (VDU). Most programs are designed in such a way that you appear to enter input directly from the keyboard on to the screen. In fact, you enter it into the processor, and the processor shows you what it has received by displaying it on the screen. Most programs also give you continuous feedback on their progress, and display their output on the screen.

Mouse

Many programs present themselves on the screen as *graphical user interfaces* (GUI – pronounced, believe it or not, 'gooey'). A GUI represents programs, files and functions as pictures on the screen. The GUI includes a pointer that you can move around the screen until it is at the picture that represents what you want to do. You then indicate your intention, and the program responds accordingly.

The mouse is the tool that you use to move the pointer around the screen. The underside of the mouse houses a ball, and, as you move the mouse over your desk, this ball detects the movements, and converts them into movements of the pointer. Move the mouse left, the pointer moves left; right, and the pointer moves right; push the mouse away from you, and the pointer moves up the screen; pull it towards you, and the pointer moves down. After a very short time it becomes second nature.

Note that the ball only moves (and therefore the pointer only moves) when the underside of the mouse is in contact with the desk. So you can move the pointer a long distance in one direction by making a series of short moves in that direction with the mouse, each time lifting the mouse so that the return journey does not affect the position of the pointer.

The mouse has two or three buttons on top: these are used to signal to the computer that the pointer has arrived where you want to go. You press one or other buttons once (called a *click*), or twice in quick succession (called a *double-click*).

The mouse (or whatever pointing device you use – see *Other pointing devices* below) makes operation of the computer easy, and even intuitive, but it is seldom absolutely necessary. Most programs allow you to move the pointer around the screen and choose your options using special keys or combinations of keys on the keyboard. Some users prefer this: it means they can do all their work from the keyboard – they don't have to switch back and forth between the keyboard and the mouse.

Other pointing devices

The mouse is by far the most common pointing device, but there are other pointing devices that can be used for input:

- **Trackballs:** These are like an upside-down mouse: you move the pointer by manipulating a ball in a special housing. They are useful in situations where desk space is limited.
- **Joysticks and games controllers:** These fulfil the same function as the mouse or trackball, but are designed especially for games and simulation.
- **Touchpad:** Most portable computers have a device built in to the keyboard for moving the pointer, either in the form of a miniature joystick, or a pressure-sensitive *touchpad* that detects movements of your finger.
- **Light pens:** These are pen-shaped devices that, when placed close to the screen, can be used both to draw and to control icons or choices shown on the screen.
- **Touchscreens:** You will often see these in public information kiosks: the user simply touches the screen at the point of interest in order to exercise a choice from the options displayed. Touchscreens are both *input* and *output* devices.
- **Graphics tablets:** These are flat surfaces that detect the movement of a plastic stylus (pen) across them. They are typically used for art and design applications, but smaller versions are becoming common in pocket, hand-held and palmtop computers. These devices (known as *personal digital assistants*, or *PDA*s) are generally too small to allow typing.

Out of the box: optional extras

Without the components described above, it would be hard to get the computer to do anything useful. There are a number of other devices that, although they are not essential, are normal parts of the system in the home, school or office. These include output devices such as printers and loudspeakers, input devices such as scanners, digital cameras and microphones, and other devices that function as both input and output devices, such as modems.

Printers

There are several kinds of printer on the market: the two most common are *laser printers* and *inkjet printers*.

- **Laser printers** use a technology similar to that used in photocopying to transfer the image of a page on to paper. The image is 'drawn' under instruction from the computer.
- **Inkjet printers** have a moving 'pen' (the *write head*) that holds an ink cartridge. This moves back and forth over the page and, under computer control, ejects a minute quantity of ink at the precise point where it is required on the page.

You will occasionally come across a third category of printer: *impact printers*. These work like a typewriter: they hammer out the required characters on to the page through an ink-impregnated (or carbon-covered) ribbon. There are several kinds, using slightly different techniques for making the marks on the paper: dot matrix printers, daisywheel printers, line printers. Nowadays their use is confined to specialist applications (printing receipts from cash registers, printing the time of arrival on a ticket in a car park), or high-volume printouts that do not use graphics (tax forms, electricity bills).

Plotters are used in specialist applications, such as producing architectural or engineering drawings. Most of them are designed to produce large drawings accurately. They are relatively expensive.

How to choose a printer

Some of the factors you should consider when buying a printer are:

- **Speed of output:** Most laser printers can print eight or twelve pages a minute. This speed may depend on what you are printing: graphics, or text pages with a variety of different fonts, tend to be slower. If you need a faster printer, be prepared to pay a lot more.

  Inkjet printers are generally a lot slower than laser printers, but their speed doesn't depend on what you are printing. The quality of the print tends to vary, because they rely on a moving write head.
- **Colour:** If you want colour output, you have to buy a colour printer. It's that simple. Colour laser printers are expensive; colour inkjet printers are only slightly more expensive than black-and-white printers.

Some colour printers use three different inks to produce their output, and some use four. Some use a combined three- or four-colour cartridge, and some use a separate cartridge for each colour. Your choice depends on what you are using the printer for. If you are only occasionally using colour output, make sure you have a separate black cartridge: the density of the black printout from a black cartridge is much higher than that from a combination of colours. If you get a combined four-colour cartridge, you will be throwing out the almost-full colour inks just because you have run out of black.

- **Cost of consumables:** The initial cost of the printer is only one of the cost factors that you need to consider: ink cartridges (for inkjet printers) and toner cartridges (for laser printers) have to be replaced regularly, and it is worthwhile calculating the cost per page of output before making your final decision.

Modems

A *modem* is used to connect your computer to the telephone network so that you can send and receive e-mail or use the Internet. Most computers sold today include a modem already installed in the system unit, but they can also be obtained as external devices that are connected to the computer by a cable. Most modems can enable your computer to function as a fax machine (although, unless you have a scanner, you are limited to sending text-only faxes).

Multimedia

Computers can manipulate any kind of data that can be converted into numbers, including music, pictures, animated drawings, video and speech. A range of applications has grown up around this capability, in which text, video and sound are mixed to deliver instruction, information or entertainment. These applications are called *multimedia applications*, and a computer that can run them is often called a *multimedia computer*. Most computers nowadays can run these applications. However, if this is your main interest, you may want to consider a computer with a larger screen, and more advanced sound generation and video display capabilities. In addition, a number of specialized peripherals are available.

Scanners

Think of a scanner as the first half of a photocopier – it copies a photograph, drawing, or page of text into the computer, where you can use a program to manipulate it or print it out (like the second half of the photocopier). You can use the scanner to include a drawing or photograph in a newsletter, or use *optical character recognition*

(OCR) software to decipher the text, and use all or part of it in a word processing document (without having to re-type it).

Digital cameras

A digital camera works exactly like a standard camera, except that it does not use photographic film – the images are recorded digitally in the camera's memory. From there, you can transfer them to your computer and subsequently print them out, use graphics software to edit them, archive them for posterity, or e-mail them to your friends.

Loudspeakers

Loudspeakers are standard equipment on almost all new computers. They are used to play music and other sounds.

Sound cards

Again, your system unit almost certainly includes a sound card, which is used to control all the audio output (music, speech, and so on). However, if the quality of music output is important to you, you may want to upgrade from the sound card supplied as standard equipment.

Microphones

Many software applications can be controlled by speech commands. These are spoken into a microphone.

Multimedia

The use of computers to present text, graphics, video animation and sound in an integrated manner. Hardware elements include scanners, sound cards, loudspeakers and microphones.

Looking after your hardware

Modern computers are robust and reliable: once they start working, they tend to go on working. But remember that they are sensitive instruments, so avoid testing their tolerance.

DO give your computer room to breathe: it has to have access to fresh air so that the fan can keep the electronics cool.

DON'T block the air vents by stacking books or magazines or (worse) draping clothes over the back of the computer.

DO keep the computer dry. Excessive moisture can play havoc with electric circuitry.

DON'T eat or drink while using your computer: crumbs can clog up your keyboard. A spilt cup of coffee can wreck your computer and (probably worse) cause the loss of all your files stored on the computer.

DO keep your computer free of dust: you will notice that it tends to attract dust. Clean the air vents occasionally, and use an anti-static wipe on the screen.

DON'T expose your computer to extremes of temperature.

DO shut down the computer in an orderly fashion, by systematically closing the applications you have opened.

DON'T just switch it off or pull the plug from the socket.

DO keep floppy disks away from the screen: the strong magnetic field generated by the screen may erase or change some of the data.

DON'T move the system unit while the computer is in operation – you risk damaging the hard disk drive.

When something goes wrong

You are more likely to be a computer user than a computer engineer. Therefore, respect your PC as a delicate instrument – if it seems to be malfunctioning, don't try to fix it. You risk destroying it or electrocuting yourself. Always call a person qualified to deal with the problem.

Chapter summary: so now you know

The basic PC consists of a *system unit*, a *screen* and a *keyboard*. Virtually all PCs include a *pointing device* – most commonly a *mouse*.

Inside the system unit are the *processor* (*CPU*), *main memory*, *hard disk* and some removable storage – usually a *disk drive* and a *CD-ROM drive*.

Other items that are almost essential are a *printer* and a *modem*. A modem is used to connect the computer to the telephone network, so that you can send and receive e-mail or access the Internet.

Most PCs sold today are equipped for multimedia: they include loudspeakers, sound cards and microphones.

To capture images, drawings or photographs and include them in newsletters, project reports or e-mails, you need a *scanner* or *digital camera*.

Finally, you have learnt how to look after your computer, so that it gives a long life of good service.

Quick quiz: computer hardware

Answer the following multiple-choice questions about computer hardware.

Q1	Which of the following is/are essential pieces of hardware for a computer to work?
A.	Processor.
B.	Scanner.
C.	Hammer.
D.	Word processor.

Q2	The C in CPU stands for:
A.	Central.
B.	Computer.
C.	Complex.
D.	Computing.
E.	Commercial.

Q3	The speed of a computer is measured in:
A.	CPUs.
B.	MHz.
C.	MB.
D.	K.
E.	RAM.
F.	GUIs.

Q4	The R in ROM stands for:
A.	Random.
B.	Read.
C.	Regular.
D.	Right.

Q5	The R in RAM stands for:
A.	Random.
B.	Read.
C.	Regular.
D.	Right.

Q6	Correct any of the following statements that are wrong.
A.	There are exactly eight bytes in a bit.
B.	A megabyte is double the size of a normal byte.
C.	100K bytes is equal to a GB.
D.	A gigabyte is approximately equal to 1,000,000,000 bytes.

Q7	Which of the following statements is/are true?
A.	Information stored in RAM is erased when the computer is turned off.
B.	Information stored in ROM is erased when the computer is turned off.
C.	The M in RAM stands for memory.
D.	The M in ROM stands for memory.
E.	Hard disks, floppy disks and CD-ROMs are all used to store computer programs.

Q8	Name three kinds of pointing device.

Q9	Name the two most common types of printer.

Q10	Which of the following can store more information?
A.	High-density floppy disk.
B.	Zip disk.

Answers

1: A.

2: A.

3: B.

4: B.

5: A.

6: B: a megabyte is a million bytes.
C: 1,000,000,000 bytes is equal to a GB.

7: A, C, D and E.

8: Mouse, joystick, trackball, light pen, games controller, touch screen.

9: Laser and inkjet.

10: B.

Chapter 4: Software and data

In this chapter

In this chapter you will learn more about the different kinds of software and how they are made. You will also learn what the most valuable part of a computer system is – the data.

New skills

At the end of this chapter you should be able to:

- Distinguish between system software and application software.
- Describe the process of software development.
- Discuss software licensing and the different types of licence.
- Describe how to protect software and data from unauthorized access, loss or damage, and computer viruses.
- State the principles of data copyright.
- State the principles of data protection and the main provisions of the European Data Protection Directive.

New words

At the end of this chapter you should be able to explain the following terms:

- System software
- Graphical user interface
- Freeware
- Systems analyst
- Copyright
- Application software
- Licensed software
- Shareware
- Programmer
- Data protection

Software

Software is the intangible side of computing: it is the generic name given to all the programs – the sets of instructions – that determine how the computer behaves.

We distinguish between two kinds of software: *system software* and *applications software*.

- System software is concerned with the computer itself – what devices it can control, how it manages files and storage, and how it deals with exceptional conditions.

- Applications software is concerned with the world outside the computer – the world of business, entertainment or education.

Software
The programs (sets of instructions) that determine how the computer behaves.

System software

The main piece of system software that we are concerned with is the *operating system* (OS). This is the driving program of the PC: without it, the PC would be virtually unusable. All other programs depend on the operating system to communicate with and control the hardware. The operating system also controls the timing of different events to make sure they happen in the correct sequence, and manages access to data to ensure security and integrity.

The most popular operating system is Microsoft Windows, of which there are a number of versions, including Windows 98, Windows Me and Windows XP. Other popular operating systems include Mac OS (for Apple Macintosh), UNIX and Linux.

When you add a new piece of hardware to your system, you might have to load a special piece of software called a *driver* to enable the operating system to control the hardware. Older PCs use an operating system called DOS (Disk Operating System). To use DOS, you have to type in commands such as DIR, COPY or REN.

System software (operating system)
Software that performs such tasks as recognizing input from the keyboard and mouse, sending output to the screen, communicating with printers and other peripherals, and keeping track of files.

Graphical user interface

More recent computers present their operating system through a *graphical user interface* (GUI). The GUI represents all the computer's resources – the hardware resources such as disks and printers, the software resources, including both system software and application programs, and the data files on which you can work – as small pictures or symbols called *icons*. You use the mouse to move the pointer to the icon representing the object you want to use, and press (or *click*) the mouse button to signal your request. This is considerably easier than having to remember a command and type it accurately. Examples of GUIs include Windows (all versions), Mac OS and Sun OS.

Application software

Nobody wants to use a lawnmower or a telephone or a satellite: what they want to do is cut the grass, talk to their friends, or predict the weather. Similarly, you don't really want to use a computer: you want to use a computer to do *something else*. That 'something else' is your application, and the program that enables you to do it is called the *application program*. By the time you have finished this book you will be able to use several application programs: word processing, spreadsheets, electronic mail (e-mail), and so on. Some application programs are very common – for example, it is hard to find an office that doesn't use a word processor (for typing reports and letters), a spreadsheet (for manipulating numbers), and a web browser for accessing the Internet. Many computers are sold with these applications pre-loaded.

Application software
Programs that do the real work for users. For example, word processors, spreadsheets and database management systems.

Other applications are developed for more specialized tasks. People and organizations purchase them in accordance with their particular needs. Accounting software helps them to keep books of accounts and issue invoices. Database applications enable them to keep track of customers, suppliers and products. Desktop publishing applications enable them to produce high-quality brochures and newsletters. Computer-aided design packages enable them to design houses. Project management software helps them to control work on large contract. In Chapter 6 we will look in more detail at the types of applications in daily use in business, administration, education, entertainment and communication.

How software is made

The development of any software system involves a cycle of research, analysis, development and testing, involving the following types of people:

- **Systems analysts:** They study the business processes that the software is intended to support, and produce the design for the software. They decide what the software should do (but not necessarily how it should do it). You can think of the systems analyst as the software architect. Systems analysts are focused on the needs of the users and the application area.
- **Programmers:** They translate the design into a working program. They write instructions that tell the computer what to do in order

to accomplish the task for which the system is intended. You can think of the programmer as the software builder. Programmers are focused on the computer, its capabilities and its limitations.

Software copyright

In general, software is *licensed* rather than sold. When you buy a software package, you don't own the software: you gain the right to use it under specified conditions.

In general, software is easy to duplicate, so it is easy for unscrupulous people to make unauthorized copies. Don't do it! It's piracy; it's illegal; and it deprives an individual developer or a company of their rightful income, which they need to produce the next version of that piece of software, or the next application that you will want to use.

Don't accept software from dubious sources, whether in person, by mail order or over the Internet. You are responsible for the legality of the software that you use.

Licensed software
Software that may be used only when the relevant user organization or individual has purchased the right to do so under certain conditions.

Some software, called *freeware*, is distributed without charge: you can find it on disks given away with magazines, or download it from the Internet. Again, you should be clear about the terms of use: in most cases, you can use it, but you may not, for example, sell it for profit, change it in any way, or label it as if it was your own product.

Freeware
Copyrighted software given away without charge by the author. Typically, the author allows people to use the software, but not to sell it.

Other software is called *shareware*. It is distributed widely in much the same way as freeware. You can try it out, but if you decide to use it you are expected to send a licence fee to the developer. In some cases, this is based on honour; in other cases, the shareware version will not function after a time period (typically thirty days), or certain functions are disabled in some way. When you register with the developer and send the licence fee, you are given a fully working copy of the software, or a password to unlock the disabled functions.

Shareware
Software that is typically available free of charge, but the author usually requests that you pay a small fee if you like the program and use it regularly. Registered users can receive service assistance and updates.

Software versions

Software developers don't like saying that they have finished an application – they prefer to say that they have brought it to a certain point in its development, so that it can be sold to the public. But as soon as the first version of a software application is released, you can be sure that the developers are already busy working on the next version.

Most developers use a numbering system to identify software versions. Version 1.0 becomes version 1.0.1, 1.0.2 ... and so on; then version 1.1.0, 1.1.1 ... and so on; then 1.2, 1.3, then 2.0, and so on.

Usually you can find out what version of a software application you have by choosing **Help | About**. The screen below shows the About information for Adobe Acrobat 5.0. In this case, the exact version number is 5.0.5. The About information usually includes the product ID or serial number of your software.

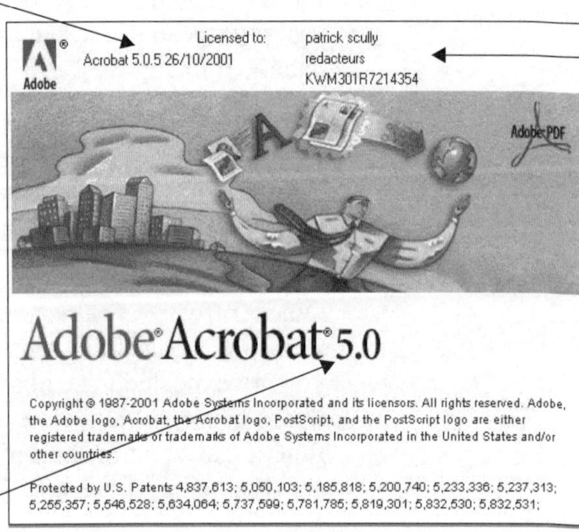

Problems with software

Software – even the smallest piece of application software – is complex. It is difficult to test thoroughly, because it is difficult to imagine every possible input in every possible combination. Sometimes mistakes are made, or unusual circumstances are not catered for adequately by the designers or programmers.

When the software produces incorrect or unexpected results, it is said to have a *bug*. Bugs can range from minor irritations, where, for example, the screen displays are inconsistent, through significant errors, such as incorrect totals on invoices, to total collapse.

When the computer 'freezes' – it ceases to function, refuses to accept any input, won't produce any output – we say that it *hangs*. When this happens, you may be able to resort to an old trick: press three of the keyboard keys simultaneously – **Ctrl**, **Alt** and **Del**. Most of the time, this will enable you to shut down the offending program and continue working on something else. Pressing this key combination *twice* generally causes your computer to restart.

Infrequently, a bug will cause the whole system to *crash*. The only solution is to turn off the power, wait a minute, and then turn it on again. A quicker way to achieve the same end is to press the **Reset** button on your system unit. Treat this as a last resort, however – you will lose any work done since you last saved in all the applications that you have open at the time.

Data

We haven't yet dealt in any detail with data. Data is another intangible in a computer system, but it is not generally built by the software developer. It's built by users – people like you.

So, to write a letter, you need a keyboard, a screen and a printer (hardware), and you need a word processing program (software). The letter itself, and the name and address of the recipient, are *data*.

Data is held on a computer system in *files*. Files are organized into *directories* (otherwise known as *folders*). Files and directories are given *names*, so that you can find them and recognize them when you need them, and so that the operating system can find them and work on them when it needs to.

Data copyright

Remember that computer data – including graphics, text, audio files and video files – carries the same copyright rights and responsibilities as printed works or musical compositions: someone created it, and that person owns it. If you download a file from the Internet or have it on CD or disk, you may not have the right to include it in your own publications or to copy it without the consent of the author or creator.

Data protection

We all appear in numerous databases: banks, insurance companies, educational institutions, employers and governments all hold files full of personal information. Our dates of birth, addresses and marital statuses, our incomes, credit and educational records, our health, criminal and bill-paying histories are all known by various institutions. This information is sometimes general, sometimes specific. It may be sensitive and, in the wrong hands, damaging or dangerous.

Marketing departments are willing to pay large sums of money for name-and-address databases of specific categories of people. This enables them to target products and services at precise sectors of the population.

It follows that the collection, maintenance and protection of information is a responsibility that demands great respect. Wrong or misleading information could lead to a person being refused a mortgage, a job, an overseas work visa or medical insurance. It could ruin their life. Holding personal information thus demands sensitivity and respect. This is reflected in the *data protection laws*.

Data protection
The conception that information relating to individuals (personal data), collected and used by organizations, is subject to certain regulations.

The European Data Protection Directive

All EU states either have already adopted laws to give effect to this EU Directive or will shortly do so.

The Directive requires that all computer-based data be:

- Processed fairly and lawfully.
- Collected for specified and explicit purposes.
- Adequate, relevant and not excessive.
- Accurate and up to date where necessary.

- Maintained in a form that means that the data subject (that is, the person about whom the data is gathered) cannot be identified once their identification is no longer necessary.

It is quite common for data to be gathered about Internet users – this enables online businesses to target their marketing more effectively. Such information is also subject to the rules on data protection. The EU Directive sets out the information that must be provided to web users when such details are collected, including the identity of the collecting body, the purposes for which the data is intended, the likely recipients of the data, and the right to access the information and correct it if it is inaccurate. Each EU member state must ensure that controllers of information respect the above rules.

Hacking has worrying implications for data protection. Controllers are required to implement adequate security measures to protect data against accidental or malicious disclosure or access, in particular where the information is being transferred over a network as in the case of the Internet.

One difficulty with the Internet is that it is transnational. Data can be transferred from the EU website to the USA at the click of a button. However, the EU Directive prohibits the transfer of information to countries outside the EU unless they have similar protection in place.

Chapter summary: so now you know

A computer *is* hardware, but it *does* software. Software determines how the computer behaves – the particular problems it solves at any given time.

System software is inward-looking – it is software that controls the computer itself.

Application software is software that addresses a 'real world' problem – it does something that users want done.

Software is developed by *systems analysts* and *programmers* in a process that involves detailed research, analysis, program development and testing. Testing is almost never comprehensive, so errors and problems (called *bugs*) sometimes occur.

Licensed software must be purchased and used only under specified conditions.

Software versions are identified by version numbers.

Shareware is typically available without charge, but a small payment must be made if it is used regularly. Registered users typically receive service assistance and updates.

Freeware is software that, although copyrighted, is given away without charge by its author.

Software belongs to the authors, and, in general, copying it is illegal.

Data is often the most valuable part of a computer system, because it is the least easily replaced. For that reason, you should protect your data against loss or damage by using passwords and anti-virus software. You should also save your work frequently and make *backups* at regular intervals.

Quick quiz: software and data

Answer the following questions about software and data.

Q1	What is a word processor system?
A.	Software.
B.	Application software.

Q2	What is a Windows system?
A.	Software.
B.	Application software.

Q3	What is the difference between freeware and shareware?

Q4	Which of the following statements is/are true?
A.	A folder is another name for a floppy disk.
B.	A file can contain any number of folders.
C.	Records have been made obsolete by CDs.
D.	Files contain records.

Q5	You edit the newsletter for your local community. Are you entitled to sell the mailing list to a marketing company? State why.

Answers

1: B.

2: A.

3: No payment is required for freeware.

4: D.

5: No. The list was collected for one purpose and may not be used for another without the consent of everyone on the list.

Chapter 5: Networks and the Internet

In this chapter

Networking of computers, as you will discover in this chapter, opens up productive and exciting opportunities for sharing resources and information.

As you will learn, the world's largest network is the Internet, which connects millions of computers. Unlike smaller, private networks, which are controlled centrally, the Internet is decentralized by design.

New skills

At the end of this chapter you should be able to:

- Describe the advantages of computer networking.
- Describe the use of the telephone network in computing.
- Describe the uses of e-mail, the Internet and the World Wide Web.
- Describe how e-commerce is changing business practices.

New words

At the end of this chapter you should be able to explain the following terms:

- Network
- LAN
- PSTN
- E-mail
- World Wide Web
- Search engine
- SMS
- WAN
- ISDN
- DSL
- Internet
- Browser
- E-commerce

Networks

Computers can function quite happily on their own (*stand-alone computing*), but increasingly they are being connected together into *networks*.

The advantages of networking

When your computer is connected to other computers – whether they are in the same building or on the other side of the world – it is part of a computer network. You can still use it to do your own work as usual, but several new possibilities open up:

- **Sharing hardware:** In a stand-alone world, people can print only if a printer is attached directly to their computer. By connecting one or more printers to a computer network, everyone whose computer is also attached to the same network can print their documents. Printer-sharing means that everyone can print (although not at the same time) without everyone having an individual printer. The same is true of other hardware resources, such as modems, scanners and plotters.
- **File sharing:** On a stand-alone computer, you can work with all the files stored on your computer's hard disk. On a network-connected computer, you may be able to work with files (data files or application software) stored on other people's computers too. Rather than have network users rummaging through each other's hard disks, information that is needed by everyone in a particular department (in accounts, for example, or in a warehouse) is usually stored on a single, powerful, permanently switched-on computer called a *file server.*
- **E-mail:** Meetings, telephone conversations, letters and memos – typically, these are the ways in which people in an organization communicate with one another. Computer networks make possible another form of communication called electronic mail, or e-mail for short. This is the exchange of (usually plain-text) messages between users of computers that are connected to a common network.
- **Data exchange:** Users connected to a computer network can exchange files: one person can write an article for the newsletter, another can edit it, a third can lay it out, while a fourth can contribute a drawing or a scanned photograph. This kind of cooperative work over a network is known as *workgroup computing*, or *groupwork*.

Computer network

Two or more computers that are connected together by some means to provide their users with such services as printer-sharing, file-sharing and electronic mail.

Networking: the risks and disadvantages

Networking is not without its risks and disadvantages.

- You have to take your turn in the queue for printers and other shared network resources.
- You might feel less in control when you are sharing documents, databases and information with other users of your network. For documents with multiple authors and editors, you might need to put a document change and tracking system in place.
- Even small office networks can be technically quite complex. Not every company has the in-house networking expertise necessary when things go wrong – and buying in network consultancy can be expensive. So for very small networks, the cost of ownership can be quite high compared with that of stand-alone PCs.

LANs and WANs

Networks come in two sizes: big and small. A local area network, or LAN, is the kind that connects the computers in a single office, building or group of adjoining buildings.

Local area network (LAN)
A network that connects computers located within a small area.

Large corporations operate computer networks that connect offices at locations within the same or different countries. Such wide area networks, or WANs, can enable, for example:

- The Frankfurt office to exchange e-mails with the Sydney office.
- The Tokyo office to read files that are stored on a computer in the New Orleans office.
- The Cape Town office to print a report on a printer that is located in the Bombay office.

Wide area network (WAN)
A network that connects computers over a wide area, typically across international boundaries.

In reality, most networks are bigger than LANs but smaller than WANs. But, for some reason, no one has thought up a name for them.

Computer networks can be open to everyone or restricted to the chosen few. An example of a *private access* network is one operated by a company or government agency for its own personnel only. An example of a *public access* network is the Internet.

Client/server systems

The term 'client/server computing' defines the relationship between two computer programs where one program (the server) fulfils requests made by another program (the client). Typically, the server resides on a larger or more powerful computer, and processes requests from many clients. Most large companies use client/server computing to enable dispersed computers to communicate with and access central resources.

Every time you connect to the Internet, you are using client/server computing. Your browser (the client) requests web pages, files and other services from a server somewhere on the Internet.

Making the connection

How do the computers in a network actually connect with one another? Well, in a LAN it's relatively simple: the computers (and printers) are connected together with a special cable. However, in a WAN, that isn't an option. It would be quite impractical to run cables from one side of the country to another, or from one continent to the next.

The telephone network

The solution is that WANs use cables already in place – the cables of the national and international telephone system (the PSTN, or public switched telephone network). They also use all the other technology of the telephone network – satellites, microwaves, optic fibres and so on. This has advantages, and one major disadvantage too:

- **Advantages:** It's already in place (so there is no need to run WAN cables across rivers and over mountains), and its connection points are never far away (the phone system reaches into every workplace and virtually every home).
- **Disadvantage:** Computer signals (the ones that travel around inside a computer) are a different 'shape' from the signals accepted by the phone system (ones resulting from the sound of the human voice). Computer signals are 'digital'; voice signals are 'analogue'.

We therefore have a problem: a *signal shape* problem. To connect a computer to a phone line, we need a device that can do two jobs. Which job it does at any particular time depends on the direction of the information transfer:

- **Outgoing information:** When your computer sends data (such as an e-mail) down the phone line, the device must 'shape' the signal

– convert it from computer-shape to phone-shape (digital to analogue).

- **Incoming information:** When you receive data (such as a file from a distant computer), the device must 'deshape' the signal – reconvert it back from phone-shape to its original computer-shape (analogue to digital).

Another, rather poetic, word for the act of shaping anything in this way is *modulation*. A device that shapes (*mod*ulates) and deshapes (*dem*odulates) a signal is called – guess what? – a modem.

Modem

A device that enables computers to communicate over the telephone system. At the sending computer, the modem converts the outgoing data to the format acceptable to the phone system. At the receiving computer, another modem reconverts the data back to its original computer format.

Most modern computers have built-in modems. To connect such a computer to the telephone system you plug the phone line into the socket at the back of the computer. If your modem is a separate unit you plug the telephone line into the modem and use another cable to connect the modem to the serial port on the computer. The modem may be battery-powered or may need to be plugged into the mains.

Modems are rated according to the speed at which they can transmit and receive data. The *baud rate* is the number of times the signal changes in one second. However, each change in the signal can carry more than one bit of data, so the measure more commonly used nowadays is *bits per second* or *bps*. The top speed of current modems is around 56 kbps (kilobits per second, or thousands of bits per second).

ISDN

An alternative to using modems and the normal telephone network (PSTN) is to use ISDN, or integrated services digital network. As its name suggests, this network is designed to carry digital signals. In the past it has been used mainly by businesses that need frequent high-volume communication with other offices, and has been relatively expensive for low-volume users. This is beginning to change – the cost of ISDN is now within the reach of small businesses and home users.

ISDN gives access to two 64 kbps channels; these can be used separately or combined to exchange data at 128 kbps.

DSL

Digital subscriber line (DSL) technology is a technique for squeezing more bandwidth out of ordinary copper telephone lines. The effects can be stunning, with typical transmission speeds of up to 15 mbps – that's more than twenty times the speed of the fastest modem.

Depending on the particular flavour of DSL installed, there can be a difference between the upload speed and the download speed – usually downloading is much faster, and this is the case with asymmetric DSL (ADSL), the most widespread type of DSL.

One of the main advantages of DSL is that it is *always on*, and you don't need to dial up to connect to the Internet. On the downside, however, DSL is usually only available to users located within five kilometres of a DSL-enabled telephone exchange.

E-mail

Networks enable users to exchange personal messages with one another: this is the idea behind *e-mail*.

To send someone an e-mail message, you need to have a computer connected to a network, and the recipient has to have a computer connected (directly or indirectly) to the same network. You also need e-mail software, and the unique 'address' of the recipient. That's the minimum.

In practice, this means that both of you have:

- A PC.
- A modem.
- A telephone line.
- A subscription to an Internet service provider (ISP).

The ISP maintains a continuous connection to the Internet and stores on its computer all e-mail that is sent, from anywhere in the world, to your *mailbox*, until you collect it after submitting a password to prove your entitlement to it.

This system means that you can send a message to your friend even when their computer is turned off: it is stored for them, by their ISP, until they collect it.

Thus, you can carry on an electronic conversation over a period of time, during which neither you nor your friend are ever talking at the same time. This is particularly useful if you live in different time zones.

E-mail
The exchange of (usually plain-text) messages between users of computers that are connected to a common network.

E-mail has largely taken over from two earlier technologies that used the telephone network to send and receive written messages:

- **Fax** can be thought of as remote photocopying. The sender uses a fax machine to scan a letter, drawing, map or whatever. The fax machine encodes it so that it can be sent down the telephone line. The recipient's fax machine decodes the message and provides a printout.
- **Telex** was a much more primitive technology, which acted like a remote typewriter. It accepted only text typed on a special Telex machine (no pictures). At the receiving end, the Telex machine responded by typing out the same letters and numbers.

Mobile phone text messaging (SMS)

But you don't even need a computer or a connection to the Internet to exchange short text messages with your friends and colleagues – you can use your mobile phone's short messaging service (SMS). SMS messages can be up to 160 characters long which is usually long enough to tell your friends where you'll meet them, or what time you'll be home at.

SMS or *texting* has been hugely successful, particularly with younger people, and a language subculture of phrases and abbreviations has grown up around it.

CUL8R	see you later	BFN	bye for now
BTW	by the way	NRN	no reply necessary
PCM	please call me	B4	before

You can also use text messages to exchange ringtones and small graphics such as logos and icons.

The Internet

The *Internet* – everyone's talking about it. It may even be one of the main reasons you decided to learn about computers.

Internet
The Internet is a worldwide network of interconnected networks.

If you connect to the Internet, you can:

- Send e-mail to other users.
- Access information stored on computers all around the world.

Millions of users have access to the Internet; hundreds of thousands of computers are connected to it permanently – computers owned by governments, universities, companies, retailers, voluntary organizations and private individuals. Any user, anywhere, can send a message to any other user, and can access files on the other computers. This rich resource can be used for research, news, entertainment, education, information, sports, current affairs, shopping and art.

The Internet has become by far the most popular network for carrying e-mail, for a number of reasons:

- The network is already in place: there is no need to create a new physical network connecting all the people you want to communicate with.
- It has a huge population of already-connected users: the chances are high that the person you want to communicate with has an Internet connection.
- It is designed so that there is no single point of failure – if one computer on the network breaks down, or one phone line fails, the message is routed a different way to avoid the problem.
- It uses common standards: messages sent from one computer system in one country can be received and interpreted correctly by a different computer system in a different country.

The World Wide Web

The term *World Wide Web* is used to describe documents made available over the Internet that are in a particular graphic format. The documents can be linked together, irrespective of where they are located physically, and users can follow the links from document to document. This enables you to pursue a research topic from the general to the specific, from detail to 'big picture', from graphic to text, from text to sound. These links are called *hyperlinks*, and documents constructed with hyperlinks are called *hypertext*, or *hypermedia* if sound, graphics or video are involved.

The software used to display World Wide Web documents (or *web pages*) is called a *browser*. The two most frequently used browsers are Microsoft Internet Explorer and Netscape Navigator.

World Wide Web
The entire range of documents published on the Internet in a format that enables them to be displayed using a browser.

Browser
A program that enables you to display web pages and follow links from one web page to another.

However, with hundreds of thousands of computers connected to the Internet, each with thousands of pages of information available to you, how do you find anything of value?

You use a *search engine* – a program that trawls the Internet looking for documents that contain information of interest to you: the share price of a company, flight times from Rome to Athens, comparisons of different brands of vacuum cleaner, the correct spelling of a word in German, the prognosis for a medical condition, tonight's TV listings ... it's all there – somewhere.

Search engine
A program that searches the World Wide Web for documents that match your criteria.

Another term used to describe the Internet and the World Wide Web is the *information superhighway*.

Intranets and extranets

When is the Internet not the Internet? When it's an intranet. An intranet is like a private Internet within a company or department. You can move around the intranet in much the same way as you would around the Internet, using the same familiar browser software and the same interface, but access to and from the outside world is restricted. Many companies use an intranet to make internal and operational documents available to their staff.

But there are times when you want *some* people to come and visit *some parts* of your intranet – for example, authorized suppliers and key customers. An intranet that allows controlled and authorized access from outside is known as an *extranet.* Extranets have wide application in the area of supply chain management.

E-commerce

Booking airline and rail tickets, buying books or CDs, checking your bank statements, booking concert tickets, topping up your mobile phone credit – these are examples of the kinds of things that more and more of us are doing online now. This move of business to the Internet is known as *e-commerce* (or electronic commerce).

The Internet can change the way you shop. You can shop 365 days a year, 24 hours a day, you can compare prices from different suppliers, buy direct from the manufacturer or from a supplier anywhere in the world, and communicate with other buyers to get their views on quality and suitability.

On the downside, you can't discuss the purchase with the salesperson, or touch and feel the goods before you buy them, and not everybody feels secure about giving their personal details and credit card number over the Internet. Make sure that the organization you are buying from is reputable, and offers a secure connection. Check that it has a returns policy, in case the goods are unsatisfactory, and remember that your statutory consumer rights are the same as if you were buying in a shop or by mail-order. (However, it may be difficult to enforce your rights if the supplier is on the other side of the world.)

When you are making a trip, you can plan your itinerary, find the cheapest flights, look at alternative hotels and compare their facilities and prices, check out special offers, look at maps and check event listings. You can book flights, hire cars, reserve hotel or guest-house accommodation, order tickets for concerts and sporting events, and even book a table in your favourite restaurant.

E-commerce
Business conducted over a network or the Internet. The products and services offered may or may not be available in digital form.

If you are buying over the Internet, the most common way of paying is by credit card. You should make sure that the organization you are buying from is reputable,

E-banking and e-government

Banks now increasingly offer e-banking services where customers can access their accounts online: checking statements and balances, transferring funds, buying and selling shares, and paying utility bills. Governments are also getting in on the act and are moving towards *e-government,* making government services available online and giving the public increased access to information.

Chapter summary: so now you know

Computer *networking* enables users to share resources such as hardware and data and to exchange messages. This kind of cooperative work over a network is known as *workgroup computing*, or *groupwork*. Networks may cover a small area (*local area networks* or *LANs*) or a larger region (*wide area networks* or *WANs*).

WANs typically use the telephone system (the PSTN) to establish connections between distant computer users. This requires the use of a modem. Telephone companies increasingly offer *ISDN* and *DSL* services for high-speed computer communications.

To use *e-mail*, the sender and the receiver must each have a PC, a modem, access to a telephone line, and a subscription to an *Internet service provider* (or other e-mail carrier). To send SMS messages, all you need is a mobile phone.

The *Internet* is a worldwide network of interconnected networks. It is by far the most common medium for e-mail, and it also provides the infrastructure for the *World Wide Web*. The World Wide Web is a vast array of documents that are available over the Internet in a particular format – a format that enables them to be displayed with a browser. The *browser* enables you to display the document of your choice, and to follow hyperlinks from one document to another. A *search engine* is a program that trawls the Internet looking for documents that contain information of interest to you.

The Internet is enabling many businesses to reach new markets and offer new services to customers around the world. This is known as *e-commerce*.

Quick quiz: networks and the Internet

Answer the following questions about networks and the Internet.

Q1	Give two reasons for connecting your computer to a network.

Q2	The L in LAN stands for:
A.	Leading.
B.	Local.
C.	Long.
D.	Linked.

Q3	The A in WAN stands for:
A.	Access.
B.	Attached.
C.	Area.
D.	Aerial.

Q4	Comment on each of the following statements, indicating whether each is true or false.
A.	Computer networks will shortly make the telephone system obsolete.
B.	Modems are used to increase the speed at which computers can communicate.
C.	The telephone system is ideally suited for communication between computers.
D.	E-mail is another name for the Internet.

Q5	What is the Internet? State two of its most common uses.

Q6	**What is the World Wide Web? What kind of software do you need to use it?**

Q7	**What is a search engine?**

Q8	**Give some examples of e-commerce.**

Q9	**What kinds of goods and services are traded most easily over the Internet?**

Q10	**For one of the following businesses, say how its business could be changed by e-commerce: travel agent, record company, supermarket, restaurant, hairdresser.**

Answers

1: To exchange e-mail; to exchange or share files; to share hardware resources.

2: B.

3: C.

4: A – False – computers are a major part of modern telephone systems, and major users of them.
B – False – modems are *necessary* for computers to communicate over the telephone network.
C – False – not ideal – while the telephone system has the advantage of being in place, it was designed for voice communication.
D – False – e-mail is one of the major uses for the Internet.

5: A vast network of interconnected networks.

6: A vast range of documents available on the Internet in a format that enables them to be displayed with browser software.

7: A program that searches the World Wide Web for documents that match your criteria.

8: Sales of books or CDs over the Internet; electronic banking; comparing the price of goods using online catalogues; booking tickets on the Internet.

9: Non-perishable goods; goods with high value-to-weight ratio; information services; digital content.

10: *Travel agent* – Accept bookings by e-mail or via a website, reserve airline tickets, hotel rooms, hire cars, etc., via the Internet; provide better customer services to a wider client base via a website.

Record company – Use website to promote artists and releases, provide samples on website; deliver albums or individual tracks as MP3 files; run competitions and promotions.
Supermarket – Provide online ordering facility backed up by home delivery service; attract loyal customers with special promotions, etc.; link sales to supplier orders to ensure just-in-time replenishment of stock.
Restaurant – Promote via website showing menu, special offers, etc.; take reservations online – including letting customers choose their own table; keep in touch with customers via e-mail.
Hairdresser – Promote new styles, products, special offers, etc. on a website; allow customers to make appointments with their preferred hair stylist; generate customer loyalty by keeping in touch by e-mail.

Chapter 6: What computers are used for

In this chapter

In this chapter we take a look at some of the ways in which computers are used, and the effects they have on our lives. This isn't comprehensive – it can't be, as new uses are being found every day. However, by the end of the chapter, you should appreciate that the range of applications is very wide indeed.

New skills

At the end of this chapter you should be able to:

- Discuss the widespread use of information technology (IT) in modern society.
- Offer examples of IT applications in business, industry, schools, health care and the home.
- Discuss appropriate and inappropriate uses of computers.
- Discuss the information society.

New words

At the end of this chapter you should be able to explain the following terms:

- Teleworking
- E-learning
- CBT
- Information technology

Business and administration

Most offices today depend on computers. Computers are used to keep accounts, to send invoices, to maintain records of customers and suppliers, to hold details of stock, to calculate payroll, to write and edit letters, memos and reports, to design sales presentations, to communicate with other companies, to collect market intelligence, and to collaborate with others in research activities.

Computers are also used in more complex business processes such as resource planning, scheduling, route planning, customer relationship management, insurance claims processing, sales analysis and simulation.

Computers are particularly useful where there are large volumes of data to be maintained, analysed, stored and filtered, or where complex or repetitive calculations have to be performed.

Industry

In manufacturing industry, the range of applications includes all of the administrative functions mentioned above, and a whole lot more besides. Computers are used to schedule production, to monitor raw material usage and finished product quality, to control machine tools, to design new products, to minimize waste and to determine optimum stock levels.

In most automated plants, computers are used to collect orders from customers, to issue instructions to build the required products to the customer's specifications, to order the parts and materials automatically from the relevant suppliers (having first checked that they can deliver on time), and to schedule the plant and personnel necessary for satisfying the customer's order.

Retailing

In supermarkets, and increasingly in smaller shops, computers are used at the checkout to scan the bar codes on your purchases, and to calculate your bill. In many stores the information on your purchases is passed immediately to the warehouse, and orders for replacement stock are generated automatically when stock falls below a given point. Instructions can also be generated for the personnel responsible for stacking the shelves, so that the products are always available. This technology enables the supermarket to keep its stock to the minimum necessary to satisfy its customers, instead of having money tied up unnecessarily in stock and storage space.

Computers can also be used to control moving-message advertising panels. These displays are made up of hundreds of *light-emitting diodes* (LEDs) that are turned on and off rapidly to create text and pictures.

Home

In the home, computers have found a wide variety of uses – for playing games (most often), for keeping household accounts, for getting information over the Internet (for example, to research ancient history for a homework project or for checking the scores in the Italian football league), and for sending e-mail to friends and relatives abroad. The list grows every day, and the only limit is imagination.

Teleworking

But we don't just use computers at home to have fun. Information technology – the technology used to create, store, exchange, and use all kinds of information – now makes it possible for people to work from home, or *telework*. What are the tools of your trade? A computer? Access to the Internet? Printers, scanners, telephones? Well, you can have all of these at home, and be just as productive as you are at the office. You don't have to commute, and you can set your schedules to suit your home life better. There are also significant advantages and savings for companies who can reduce their office space requirements and attract quality staff from a wider pool.

On the downside, some people can find teleworking quite isolating – you don't have the interaction of working with other people in an office, and teamwork can suffer.

Running your own business from home

Many people have established professional design studios and desktop publishing businesses at home using PCs. Others have managed to use their PC to offer desktop video or sound editing comparable to that offered by expensive and sophisticated dedicated equipment. Bookkeepers and accountants, journalists and editors, and database designers are also able to work from home nowadays, thanks to PCs and the Internet.

Schools and education

Computers are used in school administration to register students and record attendance, and to devise timetables.

When you hear about young people using computers in schools, you may think they are doing something very technical, like programming or electronics. They seldom are.

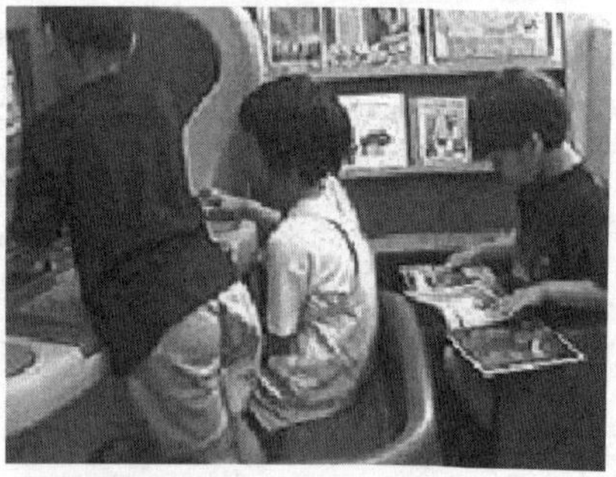

The main uses for computers in schools are in the traditional subject areas. There is a lot of educational software available that presents school subjects in a structured and entertaining way. Some students respond better to information presented this way, and computers also enable each student to progress at his or her own pace – the computer will repeat lessons as often as necessary, without losing patience.

In addition, the computer opens up the school to the outside world. Students can retrieve information from libraries, universities, government agencies, voluntary bodies, news organizations and other sources. They can communicate with students in other countries, and cooperate with them on research projects. They can take lessons from world experts without leaving their classroom.

In some science subjects, computers can be used to simulate experiments that are either dangerous or expensive. This enables students to learn without exposing themselves to the dangers, or without incurring the costs of the materials of equipment involved in the experiment.

Students can also use computers to write reports, produce school newsletters and design posters.

Education at work: e-learning and CBT

In a knowledge-based economy, we need to keep learning all the time. But where do we find the time? Evening classes and day release training can be expensive and difficult to schedule. One alternative that is increasingly popular in both the business and academic worlds is *e-learning* or computer-based training (CBT). Typically e-learning courses are available on CD, via a company intranet or over the Internet, and students access them from their PCs. Students can set their own pace, and can monitor their own progress through the course material. They can sit pre-assessment tests before they begin, and when they are finished they can confirm their competence by taking a mastery test.

In many organizations, e-learning is integrated into a training programme that includes some elements of classroom and teacher-led instruction. E-learning works particularly well where it offers simulated or protected environments where students can practise their skills before going live.

E-learning doesn't always work, however. Some students learn better in an environment where there is social interaction with teachers and other students. And from the trainer's point of view, there is less feedback on the effectiveness of the training.

Health care

The administration of hospitals depends more and more on computers. In fact, many of the applications are similar to manufacturing: scheduling expensive and scarce equipment, drawing up rosters, making appointments for patients, controlling ambulance fleets, and so on. In addition, computers are used for monitoring patients' conditions and alerting staff when abnormalities arise. Computers also allow doctors to keep comprehensive patient records, and to conduct research into the effectiveness of different treatments.

Research is also heavily dependent on computing power: most modern drugs are designed with the aid of computers and manufactured under computer control. The human genome project, which promises major breakthroughs in the treatment of genetic disorders, would be impossible without powerful computers.

Computers and communications technology are also being used to deliver health services to remote regions: the patient can connect to a major centre (or a centre of specialist expertise) for diagnosis and, in some cases, for treatment. This development is expected to yield significant cost savings and better treatment for patients in the coming years.

Government and public administration

Government agencies use computers for a wide range of purposes, in the same way as businesses – for accounting, stock control, project management, budgeting, forecasting, and so on. The main difference is one of scale: in general, governments need to maintain very large bodies of information – for example, registers of births, marriages and deaths, tax and social welfare records, vehicle registration, census of population data and voting registers. It would be almost impossible to maintain these records in a usable condition without computers.

Everyday life

You would recognize the computers used in the applications outlined so far. However, computer technology is also used in less visible ways. Computers control the cycles in your washing machine, the timer in your video recorder, the sequences of traffic lights, the delivery of money through an automatic teller machine, and the supply of fuel to your car engine. Almost anywhere you see something happening 'automatically', there is a computer at its heart, monitoring the outside world and responding to it.

Speech synthesizers are programs that produce computer-generated speech in imitation of the human voice. They are used increasingly in telephone applications such as in directory enquiries, in voicemail systems, in telephone banking and in travel information systems. They are also used to enable blind or partially sighted people to use computers: the speech synthesizer 'reads' aloud any text that appears on the screen.

Information technology and society

Some people find this proliferation of IT somewhat disturbing. Is there no aspect of our lives that is untouched by computers? Are computers replacing people and creating unemployment? Are all uses of computers good, or are computers being used to manipulate and control us? Are all computer-assisted services and all computer-manufactured goods better than their predecessors?

These questions don't have clear-cut answers.

From the discussion in this chapter, you probably agree that the society we live in uses computers a lot, and that many of the goods we consume and many of the services we use would not be available without computers. Like it or not, we are living in the Computer Age, or the Information Age, or the Digital Age (take your pick), and our society can justifiably be called an *information society*. In essence this means that value in society comes from information.

In the Age of Agriculture, most of the work, and most of the value, related to food production. In the Industrial Age, it was manufacturing that defined the society. The availability of food was almost taken for granted; proportionately less time and effort went into ensuring the food supply to the individual. Value, wealth and incomes depended more on manufactured goods.

In recent years, the balance has shifted again, this time towards service occupations – office-based occupations, in which information, knowledge and intelligence play the key role. The emphasis has been transferred from brawn to brain. And in this new economy, computers play a critical, central role.

It is worth asking, however, whether all uses of IT are good. We can see the benefit of using computers, for example, to process bank transactions. Routine administration of, say, parking fines could usefully be delegated to computers, but what about putting computer systems in the role of judges in court? In medicine and health care, there are many obvious useful applications, and there are other applications that make many people uncomfortable.

In the world of art, there are also difficulties: does computer-generated 'art' deserve the name? Can a computer write poetry, make paintings, compose music? And should we judge these 'creations' by the same criteria that we judge work made by humans?

As we said, these questions do not have clear-cut answers. But it is worth thinking about them, because they are becoming increasingly relevant to everyday life.

Participation in the information society

Computers and related technologies are touching our lives from the time our electronic alarm clock wakes us up to the time we use the remote control to turn off our television at night. We can respond as passive consumers of entertainment and advertising, or by becoming active participants in this society.

Participation means exercising choice: choice about what information we get, when we get it, in what form we get it, and how we use it. It means analysing the information for relevance, salience and accuracy. It means deciding what to keep, and what to discard. It means deciding what to produce, what to publish, to whom you publish it, in what form and at what time.

The idea of the ECDL – and the idea of this book – is to enable you to use some of the tools necessary for this kind of active participation in the information society.

However, you already have the most important tools, and you know how to use them: your natural intelligence, your critical faculties, the ability to judge whether something makes sense. No amount of technology can replace these, and you should never be so blinded by technological wizardry that you doubt these innate talents.

Chapter summary: so now you know

Computers are used in business, in industry, in retailing, in the home (both for business and for leisure use), in schools and colleges, in health care, in public administration, and in almost every aspect of everyday life.

It is worthwhile pausing every so often to consider whether every possible application of computers is necessarily a good one. Some things are best left to human beings, exercising human judgement and bringing human values to bear.

And it is also worth considering what this proliferation of computers into every aspect of modern life means for society. There is a danger that society will be divided into those who have access to computers and know how to use them (the 'information-rich'), and those that have no access to computers or don't know how to use them (the 'information-poor').

The ECDL will equip you with the skills to participate in the information society, but you will increasingly need to exercise your critical faculties: remember that all the information available on the Internet, for example, was created and input by someone, somewhere. And that 'someone' could be biased, misguided, prejudiced, or just plain wrong.

Quick quiz: what computers are used for

Answer the following questions about what computers are used for.

Q1	Which of the following statements do you agree with, and why?
A.	Computers are faster than humans at mathematical calculations.
B.	Humans have more reliable long-term memory than computers.
C.	Computers can be programmed to write poetry.
D.	Computers can diagnose and treat medical conditions better than doctors.

Q2	Name some of the ways in which your local supermarket uses computers. Say how each of these affects the management, the staff, and the customers.

Q3	What does the term 'information society' mean?

Q4	Who benefits from the transition to an information society? What problems might arise?

Q5	'The information society will involve gross invasions of personal privacy.' Discuss.

Answers

(Note: Answers to this test should not be treated as absolute. Discuss them with your friends and fellow students. Disagree. Debate.)

1: A – Agree, under most circumstances.
B – Disagree, again under most circumstances – but when a computer fails, it fails completely.
C – Disagree – it may look like poetry, it may sound like poetry ... but is it poetry?
D – Disagree – as long as the condition is complex, human judgement is required.

2: *Checkout scanning* – Makes stock control easier; makes life very tedious for staff; customers are checked out quicker, with fewer errors.
Stock control – Ensures that products are always available, without keeping excess stock; helps staff to identify products that are running low and need to be restocked; customers should benefit from product availability and lower prices.
Office administration – Rostering staff, payroll, accounting; staff benefit from a smooth running organization; customers don't really see the benefit, but they benefit indirectly from the smoother operation.

3: The term is used to describe a society in which most of the value relates to information products and services.

4: Those who benefit are those who are involved with the production of information products and services, or who can afford to consume them. Problems can arise if the benefits are concentrated in the hands of relatively few people, or if significant segments of society are excluded by not having access to or the ability to use the information goods or services.

5: *Discuss.*

Chapter 7: Looking after number one: health and safety

In this chapter

This chapter deals with something even more valuable than hardware, software or data. Something irreplaceable – you.

Just as we have accustomed ourselves to using safety belts and child-proof locks in cars, we need to adopt safe computing practices. Problems can arise in a number of areas, but sensible precautions can help you avoid them.

New skills

At the end of this chapter you should be able to:

- Describe some of the hazards associated with using a computer.
- Describe sensible computing practices.

New word

At the end of this chapter you should be able to explain the following term:

- Repetitive strain injury

Health warning!

In general, computers are clean, quiet and safe to use. You should be aware, however, of a number of potential dangers, and how to avoid them.

Repetitive strain injury (RSI)

If you do any physical activity for a long time without a break, you risk straining or injuring yourself. Using a keyboard or mouse for a prolonged period can lead to the computer user's equivalent of tennis elbow. It can affect the fingers, hands, wrists, elbows, or even the back. The best way to avoid this problem is to take a break every fifteen or twenty minutes to allow your muscles to rest and recuperate. A mouse mat makes it easier to move the mouse without having to apply undue pressure.

Repetitive strain injury (RSI)
Damage to tendons, nerves, muscles and other soft body tissues resulting from repeated physical movements.

You should also make sure your desk and chair are at a suitable height, and that your keyboard is at a comfortable angle (see below).

Eyesight

Extended periods of staring at a PC screen can lead to fatigue and ultimately to eye strain. Avoid locking your eyes into a fixed screen stare. Look away frequently and focus your eyes on objects on the other side of the room or out the window. Make sure that your work area is adequately lit and ventilated. If your screen is positioned so that it reflects light, use a screen filter to reduce the reflection.

Posture

Simple ergonomics are often so obvious that they are overlooked. You should arrange the hardware elements of your PC in such a way as to provide the easiest and most physically comfortable access. Your desk should support your screen at the correct eye level. Your chair should be comfortable and adjustable and provide adequate lumbar support.

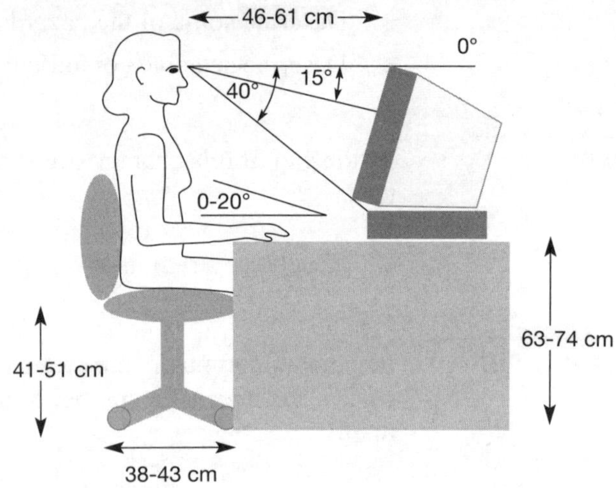

Accidents

Your computer system includes a number of different physical devices that are connected together by cables. The system unit is plugged into the mains electricity socket. On some models the screen takes its electricity supply from the system unit; in others it plugs directly into the mains. The loudspeakers are usually plugged into the mains. The modem is connected to the telephone socket.

That's a lot of cables and wires. Make sure that the cables connecting the components are kept tidy, secure and out of the way, so that there is no danger of tripping over them. Also make sure that the mains electricity sockets you use are capable of handling the load safely:

don't plug all the appliances into a single adaptor or you risk overloading the circuit.

Environmental issues

Information technology has impacted the environment in all kinds of ways, some good and some bad. There are a number of ways in which you can help to reduce the negative impact of computers on the environment:

Reducing power consumption	■ Use the Power Options (found in the Control Panel of your PC) to eliminate any unnecessary power consumption. ■ Turn off your computer and peripherals when you are not using them. ■ Ensure that any computer you buy is Energy Star compliant – Energy Star is an internationally recognized energy efficiency standard.
Printer toner and cartridges	Some charities now collect used printer toner cartridges and pass them on to specialist companies who can remanufacture or refill them. This brings the charities some revenue and reduces the difficulty of disposing of the cartridges.
Saving paper	■ Use recyled paper and reduce the volume of paper that you use. ■ If your printer has a duplex option (can print on both sides of the page), then set that as your default. ■ Recycle unwanted printouts.

Chapter summary: so now you know

While using a computer is generally safe, there are a number of hazards, and all of them are avoidable. Most of them – in particular *repetitive strain injury* and eye-strain – arise only if you use the computer for long periods without a break. Others arise from bad posture or inappropriate positioning of equipment. Cabling also presents a potential source of accidents: you should make sure that cables are tidy and out of the way.

Quick quiz: health and safety

Answer the following questions about health and safety.

Q1	Which of the following is/are true?
A.	It is best to get all your data entry done in the morning, while you are fresh.
B.	You should sit as close to the screen as possible, so that you don't strain your eyes.
C.	If you sit too close to the screen, you can catch a computer virus.
D.	The best way to avoid repetitive strain injury (RSI) is to continue working after you feel pain. That way, your arm muscles develop faster.

Q2	If you are using a computer for a long time, the best kind of chair is:
A.	An office chair that can be adjusted for height.
B.	A dining chair with arm supports.
C.	A comfortable sofa.

Q3	In winter, it is a good idea to cover the system unit with a blanket so that it doesn't get cold.
A.	True.
B.	False.

Q4	State some of the dangers associated with using a computer, and explain how to minimize them.

Answers

1: None are true.

2: A.

3: B.

4: Repetitive strain injury (take regular breaks; choose suitable furniture); eye strain (rest your eyes by looking away from the screen frequently); accidents (make sure cables are secure and tidy; don't overload electricity sockets).

Chapter 8: Keeping your information safe

In this chapter

You might not know it, but there is always someone who wants your data, who wants to access your computer, or who wants to read your e-mail. And you need to take some simple security measures to ensure that what's yours remains yours.

The security risks to our computers and to the intellectual property in our data come from a variety of sources, and we have ways of tackling each of these:

- Theft of data.
- Unauthorized access to data.
- Loss due to systems failure or power failure.
- Loss due to virus attack.

In this chapter we look at some of the information security measures we can take to protect our data against theft or loss. Don't wait until it's too late: ask anyone who has lost data due to a virus – put basic information security measures in place today.

New skills

At the end of this chapter you should be able to describe how to protect your workplace, your software and your data from unauthorized access, loss or damage, and computer viruses.

New words

At the end of this chapter you should be able to explain the following terms:

- Password
- Computer virus
- Backup

Looking after your data

In most computer systems, the data is the most important element. Hardware and software are easily replaced if they break down or are lost or stolen. Data, on the other hand, can represent years of work, and may be irreplaceable.

You have such data in your computer, but you may also have important, private or confidential data in your mobile phone or PDA. If your laptop, mobile phone or PDA is stolen, you might lose your only source of such data (contact details, telephone numbers or diary, for example), the thief might try to profit from information in the confidential files, or use the contact details or telephone numbers.

So it makes sense to protect your data, wherever it is, against the many ways in which it can be lost, corrupted, damaged or abused, accidentally or deliberately.

Security and passwords

Whether you're withdrawing money from an ATM machine, accessing your e-mail, or entering the building where you work, chances are you need to enter some kind of password or PIN number. You can also use passwords to protect your data against theft, corruption and prying eyes by using a system of *user IDs* and *passwords*. Tyically, your user ID identifies you to a computer, while your password is a security device to restrict access. Depending on the application, you can use passwords to decide who can see and who can change the data.

Most applications allow you to choose your own password, and encourage you to change it frequently. Choose a password that is not too obvious – if it is easy to guess, its purpose may be defeated. However, choose a password that is easy to remember. If you forget it, you may not be able to get at your own data, and if you write it down, it may be discovered and used by someone else. The best passwords include both numbers and letters, so that unauthorized persons will find them harder to guess – there are over two billion possibilities for a non-case-sensitive password consisting of six letters and/or numbers.

Password
A string of letters and/or numbers and/or punctuation marks that you use to authenticate your identity to a computer system.

Access rights

You can grant other people *access rights* to your computer, subject to them identifying themselves and entering a valid password. If you work in a networked environment, you can define certain parts of your computer as *shared* – and you can grant access to colleagues on the network.

Backups

Files can be lost or destroyed accidentally. The hard disk may develop problems, a laptop could be stolen, or the whole office might be destroyed by fire. You can protect yourself against these nightmare scenarios by keeping backup copies of all your data files, on floppy disk or another removable medium, and storing them safely at home or at another location. That way, even in the worst situation, you can be up and running very quickly after a disaster.

Backups
Copies of software or files on a second storage medium, such as disk, tape or CD, as a precaution in case the first medium fails.

Save frequently

You should also save your work at regular intervals while you are working. Remember that the computer works on your data in working storage (RAM), which is volatile. If there is a power cut, or if someone accidentally unplugs your PC, everything you have done since you last saved will be lost. It is a good discipline to save after every paragraph of text, or after you have done any complex operation.

Printing, faxing and copying

Whatever the dangers of intrusion or unauthorized access to your computer system, remember that once you commit data to paper, it becomes susceptible to different kinds of security risks. If your data is of a sensitive nature, make sure that your paper security is just as robust as your electronic security.

Viruses

Computer viruses are attempts at sabotage. They are clever but poisonous programs written by malicious software developers and amateur hackers. They attack the integrity of your files, and are designed to transfer easily and stealthily from one computer to another. There are many different types of virus, using different techniques to replicate themselves. Their effects vary from minor irritation (where a message is displayed on your screen, but no files are damaged), through inconvenience (where one or more files are affected), to total disaster (where the entire hard disk is rendered unusable).

Viruses are spread through programs downloaded from the Internet, e-mail attachments and infected floppy disks. To protect yourself against infection, take the following simple precautions:

- Don't open e-mail messages that are from a source you don't recognize.
- Never open an e-mail attachment unless you know what it is. You are more likely to receive viruses from people you know. Many viruses replicate by e-mailing themselves to regular correspondents of the person they attack.
- Never download a file from the Internet unless it is from a reputable organization.
- Always use the most recent virus-scanning software to check any floppy disk that comes from outside your organization.

Computer virus
A program that is loaded on to a computer without the user's knowledge and that damages software or data files in some way. Most viruses have the ability to replicate themselves.

Anti-virus software

Prevention is better than cure: make sure that you install reputable anti-virus software on your computer that will automatically scan your disks (hard drive and floppy disk), and detect and remove any viruses found. In some cases it is possible to *disinfect* files that have been infected – to remove the malicious code from them.

Anti-virus software usually consists of a number of components:

Periodic complete checkup	As a regular housekeeping action, you should perform regular and complete anti-virus checkups on your PC.
E-mail scanning	As far as viruses are concerned, e-mail is a form of first-class travel. Make sure your anti-virus software is set up to check your incoming e-mails and attachments.
Background scanning	Every time you place a floppy disk in your computer, you are opening up your defences. To protect yourself in the course of your normal working day, you need to enable background scanning.

Anti-virus software must be kept up to date – new viruses are being concocted all the time, and the software used to detect and remove them needs to be the very latest. The exercises that follow use VirusScan, a popular virus protection software packages.

Exercise 8.1: Using VirusScan software to scan your system

1) Choose **Start | All Programs | Network Associates | VirusScan.** The *VirusScan* dialog box is then displayed.

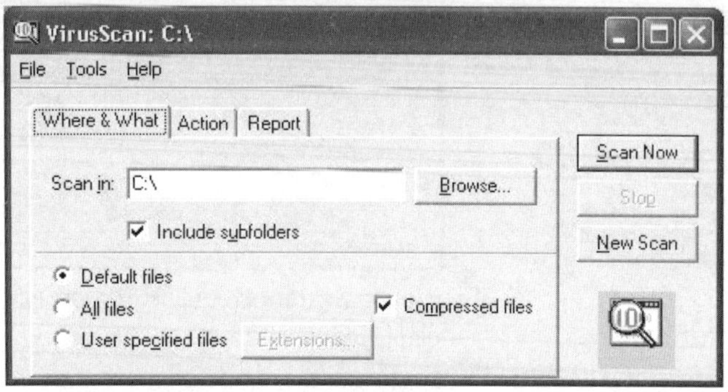

2) Specify what you want to scan – in this example, drive C, *Include Subfolders*, *All Files* and *Compressed Files*.

3) Click **Scan Now** to begin the scanning.

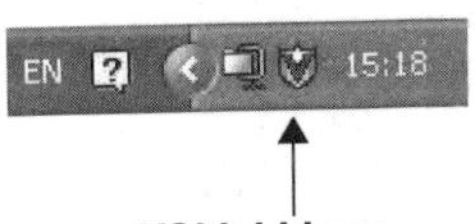

VShield icon

You can configure VirusScan so that it runs in the background all the time, checking your files for virus infection. This utility is called VShield. If VShield is running, you see its icon in the taskbar.

If the VShield icon is not in your taskbar, it means that background scanning is not in place. Follow these steps to set up background scanning with VShield.

Exercise 8.2: Background scanning with VirusScan

1) Choose **Start | All Programs | Network Associates | VirusScan Console**. The *VirusScan Console* dialog box is displayed.

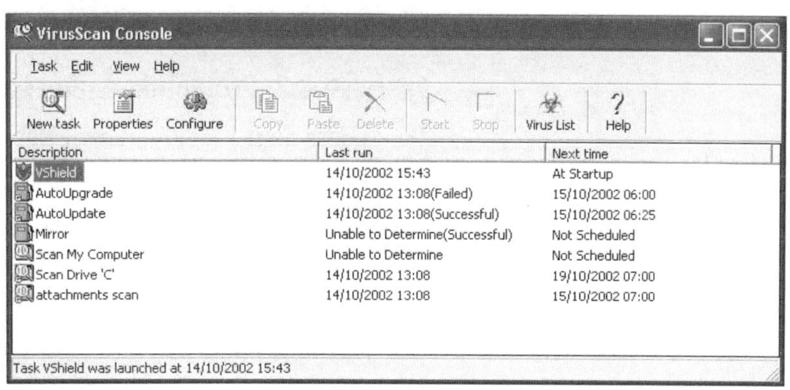

2) Select *VShield* and then choose **Task | Properties**. The *System Scan Status* dialog box is then displayed.

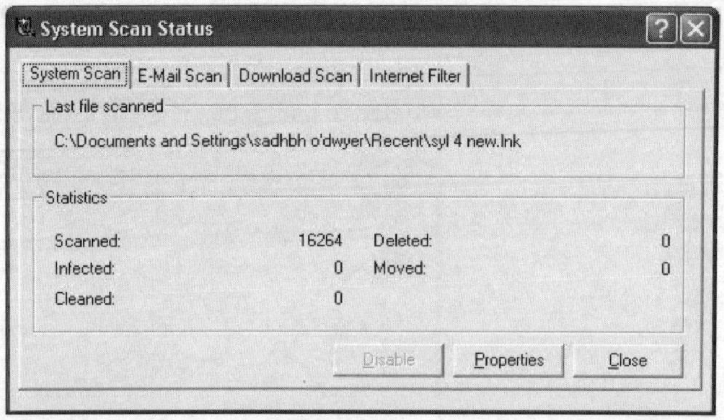

3) On the **System** tab, click *Properties*. The *Scan Properties* dialog box is then displayed.

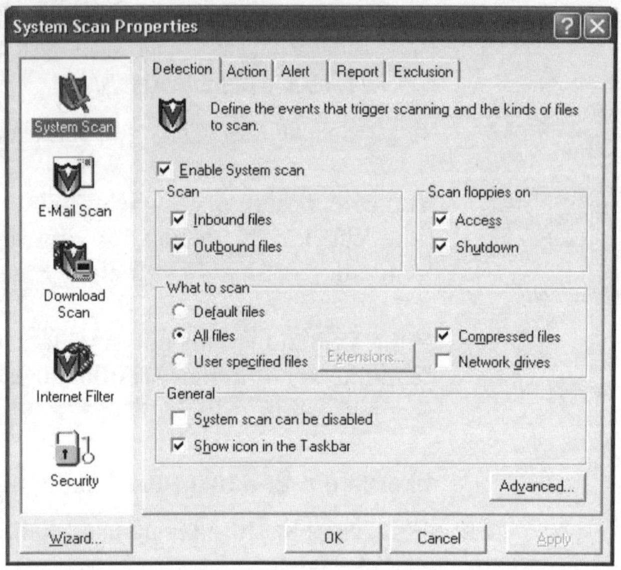

4) Select *Enable System scan* and any other options you want.

Exercise 8.3: Protecting against e-mail-borne viruses

1) Choose **Start | All Programs | Network Associates | VirusScan Console**.
2) Select *VShield* and then choose **Task | Properties**. The *Scan Status* dialog box is then displayed.

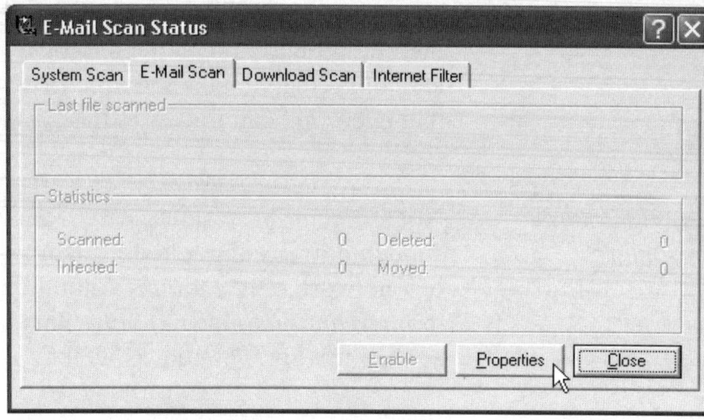

3) On the **E-mail Scan** tab, click *Properties*. The *E-Mail Scan Properties* dialog box is then displayed.

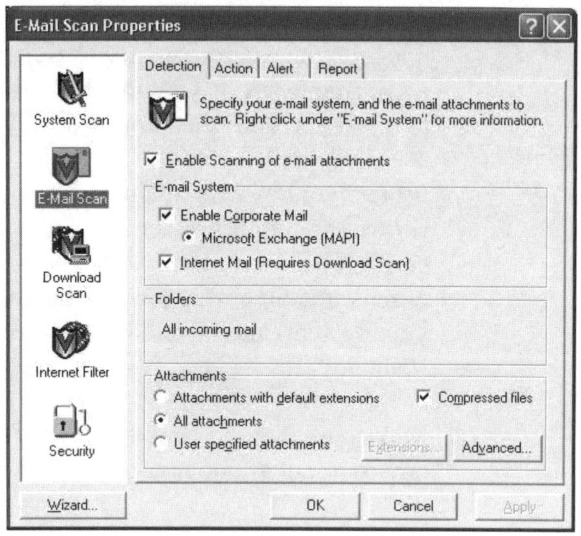

4) Select *Enable Scanning of e-mail attachments* and any other options you want.

Protecting the workplace

There's not much point arming your computer and your sensitive data files with logon verification and password protection if you don't also secure the physical environment where your computers are located. You and your colleagues need to be aware of the potential risks from *visitors*, both invited and uninvited. You only allow authorized users to access the sensitive data on your intranet and extranets – you need to do the same with visitors who arrive at your building, and most companies now use a visitor sign-in and pass system.

Your security is only as strong as its weakest point. Staff members, including teleworkers, need to be aware of their responsibilities in the area of security – take the time to develop simple reporting procedures that everyone can follow in the event of a suspected breach of security.

Protecting against power failure

Not all security breaches arise from malice. Think of the damage that a sudden power cut could do to your organization: unsaved data files, lost network connections. You might consider investing in an *uninterruptible power supply.* This is a device that protects your PC against total power cuts as well as sudden surges or drops in voltage.

Chapter summary: so now you know

Your data is the most valuable part of your computer system: make sure you protect it against loss or damage. Use *user IDs* and *passwords* to restrict who has access to your data. Make sure that you *back up* your data regularly to floppy disk, CD or Zip disk. Save your work frequently as you go – this will protect you from loss of data due to unexpected crashes or power failures.

Protect your system against *computer viruses*. Install *anti-virus software* on your system and make sure it is kept up to date. You can configure your anti-virus software to protect against viruses carried in e-mail attachments. Do a regular and complete anti-virus checkup on your system, and install a background checking utility such as VShield.

Make sure that the general security arrangements in your work environment are not exposing your system to risk.

Quick quiz: keeping your information safe

Answer the following questions about software and data.

Q1	Which of the following would be the best password?
A.	mary
B.	xd7idZ
C.	1234
D.	nottsforest

Q2	What is a computer virus?

Q3	State ways to protect your data against loss or corruption.

Answers

1: B.

2: A malicious program designed to disrupt the normal operation of a computer or corrupt its files.

3: Save frequently; use password protection; make regular backups; use up-to-date anti-virus software.

2

Using a Computer and Managing Files

Module 1 was the tourist guidebook to prepare for your visit to computer land. Module 2 is where you get to meet the natives in the flesh.

And what exotic creatures they are! The citizens are called files. They reside in houses called folders. And folders are built on areas called drives. (Files inside folders, and folders on top of drives – you have learnt quite a lot already!)

And such obedient citizens too! You can change their names, move them to a different location, alter their appearance, get rid of ones you don't want any more – you can even create new ones out of nothing.

But remember this: files are delicate. So treat them with care. You do this by saving them regularly and by making copies of them every so often – just in case something bad happens to the originals. It's always the files you like and need most that seem to disappear the quickest. Better to learn this lesson from the book than from real life in computer land.

Chapter 9: Starting up, clicking around, shutting down

In this chapter

Are you ready to take your first practical steps in computing?

This chapter guides you through the basics. You will learn the correct ways of starting and turning off a computer, discover the meaning of the various little pictures on the Windows screen, and find out how to start and close Word, Excel and other software applications that you will meet in later ECDL modules.

New skills

At the end of this chapter you should be able to:

- Power up and power down a computer.
- Use the **Start** menu to open software applications.
- Switch between open applications.
- Click, double-click, right-click, and drag with the mouse.
- Use the three control buttons at the top right of a window.
- Move, resize and scroll windows.
- Restart a computer when problems occur.

New words

At the end of this chapter you should be able to explain the following terms:

- Powering up/Booting
- Clicking
- Taskbar
- Close button
- Folder
- Application window
- Minimize button
- Double-clicking
- Cursor
- Menu
- Restore button
- Desktop window
- Maximize button
- Dragging
- Pop-up/shortcut menu
- Dialog box

Starting your computer

Before you start your computer, check that it is plugged into the electricity socket. Now, press the button to switch on the computer.

- On some computers, a single button switches on both the computer and the screen.
- Other computers have two buttons: one for the computer itself and a second for the screen.

Your computer will make some humming noises and some messages will flicker on your screen. Don't worry: this is just your computer warming up and checking that everything is in working order.

If you have multiple users set up on your computer, you need to click your user name to begin.

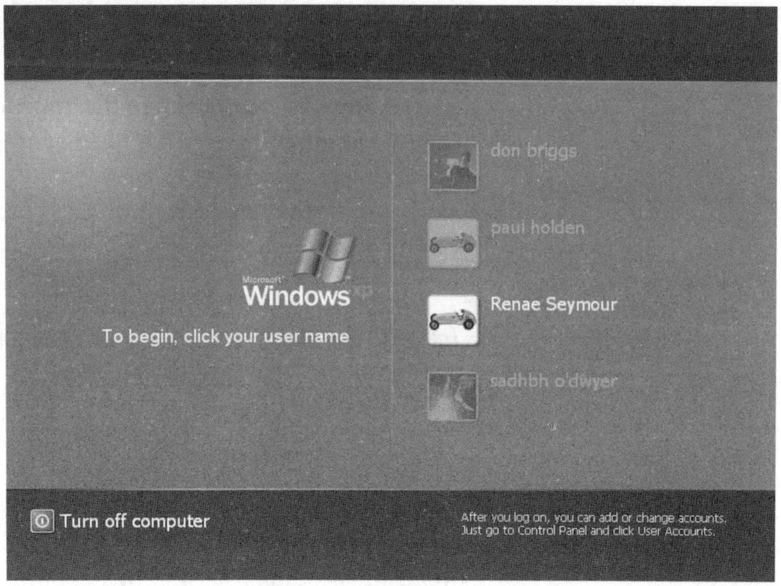

The Windows desktop

The Windows desktop appears – little pictures set against a coloured background. These pictures are called *icons*. Along the bottom of your screen you will see a blue bar, with a button named **Start** in its left corner and a clock in its right. This is called the taskbar.

A sample Windows desktop

The little pictures are called icons

The blue bar along the bottom is called the taskbar

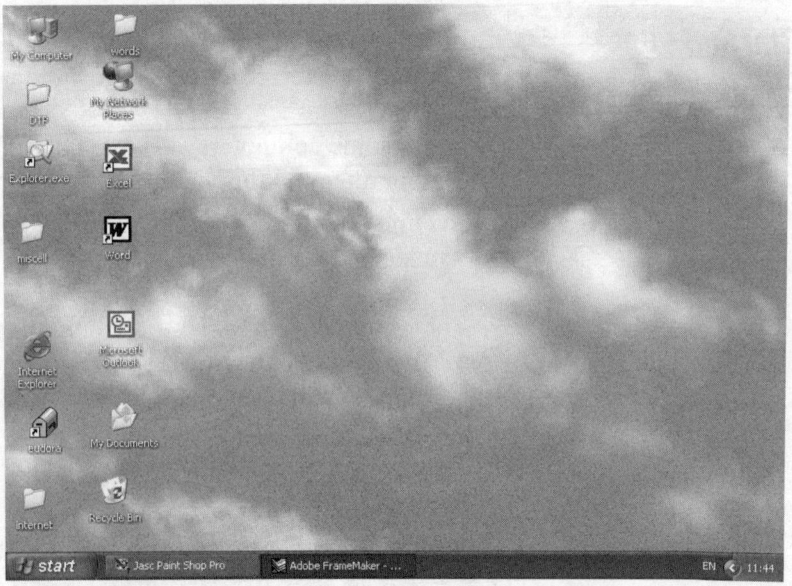

You will learn more about icons and the taskbar later. You will also discover how you can change the appearance of your Windows desktop to suit your working needs and personal taste.

Congratulations. You have now powered up your computer.

Powering up/booting
The technical terms for starting a computer and displaying the Windows desktop on the screen. You don't 'switch on' a computer; you 'power up' or 'boot' a computer.

Starting applications

Software applications are useful programs such as Microsoft Word, Excel, Access and PowerPoint that enable you to create documents, spreadsheets, databases and presentations. You will learn a lot about these in Modules 3, 4, 5 and 6 of this ECDL course. Your first step in working with applications is to learn how to start them.

Using the mouse

Place your hand over the mouse and move it around your (physical) desktop. As you move the mouse, the cursor moves around the Windows desktop, allowing you to point to the item you want to work with.

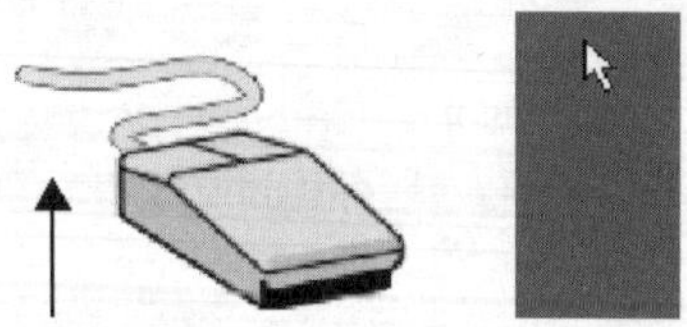

To move the cursor up the screen, move the mouse in the up direction

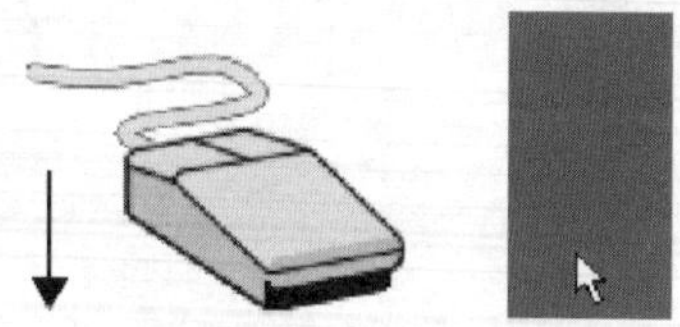

To move the cursor down the screen, move the mouse in the down direction.

Cursor
A symbol, usually an arrow, that you move around the computer screen by moving the mouse across your (physical) desktop.

The Start button

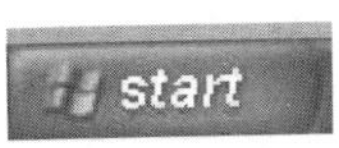

Move the cursor down to the bottom-left of your screen so that it is over the **Start** button. Now, press down the left mouse button and then release it. You don't need to hold down the button for more than a second. This is called *clicking*.

Clicking with the mouse
This means briefly holding down the left mouse button. By clicking an item on the screen, you tell your computer: 'I want to select this item.'

Your mouse-click causes the **Start** button to display the start-up menu. This includes the applications that you use most often. Move the cursor up over the item called **All Programs**. As you do, another menu appears to its right listing all the programs installed on your computer. On this second menu or sub-menu, move the cursor over the item called **Microsoft Word** and click on it. This opens the Microsoft Word application.

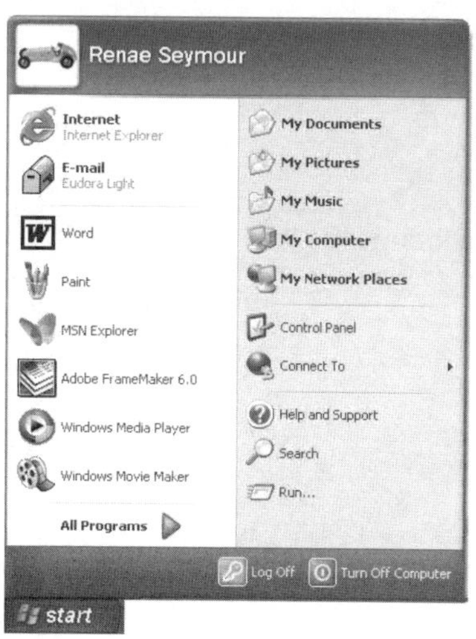

Menu
A list of items displayed on the computer screen that allows you to work with applications and files, and get more information. Some menus offer sub-menus of further options.

Multi-tasking with Windows

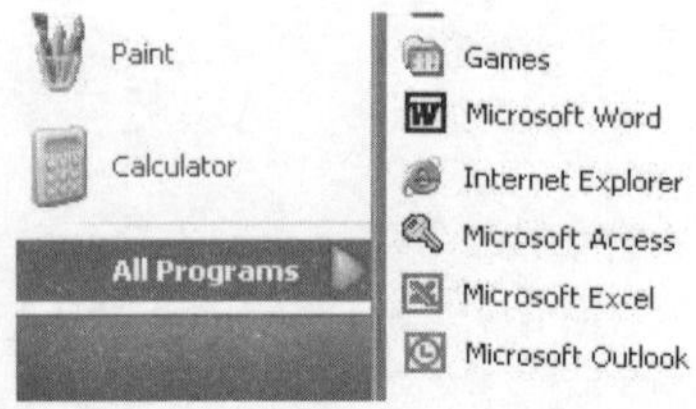

You can open more than one application at one time – this is called multi-tasking. Move the cursor back down over the **Start** button and click it. Next, move the cursor over the menu item called **All Programs**. On the next menu displayed, move the cursor over the item called **Microsoft Excel** and click it. You have now started a second application.

Why stop at two applications? Exercise 9.1 takes you through the steps of starting a third application, **Notepad**.

Exercise 9.1: Opening the Notepad application

1) Click the **Start** button.
2) Click **Start | All Programs** to display the start-up menu.
3) Click **Start | All Programs | Accessories** to display the **Accessories** sub-menu.
4) Click **Start | All Programs | Accessories | Notepad** to open the **Notepad** application.

Congratulations. You now have three applications open on your screen.

The expression **Start | All Programs** is a shorthand way of saying 'Open the start-up menu and select the option named All Programs.' And **Start | All Programs | Accessories | Notepad** means: 'Open the start-up menu and select the option called **All Programs**. Next, on the **All Programs menu**, choose the option named **Accessories**, and from the **Accessories** menu, choose **Notepad**'.

Although you can have lots of applications open at one time, only one can be in the foreground; the others wait behind it in the background. How do you tell Windows which application you want to bring to the foreground?

Take a look at the taskbar along the bottom of your Windows desktop. Notice how it displays the names of all your open applications.

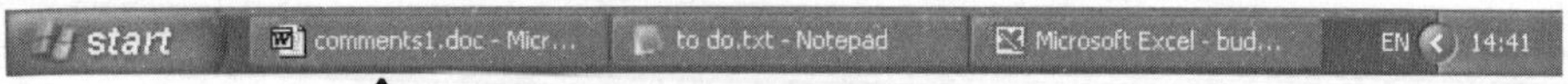

Click an application's name to display it in the foreground

To select one, for example Word, click Word (shown on the left in the above figure). Or, to select Excel, click Excel. You use the taskbar to switch between open applications and display a particular one in the foreground.

Taskbar
*A horizontal bar across the bottom of the Windows desktop that displays the **Start** button, plus the names of any open applications. Click an application's name to display it in the foreground.*

You will find Windows' ability to open several applications at one time very useful. For example, you could have the following open on your computer: a Word letter (see ECDL Module 3), an Excel spreadsheet (Module 4), and an e-mail (Module 7). As you will also learn, you can copy items from one application to another.

Multi-tasking
The ability of Windows to have several applications and files open at the same time.

The control buttons

Using the taskbar, switch to Notepad. Notice the three buttons at the top right? These are called control buttons. You can use these to perform various actions, as the following exercises show.

Exercise 9.2: Using the Close button to close Notepad

Close button

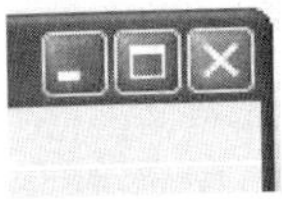

1) Is Notepad in the foreground? If not, click its name on the taskbar.
2) Move the mouse to the top-right of the Notepad screen, and right-click the button that contains an X.

   You have closed the Notepad application by clicking on one of the control buttons – the **Close** button.

Close button
A button at the top right of an application window that, if selected, closes the application.

In the next two exercises you will learn how to use the **Restore** and **Maximize** control buttons.

Exercise 9.3: Using the Restore button to reduce a window's size

1) Is Excel in the foreground? If not, click its name on the taskbar.
2) Move the mouse to the top-right of the Excel screen and click the **Restore** button. This reduces the size of the Excel screen, so that it no longer fills the entire Windows desktop.
3) Using the taskbar, switch to Word. Click Word's **Restore** button.

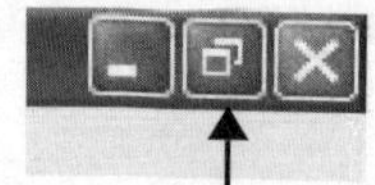

Restore button

You should now be able to see both applications on your screen, with the currently selected application (Word) overlapping the other (Excel). Each application appears within its own *window*.

Overlapping application windows of Microsoft Word and Microsoft Excel

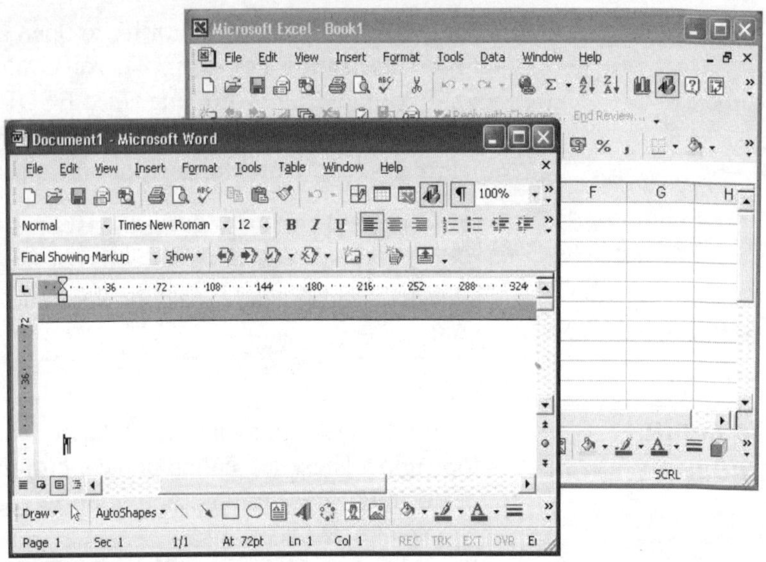

Restore button
*A button beside the **Close** button that reduces the size of the application screen area.*

To bring Excel to the foreground, click any part of its window. You do not need to click its name on the taskbar. The Excel window now overlaps the Word window. To return the Word window to the foreground, click any part of it.

Application window
A rectangular area that can display a file or files from an application. All application windows, regardless of their content, share common components and features.

When you click the **Restore** button to reduce the size of a window, the **Restore** button disappears and is replaced by another button called the **Maximize** button.

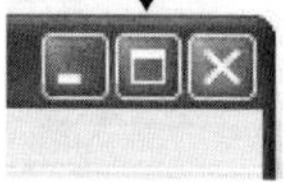

Clicking on this button reverses the effect of **Restore**: that is, it increases the size of the window so that it again fills the Windows desktop.

Maximize button
A button that increases the size of a previously reduced window so that it fills the entire Windows desktop.

One control button remains: the **Minimize** button. Exercise 9.4 provides an example of the **Minimize** button in use.

Exercise 9.4: Shrinking a window with the Minimize button

1) Is Word in the foreground? If not, click any part of its window.
2) Click Word's **Minimize** button.

   This 'shrinks' Word so that it appears on the taskbar and nowhere else.
3) Click any part of the Excel window to select it, and then click its **Minimize** button.

   Both applications now appear only on the taskbar. To display Word and Excel again, click their names on the taskbar.

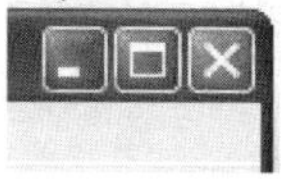

Minimize button
A button that shrinks an application window to remove it from the desktop to the taskbar only.

You will find the **Close**, **Restore** or **Maximize**, and **Minimize** buttons at the top-right corner of every window.

Moving windows with the title bar

Another feature that every window shares is a title bar – the identifying bar that runs across the top of the window. You use the title bar to move a window to a different position on the desktop as follows:

- Click on the window's title bar – but do not release the mouse button.
- With your finger still on the mouse button, move the mouse to reposition the window.
- When you have positioned the window where you want it, release the mouse button.

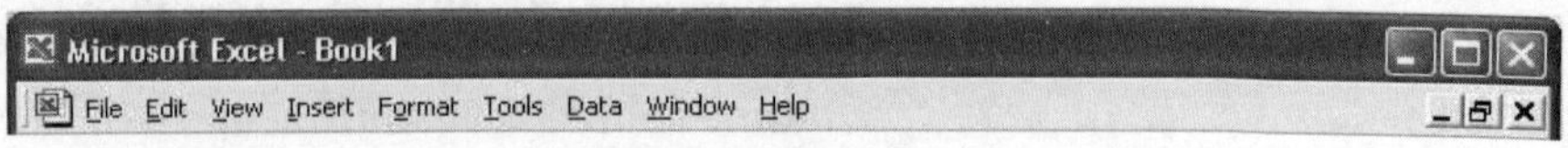

Click on the title bar and drag to reposition the window

This series of click–move–release actions is called *dragging*.

Dragging with the mouse
Moving a selected item on the desktop by clicking on it with the left mouse button, and holding down the button as you move the item.

Using the **Close** box, close Excel. You now have only the Word application open on your desktop.

Working with desktop windows

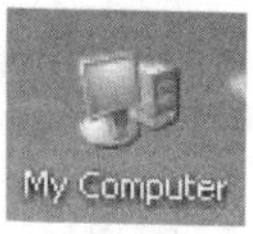

On the Windows desktop, move your cursor over the icon (little picture) named **My Computer** and click. Notice that the icon is highlighted. Your single click selects it – but does not perform any action on it. **My Computer** is also available from the **Start** menu.

Now, click anywhere on the desktop to deselect the **My Computer** icon.

Once again, move the cursor over the **My Computer** icon. Now, click once and then, very quickly, click a second time on **My Computer**. This two-click action (called double-clicking) opens the **My Computer** icon so that you can see its contents.

A sample My Computer desktop window

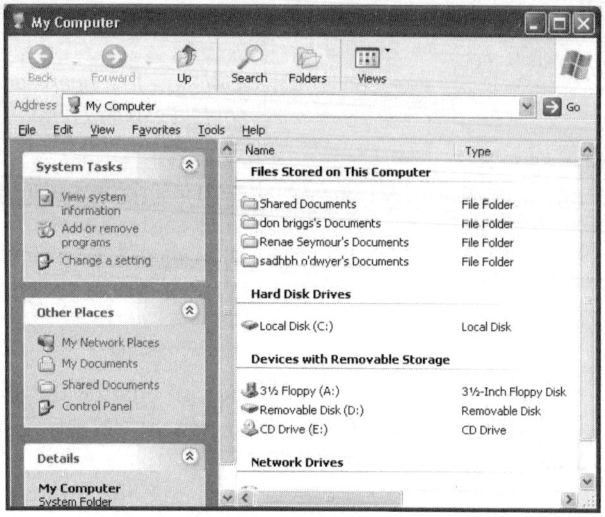

Double-clicking with the mouse
To tell Windows to perform an action on a selected item, press the left mouse button quickly twice.

Click on the **Close** box at the top right of the My Computer window to close it. My Computer is an example of a desktop folder – an icon that represents a number of items grouped together.

Except for My Computer, every other folder on your desktop looks like a 'real' folder. Here are some examples.

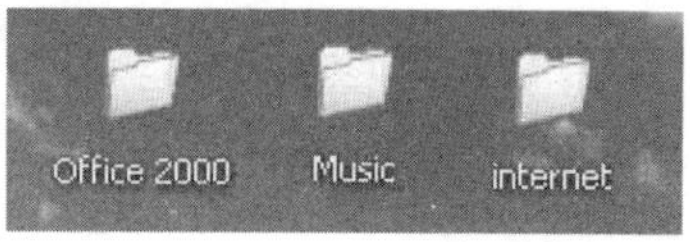

Folder
An icon on the Windows desktop that contains within it one or more icons representing applications, files or physical devices.

A window that opens when a folder is double-clicked is called a desktop window. Desktop windows look and can be used in a similar way to applications windows – so much so that the term 'window' is commonly used to describe either type.

Desktop window
A window that opens when a folder is double-clicked. Desktop windows contain similar components and features to application windows.

Practise opening folders on your desktop by double-clicking on them. Some folders, you may find, contain subfolders. (A subfolder is no different to a folder; it's just a folder that happens to be inside another folder.) Close any folders you open by using their **Close** box.

Changing the shape and size of a window

You can change the shape and size of an application or desktop window by selecting it and then dragging any of its four sides.

To change the width of a window, click its left or right edge. The cursor changes to a double-headed arrow. Then drag with the mouse. As you drag the window, its edges change to dashed lines.

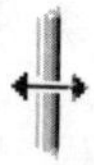

To make a window taller or shorter, click its top or bottom edge. Again, the cursor changes to a double-headed arrow. Drag the edge with the mouse.

To change both window height and width, click in the bottom right corner of the window. The cursor changes to a double-headed, diagonal arrow. Drag the corner with the mouse.

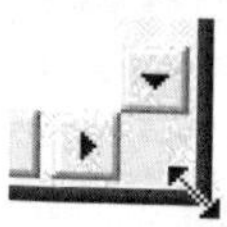

Practise your window resizing skills with the My Computer folder window.

Scrolling a window

Sometimes a window may not be large enough to display all its contents. In such cases, scroll bars appear on the right and/or along the bottom of the window. To view a different part of the window:

- The *position* of the scroll box in relation to the scroll bar indicates which area of the window you are viewing. When the scroll box is in the middle of the scroll bar, for example, the window is positioned halfway through its contents.
- The *size* of the scroll box indicates how much of the window's contents you can see at one time. For example, if the scroll box is half the length of the scroll bar, you can see half the contents.

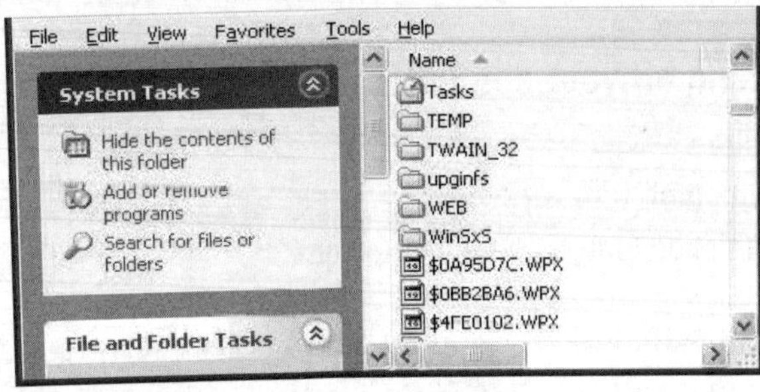

Click the arrow to scroll one line at a time

Drag the scroll box to scroll the window directly

Click the scroll bar to scroll one window-full at a time

Right-clicking and pop-up menus

In addition to clicking (to select), dragging (to move) and double-clicking (to perform an action), Windows offers a fourth kind of mouse movement: right-clicking.

To right-click something is to click it once with the right mouse button.

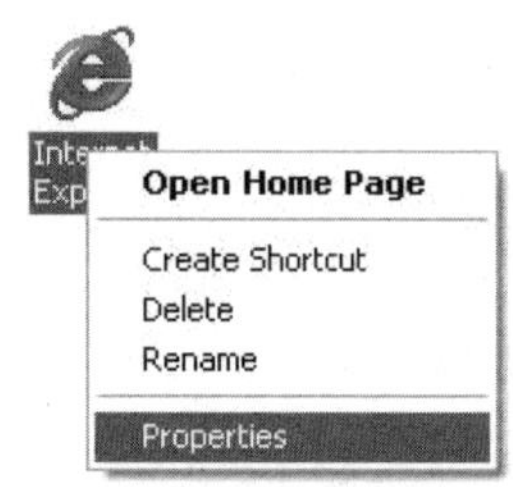

Right-clicking on anything – whether a folder, application or file icon, or even the desktop – displays a pop-up menu. The menu options shown depend on the item you right-click.

Right-clicking with the mouse
Briefly holding down the right mouse button. Windows responds by displaying a pop-up menu of options.

One option that a right-click always displays is called **Properties**. Select this option from the pop-up menu to view details about the item.

Practise right-clicking on icons and on the desktop background. In each case, click the **Properties** option on the pop-up menu.

Pop-up or shortcut menu
A small menu that appears temporarily, typically when you right-click an item. When you select an option from a pop-up menu, the menu usually disappears.

Switching off

The opposite of powering up a computer is powering down or turning it off. Never just switch off your computer – you may lose unsaved information and damage your computer's hard disk drive (thereby losing saved information too).

To turn off your computer properly, follow the steps in Exercise 9.5.

Exercise 9.5: Turning off your computer

1) Click the **Start** button.
2) Click **Turn Off Computer**.
3) Click the **Turn Off** option to turn off the computer.

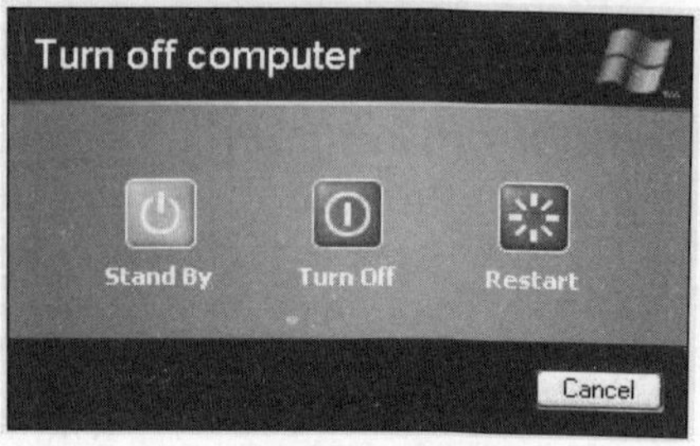

Some computers can switch themselves off automatically. On others, you need to press the on/off button after you see the message: 'It is now safe to turn off your computer'.

Now, power up your computer again – *but wait at least twenty seconds*. Otherwise, you may damage your computer's hard disk drive.

Restarting your computer

The **Restart** command has the same effect as powering down the computer and powering it up again very quickly – but without the risk of damage to the computer hardware.

Exercise 9.6: Restarting your computer

1) Click **Start | Turn off computer**.
2) Click the **Restart** command to restart the computer.

When your computer hangs

Sometimes, an application open on a computer may 'hang' or 'freeze'. This means that it does not respond to the pressing of any keys or any clicking with the mouse. On other occasions, Windows itself may fail to respond to any user action, with the result that the entire computer hangs. What do you do? This topic provides the answers.

Application problems

When a particular application fails to respond to any action you take, press the following three keys simultaneously: **Ctrl**, **Alt** and **Delete**. Most computer users do this by holding down the **Ctrl** and **Alt** keys with the fingers of their left hand, and then pressing the **Delete** key with a finger of their right.

The shorthand way of writing 'Press the **Ctrl**, **Alt** and **Delete** keys simultaneously' is **Ctrl+Alt+Delete**.

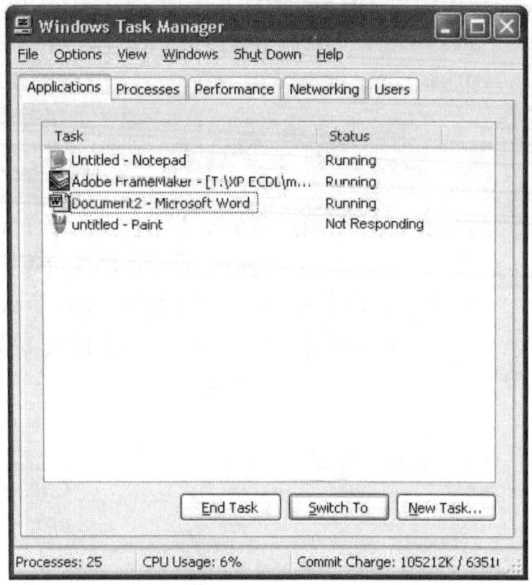

You are then shown a window similar to this one, which lists all the applications currently open on your computer. The frozen application is indicated by the message 'Not Responding':

Click on the frozen application, and then click the **End Task** button. You can then reopen the application in the usual way.

Windows problems

If Windows hangs and your computer freezes, press **Ctrl+Alt+Delete** *twice* in quick succession. This has the effect of powering down the computer and powering it up again very quickly – but without the risk of damage to the computer hardware. In fact, it has the same effect as selecting the **Restart** command from the *Turn off computer* window.

After improper shutdowns

If you power down your computer in any way other than using **Start | Turn off computer**, Windows will automatically check your file system when you next power up the computer. This checks your hard disk drive(s) for errors. Windows starts as normal once the check is completed.

Dialog boxes

The *Close Program* window described in the previous topic is an example of a Windows *dialog box*. You will meet many such dialog boxes when you use Windows Explorer, Word, Excel and other applications.

Dialog box

A rectangular box that Windows displays when it needs further information before it can carry out a command, or when it needs to provide you with more information.

Dialog box components

Dialog boxes typically contain some or all of the following components:

- **Command button:** A button that performs or cancels an action. **OK** and **Cancel** are the two most common buttons. Here are some more:

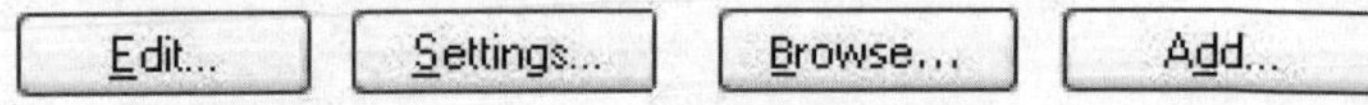

- **Drop-down list box:** A list of options that you can select from. Click the arrow on its right to view all the choices available. The example below is taken from the *Font* dialog box in Word – it shows the underline style choices available to you. You click to select the one you require.

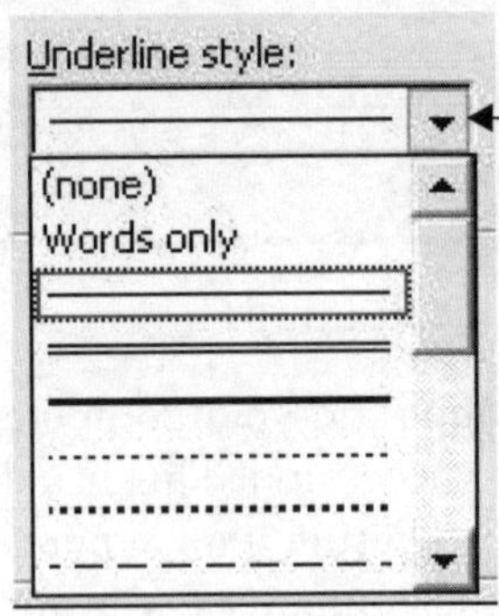

Click here to view the options on the drop-down list

- **Option buttons:** A group of *round buttons* indicating alternative choices. The example below is from the *Print* dialog box.

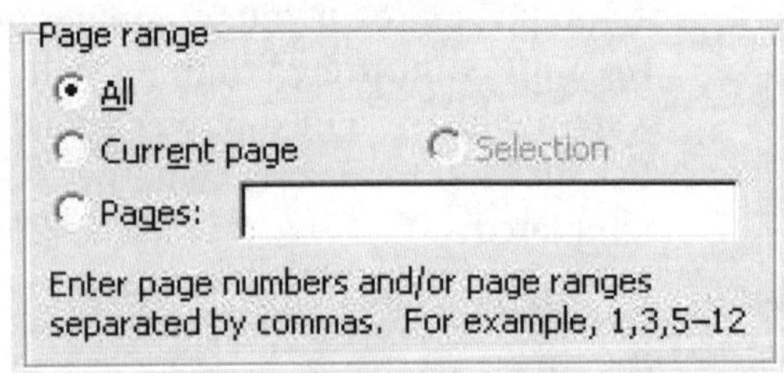

- **Check boxes:** A set of *square boxes* that you can select or clear (deselect) to turn options on or off. More than one check box can be selected at one time.

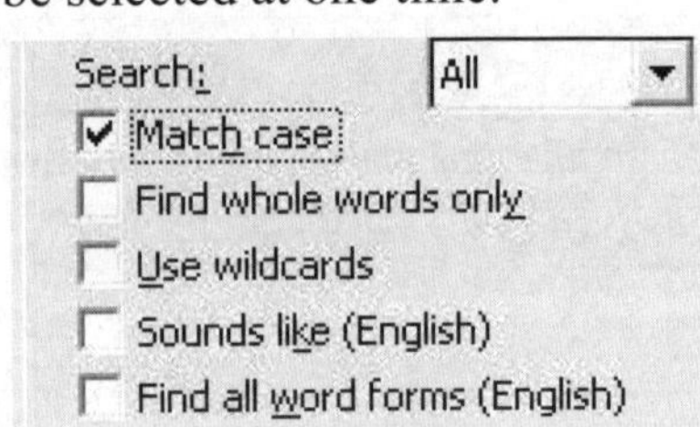

Default options

Most dialog boxes offer preselected or default settings. Unless you choose otherwise, the default settings decide which options and actions are performed. When you choose to print a Word document, for example, the default option is to print all pages in the document. To accept the defaults, simply press the **Enter** key.

Chapter summary: so now you know

To power up a computer, switch on the system box. If the screen has a separate on/off switch, switch this on as well. Windows starts and displays icons on the *desktop*.

Use the **Start | All Programs** menu to start software applications such as Word or Excel, and the *taskbar* to switch between open applications.

The *control buttons* at the top left of a window enable you to *restore* (decrease the size of), *maximize*, *minimize* and *close* that window. To *move* a window across the desktop, drag it by its *title bar*. To resize a window, drag its edges.

Icons on the desktop represent drives, applications, files and folders.

Clicking an item selects it. *Double-clicking* performs an action on it. *Right-clicking* displays a small *pop-up menu* of relevant options.

Where a window is too small to display all its contents, *scroll* to view different parts of that window. When Windows needs further information before carrying out an action, it displays a *dialog box*.

Always use the *turn off* procedure when switching off your computer. To restart a 'hung' application, press **Ctrl+Alt+Delete**. Press the three keys twice in quick succession if Windows itself hangs.

Quick quiz: starting up, clicking around, shutting down

Circle the correct answer to each of the following multiple-choice questions about starting up, clicking around and shutting down.

Q1	To open an application such as Notepad you choose ...
A.	Start | All Programs | Microsoft Office Tools.
B.	Start | All Programs | Accessories | Notepad.
C.	Start | Control Panel | Add or Remove Programs.
D.	Start | My Documents.

Q2	To shrink a window you press ...
A.	The **Minimize** button.
B.	The **Maximize** button.
C.	The **Close** button.
D.	The **Restore** button.

Q3	How do you shut down your computer?
A.	Click the **Start** button and click **Log Off**. Click the **Log Off** option to shut down the computer.
B.	Click the **Start** button and click **Turn Off Computer**. Click the **Stand By** option to shut down the computer.
C.	Click the **Start** button and click **Turn Off Computer**. Click the **Restart** option to shut down the computer.
D.	Click the **Start** button and click **Turn Off Computer**. Click the **Turn Off** option to shut down the computer.

Q4	If your computer hangs you should press ...
A.	**Ctrl+Alt+Enter**.
B.	**Ctrl+Alt+Esc**.
C.	**Ctrl+Alt+Delete**.
D.	**Ctrl+Alt+Insert**.

Q5	To make a window bigger you press ...
A.	The **Minimize** button.
B.	The **Maximize** button.
C.	The **Close** button.
D.	The **Restore** button.

Answers

1: B, **2:** A, **3:** D, **4:** C, **5:** B.

Chapter 10: Exploring your computer

In this chapter

Ever wondered what information was stored on your computer? Or on someone else's computer? After reading this chapter, you will be able to answer questions such as: what drives are installed on a computer? what are the names of its folders and files? and what processor chip and how much memory does it have?

You will also discover how to find a particular file when you don't know its name, and how to use the Windows online help system.

New skills

At the end of this chapter you should be able to:

- Distinguish between files, folders and drives.
- Use My Computer to view drives, folders and files.
- Change the order in which folders and files are displayed in My Computer.
- Explain file name extensions and recognize the most common types.
- Search for folders and files.
- Use the Windows Help and Support Center.

New words

At the end of this chapter you should be able to explain the following terms:

- File
- Folder
- Subfolder
- Drive
- My Computer
- Recycle Bin
- File name extension
- Windows Search
- Wildcard
- Properties

How your computer stores information

If you throw all your belongings together in a heap on the floor, you will have a difficult time finding anything. It is much easier to sort your valuables beforehand, dividing them neatly between shelves or drawers. When you need to find something, you know exactly where it is.

As with your belongings, so with information stored on a computer. In this chapter you will learn about files, folders and drives – the three levels at which information is organized on a computer.

Files

All the information and applications on your computer are stored in individual files. Think of a file as the computer's basic unit of storage.

File
The computer's basic unit of information storage. Everything on a computer is stored in a file of one type or another.

Folders

A computer may contain many thousands of files. To make it easier for you (and the computer) to find and keep track of files, you can group files together in folders.

Folder
A group of files. Files grouped into folders are easier to find and work with.

A folder can also contain one or more folders, thereby forming a tree-like hierarchy.

Subfolder
A folder located within another folder.

In this example, the folder named Word Documents contains two subfolders: Letters and Reports.

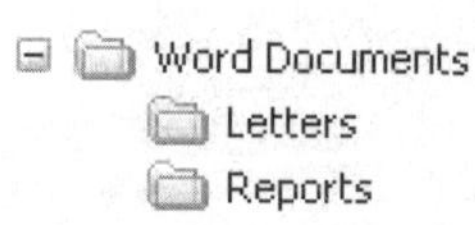

Another advantage of placing files in a folder or subfolder is that you can work with the files as a group. For example, you can copy or delete all files in a folder in a single operation.

Drives

A drive is a device that stores folders and files. Typical PCs have a hard disk drive named the C: drive. On some computers, the hard disk is divided ('partitioned') into two – a C: drive and a D: drive.

The next available letter after the hard disk is given to the CD-ROM drive. This can be D: or E:, depending on whether your hard drive is partitioned. The floppy disk drive is named the A: drive.

Drive
A physical storage device for holding files and folders. Typically, A: is the floppy disk drive, C: the hard disk and D: the CD-ROM drive.

Where is the B: drive? Early personal computers had just two floppy disk drives, A: and B:. The advent of hard disks (C: drives) eliminated the need for a second floppy drive.

Using My Computer

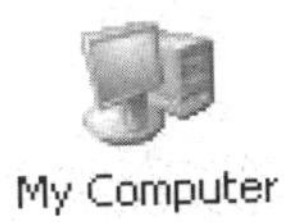

Take a look at your Windows desktop. Can you see a folder named My Computer? If not, resize or minimize any open windows until the My Computer icon is visible. Alternatively, choose **Start | My Computer**.

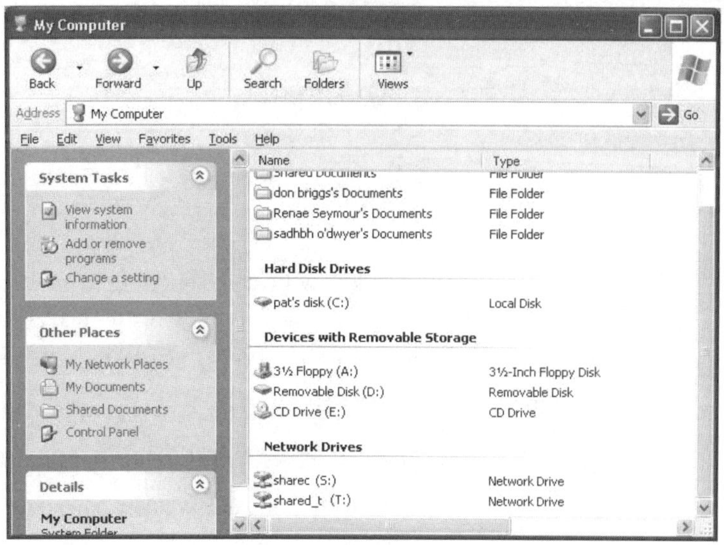

My Computer displays icons showing the hard disk, floppy disk and CD-ROM drives on your PC. .

My Computer
A desktop folder in which you view almost everything on your computer, including drive contents, and computer, printer and Internet settings.

Exploring drives with My Computer

What disk drives does your computer contain? Find out in Exercise 10.1.

Exercise 10.1: Exploring drives with My Computer

1) Double-click the **My Computer** icon on the Windows desktop. In the example below, you can see six drives: a floppy disk drive (A:), a hard disk drive (C:), a CD-ROM drive (E:), a removable drive (D:), and two network drives (S: and T:).

   What drives are on your computer?

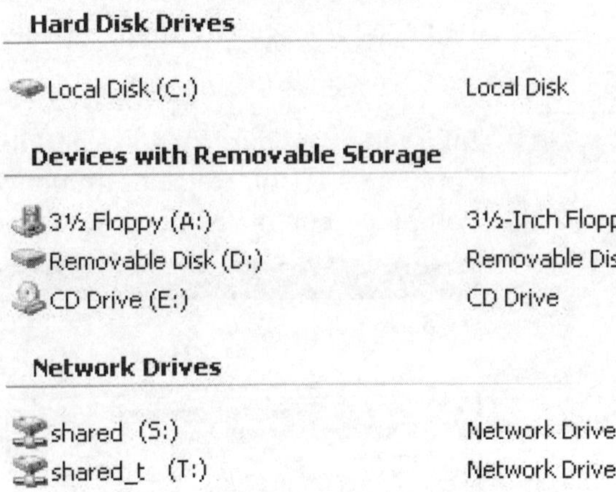

Now you know how to discover what drives are installed on your PC – or on any other PC you encounter. In Exercise 10.2, you will learn how to view the properties or basic information about an installed drive.

Exercise 10.2: Viewing drive properties

1) With the My Computer window open, right-click the C: drive icon.

   On the pop-up menu displayed, click the last option, **Properties**. You are now shown a dialog box similar to the one here.

   You can see how much space is occupied on your hard disk, and how much is still free. You can also use this dialog box to give a name ('label') to your hard disk drive.

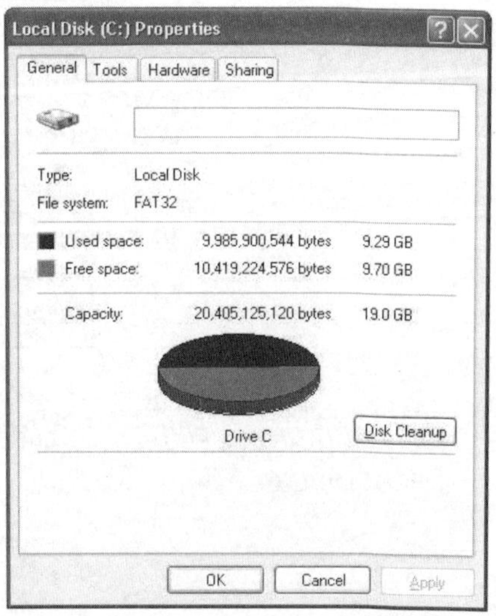

2) When finished, click **OK**.

   As further practice, perform this exercise on your other drives.

Leave the My Computer window open on your desktop. Note that an icon for the My Computer window is displayed on your taskbar.

Exploring folders and files with My Computer

You can use My Computer to display the folders and files contained on any drive of your computer. Just double-click a drive icon – for example, the C: icon – and My Computer opens a second window showing the selected drive's contents.

My Computer can display folders and files within a drive in a number of ways. Click the **View** menu to display the options available.

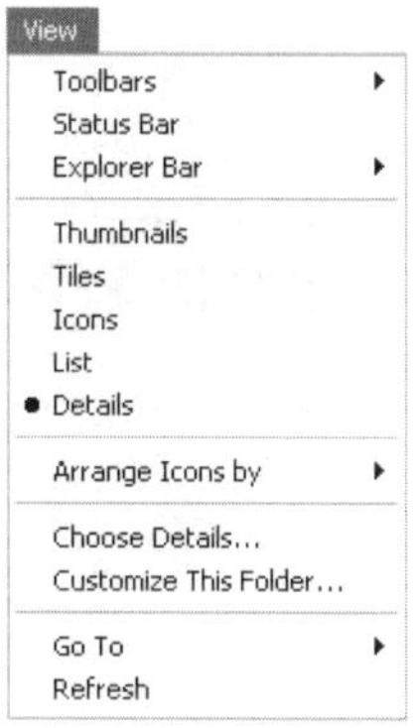

For the exercises in this book, choose **View | Details**. This viewing option provides the most information about your drive's contents.

Along the bottom of the My Computer window, in the Status Bar, you can see the number of items in the window, and the disk space that they occupy. Can't see the Status Bar or toolbar? Choose **View | Status Bar**.

Sorting folders and files

You can change the order in which My Computer displays your folders and files. By default, folders and files are listed alphabetically by name. To view them in order of size, for example, click **Total Size** in the bar across the top of the window – you might need to scroll right to see this. Alternatively, you can sort them by **Type** or **Date Modified**.

Exercise 10.3: Sorting folders and files in My Computer

1) Use My Computer to display the contents of your C: drive.

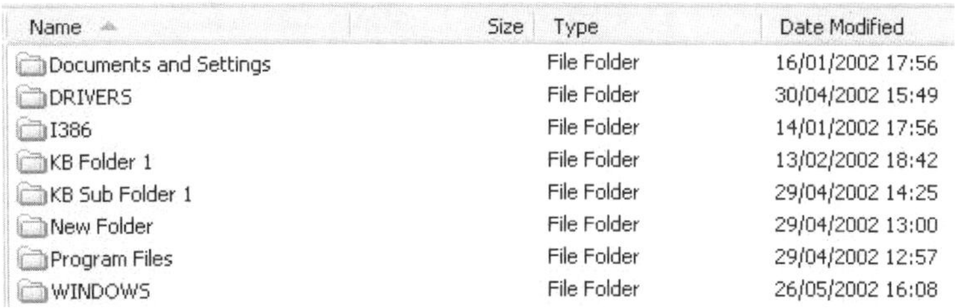

Name	Size	Type	Date Modified
Documents and Settings		File Folder	16/01/2002 17:56
DRIVERS		File Folder	30/04/2002 15:49
I386		File Folder	14/01/2002 17:56
KB Folder 1		File Folder	13/02/2002 18:42
KB Sub Folder 1		File Folder	29/04/2002 14:25
New Folder		File Folder	29/04/2002 13:00
Program Files		File Folder	29/04/2002 12:57
WINDOWS		File Folder	26/05/2002 16:08

2) Click **Name** in the window heading. My Computer sorts the folders and files in reverse alphabetical order. Click again on **Name** to resort them in their original order.

3) Click **Size** in the window heading. My Computer sorts the folders and files in order of decreasing size, with the largest shown first. Click **Size** again to resort them so that the smallest files are listed first.
4) Click **Date Modified** in the window heading. My Computer sorts the folders and files so that the most recently created or changed are shown first. Click **Date Modified** again to resort them so that the oldest are listed first.

You can make any column narrower or wider by clicking the boundary line and holding down the mouse button. The cursor changes to a cross-hair. Next, drag the boundary left or right.

File name extensions and icons

A file, as stated at the beginning of this chapter, is the basic unit of information storage on a computer. When you look at files in My Computer windows, you can see that different files are represented by different icons.

The icon that Windows uses to represent a file depends on the file's three-letter file name extension. Application files have the extension .exe or .dll. A file name extension is separated from the remainder of the file name by a full stop.

When you name and save a file (for example, a Word document within Microsoft Word), Windows automatically attaches the appropriate three-letter extension to that file.

File name extension
A three-letter addition to a file name that indicates the type of information stored in the file. A full stop separates the extension from the remainder of the file name.

Here are some common file name extensions and their icons:

Application file type	Extension	Icon
Microsoft Word document	.doc	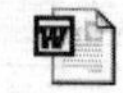
Microsoft Excel spreadsheet	.xls	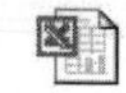
Microsoft PowerPoint presentation	.ppt	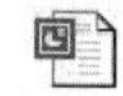
Adobe Acrobat document	.pdf	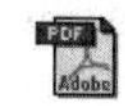
Plain text file	.txt	
Online help file	.hlp	
Temporary file	.tmp	
Web page file	.htm	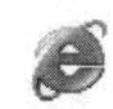
Bitmap image file	.bmp	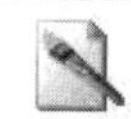
Video/audio files	.mpg	
	.wmv	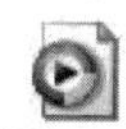

Searching for folders and files

The quickest way to locate a folder or file on your (or anyone else's) computer is to use the Windows Search feature. Most Search actions are based on all or part of the folder or file name. But Search also allows you to perform sophisticated searches based on date ranges, content or size.

To find a folder or file on a drive, choose the **Start | Search** command.

You can then specify what you want to search for: pictures, documents, or all files, and so on. As you progress with your search, you progressively narrow down the criteria for your search.

The content of the next dialog box you see depends on what you are looking for – in this example, the dialog box on page 100 shows what you see when you are looking for a document: here you can specify how long it is since you last modified the file, and you can include all or part of the document's name.

The following example shows a search for a document called report.doc. Click **Search**, and the results are then displayed.

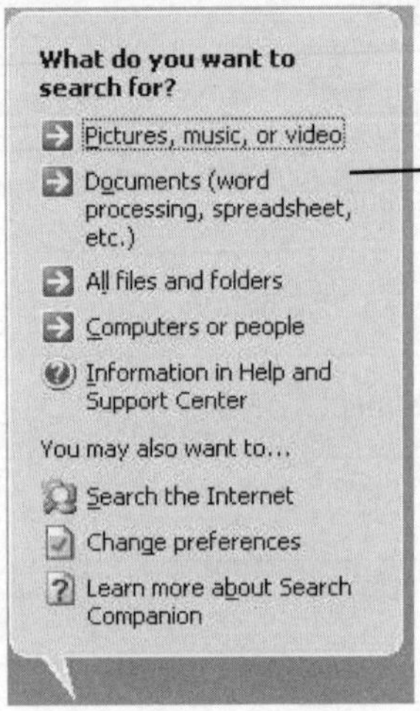

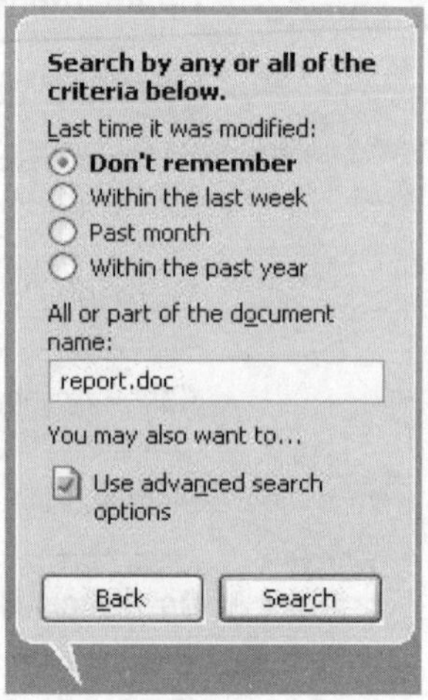

Wildcard searches

When searching for folders and files, you can use the asterisk character (*) as a *wildcard* – this means that it can represent one or several characters. If you cannot remember the full name of the item you want to search for, type the wildcard character in place of the missing letter(s).

For instance, report*.doc finds all files that begin with 'report' and have the .doc extension. Examples might be report3.doc, reportnew.doc and report-a.doc.

If you search for *.xls, Windows finds all files on your computer that have the Microsoft Excel file name extension. Try it and see!

Wildcard
The asterisk character (*) that can stand for one or a combination of characters when performing a search for a folder or file.

Exercise 10.4: Finding all Word documents using a wildcard

1) Choose **Start | Search | All files or folders**.
2) In the *All or part of the file name* box, type *.doc.
3) In the *Look in* box, select the C: drive.
4) Click **Search**.

Windows displays all files ending in .doc in a My Computer-style window. You can open any listed file by double-clicking it. To close the *Search Results* dialog box, click the **Close** button in the top-right corner.

Date-based searches

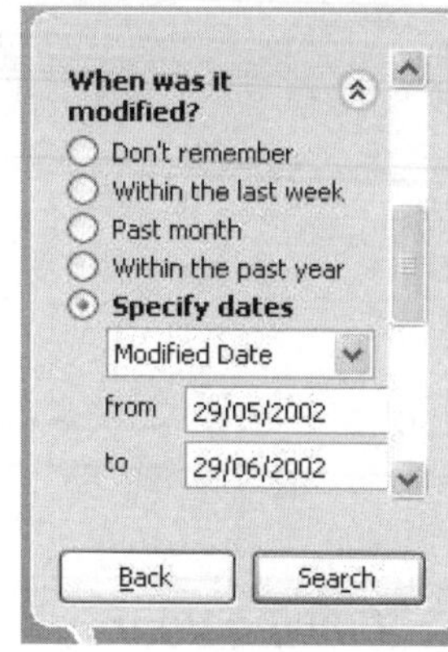

You can use the *When was it modified?* options to limit your search to only those folders or files created or changed between certain dates, or during a specified number of days or months.

Choose the **Specify Dates** check box and then specify the date or date range.

You can also search for the files by the date they were created or the date they were last accessed: click on the drop-down arrow to the right of Files Modified to access the Files Created and Files Last Accessed options.

Content-based searches

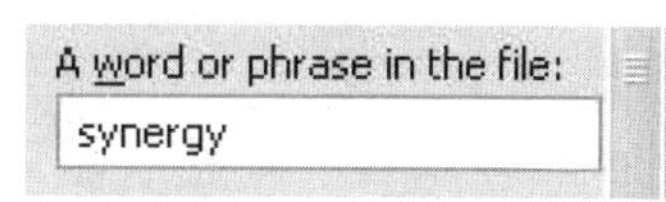

If you have absolutely no idea of the name of the item that you are looking for, or when it was created or modified, you can search by content.

In the *Containing text* box, type in one or more words you think might be contained within the files you are searching for.

The Recycle Bin

Windows stores files that you delete in an area it calls the Recycle Bin. Can you see its icon on your Windows desktop? If not, resize or minimize some open windows.

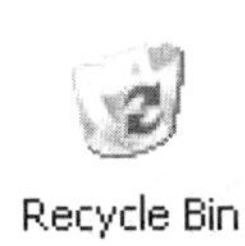

Bin containing files marked for deletion

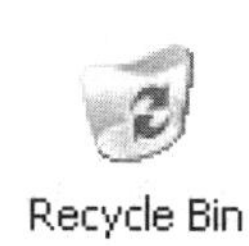

Empty bin

If you delete a file or a folder in error, double-click the **Recycle Bin** icon, click the file to select it, and choose **File | Restore**.

You can delete a file or a folder from the Recycle Bin by selecting it and then choosing **File | Delete**. Or you can empty the Recycle Bin entirely by choosing **Empty the Recycle Bin**. Once you delete an item from the Recycle Bin, you cannot subsequently restore it.

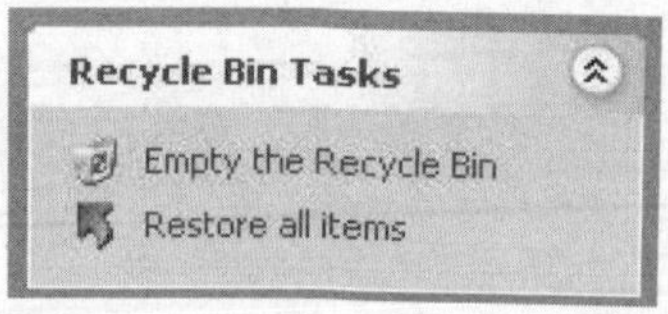

Emptying your bin increases the free space available on your C: drive.

Recycle Bin
A storage area where Windows holds deleted files. You can retrieve items that you deleted in error, or empty the bin to free more disk space.

Viewing your system information

What are your computer's specifications? To find out, follow these steps:

Choose **Start | Control Panel | Performance and Maintenance**. Then pick the **See basic information about your computer** option.

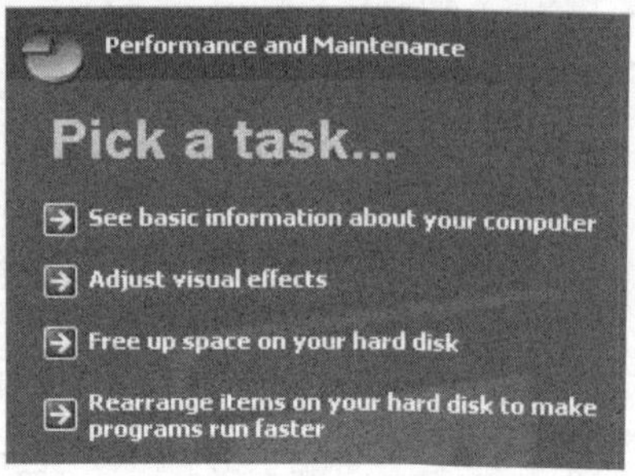

You are now shown the *System Properties* dialog box. Its **General** tab displays your computer's operating system type, processor type and amount of RAM.

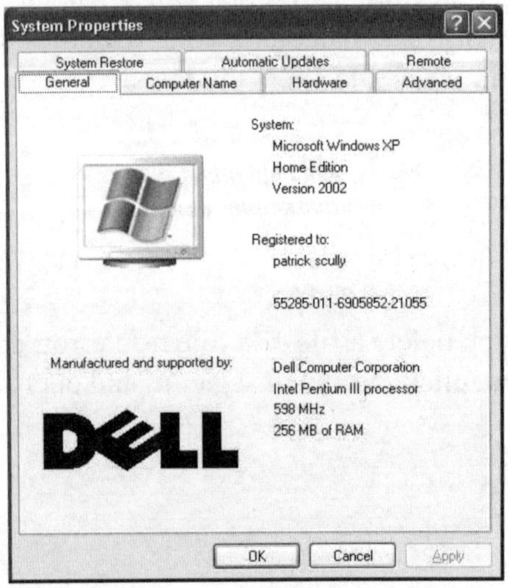

Help and Support Center

The Windows Help and Support Center gives you access to a wide range of online help information on all aspects of using Windows.

- The 'help' means that the information is there to assist you understand and use the operating system.
- The 'online' means that the material is presented on the computer screen rather than as a traditional printed manual.

You can search through and read online help by choosing **Start | Help and Support**. Alternatively, when using My Computer, choose **Help | Help and Support Center**. In both cases, you now see the Help and Support home page.

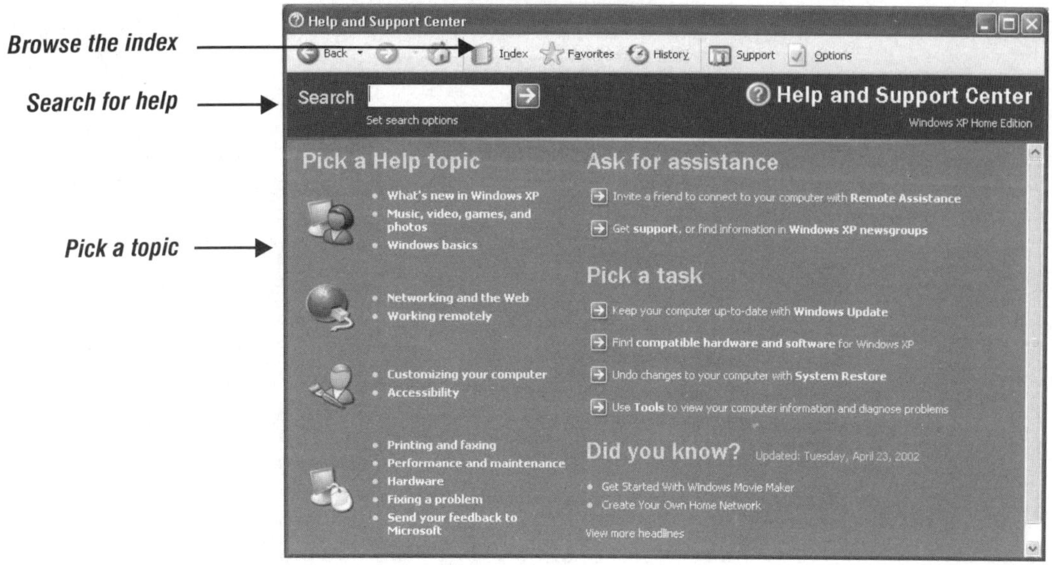

You can then access the help you need in the following ways:

- By searching for the topic you are interested in.
- By using the Help Index.
- By picking one of the topics on the Help and Support Center home page.

Searching for help

Enter the word or phrase that you want to search for in the *Search* field. The search results are then displayed, and you can choose the most appropriate article for your needs.

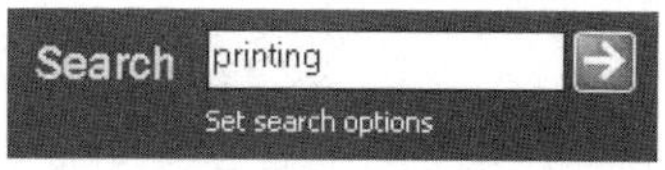

Use the **Back** and **Forward** buttons on the top-left of the toolbar to navigate through the Help pages.

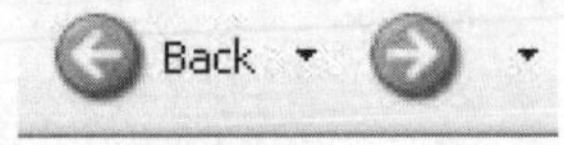

Using the Help Index

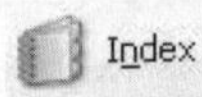

Click the **Index** button to view a table of contents or index of the help contents. Type in the keyword that you want to search for, or browse through the list.

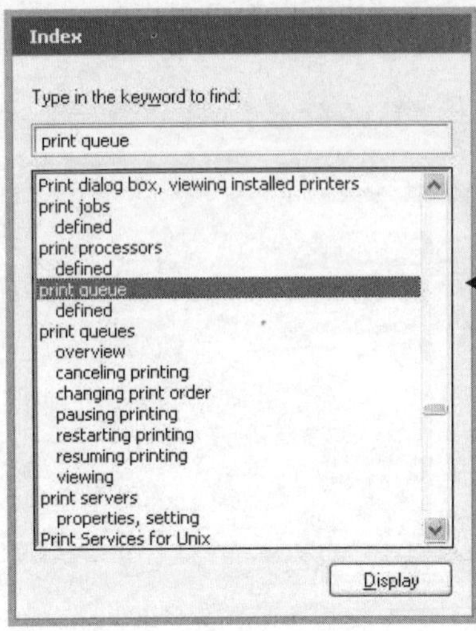

Double-click the article you want to read

Picking a topic

The Help and Support Center window offers you a selection of the most popular help topics, plus a range of support options that you can choose. These include access to support via the Internet, access to updates for your operating system, and diagnostic and maintenance tools.

Chapter summary: so now you know

A *file* is the computer's basic unit of information storage. A folder is a group of files (and perhaps subfolders too). Grouping files into folders makes them easier to find and work with.

A *drive* is a physical storage device for holding files and folders. Typically, A: is the floppy drive, C: the hard disk and D: the CD-ROM drive.

Use *My Computer* to view the hierarchy of folders on your computer, and to see all the files and subfolders in any selected folder.

To display the details of a drive, folder, file or range of files, right-click and select the *Properties* option.

Windows adds a three-letter *file name extension* to every file to indicate the file type. A full stop (.) separates the extension from the remainder of the file name. Common file name extensions are *.doc* (Word), *.xls* (Excel), *.mdb* (Access) and *.ppt* (PowerPoint).

To find a file on a drive, choose the **Start | Search | All files or folders** command. Windows allows you to use *wildcards* to represent missing letters. You can also restrict your search to files of a certain date or date range, or to files that contain the specified keywords.

The Windows *Help and Support Center* provides a comprehensive and searchable guide to the system's features and procedures.

Quick quiz: exploring your computer

Circle the correct answer to each of the following multiple-choice questions about exploring your computer.

Q1	You can explore the drives on your PC by clicking My Computer.
A.	True.
B.	False.

Q2	How do you view the remaining space on your hard disk?
A.	Double-click **My Computer**. Right-click on the floppy disk drive (A:) and select **Properties** from the menu displayed.
B.	Double-click **My Computer**. Right-click on the hard disk drive (C:) and select **Explore** from the menu displayed.
C.	Double-click **My Computer**. Right-click on the floppy disk drive (A:) and select **Explore** from the menu displayed.
D.	Double-click **My Computer**. Right-click on the hard disk drive (C:) and select **Properties** from the menu displayed.

Q3	How do you use My Computer to sort by size in the C: drive?
A.	Double-click **My Computer**, and click the A: drive. Click **Size** in the window heading.
B.	Double-click **My Computer**, and click the C: drive. Click **Type** in the window heading.
C.	Double-click **My Computer**, and click the C: drive. Click **Size** in the window heading.
D.	Double-click **My Computer**, and click the A: drive. Click **Date Modified** in the window heading.

Q4	How do you find a Word document using a wildcard?
A.	Choose **Start | Search | All Files or Folders**. Type *.xls in the *All or part of the document name* box and select the drive. Click **Search**.
B.	Choose **Start | Search | All Files or Folders**. Type *.doc in the *All or part of the document name* box and select the drive. Click **Search**.
C.	Choose **Start | Search | All Files or Folders**. Type *.ppt in the *All or part of the document name* box and select the drive. Click **Search**.
D.	Choose **Start | Search | All Files or Folders**. Type *.txt in the *All or part of the document name* box and select the drive. Click **Search**.

Q5	You can restore files from the Recycle Bin.
A.	True.
B.	False.

Answers

1: A, **2:** D, **3:** C, **4:** B, **5:** A.

Chapter 11: Working with folders and files

In this chapter

In the previous chapter you used My Computer to explore the folders and files on your PC. Now, you will learn how to perform actions on folders and files – how to create, name and rename, move and copy, and delete and undelete them – using Windows Explorer.

New skills

At the end of this chapter you should be able to:

- Create, save, rename and delete folders.
- Create, save, rename and delete files.
- Move and copy folders and files.
- Select several folders or files, whether adjacent or non-adjacent.

New words

At the end of this chapter you should be able to explain the following terms:

- Windows Explorer
- Drop-down menu
- File association
- Clipboard
- Toolbar
- Compression (zipping)

About Windows Explorer

Think of a Windows application and names such as Word, Excel and PowerPoint are probably the first to come to mind. But included with the Windows operating system is another, powerful application. It's called Windows Explorer and you can use it to:

- View the folders on your computer, and the hierarchy of subfolders and files within any folder.
- Perform operations on various folders and files, such as renaming, copying, moving and deleting.

You can open Windows Explorer in two ways:

- Choose **Start | All Programs | Accessories | Windows Explorer**, -or-
- Right-click the **Start** button, and click **Explore.**

The two panes of Windows Explorer

Windows Explorer differs from My Computer in that its window is divided into left and right sub-windows called panes.

- You use the *left pane* to select a particular drive or folder. You cannot view files in the left pane.
- You use the *right pane* to view the folders and files in the drive or folder selected in the left pane.

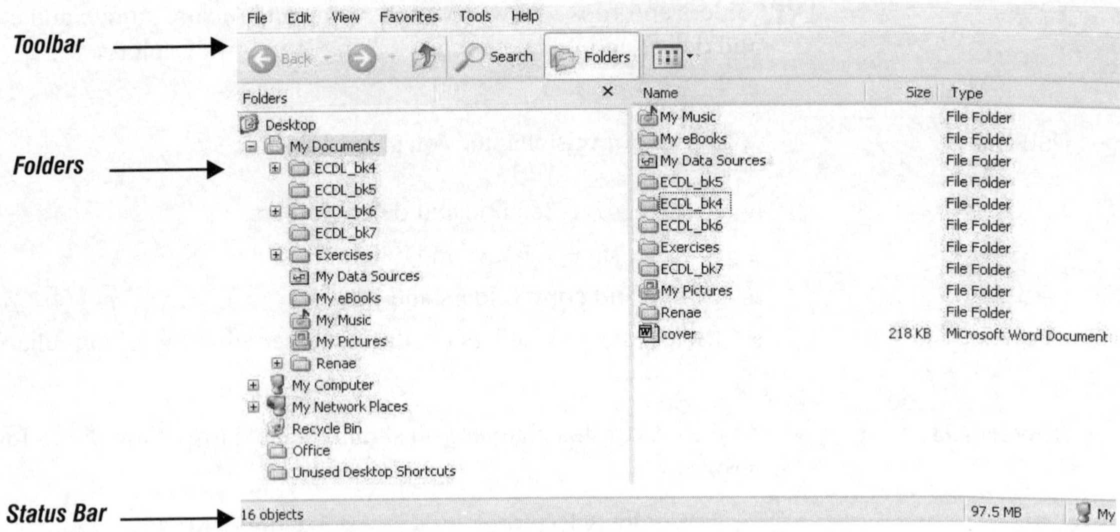

In the Windows Explorer left pane, you can see a hierarchical diagram of your computer's storage space:

- **Top level:** The Windows Desktop.
- **Second level:** System folders such as My Documents, Recycle Bin, and any user-created desktop folders.
- **Third level:** User-created desktop folders.

The right pane looks and works in a similar way to My Computer.

- Click on any drive in the left pane to display, in the right pane, the folders and files stored on that drive.
- Double-click on any folder in the right pane to view any subfolders and files contained within that folder.

Windows Explorer
A Windows application for viewing the hierarchy of folders and files, and for performing such actions as renaming, moving and deleting.

Viewing options

As with My Computer, Windows Explorer offers a number of options that let you control how you view your drives, folders and files. Click the **Views** button on the toolbar and choose **Details** (or **View | Details**). This option provides the most information in the smallest screen space.

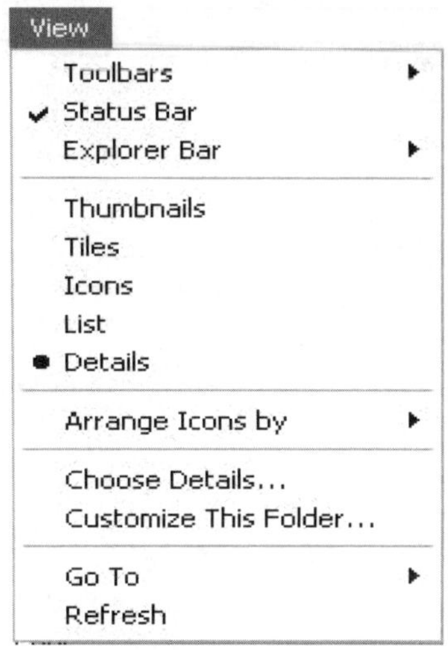

Along the bottom of the Windows Explorer window, in the Status Bar, you can see the number of items in the currently open folder (the one whose contents are shown in the right pane), the disk space occupied by the folder's contents, and the remaining free space on the drive.

Can't see the Status Bar or Toolbar? Choose **View**, and click the relevant options on the **View** menu to display them.

Follow Exercise 11.1 to practise your Windows Explorer skills.

Exercise 11.1: Viewing the Windows folder

1) If Windows Explorer is not already open, open it now.
2) In the left pane, click the C: drive icon.
3) In the right pane, scroll down until you see the Windows folder. Double-click it.

   You can now see the folders and files stored within it. Folders are listed first. Scroll down through the Windows folder to see what files are within it.

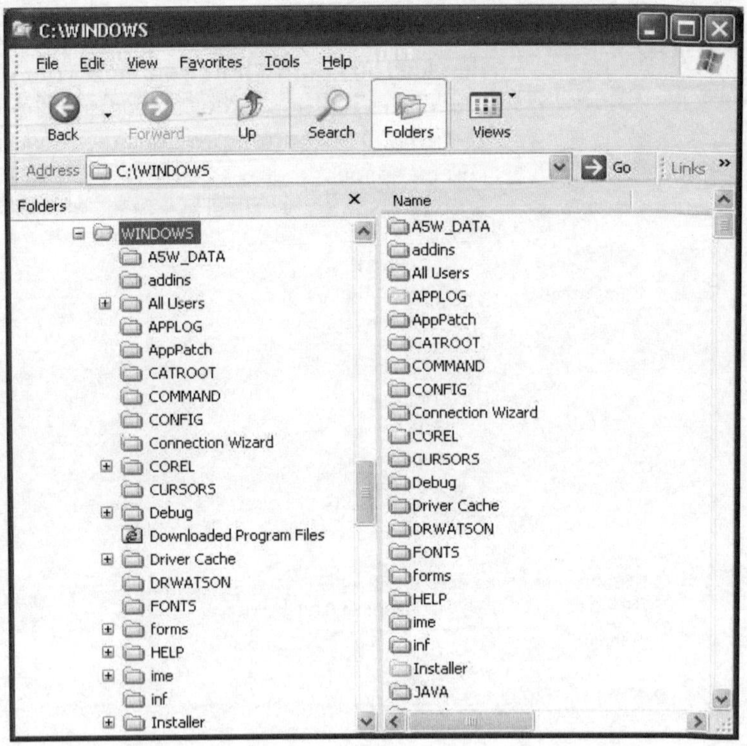

Explorer's plus and minus signs

In Windows Explorer, a folder without a plus (+) or a minus (-) sign in front of it is either empty or has only files inside it.

A folder with a plus sign has folders inside it, and perhaps files too. To open it, click on the folder name or the plus sign.

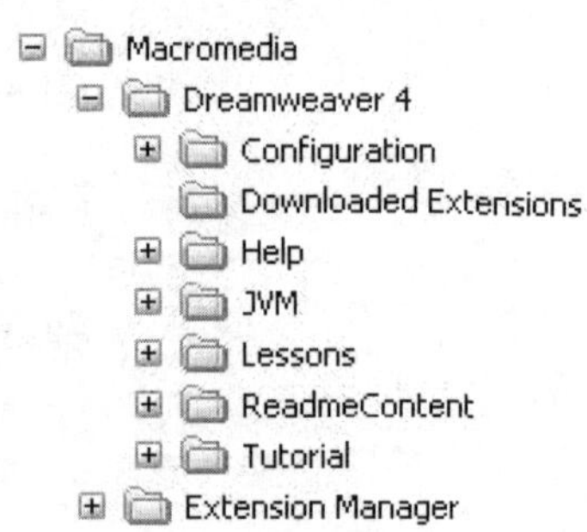

A minus sign in front of a folder indicates that the folder is open – its subfolders and files are currently displayed on the screen.

Click on a plus sign to display ('expand') or a minus sign to hide ('collapse') your view of a folder.

Working with folders

In the next few exercises you will use Windows Explorer to create folders and subfolders, and to rename, delete and restore (undelete) folders.

Exercise 11.2: Creating two new folders

1) In the left pane of the Windows Explorer window, click on the C: drive.

2) Choose **File | New | Folder**. Window displays a new folder at the bottom of the list in the right pane. It gives it the default name of 'New Folder'.

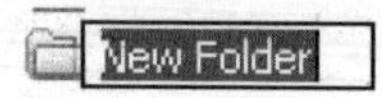

3) Type a name for your new folder. If your initials are KB, for example, call it KB Folder 1.

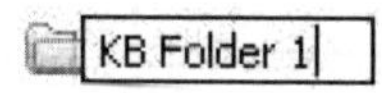

4) Repeat steps 1, 2 and 3. Name your second folder (say) KB Folder 2.

Exercise 11.3: Creating a subfolder

1) In the right pane of the Windows Explorer window, double-click on the first folder that you created in Exercise 11.2 – in this example, the folder named KB Folder 1.
2) Choose **File | New | Folder**. Windows displays a new subfolder.
3) Type a name for your new folder. If your initials are KB, for example, call it KB subfolder 1.

Changing a folder's name

You can change a folder's name at any stage. Exercise 11.4 shows you how.

Exercise 11.4: Changing a folder's name

1) Right-click on one of your new folders to display a pop-up menu.
2) Choose **Rename**.
3) Type a new folder name. For example, KB New Folder.
   Well done! You have given your folder a new name.

Deleting a folder

Suppose that you don't need a folder any more? Here is how to delete an unwanted folder.

Exercise 11.5: Deleting a folder

1) In the left pane of the Windows Explorer window, click on the first folder that you created in Exercise 11.2. It should contain the subfolder you created in Exercise 11.3.
2) In the left pane of the Windows Explorer window, right-click on the subfolder. From the pop-up menu, select **Delete.**

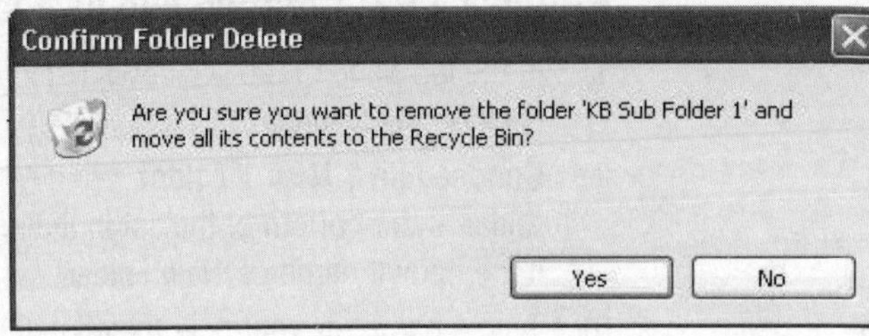

3) Click **Yes** to confirm that you want to remove the folder.

The folder is deleted, as are any subfolders and files it may have contained.

Looking at a folder's properties

To display information about a folder in My Computer – for example, the Windows folder – right-click it. From the pop-up menu displayed, click the **Properties** option. You are shown a dialog box similar to the one here.

Among other details, this tells you the number of folders and files within the Windows folder.

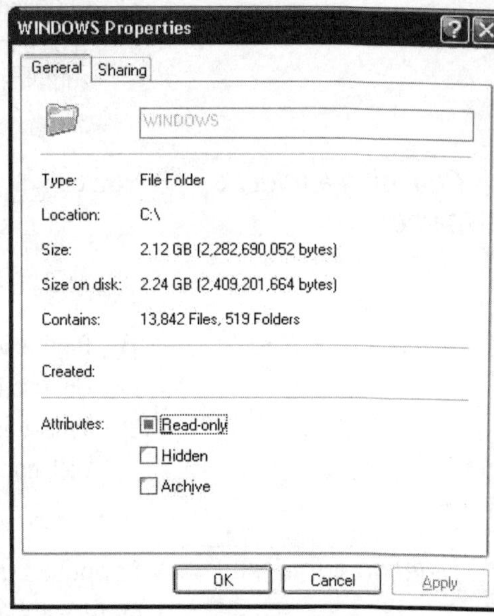

It also shows the drive where the folder is located (in this case, C:), the size of the folder (in this case, 2.12 Gigabytes), and file attribute information – you can change the file attributes by checking or unchecking the boxes.

Exercise 11.6: Viewing properties of a range of files

1) Use Windows Explorer to open the folder containing the files you want to enquire on.
2) Click on the **Type** column heading to sort the files by type.
3) Select all the files of the type you want to enquire on.

4) Right-click on the selected files, and then choose **Properties**. The *Properties* dialog box tells you the properties of the selected files. The example on the right shows properties for a range of .jpg files.

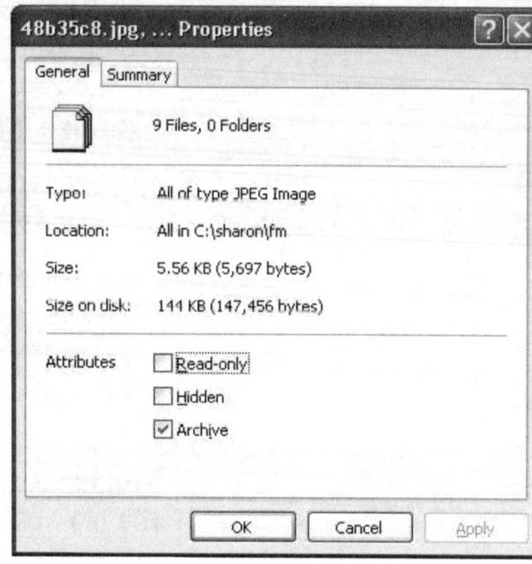

Restoring a folder's files

Where did your deleted folder go? If it contained no files, it has been deleted permanently by Windows. If it contained files, Windows has moved the files to the Recycle Bin. Follow the steps in Exercise 11.7 to bring your deleted folder and files back to life.

Exercise 11.7: Restoring a folder's files

1) In the left pane of the Windows Explorer window, scroll down until you can see the Recycle Bin, and click on it.

   Windows Explorer now displays the contents of the Recycle Bin in the right pane.

2) Choose **Edit | Undo Delete** to restore the files and the folder that contained them.

Working with files

A file, as you learnt in Chapter 10, is the basic unit of information storage on a computer. In the next few exercises you will discover how to create, name and save, delete and restore a file.

Creating a file

Files are created by applications. For example, you can create a letter in Microsoft Word and a spreadsheet in Microsoft Excel.

The simplest type of file that you can create on a computer is a plain text file. A file of this kind contains just words, numbers and punctuation marks – and no fancy formatting or graphics of any kind.

The Windows application for creating plain text files is called Notepad.

Exercise 11.8: Creating a file

1) Choose **Start | All Programs | Accessories | Notepad**. A blank Notepad window appears on your screen, ready to accept text.
2) Type the following words: Just testing

You have now created a file and entered content in that file. But your file is not saved on your hard disk. It exists only in the computer's memory. If the computer were to switch off for any reason, your file would be lost.

Naming and saving a file

The first time you save a file, Windows asks you to give that file a name. Follow the steps in Exercise 11.9 to discover how.

Exercise 11.9: Naming and saving a file

1) Choose **File | Save** to view the *Save As* dialog box. By displaying this dialog box, Windows is asking:
   - What drive do you want to save your folder in?
   - What folder (or subfolder) do you want to save your file in?
   - What name do you want to give your new file?
2) Click the arrow at the right of the *Save in* drop-down list box.

   Scroll up until you see the C: drive icon. Click it.

   The *Save As* dialog box now displays a list of the folders on your C: drive.

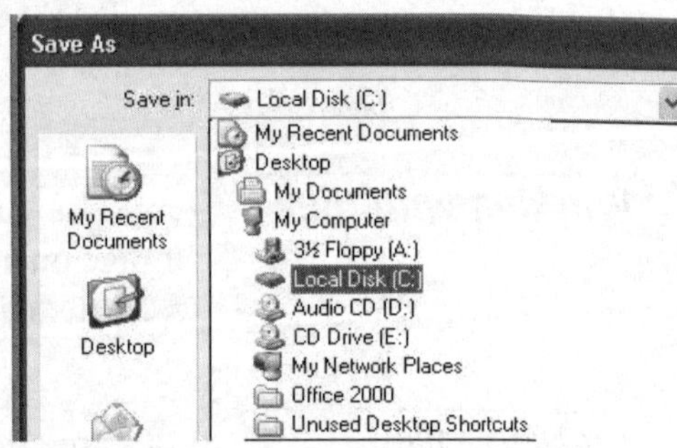

3) Locate the folder that you renamed in Exercise 11.4. Double-click it.

   You have now told Windows the drive and folder where you want to save your file. All that remains is for you to give your new file a name.
4) Click in the *File name* box, delete any text there, and type a name for your new file. If your initials are KB, for example, name it KB New File.

   When you are finished, click **Save**.

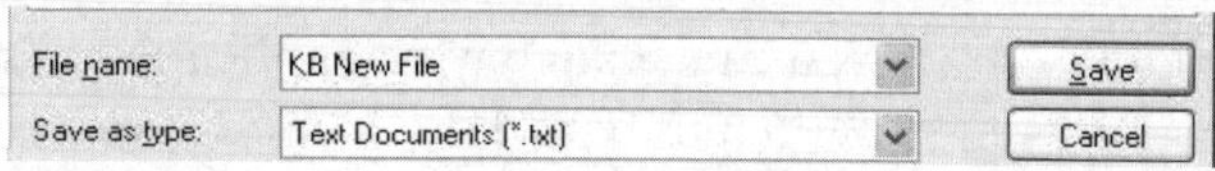

Windows automatically adds the three-letter file name extension of .txt to all plain-text files created with the Notepad application.

Well done! You have learnt how to name and save a file.

Move the mouse to the top-right of the Notepad window, and click the **Close** button to close it.

Opening a file directly

You can open a file directly from its location by double-clicking on it in Windows Explorer. This saves you having to first open the application and then the file.

Windows recognizes all the common file types by their three-letter file extension, so that it knows what application to use when you choose the file – this is known as the *file association.* For example, when you double-click on a file with the .xls extension, Windows uses Microsoft Excel to open it. Similarly, when you double-click on a file with the extension .txt, Windows uses Notepad to open it.

Exercise 11.10: Opening a file directly

1) Using Windows Explorer, go to the folder containing the file you saved in Exercise 11.9.
2) Double-click on the file to open it with Notepad.

Opening a file with an alternative application

Certain types of file can be opened with a number of applications. For example, HTML files can be opened with Internet Explorer or with Netscape Navigator. Similarly, text files can be opened with Notepad, Wordpad or any word processor.

To choose an application other than the default, right-click on the file, choose **Open With**, and then choose the application you want. This example shows the range of applications offered for a HTML file.

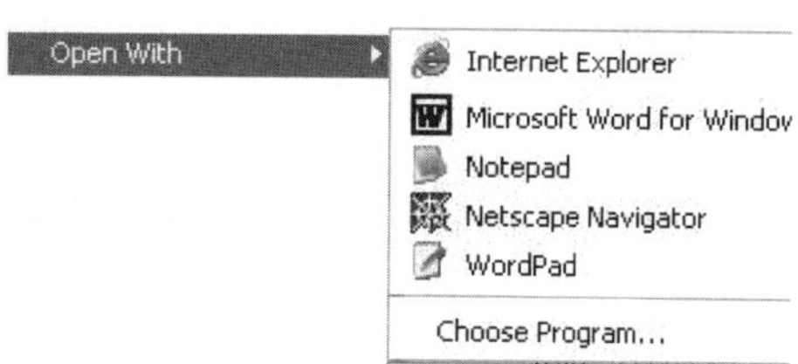

File associations

You can change what application is used to open all files of a particular type. For example, you might decide that you prefer to use Wordpad (instead of Notepad) to open .txt files.

Exercise 11.11: Changing the file association for all files of the same kind

1) Using Windows Explorer, go to the folder containing the file you saved in Exercise 11.9.
2) Right-click on the file, and then choose **Open With | Choose Program.**
3) You now see the *Open With* dialog box where you can specify what program you want to use to open the file.

Check this box if you want all files of this kind to be opened with the selected program

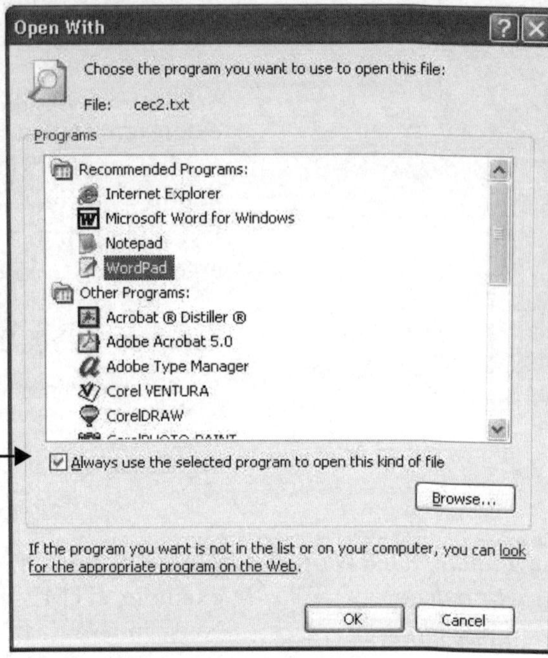

Changing a file's name

You can change a file's name at any stage. Exercise 11.12 shows you how.

Exercise 11.12: Changing a file's name

1) Using Windows Explorer, open the folder containing the file you saved in Exercise 11.9.
2) Right-click on the file to display a pop-up menu.
3) Choose **Rename**.

4) Type a new file name. For example, KB Renamed File. Do not change or delete the file name extension (in this case, .txt).

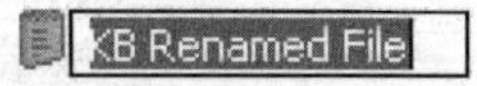

You have given your file a new name. Another exercise completed!

Deleting a file

When you have been working on your computer for a while, you may find that its hard disk is taken up by files and folders you no longer use or need.

You can delete these files, but be careful not to delete any files that your computer needs to run programs! If in doubt, don't delete!

Exercise 11.13 shows you how to delete an unwanted file.

Exercise 11.13: Deleting a file

1) Using Windows Explorer, display and right-click on the file that you renamed in Exercise 11.10.
2) From the pop-up menu, select the **Delete** command.
3) Click **Yes** to confirm that you want to remove the file to the Recycle Bin.

Restoring a file

Follow the steps in Exercise 11.14 to restore your deleted file.

Exercise 11.14: Restoring a file

1) In the left pane of the Windows Explorer window, scroll until you can see the Recycle Bin, and click on it.

   Windows Explorer now displays the contents of the Recycle Bin in the right pane.
2) Click the file to select it, and then choose **File | Restore**.

Looking at a file's properties

To display information about a file, right-click it. From the pop-up menu displayed, click the **Properties** option.

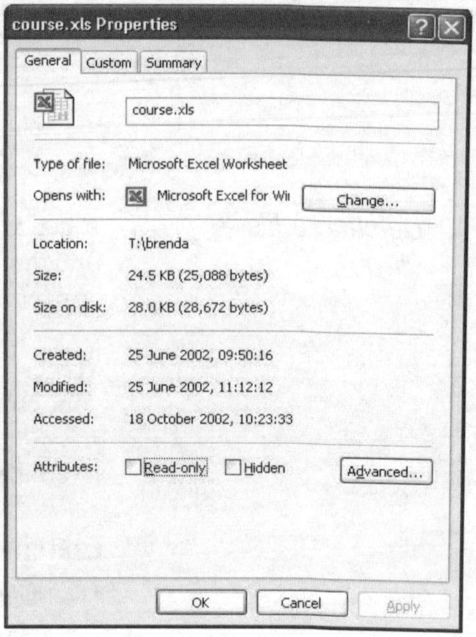

You are shown a dialog box similar to the one on the right.

Among other details, this tells you the size of the file, the application that was used to create the file, when it was created, when it was last modified, and so on.

You can also change the file's attributes.

Viewing a list of recent files

To see a list of files you have used recently, choose **Start | My Recent Documents.**

The Windows clipboard

Suppose you want to place a folder or file in a different location on your computer. Or reproduce a folder or file so that two copies of it appear in different locations. Can you do it? Yes. This is a two-step process:

- **Copy:** You select and then copy the folder or file to the clipboard, a temporary storage area. The selected folder or file remains in its original location.

  -or-

- **Cut:** You select and then cut the folder or file to the clipboard. The selected folder or file is no longer in its original location.

- **Paste:** You paste the folder or file from the clipboard into a different part of your computer – into a different folder, or on to a floppy disk, a Zip disk or a writeable CD.

Clipboard
A temporary storage area to which you can copy or cut folders or files. You can paste from the clipboard to any location within the same or a different drive.

About the clipboard

Points you should remember about the Windows clipboard:

- The clipboard is temporary. Turn off your computer and the clipboard contents are deleted.
- The clipboard can hold only a single copied item at a time. If you copy or cut a second item, the second overwrites the first.
- Items stay in the clipboard after you paste from it, so you can paste the same folder or file into as many locations as you need.

Copying and moving folders

To copy a folder means to make a copy of it, and to place that copy in a new location. Exercise 11.15 takes you through the steps by using the *Copy to Folder* option.

Exercise 11.15: Copying a folder

1) In the left pane of Windows Explorer, click the folder that you renamed in Exercise 11.12.
2) Choose **Edit | Copy to Folder**.
3) Select the Windows folder in the *Copy Items* dialog box.
4) Double-click the Windows folder to open it.
5) Click **Copy**.

   This places a copy of your folder within the Windows folder.

To move a folder means to place it in a new location – and to remove it from its original location. Exercise 11.16 shows you a way to do this by using the *Move to Folder* option.

Exercise 11.16: Moving a folder

1) In the right pane, display the folder that you copied to the Windows folder in Exercise 11.15. Click on it to select it.
2) Choose **Edit | Move to Folder**.

3) Select the Systems folder in the *Move Items* dialog box.
4) Double-click on the System folder to open it.
5) Click **Move**.

   This places your folder within the System folder of the Windows folder.

Copying and moving files

To copy a file means to make a copy of it, and to place that copy in a new location. To move a file means to remove a file from one location and place it in another location.

In Exercise 11.17 you will make a copy of your plain text file, and place that copy in a different folder on your hard disk. In Exercise 11.18 you will move the file from its current folder to a new one.

You can also copy and move files from one drive to another – for example, from a hard drive to a removable drive such as a floppy disk or a writeable CD.

Exercise 11.17: Copying a file to another folder

1) In the left pane, the folder containing the file that you created in Exercise 11.8 will be shown. Double-click the folder to display its contents in the right pane.
2) Choose **Edit | Copy**.
3) In the left pane, scroll down to locate the folder called Windows.
4) Click on the Windows folder to open it. Its contents are now listed in the right pane.
5) Choose **Edit | Paste**.

   You have now placed a copy of your file within the Windows folder.

Exercise 11.18: Moving a file to another folder

1) In the right pane, display the file that you copied to the Windows folder in Exercise 11.15. Click it to select it.
2) Choose **Edit | Cut**.
3) Scroll back up the right pane to locate the folder named System.
4) Double-click the System folder to open it.
5) Choose **Edit | Paste**.

   You have now moved the file to the System subfolder of the Windows folder.

Working with multiple files

Windows Explorer provides an easy method of copying or moving several files in a single operation. This method works only when:

- The files you want to copy or move are currently located in the *same* folder.
- The place you want to copy or move them to is also a single folder.

When you list the files to copy or move in Windows Explorer, two situations are possible:

- The files are *adjacent*. They are positioned immediately below or above one another.
- The files are *non-adjacent*. They are not positioned immediately below or above one another.

If the files are adjacent, follow these steps:

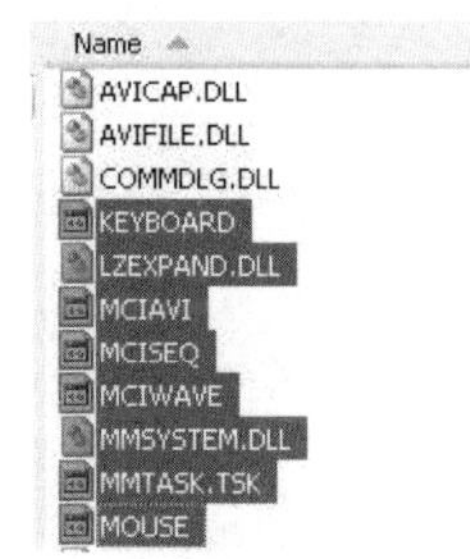

- Click on the first file.
- Press and hold down the **Shift** key.
- Click on the last file.

All the files – the first, last and in-between – are now selected, and you can copy or cut them in a single operation.

If the files are non-adjacent, follow these steps:

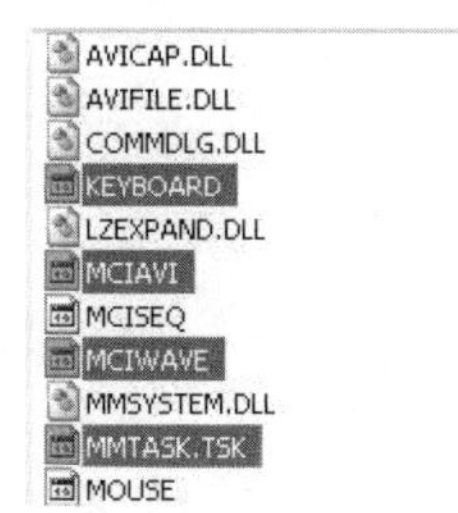

- Click on the first file.
- Press and hold down the **Ctrl** key.
- Click the relevant files, one after the other, to select them.

Again, all the files are now selected, and you can copy or cut them in a single operation.

When selecting several files, you can scroll up or down as you make your selection. This method works for folders as well as files. Another operation that you can perform on selected folders or files is deletion. Simply select the adjacent or non-adjacent files or folders, and press the **Delete** key.

Compressing and archiving files

Windows XP includes a compression utility that enables you to compress files and folders on your computer. Compressed files and folders take up less space on your disk, and they are easier and quicker to send as e-mail attachments.

Often, files that you download from the Internet are in compressed (zip) format, and you need to *unzip* them before you can use them.

Exercise 11.19: Creating a compressed folder and adding files to it

1) Within Windows Explorer or My Computer, go to the folder where you want to create the new compressed folder (in the example below this is C:\BACKUP), and choose **File | New | Compressed (zipped) Folder.**
2) Give the folder the name of your choice – in this example, the folder is called jpg.zip.

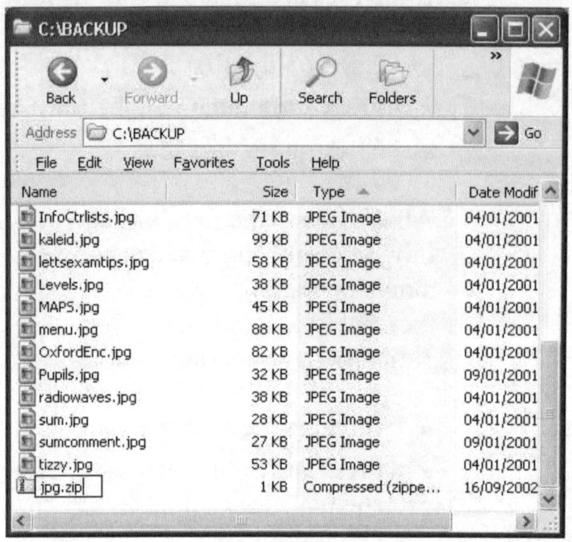

3) Drag the files you want to compress into the compressed folder.
4) Delete the files from their original location.

   To unzip a compressed folder, simply double-click on it.

Menu bars, toolbars and shortcuts

In the final part of this chapter, you will discover the three ways that you perform actions in a Windows application: menu commands, toolbar buttons and keyboard shortcuts.

Menu bars

Start the Microsoft Word application. Take a look at the line of words that runs just under the title bar. Each of these words represents a drop-down menu.

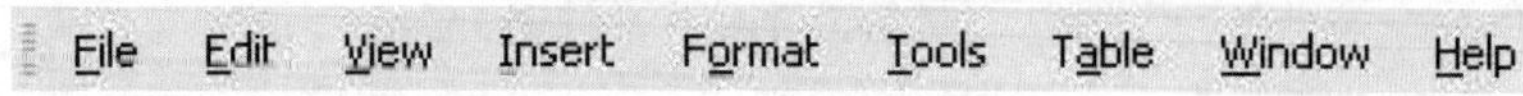

Click the **File** menu name to display the commands (actions) available on this menu. You tell Word that you want to perform a particular action by clicking the action's name on the drop-down menu. Click the **Exit** command to close Word.

Drop-down menu
A list of options that appears when you click on a menu name. The menu name is generally on a menu bar along the top of the window, and the menu appears below that bar, as if you have pulled it down.

Whenever you see an arrow to the right of a menu option, selecting that option displays a further sub-menu of choices.

All Windows applications share a number of common menus. Understand their general purpose and you will be able to use most applications. The common menus are:

- **File:** Use the commands on this menu to create a new (blank) file, open an existing file, save the current file, save the current file with a new name (Save As), print the current file, and quit the application.

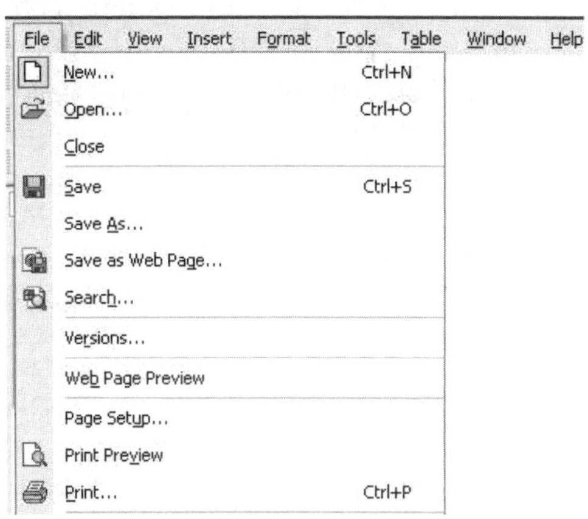

Word's drop-down File menu

- **Edit:** Use the commands on this menu to copy and move selected files, or items (such as text or graphics) within files.
- **View:** Use the commands on this menu to display your file in different ways, including a zoomed-in (up-close) view or zoomed out (bird's-eye) view.
- **Help:** Use the commands on this menu to display online help information about the application you are using.

Toolbars

A second way of performing an action is to click a button on a toolbar. Instead of choosing **File | Save** to save a file, for example, you could click the **Save** button on the toolbar.

Not every menu command has a toolbar button equivalent, but the most commonly used commands do.

> ***Toolbar***
>
> *A collection of buttons that you can click to perform frequently used actions, such as creating, opening or saving files, and for clipboard operations.*

Here are the toolbar buttons that you will find on almost every Windows application:

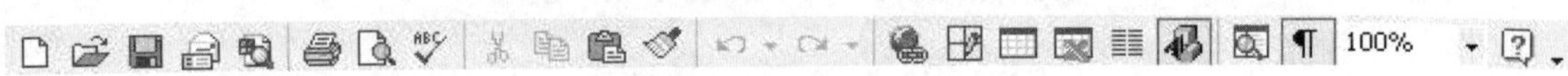

Keyboard shortcuts

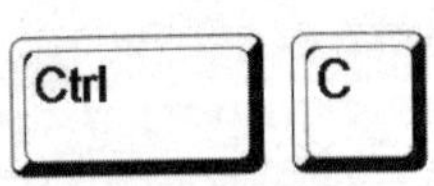

Keyboard shortcut for copying a selected item to the clipboard

A third way of performing actions in Windows is to use keyboard shortcuts. You may find using these faster than either menu commands or toolbar buttons, as you don't need to take either hand away from the keyboard.

An example of a keyboard short cut is **Ctrl+c**, which means 'Hold down the **Ctrl** key and press the letter **c** key.' This has the same effect as choosing **Edit | Copy**. Here are the most commonly used shortcut keys:

Keyboard shortcut	Action performed	Menu command
Ctrl+o	Opens an existing file	**File | Open**
Ctrl+n	Opens a new file	**File | New**
Ctrl+s	Saves the current file	**File | Save**
Ctrl+c	Copies selected item to the clipboard	**Edit | Copy**
Ctrl+x	Cuts selected item to the clipboard	**Edit | Cut**
Ctrl+v	Pastes selected item from the clipboard	**Edit | Paste**

Protecting against viruses

Computer viruses are clever but poisonous programs written by malicious software developers and amateur hackers. They attack the integrity of your files, and are designed to transfer easily and stealthily from one computer to another: via e-mail attachments, through programs downloaded from the Internet and infected floppy disks.

There are many different types of virus, using different techniques to replicate themselves. Their effects vary from minor irritation (where a message is displayed on your screen, but no files are damaged), through inconvenience (where one or more files are affected), to total disaster (where the entire hard disk is rendered unusable).

See **Viruses** *in Chapter 8: Keeping your information safe* (page 67) for more detailed information on:

- What precautions to take against viruses.
- The different functions of virus scanning software – see Exercises 8.1, 8.2 and 8.3 for details on how to use virus scanning software.
- Why it is so important to keep your virus scanning software up to date.
- How to use anti-virus software to scan your PC for viruses.
- How to *disinfect* any files that have been affected.

Chapter summary: so now you know

Use *Windows Explorer* to view the hierarchy of folders on your computer, and to view and work with the drives, folders and files on your computer. Windows Explorer displays two sub-windows or panes. You use the *left pane* to select a particular drive or folder. You use the *right pane* to view the folders and files in the drive or folder selected in the left pane. See Exercise 11.1 for an example of how to do this.

Windows Explorer enables you to *copy*, *move*, *rename* and *delete* folders and files. You can also create folders with Windows Explorer. See Exercises 11.2, 11.3, 11.4 and 11.5 for examples of how to do these tasks. You can view a folder's properties and you can restore a folder you have moved to the Recycle Bin – see Exercises 11.6 and 11.7.

You create files with software applications. See Exercise 11.8 for an example of how to do this. You can change the *file association* for a type of file. The *clipboard* is a temporary storage area to which you can copy or cut folders or files. You can change a file's name, delete a file, and restore a file you have deleted – see Exercises 11.12, 11.13 and 11.14. You can paste from the clipboard to any location within the same or a different drive. See Exercises 11.15 and 11.16 for examples of how to do these tasks.

You can select *multiple* files, and then copy, cut, paste or delete them in a single operation. See Exercises 11.17 and 11.18 for examples of how to do these tasks. If the files are *adjacent*, click the first file, hold down the **Shift** key, and then click the last file. If they are *non-adjacent*, click the first file, hold down the **Ctrl** key, and then click the individual files to select them.

You can *compress* (or *zip)* files and folders so that they take up less space. See Exercise 11.19.

A *drop-down* menu is a list of options that appears when you click a menu name on a menu bar. When you see an arrow to the right of a menu option, selecting that option displays a further *sub-menu* of choices. You tell Word that you want to perform a particular action by clicking the action's name on the drop-down menu.

A second way of performing an action is to click a button on a toolbar. Most applications have toolbar buttons for creating, opening or saving files, and for clipboard operations.

A third option is to press the **Ctrl** key in combination with a particular letter key. Examples of such keyboard shortcuts include **Ctrl+c** to copy to the clipboard and **Ctrl+v** to paste from it.

Quick quiz: working with folders and files

Circle the correct answer to each of the following multiple-choice questions about working with folders and files.

Q1	To save a file you choose ...
A.	**File | Save As.**
B.	**File | Save.**
C.	**File | New.**
D.	**File | Close.**

Q2	How do you create a new folder in the C: drive?
A.	Double-click Windows Explorer. Click the C: drive and in the left pane choose **File | New | Folder**. Type a name for your new folder.
B.	Double-click Windows Explorer. Click the C: drive and in the left pane choose **File | New | Briefcase**. Type a name for your new folder.
C.	Double-click Windows Explorer. Click the C: drive and in the left pane choose **File | New | Microsoft Word Document**. Type a name for your new folder.
D.	Double-click Windows Explorer. Click the A: drive and in the left pane choose **File | New | Folder**. Type a name for your new folder.

Q4	How do you change a file's name?
A.	Double-click on Windows Explorer to open the folder containing the file. Right-click the file and choose **Properties** from the pop-up menu displayed. Type the new file name.
B.	Double-click on Windows Explorer to open the folder containing the file. Right-click the file and choose **Create Shortcut** from the pop-up menu displayed. Type the new file name.
C.	Double-click on Windows Explorer to open the folder containing the file. Right-click the file and choose **Rename** from the pop-up menu displayed. Type the new file name.
D.	Double-click on Windows Explorer and select the folder containing the file. Right-click the folder and choose **Rename** from the pop-up menu displayed. Type the new folder name.

Q3	The keyboard shortcut for saving a file is c...
A.	**Ctrl+v.**
B.	**Ctrl+x.**
C.	**Ctrl+n.**
D.	**Ctrl+s.**

Q5	If you turn off your computer, the contents of the clipboard are deleted.
A.	True.
B.	False.

Answers

1: B, **2:** A, **3:** D, **4:** C, **5:** A.

Chapter 12: Mastering Windows

In this chapter

Now that you are familiar with Windows basics, you are ready to move on to the more advanced features.

You will discover how to take control of your Windows desktop, enabling you to customize it to reflect your working needs and your personal taste. You will also learn how to make backup copies of your files on floppy disks.

New skills

At the end of this chapter you should be able to:

- Personalize your desktop by moving icons and creating folders to hold application and file icons.
- Create shortcuts that take you directly to a particular application, file or folder.
- Select a screen saver.
- Customize your wallpaper, background pattern, scheme and screen resolution.
- Change your computer's date and time settings.
- Adjust your computer's sound volume.
- Change your computer's regional settings.
- Format a floppy disk.
- Copy a file to a floppy disk.
- Save a file to a floppy disk.
- Use various print features and options.

New words

At the end of this chapter you should be able to explain the following terms:

- Desktop shortcut
- Screen saver
- Print queue

Managing your desktop

You can arrange your Windows desktop to suit your working needs and personal taste:

- To reposition your icons, simply drag them to where you want them.
- To make your screen look tidier, create desktop folders and place application and file icons in them.

You create a desktop folder as follows:

- Right-click on the desktop to display a pop-up menu.
- Choose **New | Folder**. Windows creates a desktop folder with the default name New Folder.
- Type your folder name, and press **Enter**.

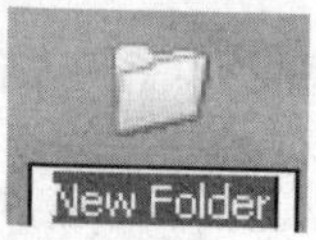

Next, double-click the folder to open it, and drag icons into it, either from the desktop or from other desktop folders.

Creating desktop shortcuts

You will use some applications more frequently than others. You can save yourself time by creating a shortcut to these programs from your desktop (or from a folder on your desktop). As a result, you won't have to take the **Start | All Programs** route every time you want to start that application.

Follow the steps in Exercise 12.1 to create a desktop shortcut for Notepad.

Exercise 12.1: Creating a desktop shortcut for Notepad

1) Chose **Start | All Programs | Accessories | Windows Explorer**. If the Explorer window occupies the full Windows desktop, click the **Restore** button (top right).
2) Display the application for which you want to create a shortcut. You will find Notepad in the Windows folder.

3) Right-click the Notepad icon and choose **Create Shortcut** from the pop-up menu displayed. Drag the Shortcut icon to the Desktop in the left pane of Windows Explorer.

   If you don't like your shortcut's default name, right-click it, choose **Rename**, type a new name, and press the **Enter** key.

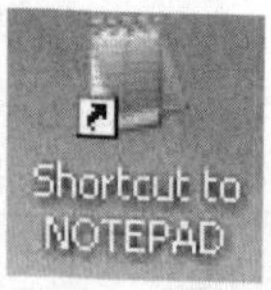

You can also create shortcuts for frequently used folders and files. You can leave the Notepad icon on your desktop, or drag it to a desktop folder.

Desktop shortcut
A user-created icon that, when clicked on, takes you directly to an application, folder or file. It is a fast, convenient alternative to using the Start menu.

In Exercise 12.2 you will create a desktop folder named Office 2002, and create desktop shortcuts for three Office applications within it.

Exercise 12.2: Creating an Office 2002 desktop folder containing shortcuts

1) Right-click on your desktop. On the pop-up menu displayed, choose **New | Folder**. Windows creates a folder with the default name New Folder.
2) Type 'Office 2002' as the new folder name, and press **Enter**.
3) Double-click your new folder to open it. You are now ready to create desktop shortcuts and place them within the folder.
4) Let's start with a shortcut to Microsoft Word. Choose **Start | Search** to display the *Search Results* dialog box.
5) Click *All files and folders*. In the *All or part of the file name* box, type winword.exe. Select the drive and click **Search**.
6) When winword.exe is found, right-click on its icon, and drag it from the *Search Results* dialog box into your Office 2002 desktop folder.
7) Click on the *Search Results* dialog box again. Repeat steps 5 and 6 for the following other Office 2002 application files: excel.exe, powerpnt.exe and msaccess.exe.

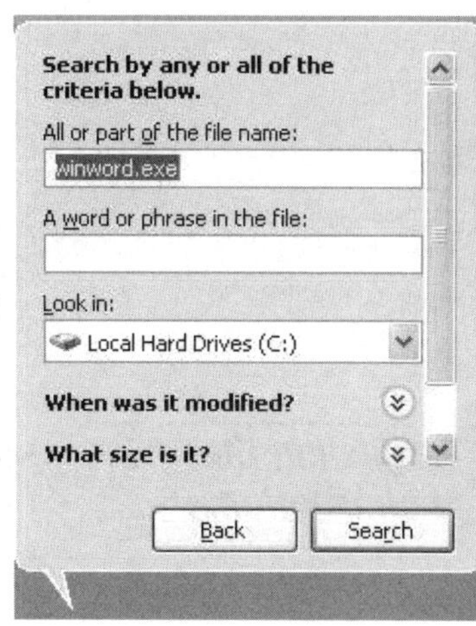

When finished, you may wish to rename the shortcut icons as shown.

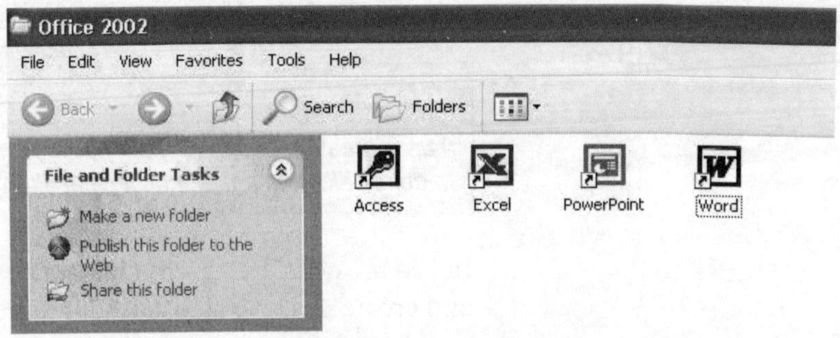

You can now close the new Office 2002 desktop folder.

Setting the time and date

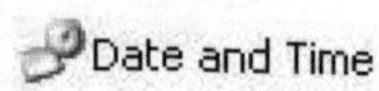

Is your computer set to the correct date and time? If not, the files you create and edit, and e-mails you send, will show misleading dates or times. Exercise 12.3 shows you how to set the date and time on your computer.

Exercise 12.3: Setting your computer's date and time

1) Choose **Start | Control Panel**.
2) On the folder displayed, double-click the Date and Time icon.
3) Make the changes you want. Click **Apply** and then **OK**.

A small battery inside your computer ensures that Windows remembers the date and time settings, even when your computer is turned off.

Adjusting the sound volume

Modern PCs have the ability to play sound files through attached loudspeakers or headphones. Follow Exercise 12.4 to discover how to adjust the playback volume setting on your computer.

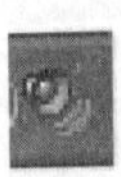

Volume control icon

Exercise 12.4: Changing the playback volume

1) Click the **Volume Control** icon displayed towards the right of the taskbar. The icon's appearance depends on the type of sound card installed on your computer. Typically, it looks like a small loudspeaker.

   If you are unsure which taskbar icon is the **Volume Control**, position the cursor over each icon until you see a text box telling you the icon's purpose.

2) On the pop-up menu shown, drag the Volume Control slider up to raise the volume or down to lower it.

   You can switch off sound completely by selecting the *Mute* box.

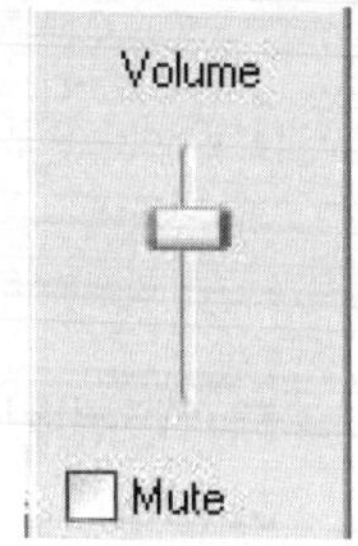

3) When finished, click on any other part of your screen to close the Volume Control.

Setting the screen saver

A screen saver is a program that takes over the computer's display screen if there are no keystrokes or mouse movements for a specified amount of time.

They were originally developed to prevent damage to monitors that could arise if one fixed image was displayed continuously over a long period. Screen savers prevented this by either blanking out the screen entirely or by displaying a series of constantly moving images.

Today's monitors are less likely to suffer from the problem that screen savers were designed to prevent, and they are now mostly an adornment.

Exercise 12.5 shows you how to set up or change your computer's screen saver.

Screen saver
A program that takes over the computer's display screen if there are no keystrokes or mouse movements for a specified length of time. They either blank out the screen entirely or display a series of continually moving images.

Exercise 12.5: Setting up or changing your screen saver

1) Right-click on the Windows desktop, choose **Properties** from the pop-up menu, and select the **Screen Saver** tab.
2) Click the arrow to the right of the *Screen saver* drop-down list box to display a list of screen savers installed on your computer.

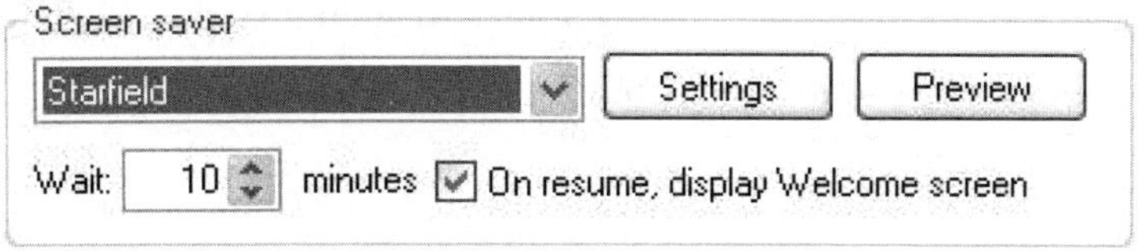

3) Click to select the screen saver you require from the list.

4) In the *Wait* box enter the number of minutes before which the screen saver will activate, and click **OK**.

To clear the screen saver after it has started, move your mouse or press any key.

Customizing your screen

The appearance of Windows on your computer is controlled by the setting of the following two items, each of which you can change to suit your working needs or personal taste:

- Wallpaper.
- Scheme.

Wallpaper

You can insert an image, such as a scanned photograph or a picture downloaded from the Internet, on your desktop background. Follow these steps to do so:

- Right-click on the desktop, choose **Properties** from the pop-up menu, and select the **Desktop** tab.
- Select your required wallpaper from the *Background* list.

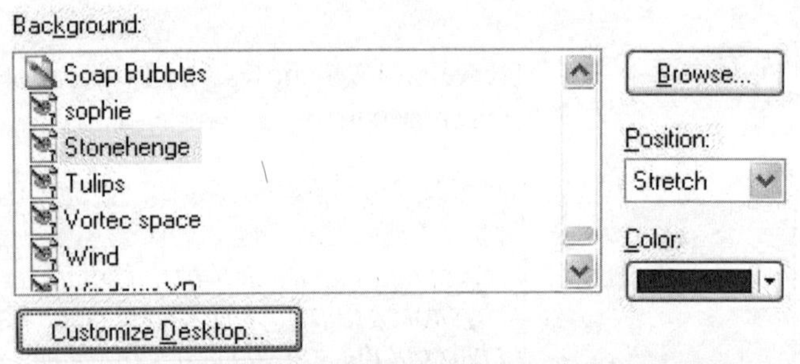

- From the *Position* drop-down list, select *Center* to position the image in the middle of your desktop, *Stretch* to position the image all across the screen, or *Tile* to repeat the image horizontally and vertically until it fills the entire screen. Click **OK**.

Scheme

This is the combination of colours, fonts and spacing that controls the appearance of such items as title bars, scroll bars and icons. To view or adjust your scheme:

- Right-click on the desktop, choose **Properties** from the pop-up menu, and select the **Appearance** tab.
- Select a colour scheme from the *Color scheme* drop-down list box. Select your required windows and buttons scheme from the *Windows and buttons* drop-down list box. Select your required font size, and click **OK**.

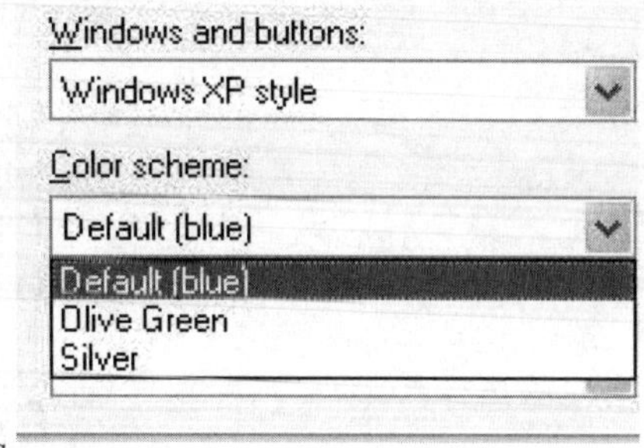

You can change your wallpaper and scheme as often as you wish. The relevant dialog boxes offer a preview area where you can view the effect of any changes before you apply them. Don't be afraid to experiment with different settings.

Changing your screen resolution

Everything you view on your screen is composed of tiny square dots called pixels. The number of pixels displayed is determined by your screen resolution.

- Lower-resolution settings (such as 640 x 480) result in fewer, larger pixels, so that everything on your screen appears bigger and blockier.
- Higher-resolution settings (such as 1024 x 768) use more, smaller pixels, so that everything appears smaller and more defined.

To change your screen resolution:

- Right-click on the desktop, choose **Properties** from the pop-up menu, and select the **Settings** tab.
- Drag the *Screen resolution* slider left to decrease the resolution or right to increase it.

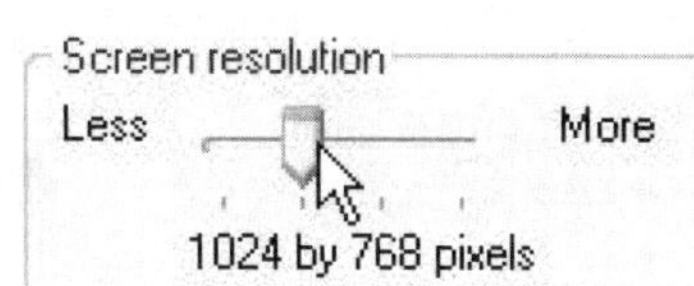

You can see the effect of a new screen resolution in the preview area. When finished, click **OK** to save your new settings and close the dialog box.

Changing your regional and language options

The options you select in the Windows Regional and Language Options decide the default currency symbol shown in your applications, and which conventions Windows uses when displaying times, dates and numbers. You can also change the keyboard language.

To change your regional and language options:

- Choose **Start | Control Panel**, and click the **Regional and Languages Options** icon.

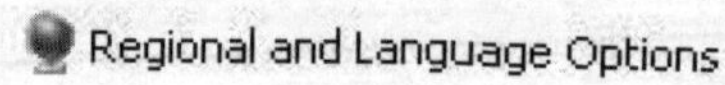

- On the **Regional Options** tab, select the relevant region from the drop-down list.

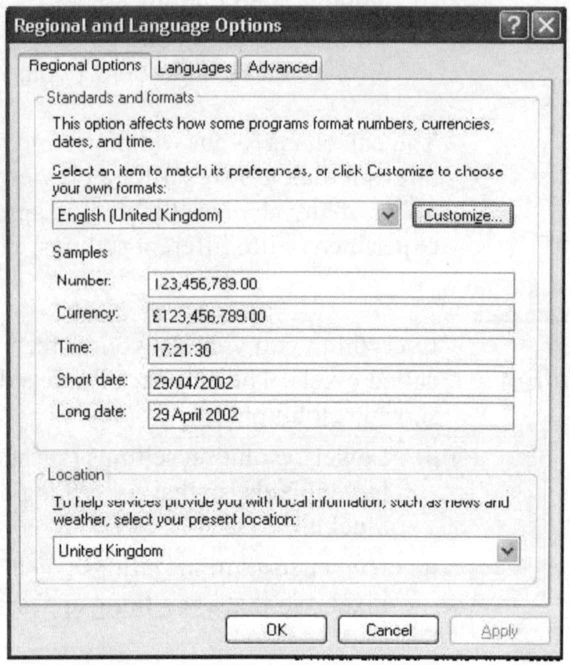

- To override the default conventions for your selected region, click the **Customize** button. Fill in the required details on the **Number**, **Currency**, **Time** and **Date** tabs.
- When finished, click **OK** to save your new options and to close the dialog box.

If you work a lot in a language other than English, you might find it useful to change your keyboard language. This makes it easier for you to use accented characters and characters not used in English. This is a two-stage procedure:

- First, you set up the language or languages you want to use using the **Languages** tab of the *Regional and Language Options* dialog box.
- Second, you choose the language from the taskbar.

To set up a new language/keyboard, follow these steps:

- Select the **Languages** tab, and then click on **Details**. Currently installed languages are listed under *Installed Services*.

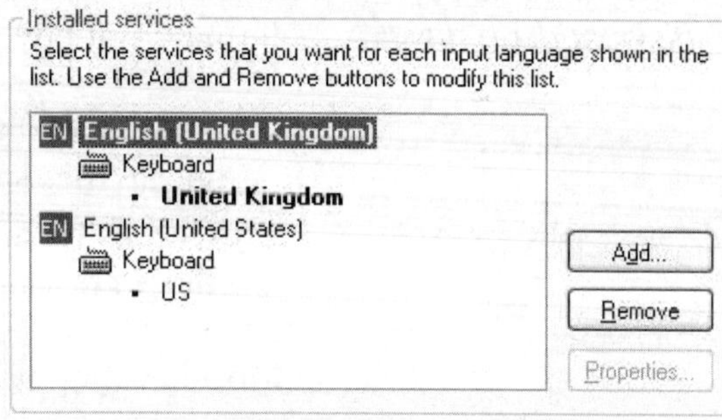

- Click on the **Add** button to add a new language/ keyboard. Then select the language and the keyboard layout you want from the *Add Input Language* dialog box. Click **OK**. The example here shows Greek being chosen for both input language and keyboard layout.

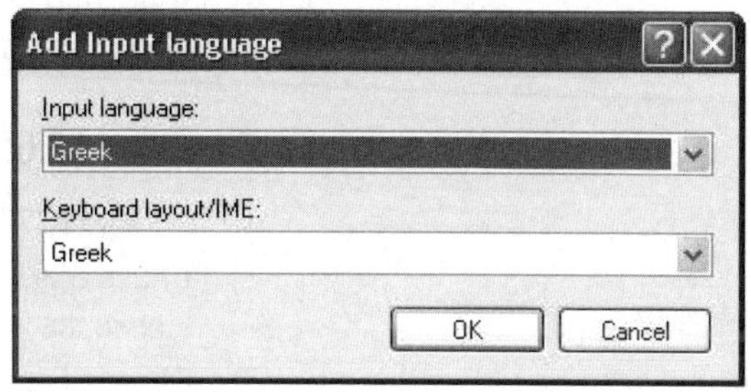

To change the language/keyboard you use, click on the language bar icon on the taskbar – this is indicated by a two-letter abbreviation for the current language (EN for English). Click on the language you want to use.

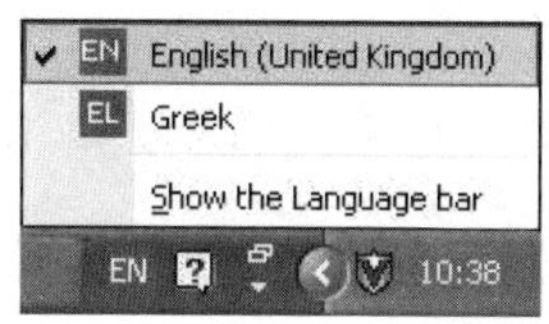

Working with floppy disks and other removable media

You can copy files and folders from your hard disk to a floppy disk or to other removable media such as a Zip disk or a writeable CD. You can do this to:

- Make a copy of a file that you can give to a colleague or friend.
- Have a second, backup copy of your work just in case your computer is somehow damaged and the files on it are ‘lost’.

The more regularly you make backups, the more up-to-date your files will be if your computer fails.

Formatting floppy disks and Zip disks

You can only copy files to a disk that is formatted. When Windows formats a floppy disk or Zip disk, it:

- Sets up a 'table of contents' on the floppy disk that it later uses to locate files stored on the disk.
- Checks for any damaged areas, and, when it finds them, marks those areas as off-limits for file storage.

Most new floppy disks and Zip disks come already formatted. But you can also buy unformatted ones and format them yourself. The ECDL syllabus also specifies that you must know how to format floppy disks and Zip disks. Exercises 12.6 and 12.7 show you how.

Exercise 12.6: Formatting a floppy disk

1) Insert the floppy disk you want to format into the disk drive.
2) Chose **Start | All Programs | Windows Explorer** and right-click the A: drive icon in the left-hand pane.
3) Choose **Format** and then click **Start**.
4) Windows lets you know when the formatting has been completed. Click **OK**.

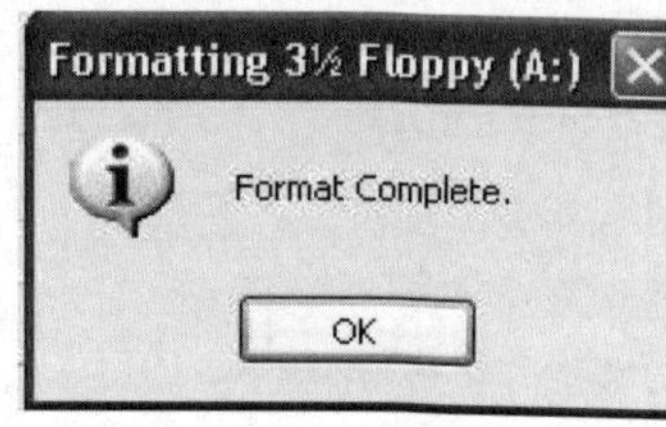

Exercise 12.7: Formatting a Zip disk

1) Insert the Zip disk you want to format into the disk drive.
2) Chose **Start | All Programs | Windows Explorer** and right-click the Zip drive icon in the left-hand pane.
3) Choose **Format** and then click **Start**.
4) Windows lets you know when the formatting has been completed. Click **OK**.

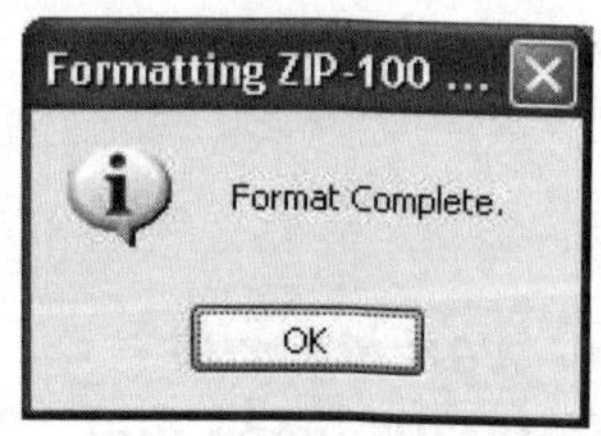

Formatting a disk overwrites any table of contents there may previously have been on the disk, making it impossible for Windows to find files that were saved on the floppy disk before it was formatted.

For that reason, don't even think about formatting your computer's hard disk.

You cannot format a disk if there are files on that disk that are open.

Copying a file to a floppy disk

You can copy a file to a floppy disk using the copy and paste option available with Windows Explorer. See Exercise 12.8.

Exercise 12.8: Copying a file to a floppy disk

1) Place a formatted floppy disk in the A: drive of your computer.
2) Choose **Start | All Programs | Accessories | Windows Explorer** and, in the right-hand pane, display the file that you want to copy – for example, the FaxSetup.txt file from the Windows folder.

3) Click the file and choose **Edit | Copy** or press **Ctrl+c**.
4) In the left pane, click the A: drive icon.

   If there are currently any files on the floppy disk, Windows Explorer lists them in its right pane.

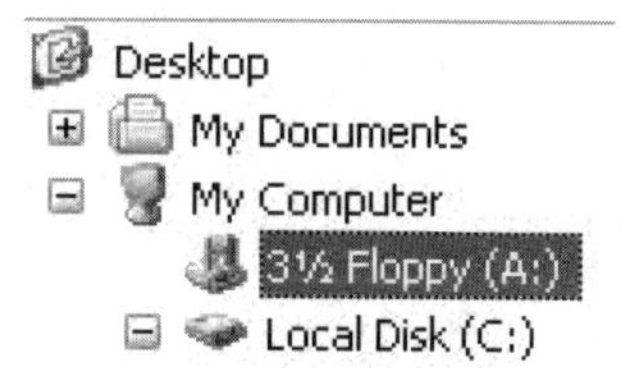

5) Choose **Edit | Paste** or click **Ctrl+v** to copy the file to the floppy disk.

Saving a file to a floppy disk

A second way to copy a file to a floppy disk is to use the **File | Save As** command of the application in which you created and work with the file. If you currently have the application open on your screen, this is faster than using Windows Explorer. See Exercise 12.9.

Exercise 12.9: Saving a file to a floppy disk

1) Choose **Start | All Programs | Accessories | Notepad**.
2) Choose **File | Open**, locate the file you saved in Exercise 12.8, and click **Open**.
3) Choose **File | Save As**, locate the A: drive, and click **Save** to save the file.

   A copy of the Notepad file is now stored on the floppy disk.

Installing software applications

There are a number of different ways of installing new software on your PC. Usually, however, the manufacturer will have taken steps to make installation easy – after all, they want you to get up and running as quickly and easily as possible.

Software that is distributed on CD is usually installed via an *autorun* feature – this means that the installation procedure launches automatically as soon as you place the CD in the CD drive. You are then prompted to answer some questions: usually you have to indicate that you accept the licensing conditions, and you have to specify where on your PC you want the installed application to reside.

Note: It's a good idea to close down all open applications on your PC before you install a new software application. This limits the possibility of any conflicts arising.

If the CD does not have an autorun feature, then use My Computer to navigate to the CD and look for the installation file – this is usually called **setup.exe** or **install.exe**. Double-click on this file to launch the installation procedure. Again, you will probably be asked to agree to the licensing conditions and to specify where you want to install the application.

If you download software from the Internet, it will probably come in the form of a *self-extracting executable* – this means that the installation procedure is launched when you double-click on the file in My Computer.

For example, when you download WinZip from the Internet, you can install it by double-clicking on the downloaded file.

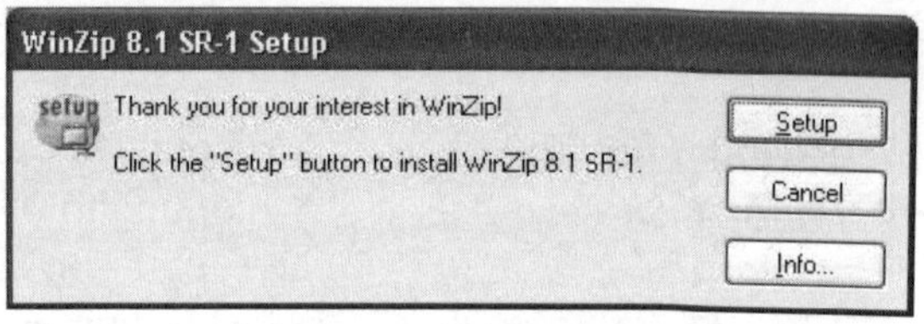

You are then prompted to specify where you want to install it – the default is usually a subfolder in Program Files.

See Exercise 43.8 in Module 7 for details of how to download WinZip from www.ecdl.com.

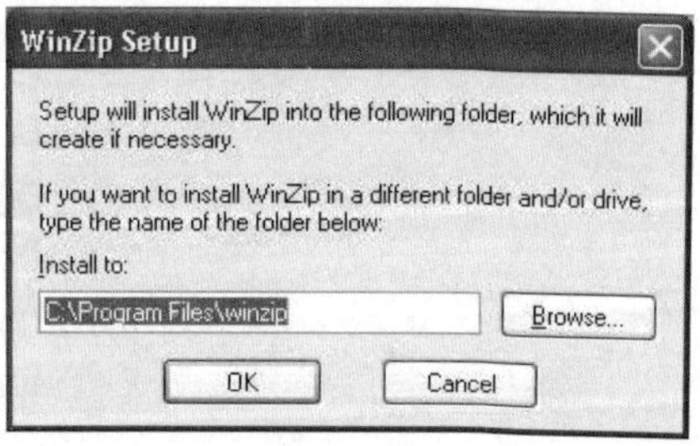

Uninstalling software applications

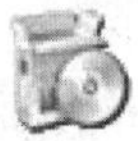

When you install a software application, different files are placed in different folders on your PC's hard drive. So, when you want to remove an application it's not enough to just delete the application folder.

The best way to remove unwanted software is to *uninstall* it using the **Add or Remove Programs** function in the Control Panel.

When the list of installed applications is displayed, select the one you want to uninstall and click **Change/Remove**.

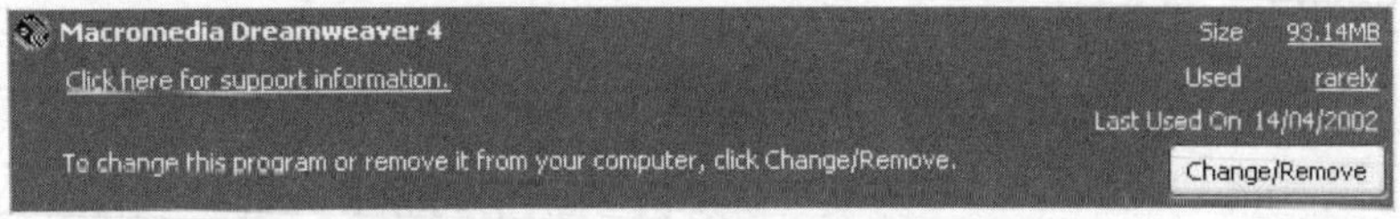

Printing files

Now that you can open and work with files, you will want to print copies of your work so you can see it on paper.

Exercise 12.10: Printing a file

1) Open a file – for example, a Word document.
2) Select **File | Print**.
3) Click **OK** in the *Print* dialog box.

If your printer is connected and set up correctly, your file should print.

You can also print by dragging a file icon on to a desktop printer icon.

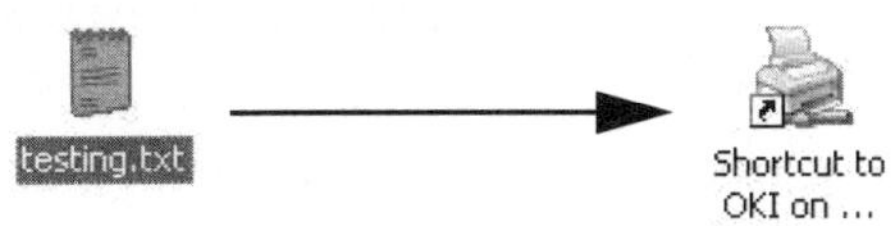

The print queue

What happens to a file after you choose to print it with the **Print** command? The answer is that it goes to a file called a print queue, and is then taken from the print queue by the selected printer.

The print queue can store a number of files, which the printer then collects in turn as it becomes ready to print them. The time it takes to print a file depends on the number and size of the other print jobs in the print queue.

You can view your print queue to see what print jobs are waiting in it, delete print jobs from the queue, and reorder the sequence in which print jobs are listed.

Print queue
A list of files (print jobs) that are waiting to be printed. The printer pulls the files off the queue one at a time.

Viewing the print queue

What jobs are currently in the print queue? See Exercise 12.11 to find out.

Exercise 12.11: Viewing the print queue

1) Choose **Start | Control Panel | Printers and Faxes**.
2) Double-click the icon of the printer you want to look at.
   Windows displays a list of all the print jobs in the queue.

Cancelling a print job in the queue

There are many reasons why you may decide to cancel a print job – you may discover that the job is not printing correctly, you may realize that you already have a copy of the printout, or you may simply change your mind about printing the file.

Follow the steps in Exercise 12.12 to cancel a job.

Exercise 12.12: Removing a job from the print queue

1) Choose **Start | Control Panel | Printers and Faxes**.
2) Double-click the icon of the printer you want to look at. Windows displays a list of all the print jobs in the queue.
3) Select the document you want to cancel printing.
4) Choose **Document | Cancel**.

Pausing and then restarting a print job in the queue

Follow the steps in Exercises 12.13 and 12.14 to pause and then restart printing.

Exercise 12.13: Pausing a job from the print queue

1) Choose **Start | Control Panel | Printers and Faxes**.
2) Double-click the icon of the printer you want to look at. Windows displays a list of all the print jobs in the queue.
3) Select the document you want to pause printing.
4) Choose **Document |Pause**.

Exercise 12.14: Restarting a job from the print queue

5) Choose **Start | Control Panel | Printers and Faxes**.
6) Double-click the icon of the printer you want to look at. Windows displays a list of all the print jobs in the queue.
7) Select the document you want to restart printing.
8) Choose **Document |Restart**.

Changing the order of jobs in the print queue

You can change the sequence of jobs in the print queue. Here's how.

Exercise 12.15: Reordering the jobs in a print queue

1) Choose **Start | Control Panel| Printers and Faxes**.
2) Double-click the icon of the printer you want to look at. Windows displays a list of all the print jobs in the queue.
3) Right-click the file you want to move, and select **Properties**. On the **General** tab, drag the **Priority** slider to raise or lower the document priority.
4) Click **OK**. The documents will print in the order you selected, but this order may not be shown in the list of documents.

You can't move a file that is already printing.

Deleting all documents from the print queue

Follow the steps in Exercise 12.16 to remove all pending print jobs from the print queue.

Exercise 12.16: Deleting all jobs in the print queue

1) Choose **Start | Control Panel | Printers and Faxes**.
2) Double-click the icon of the printer you want to look at. Windows displays a list of all the print jobs in the queue.
3) Choose **Printer | Cancel All Documents**.

The Print dialog box

When you choose the **File | Print** command within an application, you are shown a dialog box that typically offers the following options:

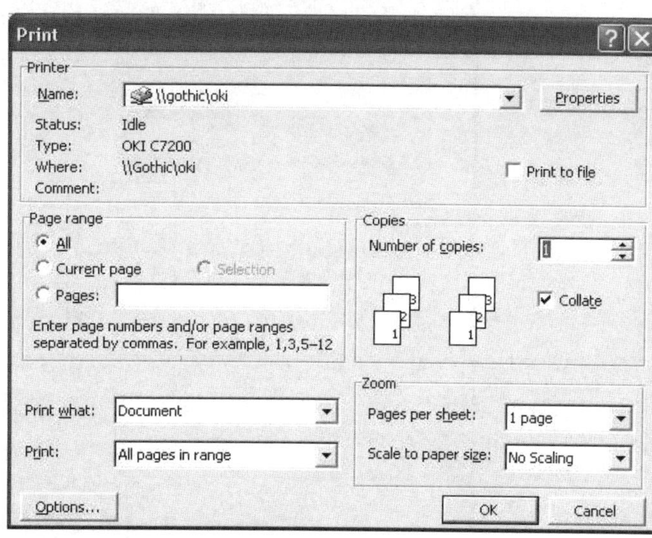

Name

To choose a different printer, click on the arrow on the right of the *Name* drop-down list box, and then click the printer you require.

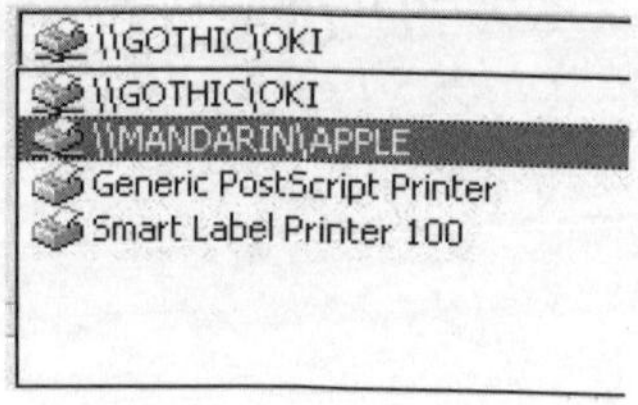

Print range

You can choose to print all pages, the currently displayed page only, or a range of pages.

To print a group of continuous pages, select the *Pages* option button. Enter the first and last page number of the group, separated by a hyphen. For example, 2-6 or 12-13.

To print a non-continuous group of pages, enter their individual page numbers, separated by commas – for example, 3,5,9 or 12,17,34. You can combine continuous with non-continuous page selections.

Copies

You can specify how many copies of the file you want to print. For multiple copies, ensure that the *Collate* check box is selected.

The Properties button

Clicking the **Properties** button displays some further print choices that will vary with the type of printer selected – colour or black and white, inkjet or laser.

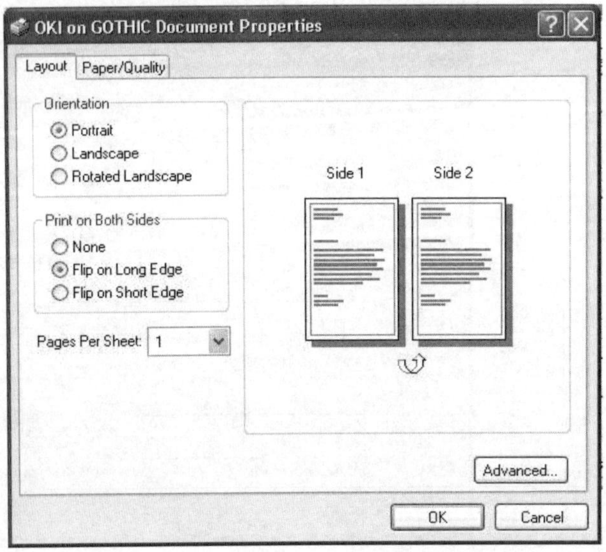

All printers offer choices about paper size (A4 is standard) and orientation (portrait means 'standing up', landscape means 'on its side').

When you have selected your options, click **OK** to print your file.

Print Preview

Most Windows applications have a **Print Preview** command on their **File** menu that lets you see on screen how the file contents will look when printed on paper.

Print to file

In certain circumstances you might find it useful to *print to file*. In other words, your file is printed in a particular printer language such as PostScript. You might need to do this if you are handing your document over to a commercial printer.

Click on the *Print to File* box before you click on **OK**. You are then asked to specify the file name and location for the print file. The example below the destination print file is called chapter1.prn.

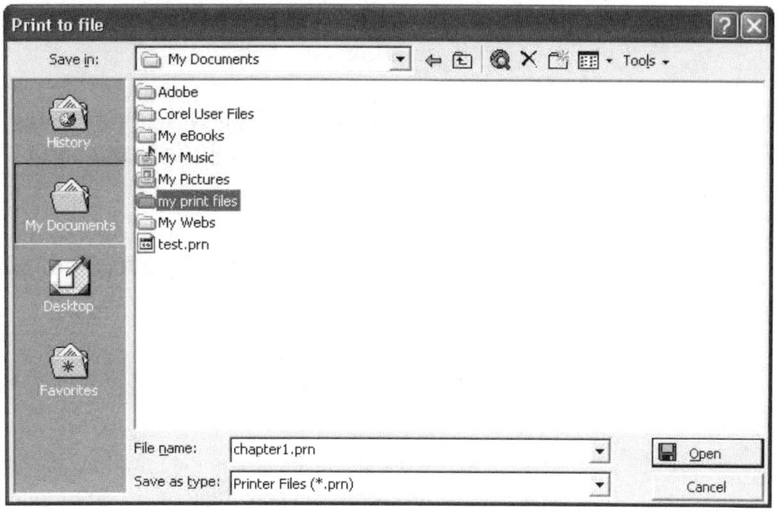

Changing the default printer

If your PC is attached to a network, you may have a number of printers available to you. It's a good idea to set the printer you use most often as the default printer. When you choose the **File | Print** command in Word or other Windows applications, your file outputs on the default printer unless you specify otherwise.

Follow this procedure to set a printer as the default printer:

- Choose **Start | Control Panel | Printers and Faxes.**
- Right-click the icon of the printer you want to set as the default.
- Select the **Set as Default Printer** command from the pop-up menu.

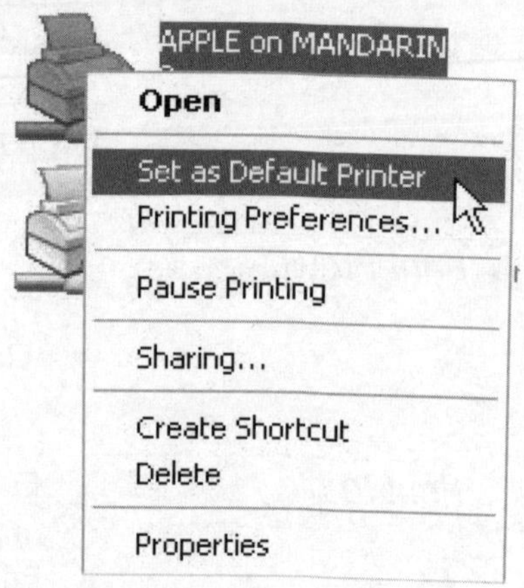

If there is a check mark beside the printer icon, the printer is already selected as the default printer.

Using the Print Screen utility

There may be occasions where you wish to take a snapshot of what's on your computer screen.

- Press **Print Screen** to take a snapshot of the entire screen.
- Press **Alt+Print Screen** to take a snapshot of the currently active window.

You can then paste the screen into an application such as Microsoft Word. Exercise 12.17 shows how to save a snap of the Windows Calculator for later use.

Exercise 12.17: Saving a screen snapshot of the Windows Calculator

1) Click on the **Start** button.
2) Choose **All Programs**, and then choose **Calculator** from the **Accessories** menu.
3) While the calculator is the currently active window, press **Alt+Print Screen**. Click on the **Start** button.
4) Choose **Paint** from the **Accessories** menu.

5) When Paint opens, press **Ctrl+v** to paste the saved snapshot into Paint. The figure below shows the screenshot of the Calculator pasted into Paint.

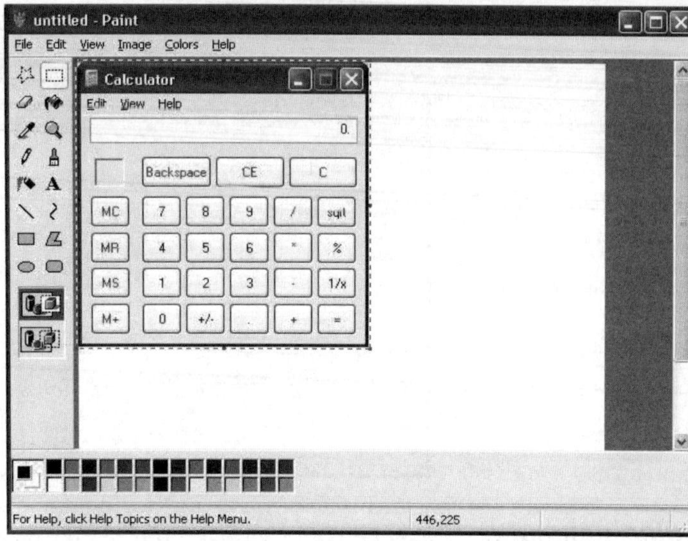

6) Choose **File | Save** to save the image with a file name of your choice. You can subsequently insert the image into another application.

Installing a new printer

Most printers available on the market today are *plug and play* – this means that once you connect one to your computer, your computer recognizes that you have a new printer and leads you through the appropriate steps to install it.

If your printer does not support plug and play or if for some reason your computer does not recognize the new printer, then use the *Add New Hardware* wizard. To do this, choose **Start | Control Panel | Printers and Faxes**. Then click on the **Add Printer** icon to start the wizard. You are then led through the steps required to install the printer.

Your version of Windows includes printer drivers for most popular makes of printer. Choose your printer from the list. Alternatively, use the disk or CD supplied with the printer: place the disk in the drive, click on **Have Disk**, and navigate to it.

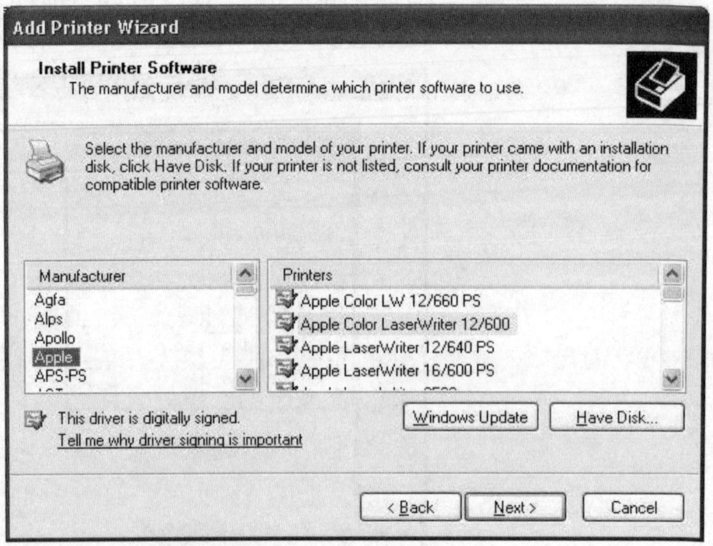

Chapter summary: so now you know

You can *personalize* your Windows desktop by repositioning icons, creating new folders, and placing application and file icons in them. See Exercises 12.1 and 12.2 for examples of how to do these tasks.

You can create desktop *shortcuts* – icons that take you directly to a particular application, file or folder. See Exercise 12.3 for an example of how to do this. You can also customize your *wallpaper*, *scheme* and *screen saver*.

You can adjust the *date* and *time* settings on your computer so that Windows attaches the correct date and time to the files you create and edit, and to e-mails you send. See Exercise 12.4 for how to do this. You can also adjust the *sound volume*.

By either blanking out the screen or showing a series of continually moving images, a *screen saver* program takes over the computer's display screen if there are no keystrokes or mouse movements for a specified length of time. See Exercise 12.5 for an example of how to do this.

Your *Regional and Language Options* decide the language, the default currency symbol shown in your applications, the keyboard/language combination, and which conventions Windows uses when displaying times, dates and numbers.

Your *screen resolution* is the number of pixels it displays. Lower-resolution settings make everything appear bigger and 'blockier'.

Higher-resolution settings make everything appear smaller and more defined.

Before you can copy files to a floppy disk, you must format the disk. If you format a previously used floppy disk, any files that may have been on the disk are no longer accessible. See Exercise 12.6 for an example of how to do this.

Anything you print goes first to a file called a *print queue* that can hold multiple print jobs. It is then taken from the print queue by the selected printer. You can view your print queue to see what jobs are waiting in it, delete jobs from the queue, and reorder the sequence in which jobs are listed. You can also pause and restart print jobs. See Exercises 12.11–12.16 for examples of how to do these tasks.

You have now completed the final section of ECDL Module 2. Congratulations.

Quick quiz: mastering Windows

Circle the correct answer to each of the following multiple-choice questions about mastering Windows.

Q1	How do you create a desktop shortcut for Word?
A.	Select Word in Windows Explorer. Right-click the **Word** icon and choose **Rename** from the pop-up menu displayed. Drag the Shortcut icon to the Desktop in the left pane of Windows Explorer.
B.	Select Word in Windows Explorer. Right-click the **Word** icon and choose **Create Shortcut** from the pop-up menu displayed. Drag the Shortcut icon to the Desktop in the left pane of Windows Explorer.
C.	Select Word in Windows Explorer. Right-click the **Excel** icon and choose **Rename** from the pop-up menu displayed. Drag the Shortcut icon to the Desktop in the left pane of Windows Explorer.
D.	Select Word in Windows Explorer. Right-click the **Word** icon and choose **Properties** from the pop-up menu displayed. Drag the Shortcut icon to the Desktop in the left pane of Windows Explorer.

Q2	How do you copy a file to a floppy disk?
A.	Open the file and choose **File | Save**. Locate the A: drive, and click **Save** to save the file.
B.	Open the file and choose **File | Save As**. Locate the C: drive, and click **Save** to save the file.
C.	Open the file and choose **File | Save As**. Locate the A: drive, and click **Save** to save the file.
D.	Open the file and choose **File | Save**. Locate the C: drive, and click **Save** to save the file.

Q3	How do you remove a job from the print queue?
A.	Choose **Start | Control Panel | Printers and Faxes**. Double-click the icon of the printer you want to look at. Windows displays a list of all the print jobs in the queue. Select the document you want to cancel printing and choose **Document | Cancel**.
B.	Choose **Start | Control Panel | Printers and Faxes**. Double-click the icon of the printer you want to look at. Windows displays a list of all the print jobs in the queue. Select the document you want to cancel printing and choose **Printer | Pause Printing**.
C.	Choose **Start | Control Panel | Printers and Faxes**. Double-click the icon of the printer you want to look at. Windows displays a list of all the print jobs in the queue. Select the document you want to cancel printing and choose **Printer | Cancel All Documents**.
D.	Choose **Start | Control Panel | Printers and Faxes**. Double-click the icon of the printer you want to look at. Windows displays a list of all the print jobs in the queue. Select the document you want to cancel printing and choose **Document | Restart**.

Q4	How do you set the date and time on your computer?
A.	Choose **Start | Control Panel** and double-click the **Display** icon. Make the changes you want. Click **Apply** and then **OK**.
B.	Choose **Start | Control Panel** and double-click the **Scheduled Tasks** icon. Make the changes you want. Click **Apply** and then **OK**.
C.	Choose **Start | Control Panel** and double-click the **Keyboard** icon. Make the changes you want. Click **Apply** and then **OK**.
D.	Choose **Start | Control Panel** and double-click the **Date and Time** icon. Make the changes you want. Click **Apply** and then **OK**.

Q5	How do you set up a screen saver?
A	Right-click the Windows desktop, choose **Properties** from the pop-up menu, and select the **Desktop** tab. Make your selections and click **OK**.
B	Right-click the Windows desktop, choose **New | Shortcut** from the pop-up menu, and select the **Screen Saver** tab. Make your selections and click **OK**.
C	Right-click the Windows desktop, choose **Properties** from the pop-up menu, and select the **Screen Saver** tab. Make your selections and click **OK**.
D	Right-click the Windows desktop, choose **Properties** from the pop-up menu, and select the **Appearance** tab. Make your selections and click **OK**.

Answers

1: B, **2:** C, **3:** A, **4:** D, **5:** C.

3

Word Processing

Back in the days when people thought they could predict the future, someone came up with the phrase 'paperless office'.

As computers found their way into more and more workplaces, the theory was that paper-based communication would disappear. Forever.

But alongside affordable computers came affordable printers. As a result, computerization has led to more rather than less paper usage. The office-supplies people have never been busier.

In this word processing module, you will learn how to add to the world's output of computer-generated paperwork.

You will discover how to create formal business letters and reports, and produce stylish posters and restaurant menus. We will even share with you the secrets of generating personalized form letters, (un)popularly known as junk mail.

Good luck with it!

Chapter 13: Your first letter in Word

In this chapter

There is a lot more to word processing than just typing and editing text, but these are the two basics. Read the material and follow the examples in this chapter and you will have the foundation skills to move on to more advanced tasks.

You will also learn how to access and search through Word's online help, which is a great place to find answers and advice on using any of the program's features.

New skills

At the end of this chapter you should be able to:

- Start and quit Word.
- Enter and edit text.
- Recognize Word's non-printing characters.
- Use the **Shift**, **Backspace**, **Delete**, arrow and **Tab** keys.
- Type and print a standard letter.
- Use Word's Insert Date feature.
- Reverse typing and editing actions with Word's Undo feature.
- Save, name, open, create and close Word documents.
- Use online help to learn more about Word.

New words

At the end of this chapter you should be able to explain the following terms:

- Document
- Paragraph mark
- Wrap-around
- Non-printing characters

Starting Word

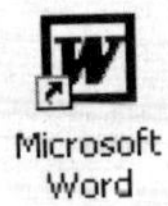

Double-click the Microsoft Word icon or choose **Start | All Programs | Microsoft Word**. Word starts and displays a new window containing a new, blank document ready for you to type into.

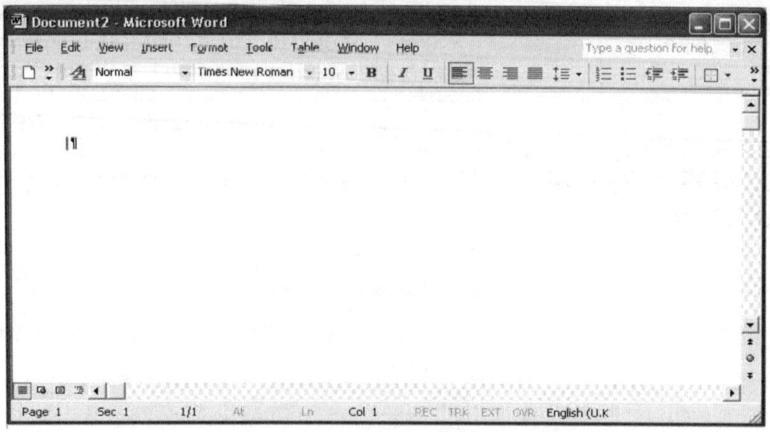

A blank Word document ready to accept your text

Word document
A Microsoft Word file. For example, a letter or a report.

No new, blank document?

If starting Word did not automatically open a new, blank document, click the **New** button at the top left of your screen.

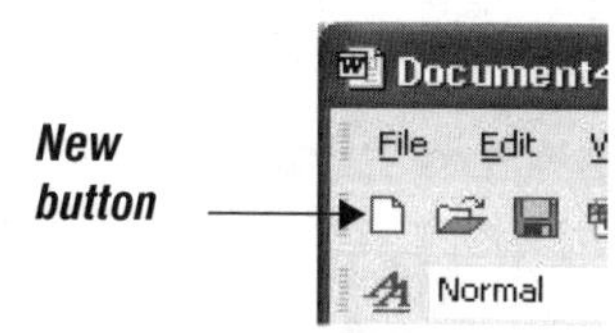

Text cursor and paragraph mark

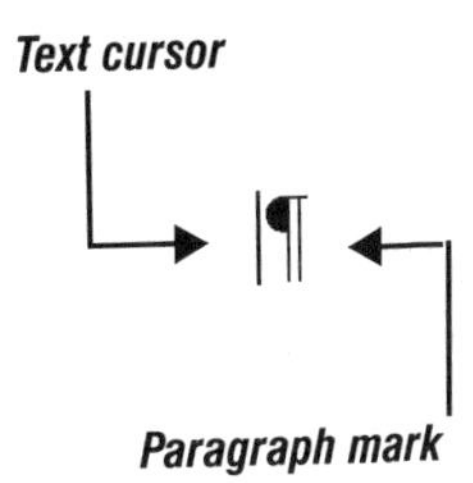

Near the top-left corner of your document you can see two items:

- **Text cursor:** A blinking vertical line. Whenever you type text, Word places the text at the text cursor's location. Think of the cursor as a 'you are here' indicator, telling you where you are in a document.
- **Paragraph mark:** Every new Word document contains one of these (it looks like a backward-facing letter P). Whenever you press the **Enter** key to begin a new paragraph, Word inserts another one at that point. The paragraph mark only appears on the screen, not on printouts.

If Word does not display the paragraph mark in your document, press **Ctrl+Shift+***.

Paragraph mark
A symbol shown on the screen (but not printed) to indicate the end of a paragraph. Word displays one each time you press the ***Enter*** *key.*

Actions you need to know

Here are the four basic operations in Word that you need to know:

- Typing text.
- Editing (changing) text you typed previously.
- Using the **Shift** key to type upper-case (capital) letters.
- Using the **Enter** key to type new paragraph marks.

You will practise each one in the following four exercises.

Exercise 13.1: Typing text in Word

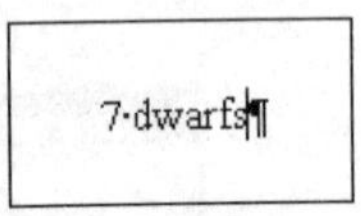

1) Type the following number: 7
2) Press the **Spacebar**. Word displays a dot on the screen. This is Word's way of telling you that you have typed a space. Word will not print the dot.
3) Type the following word: dwarfs

   That's it. Congratulations! You have typed your first text in Word.

Exercise 13.2: Editing previously typed text

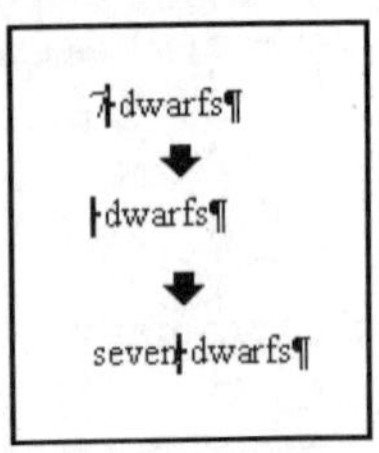

Often you will want to change – or, perhaps, remove completely – text that you have typed. This is called editing.

1) Using the mouse, click to the right of the 7.
2) Press the **Backspace** key. (You will find it directly above the **Enter** key.)
3) Type the following word: seven

   You have completed the editing exercise.

Exercise 13.3: Using the Shift key

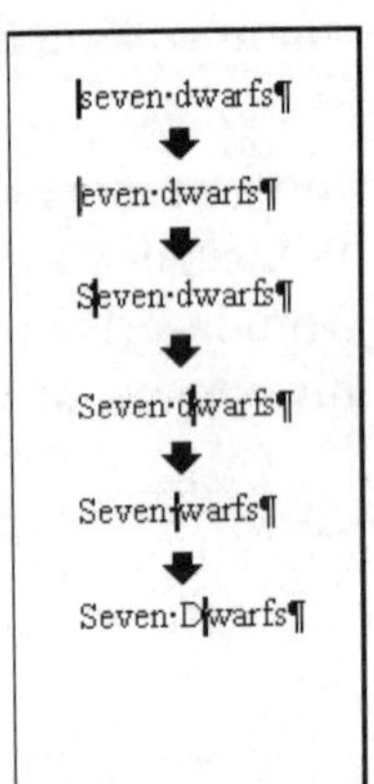

1) Click to the left of the letter 's' in 'seven'.
2) Press the **Delete** key to delete the letter 's'.
3) Hold down the **Shift** key and type the letter 's'. Word displays an upper-case 'S'.
4) Move the cursor to the right of the letter 'd' in 'dwarfs'.
5) Press the **Backspace** key to delete the letter 'd'.

6) Hold down the **Shift** key and type the letter 'd'. Word displays an upper-case 'D'.

   Well done! Another exercise completed.

Exercise 13.4: Using Enter to type new paragraph marks

Now you will use the **Enter** key to end one paragraph and begin another.

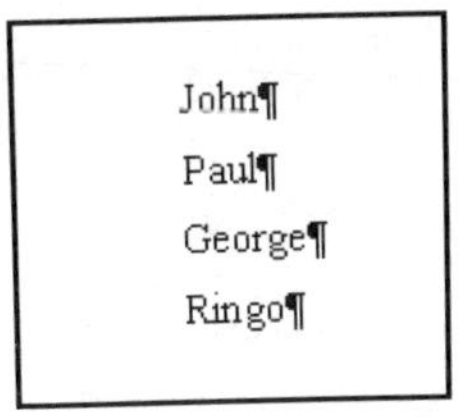

1) Click to the right of the word Dwarfs, and press **Enter**. This creates a new paragraph. Word places the cursor at the start of a new line.
2) Type 'John' and press **Enter**.
3) Type 'Paul' and press **Enter**.
4) Type 'George' and press **Enter**.
5) Type 'Ringo'.

   You will not need this text for future exercises. So delete it as follows:
6) Click to the right of the word 'Ringo'.
7) Press and hold down the **Backspace** key until Word has removed all the text from the document.

Keys you need to know

Now is a good time to summarize the roles of these important keys:

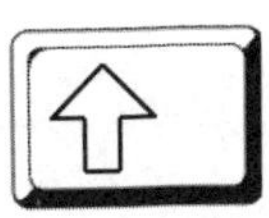

- **Shift:** Pressed in combination with a letter, this creates an upper-case letter. Pressed in combination with a number or symbol key, it creates the upper symbol shown on the key. You will find a **Shift** key at both sides of the keyboard.

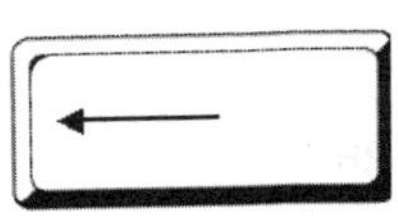

- **Backspace:** Deletes the character to the *left* of the cursor. You will find the **Backspace** key at the top-right of the keyboard, just above the **Enter** key.

- **Delete:** Deletes the character to the *right* of the cursor. You will find the **Delete** key in a group of six keys to the right of the **Enter** key.

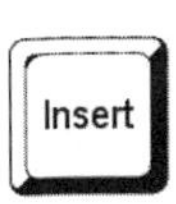

- **Insert:** Switches between Insert and Overtype editing modes. In Insert mode, typing causes existing text to move to the right and down, to make room for the new characters you are typing. In Overtype mode, characters you type replace existing characters.

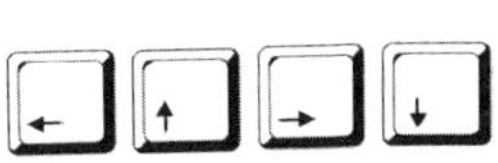

- **Arrow:** Rather than use the mouse to move the cursor around your document, you can press any of the four arrow keys, located to the right of the **Enter** key. You may find this method faster than moving and clicking the mouse, because you need not take either hand away from the keyboard.

Typing a letter

Now you are ready to type a longer piece of text.

Exercise 13.5: Typing a paragraph of a letter

1) Type the following text:

   I am writing to you in relation to our annual Sale of Work, which will take place in our local Scout Hall on 17 October next.

   Your screen should look as follows:

   I·am·writing·to·you·in·relation·to·our·annual·Sale·of·Work·which·will·take·place·in·our·local·
   Scout·Hall·on·17·October·next.¶

Notice how Word moved the cursor to the beginning of the next line when the text you were typing reached the right-hand edge of the page.

On an old-style typewriter, you would have needed to press the **Enter** (also called **Return**) key to move down to the next line. Word does this for you automatically. This feature is called wrap-around, and Word is said to 'wrap' the text to a new line once the previous line is full.

Wrap-around
Word's automatic moving of the cursor to the beginning of a new line when the text reaches the end of the previous one.

Exercise 13.6: Typing more text in your letter

In this exercise, you will type more text in the letter, and type your name at the bottom.

1) Click at the beginning of the first line, so that the cursor is just to the left of the letter 'I'.
2) Press the **Enter** key to insert a new paragraph, and then the **Up Arrow** key to position the cursor at the start of the new paragraph.
3) Type the following and press **Enter**:

   Dear Ms Smith

   Your letter should look as shown.

   Dear·Ms·Smith¶

   I·am·writing·to·you·in·relation·to·our·annual·Sale·of·Work·which·will·take·place·in·our·local·
   Scout·Hall·on·17·October·next.¶

4) Click at the end of the last line, so that the cursor is just to the right of the full stop and to the left of the paragraph mark.

I·am·writing·to·you·in·relation·to·our·annual·Sale·of·Work·which·will·take·place·in·our·local·Scout·Hall·on·17·October·next.¶

Click here

5) Press **Enter** twice.
6) Type the following and press **Enter** twice:
   In previous years your company was kind enough to donate a prize for our wheel of fortune.
7) Type the following and press **Enter** twice:
   Could we ask you to be as generous again?
8) Type the following:
   Ken Bloggs
   Your letter should look as shown.

Dear·Ms·Smith¶

I·am·writing·to·you·in·relation·to·our·annual·Sale·of·Work·which·will·take·place·in·our·local·Scout·Hall·on·17·October·next.¶

¶

In·previous·years·your·company·was·kind·enough·to·donate·a·prize·for·our·wheel·of·fortune.¶

¶

Could·we·ask·you·to·be·as·generous·again?¶

¶

Ken·Bloggs¶

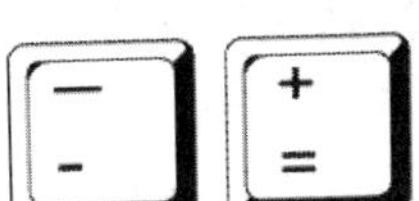

The Hyphen key (left of the Equals key)

9) Click at the beginning of the sender's name, so that the cursor is just to the left of the letter 'K' in 'Ken'. Press **Enter** to insert a new line and then move the cursor to the start of the new line.
10) Hold down the **Shift** key and press the **Hyphen** key about twenty times. (The **Hyphen** key is the second key to the left of the **Backspace** key.)

____________________________¶

Ken·Bloggs¶

Release the **Shift** key. When you print the letter, you can write your signature on the line created by the repeated pressing of the hyphen.

That's it. You have completed the exercise.

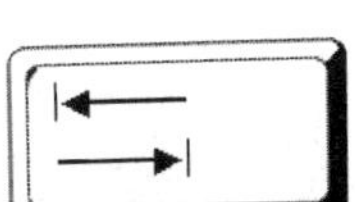

Tab key

No letter is complete without an address and a date. In the next two exercises, you will discover how you can use Word's **Tab** key to position an address, and the **Date and Time** command on the **Insert** menu to insert today's date in a letter or other document.

Exercise 13.7: Entering an address on a letter

1) Click at the beginning of the line containing 'Dear Ms Smith', so that the cursor is just to the left of the letter 'D'.
2) Press **Enter** seven times to create new lines at the top of your letter. This is where you will type the address and, in Exercise 13.8, the date.
3) Click at the beginning of the first line, so that the cursor is at the top-left of your letter.
4) Press the **Tab** key eight times, and type the following:

   24 Main Street
5) Click at the beginning of the second line, press the **Tab** key eight times, and type the following:

   Anytown
6) Click at the beginning of the third line, press the **Tab** key eight times, and type the following:

   333444

   The top of your letter should now look as shown.

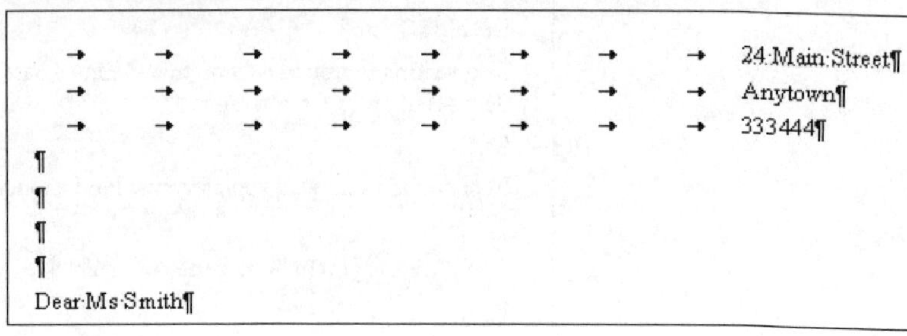

Exercise 13.8: Entering a date on a letter

1) Click at the beginning of the line containing 'Dear Ms Smith', so that the cursor is just left of the letter 'D'.
2) Press the **Up Arrow** key three times, and then press the **Tab** key eight times. You are now ready to insert a date on the letter.
3) Choose **Insert | Date and Time**.

   Word displays a dialog box that shows today's date in a variety of formats.
4) Select the date format you want, and click **OK**.

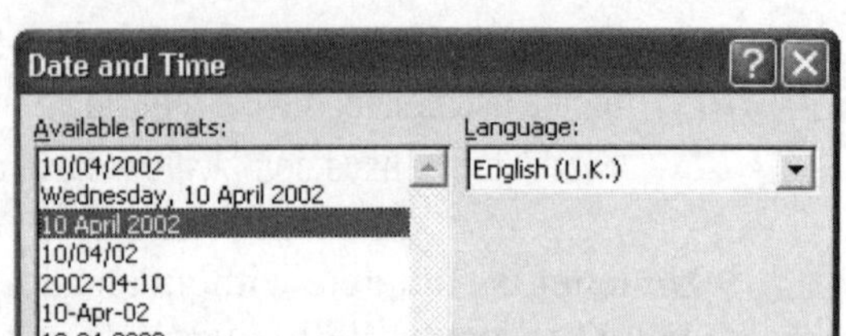

This inserts the date in your letter and closes the dialog box.

Well done. The heading of your first letter in Word should look as follows.

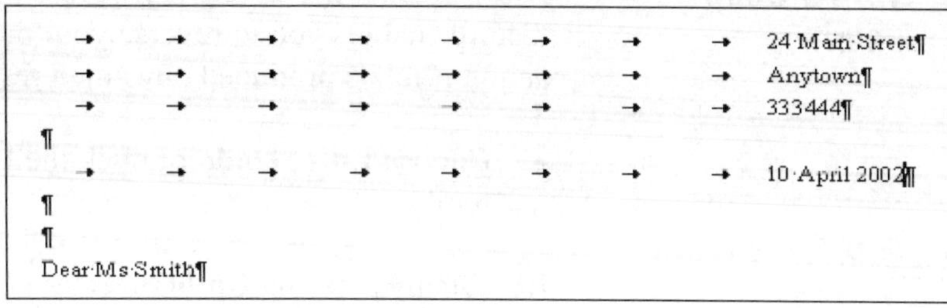
→ → → → → → → → 24·Main·Street¶
→ → → → → → → → Anytown¶
→ → → → → → → → 333444¶
¶
→ → → → → → → → 10·April·2002¶
¶
¶
Dear·Ms·Smith¶

Non-printing characters and wavy underlines

Each time you press the **Tab** key, Word inserts an arrow symbol on the screen. Like the paragraph mark that indicates a paragraph ending, and the dot between words that represents a blank space, the tab symbol is a non-printing character.

Non-printing characters
Symbols that Word displays on the screen to help you type and edit your document, but that are not printed.

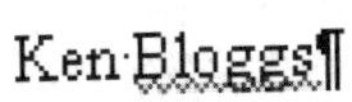

Wavy underlines indicate possible spelling or grammar errors

Depending on how Word is set up on your computer, you may see green and/or red wavy underlines beneath certain words or phrases. These are to do with Word's spell- and grammar-checking features, which are explained in Chapter 15. Until then, ignore them.

Insert or overtype?

By default, text is *inserted* as you type, and existing text is *pushed* to the right. If you prefer, you can *overtype* existing text.

Press the **Insert** key, or double-click on OVR on the status bar, to toggle between Insert and Overtype modes.

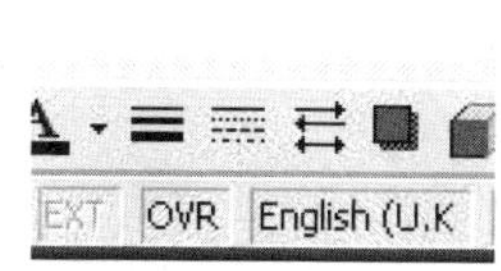

Printing your letter

Your letter is ready to be printed out. Choose **File** | **Print**. If your printer is set up correctly all you need to do is click **OK** on the *Print* dialog box. You will learn more about printing in Chapter 15.

Word's Undo feature

Did you enter the wrong text? Press the wrong key? Word's Undo feature enables you to reverse your most recent typing or editing action if it has produced unwanted results:

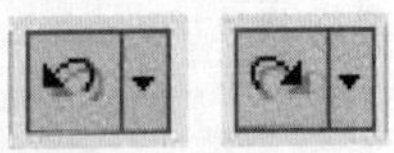

Undo Redo

- Choose **Edit | Undo** or click the **Undo** button on the *Standard* toolbar.

Repeatedly pressing **Undo** reverses your last series of actions. To view a list of recent actions that you can undo, click the arrow at the right of the **Undo** button. If you undo an action and then change your mind, click the **Redo** button (to the right of the **Undo** button).

Word's Repeat feature

Do you want to do the same thing again? Use Word's **Repeat** feature:

- Choose **Edit | Repeat** or press **Ctrl+y**.

Word's toolbars

Word's toolbars give you convenient, one-click access to the commands that you use most often. By default, Word displays two toolbars, the *Standard* and *Formatting* toolbars, on a *single* row across the top of the screen.

To display them as two, individual toolbars, follow these steps:

- Choose **Tools | Customize** and click the **Options** tab.

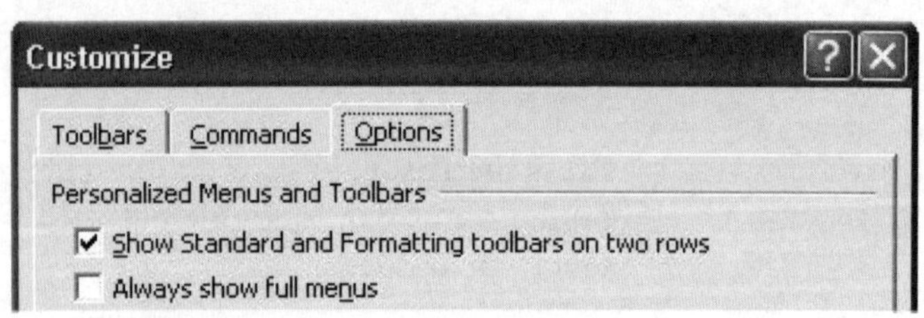

- Select the *Show Standard and Formatting toolbars on two rows* check box, and choose **Close**.

Hiding and displaying toolbars

You can display or hide Word's various toolbars by choosing the **View | Toolbars** command, and then selecting or deselecting the various toolbar options from the menu displayed. Right-clicking anywhere on a toolbar displays the same menu.

The check marks beside the **Standard** *and* **Formatting** *choices indicate that they are already selected for display on screen*

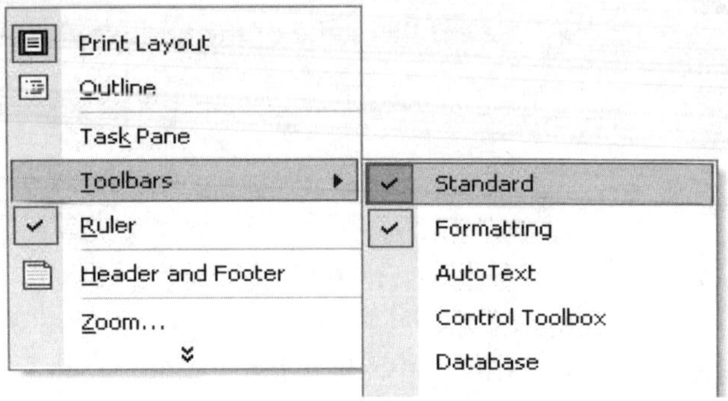

The Standard and Formatting toolbars

Only two of Word's toolbars are relevant to this ECDL module: the *Standard* toolbar and the *Formatting* toolbar.

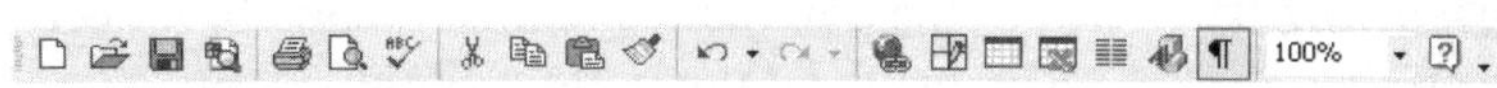

Word's **Standard** *toolbar*

The *Standard* toolbar includes buttons for managing files – that is, Word documents – and for working with tables.

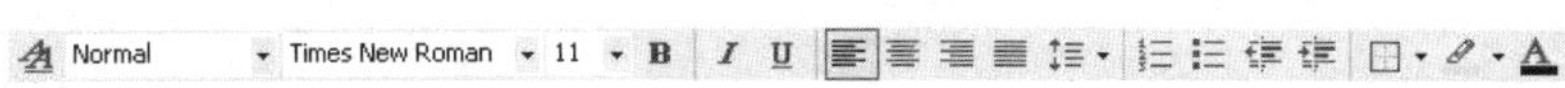

Word's **Formatting** *toolbar*

The *Formatting* toolbar includes buttons for changing the appearance of text and for inserting bullets.

Rather than introduce all these buttons at once, we will explain the ones you need to know about as they become relevant through the remainder of this ECDL word processing module.

Hiding and displaying toolbar buttons

You can remove one or more buttons from a toolbar. Follow these steps:

- Display the toolbar that you want to change.
- Hold down the **Alt** key and drag the button off the toolbar.
- Word removes the selected button from the toolbar.

Want the button back again? Follow this procedure:

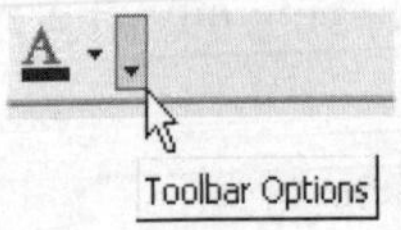

- Display the toolbar. Click the **Toolbar Options** button at the very end of the toolbar, and then select **Add or Remove Buttons** on the drop-down menu.
- Select the name of the toolbar you want to edit.

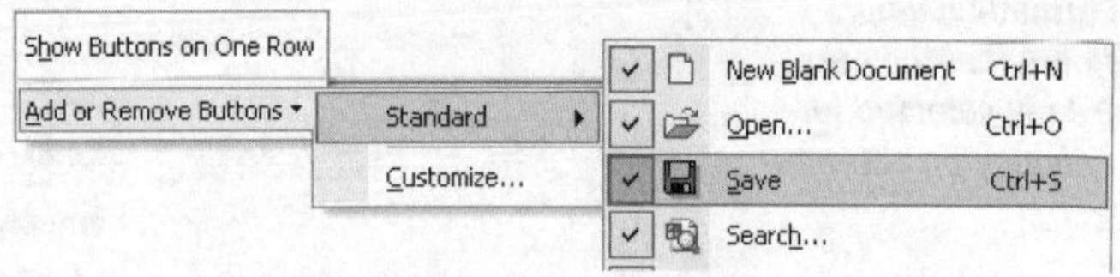

- Click the button you want to display again.
- Click anywhere outside the menu to close it.

Word redisplays the button on the toolbar.

Word's personalized menus

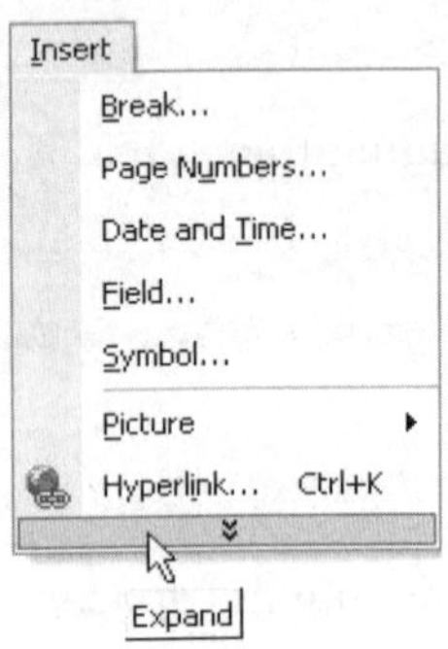

By default, when you first choose a menu, Word displays only some of the commands on that menu. To view a complete list, click the double-arrow at the bottom of the menu.

If you choose a command that is not displayed by default, Word adds it to the displayed list the next time you choose the menu.

To view all commands each time you choose a menu, follow these steps:

- Choose **Tools | Customize** and click the **Options** tab.

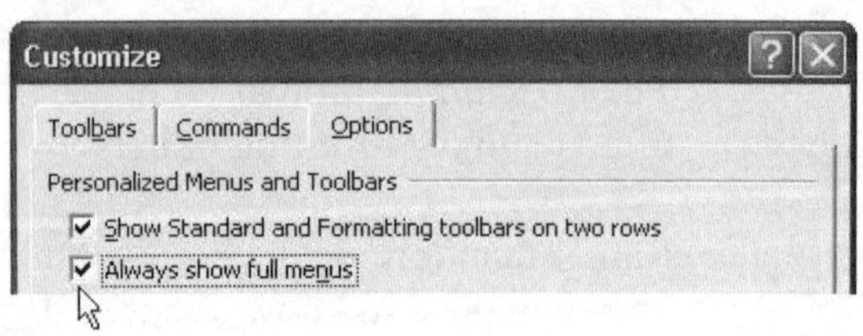

- Select the *Always show full menus* option and choose **Close**.

Modifying basic options

You can customize the way Word works and set your own personal preferences. Choose **Tools | Options** to see the range of options available.

For example, to change the name that appears on document property sheets and for tracking changes and comments, choose the **User Information** tab and enter your name.

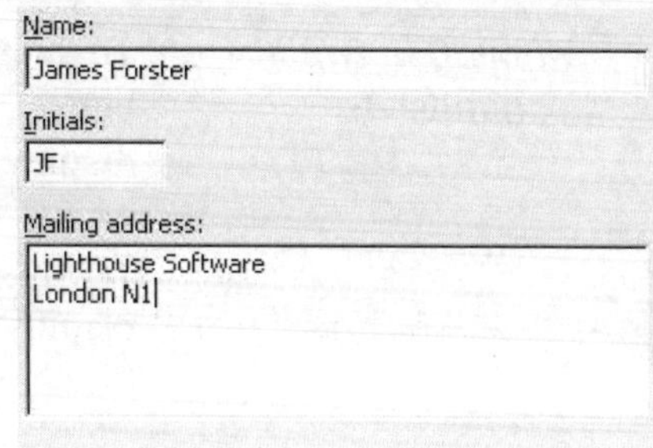

Word's task pane

While Word's toolbars provide one-click access to the commands that you use most often, Word's task pane collects in one place the various commands you may need to perform important tasks such as creating and opening documents, formatting documents and mail merge.

The task pane is located on the right side of your screen and can be opened and closed as required.

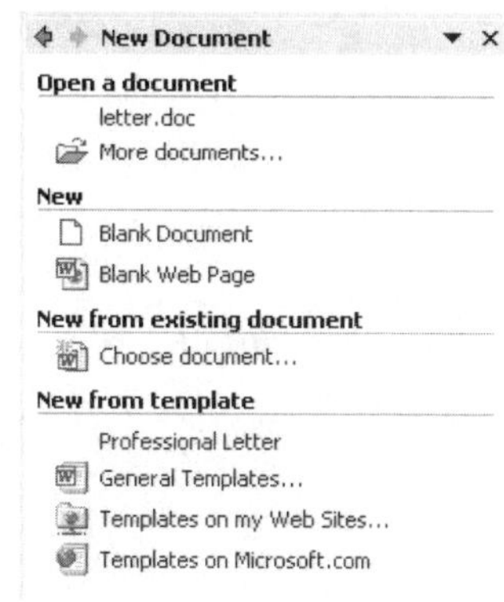

Task panes are available for many tasks. The task pane illustrated here is the *New Document* task pane, which presents the various options for creating new documents and opening existing ones. We will explain each task pane as it becomes relevant through the remainder of this ECDL word processing module.

Opening and closing the task pane

The relevant task pane automatically opens when you begin a task for which a task pane exists. To display the task pane at any other time, choose **View | Task Pane**.

To close the task pane, click the **Close** button on its title bar.

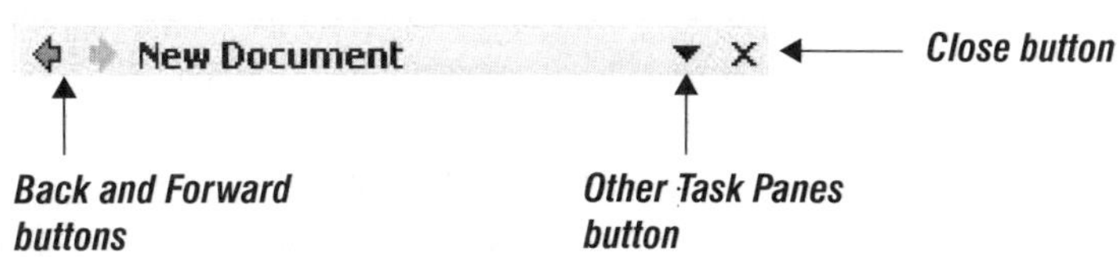

Switching between task panes

To switch from one task pane to another, click the **Other Task Panes** button on the title bar. Then select a task pane from the drop-down list displayed.

To move back and forwards through task panes you have previously displayed, use the **Back** and **Forward** buttons on the left side of the title bar.

Online help

Like Excel, Access, PowerPoint and other Microsoft applications, Word offers a searchable online help system.

- The word 'help' means that the information is there to help you understand and use the application.
- The word 'online' means that the material is presented on the computer screen rather than as a traditional printed manual.

You can search through and read online help in various ways: from the Help window, from dialog boxes, and by using the Office Assistant.

Using the Office Assistant

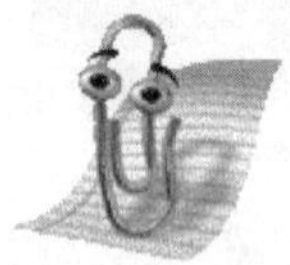

Office Assistant

The Office Assistant is a friendly, animated tool that allows you to type a topic or question about what you are looking for. It then presents a list of relevant help topics for you to choose from, as Exercise 13.9 demonstrates.

Exercise 13.9: Using the Office Assistant to get help

1) Click the Office Assistant.

   If the Office Assistant is not visible on your screen, choose **Help | Show the Office Assistant**.
2) In the search balloon displayed, type: 'help'.

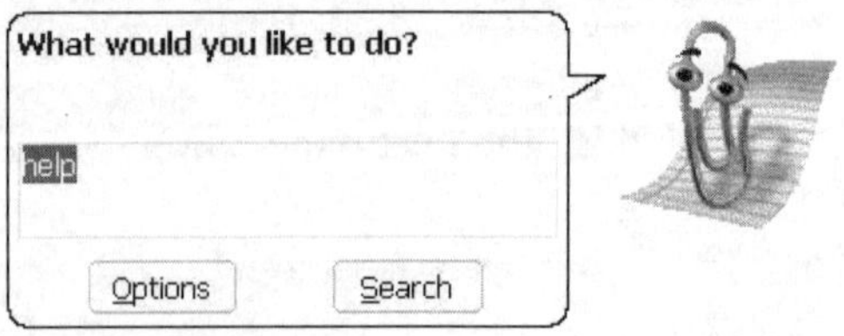

3) Click the **Search** button.
4) Click any topic in the list retrieved by the search. That topic is then displayed in the Microsoft Word Help window.

   This window is explained further in 'Using the Help window to get help' below.

5) Close the window by clicking the **Close** button in its top right corner.

Using Ask a Question *to get help*

The *Ask a Question* box on the right side of Word's menu bar allows you to type a topic or question to get help without using the Office Assistant.

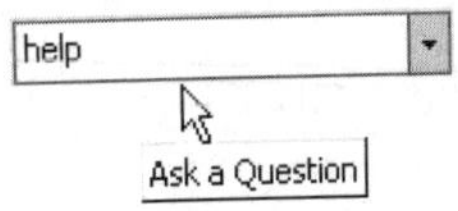

- Type your topic or question in the box and press **Enter**. Word displays a list of topics that you can choose from in the same way as you do when using the Office Assistant.

Using the Help window to get help

To use the Help window directly to get help, you must first turn off the Office Assistant. Follow these steps:

- Right-click the Office Assistant and choose **Options** from the drop-down menu.
- Deselect the *Use the Office Assistant* option and click **OK**.

To open the *Microsoft Word Help* window, choose **Help | Microsoft Word Help** or click the **Microsoft Word Help** button on the *Standard* toolbar. The Help window presents three tabs that allow you to search for help in different ways.

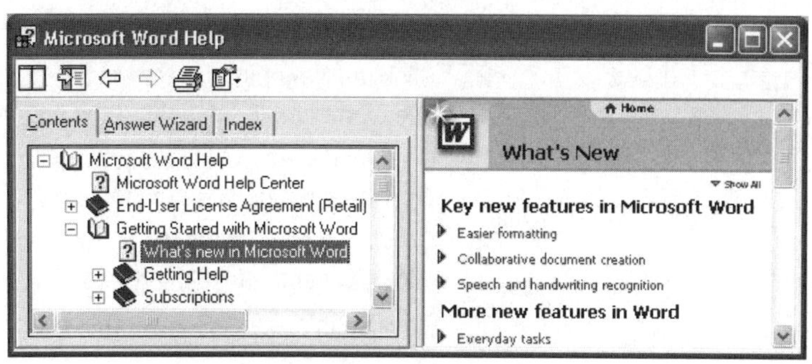

- **Contents tab:** This offers short descriptions of Word's main features.

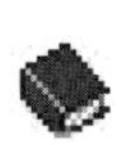

  Where you see a heading with a book symbol, double-click to view the related sub-headings.

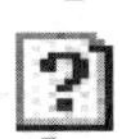

  Double-click on a question mark symbol to read the help text.

- **Answer Wizard tab:** Type your question in the *What would you like to do?* box, and click **Search**. Word displays all matches from the online help.

  Click a topic to display the associated text in the right-hand pane.

- **Index tab:** Type the word or phrase you are interested in, or choose a keyword from the list displayed. Then click **Search**. Word displays a list of suggested help topics in the lower-left of the window.

  When you find the topic that you are looking for, click it to display the associated text in the right-hand pane.

As you search through and read online help topics, you will see the following buttons at the top of the online help window:

- **Hide/Show:** Hides or displays the left pane of the *Help* window.
- **Back/Forward:** Moves you backwards and forwards through previously visited help topics.
- **Print:** Prints the currently displayed help topic.
- **Options:** Offers a number of display options.

Take a few minutes to look through Word's Online Help system.

Using help from dialog boxes

You can also access online help directly from a dialog box, as Exercise 13.10 demonstrates.

Exercise 13.10: Using online help in a dialog box

Help button

1) Choose **Edit | Find** to display the *Find and Replace* dialog box.
2) Click the **Help** button near the top-right of the dialog box. Word displays a question mark to the right of the cursor.
3) Click anywhere in the *Find what* box. Word displays online help text telling you about the purpose of the *Find what* box.
4) Click anywhere on the Word window to remove the online help text, and then click **Cancel** to close the dialog box.

   Practise this exercise with other dialog boxes in Word.

Working with Word documents

A Word document is a file containing text (and sometimes graphics too).

Saving your document

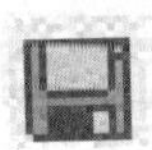

Save button

In Word, as in other applications, always save your work as you go along. Don't wait until you are finished! To save a document:

- Choose **File | Save** or click the **Save** button on the *Standard* toolbar.

The first time that you save a file in Word you are asked to specify:

- The location on your PC where you want your file saved.
- The name of your new file.

Exercise 13.11 leads you through the steps.

Word file name extensions

The file names of Word documents end in .doc. This helps you to distinguish Word files from other file types, such as Excel (.xls) or PowerPoint (.ppt) files.

Exercise 13.11: Saving and naming a new document

1) Choose **File | Save** or click the **Save** button on the *Standard* toolbar.
2) The first time that you save a document, Word prompts you to select a location. By default, Word suggests that you save your files in the My Documents folder. Accept or amend this location, as required.

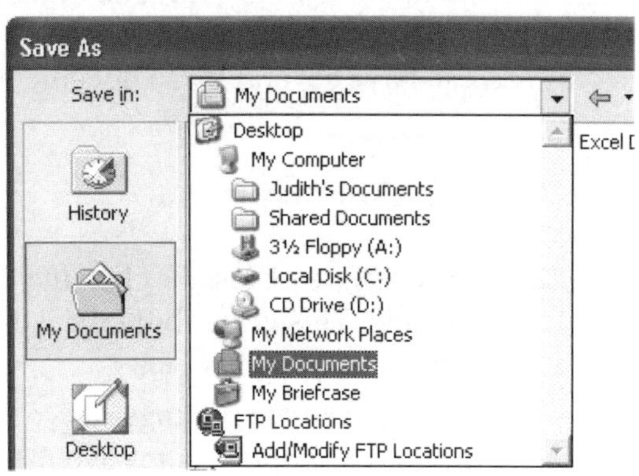

3) Word prompts you to give a name to your new file. Type a name that you will find easy to remember and recognize. If your initials are KB, for example, call it KBletter.

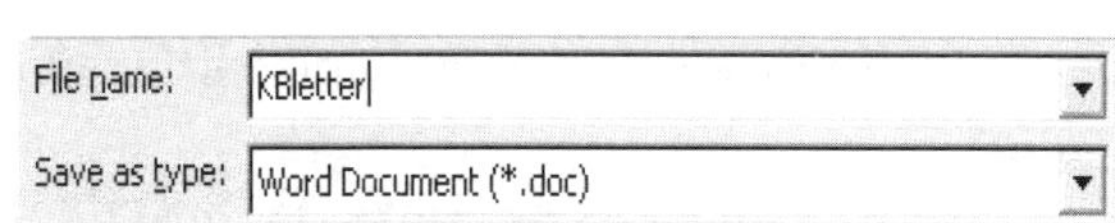

You need not type '.doc' after your file name when saving a file. Word adds the three-letter file name extension automatically.

4) Click the **Save** button.

Creating a new document

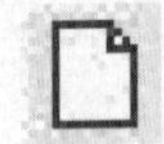

New button

To create a new Word file:

- Choose **File | New**.
  -or-
- Click the **New** button on the *Standard* toolbar.

The **New** button creates a new blank document in Word. The **New** menu option displays the *New Document* task pane in which you select the type of document you want to create.

Opening an existing document

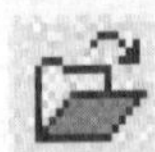

Open button

To open an existing Word file:

- Choose **File | Open**.
  -or-
  Click the **Open** button on the *Standard* toolbar.
- Select the file you want from the dialog box and click the **Open** button in the dialog box
  -or-
  Double-click the file name in the dialog box.

You can have several Word documents open at the same time.

Closing a document

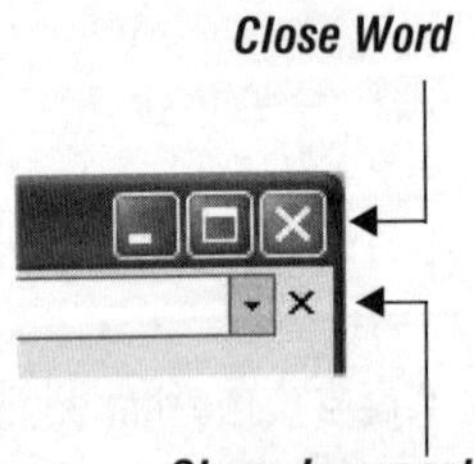

To close a Word document:

- Choose **File | Close** or click the **Close** button on the document window. This closes only the current document. Any other open documents remain open.
  If you have made changes to your document since you last saved it, Word prompts you to save the changes before it closes the file.

Saving a document with a different name

To save a document with a different name or in a different location:

- Choose **File | Save As**. Specify the drive and folder where you want to save the file, and specify the file name.

Changing the default folder

You can specify what folder you want Word to use as the default folder for opening and saving files.

- Choose **Tools | Options**, and then choose the *File Locations* tab. Highlight the file type whose default location you wish to change, and click **Modify**. Then navigate to the folder you wish to use.

Quitting Word

To leave Word:

- Choose **File | Exit** or click the **Close** button on the Word window.

If you have left open any files containing unsaved work, Word prompts you to save them.

Well done. You have now completed the first chapter of the ECDL word processing module. You can close your letter document and close Microsoft Word.

Chapter summary: so now you know

A Word *document* is a file containing text (and sometimes graphics too). Every new Word document contains a *text cursor*. Whenever you type text, Word places the text at the text cursor's location. You can move the text cursor with the mouse or with the arrow keys.

Every new document also contains a *paragraph mark*. Whenever you press the **Enter** key to type a new paragraph of text or insert a blank line, Word inserts another paragraph mark at that point.

You can edit text with the following two keys:

- **Backspace:** Removes text to the *left* of the text cursor.
- **Delete:** Removes text to the *right* of the text cursor.

Press the **Shift** key in combination with a letter, number or symbol key to type an *upper-case* (capital) character or symbol.

Press the **Tab** key repeatedly to move text to the right. When typing a letter, for example, use **Tab** to position the address and related details at the top-right of the letter.

Word's *Insert Date* feature inserts the current date in a document. You can choose from a wide range of date formats.

Word's *non-printing characters*, such as a single dot to represent a space, do not appear on printouts. They are displayed on the screen only as a guide to typing and editing.

Word's *Undo* feature enables you to reverse your most recent typing or editing actions if they have produced unwanted results.

In Word, as in other applications, always save your work as you go along. The first time you save a document file, Word prompts you to give it a *file name.* Word automatically adds the file name extension *.doc* to all saved documents.

Word offers a searchable *online help* system that you can access in various ways, including from the Help window, from dialog boxes, and by using the Office Assistant.

Quick quiz: your first letter in Word

Circle the correct answer to each of the following multiple-choice questions about creating your first letter in Word.

Q1	To turn off the Office Assistant, you ...
A.	Choose **Help | Hide the Office Assistant**.
B.	Click the Office Assistant and choose **Hide the Office Assistant** from the pop-up menu.
C.	Right-click the Office Assistant, choose **Options** from the pop-up menu, and deselect *Use the Office Assistant*.

Q2	The New button on the Standard toolbar creates a new blank Word document.
A.	True.
B.	False

Q3	The Delete key deletes the character to the left of the cursor.
A.	True.
B.	False.

Q4	When you press the Tab key, which non-printing character does Word display in your document?
A.	A dot.
B.	A hyphen.
C.	An arrow.

Q5	To insert today's date in a document, you ...
A.	Choose **Insert | Date and Time**.
B.	Choose **Insert | Symbol** and then select the date format you want from the list displayed.
C.	Choose **Insert | Date and Time** and then select the date format you want from the list displayed.

Answers

1: C, **2:** A, **3:** B, **4:** C, **5:** C.

Chapter 14: Formatting, positioning and copying text

In this chapter

In addition to typing and editing text, you can use a word processor to:

- Change the *appearance* of the text. This is called formatting. It includes such actions as making text bolder (heavier), placing a line under it, and putting it in italics. You can also change the text font and font size, format text as bullets, and apply shading (coloured backgrounds) and borders to text.
- Change the *position* of text on the page. You have already learnt how to reposition text using the **Tab** key. Now you will discover two other methods: alignment and indenting.

In this chapter you will also learn how to copy text within and between documents, and how to insert symbols and special characters.

New skills

At the end of this chapter you should be able to:

- Select text.
- Format text (bold, italic and underline).
- Copy, cut and paste text.
- Indent text from the left and right page margins.
- Align text (left, right, centre and justified).
- Create text bullets.
- Explain fonts and font sizes.
- Add borders and shading to text.
- Use Word's Zoom feature to enlarge and reduce the document display.
- Save a Word document to a floppy disk.
- Insert symbols and special characters.
- Use Word's Format Painter feature to copy formatting.

New words

At the end of this chapter you should be able to explain the following terms:

- Select
- Bulleted text
- Clipboard
- Font
- Indent
- Alignment
- Format Painter

Selecting text

Typically, when you want to format or position some text, it is only a particular character, word, group of words or paragraph that you want to change.

You tell Word which part of the document you want to change by first selecting that text. Selecting a piece of text is sometimes called highlighting.

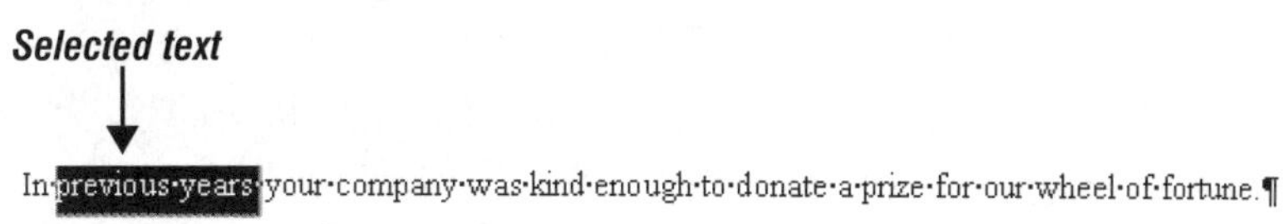

When you select text, Word displays that text in reverse (white text on a black background), rather like the negative of a photograph.

Selecting text
Highlighting a piece of text in order to perform an action on it such as formatting or alignment.

Formatting and alignment are just two of the actions that you will learn how to perform on selected text. In later chapters, you will learn how to find and replace, and spellcheck, selected text.

- To select text on a single line, drag the mouse to the right until you have selected the characters or words.
- To select text that is on more than a single line, drag the mouse to the right and down the page.
- To select a single word, double-click the word.
- To select a sentence, hold down the **Ctrl** key, and then click anywhere in the sentence.
- To select a paragraph, triple-click anywhere in the paragraph.

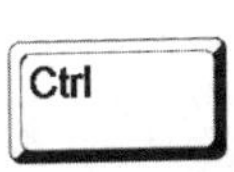

Ctrl (Control) key

- To select a whole document, hold down the **Ctrl** key and click anywhere in the left margin.
- To select non-contiguous pieces of text, select one piece of text, then hold down the **Ctrl** key while selecting the others.

Exercise 14.1: Selecting text

In this exercise you will learn how to select text – characters, words, sentences and paragraphs.

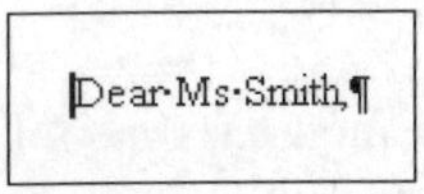

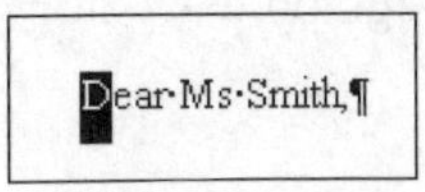

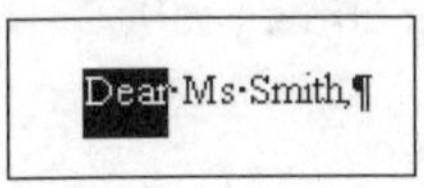

1) Open Word, and open the letter you saved in Exercise 13.11.
2) Position the cursor to the left of the letter 'D' in 'Dear Ms Smith'.
3) Drag the mouse to the right until you have selected the letter 'D'. Release the mouse button.

   You have learned how to select a single character. Now click anywhere on the page to deselect the letter 'D'. Deselecting a piece of text does not remove the text; it just means that it is no longer selected.
4) Again, position the mouse to the left of the letter 'D', but this time keep dragging with the mouse until you have selected the entire word 'Dear'. Release the mouse button.
5) Click anywhere outside the selected area to deselect it. Now double-click the word 'Dear' to select it again.
6) Position the mouse to the left of the letter 'D'. Now drag the mouse down and right until you have selected the first paragraph of the letter.

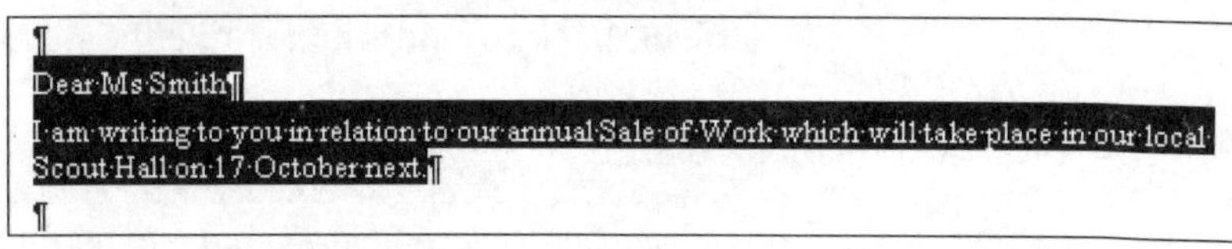

7) Click anywhere outside the selected area to deselect it. Now triple-click anywhere in the first paragraph to select it again.

That completes the exercise. But practise your text-selection skills by clicking at any point in your document, and dragging the mouse in various directions, or by double- or triple-clicking words and paragraphs.

Formatting text

Word's most commonly used formatting features are:

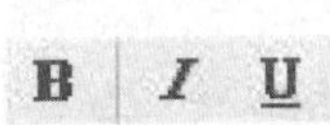

Format buttons

- **Bold**: Heavy black text, often used for headings.
- *Italic*: Slanted text, often used for emphasis or foreign words.
- <u>Underline</u>: A single line under the text, often used in legal documents and beneath signatures on letters.

You will find the relevant buttons on the *Formatting* toolbar. In the next exercises you will learn how to apply the bold and italic formats.

Exercise 14.2: Applying bold format

1) Place the cursor at the start of the first line of the address.
2) Drag right and down with the mouse until you have selected the two address lines and the phone number.
3) Click the **Bold** button or press **Ctrl+b** (hold down **Ctrl** and type **b**).
4) Deselect the lines by clicking any other area of the document.

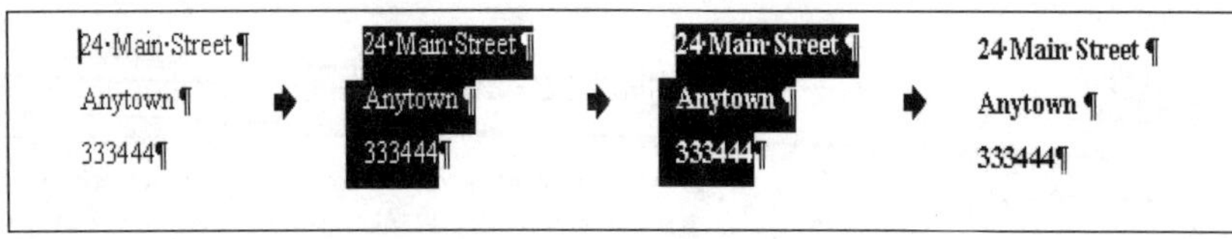

Exercise 14.3: Applying italic format

1) Place the cursor at the start of the name 'Ken Bloggs'.
2) Drag right until you have selected the name.
3) Click the **Italic** button or press **Ctrl+i**.
4) Deselect the name by clicking on any other area of the document.

   Well done. Save your letter.

Copying and pasting text

Suppose you want to use the same text – words or paragraphs – more than once in a document. Do you need to retype it each time that you need it? No.

With Word, you can type the text just once, and then insert it as many times as you need. This is a two-step process:

- **Copy:** You select and then *copy* the text to the clipboard, a temporary holding area.
- **Paste:** You insert or *paste* the text from the clipboard into a different part of the same document, or even a different document.

Clipboard
A temporary storage area to which you can copy text (or graphics). You can paste to any location within the same or different documents.

Exercise 14.4: Copying and pasting text within a document

1) Select the second paragraph of your letter.

In·previous·years·your·company·was·kind·enough·to·donate·a·prize·for·our·wheel·of·fortune.¶

Copy button

Click the **Copy** button on the *Standard* toolbar, or choose **Edit | Copy**.

2) Position the cursor at the left of the paragraph mark on the next line.

In·previous·years·your·company·was·kind·enough·to·donate·a·prize·for·our·wheel·of·fortune.¶
¶

Paste button

3) Click the **Paste** button on the *Standard* toolbar, or choose **Edit | Paste**.

In·previous·years·your·company·was·kind·enough·to·donate·a·prize·for·our·wheel·of·fortune.¶
In·previous·years·your·company·was·kind·enough·to·donate·a·prize·for·our·wheel·of·fortune.¶

4) Select the line that you have pasted from the clipboard, and press the **Delete** key. You will not need it again.

Cutting and pasting text

Sometimes, you may want to remove text from one part of a document and place it in a different part.

Rather than deleting the text and then retyping it elsewhere, Word allows you to move the text by cutting it from its current location and pasting it to the new location.

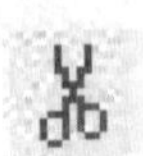

Cut button

Cut-and-paste differs from copy-and-paste in that Word removes the cut text, whereas copied text remains in its original location. You can cut selected text using the **Cut** button on the *Standard* toolbar or by choosing **Edit | Cut**.

Keyboard shortcuts

You may find it quicker to use Word's keyboard shortcuts for copy, cut and paste operations, as you need not take either hand away from the keyboard:

- To copy, press **Ctrl+c**.
- To cut, press **Ctrl+x**.
- To paste, press **Ctrl+v**.

You can also right-click on your document to get a pop-up menu displaying the available commands for copying, cutting or pasting.

About the clipboard

Points you should remember about the clipboard:

- The clipboard is temporary. Turn off your computer and the clipboard contents are deleted.
- The same clipboard is available to all Windows applications. For example, you can copy from Excel and paste into Word.
- The clipboard can hold up to twenty-four items at a time. When you copy or cut a twenty-fifth item, the first item in the clipboard is deleted.
- You can view the contents of the clipboard by opening the *Clipboard* task pane (choose **Edit | Office Clipboard)**. This lists all items in the clipboard, with the newest item at the top.

  Each item includes an icon representing the source Office program and a portion of copied text or a thumbnail of a copied graphic.

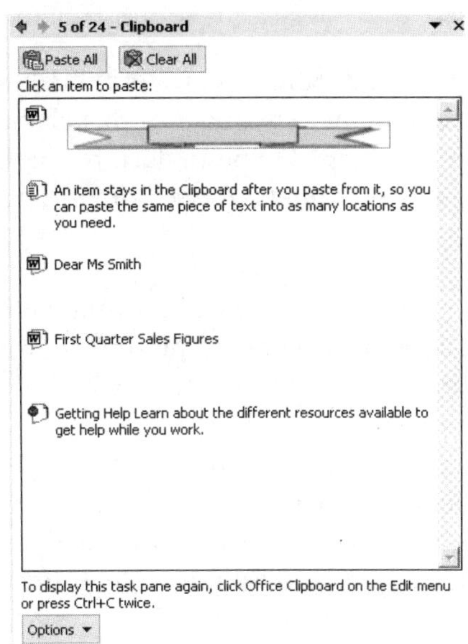

Clipboard task pane

- To paste the most recently copied/cut item from the clipboard, click the **Paste** button on the *Standard* toolbar, or choose **Edit | Paste**.

  To paste a different item, click its icon in the *Clipboard* task pane.

  To paste all previously copied/cut items, click the **Paste All** button in the task pane.
- An item stays in the clipboard after you paste from it, so you can paste the same piece of text into as many locations as you need.
- To delete an item from the clipboard, right-click on it in the *Clipboard* task pane and choose **Delete** from the pop-up menu. To

delete all items from the clipboard, choose the **Clear All** button in the task pane.

The line you copied in Exercise 14.4 is still in the clipboard. In the next exercise you will copy it to a different document.

Exercise 14.5: Copying and pasting text between documents

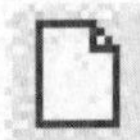

New button

1) Click the **New** button to create a new, blank Word document.
   Word places the cursor at the beginning of the document.
2) Click the **Paste** button on the *Standard* toolbar, or choose **Edit | Paste**.
3) Choose **File | Close** to close the new document. When Word asks you whether you want to save the new file, click **No**.

When you have more than one Word document open at a time, you can switch between them by choosing **Window | <document name>**.

Formatted documents

All Word documents are formatted, but some are more formatted than others. In the remainder of this chapter you will discover the Word tools that enable you to design a highly formatted poster: indents, alignment, bullets, fonts, borders and shading.

Left and right indents

The term indent means 'in from the margin'. Word's indenting feature lets you push a paragraph of text a specified distance in from the left margin, right margin, or both.

To indent a selected paragraph, choose **Format | Paragraph**, and enter the required left and/or right distances on the **Indents and Spacing** tab of the *Paragraph* dialog box.

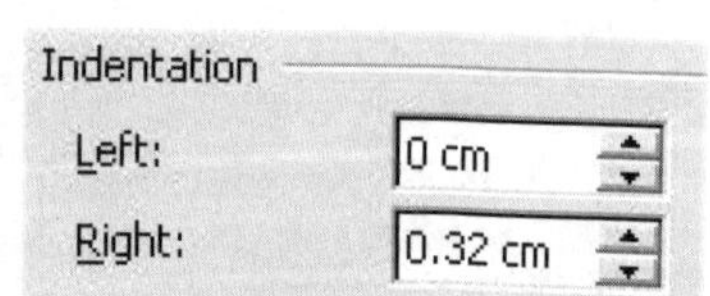

In long documents, you may sometimes see indenting used as a way of attracting attention to a particular part of the text. Here is an example that combines a left and right indent with italics:

> *Another successful year has seen revenues rise by 35% and profits by 47.5%. Our company is well placed to face the challenges of the future.*

Indent
The positioning of a paragraph of text a specified distance in from the left and/or right margin.

Aligning text

To align text means to 'line up' the text in a particular horizontal (left–right) way. Word gives you four choices:

- **Left:** The default, used for letters and business documents. Left-aligned text is generally the easiest to read.
- **Centre:** Positions the text centrally between the left and right margins. Used for headings.
- **Right:** Aligns the text against the right-hand margin of the page. Used by graphic designers for decorative purposes.
- **Justify:** Both left and right aligned at the same time. Used for narrow columns of text in newspapers and magazines.

Do not use justification when your text is in a single column across the width of the page (such as in letters), because it makes the text more difficult to read.

You can only align paragraphs. You cannot align selected characters or words within a paragraph.

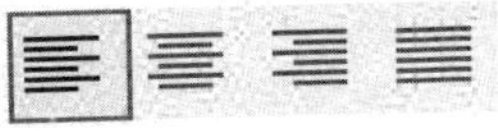

Alignment buttons

To align a single paragraph, you don't need to select the text. You need only to position the cursor anywhere within the paragraph. You will find the four alignment buttons on the *Formatting* toolbar.

Alignment
The horizontal positioning of lines in a paragraph in relation to one another. They can share a common centre-point, begin at the same point on the left, end at the same point on the right, or begin and end at the same points.

Bullets and numbered lists

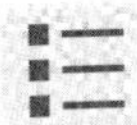

Bullets button

Lists are good ways to communicate a series of short statements or instructions. Lists are of two types:

- **Bulleted:** Used when the reading order is not critical. The bullet character is typically a dot, square, diamond, line or arrow. To make a bulleted list, select the paragraphs and click the **Bullets** button on the *Formatting* toolbar.

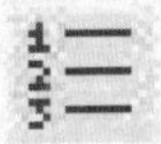

Numbering button

- **Numbered:** Used when the order of reading is important. For example, in directions and instructions. Each item is assigned a sequentially increasing number. To make a numbered list, select the paragraphs and click the **Numbering** button on the *Formatting* toolbar.

You can also apply bullets and numbering by choosing **Format | Bullets and Numbering**. Word offers you a wide range of options, such as the style of bullet or number character, and the distance between the bullet or number character and the bulleted or numbered text.

Bulleted and numbered lists
A list of short statements. The statements can be bulleted (preceded by a dot or other symbol) or numbered (preceded by a sequentially increasing number).

The following four exercises take you through the steps of applying numbering and bullets to selected text.

Exercise 14.6: Applying numbering to text

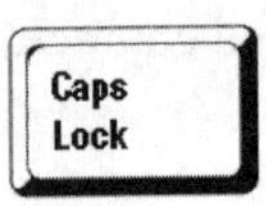

1) Open a new document, press the **Caps Lock** key once, type the following text, and press **Enter** twice:
   MY FAVOURITE FRUIT
   (The **Caps Lock** key is to the left of the 'A' key. After you press it, every letter you type is displayed as a capital letter.)
2) Press the **Caps Lock** key again to turn off capitals.
3) Select the text by clicking in front of the 'M' in 'MY', and dragging to the right with the mouse.

4) Click the **Underline** button on the *Formatting* toolbar to underline the selected text.
5) Click the last paragraph mark you entered, and type the following six fruit names, pressing **Enter** after each one: Apples, Bananas, Grapes, Kiwis, Oranges and Peaches. Your text should look as shown on the right.

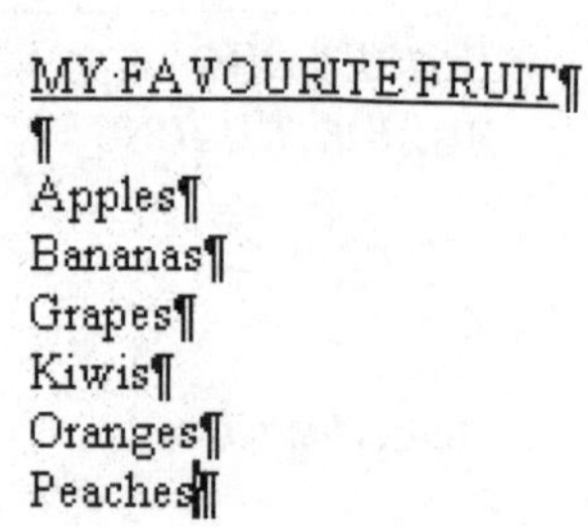

6) Select the six fruit names by clicking in front of the 'A' in 'Apples', and then dragging right and down with the mouse until you reach the final paragraph mark.
7) Click the **Numbering** button on the *Formatting* toolbar to apply numbering to the selected text.
8) Click anywhere in your document outside the selected area to deselect the text. Your text should now look as shown on the right.

   (The arrows after the numbers are non-printing characters.)

MY·FAVOURITE·FRUIT¶
¶
1.→Apples¶
2.→Bananas¶
3.→Grapes¶
4.→Kiwis¶
5.→Oranges¶
6.→Peaches¶

9) Choose **File | Save** or press **Ctrl+s** to save your document. If your initials are KB, for example, name it KBList.doc. Leave the document open.

In Exercise 14.7 you will replace the numbers in Exercise 14.6 with bullets.

Exercise 14.7: Applying bullets to text

1) Select the list of six fruit names that you entered in Exercise 14.6.

   (Notice that you cannot select the numbers. This is because they are not entered text – they are generated automatically by Word.)
2) Click the **Bullets** button on the *Formatting* toolbar. Word replaces the numbers with bullets.
3) With the list still selected, choose **Format | Bullets and Numbering**, select the **Bulleted** tab, select one of the options and click **Customize**.
4) In the *Bullet position* area, change the value in the *Indent at* box from the default to 0 cm. This aligns the bullet to the left margin.

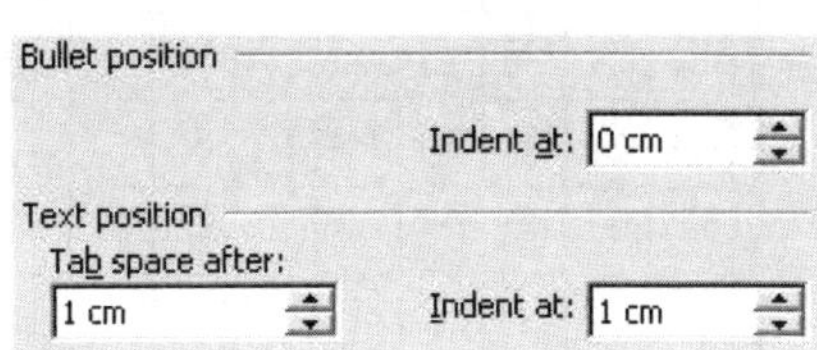

5) In the *Text position* area, change the values in the *Tab space after* and *Indent at* boxes from the defaults to 1 cm. This indents the text by 1 cm. Now click **OK**.

6) Click anywhere in your document outside the selected area to deselect the text.

   Your text should now look as shown on the right.

   (The arrows after the bullets are non-printing characters.)

MY·FAVOURITE·FRUIT¶
¶
- → Apples¶
- → Bananas¶
- → Grapes¶
- → Kiwis¶
- → Oranges¶
- → Peaches¶

Sometimes you want to apply bullets or numbering only to certain items in a list, and not to others. Exercise 14.8 provides an example.

Exercise 14.8: Choosing a custom bullet character

Word offers you a number of default bullet characters that you can choose from. If you wish, you can also choose any character you want as the bullet character or you can choose a picture bullet.

1) Select the six fruit names that you entered in the previous exercises.
2) Choose **Format | Bullets and Numbering**.
3) Click **Customize**.
4) For a character bullet, click **Character** in the *Customize Bulleted List* dialog box.
5) Choose the bullet character you want to use from the *Symbol* dialog box. To do this, you first choose the font, and then click on the character. In the example here, the chosen character is a solid diamond from the Symbol font.

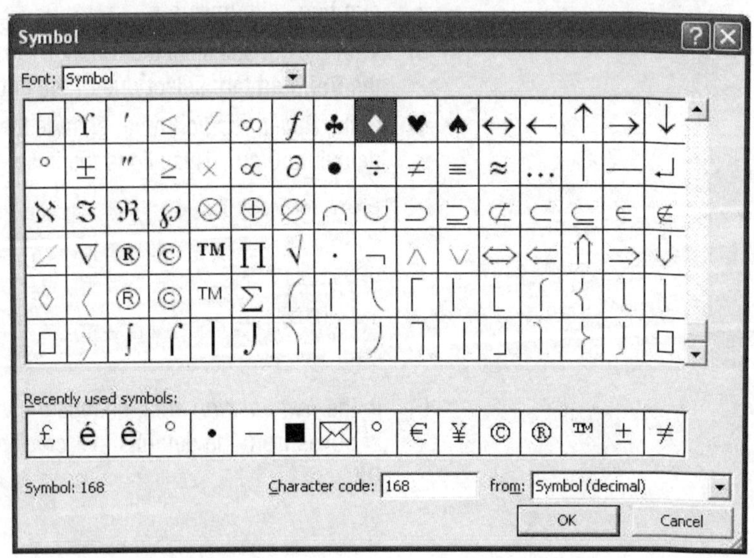

For a picture bullet, click **Picture** at step 4 and then choose the picture you want to use.

You change the style of numbering in a numbered list in exactly the same way: select the items you want to change, choose **Format | Bullets and Numbering**, and select one of the standard styles offered or click **Customize** to specify the format and style of the number. In the *Customize Numbered List* dialog box, you can also specify that you want the list to start with a number other than 1.

Exercise 14.9: Removing bullets from selected items in a list

1) Click at the paragraph mark after the word 'Kiwis', and press **Enter** to create a new line. Notice that Word places a bullet in front of the line.
2) Type the following:

   (my absolute favourite)
3) You don't want this new line to have a bullet character in front of it.

   Select the new line and click the **Bullets** button on the *Formatting* toolbar. Word removes the bullet format from the selected line.
4) Your final task is to align the new line with the other, bulleted lines.

   With the new line still selected, choose **Format | Paragraph**, choose a *Left* indent of 1 cm, and click **OK**.
5) Click anywhere in your document outside the selected line to deselect it. Your text should now look as shown on the right.

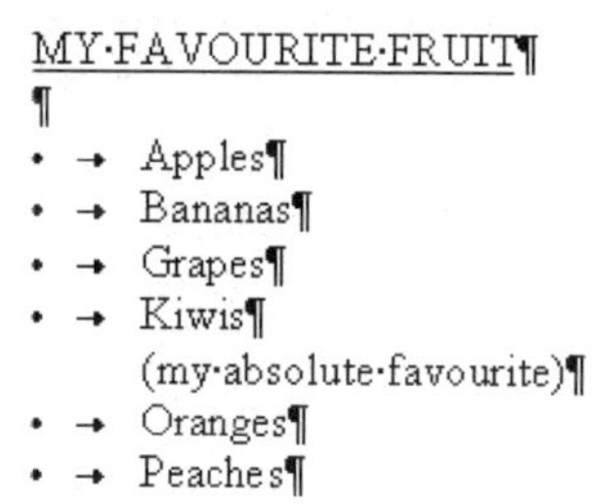

You remove numbers from items in a list in the same way: select the item you want to be unnumbered, and click the **Numbering** button on the *Formatting* toolbar.

Fonts

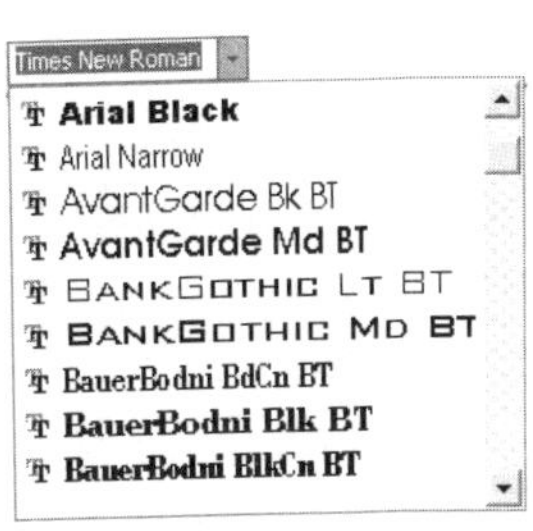

Viewing the fonts on your computer

A font or typeface is a particular style of text. What fonts are installed on your computer? Click the arrow on the drop-down **Font** box on the *Formatting* toolbar to see.

Do you need to remember the names and characteristics of all these fonts? No. You need remember only two things about fonts:

- There are really just two kinds or families of fonts: serif and sans serif. Sans serif just means without serifs (see below).
- Serif fonts are good for long paragraphs of text. Sans serif fonts are good for short pieces of text such as headlines, headers, captions, and maybe bulleted text.

You can recognize which family a font belongs to by asking: do its characters have serifs (tails or squiggles) at their edges?

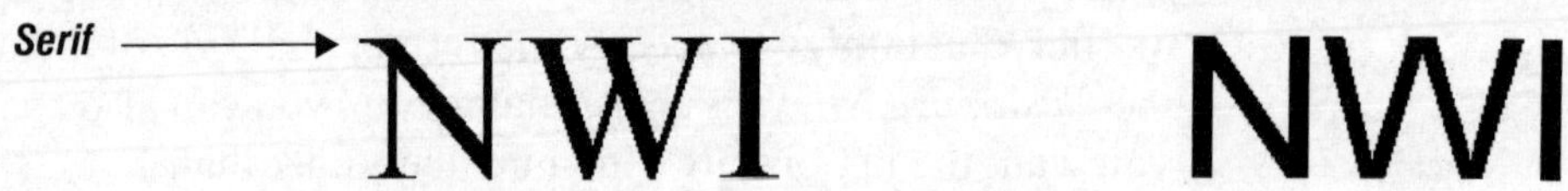

Serif font

Sans serif font

Serif fonts

Word's default font is a serif font called Times New Roman. It takes its name from *The Times* newspaper of London, where it was developed in the 1930s. Other popular serif fonts include Garamond and Century Schoolbook:

This text is written in a font named Garamond.

This text is written in a font named Century Schoolbook.

Sans serif fonts

Word's default sans serif font is Arial. It is based on another font, Helvetica. Avant Garde is another common sans serif font.

This text is written in a font named Helvetica.

This text is written in a font named Avant Garde.

Font
A typeface is a particular style of text. The two main font families are serif and sans serif.

Font sizes

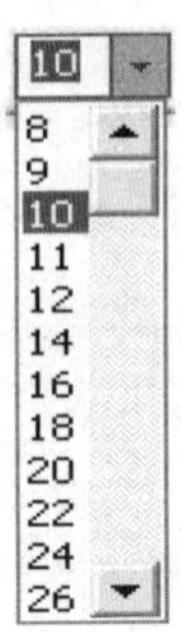

Font size is measured in a non-metric unit called the point, with approximately 72 points equal to one inch.

- For the body text of letters or longer business documents such as reports, 10, 11 or 12 points is a good choice. For headings, use larger font sizes in the range 14–28 points.
- Headers, footers, endnotes, footnotes and captions are often in 8- or 9-point font size.

To change the font size of selected text, click the required font size from the **Font Size** drop-down list box on the *Formatting* toolbar.

Changing case

The *Change Case* dialog box enables you to change the case of text, for example, from upper to lower case.

Select the text you want to change and choose **Format | Change Case**.

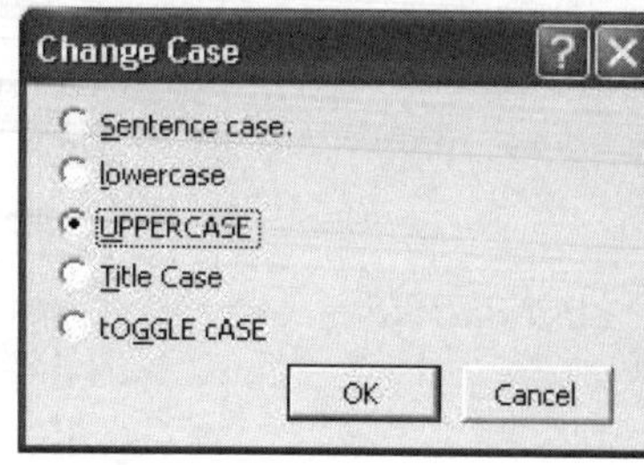

Font properties

Word's **Format | Font** command enables you to apply a number of properties to fonts: style, effects, colour and spacing.

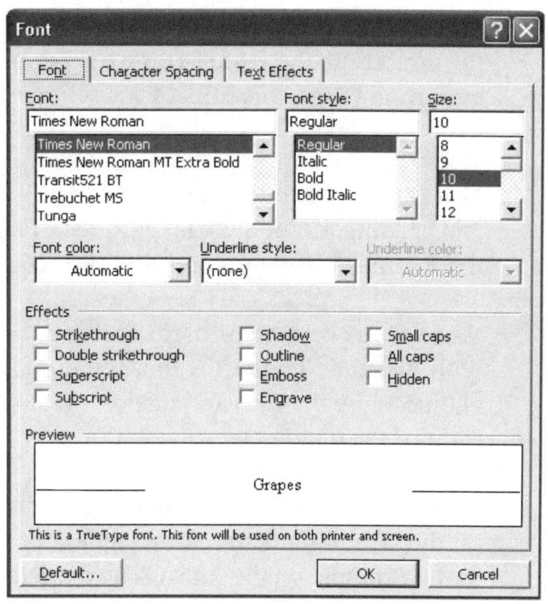

Font style

You have already applied these options using the **Bold** and **Italic** buttons on the *Formatting* toolbar.

Underline

There are a lot of choices here for the type of underlining. Single is both the simplest and most commonly used. It is also the type of underline applied with the **Underline** button on the *Formatting* toolbar. If you don't want to underline the spaces between words, choose *Words only*.

Font colour

Have you got a colour printer? Then you may want to select a text colour other than Auto. Even without a colour printer, you may want to print your headings in grey.

What colour is Auto? Auto is black, unless the background is black or a dark grey, in which case Auto switches to white.

Font effects

You can experiment with the various font effects by selecting any of the *Effects* check boxes and viewing the result in the *Preview* area at the bottom of the dialog box.

- Use subscript for chemical formulae such as H_2O.
- Use superscript in mathematical equations such as x^2.

Font spacing

You can expand or condense the space between characters by using the options on the **Character Spacing** tab of the *Font* dialog box. You may want to use this effect for document headings.

Font borders and shading

You can brighten up your document with borders (decorative boxes) and shading (coloured backgrounds), using the options available with the **Format | Borders and Shading** command.

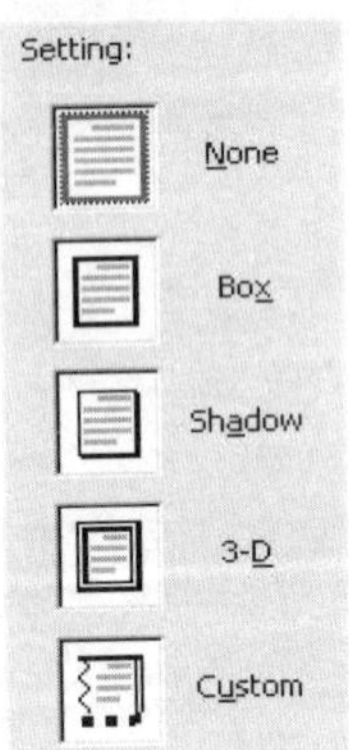

Border options

Word offers a range of border settings, with *Box* and *Shadow* the most common choices. Use the *Preview* section on the right of the dialog box to select the edges that you want bordered. So, if you only want top and bottom borders, click on the side borders to remove them (as in the example on the right). The default is borders on all four sides.

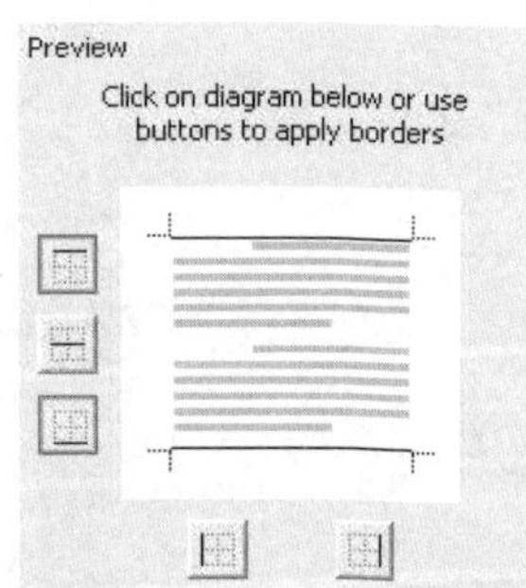

Pay attention to the *Apply to* drop-down box at the bottom right. Your choice affects how Word draws the border. See the following example.

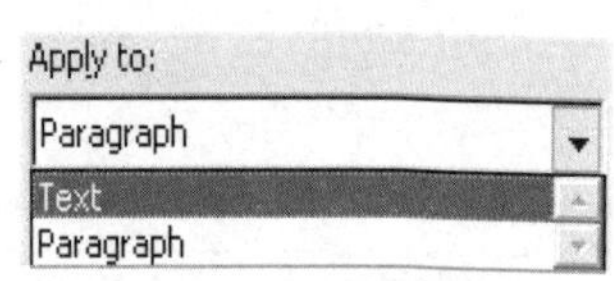

Sample Text: Apply to Text selected

Sample Text: Apply to Paragraph selected

To apply shading, select the text, choose **Format | Borders and Shading**, and then select your required *Fill*, *Style* and *Color* options from the **Shading** tab of the dialog box:

- **Fill:** This is the text background colour. If placing a grey shade behind black text, use 25% or less of grey. Otherwise, the text will be difficult to read.
- **Style:** This allows you to apply tints (percentages of a colour) or patterns of a second colour (selected in the *Color* box) on top of the selected *Fill* colour. Leave the *Style* box at its default value of *Clear* if you do not want to apply a second colour.
- **Color:** If you have selected an option in the *Style* box, select the colour of the lines and dots in the pattern here.

You can apply a border and shading to one or more characters, words or paragraphs. You do not have to apply both, but the border and shading features generally tend to be used together.

Exercise 14.10: Designing your poster

Practice makes perfect. In this exercise you will apply the formatting (fonts, bullets, borders and shading) and text positioning (alignment and indenting) skills that you have learned in this chapter. Your aim is to write and design a poster.

1) Open a new document and type the text shown.

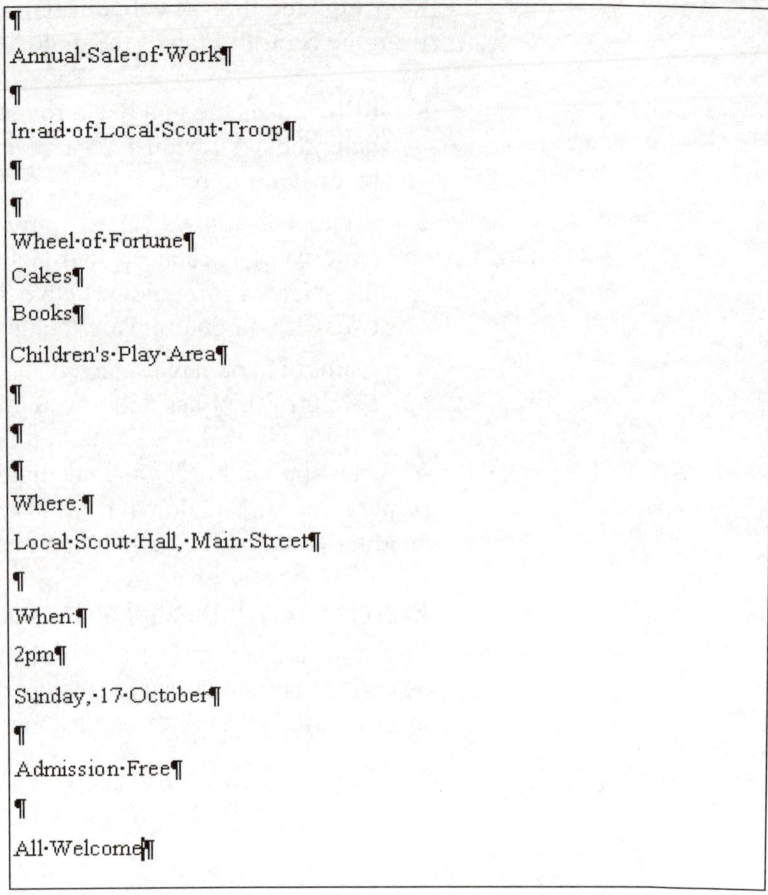
¶
Annual·Sale·of·Work¶
¶
In·aid·of·Local·Scout·Troop¶
¶
¶
Wheel·of·Fortune¶
Cakes¶
Books¶
Children's·Play·Area¶
¶
¶
¶
Where:¶
Local·Scout·Hall,·Main·Street¶
¶
When:¶
2pm¶
Sunday,·17·October¶
¶
Admission·Free¶
¶
All·Welcome¶

2) Select the text: 'Annual Sale of Work'. Using **Format | Font**, make it Times New Roman, 28 point.

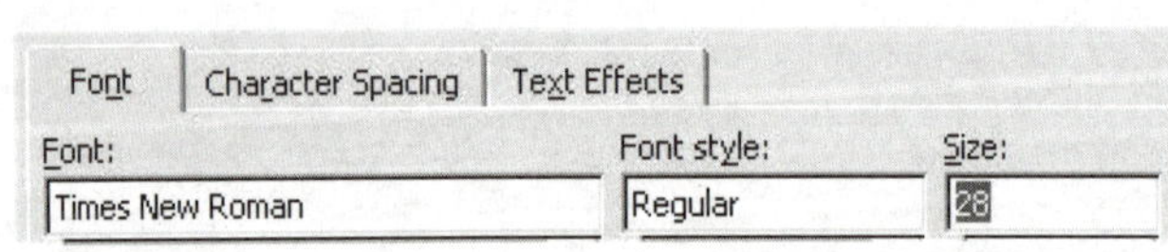

3) With the text still selected, choose **Format | Borders and Shading**, select a *Setting* of *Box* and select *Text* as the *Apply to* option.

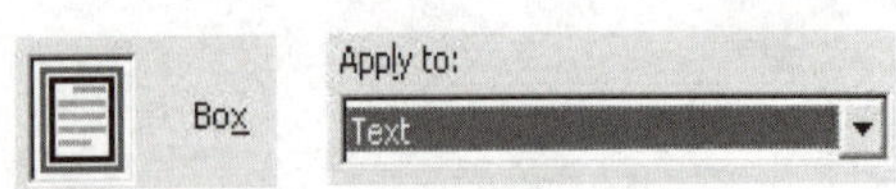

4) On the **Shading** tab, select a shading of *Gray-15%* and select *Text* as the *Apply to* option. When finished, click **OK**.

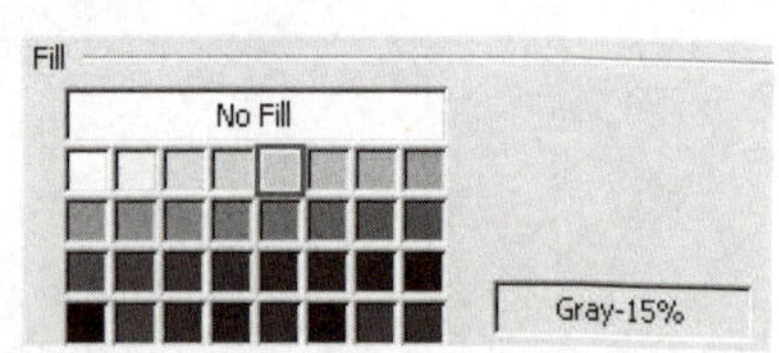

5) Again with the text still selected, click the **Centre Alignment** button on the *Formatting* toolbar.

6) Select the text 'In aid of Local Scout Troop'. Use the options on the *Formatting* toolbar to centre-align it, and make it Arial Black, 14 point.

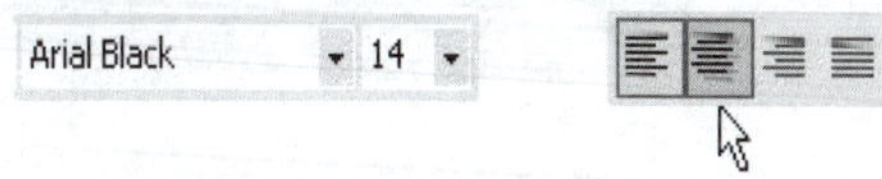

7) Select the four attractions: 'Wheel of Fortune', 'Cakes', 'Books' and 'Children's Play Area'. Make them Arial, 20 point.

   (Ensure the paragraph mark after 'Children's Play Area' is included in your selection.)

   Choose **Format | Bullets and Numbering**. On the **Bulleted** tab, select the arrow bullet character style (you may have to click **Customize** to find this option).

Arrow style bullet character

8) You want to place the bullets where they will get attention: in the centre of the page between the left and right page margins.

   But do *not* apply centre alignment, as shown on the right here, as the bullets are easier to read if they are left-aligned.

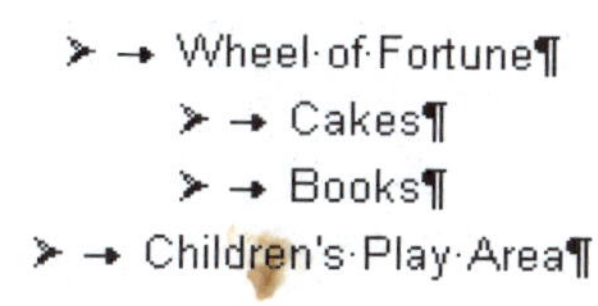

   With the four attractions still selected, select **Format | Paragraph** and apply a left indent of 4.25 cm.

   Your bulleted text remains left-aligned, but it is now in the centre of the page.

9) Select the remainder of the text, and make it centre-aligned, Arial, Regular, 20 point.

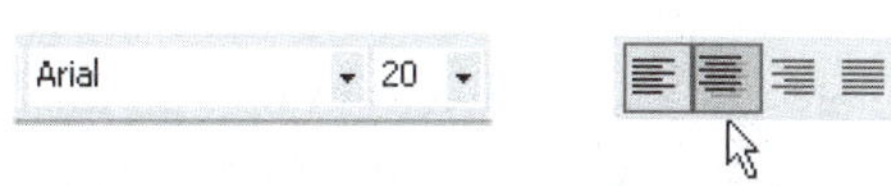

10) Select each of the following words in turn and click the **Bold** button on the *Formatting* toolbar:

    Where: When: and Admission Free

11) Select the words All Welcome and click the **Italics** button on the *Formatting* toolbar.

12) Finally, with the cursor positioned anywhere on the page, choose **Format | Borders and Shading**, and select the **Page Border** tab.

    Select a *Setting* of *Box* and, in the *Apply to* field, select *Whole Document*, and click **OK**.

Your poster is now complete and should look like that shown overleaf. Save your poster with a name that will be easy to remember and recognize. If your initials are KB, for example, save the poster document as KBposter.doc.

If you have a printer, print out your poster and inspect your work.

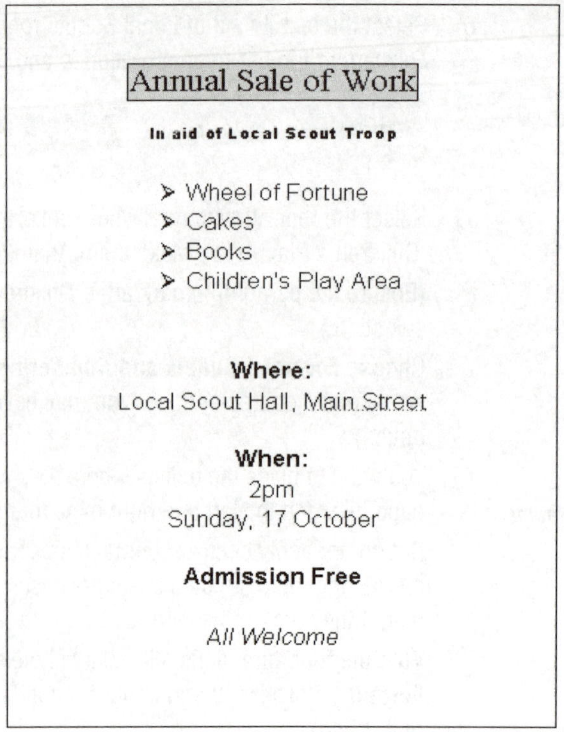
Annual Sale of Work

In aid of Local Scout Troop

- Wheel of Fortune
- Cakes
- Books
- Children's Play Area

Where:
Local Scout Hall, Main Street

When:
2pm
Sunday, 17 October

Admission Free

All Welcome

Word's Zoom views

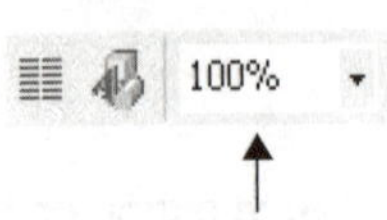

Zoom box

Word's Zoom feature enables you to magnify or reduce the document display. You can use Zoom in either of two ways:

- Click in the **Zoom** box on the *Standard* toolbar, enter a number between 10% and 500%, and press **Enter**.
- Choose **View | Zoom**, and select a magnification or reduction option from the *Zoom* dialog box.

To return from an enlarged or reduced view to normal view, select a magnification of 100%.

Zoom and printing

The Zoom feature only affects the way that Word displays a document on-screen – and not how a document is printed. (You will learn about printing documents in Chapter 15.)

Saving to a floppy disk

Have you been saving your document as you went along? You should. It is also a good idea to save a copy of your document to a floppy disk.

Follow the steps in Exercise 14.11 to learn how to save your poster to the A: drive.

Exercise 14.11: Saving a Word document to a floppy disk

1) Insert a floppy disk in the floppy disk drive of your computer:
   - If it is a new disk, ensure that it is formatted.
   - If it is a previously used one, ensure that there is sufficient space on it to hold the Word document file. Your poster file should be around 25 KB in size.
2) Choose **File | Save As**, locate the A: drive, and click **Save** to save the file. Word suggests the default file name (in this example, KBposter.doc) for you to accept or amend.

   When finished, use **File | Save As** again to resave the document to its original location on your computer.

   If you do not, saving the file in future (by clicking the **Save** button on the *Standard* toolbar or choosing **File | Save**) will save the document to the floppy disk – and not to the hard drive in your computer.

Symbols and special characters

Word allows you to insert symbols and special characters in your documents:

- **Symbols:** Among the symbols are foreign-language letters with accents (such as á, é, ä and ë), fractions, and characters used in science and mathematics.
- **Special Characters:** These include the copyright sign (©), registered mark (®) and trademark (™), plus typographic characters such as the en dash (a short dash the width of the letter ‘n’), the em dash (a longer dash the width of the letter ‘m’), and various types of opening and closing quotes.

To insert a symbol or special character:

- Click where you want to insert the symbol.
- Choose **Insert | Symbol**, and then click the **Symbols** or **Special Characters** tab.
- Double-click the symbol or character you want to insert.
- Click **Close** to close the dialog box.

Format Painter

Word's Format Painter provides a quick, convenient way to copy formatting from one piece of text to another. Follow these steps:

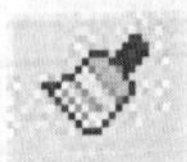

Format Painter button

- Select the text that has the formatting you want to copy.
- Click the **Format Painter** button on the *Standard* toolbar.
- Select the text to which you want to apply the formatting.

To copy the selected formatting to several locations, double-click **Format Painter**. When you have finished copying the formatting, click the **Format Painter** button again or press the **Esc** key (at the top left of your keyboard).

Exercise 14.12: Copying formatting

You begin this exercise by removing the formatting from two lines of your Annual Sale of Work poster.

1) Is the poster document from Exercise 14.10 open? If not, open it now.
2) Select the text 'Where:', choose **Format | Font**, make it 10 point, Regular, Times New Roman, and click **OK**.

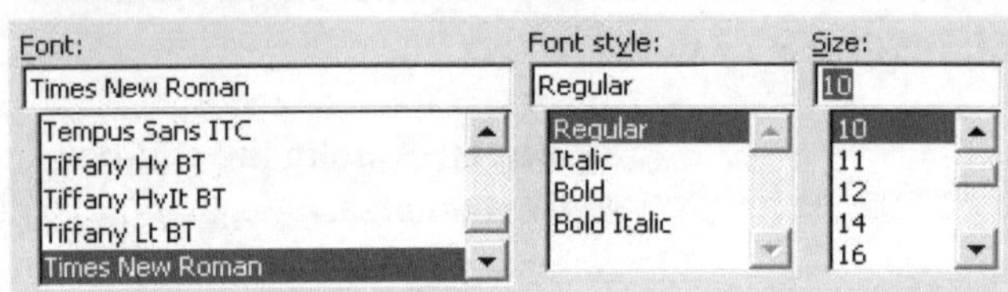

3) Select the text 'When:'. Also make it 10 point, Regular, Times New Roman.

   In the next part of this exercise, you will copy the formatting from another part of the poster to the two lines whose formatting you removed in steps 2 and 3 above.
4) Click anywhere within the words 'Admission Free'.
5) Double-click the **Format Painter** button.
6) Select the text 'Where:'.
7) Select the text 'When:'.
8) Press the **Esc** key to switch off the **Format Painter** feature.

Your poster now looks as it did before this exercise. Save the poster and close it. You can also close Microsoft Word. You have now completed this chapter of the ECDL word processing module.

Chapter summary: so now you know

Before you format or align text, you must first *select* that text. You do so by clicking and then dragging with the mouse. You can also use various double-clicking and triple-clicking options. Word displays selected text in reverse (white text on a black background). See Exercise 14.1 for an example of how to do this.

Bold, italic and underline are Word's most commonly used *formatting* features. Buttons for these options are provided on the *Formatting* toolbar. See Exercises 14.2 and 14.3 for examples of how to do these tasks.

You can *copy* text from one part of a document and then *paste* it to another part (or even to a different document) using the *clipboard*, a temporary storage area. You can also *cut and paste* text, in which case Word deletes the text from its original location. See Exercises 14.4 and 14.5 for examples of how to do these tasks.

Indenting is a way of moving text in a specified distance from the left or right margin of the page – or from both. *Alignment* is a way of positioning text in a paragraph so it lines up beside the left margin, beside the right margin, beside both left and right margins (justification) or away from both left and right margins (centred). Buttons for the alignment options are provided on the *Formatting* toolbar.

Use lists to communicate short statements or instructions. *Bulleted lists*, in which each item is preceded by a symbol such as a square or diamond, are suitable when the reading order is not critical. *Numbered lists*, in which each item is preceded by a sequentially increasing number, are used for instructions and directions, where the order of reading is important. See Exercises 14.6, 14.7, 14.8 and 14.9 for examples of how to do these tasks.

Fonts (typefaces) are styles of text. Serif fonts are better for long paragraphs. Use sans serif fonts for shorter text items, such as headlines or captions.

You can brighten up your documents by adding decorative *borders* and background *shading*. See Exercise 14.10 for an example of how to do this.

Word's *Zoom* feature enables you to magnify or reduce the document display – without affecting how the document is printed.

You can insert *symbols* and *special characters* in a document to represent such items as foreign-language letters with accents, fractions, characters used in scientific and mathematical texts, and typographic characters such as dashes and quotes.

Word's *Format Painter* provides a quick, convenient way to copy formatting from one piece of text to another. See Exercise 14.12 for an example of how to do this.

Quick quiz: formatting, positioning and copying text

Circle the correct answer to each of the following multiple-choice questions about formatting, positioning and copying text.

Q1	To select an entire paragraph of text, you ...
A.	Double-click anywhere in the paragraph.
B.	Triple-click anywhere in the paragraph.
C.	Hold down the **Ctrl** key and double-click anywhere in the paragraph.

Q2	You can apply bold, italic and underline formatting using buttons on the *Formatting* toolbar.
A.	True.
B.	False.

Q3	The keyboard shortcut for copying text is:
A.	**Ctrl+v.**
B.	**Ctrl+p.**
C.	**Ctrl+c.**

Q4	Which two of the following procedures can you use to apply bullets to a list?
A.	Click the **Bullets** button on the *Formatting* toolbar, type your list, and then click the **Bullets** button again to deselect it.
B.	Type your list, select it, and then click the **Bullets** button on the *Formatting* toolbar.
C.	Type your list and select it. Then choose **Format | Bullets and Numbering**, select a bullet style, and click **OK**.
D.	Type your list, click anywhere on the list, and then click the **Bullets** button on the *Formatting* toolbar.

Q5	To add a border around a paragraph, you...
A.	Click anywhere in the paragraph, choose **Format | Borders and Shading**, and click **OK**.
B.	Click anywhere in the paragraph, choose **Format | Borders and Shading**, and select the type of border you want. Then select *Paragraph* in the *Apply to* box and click **OK**.
C.	Choose **Format | Borders and Shading**, select the type of border you want and click **OK**. Then select the paragraph to which you want to apply the border.

Answers

1: B, **2:** A, **3:** C, **4:** B and C, **5:** B.

Chapter 15: Long documents, little details

In this chapter

Long documents present problems that shorter ones do not for both writer and reader. Word offers features to make life easier for both.

To help you edit long documents, Word includes a spellchecker, a grammar-checker and a find-and-replace feature.

You can help readers navigate their way through long documents by inserting page numbers and other details in the header or footer.

Also in this chapter, you will discover how to control vertical spacing between lines and paragraphs, how to create new types of indents to highlight breaks between paragraphs, and how to insert line and page breaks.

New skills

At the end of this chapter you should be able to:

- Change the spacing between lines and between paragraphs.
- Apply a first-line indent to a paragraph.
- Apply a hanging indent to a paragraph.
- Find and replace text, text with formatting, and special characters.
- Adjust page margins and page orientation.
- Create and format headers and footers.
- Insert page numbers and document details in a header or footer.
- Insert manual line breaks and page breaks.
- Use Word's spelling and grammar checkers.
- Use Word's printing options.

New words

At the end of this chapter you should be able to explain the following terms:

- Inter-line spacing
- Margin
- Inter-paragraph spacing
- A4
- First-line indent
- Header and footer
- Hanging indent

Creating your long document

To learn how to work with long documents in Word, you need a sample long document to practise on. You begin this chapter by copying some text from Word's online help.

Exercise 15.1: Copying text from Word online help

1) Open Word, type 'autosummarize' in the **Ask a Question** box at the top right of the Word window and press **Enter**.

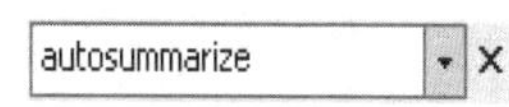

   Word displays a list of suggested help topics.

2) Click the topic named: Automatically summarize a document.

   Word displays the Microsoft Word Help window with the selected topic displayed in its right pane.

3) Select the title and first two paragraphs of the topic by dragging the mouse over them.

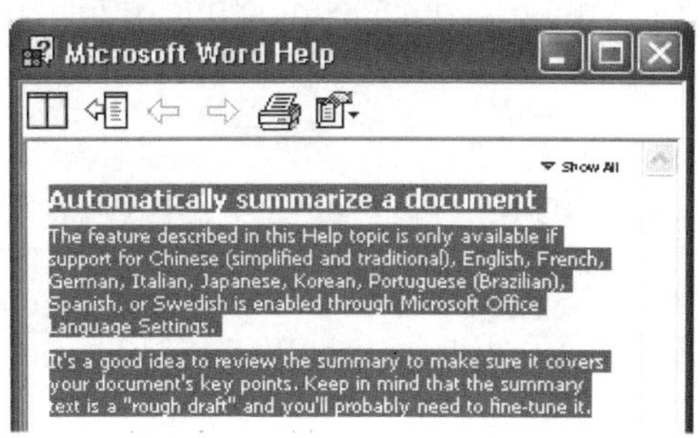

4) Right-click the selected text, and choose **Copy** from the pop-up menu. Close the online help window by clicking on the close box in the top-right corner.
5) Click the **New** button on the *Standard* toolbar to create a new Word document. The cursor is positioned at the start of the first line.
6) You now want to insert the Help text into the document, but without the formatting it had in the Help window.
7) Choose **Edit | Paste Special**, select *Unformatted Text* in the *As* box and click **OK**.

8) Delete the spare paragraph marks between the two paragraphs and at the end of the document by clicking at each one and pressing the **Backspace** key.

9) Select all the text in the document by dragging the mouse over it; do *not* include the paragraph mark at the end of the document.

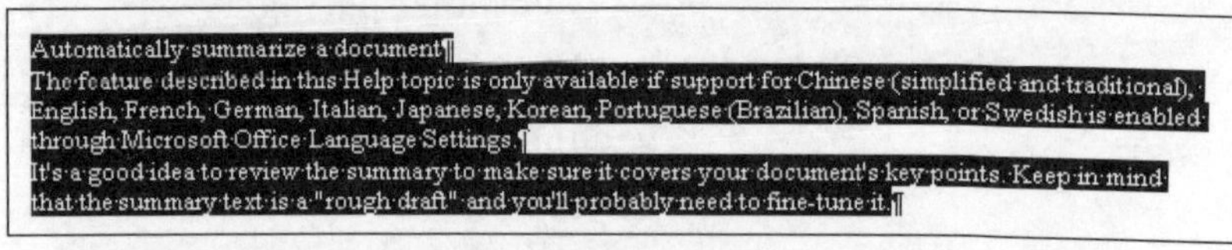

10) Choose **Edit | Copy** to copy the text to the clipboard. Deselect the text by clicking anywhere on the page outside the selected area.

11) Move the cursor down to the end of the second paragraph, and press **Enter** twice to move the cursor down a further two lines.

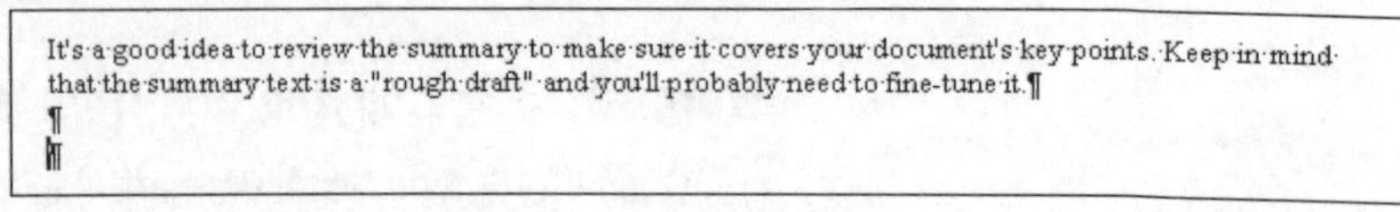

12) The text you copied in step 10 is still in the clipboard. Choose **Edit | Paste** to paste it again.

13) Repeat steps 11 and 12 seventeen times to create three pages of sample text.

14) Choose **File | Save** to save the document with a name that you will find easy to remember. If your initials are KB, for example, call it KBlong.doc.

Congratulations! You have created a three-page document in Word without typing a single line of text. You will use this sample document in other exercises in this chapter.

Inter-line spacing

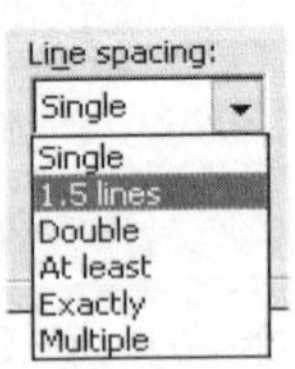

Inter-line spacing is the vertical space between lines within a paragraph of text. By default, Word applies single inter-line spacing. You can increase the inter-line spacing of a selected paragraph by choosing **Format | Paragraph**, and, in the *Line spacing* box, selecting *1.5 lines* or *Double*.

Alternatively, enter a font size in the *At* box, and select *At least* in the *Line spacing* box. A good rule is to make inter-line spacing one point size larger than the font size. If your text is 10 points, for example, make inter-line spacing 11 points.

Inter-line spacing

The vertical space between lines within a paragraph of text. Word's default is single line spacing.

Examples of single, 1.5 and double inter-line spacing

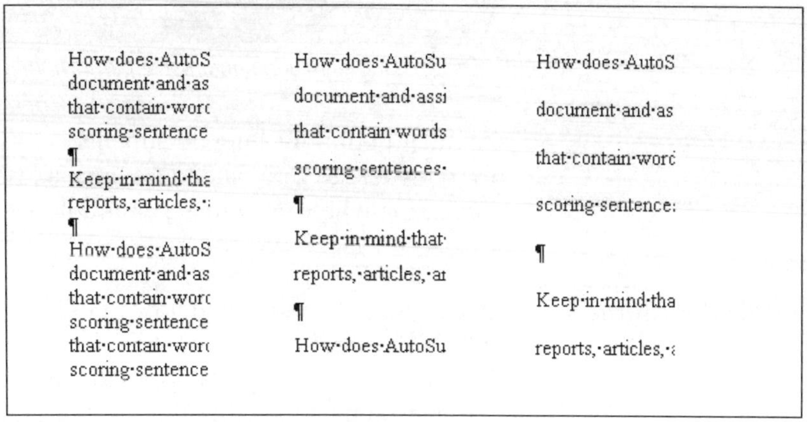

Inter-paragraph spacing

Pressing the **Enter** key to add a blank line between paragraphs of text is a crude – if effective – way of controlling the inter-paragraph spacing (spacing between paragraphs) in your documents.

For longer documents, you may instead wish to use the **Format | Paragraph** command, and enter an inter-paragraph spacing value in the *Before* and/or *After* boxes:

- For body text, enter a spacing value in the *After* box (slightly larger than the text font size) to separate the next paragraph from the current one.
- For headings, enter a spacing value in the *Before* box to place an extra area of blank space above the headings. This helps your headings to stand out from the rest of the text.

Inter-paragraph spacing created with and without extra paragraph marks

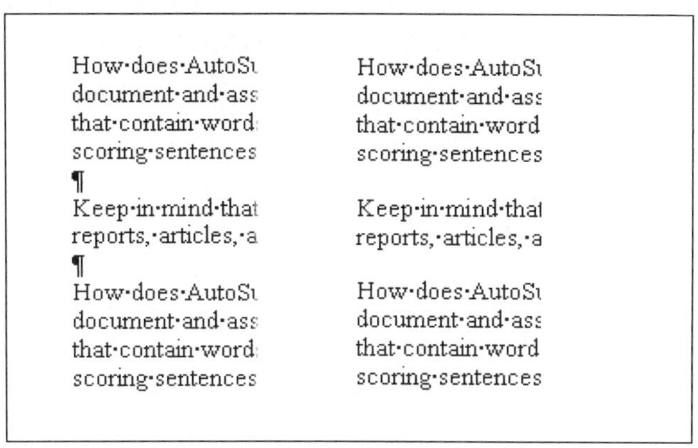

Inter-paragraph spacing
The spacing between successive paragraphs of text.

Another option for long documents is to set inter-paragraph spacing for body text to zero, and to use instead first-line indenting as a way of indicating where each new paragraph begins.

First-line indents

In Chapter 14 you learned how to indent a selected paragraph from the left and/or right margins of the page. Word also lets you indent the first line of a paragraph only, so that it is a greater distance in from the left margin than the other lines of the same paragraph.

Exercise 15.2: Creating a first-line indent

Here you will use a first-line indent to separate two paragraphs of body text.

1) Select the second paragraph of your sample text.

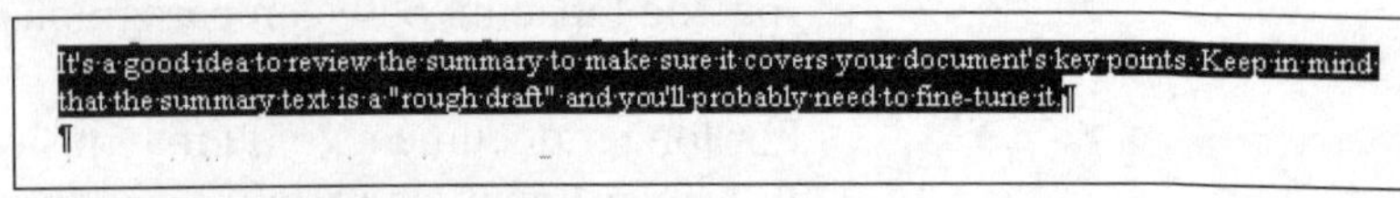

2) Choose **Format | Paragraph**.
3) On the **Indents and Spacing** tab, in the *Special* box, select *First line.* In the *By* box, enter a value of 1 cm. Click **OK**.

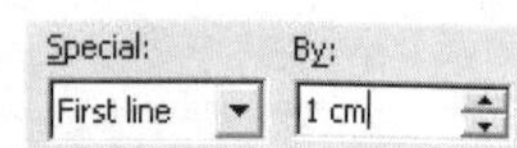

Your text should now look as shown.

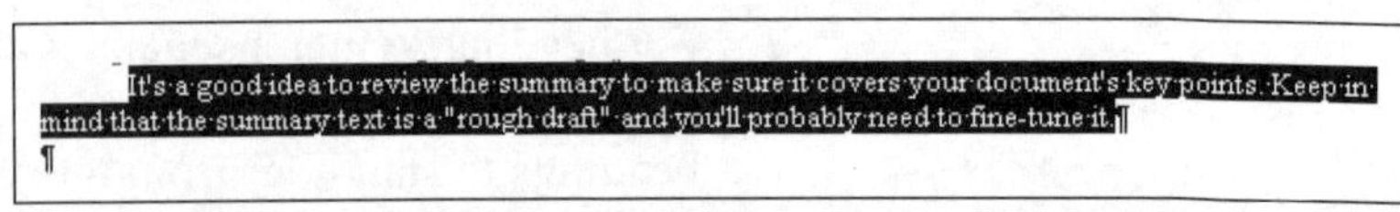

4) Undo the first-line indent change by choosing **Edit | Undo**. Your sample text should look as it was before this exercise.

First-line indent
The positioning of the first line of a paragraph a greater distance in from the left margin than the remaining lines of the same paragraph.

If using first-line indents to separate paragraphs, set inter-paragraph spacing to zero or to just one or two points. Do not use first line indents for the first paragraph after a heading.

Hanging indents

A hanging indent is where all the lines of a paragraph are indented – except the first one. Hanging indents are sometimes used for lists such as bibliographies. Below is an example.

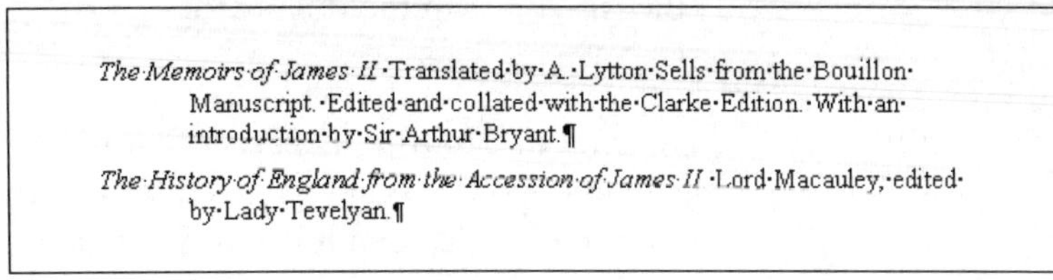
The·Memoirs·of·James·II·Translated·by·A.·Lytton·Sells·from·the·Bouillon·Manuscript.·Edited·and·collated·with·the·Clarke·Edition.·With·an·introduction·by·Sir·Arthur·Bryant.¶

The·History·of·England·from·the·Accession·of·James·II·Lord·Macauley,·edited·by·Lady·Tevelyan.¶

Practise creating a hanging indent with the sample text by selecting a paragraph, choosing **Format | Paragraph**, selecting *Hanging* from the *Special* box, and entering a value in the *By* box. Undo any changes that you make.

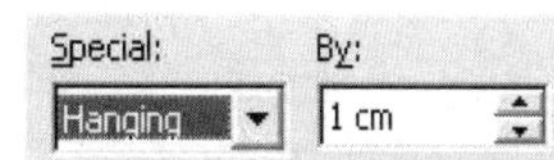

Hanging indent
Where all the lines of a paragraph are indented – except the first one. Sometimes used for lists.

Finding text

Do you need to quickly locate a particular word or phrase in a long document? Word's Find feature can take you straight to the text that you are looking for.

By default, Word searches the whole document. To limit the text that Word searches through, first select only that part of the document. When Word has finished searching the selected text, it asks whether you want to search the remainder of the document.

The basics

Choose **Edit | Find** to display the *Find and Replace* dialog box. In the *Find what* box, type (or paste in from the clipboard) the text you want to find, and choose **Find Next**.

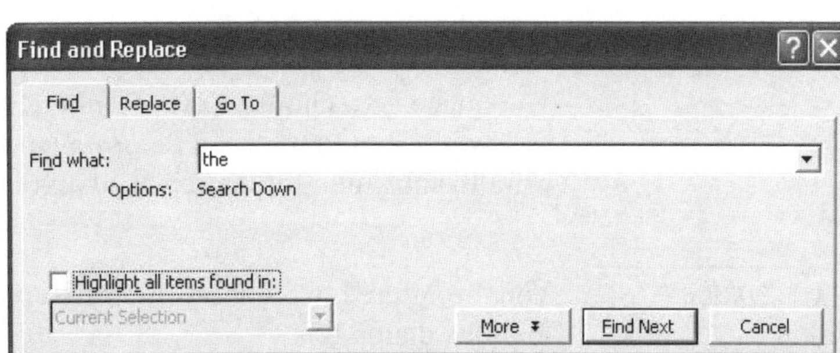

Word takes you to the first occurrence of the search text in your document. The dialog box stays open on your screen. Click **Find Next** to continue searching for further occurrences, or click **Cancel** to close the dialog box and end your search. Practise by searching for the word 'the' in your sample document.

Special options

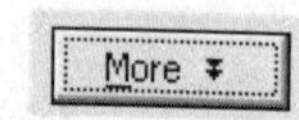

By default, Word finds parts of words as well as whole words. When you search for 'the', Word also finds 'then'. You can tell Word to find only whole words by clicking the **More** button, and then selecting the *Find whole words only* check box.

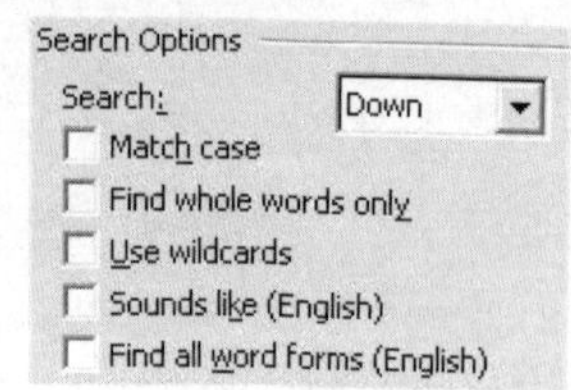

Another option is to select the *Match case* check box. So, for example, a search for 'The' does not find 'the' or 'THE'.

To find paragraph marks, tabs or other special or non-printing characters, choose the **Special** button and click the relevant character.

Formats

You can tell Word to find only occurrences of text in a certain format. Click the **Format** button, and select the formatting option that you require.

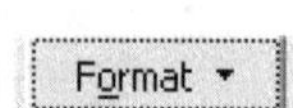

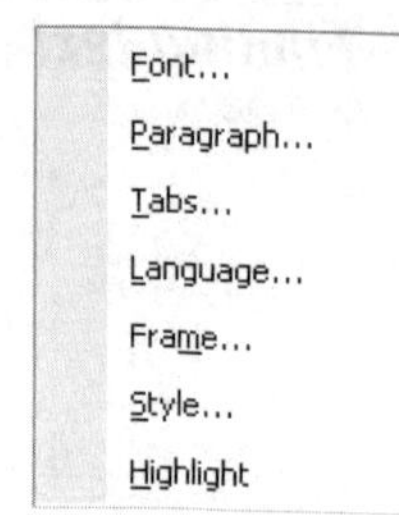

Finding and replacing text

Sometimes you will want to find and replace all occurrences of a word or phrase in a document with a different word or phrase. You might have misspelled a word consistently throughout a document, for example, or maybe you want to substitute 'person' for 'man' or 'woman'.

To replace text, choose **Edit | Replace**. On the **Replace** tab, enter the text you want to replace in the *Find what* box, and the new text you want to substitute for the replaced text in the *Replace with* box.

The two replace methods

You are offered two options by the **Replace** tab of the *Find and Replace* dialog box.

- Use the **Replace** button to replace your text one occurrence at a time. At each occurrence, you are asked whether you want to make the replacement or not. This is the 'safe' option.

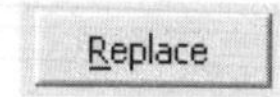

- Use the **Replace All** button to replace all occurrences in a single operation. Use this option only if you are certain that you want to replace every instance of the text you are searching for.

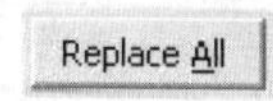

Special options

Anything that you can locate with the **Find** command, you can replace with **Edit | Replace** – including formatting, tabs, and other special and non-printing characters.

Exercise 15.3: Finding and replacing text

In this exercise you will practise finding and replacing text in your sample long document.

1) Look at the heading that you pasted in from the online help text.

   Copy the following to the clipboard:

   summarize

2) Move the cursor to the start of the first line of the document. Choose **Edit | Replace**.
3) On the **Replace** tab, paste the copied text in the *Find what* box.

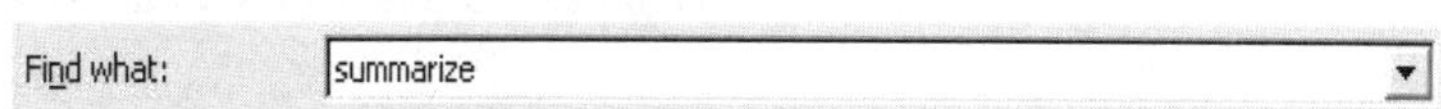

4) Type this in the *Replace with* box: summarise

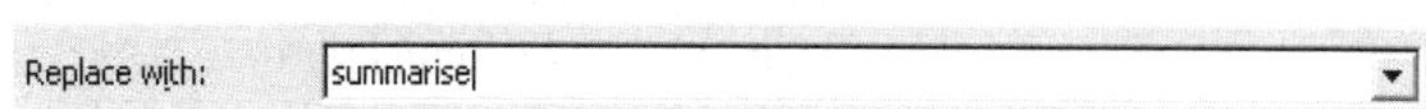

5) Choose the **Replace All** button.

   Word performs the find-and-replace operation through the entire document. So much easier than correcting each occurrence of the error!

6) When finished, Word displays a dialog box similar to the one shown. Click **OK** to close this dialog box.

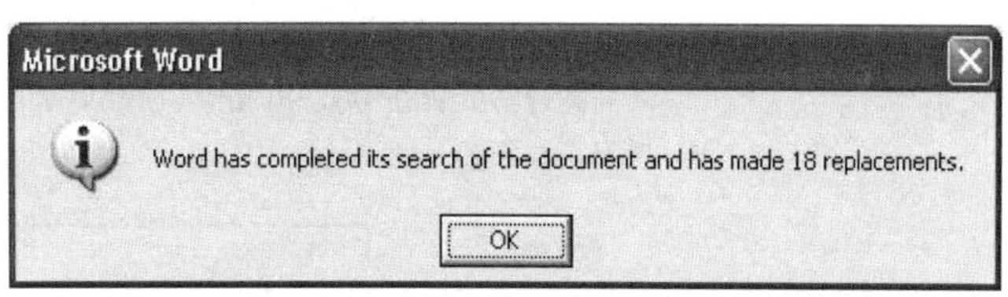

7) Close the *Find and Replace* dialog box by clicking **Close**.

Exercise 15.4: Finding and replacing formatting

In this exercise you will use Word's find-and-replace feature to reformat all occurrences of a heading in your sample long document.

1) Move the cursor to the start of the first line of the document. Choose **Edit | Replace**.
2) On the **Replace** tab, notice that the *Find what* box still contains the text from Exercise 15.3. Click in the *Find what* box, delete the previous text, and type the following: Automatically summarize a document
3) Click in the *Replace with* box, delete the text from Exercise 15.3, and type the following: Automatically summarize a document
4) With the cursor in the *Replace with* box, click the **More** button and then the **Format** button.
5) Select the **Font** option, and specify a font of Arial, a font style of Bold, and a size of 14. Then click **OK**.

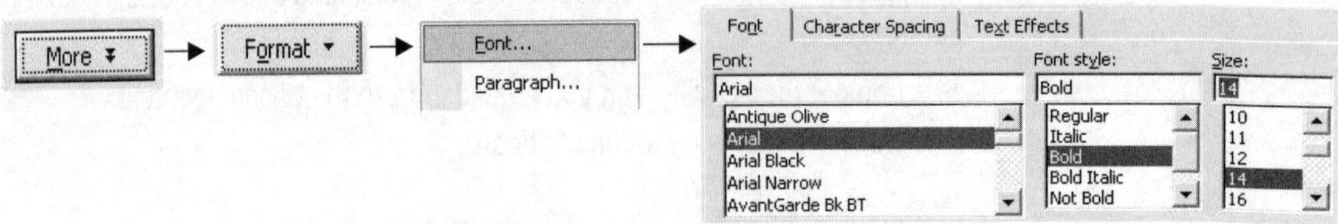

6) Click the **Replace All** button.

   Word reformats every occurrence of the heading. Click **OK** to accept the replacements and click **Close** to close the dialog box.

Exercise 15.5: Finding and replacing special characters

In this exercise you will remove the extra paragraph mark that separates the paragraphs of the sample text.

1) Move the cursor to the start of the first line of the document. Choose **Edit | Replace**.
2) On the **Replace** tab, click in the *Find what* box and delete the text from Exercise 15.4.
3) With the cursor in the *Find what* box, click the **Special** button and select *Paragraph Mark* from the pop-up menu. Click **Special** again and click *Paragraph Mark*.

   The *Find what* box should contain Word's paragraph mark symbol twice (^p^p).

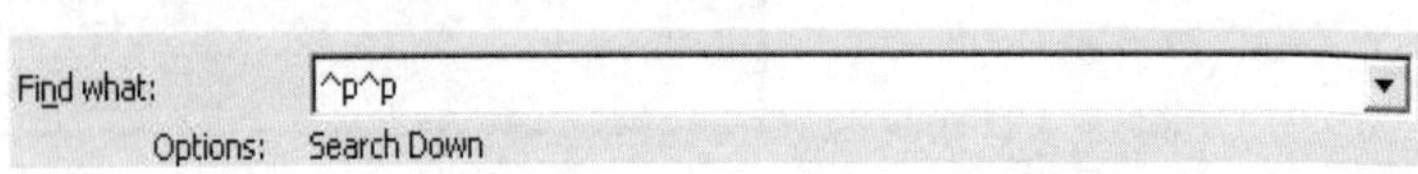

4) Click in the *Replace with* box and delete the text from Exercise 15.4. Also, click **No Formatting** to remove the formatting that you specified in Exercise 15.4.

5) With the cursor in the *Replace with* box, click the **Special** button and select *Paragraph Mark* from the pop-up menu.

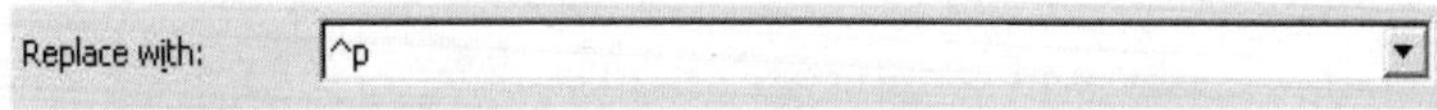

6) Click **Replace All.**

   Word replaces all occurrences of two consecutive paragraph marks with a single paragraph mark. Click **OK** to accept the replacements and click **Close** to close the dialog box.

Exercise 15.6: Finding and replacing text positioning

In this exercise you will apply a first-line indent to all occurrences of the second paragraph of sample text.

1) Move the cursor to the start of the first line of the document. Choose **Edit | Replace**.
2) On the **Replace** tab, click in the *Find what* box. Delete the text from Exercise 15.5 and type the first two words of the second paragraph of the sample text:

   It's a
3) Click in the *Replace with* box, delete the text from Exercise 15.5, and type the same words as are in the *Find what* box.
4) With the cursor still in the *Replace with* box, click the **Format** button (you may have to click the **More** button to find this), then the **Paragraph** option, and specify a first line indent of 1 cm. Click **OK**.

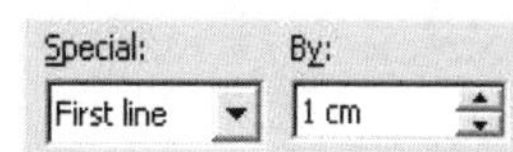

   The *Find and Replace* dialog box should look as shown:

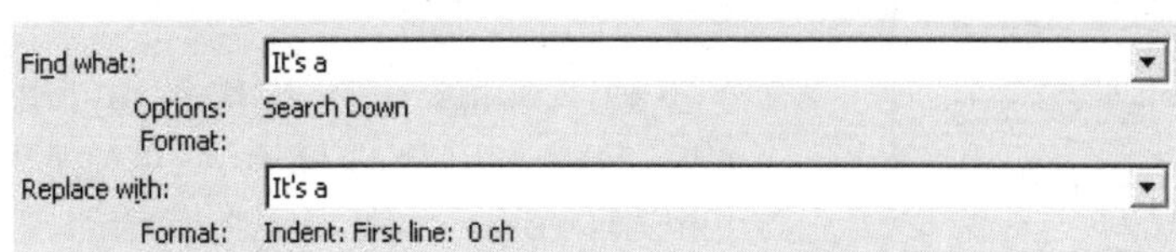

5) Click **Replace All.**

   Word indents the first line of every occurrence of the second paragraph.
6) Click **OK** to accept the replacements and click **Close** to close the dialog box. Your document should look like the sample shown below. (The inter-line spacing may be different on your PC.)

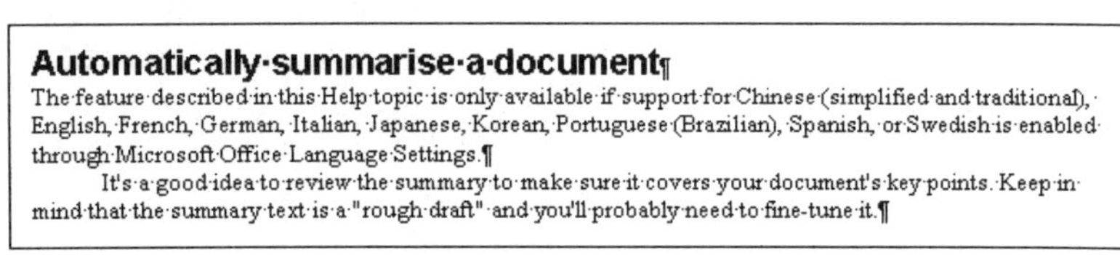

You have completed the find-and-replace exercises. Save your long document and leave it open.

Page setup

You have learnt how to control where text appears on the printed page, using text alignment, indenting, inter-line spacing and inter-paragraph spacing.

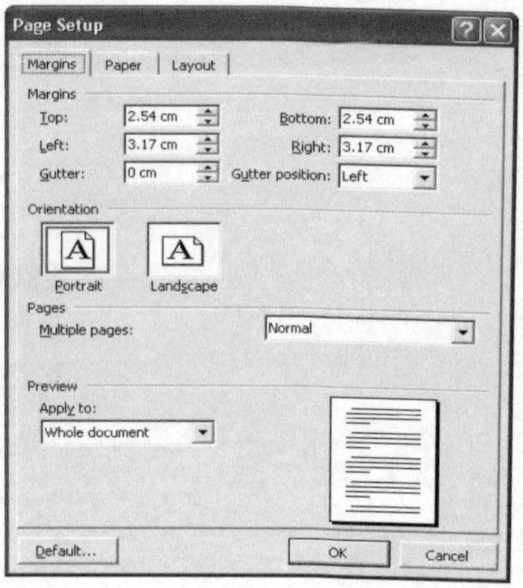

But what about the page on which the text appears? What options does Word offer you?

Choose **File | Page Setup** to view the three tabs of page setup options. Only two of these tabs are relevant at this stage: **Margins** and **Paper**.

The **Margins** tab

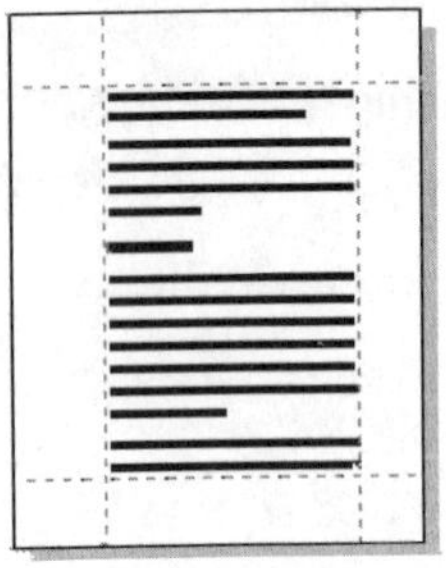

Margins indicated by dashed lines

A margin is the distance that the text and graphics are positioned in from the edge of the printed page.

Word's default margin values – top and bottom, 1 inch (2.54 cm), left and right, 1.25 inches (3.17 cm) – are acceptable for most letters and business documents.

You can change the top, bottom, left and right margins at any stage, and make your new values the new defaults by clicking the **Default** button.

Margin
The distance of the text and graphics from the edge of the printed page. Word lets you specify separate top, bottom, left and right margins.

Orientation is the direction in which the page is printed. Your options are *Portrait* ('standing up') and *Landscape* ('on its side'). Letters and most other business documents are printed in portrait.

The **Paper** tab

For the *Paper size* box, select the *A4* option. This is the European standard paper size (21 cm wide and 29.7 cm high). A4 is used for almost all letters and other business documents.

A4
The standard page size for letters and most other business documents throughout Europe.

Headers and footers

Headers and footers are pieces of text that appear on the top and bottom of every page of a document (except the title and contents pages).

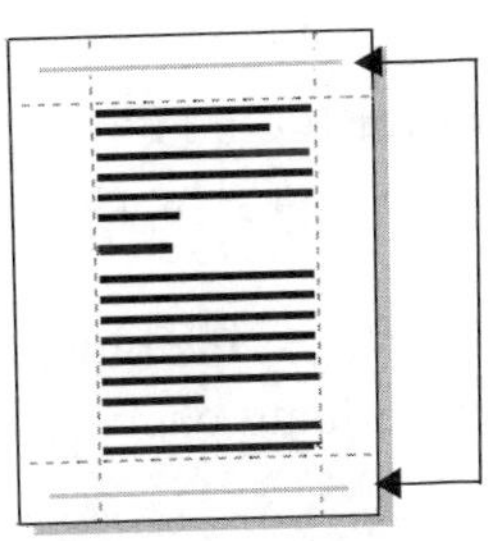

Word places headers and footers in the top and bottom page margins

Looking at examples of published documents, you will see that headers and footers typically contain such details as document title, organization name, author name, and perhaps a version or draft number. Usually, headers and footers also contain page numbers. You will learn about page numbering in the next topic.

With Word, you need only type in header and/or footer text once, and the program repeats the text on every page. Any formatting that you can apply to text in your document – such as bold, italics, alignment, borders and shading – you can also apply to text in the headers and footers. You can also insert graphics, such as a company logo, in a header or footer.

Headers and footers
Standard text and graphics that are printed in the top and bottom margins of every page of a document.

Here are a few facts about headers and footers in Word:

- You insert them with the **View | Header and Footer** command.
- This command displays the header or footer area (surrounded by a dashed border), the document text (which you cannot edit when working with headers and footers), and a *Header and Footer*

toolbar (giving you quick access to the commonly used commands).

Word's header area with toolbar

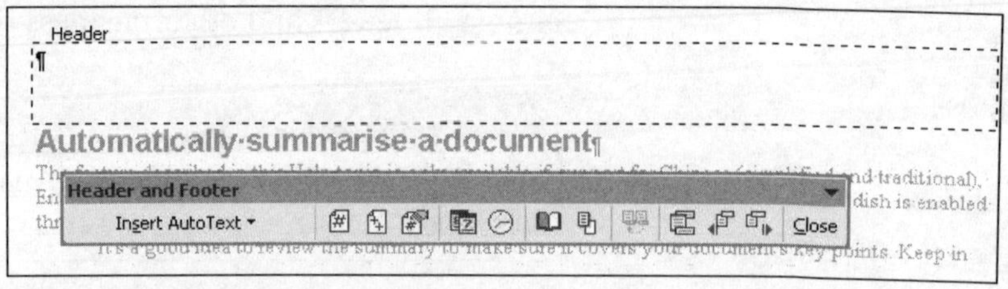

- Word positions the paragraph mark at the left of the header or footer area, ready for you to type text.
- Word inserts two preset tab stops to make it easy for you to centre-align or right-align headers or footers. Press **Tab** once to centre a header or footer, and press **Tab** twice to line it up against the right margin.
- Click the **Switch Between Header and Footer** button to view the footer area when in the header area, and vice versa. The two areas are similar in appearance and operation.

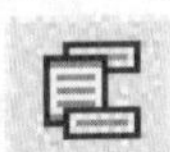

Switch Between Header and Footer button

- Place page numbers (discussed in the next topic) at the outside margin (left for left-hand pages, right for right-hand pages) or at the centre of the header or footer area.
- Place text at the centre or at the inside margin of the header or footer area.

Exercise 15.7: Creating a header

In this exercise you will insert header text in your sample document.

1) Choose **File | Page Setup**, select the **Layout** tab, ensure that the *Headers and footers* check boxes are as shown on the right, and click **OK**.

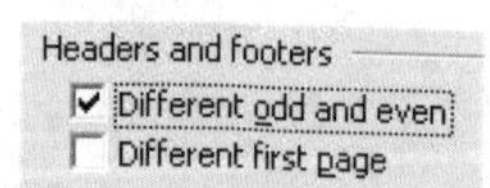

2) Choose **View | Header and Footer**. Word positions the paragraph mark at the left of the header area, ready for you to type text.
3) Type the following text: Annual Report

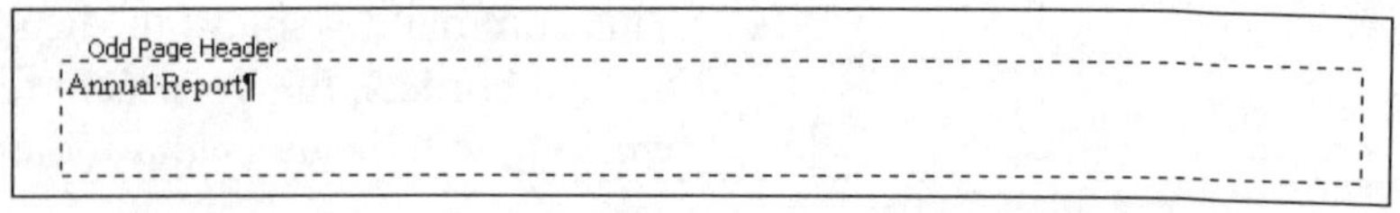

4) Click the **Show Next** button on the *Header and Footer* toolbar. Word takes you to the next page, the first even (left-hand) page of the document.

5) Press the **Tab** key twice to move the paragraph mark against the right-hand margin. Type the following text: ABC Limited

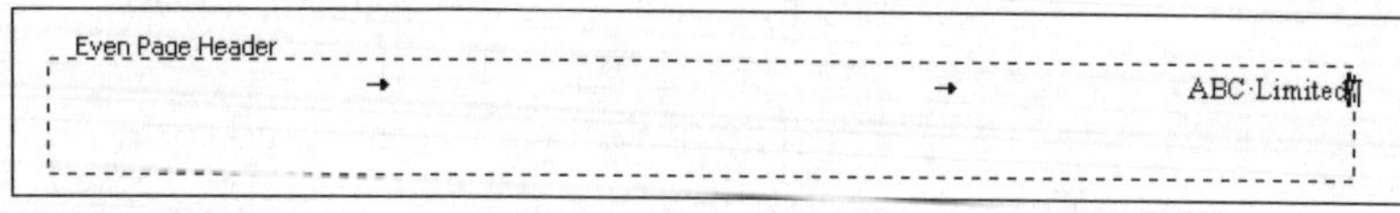

6) Click the **Close** button on the *Header and Footer* toolbar. Save your document.

Because you began this exercise by selecting the *Different odd and even* check box on **File | Page Setup**, Word allowed you to type separate headers for odd (right-hand) and even (left-hand) pages.

In the next exercise you will place a border under the header text to help separate it from the main body of the document. You will also change the font and font size. Typically, the header font is two or three point sizes smaller than the body text. At that size, sans serif fonts such as Arial are easier to read than serif fonts.

Exercise 15.8: Formatting a header

1) Display the first page of your document and choose **View | Header and Footer**. Alternatively, double-click inside the header area.
2) Select the header text.

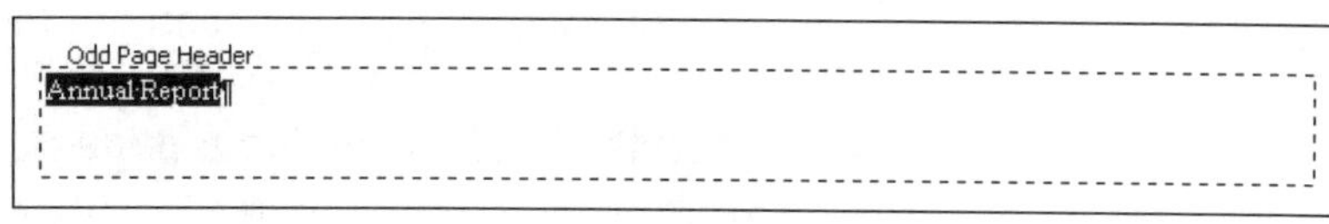

3) Chose **Format | Font**, and select Arial, Regular, 8 point.
4) With the text still selected, choose **Format | Borders and Shading**.
5) On the **Borders** tab, do the following:
   - Select *None* for *Setting*.
   - In the *Preview* area of the dialog box, click on the *Apply to* drop-down list and select *Paragraph*.

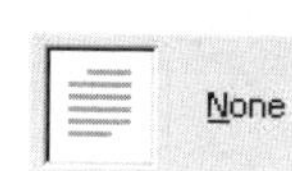

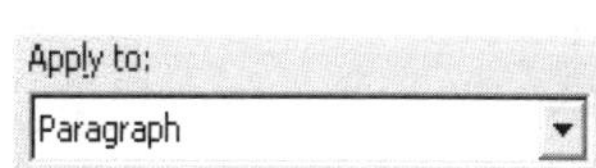

   - Also in the *Preview* area, click the **Border Beneath** button.

   - Finally, click **OK** to close the dialog box and apply the header border.

Note: Click the **Show Next** button on the *Header and Footer* toolbar. Repeat steps 2–5 for the left-hand page.

6) Click the **Close** button on the *Header and Footer* toolbar.

The top of your right-hand (odd-numbered) pages should now look as below.

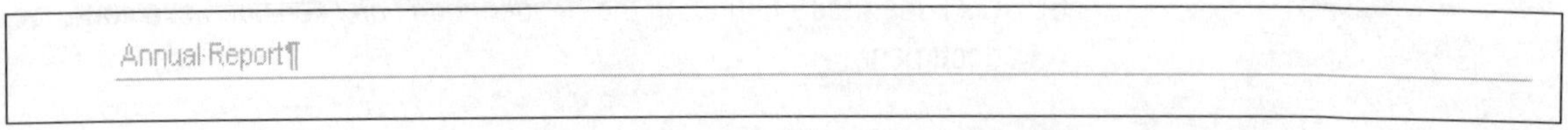

The top of your left-hand (even-numbered) pages should now look as below.

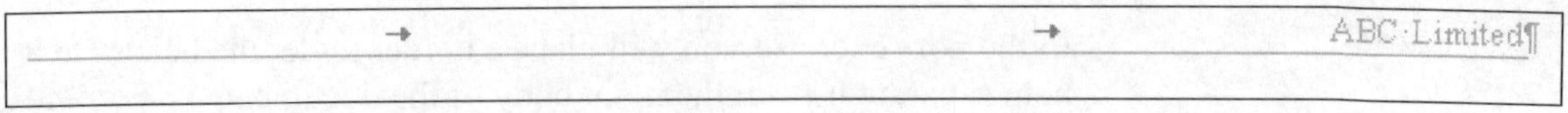

Notice that the header text is 'greyed out', indicating that you cannot edit it when working with the main body of the document.

Page numbering

You can insert a page number in the header or footer of a document. Word updates the page numbers as you add or remove document pages. The same formatting options are available for the page number as for header and footer text. You can align a page number at the left or right margin, or in the centre of the header or footer area.

Exercise 15.9: Inserting a page number

In this exercise you will insert a centre-aligned page number in the footer of your sample document.

1) Display the first page of your document, choose **View | Header and Footer**, and click the **Switch Between Header and Footer** button.
2) Click in the footer area, and press the **Tab** key once to move the cursor to the centre-aligned position.

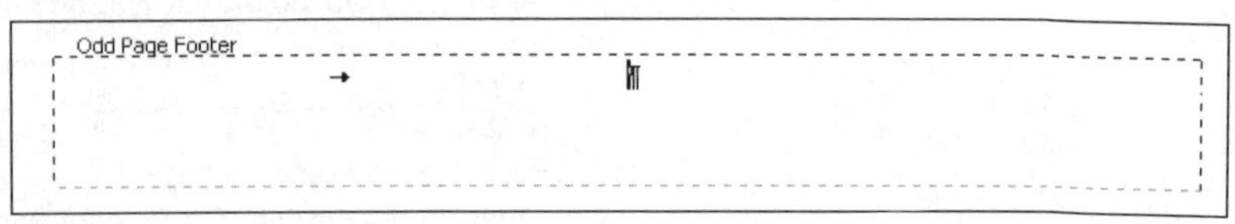

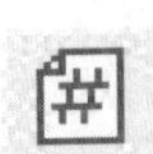

Insert Page Number button

3) Click the **Insert Page Number** button on the *Header and Footer* toolbar. Word inserts the page number.

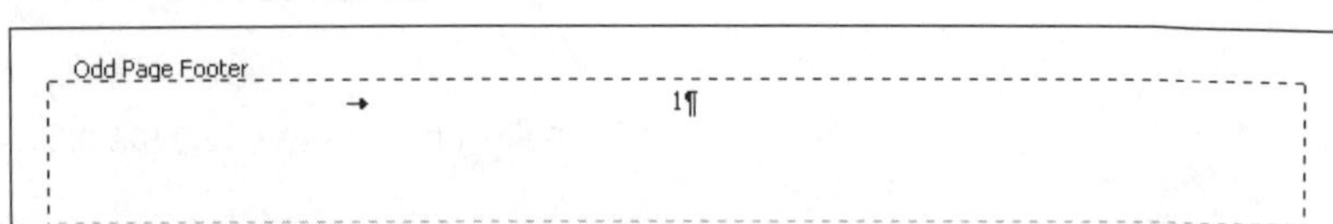

4) Click the **Show Next** button on the *Header and Footer* toolbar to move to the second page, the first even (left-hand) page of your document.
5) Repeat steps 2 and 3 to insert the page number in the centre-aligned position.

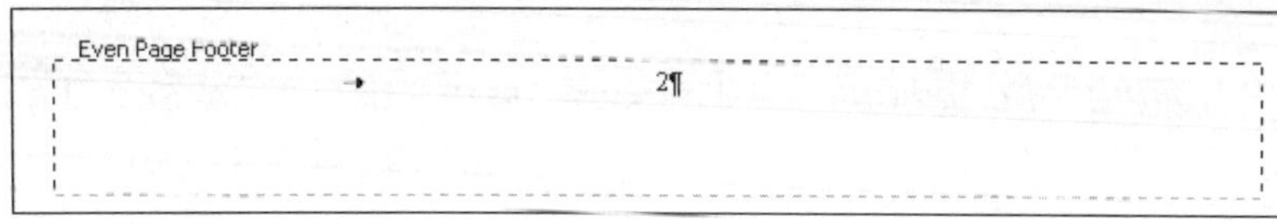

6) Click the **Close** button on the *Header and Footer* toolbar. Save your document.

Page numbering options

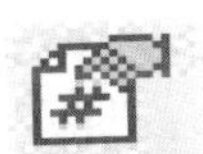

Format Page Number button

Click on the **Format Page Number** button on the *Header and Footer* toolbar to display the page numbering options.

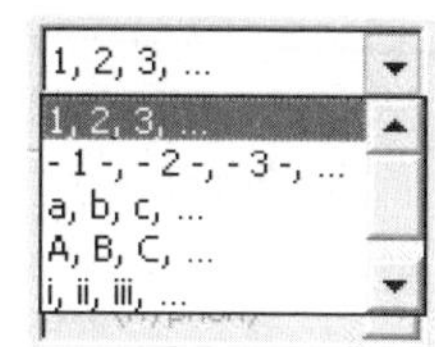

You can number the pages using numbers, letters or Roman numerals. You can also start at a number other than one.

Dates in documents

Your PC has an in-built clock and calendar, so you can choose to insert date and time details by reference to these. This saves you having to type the time and date manually.

You can also choose to update the date and time automatically. This means that when you subsequently open the document, the date and time entries will be current.

Exercise 15.10: Inserting a date

1) Position the cursor where you want to insert the date or time.
2) Choose **Insert | Date and Time**.
3) In the *Date and Time* dialog box, choose the format you want to use.
4) Check the *Update automatically* box if you want the date and time to be updated automatically.

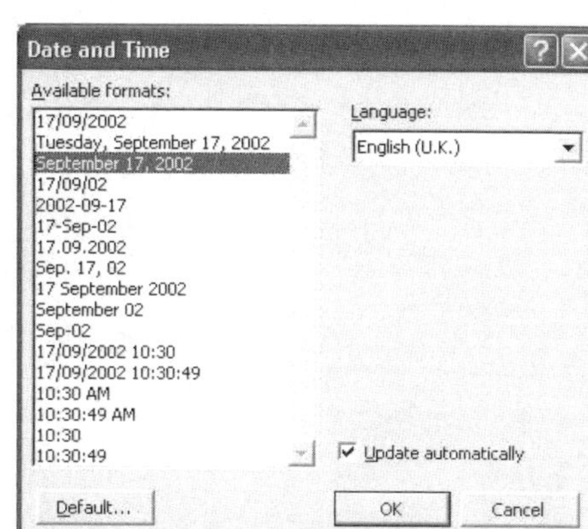

Document details

Word offers special features to make it easier for you to insert details such as today's date, your own name, and the file name and location in a header or footer.

Document creation date

To insert today's date (as recorded on your computer) in a header or footer, follow these steps:

Insert Date button

- Choose **View | Header and Footer**.
- Position the cursor where you want to insert the current date.
- Click the **Insert Date** button on the *Header and Footer* toolbar.

File name and location

To insert the file name and location in the header or footer:

- Choose **View | Header and Footer**.
- Position the cursor where you want to insert the file details.
- Choose **Insert | AutoText | Filename and path**.

Document author name

To insert the author's name (that is, your name), follow these steps:

- Choose **File | Properties**, and check that your name is displayed in the *Author* box on the **Summary** tab.

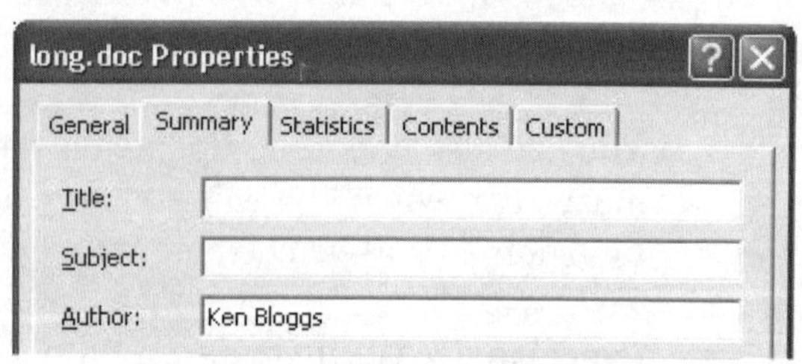

  Word displays in this box the user name entered when Windows was installed on your computer. If yours is not the name shown, delete the displayed name, type in your name, and select **OK**.
- Choose **View | Header and Footer**.
- Position the cursor in the header or footer area where you want to insert the author name.
- Choose **Insert | Field** to display the *Field* dialog box.

- In the *Field Names* list, select *Author,* and in the *Format* field, select *First capital*. Click **OK**.

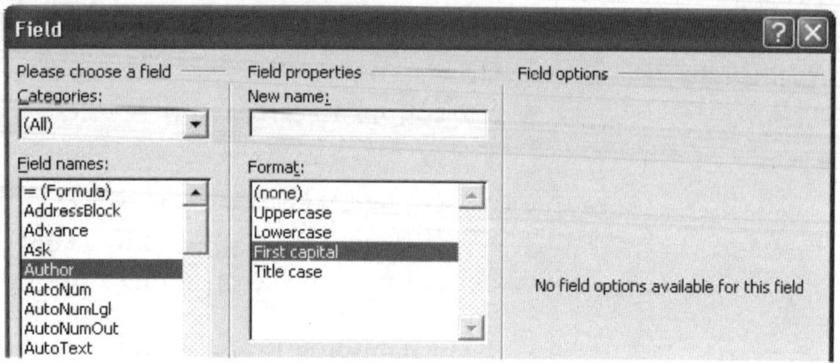

Manual line and page breaks

Pressing **Enter** at any stage inserts a new paragraph mark, and causes Word to begin a new paragraph. To insert a line break within a paragraph, press **Shift+Enter**.

Example of three line breaks

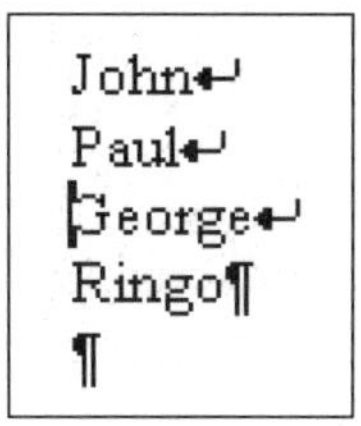

When text fills a page, Word automatically creates another page to hold the additional text. You can insert a page break manually at any point in a document by pressing **Ctrl+Enter**. Alternatively, choose the **Insert | Break** command, select the *Page break* option, and click **OK**.

Word's manual page break indicator

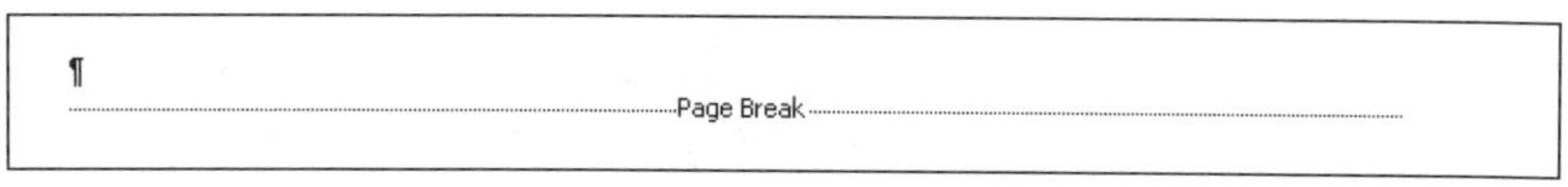

To delete a manual break, place the cursor before it and press **Delete**. If you cannot see the break marks, click on the **Show/Hide** button.

Proofing your document

Before you send your document off into the world, it's very important to proof it. Proofing your document will normally include the following quality checks:

- Are the formatting, page layout, and margin settings suitable for your intended audience?
- Are fonts and graphics used consistently?

You should also check the spelling and grammar – the options for doing this are described below.

Checking your spelling

How's your spelling? Word can check your spelling and suggest corrections to errors in two ways:

- As you type and edit your document (the automatic option).
- Whenever you choose the **Tools | Spelling and Grammar** command (the on-request option).

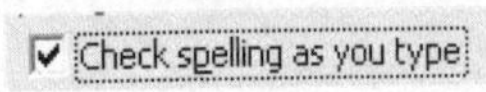

To turn automatic spellchecking on or off, select or deselect the *Check spelling as you type* check box on the **Spelling & Grammar** tab of the *Options* dialog box. You display this dialog box with the **Tools | Options** command.

Spellchecking: the automatic option

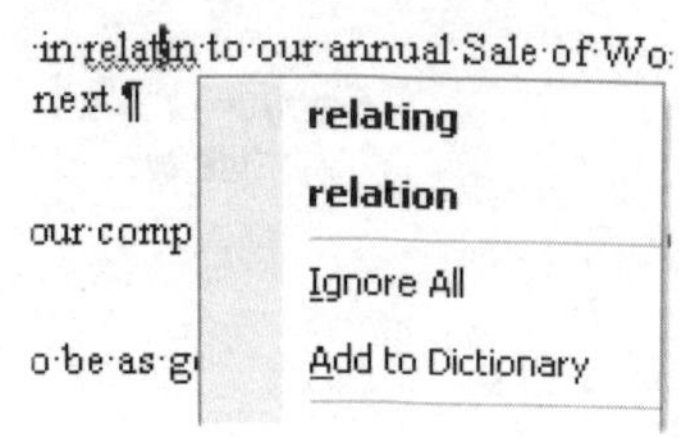

As you type and edit, a wavy red line under words indicates possible spelling errors.

To correct an error, right-click the word with a wavy underline, and then select the correction you want from the pop-up menu. Selecting **Spelling** from the pop-up menu displays Word's *Spelling and Grammar* dialog box.

The Spelling and Grammar *dialog box*

Whether automatic spellchecking is selected or not, you can spellcheck your document at any stage by choosing the **Tools | Spelling and Grammar** command.

If Word's spelling checker finds no errors, it displays a box telling you that the spellcheck is complete.

If Word finds something it does not recognize, it displays the *Spelling and Grammar* dialog box, and highlights the relevant word in red ('relatin' in our example below).

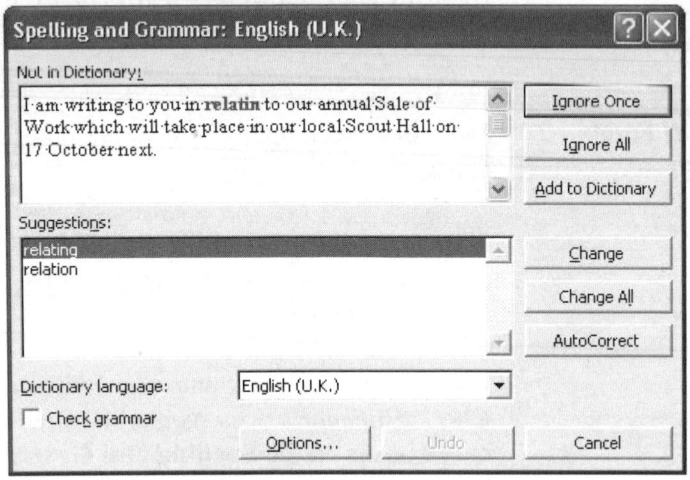

The dialog box includes a *Suggestions* area that offers likely alternatives to queried words. Click any suggested word to substitute it for the incorrect one. If none of the suggestions is appropriate, you can type your correction directly in the *Not in Dictionary* box.

Whenever the spelling checker queries a word, your options include:

- **Ignore:** Leave this occurrence of the word unchanged.
- **Ignore All:** Leave this and all other occurrences of the word in the document unchanged.
- **Add:** Add the word to the spelling dictionary, so that Word will recognize it during future spellchecks of any document. Use this option for the names of people or places, or abbreviations or acronyms that you type regularly.
- **Change:** Correct this occurrence of the word to that selected in the *Suggestions* area or entered in the *Not in Dictionary* area, but prompt again on further occurrences.
- **Change All:** Correct this occurrence of the word – and all other occurrences without further prompting.

A word of caution: if what you have typed is a correctly-spelt word but is inappropriate in this setting – for example, 'their' instead of 'there' – your spelling checker will not detect it as an error. Therefore, you should always read through the final version of the document to ensure that it doesn't contain any errors.

Watch your language

Before spellchecking your documents, choose **Tools | Language | Set Language** to display the current dictionary language. If it is incorrect (perhaps US English instead of UK English), select your required language and choose **Default**.

Checking your grammar

Word can check your grammar and suggest corrections to errors in two ways:

- As you type and edit your document (the automatic option).
- Whenever you choose the **Tools | Spelling and Grammar** command (the on-request option).

To turn automatic grammar-checking on or off, select or deselect the *Check grammar as you type* or the *Check grammar with spelling* check boxes on the **Spelling and Grammar** tab of the *Options* dialog box. You display this dialog box with the **Tools | Options** command.

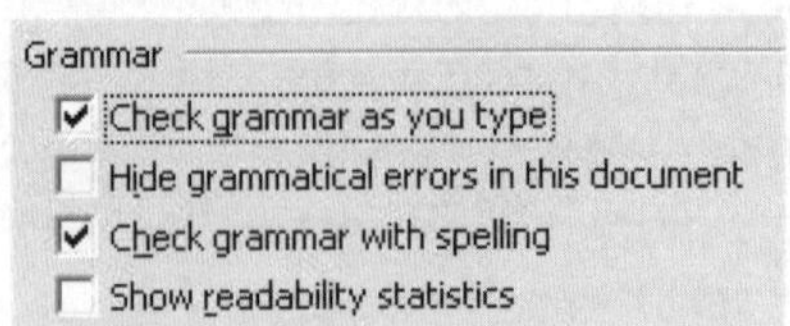

If automatic grammar-checking is turned on, a wavy green line under words indicates possible errors. You use Word's grammar-checking features in the same way as the spelling checker.

Printing options

Word offers a wide range of printing options. These include the ability to preview a document on your screen before you print it, and the choice of printing all your document, the current page, selected continuous or non-continuous pages, or the currently selected text.

Print preview

This displays each page as it will appear when it is printed on paper. To preview your document:

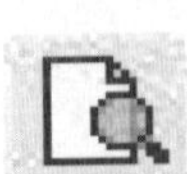

Print Preview button

- Choose **File | Print Preview** or click the **Print Preview** button on the *Standard* toolbar. Click **Close** to return to your document.

Print range options

When you choose **File | Print**, you have the following options regarding which pages of your document you may print:

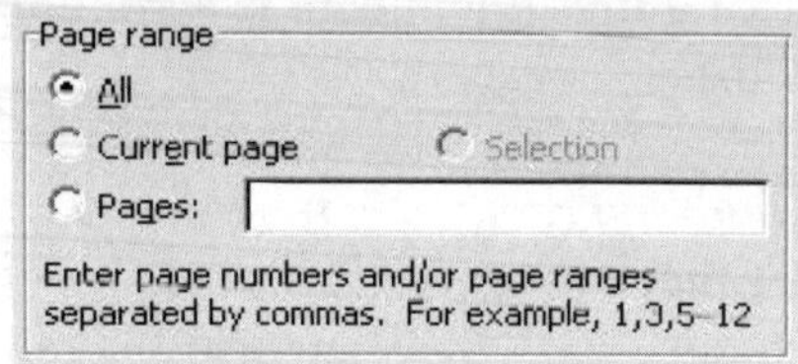

- **All:** Prints every page of your document.
- **Current page:** Prints only the currently displayed page.
- **Selection:** Prints only the currently selected text (and/or graphic).
- **Pages:** To print any single page of your document, enter its page number here.

  To print a group of continuous pages, enter the first and last page numbers of the group, separated by a dash; for example, 2-6 or 12-13.

  To print a non-continuous group of pages, enter their individual page numbers, separated by commas; for example, 3,5,9 or 12,17,34. You can combine continuous with non-continuous page selections.

Other options on the *Print* dialog box allow you to specify how many copies you want to print, whether you want to collate them, and whether you want to print only left or right pages.

If you have more than one printer installed, you select the printer you want to use from the *Name* drop-down list. If you want to change any of the default settings for that printer (for example, turn on or off duplex (two-sided) printing, print in reverse order, or change from colour to monochrome), click **Properties** and specify your requirements.

Save and close your long document, and close Microsoft Word.

You have now completed Chapter 15 of this ECDL word processing module.

Chapter summary: so now you know

You can increase or decrease Word's default *inter-line spacing* and *inter-paragraph* spacing.

You can highlight the start of each new paragraph by typing an extra paragraph mark (crude, but effective), by increasing inter-paragraph spacing, or by applying a *first-line indent* – see Exercise 15.2. The opposite of a first-line indent is a *hanging indent*, which is sometimes used for lists.

Word's *find and replace* feature enables you to quickly locate a particular piece of text, and replace it with an alternative piece of text – see Exercise 15.3. You can also find and replace text with specific formatting, and special characters such as paragraph marks and tabs – see Exercises 15.4, 15.5 and 15.6.

The standard page size is A4, and pages can be oriented in *portrait* or *landscape*. A *margin* is the distance of the text (and graphics) from a particular edge of the page.

Headers and footers are small text items that recur on every (or every second) page, and typically contain such details as the *document title* and *author name*. Either can also contain automatically generated *page numbers*. See Exercises 15.7, 15.8 and 15.9.

Word contains a *spelling checker* and a *grammar checker*. You can set up these checkers so that they are permanently switched on, or you can run them only as you require.

Word's *print options* include a Print Preview feature and the ability to print one or a range of pages.

Quick quiz: long documents, little details

Circle the correct answer to each of the following multiple-choice questions about working with long documents.

Q1	To change inter-paragraph spacing, you ...
A.	Choose **Format | Paragraph**, and use the *Special* options to change the inter-paragraph spacing.
B.	Choose **Format | Paragraph**, and use the *Line spacing* options to change the inter-paragraph spacing.
C.	Choose **Format | Paragraph**, and enter a value in either the *Space Before* box or the *Space After* box or both.

Q2	You can reformat all occurrences of a word or words by using the *Special* button in the *Find and Replace* dialog box.
A.	True.
B.	False.

Q3	To change a document's margins, you ...
A.	Use the **File | Properties** command.
B.	Use the **File | Page Setup** command.
C.	Use the **Format | Background** command.

Q4	To insert headers and footers in a document, you ...
A.	Choose **Insert | Headers and Footers**.
B.	Choose **View | Headers and Footers**.
C.	Choose **Format | Headers and Footers**.

Q5	To insert page numbers in a footer, you ...
A.	Use the **Insert Page Number** button on the *Headers and Footers* toolbar.
B.	Use the **Insert Number of Pages** button on the *Headers and Footers* toolbar.
C.	Use the **Format Page Number** button on the *Headers and Footers* toolbar.

Q6	To turn on automatic spellchecking, you ...
A.	Choose **Tools | Spelling and Grammar**.
B.	Choose **Tools | Options** and select the *Check grammar with spelling* option.
C.	Choose **Tools | Options** and select the *Check spelling as you type* option.

Answers

1: C, **2:** B, **3:** B, **4:** B, **5:** A, **6:** C.

Chapter 16: Tables, tabs and graphics

In this chapter

On most Word documents, you want text to flow left to right across the width of the page. Sometimes, however, you may want to create narrow, side-by-side columns of text, numbers and graphics.

In this chapter you will learn about Word's two options for creating such side-by-side columns: tables and tabs.

You will also discover how to insert and manipulate graphics and AutoShapes in Word.

Finally, you will be introduced to hyphenation – a way of splitting long words across lines to improve the appearance of text.

New skills

At the end of this chapter you should be able to:

- Create and format tables.
- Insert and edit tabs.
- Paste and insert graphics.
- Create AutoShapes.
- Move, reshape and resize graphics and AutoShapes.
- Apply automatic and manual hyphenation to text.

New words

At the end of this chapter you should be able to explain the following terms:

- Table
- Tab
- AutoShape
- Hyphenation

Using tables in Word

A table consists of rectangular cells, arranged in rows and columns. Inside cells, text wraps just as it does on a page. As you type text into a cell, the cell expands vertically to hold each new line.

You can create a new, blank table, and enter text and graphics in its empty cells. Alternatively, you can convert existing paragraphs of text to a table.

Table
An array of cells arranged in rows and columns that can hold text and graphics.

Exercise 16.1: Creating a new table

In this exercise you create a table, and enter text in it.

1) Open Word and click the **New** button on the *Standard* toolbar to create a new document. Click the **Save** button to save it. Give your new document a name that you will find easy to remember. If your initials are KB, for example, name it KBtable.doc.
2) Choose **Table | Insert | Table**. In the *Insert Table* dialog box, select *2* columns and *4* rows, and click **OK**. You can add or remove columns and rows later, as required.

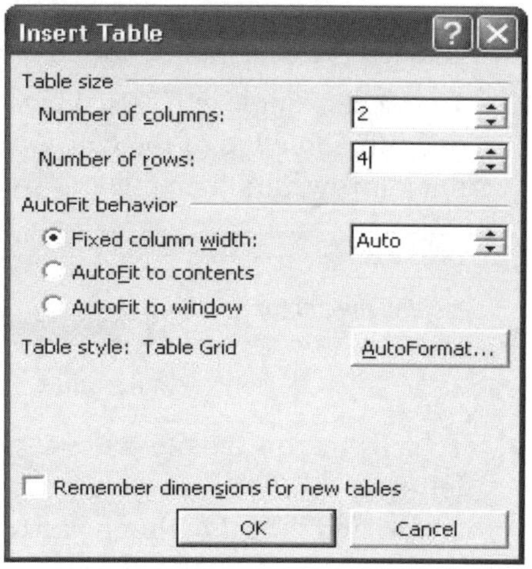

Accept the column width default of *Auto*. This creates columns of equal size across the width of your page. Word displays a blank table as shown below.

¤	¤
¤	¤
¤	¤
¤	¤

3) Click in the top-left cell, and type: Sales Region
4) Press the **Tab** key. In a table, pressing **Tab** does not insert a tab stop. Instead, it moves the cursor to the next cell. **Shift+Tab** moves the cursor back to the

previous cell. You can also use the arrow keys or the mouse to move the cursor between different cells. (To insert a tab in a table, press **Ctrl+Tab**.) With the cursor in the top-right cell, type the text: Number of Units Sold

5) Continue moving the cursor and typing text until your table looks as shown below.

Sales Region	Number of Units Sold
Europe	1234
Latin America	5678
China	4321

Congratulations. You have created your first table in Word. Save the table document and leave it open.

Selecting table cells

You can format and align table text in the same way as text outside a table. Here are the rules on selecting table text:

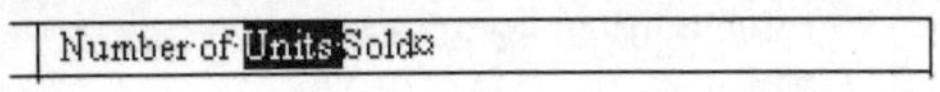

- To select text in a cell, drag the mouse across the text.
- To select a single cell, use the mouse pointer to position the cursor over the left edge of the cell, wait for the cursor to change to a thick arrow, and then click to select the cell.

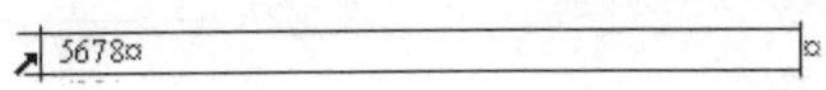

Position the cursor ...

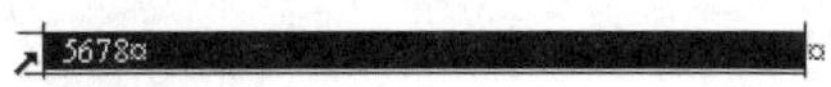

... and click

- To select a row, position the cursor over the left edge of the leftmost cell in the row, wait for the cursor to change to a thick arrow, and then double-click to select the row. (Clicking once selects the left-most cell only.)

  Alternatively click in any cell of the row and choose **Table | Select | Row**.
- To select a column, position the cursor at the top edge of the column, wait for the cursor to change to a thick, downward arrow, and then click to select the column.

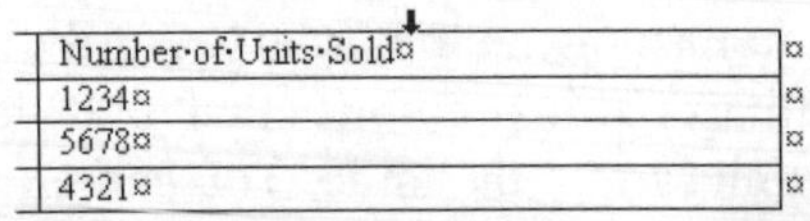

Position the cursor ...

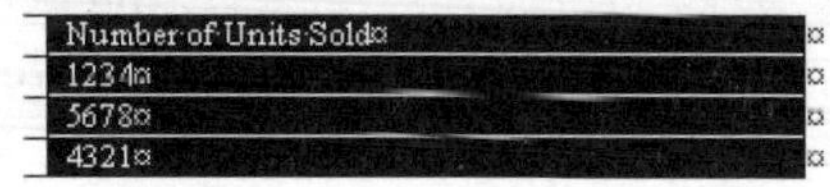

... and click

Alternatively, click in any cell of the column and choose **Table | Select | Column**.

- To select the entire table, position the cursor anywhere on the table. Notice that Word displays the table's move handle at the top-left of the table. Click the move handle to select the entire table.

Move handle →

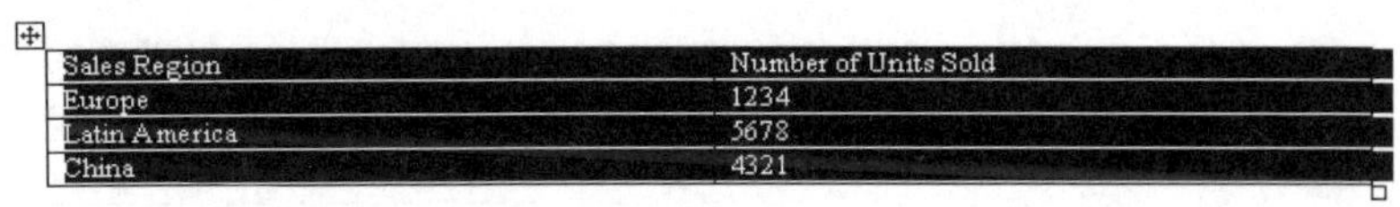

Alternatively, you can select a table by clicking in any of its cells and choosing **Table | Select | Table**.

Making changes to a table

Here are the rules for making changes to a table:

- To add a new row, select the row beneath or above the position where you want to insert the new row, and choose **Table | Insert | Rows Above** (or **Rows Below**).
- To add a new column, select the column to the right or the left of where you want to insert the new column, and choose **Table | Insert | Columns to the Left** (or **Columns to the Right**).
- To delete a row or column, select it, and choose **Table | Delete | Rows** or **Table | Delete | Columns**.
- To merge two or more selected cells from the same row into a single cell, choose **Table | Merge Cells**.
- To split a single, selected cell into two or more cells, choose **Table | Split Cells**, enter the required values in the dialog box displayed, and click **OK**.
- To apply borders and shading, select the cells, rows, columns or entire table, and apply the **Format | Borders and Shading** command.

Table gridlines

If you turn off table borders, Word displays table non-printing gridlines – thin grey lines that make it easier to see where the rows and columns are in the table. You can turn gridlines off and on with the **Table | Hide/Show Gridlines** command. This command applies to your entire document, and not just a particular table.

Exercise 16.2: Formatting and changing your table

1) Select the top row of the table you created in Exercise 16.1, choose **Format | Font**, select Arial, 12 point, Bold, and click **OK**.
2) With the top row still selected, click the **Center Align** button on the *Formatting* toolbar.

Sales·Region¤	Number·of·Units·Sold¤	¤
Europe¤	1234¤	¤

3) Place the cursor in the cell that contains Latin America. Choose **Table | Insert | Rows Above**. Type the following text into the new row.

South·Africa¤	581¤	¤

4) Select the top row of the table, and choose **Table | Insert | Rows Above**.
5) With the new, inserted top row still selected, choose **Table | Merge Cells**.
6) Type the following text in the merged row: Sales Figures
7) Select the top, merged row, choose **Format | Font**, select Arial, 14 point, Bold Italic, and click **OK**.
8) By default, Word places a ½-point black, single solid-line border around each cell. Select the top row, choose **Format | Borders and Shading** and place a double-line border under the first row.

   To do this, first of all remove the single underline under the row by clicking it in the *Preview* box. Then select the double-line border in the *Style* box, click the lower border in the *Preview* box and click **OK**.

   In the same dialog box, you can also specify a different width and colour for the border around the selected cell or group of cells by specifying your preferences in the *Width* and *Color* boxes.

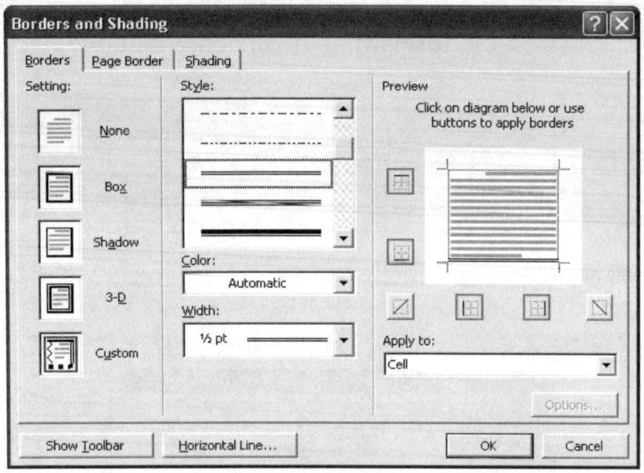

9) Select all the rows except the top one, choose **Format | Borders and Shading**, click on the **Shading** tab, select *Gray-15%* background, and click **OK**.

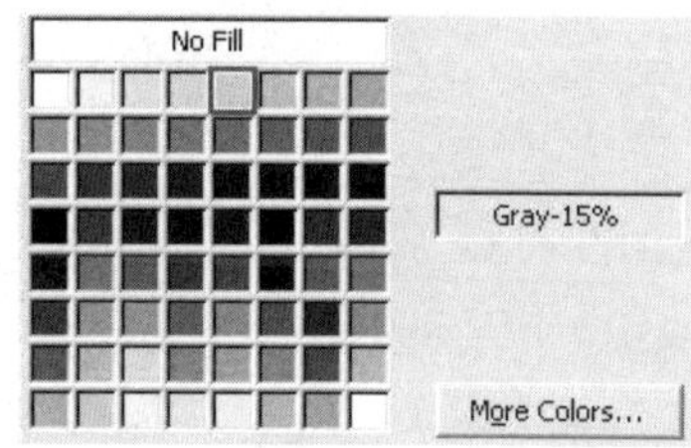

Your table should look as shown below. Save your table document again and leave it open.

Sales·Figures	
Sales·Region	**Number·of·Units·Sold**
Europe	1234
South·Africa	581
Latin·America	5678
China	4321

Column width, spacing and row height

To change the width of a column, use the mouse to position the cursor over the left or right vertical edge of the column. The cursor changes shape. Then drag with the mouse until the column is the width that you require.

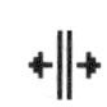

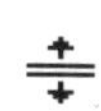

You can change the height of cells in a similar way.

The Table AutoFormat option

Word's AutoFormat option offers a range of predefined formats for your table, including borders and shading. To apply AutoFormat, select your table and choose **Table | Table AutoFormat**. The *Table*

AutoFormat dialog box offers a preview area where you can view the formatting effects on your table.

Preview

	JAN	FEB	MAR	TOTAL
East	7	7	5	19
West	6	4	7	17
South	8	7	9	24
Total	21	18	21	60

Preview

	Jan	*Feb*	*Mar*	*Total*
East	7	7	5	19
West	6	4	7	17
South	8	7	9	24
Total	21	18	21	60

Preview

	Jan	Feb	Mar	**Total**
East	7	7	5	**19**
West	6	4	7	**17**
South	8	7	9	**24**
Total	**21**	**18**	**21**	**60**

Preview

	Jan	**Feb**	**Mar**	**Total**
East	7	7	5	19
West	6	4	7	17
South	8	7	9	24
Total	21	18	21	60

Practise by selecting your table and applying a series of AutoFormats. When finished, save and close your table document.

Introduction to tabs

Old-style typewriters had a key called **Tab** that, when pressed, changed the position at which the letter keys struck the page and printed text. Typically, there were about ten tab positions – called tab stops – usually about half an inch apart.

Pressing the **Tab** key once advanced the text position to the first tab stop, pressing **Tab** again moved it to the second tab stop, and so on.

By typing text at the same tab position on successive lines, the typist could create vertical columns of text.

1	2	3	4	5	6	7	8	9	10
	Cajun·Heat·Fries				£1.45				
	Onion·Rings				£1.65				
	Bread·Sticks				£1.25				
	Fried·Cheese·Ravioli				£2.75				
	Primo·Mozzarella·Poppers				£3.25				
	Cream·Cheese·Poppers				£3.95				
	Breaded·Mushrooms				£2.95				
	Breaded·Zucchini·Sticks				£2.75				

This example shows the second tab stop used to position menu items, and the sixth tab stop used to position menu prices.

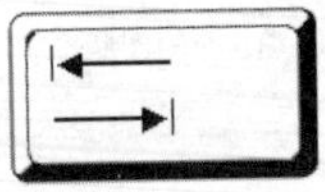

Tab key

As computers and word processing software replaced the typewriter, the idea of tabs continued. Computer keyboards include a **Tab** key, and Word, like other word-processing applications, offers a tab feature.

The effect of using tabs is similar to using tables: text appears in side-by-side columns rather than running continuously from the left to the right margin on the page.

Tabs
Predefined horizontal locations between the left and right page margins that determine where typed text is positioned. Using tabs on successive lines gives the effect of side-by-side columns of text.

If you want to position small amounts of text such as the address lines at the top of a letter, tabs are quicker to use than tables. Also, tabs have a feature called *leaders* that tables do not have, which can make it easier to read text that is separated into different columns.

Using tabs in Word

Word automatically positions tab stops at intervals of 1.27 cm (0.5 inches) from left to right. You can see this for yourself by pressing the **Tab** key repeatedly in a document; each time you press **Tab**, Word moves the cursor 1.27 cm to the right.

Exercise 16.3: Using tab stops

1) Open the letter that you created and saved in Chapter 13.

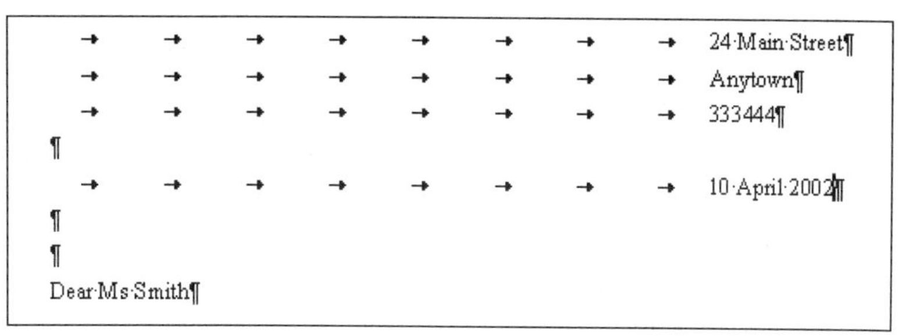

2) Move the cursor to the start of the first line and type: ABC Limited
3) Move the cursor to the start of the second line and type: Unit 32A
4) Move the cursor to the start of the third line and type: Smithstown Business Park

   If your new text pushes any of the sender's address lines to the right or onto the next line, use the **Delete** key to remove the tab stops from the line until that address line returns to its original position.

5) Your new text picks up the bold formatting of the sender's address. Change its formatting back to normal. Your letter should now look as below.

```
ABC·Limited →  →  →  →  →  →  →  24·Main·Street ¶
Unit·32A  →  →  →  →  →  →  →  Anytown ¶
Smithstown·Business·Park. →  →  →  →  →  333444¶
¶
→  →  →  →  →  →  →  →  1·October·2000¶
```

Save and close your letter document.

In the next exercise you will use Word's tabs to create a restaurant menu.

Exercise 16.4: Creating a restaurant menu with tabs

1) Open a new document and enter the following text:

```
Cajun·Heat·Fries·£1.45·Primo·Mozzarella·Poppers·£3.25¶
Onion·Rings·£1.65·Breaded·Zucchini·Sticks·£2.75¶
Bread·Sticks·£1.25·Fried·Cheese·Ravioli·£2.75¶
Cream·Cheese·Poppers·£3.95·Breaded·Mushrooms·£2.95¶
```

2) Are Word's tabs measured in centimetres or inches? Find out by choosing **Tools | Options**, selecting the **General** tab, and looking at the *Measurement units* box. If the units are inches, change to centimetres. Click **OK** to close the box.

Measurement units: Centimeters

3) On the first line of your document, position the cursor at the end of the word Fries, and press **Delete** to remove the space between Fries and £1.45. Press **Tab** repeatedly to move the £1.45 rightwards to the 5.08 cm default tab stop.

4) Repeat step 3 for the remaining three lines. Your text should look as below.

```
Cajun·Heat·Fries  →  →  £1.45·Primo·Mozzarella·Poppers·£3.25¶
Onion·Rings →  →  →  £1.65·Breaded·Zucchini·Sticks·£2.75¶
Bread·Sticks →  →  →  £1.25·Fried·Cheese·Ravioli·£2.75¶
Cream·Cheese·Poppers→  →  £3.95·Breaded·Mushrooms·£2.95¶
```

5) On the first line, position the cursor after £1.45, and press **Delete** to remove the space before Primo. Press **Tab** twice to move the Primo Mozzarella Poppers rightwards to the 7.62 cm default tab stop.

6) Repeat step 5 for the remaining three lines.

7) On the first line, position the cursor after Poppers, and press **Delete** to remove the space between Poppers and £3.25. Press **Tab** repeatedly to move the £3.25 rightwards to the 13.65 cm default tab stop.

8) Repeat step 7 for the remaining three lines. Your text should look as below.

Cajun·Heat·Fries· → →	£1.45→ →	Primo·Mozzarella·Poppers →	→ £3.25¶
Onion·Rings → → →	£1.65→ →	Breaded·Zucchini·Sticks →	→ £2.75¶
Bread·Sticks → → →	£1.25→ →	Fried·Cheese·Ravioli → →	→ £2.75¶
Cream·Cheese·Poppers→ →	£3.95→ →	Breaded·Mushrooms → →	→ £2.95¶

Save your document with a memorable name, and close it. If your initials are KB, for example, call it KBtabsmenu.doc.

Tab alignment

The tabs you have used so far have all been left-aligned; that is, a tab stop of 5 cm means that the relevant text or number is positioned so that it begins 5 cm in from the left margin. Word offers three other tab alignment options:

- **Centred:** The tabbed text or number is positioned so that its centre is (say) 5 cm from the left margin.
- **Right-aligned:** The tabbed text or number is positioned so that it ends (say) 5 cm from the left margin.
- **Decimal:** If the tabbed item is a number that contains a decimal point, the number is positioned so that the decimal point is (say) 5 cm from the left margin.

If the tabbed item is a number that does not contain a decimal point, or is text, a decimal tab stop has the same effect as a right-aligned tab.

Any tab-stop positions that you insert in a paragraph of a document apply only to that paragraph. This means that different paragraphs of the same document may contain tabs of different types and tabs positioned at different intervals.

In the next exercise you will practise using all four tab stop types – left, right, centre and decimal.

Exercise 16.5: Using different tab alignment types

1) Create a new document, and type the text and numbers as shown. Make the text 'Unit Cost' bold.

```
Unit·Cost¶
.853 ¶
621¶
45¶
26.82¶
```

2) In turn, select each of the five lines (but not the paragraph mark), and copy and paste it three times to its right. Your document should now look as shown below.

```
Unit·CostUnit·CostUnit·CostUnit·Cost¶
.853.853.853.853¶
621621621621¶
45454545¶
26.8226.8226.8226.82¶
```

3) Insert four tab stops in each line in the position shown below. (The tab positions are Word's default ones.)

```
→  Unit·Cost  →  Unit·Cost  →  Unit·Cost  →  Unit·Cost¶
→  .853 → .853 → .853 → .853¶
→  621 → 621 → 621 → 621¶
→  45 → 45 → 45 → 45¶
→  26.82 → 26.82 → 26.82 → 26.82¶
```

4) Select the five lines of text, choose **Format | Tabs**, and click **Clear All** to remove all the default tabs.

5) Set the following tab positions and alignments:

Tab stop position	Alignment
2 cm	Left
6 cm	Centre
10 cm	Right
13 cm	Decimal

In each case, type the tab position, select the alignment, and click **Set**.

6) When finished, click **OK**. Your document should now look as shown.

```
→   Unit·Cost   →   Unit·Cost   →   Unit·Cost   →   Unit·Cost¶
→   .853        →     .853      →        .853   →       .853¶
→   621         →     621       →        621    →    621¶
→   45          →     45        →         45    →    45¶
→   26.82       →    26.82      →      26.82    →     26.82¶
```

Save your document with a memorable name, and close it. If your initials are KB, for example, call it KBunitcost.doc.

Using tabs with the ruler

You can display and amend Word's default tab stops by choosing **View | Ruler**. The ruler appears along the top of the document window. You can see the default tab stops, indicated by thin vertical lines, at evenly spaced positions along the base of the ruler.

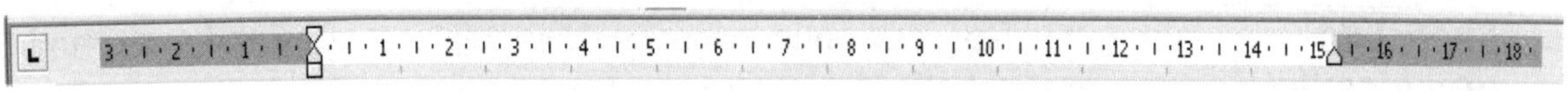

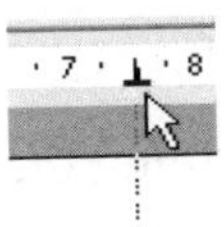

You can change the position of a tab stop by dragging it left or right to a new location on the ruler. As you drag a tab stop, Word displays a vertical, dashed line stretching down from the tab ruler to the document itself.

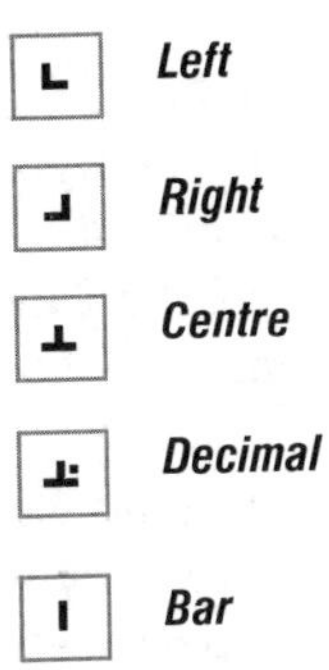

Tab alignment button

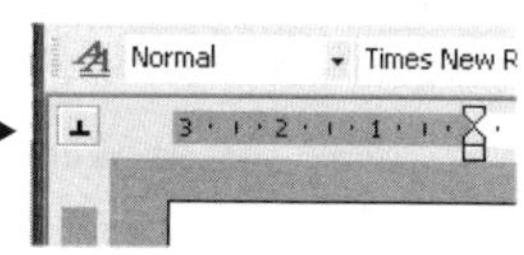

At the left of the ruler you can see the **Tab** button. As you click this button successively, it cycles through the five possible tab types: left-aligned (default), centre-aligned, right-aligned, decimal point-aligned, and bar tab.

To add a new tab stop, click the **Tab** button to display the type of tab you want, and then click the ruler where you want to place the tab. To remove a tab stop, click on it and drag it off the ruler.

Using graphics in Word

You can illustrate your Word documents with graphics of various kinds. For example:

- Charts (graphs) created in a spreadsheet applications such as Excel.
- Drawings and photographs created or manipulated in graphics applications such as Paint Shop Pro or Adobe PhotoShop.

Word contains many collections of standard or so-called Clip Art images that you can use and reuse in a wide range of documents. Examples of Clip Art would be Man Answering Phone, Woman

Sitting at Desk, Handshake, Sunset, and so on. Clip Art is also available on CD-ROMs and on the Internet.

Clip Art
Standard or stock images that can be used and reused in a wide range of documents.

Importing graphics: two options

You have two options for inserting graphics: copy and paste, and file insert. Let's look at these two in detail.

Graphics: copy and paste

This option is possible only if you can open the file containing the relevant graphic. To do so, you need to have installed on your computer a software application that can read that graphic format.

For example, to copy into Word a graphic created in Adobe PhotoShop, you need Adobe PhotoShop installed and open on your computer (or, failing that, another graphics program capable of opening Adobe PhotoShop files). To copy into Word a chart created in Excel, you need Excel installed and open on your computer.

When you have the graphic or chart open in the other program, select it (or the part of it you require), and choose **Edit | Copy** to copy it to the clipboard. Then, switch to Word, position the cursor where you want the graphic or chart to appear in your document, and choose **Edit | Paste**.

Graphics: file insert

This option enables you to include a graphic in a Word document – even if you do not have the software package in which the graphic was created installed on your PC.

Position the cursor where you want the graphic to appear in your document, and choose **Insert | Picture | From File**. Locate the relevant graphic – it may be on your hard disk, on a floppy disk in the A: drive, or on a CD-ROM – and click **OK** to insert the image.

To include any of Word's own set of Clip Art images, choose the **Insert | Picture | Clip Art** command. This displays the *Insert Clip Art* task pane, where you select the image you want to insert. Exercise 16.6 explains how you do this.

To insert a new chart, choose **Insert | Picture | Chart**. You are presented with a sample datasheet and chart. Change the numbers and captions in the datasheet, and, as you do so, the chart changes to reflect them. When you are satisfied with the result, close the datasheet. You can change the chart type and style by right-clicking in the chart and choosing from the pop-up menu.

Working with graphics

There are a number of common operations that you can perform on imported graphics, regardless of their type.

Moving a graphic

To move a graphic, first select it by clicking anywhere inside it. Next, hold down the mouse button. Word changes the cursor to a cross (see right). Then drag the graphic to its new location.

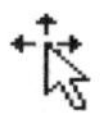

To move a graphic between documents, use the **Cut** and **Paste** commands on the **Edit** menu.

Deleting a graphic

To delete a graphic, click on it and press **Delete**.

Changing the shape and size of a graphic

You can change the shape and size of a graphic by selecting it and clicking on any of its six handles.

Hold down the mouse button and drag the handle to change the shape and size of the graphic. As you drag the object, Word changes its border to a dashed line.

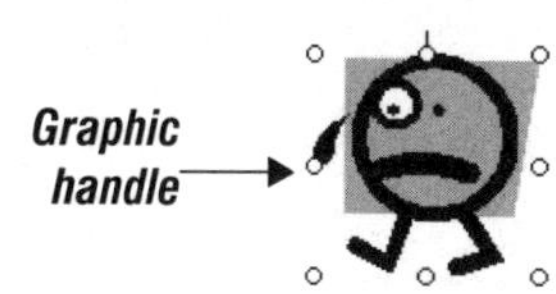

Exercise 16.6: Inserting a Word Clip Art image

1) Open the poster document that you created in Chapter 14.
2) Choose **Insert | Picture | Clip Art**. Word displays the *Insert Clip Art* task pane.

3) As you are going to insert a banner at the bottom of your poster, click the arrow at the right of the *Search in* box in the task pane, and navigate to the *Banners* collection.

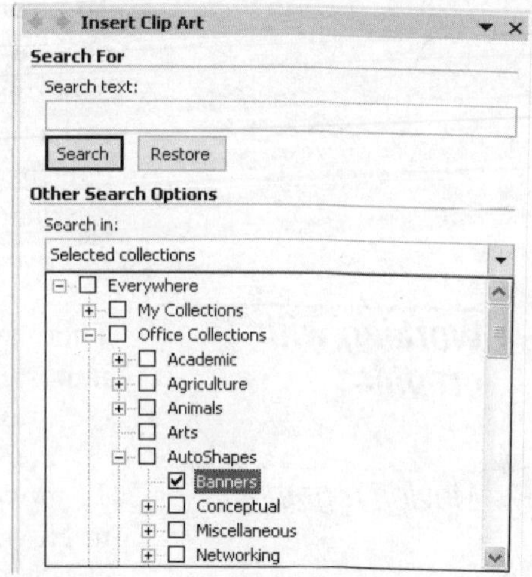

4) Click on *Banners* to select that collection.

   If all collections are currently selected, first deselect the *Everywhere* option by clicking on it.

5) Click the **Search** button in the task pane. Word displays all Clip Art images in the *Banners* collection.

6) Click the *Up Banner* (green) image and drag it to the bottom of your poster.

7) Select the image, reduce its height by about a third, and drag it until it is positioned centrally beneath the text 'All Welcome'. The bottom of your poster should now look as shown below. Save your poster.

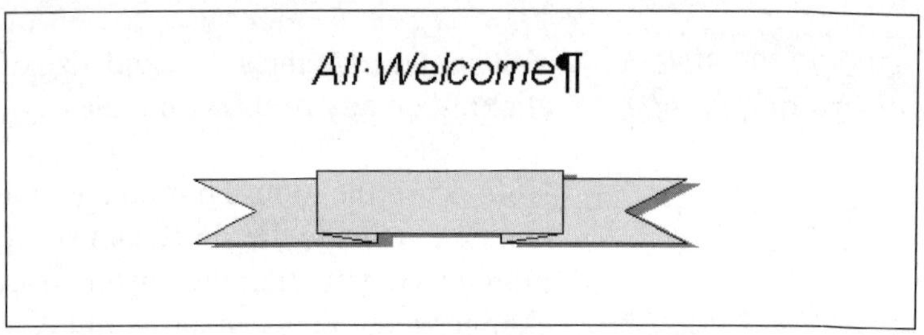

Inserting AutoShapes

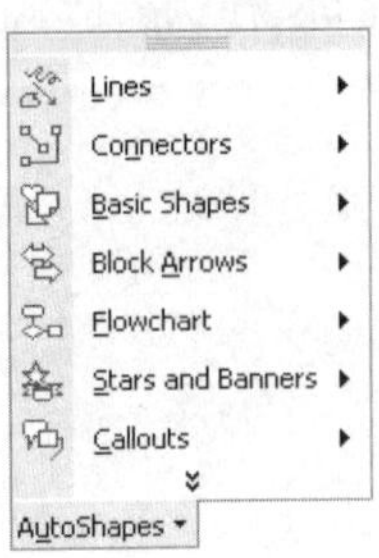

AutoShapes are categories of ready-made shapes that you can insert in your Word documents. They include lines, basic shapes, flowchart elements, stars and banners, and callouts.

When you insert an AutoShape in a document, you can reposition it, and change its size and colour, as required.

To select an AutoShape:

- Display Word's *Drawing* toolbar by choosing **View | Toolbars | Drawing**.
- Click the **AutoShapes** button on the *Drawing* toolbar.

You can then choose from the options offered by the pop-up menu.

AutoShapes
Categories of ready-made shapes, including lines, geometric shapes and flowchart elements, which you can use in your Word documents.

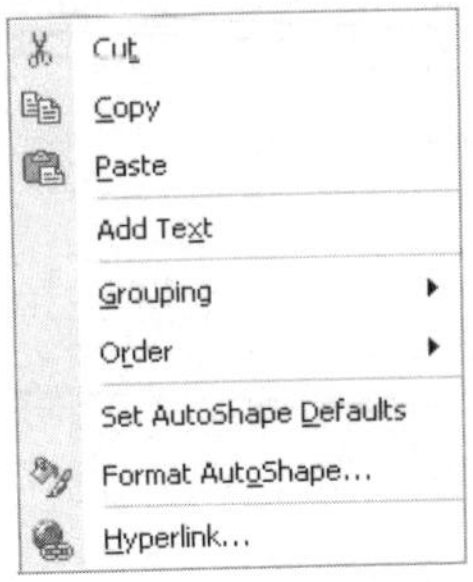

When you right-click on an AutoShape, Word offers a number of options, including:

- **Add Text:** This enables you to type characters inside the circle, square, oval, or other AutoShape. You can also paste text from the clipboard into an AutoShape.
- **Format AutoShape:** This enables you to change the border (edge) and fill (background) colours of the AutoShape.

You can move and resize AutoShapes in the same way that you can graphics.

Exercise 16.7 provides examples of creating AutoShapes and applying AutoShape features.

Exercise 16.7: Working with AutoShapes

1) If your poster document is not open after Exercise 16.6, open it now.
2) Select the text 'Admission Free' (but not its accompanying paragraph mark).

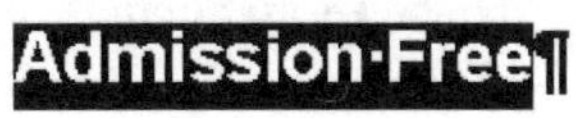

3) Cut the selected text from the poster to the clipboard and press **Enter** to insert a second paragraph mark.
4) Click the **AutoShapes** button on the *Drawing* toolbar. From the pop-up menu displayed, select **Basic Shapes**. Finally, select the *Rounded Rectangle* AutoShape.

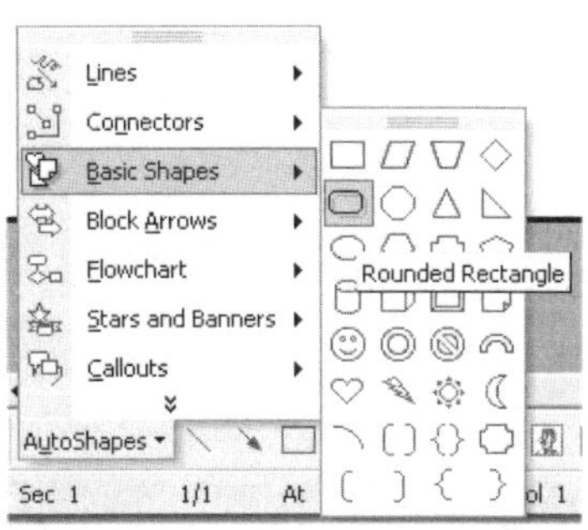

(If the *Drawing* toolbar is not open in Word, choose **View | Toolbars | Drawing** to display it.)

5) Word displays a *drawing canvas* with the words: Create your drawing here. You do not need to know about this feature for the ECDL word processing module, so press the **Esc** key (at the top left of your keyboard) to remove it.

6) Now draw the AutoShape at the location of the text you cut in step 3. Make sure the rectangle is big enough to hold the text in the clipboard. Position it so that it is centred between the left and right page margins.

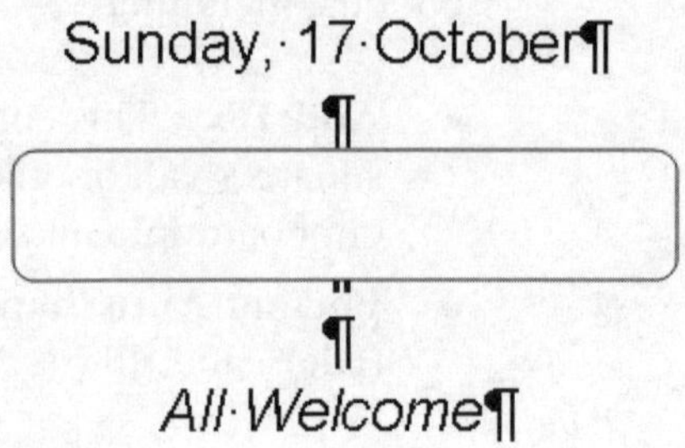

7) Right-click on the AutoShape, choose **Add Text**, and paste the text from the clipboard to the AutoShape. Select the pasted text, and click the **Centre Alignment** button on the *Formatting* toolbar. Make the text Arial, 20 point, bold.

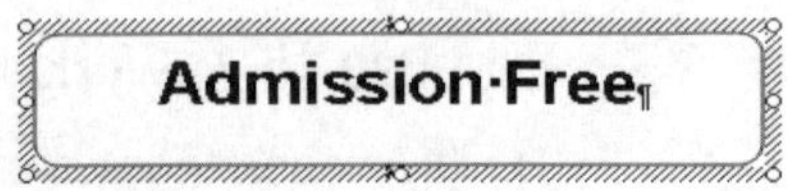

8) Click any edge of the AutoShape to select it, right-click to display the pop-up menu, and choose **Format AutoShape**.

9) On the **Colors and Lines** tab, select a *Fill Color* of yellow. Also, change the *Line Weight* to 1.5 point. Click **OK**.

10) Select the text within the AutoShape, and, using the **Format | Paragraph** command, change the *Spacing Before* until the text is centred vertically between the top and bottom edges of the AutoShape. The new poster layout should now look as shown.

When:

2pm

Sunday, 17 October

Admission Free

All Welcome

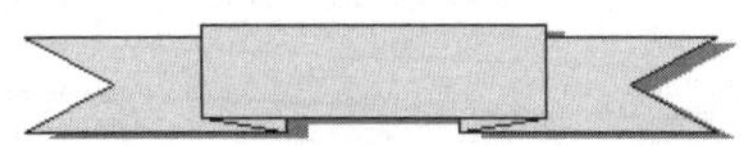

Save and close your poster document.

Hyphenating justified text

In Chapter 14 you learned about an alignment option called justification, whereby text is aligned against both the left and right margins. Justification is typically used for the narrow columns of text found in newspapers and magazines.

Justified columns can contain a lot of white (that is, blank) space, because Word spreads out the text in order to align it with both margins simultaneously. This is particularly true when the text contains a lot of long words.

Hyphenation – the process of breaking up long words and splitting them across two lines – gives justified text a more professional appearance. Consider the following two examples:

Word spreads out the text
in order to align it with
both margins
simultaneously. This is
particularly true when the
text contains a lot of long
words.

Hyphenation off

Word spreads out the text
in order to align it with
both margins simultane-
ously. This is particularly
true when the text con-
tains a lot of long words.

Hyphenation on

Word applies two rules when hyphenating text: certain words are never hyphenated, and words that are hyphenated are split only in certain places. Word allows you to hyphenate both justified and unjustified text.

Hyphenation

The process of splitting a long word across two successive lines to avoid unsightly amounts of white space. Used mostly in narrow, justified columns of text.

You can hyphenate text in two ways: automatically or manually.

Automatic hyphenation

Word can hyphenate your document automatically as you type. To use this option, choose **Tools | Language | Hyphenation**, select the *Automatically hyphenate document* check box, and click **OK**.

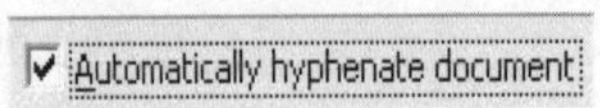

Automatic hyphenation options

If you select automatic hyphenation, Word offers you a number of options that let you control how it applies hyphenation to your document.

- **Hyphenate words in CAPS:** Typically, only headings are in capitals, so you can decide to turn automatic hyphenation off for capitalized text.
- **Hyphenation zone:** The amount of space that Word leaves between the end of the last word in a line and the right margin. It applies only to unjustified text. Make the zone wider to reduce the number of hyphens, or narrower to reduce the raggedness of the right margin.
- **Limit consecutive hyphens to:** The number of consecutive lines that Word hyphenates.

Manual hyphenation

If you don't want Word to insert hyphens in your text automatically, ensure that the *Automatically hyphenate document* check box is deselected.

A better option is to turn off automatic hyphenation, and to run manual hyphenation after you have finished writing and editing, and adding and removing text.

Running manual hyphenation

To hyphenate your document (or a selected part of it) manually, choose **Tools | Language | Hyphenation** and click **Manual**.

Word scans through your text, and when it finds a word it thinks it should hyphenate, it displays a dialog box similar to the one below.

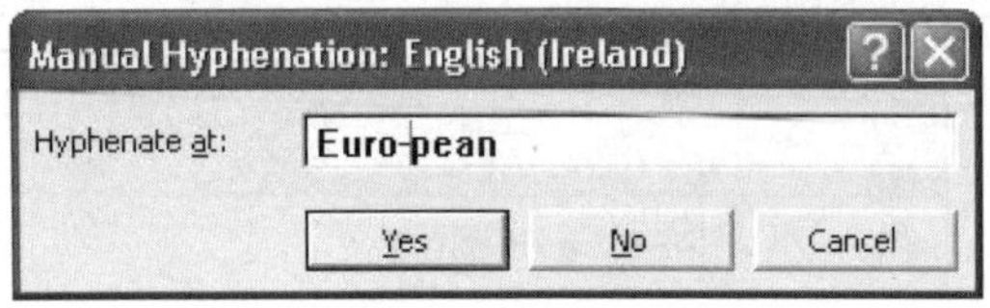

Click **Yes** if you want Word to insert a hyphen in the suggested location. If you prefer Word to insert the hyphen at a different location, move the cursor to that location, and then click **Yes**. Alternatively, click **No** to leave the word unbroken.

You can now close any open documents and exit Microsoft Word. You have completed Chapter 16 of the ECDL word processing module.

Chapter summary: so now you know

A Word *table* consists of rectangular cells arranged in rows and columns. As required, you can insert and delete rows and columns in a table, split a single cell into two cells, or merge multiple cells into a single cell.

You can also change row and column height and width, apply formatting, and add borders and shading. Word's *AutoFormat* option provides a quick way to improve the appearance of any table. See Exercises 16.1 and 16.2.

Tabs are predefined horizontal locations that, when used on successive lines, give the appearance of columns. *Tab leaders* are dashed, dotted or continuous lines that draw the reader's eye from one tabbed column to the next. See Exercises 16.3, 16.4 and 16.5.

You can add *graphics* to a Word document in two ways: by copy and paste, or by inserting the graphic as a file. You can move, reposition, resize or change the shape of any graphic. See Exercise 16.6.

AutoShapes are ready-made shapes that you can insert in your Word documents. They include lines, basic shapes, flowchart elements, stars and banners, and callouts. You can manipulate AutoShapes in a similar way to graphics. See Exercise 16.7.

You can use Word's *hyphenation* feature to remove unsightly amounts of white space by splitting long words across successive lines. Hyphenation is most often applied to narrow columns of justified text.

Quick quiz: tables, tabs and graphics

Circle the correct answer to each of the following multiple-choice questions.

Q1	In a table, you press the Tab key to ...
A.	Insert a tab stop.
B.	Move the cursor to the next cell.
C.	Move the cursor to the beginning of the table.

Q2	To insert a new row above the row where the cursor is positioned, you ...
A.	Choose **Table | Insert | Rows Above**.
B.	Choose **Table | Insert | Row**.
C.	Choose **Table | Insert Rows Above**.

Q3	To add a new tab stop to a paragraph, you ...
A.	Choose **Format | Tabs**, select the type of tab you want, and then click Word's ruler where you want to place the stop.
B.	Click the ruler where you want to place the new tab stop and choose **Format | Tabs**.
C.	Click the **Tab** button on the left side of the ruler, select the type of tab you want, and then click the ruler where you want to place the tab.

Q4	To insert a Word Clip Art image, you ...
A.	Click on the location where you want to insert the image, choose **Insert | Picture | Clip Art**, select the image you want to insert, and click **OK**.
B.	Choose **Insert | Picture | Clip Art**, use the *Clip Art* task pane to locate the image you want to insert, and then drag the image into your document.
C.	Click on the location where you want to insert the image, choose **Edit | Paste Special**, select the image you want to insert, and click **OK**.

Q5	To add an AutoShape to a document, you ...
A.	Choose **Insert | Picture | WordArt**.
B.	Click the **AutoShapes** button on the *Formatting* toolbar.
C.	Click the **AutoShapes** button on the *Drawing* toolbar.

Answers

1: B, **2:** A, **3:** C, **4:** B, **5:** C.

Chapter 17: Mail merge and templates

In this chapter

Bulk mail is the name given to mass-produced letters that contain individual names and addresses (as in 'Dear Ms Murray') but have the same basic text (as in 'Allow us to introduce our Spring Promotion ...'). A more commonly used term might be 'junk mail'.

How is it done? Each letter is basically the same, but clearly no one letter is just a copy of another, as each is slightly different. Read this chapter to find out.

Hint: each letter is the result of combining or merging two separate files: the form letter, which contains the basic text, and the data source, which holds a list of names, addresses and other details.

Also in this chapter you will learn about templates and styles. These are quick, convenient ways to create documents that can contain ready-made text, images, formatting and page settings.

New skills

At the end of this chapter you should be able to:

- Create the two components of a merged letter: the form letter and the data source.
- Select the appropriate merge fields and insert them in a form letter.
- Merge a form letter with a data source to produce a mail merge.
- Explain the two possible roles of a Word template: document model and interface controller.
- Choose an appropriate Word template for a document type.
- Explain the relationship between styles and templates, and apply styles to selected text.
- Attach a different template to a document, and create a new template.
- Apply Word's document views – Normal, Page Layout, Web Layout and Outline.

New words

At the end of this chapter you should be able to explain the following terms:

- Form letter
- Data source
- Merge field
- Style
- Template
- Normal view
- Page Layout view
- Web Layout view
- Outline view

Mail merge: the components

Think of a mail merge as composed of two components: a form letter and a data source. And think of merge fields as the glue that binds the two together. Read on to discover what these three terms mean.

Form letter

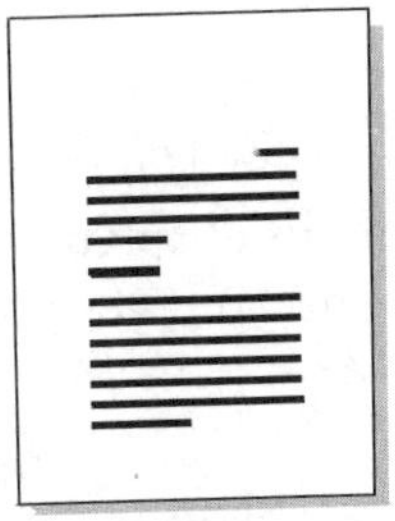

The form letter holds the text that remains the same in every letter – plus punctuation, spaces and perhaps graphics.

You never type the names or addresses in the form letter, because these will be different on each copy of the final, merged letter.

Form letter
A Word document containing information (text, spaces, punctuation and graphics) that remains the same in each copy of the merged letter.

Data source

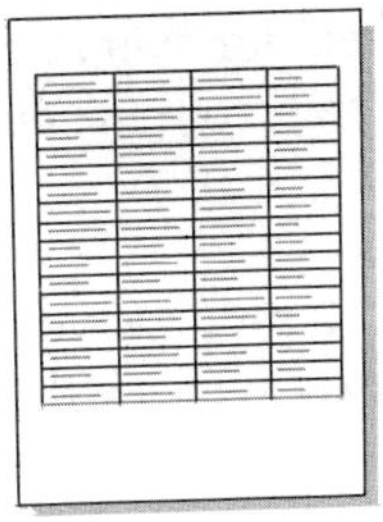

The data source holds the information that changes for each copy of the final, merged letter – the names and addresses of the people that you want to send the merged letters to.

You can create a data source in Word, or in a spreadsheet (such as Excel) or a database (such as Access). Whichever file type you use, its contents must be arranged in a table. Along the top row must be the titles identifying the information categories in the columns underneath, such as Title or Last Name.

Data source
A file containing information (such as names and addresses) that will be different in each merged copy of the final letter.

Merge fields

«FirstName»¶
«Title»·«LastName»,¶
«Company».¶

Merge fields are enclosed within double angled brackets

The merge fields are special instructions that you insert in your form letter. They tell Word which details you want to merge from your data source, and where Word is to position them in your merged letter.

Merge fields have names such as Job Title, First Name and Town. When you merge the form letter and the data source, Word replaces the merge fields in the form letter with the associated details from the data source. For example, Word might replace the merge field called Town with Bristol, Carlisle or Derby on different copies of the merged letter.

The merge field titles are the same as the column headings in the data source.

Merge field
An instruction to Word to insert a particular type of information, such as job title or a line of an address, in a specified location on the form letter.

Mail merge: the procedure

In Word, you can perform a mail merge using either the *Mail Merge Wizard* or the *Mail Merge* toolbar. The exercises in this chapter use the wizard, but when you become more familiar with mail merges you may choose to use the toolbar instead.

You can think of a mail merge as a five-step process. Steps one and two are about preparing the ingredients: the form letter and the data source.

In step three, you make the connection between the two by inserting the merge fields in your form letter – one merge field for every item of information that you want to merge to the form letter from the data source.

Step four is optional, but recommended. Before you produce your merged letters, take a preview of the first one or two to check that the merge has worked successfully.

Finally in step five, print your merged letters.

One: prepare your form letter

A form letter is simply a Word document. With the *Starting document* step of the *Mail Merge Wizard*, you can do one of the following:

- Create a new letter especially for the merge operation.
- Select a letter you have already typed as the form letter.

Exercises 17.1 and 17.2 show you how to perform these steps.

Two: prepare your data source

With the *Select recipients* step of the *Mail Merge Wizard*, you can do one of the following:

- Create a data source and enter the names, addresses and other details of the people you plan to send the merged letter to.
- Select a file created in another software application.
- Select recipients from your Microsoft Outlook contacts list.

You will learn how to create a Word data source in Exercise 17.3.

Three: insert merge fields in your form letter

With the *Write your letter* step of the *Mail Merge Wizard,* you insert in your form letter all the merge fields required for your mail merge. Exercise 17.4 shows you how to do this.

Four: preview your merged letters

Before you produce your (perhaps hundreds or thousands!) of merged letters, use the *Preview your letters* step of the *Mail Merge Wizard* to preview the first one or two merged letters.

You will learn how to preview your merged letters in Exercise 17.5.

Five: print your merged letters

If you are happy with the preview, use the *Complete the merge step* of the *Mail Merge Wizard* to complete the merge operation and print copies of your merged letters.

You will learn how to print your merged letters in Exercise 17.6.

Your mail merge exercises

Exercises 17.1 to 17.6 take you step by step through a complete, worked example of a mail merge operation.

The exercises are all part of a single process and are intended to follow on directly from each other. However, if you need to stop working on the mail merge, you can save the form letter. Then the next time you open that letter and start the *Mail Merge Wizard*, it resumes at the step where you left off.

For these exercises, we will assume that the merged letters are produced on pre-printed paper that already contains the sender's name and address. Only the recipients' names and addresses need therefore be inserted.

Do you still have the letter you saved from Exercise 16.3? If you do, Exercise 17.1 shows you how to use that text as a basis for your form letter. If you don't, proceed to Exercise 17.2 to create a new form letter from scratch.

Exercise 17.1: Using an existing document as a form letter

1) The mail merge facility is available only when there is a document open in Word, so open a new document now by clicking the **New** button on the *Standard* toolbar.
2) Choose **Tools | Letters and Mailings | Mail Merge Wizard**. Word starts the *Mail Merge Wizard* in the *Mail Merge* task pane, as shown below.

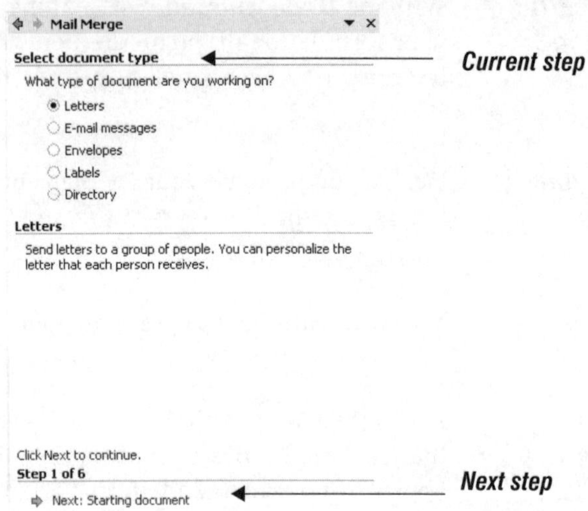

3) In the first step of the wizard, Word prompts you to select the type of document you want to mail merge. Select *Letters* and then click the link to the next step of the wizard (*Starting document*) at the bottom of the task pane.
4) Under *Select starting document*, select the *Start from existing document* option, select your letter in the *Start from existing* box, and click **Open**.

If your letter is not listed, double-click the (*More files...*) option to open the standard Word *Open* dialog box. Locate and open your letter from there.

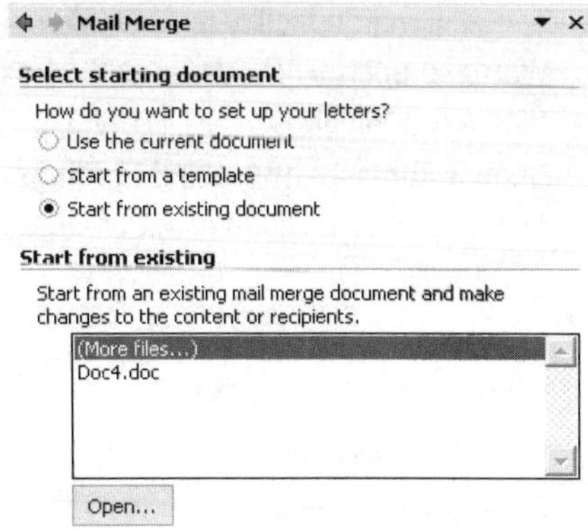

The wizard now opens your letter document and automatically moves to the next step in the wizard, which is explained in Exercise 17.3. Before that, however, you need to make some changes to your letter.

5) Remove the recipient's name and address from the top left of the letter, and remove the sender's address from the top right. Also delete 'Ms Smith' after the word 'Dear'.

6) At the top left, type 'To:' and press **Tab**. Insert three new lines, each with a tab stop, under the 'To:'. Your letter should look like that shown.

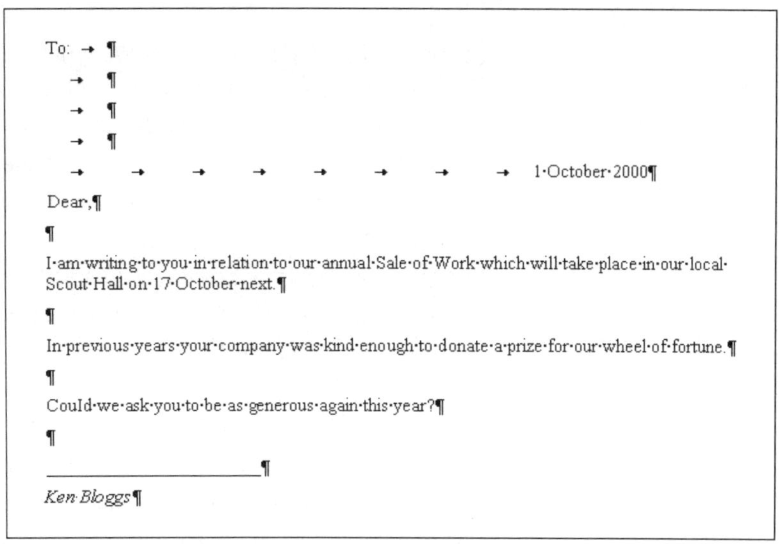

To: → ¶
→ ¶
→ ¶
→ ¶
→ → → → → → → → 1·October·2000¶
Dear,¶
¶
I·am·writing·to·you·in·relation·to·our·annual·Sale·of·Work·which·will·take·place·in·our·local·Scout·Hall·on·17·October·next.¶
¶
In·previous·years·your·company·was·kind·enough·to·donate·a·prize·for·our·wheel·of·fortune.¶
¶
Could·we·ask·you·to·be·as·generous·again·this·year?¶
¶
______________________¶
Ken·Bloggs¶

7) Save the new letter and give it a name that you will find easy to remember. If your initials are KB, for example, name it KBformlet.doc.
Proceed to Exercise 17.3.

Exercise 17.2: Creating a new form letter

Follow this exercise to create a new form letter for a mail merge operation.

1) The mail merge facility is available only when there is a document open in Word, so open a new document now by clicking the **New** button on the *Standard* toolbar.
2) Choose **Tools | Letters and Mailings | Mail Merge Wizard**. Word starts the *Mail Merge Wizard* in the *Mail Merge* task pane, as shown below.

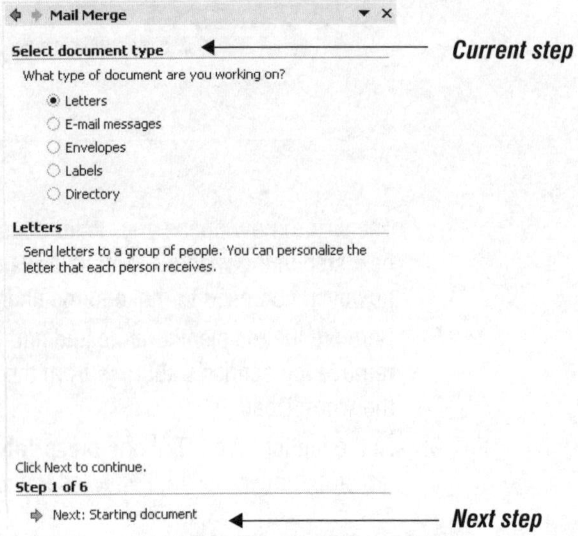

3) In the first step of the wizard, Word prompts you to select the type of document you want to mail merge. Select *Letters* and then click the link to the next step of the wizard (*Starting document*) at the bottom of the task pane.
4) Under *Select starting document*, select the *Use the current document* option.
5) In the new document you created in step 1, type the text as shown in Exercise 17.1.
6) Save the new letter and give it a name that you will find easy to remember. If your initials are KB, for example, name it KBformlet.doc.

   Proceed to Exercise 17.3.

Exercise 17.3: Creating a data source

In this exercise you create your data source with the names, addresses and other information that will be different on each copy of the final, merged letter.

Do not begin this exercise until you have completed either Exercise 17.1 or Exercise 17.2.

1) If Word has not automatically taken you to the *Select recipients* step of the wizard, display it now by selecting the *Next: Select recipients* option at the bottom of the task pane.

2) Under *Select recipients*, select *Type a new list*, and click **Create**.

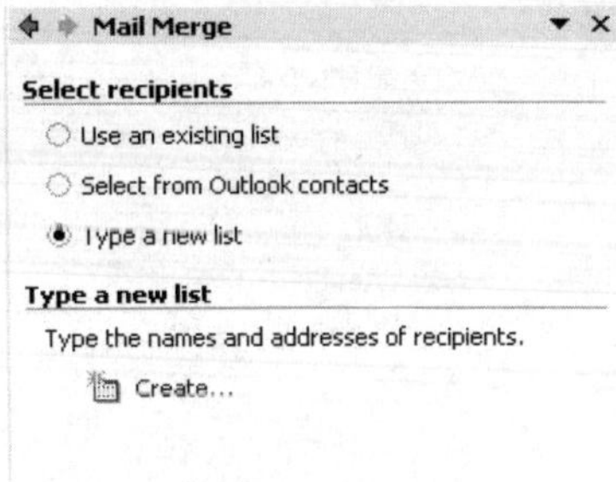

Word now displays the *New Address List* dialog box.

3) Click **Customize**. Word displays the *Customize Address List* dialog box where you can select which merge fields are relevant for your mail merge.

4) In the case of each of the following merge fields, click the field name in the list displayed and then click the **Delete** button to delete them: City, State, ZIP Code, Country, Home Phone, Work Phone and E-mail Address. When Word asks you to confirm that you want to delete a field, click **Yes**.

The list of fields should now look as shown:

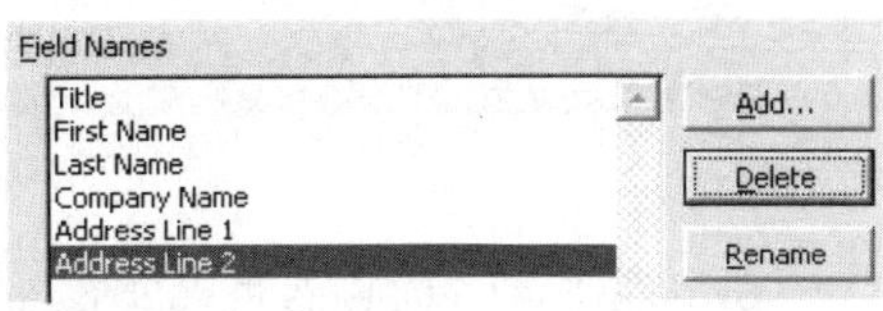

5) You now have all the merge fields that you need. Click **OK**.

Word returns you to the *New Address List* dialog box, where you can start entering details of each recipient for your mail merge.

6) Enter the information as shown below.

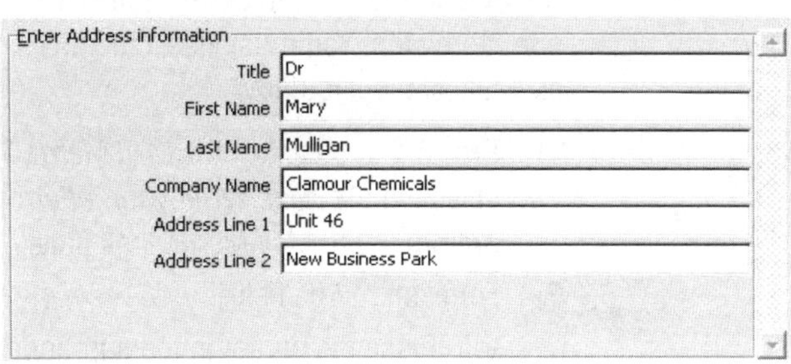

7) Click **New Entry** and enter a second set of details as shown below.

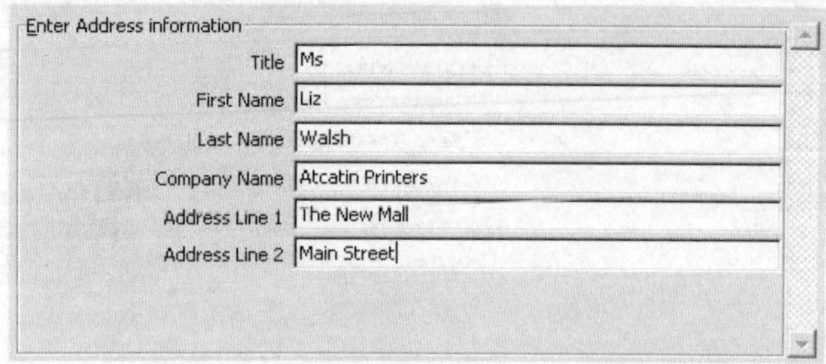

You have now created a data source with two records – enough for this exercise. But you can easily imagine a data source with hundreds or thousands of records, each record holding the name, address and other information regarding a particular person or organization.

8) Click **Close**. Word now asks you to name and save your data source file. If your initials are KB, for example, name it *KBDataSource* and click **Save**.

9) Word now asks you to select which of the people in your data source you want to include in the mail merge you are currently performing.

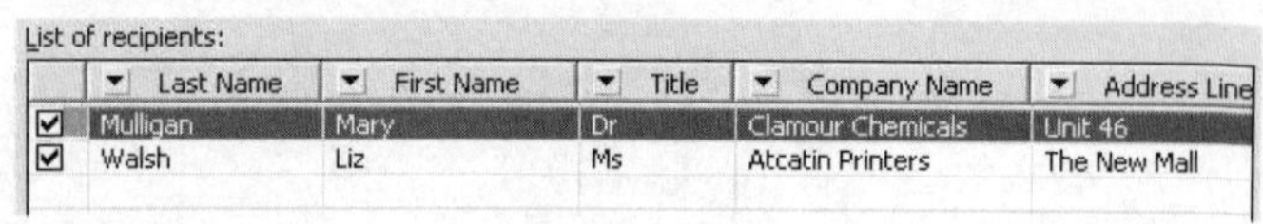

By default, all recipients in your list are selected, so you can simply click **OK** at this dialog box.

Proceed to Exercise 17.4.

Exercise 17.4: Inserting the merge field codes

Before you move on to perform the mail merge operation, you need to perform one more step. You must insert the merge field codes in your form letter. This exercise shows you how.

1) Proceed to step 4 of the *Mail Merge Wizard* by selecting the *Next: Write your letter* option at the bottom of the *Mail Merge* task pane.

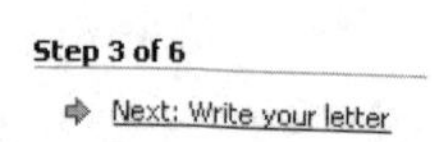

2) For each merge field:
   - Place the cursor in the appropriate position in your form letter.
   - Click the *More items* option in the *Write your letter* section of the task pane.

- In the *Insert Merge Field* dialog box, click the relevant field title, and click **Insert**.

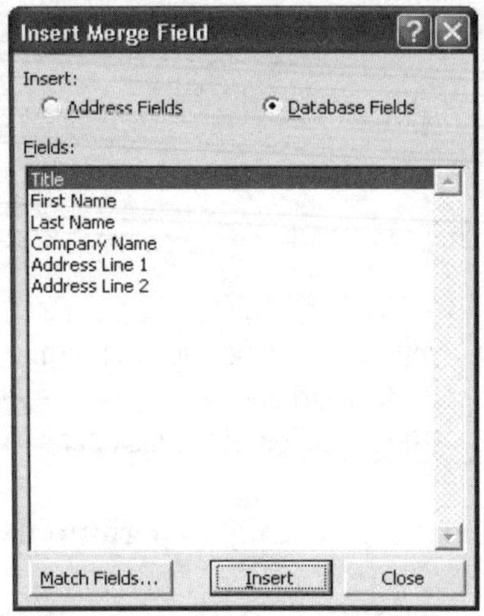

Repeat this step for each merge field you want to include on the same line and then click **Close**.

Continue until your form letter looks like the sample shown.

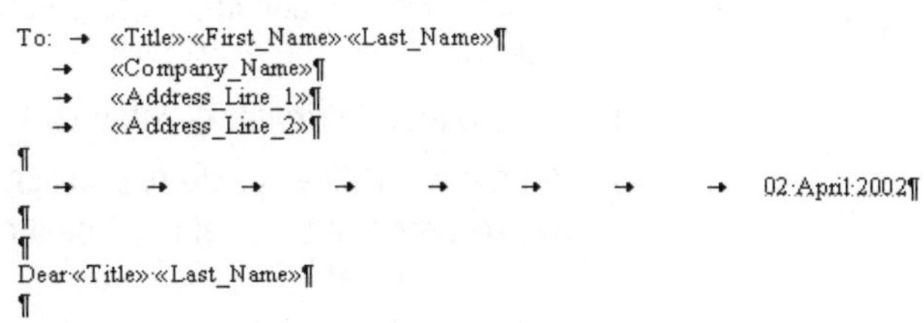
To: → «Title» «First_Name» «Last_Name»¶
→ «Company_Name»¶
→ «Address_Line_1»¶
→ «Address_Line_2»¶
¶
→ → → → → → → → 02 April 2002¶
¶
¶
Dear «Title» «Last_Name»¶
¶

Don't forget to type spaces between merge fields just as you would between words in ordinary text. Also, type the necessary commas or full stops at the end of lines.

Save your form letter when finished.

Now everything is in place for the mail merge operation.

Exercise 17.5: Previewing the mail merge

1) Proceed to step 5 of the *Mail Merge Wizard* by selecting the *Next: Preview your letters* option at the bottom of the *Mail Merge* task pane.

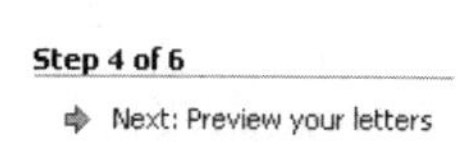

Word displays the first merged letter. It should look as shown below.

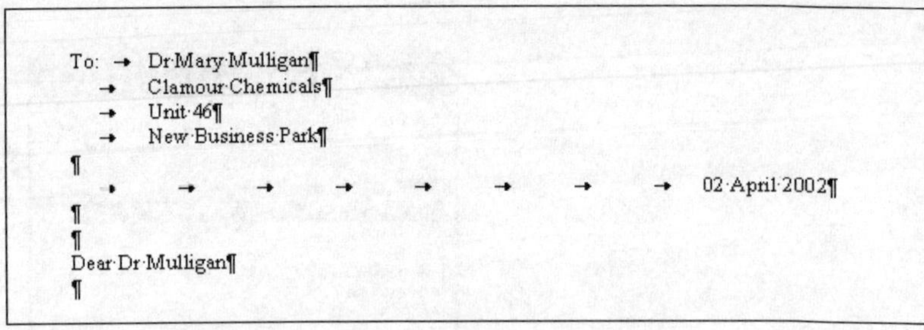

To: → Dr·Mary·Mulligan¶
→ Clamour·Chemicals¶
→ Unit·46¶
→ New·Business·Park¶
¶
→ → → → → → → → 02·April·2002¶
¶
¶
Dear·Dr·Mulligan¶
¶

2) You can view the second merged letter by clicking the forward arrow button in the *Preview your letters* section of the task pane.

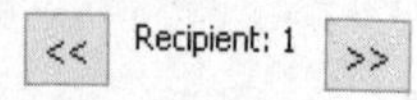

Arrow buttons

You are now ready to perform the mail merge.

Exercise 17.6: Performing the mail merge

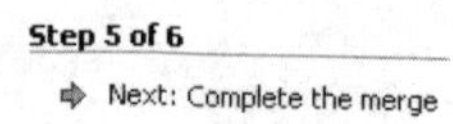

1) Proceed to step 6 of the *Mail Merge Wizard* by selecting the *Next: Complete the merge* option at the bottom of the *Mail Merge* task pane.
2) Click the *Print* option in the *Merge* section of the task pane.
3) In the *Merge to Printer* dialog box, select the *All* option and click **OK**.
4) Word now displays the *Printer* dialog box. Click **OK**. Your form letter and the two records from the data source are now merged to the printer.

Congratulations! You have performed your first mail merge in Word.

Using non-Word data sources

Does your data source have to be a Word document? No. You can also use files created in a spreadsheet such as Excel or a database such as Access. The only requirement is that the information is arranged in the same type of table format: a single row of merge field titles at the top, followed by other rows holding individual records.

Merging addresses to labels

You can use Word's *Mail Merge Wizard* to print a list of names and addresses (or any other list or structured information) on adhesive labels. Exercise 17.7 shows you how.

Exercise 17.7: Merging to address labels

1) Open a new Word document.

2) Choose **Tools | Letters and Mailings | Mail Merge Wizard**. Word starts the *Mail Merge Wizard* in the *Mail Merge* task pane.

3) In the first step of the wizard, Word prompts you to select a type of document. Select *Labels* and then click the link to the next step of the wizard (*Starting document*) at the bottom of the task pane.

4) Under *Select starting document*, select the *Change document layout* option.

5) Under *Change document layout*, click *Label options*.

6) In the *Label Options* dialog box, select the type of printer and the type of labels you want to use, and click **OK**.

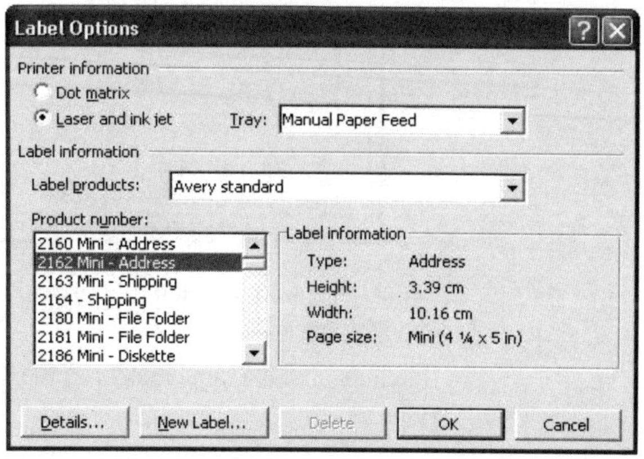

7) Proceed to step 3 of the *Mail Merge Wizard* by selecting the *Next: Select recipients* option at the bottom of the *Mail Merge* task pane.

8) Select the *Use an existing list* option and click **Browse** to locate the data source that you created in Exercise 17.3.

9) Word now asks you to select which of the people in your data source you want to include in the mail merge you are currently performing.

   By default, all recipients in your list are selected, so you can simply click **OK** at this dialog box.

10) Proceed to step 4 of the *Mail Merge Wizard* by selecting the *Next: Arrange your labels* option at the bottom of the *Mail Merge* task pane.

11) Position the cursor in the first label displayed in your document.

12) For each merge field to be included in the label:

    - Place the cursor in the appropriate position in the label.
    - Click the *More items* option in the *Arrange your labels* section of the task pane.

- In the *Insert Merge Field* dialog box, click the relevant field title, and click **Insert**.

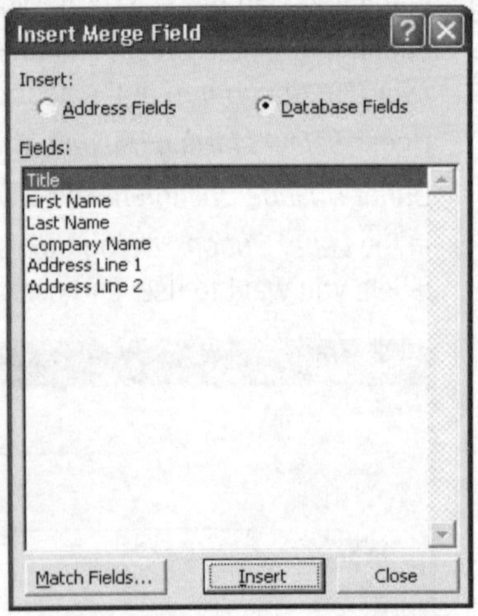

Repeat this step for each merge field you want to include on the same line and then click **Close**.

Continue until the label looks like the sample shown.

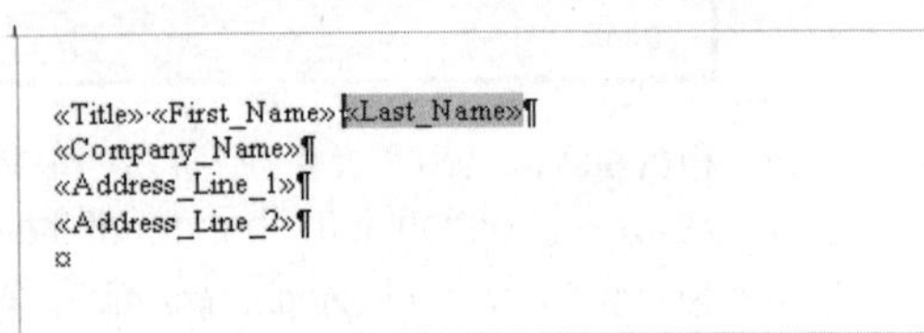

13) In the *Replicate labels* section of the task pane, click *Update all labels*.
14) Proceed to step 5 of the *Mail Merge Wizard* by selecting the *Next: Preview your labels* option at the bottom of the *Mail Merge* task pane.
15) Proceed to step 6 of the *Mail Merge Wizard* by selecting the *Next: Complete the merge* option at the bottom of the *Mail Merge* task pane.
16) Select the *Print* option in the *Merge* section of the task pane.
17) In the *Merge to Printer* dialog box, select the *All* option and click **OK**.
18) Word now displays the *Printer* dialog box. Click **OK** to print the labels.

Well done! That completes your mail merge exercises.

Word templates

Microsoft Word is made up of three components: the Word software application itself, the document files that Word produces, and a third component, which you now meet for the first time: templates.

- **Word application:** This provides the standard Word menus, commands and toolbars – the things you use to create and work with documents.
- **Document files:** Look in any of these and you will find the text, graphics, formatting and settings such as margins and page layout for that particular document.
- **Word templates:** These have two main purposes. They can provide a model for creating documents and they control Word's interface: the menus, commands and toolbars available to the user.

A template as a document model

A template can act as a document model by storing:

- Built-in text and graphics such as your company's name and logo. These are sometimes called 'boilerplate' text and graphics.
- Preset formatting (such as font settings) and text positioning (such as alignment, indents, tab stops and inter-line and inter-paragraph spacing settings).
- Preset page settings (such as margins and page orientation).

For example, you could save everyone in your organization time by creating a memo template that contained preset margins, the company logo, and text for standard headings such as 'Memo', 'To:' and 'From:'. With much of the formatting and typing already done, users simply fill in the additional text.

A template as an interface controller

A template can also store customized Word commands, menus and toolbar settings. This allows managers to remove unused and unnecessary features, and to adapt Word to meet the needs of different levels of users.

For example, you could create a template that helps new Word users by displaying a customized toolbar with buttons and menus to lead them through everyday tasks.

Templates and documents

Whether you realized it or not, every new Word document that you have created has been based on a template.

A single template can provide the basis for lots of documents. But each document can be based on only a single template at a time.

A template, like a document, is a Word file. Whereas document file names end in .doc, template file names end in .dot.

The Normal.dot template

Unless you choose otherwise, every new Word document you create is based on a template called Normal.dot.

In addition to this standard, all-purpose template, Word provides templates for specific document types such as letters, memos and reports.

Word template
A file that can contain ready-made text, formatting and page settings and interface controls. Every Word document is based on, and takes its characteristics from, a template of one kind or another.

Templates and new documents

In Chapter 13, you learned two ways to create a new document:

- Clicking the **New** button on the *Standard* toolbar.
- Choosing the **File | New** command.

If you click the **New** button, Word automatically bases your new document on the Normal.dot template.

Choose **File | New**, however, and Word opens the *New Document* task pane, which presents you with a wide range of options to choose from, including creating a new document based on a template of your choice.

Exercise 17.8: Previewing Word's templates

1) Choose **File | New** to display the *New Document* task pane.

2) Under *New from template*, click *General Templates*. This displays the *Templates* dialog box.

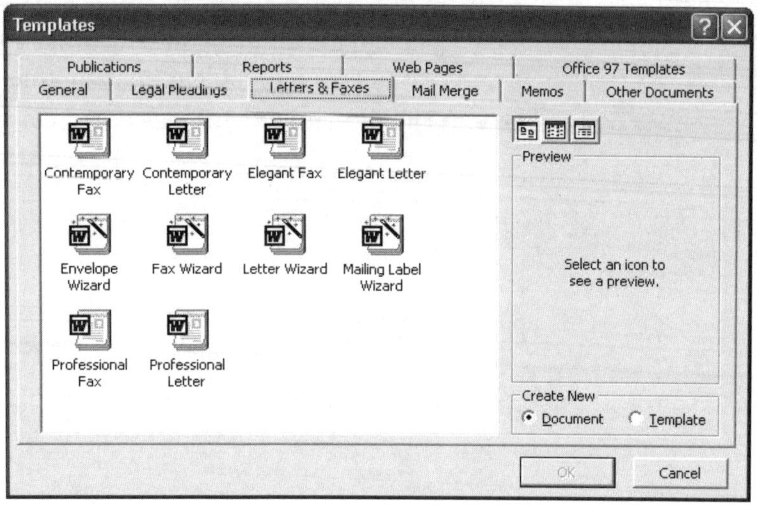

3) Click on the various tabs to view the available templates.

4) Click on the various templates to view a miniature of them in the *Preview* area on the right of the dialog box. (Note: not all templates have previews associated with them.)

Templates and styles

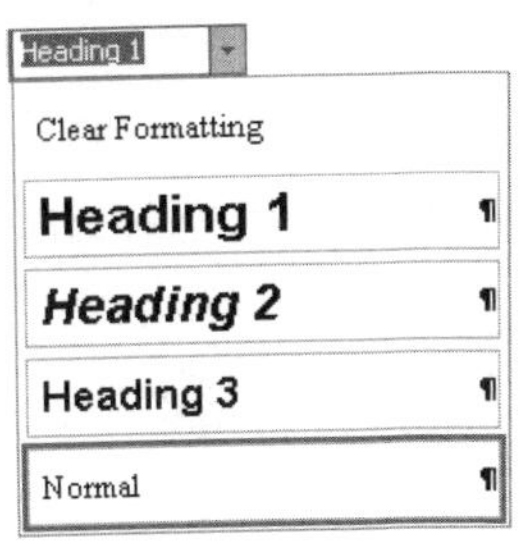

At the top-left of the *Formatting* toolbar is a drop-down list box containing items called Normal, Heading 1, Heading 2, and so on. These items are termed *styles*.

There are four things you need to know about styles:

- A style is a bundle of formatting and text positioning settings.
- You apply a style to selected text by selecting the required style from the drop-down list on the *Formatting* toolbar or from the list of styles in the *Styles and Formatting* task pane.
- Unless you choose otherwise, Word applies the style called Normal to all text you type in a document.
- Styles are linked to templates. For example, in one template the style called Heading 3 might be centre-aligned, Times, 10 point, italic. In another, Heading 3 might be left-aligned, Arial, 12 point, bold.

The Styles and Formatting *task pane*

The *Styles and Formatting* task pane provides styles and formatting information about your document, including:

- A list of the styles available in your document – for example, Normal and Heading 1.
- A list of all formatting combinations that you have directly applied to text using the **Format | Font** command or buttons on the *Formatting* toolbar, for example.
- The formatting attributes of the currently selected text.

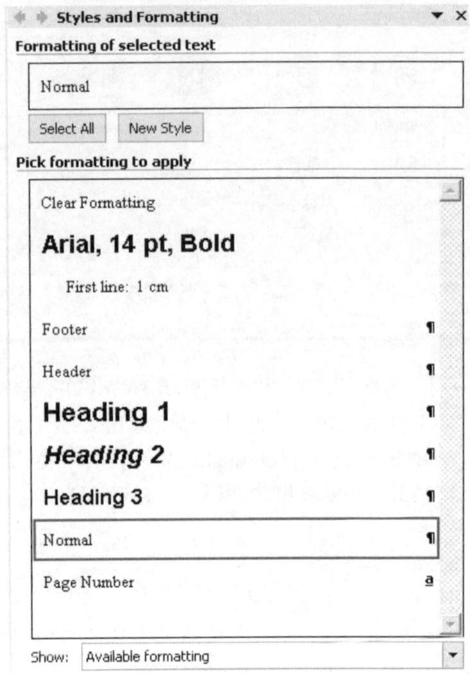

The *Show* option at the bottom of the task pane allows you to choose which items are listed in the *Pick formatting to apply* box. The options include:

- **Available formatting:** all styles and formatting available in the document.
- **Formatting in use:** all styles and formatting currently used in the document.
- **Available styles:** only the styles available in the document.

Styles and Formatting button

To open and close the *Styles and Formatting* task pane, click the **Styles and Formatting** button at the left side of the *Formatting* toolbar.

Exercise 17.9: Applying a style to text

In this exercise you will open a document that you previously created and saved, and apply a style to its headings.

1) Open the document that you saved in Exercise 15.9.
2) Open the *Styles and Formatting* task pane by clicking the **Styles and Formatting** button on the *Formatting* toolbar.
3) Click on the first heading in the document. The *Formatting of selected text* box in the task pane displays the formatting currently applied to the paragraph – that is, Arial, 14 point, Bold.
4) Click **Select All** to select all occurrences of that formatting in the document.

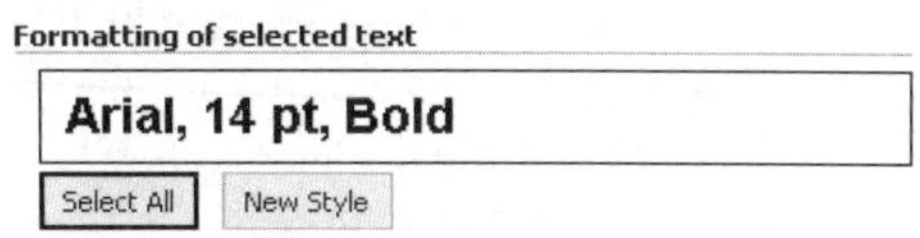

5) With all the headings still selected, click the *Clear Formatting* option in the *Pick formatting to apply* box. This removes all the formatting you applied in previous exercises.
6) Again with all the headings still selected, click the *Heading 1* style in the *Pick formatting to apply* box.

   Word now applies the style called Heading 1 to all the headings in your document. Unless you have at some stage changed the Heading 1 style that comes with Normal.dot, the Heading 1 font should be Arial, 16 point, Bold. Save the document.

Why use styles?

Using styles to control the appearance of a document has three advantages:

- You can apply a bundle of formatting and text positioning settings to a piece of selected text in a single, quick operation.
- By changing the settings of a particular style, Word can automatically apply your new settings to all occurrences of text in that style throughout the entire document.

  For example, by changing the Heading 1 style from bold to italic, all text with the Heading 1 style changes from bold to italic. This is much faster than individually selecting and then changing every heading.
- If you change the template on which a document is based, the document takes its style settings from the new template.

You can therefore change the entire appearance of a document by linking it with a different template. Exercise 17.10 illustrates this point.

Style
A collection of formatting and positioning settings that you can apply to selected text in a single operation. Styles are linked to templates, and can have different settings in different templates.

Exercise 17.10: Attaching a different template to a document

1) If the document you worked with in Exercise 17.9 is not already open, open it now. Select all the text in the document, and choose **Edit | Copy** (or **Ctrl+c**). You can now close that document.
2) Choose **File | New** to open the *New Document* task pane. Under *New from template*, click the *General Templates* option.

   In the *Templates* dialog box, click the **Reports** tab, and then click the template called Professional Report.dot. Finally, click **OK**.

3) Word opens a new document that is based on Professional Report.dot.

   This contains text and instructions which you can ignore. Hold down the **Ctrl** key and click in the left margin to select everything in the new document, and then press **Delete** to delete the new document's contents.
4) Choose **Edit | Paste** (or press **Ctrl+v**) to paste the text copied from your document into the new document. Save and name your new document.

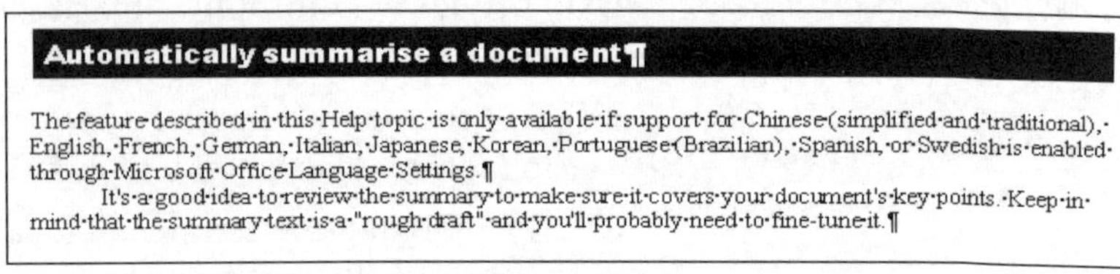

Automatically summarise a document¶

The·feature·described·in·this·Help·topic·is·only·available·if·support·for·Chinese·(simplified·and·traditional),·English,·French,·German,·Italian,·Japanese,·Korean,·Portuguese·(Brazilian),·Spanish,·or·Swedish·is·enabled·through·Microsoft·Office·Language·Settings.¶

It's·a·good·idea·to·review·the·summary·to·make·sure·it·covers·your·document's·key·points.·Keep·in·mind·that·the·summary·text·is·a·"rough·draft"·and·you'll·probably·need·to·fine-tune·it.¶

Notice how all text in your document with the Normal and Heading 1 styles changes in appearance. This is because such text is now taking its settings from the Professional Report.dot template – and not from the Normal.dot template on which the document was originally based.

You can now close the document.

Creating a new template

Word offers a number of ways of creating a new template. Here is the easiest way:

- Create a document that has the features you want in your template – some general text, perhaps, or a particular margin setting.
- With the document open on your screen, save it, not as a document, but as a template.

In future, whenever you use the **File | New** command to create a document, your new template appears as an option on the **General** tab of the *Templates* dialog box.

Exercise 17.11 takes you through an example of this procedure.

Exercise 17.11: Creating a new template

1) Create a new document and enter the following:

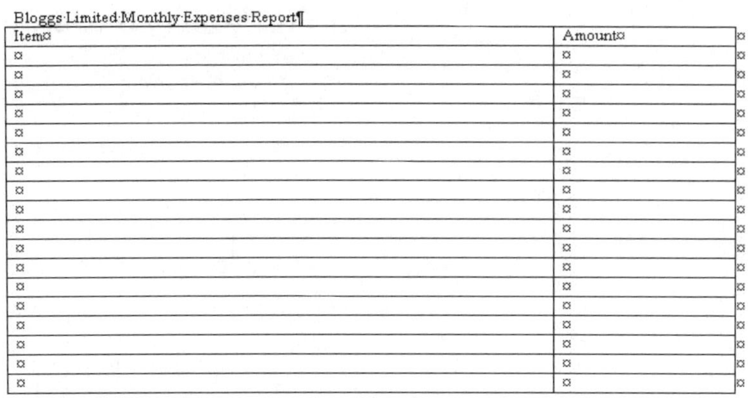
Bloggs Limited Monthly Expenses Report

Item	Amount

Apply the following settings:

- Heading: Centre-align the heading, and make it Times New Roman, 20 point.
- Table: Create a two-column, 19-row table. Select the table and, using the **Row** tab displayed by the **Table | Table Properties | Row** command, set the row height to 20 points.

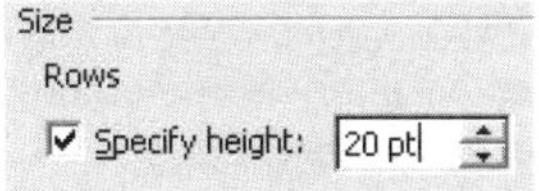

2) Choose **File | Save As**, and save the file as a template.

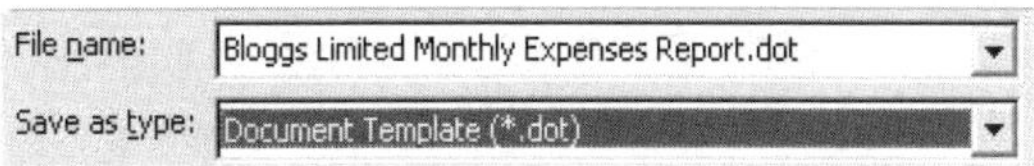

3) Choose **File | Close** to close your new template.
4) Choose **File | New** to open the *New Document* task pane. Under *New from template*, click the *General Templates* option.

5) You can now see your new template on the **General** tab of the *Templates* dialog box. Select your new template and then click **OK**.

   Word creates a new document based on your template. You can close the document.

Styles and Outline view

Using styles in your Word documents offers another advantage: it allows you to display documents in a way that reflects their structure. Such a structured view of a document is called an Outline view.

To switch to outline view, choose **View | Outline**. An Outline view of a document that is formatted using styles would typically look as follows:

- **This·is·Heading·One·Style¶**
  - This·is·body·text·(in·Normal)¶
  - **This·is·a·Heading·Two·Style¶**
    - This·is·body·text·(in·Normal)¶
- **This·is·Heading·One·Style¶**
  - This·is·body·text·(in·Normal)¶

In the above example, three styles are applied: Heading 1, Heading 2 and Normal (the default, used for body text).

Notice that Word progressively indents styled text according to its level of importance in the document, starting with Heading 1.

To change from Outline view, choose the **View** menu and select **Normal** view or **Print Layout** view. These are explained in the next topic.

Outline view
A view of a Word document that is formatted using styles. Outline view displays the structure of a document, with text indented progressively to reflect its level of importance.

Other document views

Other Word document views include Normal, Print Layout and Web Layout.

Normal view

This is the fastest view for typing, editing and scrolling. Any graphics or AutoShapes in the document are not displayed in this view. To switch to Normal view, choose **View | Normal**.

Normal view
A view of a Word document that displays only text.

Print Layout view

Print Layout view is Word's default view for all new documents. Also, if you insert a graphic or an AutoShape when in Normal view, Word automatically switches to Print Layout view. While it is necessary for manipulating graphics and AutoShapes, Print Layout view may slow down tasks such as typing, editing and scrolling. To switch to Print Layout view, choose **View | Print Layout**.

If you are working with a long document that contains a small number of graphics or AutoShapes, you may want to switch to Normal view.

Page Layout view
A view of a Word document that displays any graphics or AutoShapes in that document.

Web Layout view

Web Layout displays a document as it would appear in a web browser. Use this view when creating a web page. To switch to Web Layout view, choose **View | Web Layout**.

You can now close any open documents and exit Microsoft Word. You have completed Chapter 17 of the ECDL word processing module.

Chapter summary: so now you know

Mail merge is the process of combining a *form letter* (which holds the unchanging letter text) and a *data source* (which holds the names, addresses and other details that are different in every merged letter).

The data source can be created in Word, or in a spreadsheet (such as Excel) or database (such as Access). Whichever the file type, the data source contents must be arranged in a table. Along the top row are the titles identifying the information categories in the columns underneath, such as Title or Last Name.

Merge fields in the form letter indicate which details are taken from the data source, and where they are positioned on the final, merged letter.

Exercises 17.1 to 17.7 deal with mail merging.

A *template* can act as a *document model* by storing built-in text and graphics such as your company's name and logo, preset formatting and text positioning and preset page settings. A template can also act as an *interface controller* by specifying which of Word's menus, commands and toolbars are available to the user. A template, like a document, is a Word file. Whereas document file names end in .doc, template file names end in .dot. See Exercises 17.8, 17.10 and 17.11.

Unless you choose otherwise, every new Word document you create is based on a template called *Normal.dot.* Word also provides templates for specific document types. You can create new templates, and change the template on which a document is based.

Styles, which are linked to templates, enable you to apply a bundle of formatting and text positioning settings to selected text in a single, quick operation. See Exercise 17.9.

In *Outline* view, you can display the structure of a document that has been formatted using styles. Use *Normal* view to display only the text in a document, and *Print Layout* view to display both text and any graphics or AutoShapes that it may contain.

Quick quiz: mail merge and templates

Circle the correct answer to each of the following multiple-choice questions.

Q1	To start the Mail Merge Wizard, you ...
A.	Choose **Tools | Letters and Mailings | Show Mail Merge Toolbar**.
B.	Choose **Tools | Letters and Mailings | Letter Wizard**.
C.	Choose **Tools | Letters and Mailings | Mail Merge Wizard**.

Q2	With the Mail Merge Wizard you can create a form letter from an existing document.
A.	True.
B.	False.

Q3	To apply a new style to a paragraph, you ...
A.	Open the *Styles and Formatting* task pane, select the style you want to apply, and then select the paragraph to which you want to apply it.
B.	In the **Styles** list box on the *Formatting* toolbar, select the style you want to apply, and then select the paragraph to which you want to apply it.
C.	Click anywhere in the paragraph to which you want to apply the new style, open the *Styles and Formatting* task pane, and click the style you want to apply.

Q4	To create a new template, you ...
A.	Create a document that has all the features you want in your template, and then save it as a document template (*.dot) file.
B.	Create a document that has all the features you want in your template, and then save it as a text with layout (.ans) file.
C.	Create a document that has all the features you want in your template, choose **New Style** in the *Styles and Formatting* task pane, enter a name for the template and click **Save**.

Q5	Word's Normal view displays all graphics and AutoShapes in your document.
A.	True.
B.	False.

Answers

1: C, **2:** A, **3:** C, **4:** A, **5:** B.

Chapter 18: File formats and importing spreadsheet data

In this chapter

In this chapter you will learn how Word XP, like all other applications, uses a particular file format. You will also discover how to convert your documents into other, non-Word XP file formats, so that they can be opened and read by people who work with applications other than Word XP.

Copying and pasting within and between Word documents has been covered in previous chapters of this word processing module. This chapter takes you a step further, and shows you how to move data from a spreadsheet file to a word processor document. As you will see, you can transfer the data in either of two ways: pasting or embedding.

New skills

At the end of this chapter you should be able to:

- Save Word XP documents in the following file formats: earlier versions of Word, RTF, WordPerfect, text-only and HTML.
- Explain the difference between pasting and embedding spreadsheet data in Word.
- Paste spreadsheet data from Excel into a Word document.
- Embed spreadsheet data from Excel into a Word document.

New word

At the end of this chapter you should be able to explain the following term:

- File format

File formats

In Chapter 14, you met the term *format*, where it referred to items that affect the appearance of text in a Word document – italics, colours, bullets, and so on. When used alongside the word 'file', however, format has another, different meaning.

In Module 1, you learnt how all information stored on a computer consists ultimately of just two characters: 1 and 0. This raises two questions:

- When you open a file, how are these 1s and 0s translated into the text and graphics you see on your computer screen?
- And, when you save a file, how are the text and graphics converted back to 1s and 0s on your computer?

The answer is that the application developers apply a set of rules that translate between the 1s and 0s and the displayed text and graphics. Such a set of rules is called a file format.

File format
A set of rules that translates 1s and 0s into text and graphics on computer screens and printouts, and vice versa.

A Word file, for example, is said to be in Word file format, an Excel file in Excel file format, and so on.

Different applications, different file formats

Different software companies, however, use different rules for translating 1s and 0s into the text and graphics on screens and printouts.

Moreover, different versions of the same application often use different file formats. The Microsoft Word XP file format, for example, is different to the file format used in earlier versions of Word.

As you can imagine, these different file formats can create problems:

- In one company's file format, for example, the characters 10101010 might translate as the letter 'w' in Arial, 12 point, italic, positioned 5 cm from the left page margin.
- In another, the same characters of 10101010 might convert to a thick blue line running down the left-hand side of the page.

File name extensions

The format of a file is revealed by its three-letter file name extension, which the software application adds to the file name when the user saves the file.

The file name extension of .doc, for example, indicates a Word file, and .xls an Excel one. If you have worked with graphics files, you have probably met files with extensions such as .bmp, .gif and .jpg.

The file format used in pages on the World Wide Web is HTML, which stands for HyperText Markup Language. HTML file names typically end in .htm.

Word's file format options

Word XP offers you the ability to save your documents in a format other than its own. This feature is very useful when you want to give a file you have created to someone who uses a word processor other than Word XP.

To view the file formats in which you can save your Word XP documents:

- Open a document.
- Choose **File | Save As**.
- Click on the arrow to the right of the *Save as type* box.

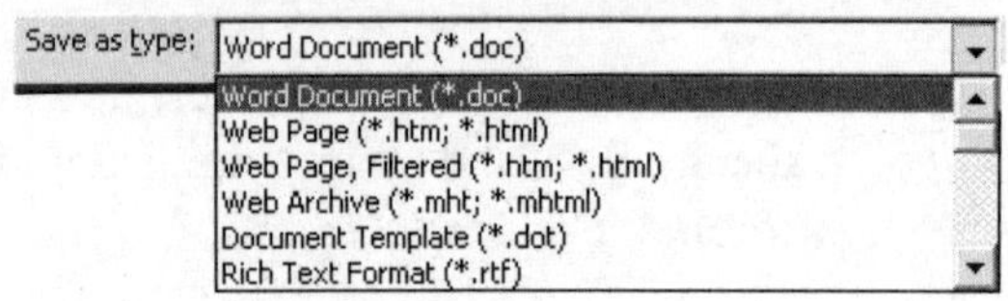

Only some of the listed options are relevant to this ECDL word processing module.

Previous Word versions

To save your Word XP document in a previous Word file format, select either Word 6.0/95 or Word 2.x for Windows, for example. Both file formats have the same file name extension as Word XP (.doc).

Saving a Word XP file in an earlier file format may result in some loss of formatting.

Rich Text Format

This is the common format of all Microsoft Office applications, including Word. A Word XP document saved in this file format looks just like one saved in Word XP's own file format. The file name extension that is added is .rtf.

WordPerfect format

Select from these options to save your document so that it can be opened and read within WordPerfect, another word processor application. Of the various WordPerfect options listed, the most commonly used is WordPerfect 5.x for Windows.

Converting a file from Word XP to WordPerfect may result in some loss of formatting. The file name extension of WordPerfect for Windows files is also .doc.

Text-only format

As its name suggests, this format saves only the text of a file. Any text formatting (such as bold or italics) or graphics contained in the Word XP file are lost. This format is also called plain-text or ASCII format.

Only two of the various plain-text options offered by Word are relevant:

- **Plain-text:** Each paragraph of the original Word document occupies a single line of the plain-text file, often resulting in very long lines of text that you can view only by scrolling horizontally. The file name extension is .txt.
- **Text with layout:** With this file format, the line width remains the same as in the original Word document, so that the text is easier to read on screen. The file name extension is .ans.

Because it is such a 'basic', no-frills format, plain-text files can be opened and read correctly by just about all software applications on virtually every type of computer. Plain-text is the file format used most commonly in electronic mail messages on the Internet.

HTML (web) format

Web pages are created using the HTML file format. The file name extension of this format is .htm (or, sometimes, .html).

You can save a Word XP file in HTML format in two ways:

- Choose **File | Save As Web Page**.

  -or-
- Choose **File | Save As**, and select the *Web Page* option.

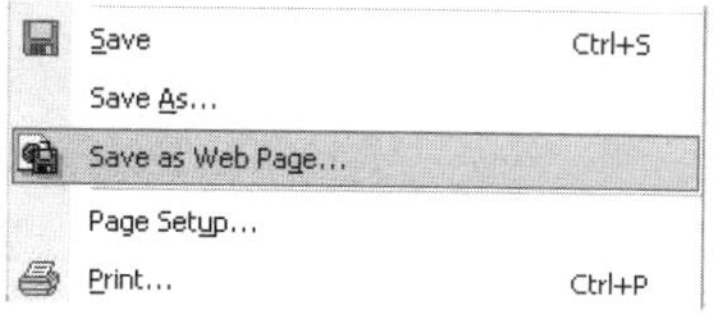

You can display and print HTML format files with a web browser application such as Microsoft Internet Explorer or Netscape Navigator.

Embedding or pasting spreadsheet data

Microsoft Office applications (and most other Windows applications) allow you to transfer information between them. For this ECDL module, you need only know how to insert data (text and numbers) into Word from the spreadsheet application, Microsoft Excel. In Excel, numbers and text are stored in little boxes called cells.

To transfer information from Excel to Word, follow these steps:

- Open the Excel file and select the required cells.
- Copy the selected Excel cells to the clipboard.
- Open the Word file and insert the Excel cells in Word.

Pasting special options

The Word command you use for embedding Excel cells is **Edit | Paste Special**.

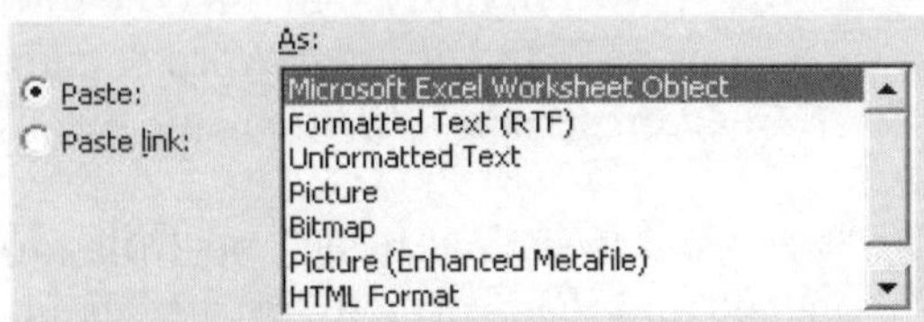

The *Paste Special* dialog box offers the following options:

- **Paste or Paste link:** Leave this as the default of Paste.
- **Display as icon:** Leave this check box unselected.
- **As:** One option is relevant here: Microsoft Excel Worksheet Object.

Pasting from Excel

When you insert with the **Edit | Paste** command, the inserted spreadsheet data:

- Becomes fully part of Word.
- Is displayed as a Word table.
- Can be edited within Word itself.

Pasting Excel data into Word in this way is similar to pasting from another Word document.

Embedding from Excel

When you insert with the **Edit | Paste Special | Microsoft Excel Worksheet Object** command, the inserted spreadsheet data:

- Is positioned within Word, but remains part of Excel.
- Behaves like an imported graphic – it can be repositioned and resized by selecting and dragging.
- Cannot be edited within Word.

If you try to edit the spreadsheet data in any way (to change a number, for example, or to apply a different border style), Word's menu and toolbars disappear from your screen and are replaced by Excel's menu and toolbars. Inserting data in this way brings with it the functionality of the application in which it was created. This is called *embedding*.

The following four exercises demonstrate pasting and embedding from Excel to Word.

In Exercise 18.1, you create two copies of an identical Word document. In Exercise 18.2, you create the Excel data for inserting into Word. In Exercises 18.3 and 18.4 you embed and paste your Excel data in the two Word documents.

Exercise 18.1: Creating a Word document that you can embed and paste data into

1) Open Word and create a new document.
2) Type the following text and press **Enter** twice:
   First Quarter Sales Figures
3) Select the text and make it Arial, bold italic, 24 point. Centre-align the text.
4) Type the following text and press **Enter** three times:
   Congratulations Everyone!!!
5) Select the text you typed in step 4 and make it Times New Roman, italic, 22 point. Centre-align the text. Your document should now look as shown.

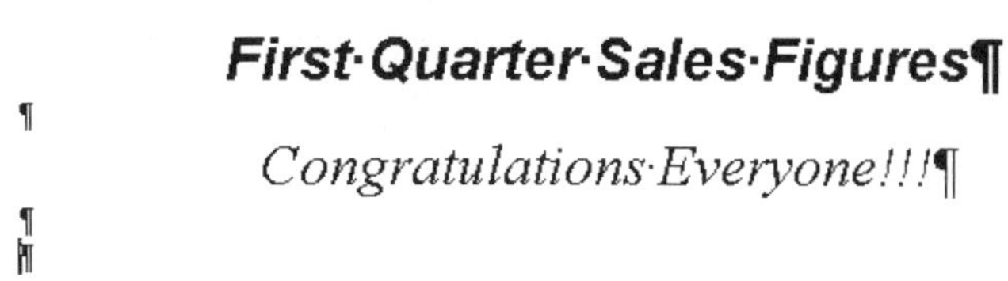

6) Save and name the Word document. If your initials are KB, for example, save it as KBsalesfigures1.doc.
7) Choose **File | Save As** to resave your Word document – but this time save it under a different name. For example, KBsalesfigures2.doc.
8) Choose **File | Open** and reopen the first saved version of your Word document.

You now have two Word documents, with identical content, open on your screen.

Exercise 18.2: Creating an Excel data source file

1) Choose **Start | All Programs | Microsoft Excel** to open a new Excel file on your screen.
2) Click on the cell at location *C3*, and type the word January.

	A	B	C	D	E
1					
2					
3			January		
4					

3) Enter more text and numbers to Excel as shown below.

	A	B	C	D	E
1					
2					
3			January	February	March
4		Product 1	213	345	698
5		Product 2	180	245	401
6		Product 3	270	389	528
7		Product 4	134	262	390
8		Product 5	90	154	310
9					

4) When finished, save the Excel file. If your initials are KB, for example, save it as KBsalesfigures.xls. Leave the Excel file open on your screen.
5) Click on cell *B3* and hold down the mouse button. Drag rightwards and down to cell *E8*.

	A	B	C	D	E
1					
2					
3			January	February	March
4		Product 1	213	345	698
5		Product 2	180	245	401
6		Product 3	270	389	528
7		Product 4	134	262	390
8		Product 5	90	154	310
9					

6) Choose **Edit | Copy** to copy the selected Excel cells to the clipboard.
Do not close the Excel file, as it must be open for Exercise 18.3 to work.

Exercise 18.3: Embedding the Excel data in Word

1) Use the **Window | <document name>** command to display the first Word document that you saved (in this example, KBsalesfigures1.doc), and then click the last paragraph mark in that document.

2) Choose **Edit | Paste Special**, select the *Microsoft Excel Worksheet Object* option, and click **OK**.

   (This option is available only when the original Excel file is open on your computer.)

   This embeds the Excel data from the clipboard to the Word document.

3) Click the bottom-right handle of the inserted data, and drag it until the inserted data is centred between the left and right page margins. Your Word document should now look like that shown below.

First·Quarter·Sales·Figures¶

¶

Congratulations·everyone!¶

¶
¶

	January	February	March
Product 1	213	345	698
Product 2	180	245	401
Product 3	270	389	528
Product 4	134	262	390
Product 5	90	154	310

¶

You can work with the embedded data area just as you can with a graphic: you can select it and reposition and resize it. You cannot edit it, however, at least not in Word.

To change the embedded data in any way – edit a number, delete a row, or add a coloured border – you must first double-click it. This action causes Word's menus and toolbars to be replaced by Excel ones. Try it and see. Your screen should look as shown.

	B	C	D	E
3		January	February	March
4	Product 1	213	345	698
5	Product 2	180	245	401
6	Product 3	270	389	528
7	Product 4	134	262	390
8	Product 5	90	154	310

Sheet1 / Sheet2 / Sheet3

To return to Word, click anywhere on the Word document, outside the embedded spreadsheet area. Save your Word document.

You may now close Excel. It does not need to be open for the next exercise.

Exercise 18.4: Pasting the Excel data in Word

1) Use the **Window | <document Name>** command to display the second Word document that you saved (in this example, KBsalesfigures2.doc), and then click the last paragraph mark in that document.
2) Choose **Edit | Paste**.

   This pastes the Excel data from the clipboard to the Word document. The spreadsheet cells have the format of a Word table.
3) Click anywhere in the table, choose **Table | Table Autoformat**, select the *Table Contemporary* option, and click **Apply**.
4) Drag the right edge of the table to the right until the table is centred between the left and right margins of the page.
5) With the cursor anywhere in the table, choose **Table | Select | Table**. Then choose **Table | Autofit | Distribute Columns Evenly**.
6) With the table still selected, change the font size to 14 point.

   Your Word document should now look like that shown.

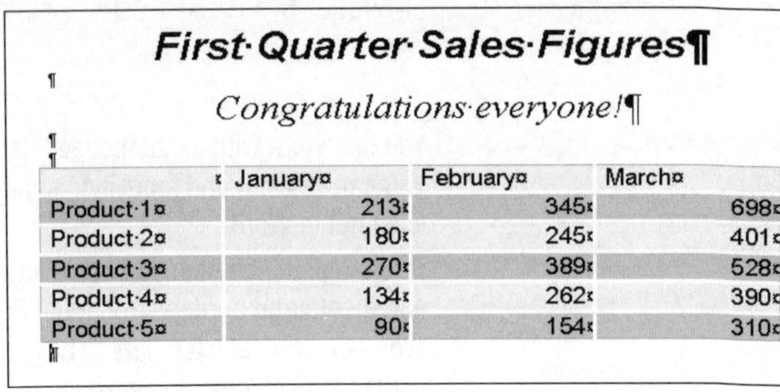

First·Quarter·Sales·Figures¶

Congratulations·everyone!¶

	January	February	March
Product·1	213	345	698
Product·2	180	245	401
Product·3	270	389	528
Product·4	134	262	390
Product·5	90	154	310

7) Save your Word document. You have finished the embedding and pasting exercises, and you can close both Word documents.

You have now completed the final chapter of the ECDL word processing module. Congratulations!

Chapter summary: so now you know

A *file format* is a set of rules that translates between the 1s and 0s used by the computer to store information and the text and graphics displayed on screens and on printouts. Different applications – even different versions of the same application – can use different and incompatible file formats.

To help you share your files with others, Word XP allows you to save your documents in a file format other than its own. The options include: earlier versions of Microsoft Word, RTF (the common

Microsoft Office file format), WordPerfect (another word processor) and HTML (the web page file format).

You can also save a Word document as a *text-only* file, so that it can be opened and read by virtually all applications on all types of computers. Any formatting or graphics in the Word document are lost, however.

You can insert spreadsheet data from Excel to Word in either of two ways: pasting or embedding.

Pasted data becomes fully part of the Word document: it is displayed as a Word table, and can be edited within Word itself. Inserting Excel data into Word in this way is similar to pasting from another Word document. See Exercise 18.4.

Embedded spreadsheet data, while positioned within the Word document, remains part of Excel: it behaves like an imported graphic and cannot be edited within Word. If you try to edit the spreadsheet data in any way, Word's menu and toolbars are replaced on screen by Excel's ones. Embedded data brings with it the functionality of the application in which it was created. See Exercise 18.3.

Quick quiz: file formats and importing spreadsheet data

Circle the correct answer to each of the following multiple-choice questions.

Q1	To save a document in HTML format, you ...
A.	Choose **File | Save As**, select *Rich Text Format* in the *Save as type* box, and click **Save**.
B.	Choose **File | Web Page Preview**.
C.	Choose **File | Save As**, select *Web Page* in the *Save as type* box, and click **Save**.

Q2	When you embed an Excel spreadsheet in a Word document it remains part of Excel and can be worked on using Excel's menus and toolbars.
A.	True.
B.	False.

Q3	**The original Excel spreadsheet must be open in Excel when you embed a copy in a Word document.**
A.	True.
B.	False.

Q4	**To embed an Excel spreadsheet in a Word document, you ...**
A.	Choose **Edit | Paste**, select the *Microsoft Excel Worksheet Object* option, and click **OK**.
B.	Choose **Edit | Paste Special**, select the *Formatted Text* option, and click **OK**.
C.	Choose **Edit | Paste Special**, select the *Microsoft Excel Worksheet Object* option, and click **OK**.

Answers

1: C, **2:** A, **3:** A, **4:** C.

4 Spreadsheets

Some things are easy to explain or describe – but difficult to use or operate. A spreadsheet is not one of those things. In fact, it's the very opposite.

At the end of this module, you will able to build number-crunching spreadsheets for recording, analysing and drawing graphs of just about any kind of numbers you can think of.

Quarterly sales commission, annual rainfall or the monthly household budget: if you can count it now, you will be able to put it on a spreadsheet later.

Along the way we will show you the shortcuts that will help you get a lot of work done on long numbers, but with little typing, and in a very short time.

But you will be no closer to being able to give a one-sentence definition of what exactly a spreadsheet is.

Perhaps it's because spreadsheets are about processing numbers rather than words that they are so hard to define.

Think of this module as your chance to count, rather than be counted. Good luck with it.

Chapter 19: Your first steps in Excel

In this chapter

'Why do I need to know all this ... What is the point?' You may find yourself asking such questions when reading this chapter.

But first lessons are like that – whether you are learning the guitar, karate or spreadsheets.

In your first hour you usually have the hard work of remembering new activities and words – but rarely the pleasure of putting your new knowledge into practice.

There is nothing in this chapter that you will find difficult or complex. We have included only the material that you absolutely need to know, and we have introduced it as gently as possible.

Halfway through Chapter 20, when you discover the power and convenience of spreadsheets, you will be asking a very different question: 'How did I ever manage to organize my work or life without Microsoft Excel?'

New skills

At the end of this chapter you should be able to:

- Start and quit Excel.
- Explain the difference between a worksheet and a workbook.
- Create and name Excel worksheets.
- Enter numbers, text and cell references to a worksheet.
- Edit and delete the contents of a cell.
- Use Excel's Undo feature to reverse commands and cell entries.
- Save, name, open, create and close Excel workbooks.
- Use Excel's online help.

New words

At the end of this chapter you should be able to explain the following terms:

- Worksheet
- Name Box
- Column
- Active Cell
- Workbook
- Dependent Cell
- Cell
- Row
- Cell Reference

Starting Excel

- Double-click the Microsoft Excel icon.

  -or-
- Choose **Start | All Programs | Microsoft Excel**.

Excel starts and displays a new workbook with three worksheets ready for you to use.

Worksheets and workbooks

This ECDL module is about spreadsheets. But Excel does not use the word spreadsheet. Instead, it uses two other words – worksheet and workbook. Let's explain what these mean.

Worksheet
A page that is made up of little boxes arranged in rows and columns. Relationships can be created between the cells so that changing the contents of one cell affects the contents of the related cells.

In Excel, a worksheet is a spreadsheet. A worksheet is much larger than your screen. You can see only a very small part of it at one time.

Workbook
A file containing worksheets.

When you create a new workbook, Excel creates three blank worksheets inside that workbook. Excel calls the worksheets Sheet1, Sheet2 and Sheet3.

An Excel worksheet

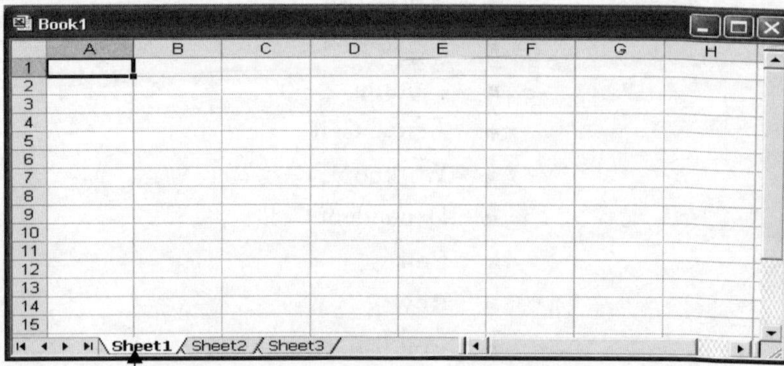

To move from one worksheet to another, click the tab that displays its name

If three worksheets are not enough, you can add more to your workbook – up to a maximum of 256. Think of worksheets as pages in a book, and the workbook as the book containing those pages.

Now you will learn the names of the important parts of a worksheet.

Cells
The little boxes that make up a worksheet.

Cells are arranged in (horizontal) rows and (vertical) columns.

Active cell
The cell in which the cursor is currently located.

Only one cell on a worksheet can be the active cell at any one time. You will always know which cell is the active cell as Excel surrounds it with a thicker border. You can make a cell active by clicking it with the mouse.

The active cell

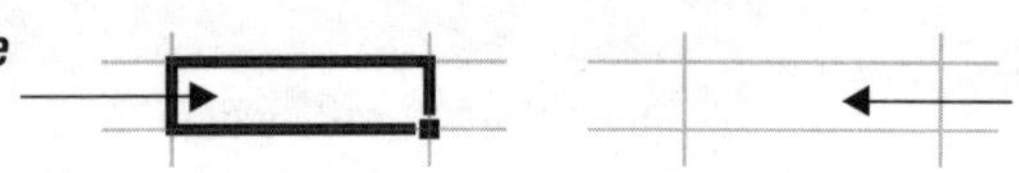

A cell that is not the active cell

When you open a new workbook, Excel makes the top-left cell of the first worksheet, *Sheet1*, the active cell.

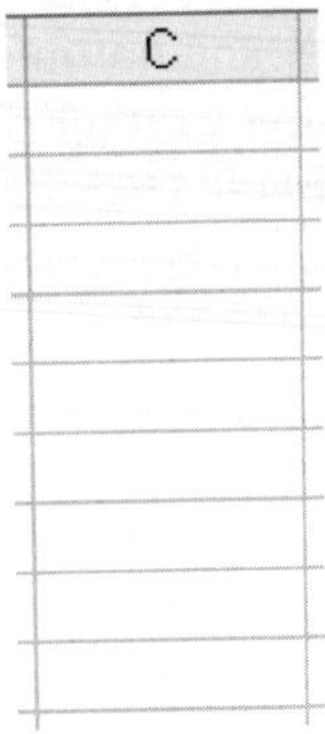

A worksheet column

Column
A vertical line of cells from the top of the worksheet to the bottom.

Each worksheet contains 256 columns. Excel names each column with a letter or group of letters. The first 26 are named *A* to *Z*. The remainder are *AA* to *AZ*, *BA* to *BZ*, and continuing through to *IA* to *IV*.

Row
A horizontal line of cells that stretches left to right across a worksheet.

Each worksheet contains 65,536 rows. Excel gives each row a number, from *1* to *65536*. The total number of cells in a worksheet is therefore 256 multiplied by 65,536 or 16,777,216!

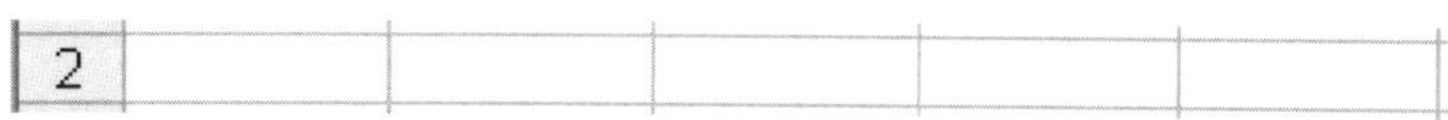

A worksheet row

Each cell in a worksheet has a unique address or location known as its cell reference.

Cell reference
The location or 'address' of a cell on a worksheet.

A cell reference is made up of two parts:

- The column letter (*A*, *B*, *C*, ...).
- The row number (*1*, *2*, *3*, ...).

When you open a new workbook in Excel, the active cell is the one on *Sheet1* with the cell reference *A1*.

Remember: column letter first, row number second – for example, *B6*, *C8* and *J12*.

Column letters: upper- or lower-case?

You will always see cell references written with the column letters in upper-case letters (for example, *A1*, *B10* and *W90*) rather than in lower-case (for example, *a1*, *b10* and *w90*). This is true for Excel's online help – and this book.

However, when you type a cell reference into Excel, as you will in Exercise 19.1, it does not matter whether you type the column letter in upper- or lower-case. Excel accepts either. You may find it easier to enter column letters in lower-case, because you need to type only the letter key, and not the letter key in combination with the **Shift** key.

Name Box
The rectangular area above the top-left corner of a worksheet in which Excel displays the cell reference of the active cell.

You can use the *Name Box* to move the cursor to any cell on the worksheet, making that cell the active cell.

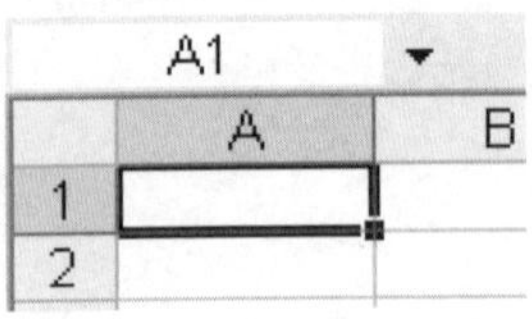

To do so, type the cell reference in the *Name Box* and press **Enter**.

Exercise 19.1: Name Box and cell references

Perform this exercise to learn how to enter a cell reference in the *Name Box*.

1) Click in the *Name Box*.
2) Type *B2* and press **Enter**.

   Excel responds by making cell *B2* the active cell.

   As further practice, repeat these two steps for the following cells: *D8*, *A3*, *H5* and *I19*.

Entering numbers in cells

When you type something into a cell and press **Enter**, Excel looks at your entry and asks:

- Is this a number?
- Is this text?
- Is this a cell reference?
- Is this a calculation?

Excel treats each type of entry in a different way. In this section, you will deal with entering numbers, text and cell references.

Excel accepts two kinds of calculations: formulas (you will learn about these in Chapter 20) and functions (covered in Chapter 21).

Exercise 19.2: Entering a number in a cell

1) Click *B3*, making it the active cell.
2) Type the number: 1274.
3) Press **Enter**.

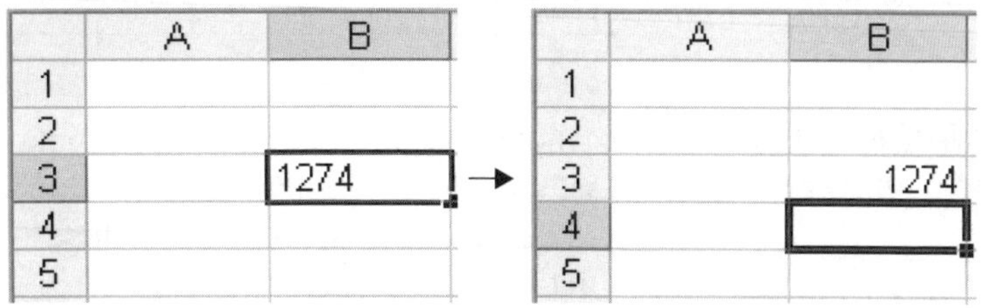

Why does Excel right-align numbers?

In Exercise 19.2, Excel did two things after you pressed **Enter**.

- It moved 1274 from the left of cell *B3* to the right. This is because Excel assumes that you will want to perform addition or another arithmetic operation on the entered number. When you write a list of numbers on paper to add them, you line up the numbers from the right. Excel right-aligns numbers for the same reason.
- It moved down the cursor to cell *B4*, the cell under *B3*. Again, this is because of arithmetic. Excel assumes that you will want to enter another number beneath the previous one.

Entering text in a cell

You can enter text in a worksheet as well as numbers. By using text to identify the meaning or source of numbers, you make your worksheet easier to read and understand.

Exercise 19.3: Entering text in a cell

1) Click *B2*, making it the active cell.
2) Type the word: Add
3) Press **Enter**.

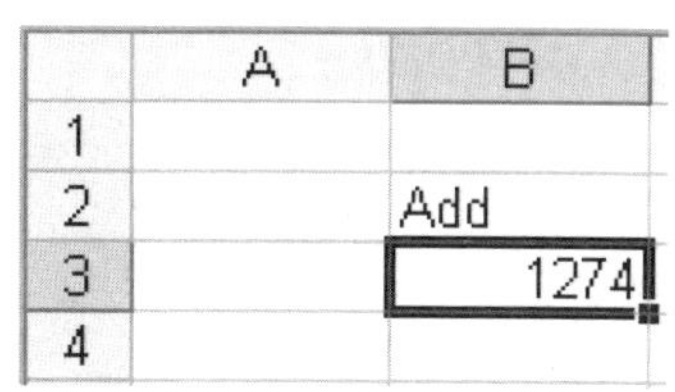

Notice how Excel responded after you pressed **Enter**.

- 'Add' remained in the left of the cell *B2*. While Excel right-aligns numbers, it left-aligns text.

- It moved the cursor down to cell *B3*, the cell under *B2*. Excel assumes that this is the next cell you will want to use.

Text that describes a number on a worksheet is known as a label.

Label
A piece of text in a worksheet cell that provides information about the number in an accompanying cell, usually either below it or to its right.

Entering a cell reference in a cell

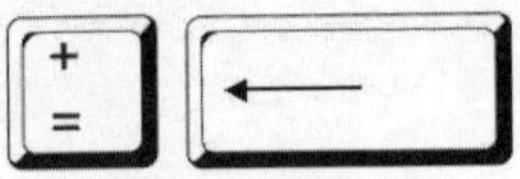

The Equals key is to the left of the Backspace key

Another type of entry you can make in a cell is a cell reference – that is, the address of another cell – preceded by the 'equals' (=) sign. When you do so, Excel reproduces the content of the other cell to the active cell.

Exercise 19.4: Entering a cell reference in a cell

If *B3* does not contain the number 1274 from Exercise 19.2, enter it now.

1) Click cell *B10*, type the following, and press **Enter**:

   =B3

   That is, an 'equals' sign (=) followed by cell reference *B3*.

   Excel responds by displaying the current content of *B3* (that is, number 1274) in *B10*.

The arrow keys

So far you have used the mouse and the *Name Box* to move the cursor around the worksheet.

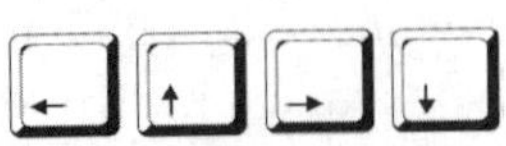

The four arrow keys

Another way of moving the cursor is by pressing the arrow keys. You may find this method faster than moving and clicking the mouse, because you need not take either hand away from the keyboard.

Editing the content of a cell

Sometimes, you will want to change the content of a cell. Exercise 19.5 shows you how.

Exercise 19.5: Editing the content of a cell

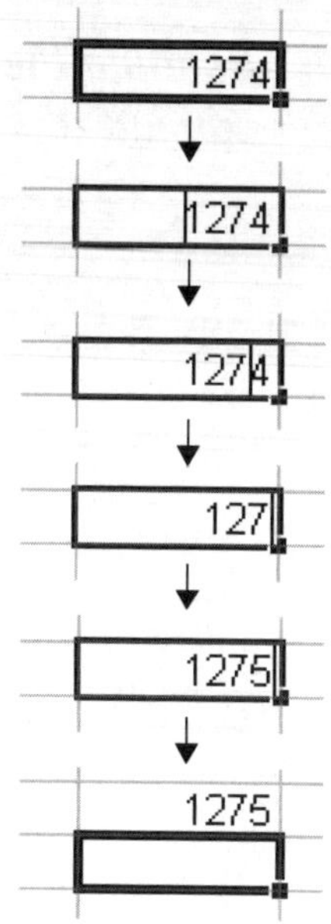

1) Double-click cell *B3*.

   Excel makes the cell border thinner and displays a blinking cursor in the cell. (The location of the cursor within the cell depends on which part of the cell you double-clicked.)
2) Using the arrow keys, move the blinking cursor to the left of the 4.
3) Press **Delete** once, deleting the 4.
4) Type 5.
5) Press **Enter**.

   This moves the cursor out of *B3* and down to *B4*. Excel has replaced 1274 with 1275. Notice that the number in *B10* also changes.

Dependent cells

Cell *B10* is an example of a dependent cell – a cell whose content depends on the content of another cell. In this case, the other cell is *B3*.

When *B3* changed from 1274 to 1275, so too did *B10*. That is because *B10* contains the cell reference of =B3.

As you will learn in later chapters of this module, cell relationships are the basis of spreadsheets.

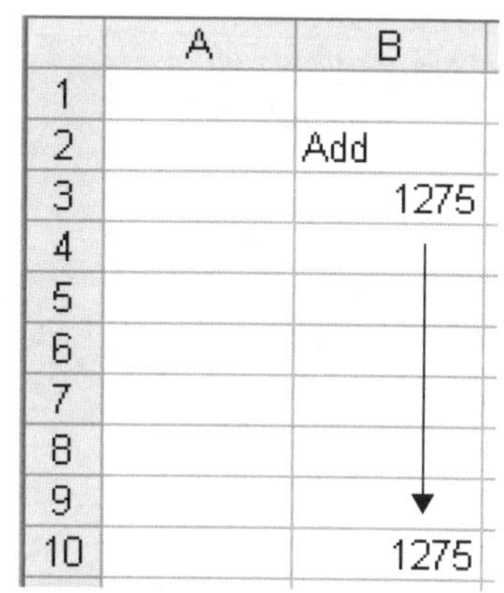

Content of B10 depends on the content of B3

F2: Excel's Edit key

In Exercise 19.5, you double-clicked cell *B3*. This made the cell editable – that is, you were able to move the cursor within the cell and change the cell content.

When a cell is already the active cell, you can make it editable by pressing **F2**. This is Excel's **Edit** key. You may find this method faster than double-clicking with the mouse.

Once the cell is editable, you can insert additional cell content or replace the existing cell content.

Deleting the content of a cell

Want to delete a number, some text or a cell reference from a cell? The following exercise shows you how.

Exercise 19.6: Deleting the content of a cell

1) Move the cursor to cell *B10*. From Exercises 19.4 and 19.5, this contains the cell reference =B3 and displays the number 1275.
2) Press **Backspace** or **Delete**.

   Excel removes the content of the cell. *B10* is now empty.

Deleting and the Enter key

When you enter something in a cell, you must press **Enter** to confirm the new content of the cell. Similarly, when you edit a cell, Excel makes the change only after you press **Enter**.

When deleting a cell's content, however, you do not need to press **Enter** to confirm the deletion. Just pressing **Backspace** or **Delete** is enough.

Deleting cell content – not the cell

Another way to delete the content of a cell is to right-click the cell and choose **Clear Contents** from the pop-up menu.

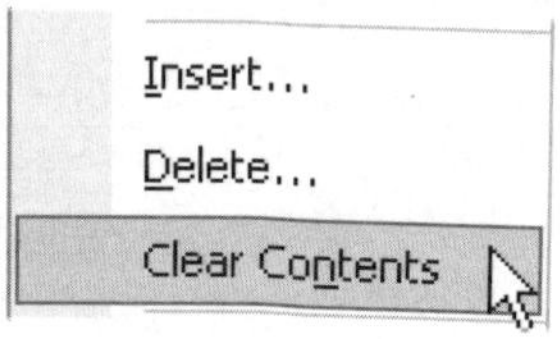

Do not choose **Delete** from this pop-up menu. This command not only deletes the cell contents – it also removes the cell itself from the worksheet! As a result, other cells must change their position to fill the space left empty.

Excel's toolbars

Excel's toolbars give you convenient, one-click access to the commands you use most often. By default, Excel displays just two toolbars, the *Standard* and *Formatting* toolbars, on a single row across the top of the screen.

To display them as two, individual toolbars, follow these steps:

- Choose **Tools | Customize** and click the **Options** tab.

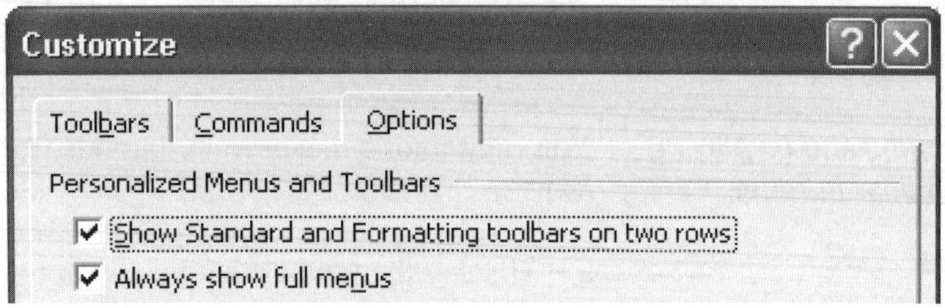

- Select the *Show Standard and Formatting toolbars on two rows* check box and choose **Close**.

Hiding and displaying toolbars

You can display or hide Excel's various toolbars by choosing the **View | Toolbars** command, and then selecting or deselecting the various toolbar options from the drop-down menu displayed.

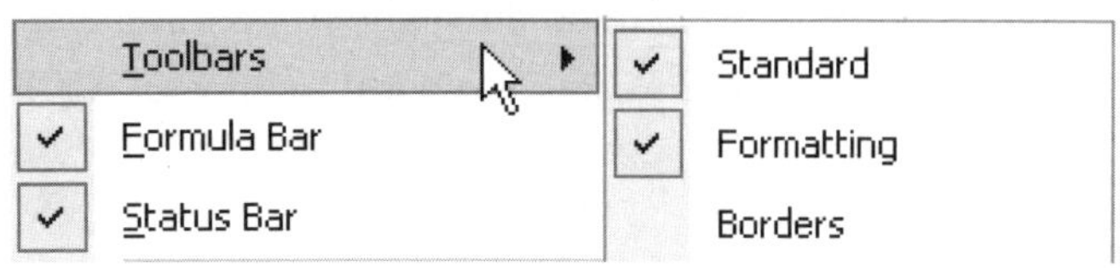

The check marks beside the *Standard* and *Formatting* toolbars indicate that they are already selected for display on screen.

The Standard and Formatting toolbars

Only two of Excel's toolbars are relevant to this ECDL module: the *Standard* toolbar and the *Formatting* toolbar.

The *Standard* toolbar includes buttons for managing files and working with numbers in cells.

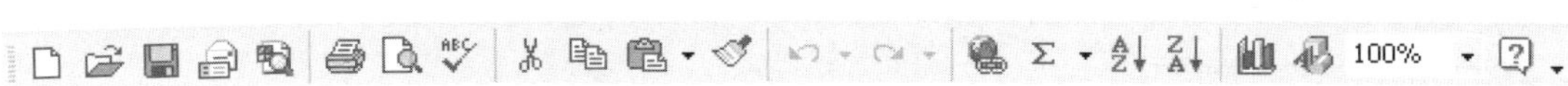

Excel's Standard toolbar

The *Formatting* toolbar includes buttons for changing the appearance of text and numbers in cells.

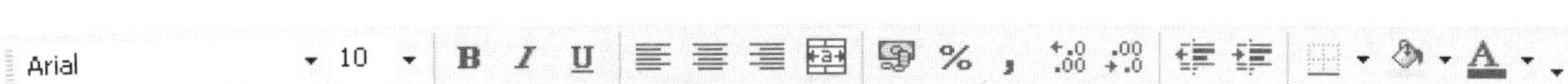

Excel's Formatting toolbar

Rather than introduce all these buttons at once, we will explain the ones you need to know about as they become relevant through the remainder of this ECDL spreadsheets module.

Hiding and displaying toolbar buttons

You can remove one or more buttons from a toolbar. Follow these steps:

- Display the toolbar that you want to change.
- Hold down the **Alt** key, and drag the button off the toolbar.

Excel removes the selected button from the toolbar. Want the button back again? Follow this procedure:

- Display the toolbar. Click **Toolbar Options** (at the very end of the toolbar), then **Add or Remove Buttons** and finally click the name of the toolbar.

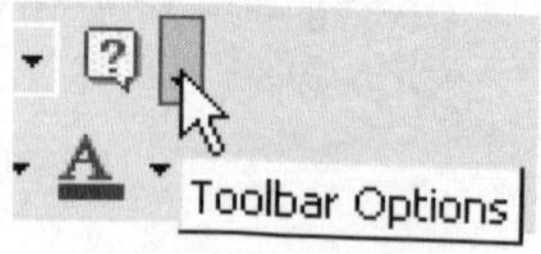

- Click the button you want to display again. Buttons with a check mark beside their names are displayed on the toolbar, and those without are not.

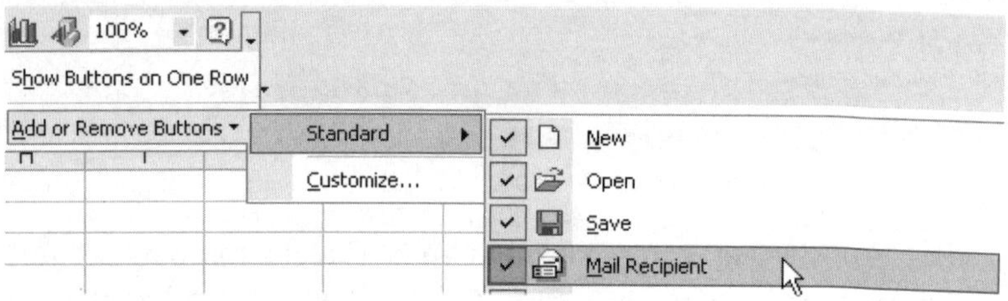

- Click anywhere outside the menu to close it.

Excel redisplays the button on the toolbar.

Excel's task pane

While Excel's toolbars provide one-click access to the commands that you use most often, Excel's task pane collects in one place the various commands you may need to perform important tasks such as creating and opening documents and copying and pasting information.

The task pane is located on the right side of your screen and is displayed by default when you first start Excel.

Task panes are available for many tasks. The task pane illustrated here is the *New Workbook* task pane, which presents the various options for creating new workbooks and opening existing ones. We will explain the task panes you need to know about as they become relevant through the remainder of this ECDL Spreadsheets module.

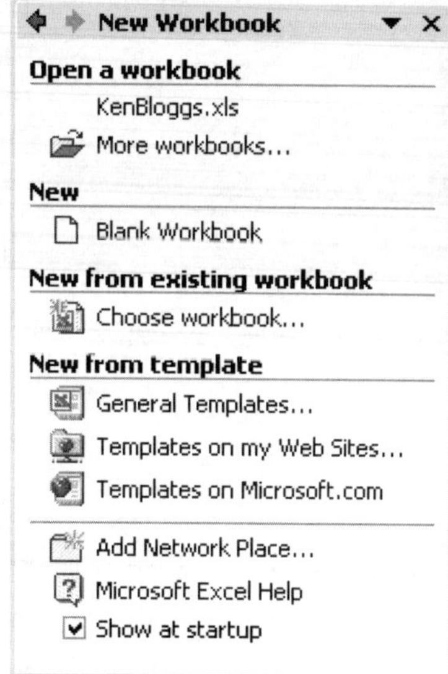

Opening and closing the task pane

The relevant task pane automatically opens when you begin a task for which a task pane exists. To display the task pane at any other time, choose **View | Task Pane**.

To close the task pane, click the **Close** button on its title bar.

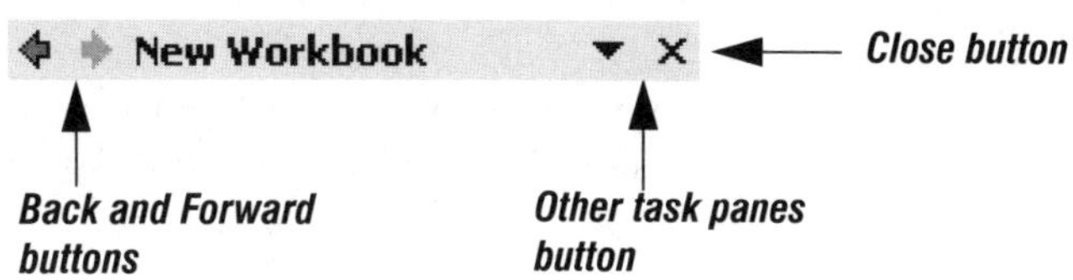

Switching between task panes

To switch from one task pane to another, click the **Other Task Panes** button on the title bar. Then select a task pane from the drop-down list displayed.

To move back and forwards through task panes you have previously displayed, use the **Back** and **Forward** buttons on the left side of the title bar.

Excel's personalized menus

By default, when you first choose a menu, Excel displays only some of the commands on that menu. To view a complete list, click the double-arrow at the bottom of the menu.

If you choose a command that is not displayed by default, Excel adds it to the displayed list the next time you choose the menu.

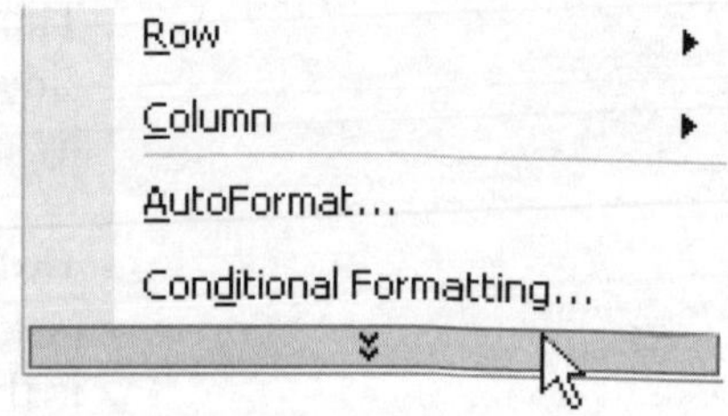

To view all commands each time you choose a menu, follow these steps:

- Choose **Tools | Customize** and click the **Options** tab.
- Select the *Always show full menus* check box, and choose **Close**.

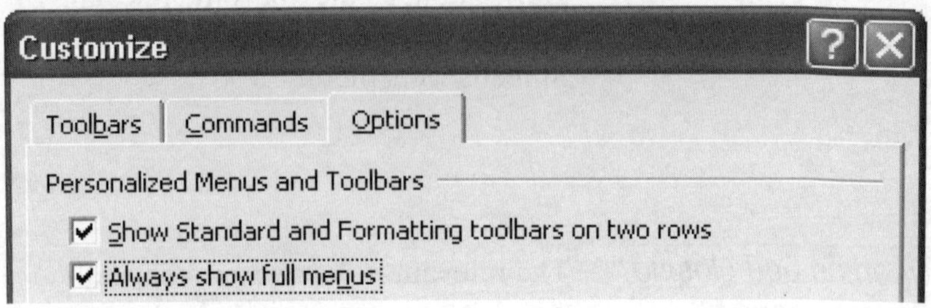

Modifying basic options

You can customize the way Word works and set your own personal preferences. Choose **Tools | Options** to see the range of options available.

Choose the **General** tab to specify the default file location for opening and saving spreadsheets and to specify the user name that will appear on spreadsheet property sheets.

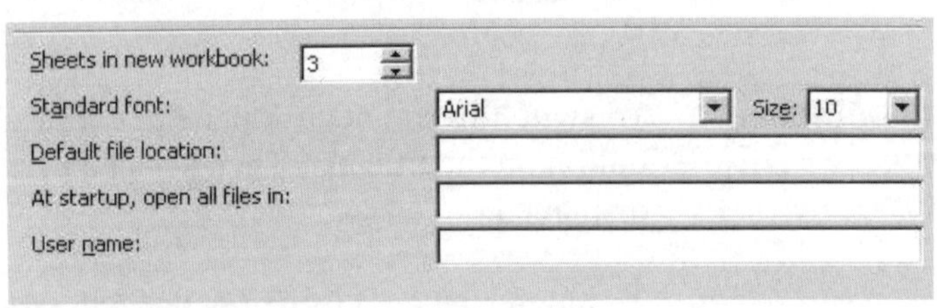

Excel's Undo feature

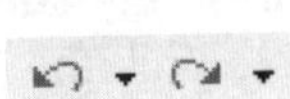

Undo and Redo buttons

Entered the wrong data? Pressed the wrong key? Don't panic. Excel allows you to undo your most recent cell entry or action if it has produced unwanted results. To undo a cell entry or action:

- Choose **Edit | Undo**.

  -or-

- Click the **Undo** button on the *Standard* toolbar.

Repeatedly pressing **Undo** reverses your last series of actions. To view a list of recent actions that you can undo, click the arrow at the right of the **Undo** button. If you undo an action and then change your mind, click the **Redo** button (to the right of the **Undo** button).

Exercise 19.7: Using the Undo feature

Perform this exercise to practise using Excel's Undo feature.

1) Click in cell *B2*, and press **Delete**.
2) Click in cell *B3*, and press **Delete**.

   Everything that you entered in the worksheet is now deleted. But you can use Undo to get it all back by reversing your two delete actions.
3) Click the **Undo** button.

   This reverses your most recent action (in step 2) above. *B3* again contains the number 1275.
4) Click **Undo** a second time.

   This reverses your second most recent action (step 1) above. *B2* again contains the word 'Add'.

Excel's Repeat feature

Do you want to do the same thing again? Use Excel's **Repeat** feature:

- Choose **Edit | Repeat** or press **Ctrl+y**.

Working with Excel workbooks

An Excel workbook is a file containing a collection of worksheets. The file names of Excel workbooks end in .xls. This helps you to distinguish Excel files from other file types, such as Word files (ending in .doc).

Saving your workbook

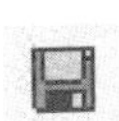

Save button

In Excel, as in other applications, always save your work as you go along. Don't wait until you are finished! To save a workbook:

- Choose **File | Save**.

  -or-
- Click the **Save** button on the *Standard* toolbar.

The first time that you save a workbook file, Excel asks you to give the file a name. Exercise 19.8 shows you how.

Exercise 19.8: Saving and naming a new workbook

1) *Sheet1* of your workbook should contain the word 'Add' in cell *B2* and the number 1275 in cell *B3*, as entered in this chapter's exercises.

If not, enter that data now.

2) Choose **File | Save** or click the **Save** icon on the *Standard* toolbar. Excel displays a dialog box with two boxes similar to the ones shown below.

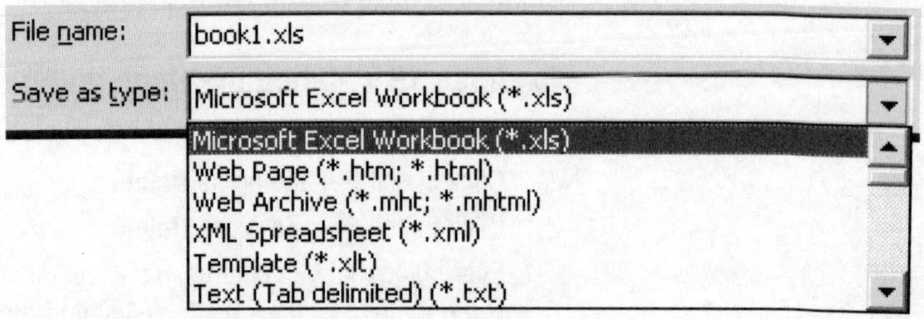

3) By default, Excel names the first workbook file you open and save as Book1.xls. Replace this file name with something that you will find easier to remember and recognize – such as your own name – and click the **Save** button.

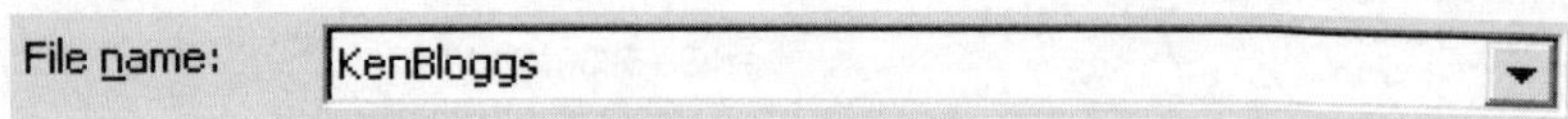

Excel adds the file name extension of .xls automatically. You need not type it.

Creating a new workbook

To create a new workbook file:

- Choose **File | New** to open the *New Workbook* task pane, where you can choose to open an existing workbook, open a new blank workbook, create a new workbook based on an existing workbook, or create a new workbook from a template.

-or-

New button

- Click the **New** button on the *Standard* toolbar to open a new blank workbook.

Opening an existing workbook

To open an existing workbook file:

- Choose **File | Open**.

-or-

Open button

- Click the **Open** button on the *Standard* toolbar. Select the file you want from the dialog box.

Closing a workbook

To close a workbook file:

- Choose **File | Close**.

  -or-

- Click the **Close** button on the workbook window.

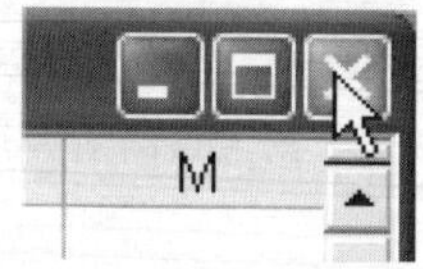

If you have made changes to your workbook since you last saved it, Excel prompts you to save the changes before it closes the file.

Exercise 19.9: Closing and reopening a saved workbook

In this exercise you will close and then reopen the workbook you saved in Exercise 19.8.

1) Choose **File | Close** or click the **Close** button at the top-right of the workbook window.
2) Choose **File | Open** or click the **Open** button on the *Standard* toolbar to display the *File Open* dialog box. Locate your workbook and open it.

Saving a workbook file with a different name

To save a workbook file with a different name or in a different location:

- Choose **File | Save As**. Specify the drive and folder where you want to save the file, and specify the file name.

Switching between workbooks

To switch between open workbooks, choose the **Window** menu to list the workbooks that are currently open. then choose the workbook you want to switch to.

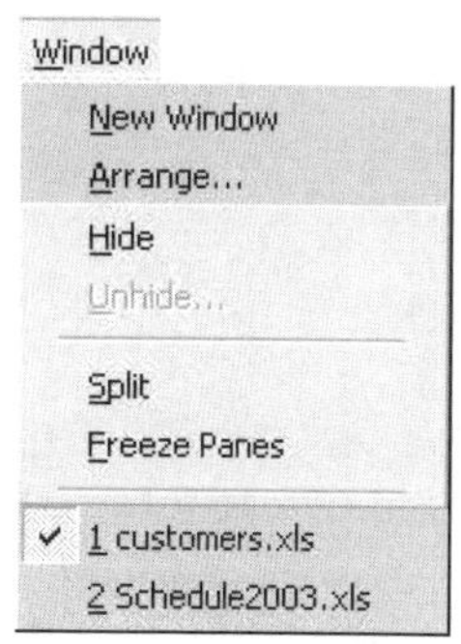

Working with Excel worksheets

A workbook consists of one or more worksheets, and you can perform all the standard management functions on worksheets: adding new worksheets, copying and moving worksheets, and deleting worksheets.

Inserting and naming a new worksheet

To insert a new worksheet, choose **Insert | Worksheet**. The new worksheet is inserted to the left of the currently open worksheet, and is given a default name such as 'Worksheet 4'.

To rename the worksheet, right-click on the worksheet title, choose **Rename,** and then enter the new name over the current name.

Copying and moving worksheets

You can copy and move worksheets within the current workbook or within any currently open workbook.

Choose **Edit | Move or Copy Sheet** while the worksheet you want to move or copy is the current one. You now see the *Move or Copy* dialog box where you can specify the following:

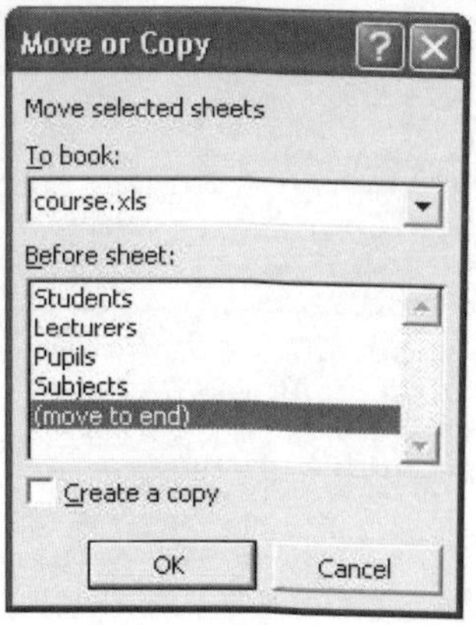

- The workbook you want to move the worksheet to. Note that you may only move or copy a worksheet to a workbook that is currently open.
- The position of the worksheet – you do this by indicating which worksheet in the target workbook you want it before.
- Whether or not you want to leave a copy of the worksheet in its current workbook – select the *Create a copy* check box to make a copy.

In the example shown here, the worksheet is moved (not copied) to the end of the workbook course.xls.

Deleting a worksheet

To delete a worksheet, right-click on the worksheet title. Then choose **Delete** from the worksheet menu.

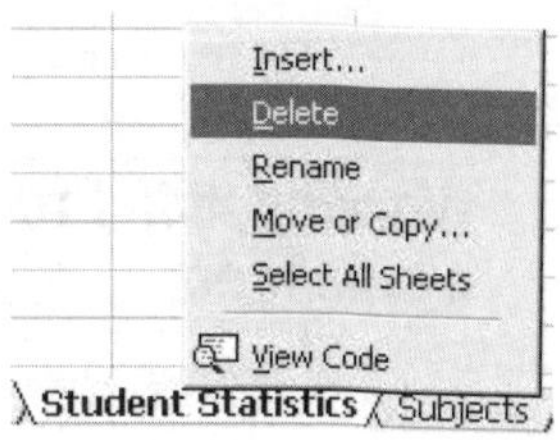

Quitting Excel

To quit Excel:

- Choose **File | Exit**.

  -or-

- Click the **Close** button on the Excel window.

If you have left open any files containing unsaved work, Excel prompts you to save them.

Online help

Like Word, Access, PowerPoint and other Microsoft Office applications, Excel offers a searchable online help system:

- The 'help' in online help means that the information is there to assist you understand and use Excel.
- The word 'online' means that the material is presented on the computer screen rather than as a traditional printed manual.

You can search through and read online help in various ways, from the Help window, from dialog boxes, and by using the Office Assistant.

Using the Office Assistant

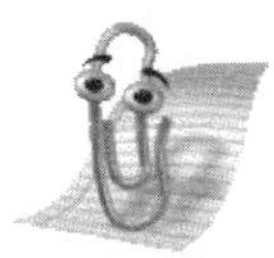

Office Assistant

The Office Assistant is a friendly, animated tool that allows you to type a topic or question about what you are looking for and then presents a list of relevant help topics for you to choose from, as Exercise 19.10 demonstrates.

Exercise 19.10: Using the Office Assistant to get help

1) Click the Office Assistant.

   If the Office Assistant is not visible on your screen, choose **Help | Show the Office Assistant**.
2) In the search balloon that Excel then displays, type the following: help

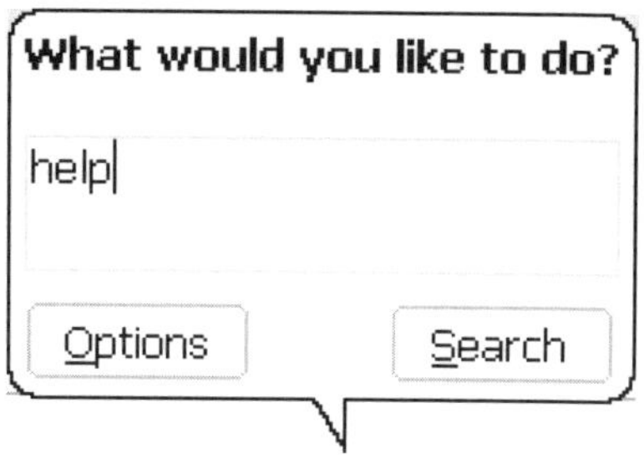

3) Click the **Search** button.
4) Click any topic in the list of help topics retrieved by the search. That topic is then displayed in the Microsoft Excel Help window.

   This window is explained further below.

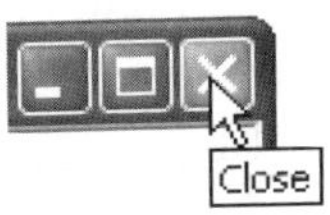

5) Close the *Help* window by clicking the **Close** button at the top right of the window.

Using Ask a Question to get help

The *Ask a Question* box on the right side of Excel's menu bar allows you to type a topic or question to get help without using the Office Assistant.

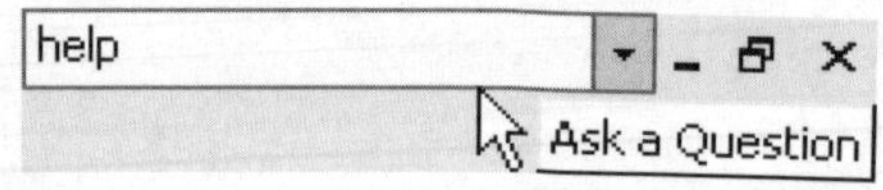

- Type your topic or question in the box and press **Enter**. Excel displays a list of topics that you can choose from in the same way as you do when using the Office Assistant.

Using the Help window to get help

To use the *Help* window directly to get help, you must first turn off the Office Assistant. Follow these steps:

- Right-click the Office Assistant and choose **Options** from the drop-down menu.
- Deselect the *Use the Office Assistant* option and click **OK**.

To open the *Microsoft Excel* Help window, choose **Help | Microsoft Excel Help** or click the **Microsoft Excel Help** button on the *Standard* toolbar.

The *Help* window presents three tabs that allow you to search for help in different ways:

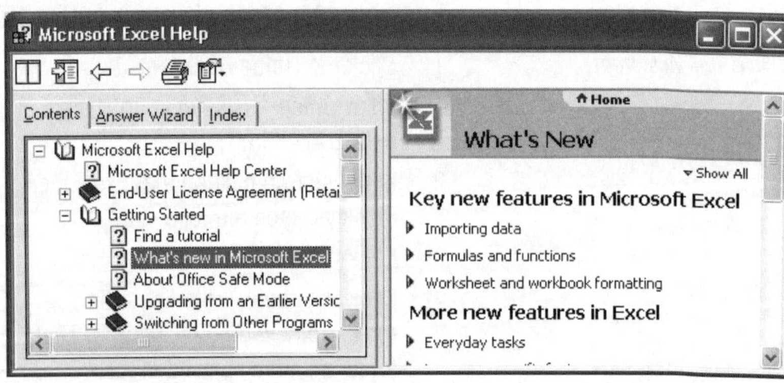

- **Contents tab:** This offers short descriptions of Excel's main features.

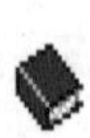

Where you see a heading with a book symbol, double-click to view the related sub-headings.

Double-click on a question mark symbol to read the help text.

- **Answer Wizard tab:** Type your question in the box at the top-left of the window, and click **Search**. Excel displays all matches from the online help in the lower-left of the window.

  Click a topic to display the associated text in the right-hand pane.
- **Index tab:** Type the word or phrase you are interested in and click **Search**. Excel displays a list of suggested help topics in the lower-left part of the window.

  When you find the index entry that you are looking for, click it to display the associated text in the right-hand pane.

As you search through and read online help topics, you will see the following buttons at the top of the online help window:

- **Hide/Show:** Hides or displays the left pane of the *Help* window.

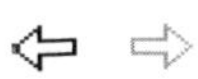

- **Back/Forward:** Moves you backwards and forwards through previously visited help topics.

- **Print:** Prints the currently displayed help topic.

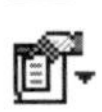

- **Options:** Offers a number of display options.

Take a few minutes to look through Excel's online help system. Remember that you are free to use online help during an ECDL test.

Using help from dialog boxes

You can also access online help directly from a dialog box, as Exercise 19.11 demonstrates.

Exercise 19.11: Using online help in a dialog box

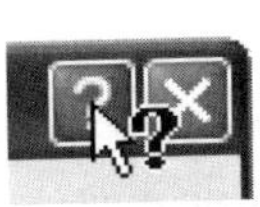

1) Choose **View | Zoom** to display the *Zoom* dialog box.
2) Click the question mark symbol near the top-right of the dialog box. Excel displays a question mark to the right of the cursor.

3) Move the mouse down and left, and click the *Fit selection* option.

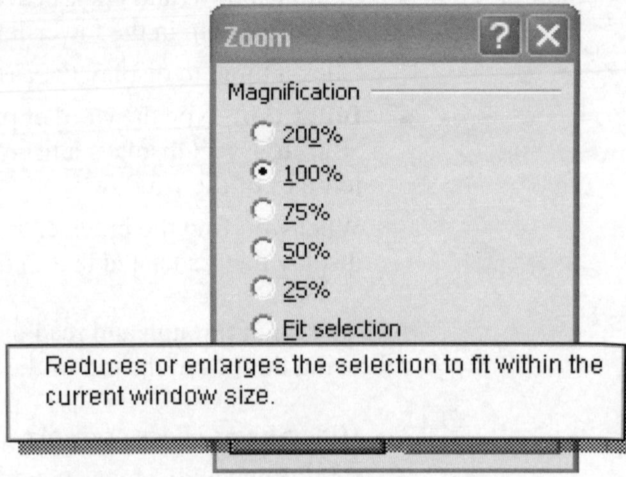

Excel displays online help text that tells you about the selected option. Practise this exercise with other dialog boxes in Excel.

When finished, you can close your workbook and Excel. You have now completed the first chapter of the ECDL Spreadsheets module.

Chapter summary: so now you know

An Excel *workbook* is a file containing *spreadsheets*, which Excel calls *worksheets*. Workbook file names end in .xls.

A worksheet is made up of cells, arranged in columns and rows. Each cell has a unique cell reference, consisting of its column letter and row number – for example, *B3* and *G47*.

Only one cell is the active cell at any one time. You make a cell active by moving the cursor to it, using the mouse, arrow keys or *Name Box*.

You can enter a number, text (to label a number) or a cell reference to any cell. Press **Enter** to confirm your entry. Excel left-aligns text but right-aligns numbers.

To edit a cell, first make it editable. You do so by double-clicking it with the mouse. Alternatively, make it the active cell and then press Excel's **Edit** key, **F2**. See Exercise 19.5 for an example of this.

You can delete the content of the active cell (but not the cell itself) by pressing **Delete** or **Backspace**. See Exercise 19.6 for an example of this.

Excel's *Undo* feature, available from a button on the *Standard* toolbar, allows you to reverse your recent cell entries or actions if they have produced unwanted results. See Exercise 19.7 for an example of this.

You can hide and display Excel's various toolbars. The two most commonly used are the *Standard* and *Formatting* toolbars.

An Excel workbook consists of one or more *worksheets*, and you can perform all the standard management functions on worksheets.

Excel's online help system, available through the *Office Assistant*, from the **Help** menu and from individual dialog boxes, provides a comprehensive and searchable guide to the program's features and procedures. See Exercises 19.10 and 19.11 for examples of this.

Quick quiz: your first steps in Excel

Circle the correct answer to each of the following multiple-choice questions about your first steps in Excel.

Q1	Excel's **Edit** key is:
A.	**Alt.**
B.	**F2.**
C.	**Insert.**
D.	**Ctrl.**

Q2	Pressing **Delete** deletes a cell's content and the cell itself.
A.	True.
B.	False.

Q3	If you remove an icon from an Excel toolbar, you can never put it back.
A.	True.
B.	False.

Q4	You will be allowed to access Excel's online help during the ECDL exam.
A.	True.
B.	False.

Q5	The *Name Box* shows:
A.	The cell reference of the active cell.
B.	The name of the workbook.
C.	The name of the worksheet.
D.	Your name.

Answers **1:** B, **2:** B, **3:** B, **4:** A, **5:** A.

Chapter 20: Arithmetic with Excel

In this chapter

Prepare to be impressed. In Chapter 19 you learned the names for the important parts of an Excel worksheet, and practised the simple operations of entering numbers, text and cell references to cells.

Now you have the basics you need to discover the power of spreadsheets in this chapter.

You will very quickly discover why people who work with numbers – such as accountants, statisticians, engineers and project managers – rely on spreadsheets to perform tedious calculations quickly, easily and accurately.

In the practical exercises you will use fewer than a dozen numbers. These simple examples differ from the multi-page financial reports of a large corporation in size only. The principles are the same. Learn the principles in this chapter and you will never meet an amount of data too large or too complex for you to master with your spreadsheet skills.

New skills

At the end of this chapter you should be able to:

- Explain what an Excel formula is, and name its components.
- Use Excel formulas to add, subtract, multiply and divide numbers.
- Apply the rules of arithmetic to calculations in Excel.
- Recognize Excel error messages.
- Use Excel's **Zoom** feature to enlarge and reduce worksheet display.
- Save a workbook to a floppy disk.

New words

At the end of this chapter you should be able to explain the following terms:

- Formula
- Argument
- Calculated cell
- Operator
- Non-adjacent cells
- Constant

Formulas in Excel

In Chapter 19 you learnt how to enter numbers, text and cell references to worksheet cells. Now it's time to discover a fourth type of cell entry, called a calculation.

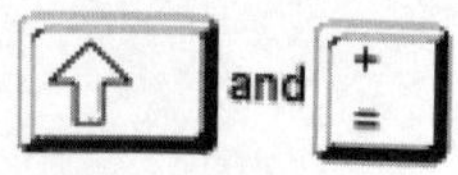

To type a plus (+), hold down the Shift key and press the Equals key (=)

Calculations are the reason that you enter numbers to cells, because calculations enable you to perform arithmetic – addition, subtraction, multiplication and division – on your entered numbers.

Excel accepts two kinds of calculations: formulas and functions. This chapter shows you how to perform calculations using formulas. You will learn about functions in Chapter 21.

Exercise 20.1: Adding two numbers with an Excel formula

1) Open the workbook that you saved in Exercise 19.8. If cells *B2* and *B3* do not contain the word 'Add' and the number '1275', enter that data now.
2) Click *B4*, and type the number: 25
3) Press **Enter**.
4) Click *B5*, and type:
   =B3+B4
   When you enter the formula, Excel highlights each cell reference in a different colour, and turns the border of the corresponding cell the same colour so that you can easily see which cells you refer to in your formula.

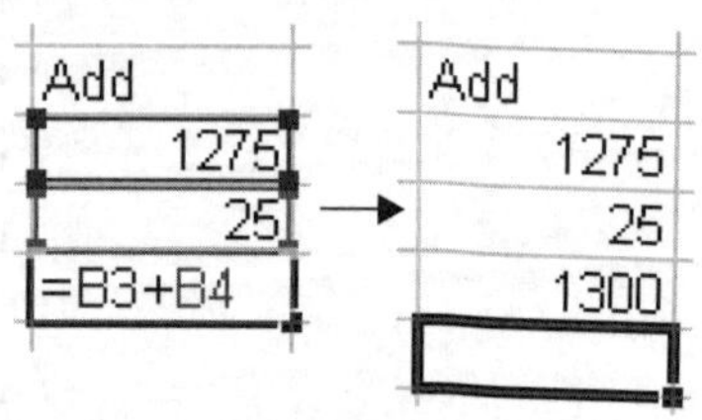

5) Press **Enter**.
   Excel displays in *B5* the sum of the contents of the two cells *B3* and *B4*.

Congratulations! You have performed your first calculation in Excel.

Formulas and arguments

'Formula' and 'argument' are two words you will meet a lot when learning about spreadsheets. So it is important that you understand what they mean.

Formula
An equation that performs operations such as addition, subtraction, multiplication or division on data that is stored in a worksheet.

In Exercise 20.1, the formula you used was =B3+B4. Note the following about formulas:

- Always begin formulas with the equals (=) sign.
- Always press **Enter** to confirm your formula.

The components of a formula are called arguments. In the formula =B3+B4, the arguments are B3 and B4. Both are cell references. As you will see, you can also use numbers as arguments.

Argument
The inputs to a calculation that generate the result.

Next, let's perform three other arithmetic operations using Excel formulas: subtraction, multiplication and division.

Exercise 20.2: Subtracting with Excel

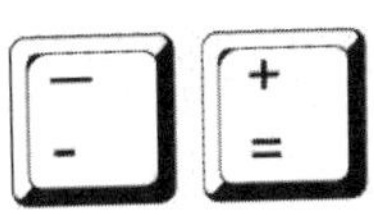

Excel's Subtraction key is the Hyphen (-) key, to the left of the Equals to key

1) In cell *D2*, type the word Subtract and press **Enter**.
2) In cell *D3*, enter the number: 1275
3) In cell *D4*, enter the number: 25
4) In cell *D5*, type the formula:

   =D3-D4

   Then press **Enter**.

   Excel displays in *D5* the result of subtracting the contents of *D4* from *D3*.

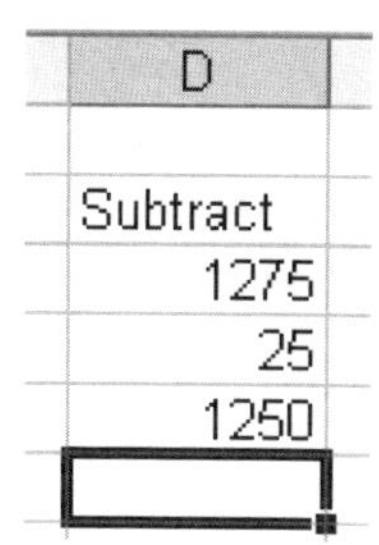

Exercise 20.3: Multiplying with Excel

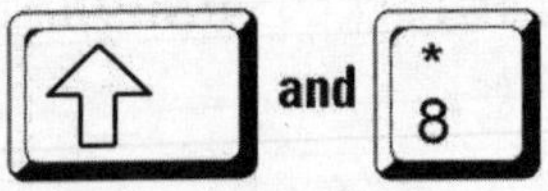

Excel's Multiplication key is the Asterisk (*) key, typed by holding down the Shift key and pressing the 8 key

1) In cell *F2*, enter the word: Multiply
2) In cell *F3*, enter the number: 1275
3) In cell *F4*, enter the number: 25
4) In cell *F5*, enter the formula:

   =F3*F4

   Excel displays in *F5* the result of multiplying the contents of *F3* by *F4*.

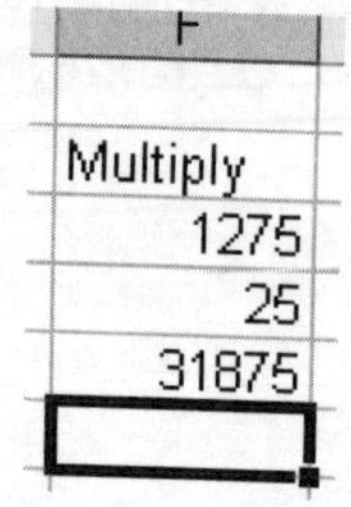

Exercise 20.4: Dividing with Excel

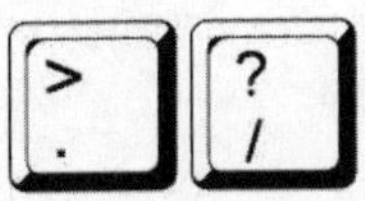

Excel's Division key is the Forward slash (/) key, to the right of the Full stop (.) key

1) In cell *H2*, enter the word: Divide
2) In cell *H3*, enter the number: 1275
3) In cell *H4*, enter the number: 25
4) In cell *H5*, enter the formula:

   =H3/H4

   Excel displays in *H5* the result of dividing the contents of *H3* by *H4*.

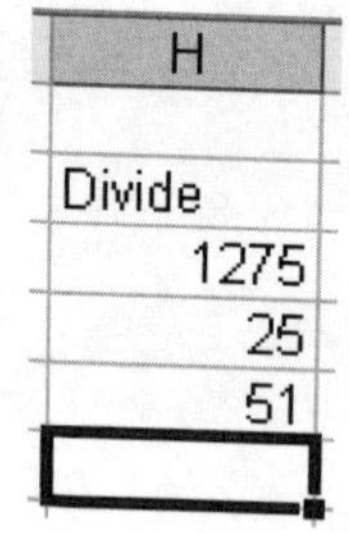

Calculated cells

In Exercises 20.1 to 20.4, the cells *B3* and *B4*, *D3* and *D4*, *F3* and *F4*, and *H3* and *H4* each:

- Contain a number, and
- Display a number.

In other words, what they contain and what they display are the same.

Cells *B5*, *D5*, *F5* and *H5*, however, contain one thing (a formula) but display another (a number). These are examples of calculated cells.

Calculated cell
A cell that contains a calculation but displays the result of that calculation.

You can think of a calculated cell as an 'answer cell'.

In addition to arguments, the other type of component in a formula is the operator.

Operators
*Symbols that specify the type of calculation you want to perform on the arguments of a formula. Excel's four main arithmetic operators are +, -, * and /.*

Excel offers other, more complex, operators that are beyond the scope of this ECDL spreadsheets module.

Adding down and across

Two of the most common arithmetic operations in spreadsheets are the addition of numbers that are arranged in vertical or horizontal lists. Exercises 20.5 and 20.6 provide examples of each.

Exercise 20.5: Adding a vertical list of numbers

1) In cells *B8*, *B9*, *B10*, *B11* and *B12*, enter the numbers: 1234, 4532, 5693, 3512, 239
2) In cell *A13*, enter the word: Total
3) In cell *B13*, enter the formula:

   =B8+B9+B10+B11+B12

   Excel displays in *B13* the result of adding the specified cells.

8		1234
9		4532
10		5693
11		3512
12		239
13	Total	15210
14		

Exercise 20.6: Adding a horizontal list of numbers

1) In cells *B16*, *C16*, *D16*, *E16* and *F16*, enter the numbers: 1234, 4532, 5693, 3512, 239 (the same numbers as in Exercise 20.5).
2) In cell *G15*, enter the word: Total
3) In cell *G16*, enter the formula:

   =B16+C16+D16+E16+F16

   Excel displays in *G16* the result of adding the specified cells.

15							Total
16		1234	4532	5693	3512	239	15210
17							

Adding non-adjacent cells

Excel can add cells even when they are not arranged in neat, vertical or horizontal lists, as Exercise 20.7 demonstrates. Cells that are not immediately adjoining one another are called 'non-adjacent cells'.

Exercise 20.7: Adding non-adjacent cells

1) Enter the following numbers:

   1234 in *B20*, 4532 in *C22*, 5693 in *D21*, 3512 in *E19* and 239 in *F20* (the same numbers as in Exercises 20.5 and 20.6).

2) In *G19*, enter the word: Total

3) In *G20*, enter the formula:

   =B20+C22+D21+E19+F20

   Excel displays in *G20* the result of adding the specified cells.

19				3512		Total
20	1234				239	15210
21			5693			
22		4532				

Non-adjacent cells
Cells that are not located immediately beside, above or below one another.

Editing formulas

In Exercise 19.5 you learnt how to edit a number in a cell. You can also edit a formula, as Exercise 20.8 demonstrates.

Exercise 20.8: Editing a formula

1) Double-click *G20*. (Alternatively, move the cursor to it with the arrow keys, and then press Excel's **Edit** key, **F2**.)

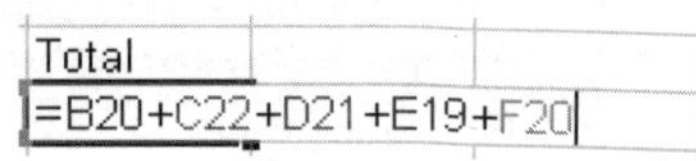

2) Using the **Backspace** or **Delete** key, delete from the formula the argument F20 and the plus operator (+) in front of it.

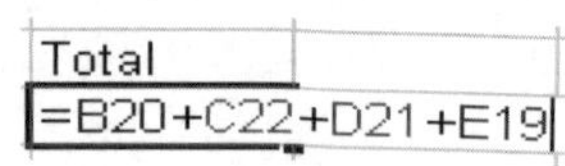

3) When finished press **Enter**.

   Excel now displays in *G20* the result of adding *B20*, *C22*, *D21* and *E19* only.

Combining operators

You can enter more than one type of operator in a single formula. In Exercise 20.9, you will enter formulas that contain both the addition and the subtraction operators.

Exercise 20.9: Formulas with multiple operators

Your company produces four products. They have fixed costs, variable costs, discounts and prices as set out in the cells shown below.

Your task is to enter formulas to calculate the total costs for each product, and to determine the profit for each product.

	A	B	C	D	E	F	G
25	Name	Fixed	Variable	Total	Discount	Price	Profit
26	Product 1	12	2		2	21	
27	Product 2	34	6		8	56	
28	Product 3	56	28		12	112	
29	Product 4	127	92		19	290	

1) Enter the numbers and text in the cells as shown above.
2) Enter the formulas shown on the right in cells *D26*, *D27*, *D28* and *D29*.

   When you press **Enter** after typing each formula, Excel displays the calculated result.

D	→	D
Total		Total
=B26+C26		14
=B27+C27		40
=B28+C28		84
=B29+C29		219

3) Enter the formulas shown on the right in cells *G26*, *G27*, *G28* and *G29*.

   When you press **Enter** after typing each formula, Excel displays the calculated result as shown.

   That is, the profit on each product is its price minus the sum of the total cost and the discount.

G	→	G
Profit		Profit
=F26-(D26+E26)		5
=F27-(D27+E27)		8
=F28-(D28+E28)		16
=F29-(D29+E29)		52

Formulas: using constants

Excel formulas can contain numbers instead of (or as well as) cell references. Excel calls these numbers 'constants'.

Constant
An argument in a formula that is a fixed number.

Here are some examples of formulas containing both cell references and constants:

26*109 =45*(A12+3) =B2/100-B3/50

You can even enter formulas that contain only constants and no cell references, as shown in Exercise 20.10.

Exercise 20.10: Entering constant-only formulas

1) Enter the following in cell *B32*: =32/4

   Excel displays the result (8) in *B32*.

Formulas: the rules of arithmetic

Excel allows you to combine addition, subtraction, multiplication and division in a single formula. For example:

=C5*(A4+A7)-(C4/C7)

Excel follows the rules of arithmetic in calculating such formulas:

- Division first, followed by multiplication, then addition, and finally subtraction.

  For example, the following formula gives a result of 11 because Excel first multiplies 2 by 3 (resulting in 6) and then adds 5.

  =5+2*3
- You can use parentheses (brackets) to force Excel to calculate your formula in a particular order.

  For example, the following formula gives a result of 21 because Excel first adds 5 and 2 (because they are within parentheses) and then multiplies that result by 3 to give 21.

  =(5+2)*3

  Ensure that you follow every opening bracket that you type with a matching closing bracket. For example:

  6/2*3+4=13

  6/(2*3)+4=5

  6/2*(3+4)=21

  6/(2*(3+4))=0.42857

Here's a way to help you remember the order of precedence among arithmetical operators:

Oh **D**ear! **M**y **A**unt **S**ally!

Fixed-factor calculations

In some calculations, you need to apply the same number or factor several times to different numbers. The fixed factor may be a currency exchange rate, for example, or an employee tax rate, or a sales commission rate.

It is best to place such a fixed factor in a cell of its own, and enter its cell reference as needed in formulas. Exercise 20.11 provides an example.

Exercise 20.11: Sales commission and tax calculations

Your company employs four sales representatives: Edgar, Sheila, Wallace and Deirdre. In addition to a basic salary, each receives commission of 20% on goods sold. All four are taxed at a rate of 15%.

Given the information displayed below, use Excel formulas to calculate the net income of each employee.

	B	C	D	E	F	G	H
34							
35	Comm. Rate		0.2				
36	Tax Rate		0.15				
37							
38							
39	Person	Basic	Sales	Comm.	Gross	Tax	Net Income
40	Edgar	1200	3000				
41	Sheila	1300	3100				
42	Wallace	1600	3500				
43	Deirdre	1700	3800				

1) Enter the numbers and text in the cells as shown above. You enter 20% as .2 and 15% as .15. Excel displays your entered numbers as 0.2 and 0.15.
2) To calculate each employee's sales commission, gross income, tax payment and net income, enter the formulas as shown below.

Comm.	Gross	Tax	Net Income
=D40*D35	=C40+E40	=F40*D36	=F40-G40
=D41*D35	=C41+E41	=F41*D36	=F41-G41
=D42*D35	=C42+E42	=F42*D36	=F42-G42
=D43*D35	=C43+E43	=F43*D36	=F43-G43

3) When you press **Enter** after typing each formula, Excel displays the calculated result as shown below.

Comm.	Gross	Tax	Net Income
600	1800	270	1530
620	1920	288	1632
700	2300	345	1955
760	2460	369	2091

Exercise 20.12 provides an example of currency conversions, which are another type of fixed-factor calculation.

Exercise 20.12: Currency conversion calculations

Your company sells a range of five products, priced at £100, £150, £200, £250 and £300, to the USA and Japan. The sterling-to-dollar exchange rate is 1.64, and the sterling-to-yen rate is 170.94.

Your task is to create a currency conversion table that shows the prices of your products in sterling, dollars and yen.

1) Enter the text labels and numbers as shown below.

	B	C	D
45			
46	GBP/USD	1.64	
47	GBP/JPY	170.94	
48			
49	Sterling	Dollars	Yen
50	100		
51	150		
52	200		
53	250		
54	300		

2) In cells *C50* to *C54*, enter formulas to calculate the price of each product in dollars, obtained by multiplying its price in sterling by the exchange rate in cell *C46*.

In cells *D50* to *D54*, enter formulas to calculate the price of each product in yen, obtained by multiplying its price in sterling by the exchange rate in cell *C47*.

The formulas are as shown.

Dollars	Yen
=B50*C46	=B50*C47
=B51*C46	=B51*C47
=B52*C46	=B52*C47
=B53*C46	=B53*C47
=B54*C46	=B54*C47

When you press **Enter** after typing each formula, Excel displays the calculated result as shown on the right.

	B	C	D
45			
46	GBP/USD	1.64	
47	GBP/JPY	170.94	
48			
49	Sterling	Dollars	Yen
50	100	164	17094
51	150	246	25641
52	200	328	34188
53	250	410	42735
54	300	492	51282

Calculations and recalculations

In Exercises 20.1 to 20.12, you learnt how to use your £1000 computer as a £10 pocket calculator! You have performed calculations using handfuls of numbers but you can imagine how you could use the same methods to record and calculate hundreds or even thousands of numbers on a worksheet.

The power and convenience of a spreadsheet is not so much the ability to calculate as the ability to recalculate. Excel will recalculate the result of an addition (or other type of operation) whenever any of the numbers that make up the operation are changed.

Let's try it and see.

Exercise 20.13: Recalculating an addition

In Exercise 20.1, you entered the number 25 in cell *B4*.

1) Click *B4*, type 52, and press **Enter**.

   Notice how Excel recalculates *B5* (the 'answer cell'), and displays the new result.

   Just two numbers are added in this exercise, but it could as easily have been hundreds or more.

B
Add
1275
52
1300

→

B
Add
1275
52
1327

Exercise 20.14: Recalculating a multiplication

In Exercise 20.12, you entered a sterling-to-dollar exchange rate of 1.64 in cell *C46*, and a sterling-to-yen rate of 170.94 in cell *C47*.

1) Click *C46*, type 1.68, and press **Enter**.
2) Click *C47*, type 170.92, and press **Enter**.

   Notice how Excel recalculates the foreign currency amounts for all five products, as shown below.

	B	C	D
45			
46	GBP/USD	1.68	
47	GBP/JPY	170.92	
48			
49	Sterling	Dollars	Yen
50	100	168	17092
51	150	252	25638
52	200	336	34184
53	250	420	42730
54	300	504	51276

To gain an appreciation of the power of spreadsheets, imagine Excel recalculating the prices for hundreds of products.

As further practice, revisit Exercise 20.11, change the commission rate (in *D35*), the tax rate (in *D36*), and note the effect on the employees' commission, gross and net income columns.

Error messages: when bad things happen

If a formula cannot calculate a result properly, Excel displays an error message in the calculated cell indicating the type of error that has taken place. Here are the main error messages that you are likely to meet when following this ECDL module.

#####
Your cell contains a number or a calculation result that is too wide for the cell to display. This is not really an error: Excel has the correct information, it just can't display it. You will learn about adjusting column width in Chapter 21.

#VALUE!
Your formula contains text (or a cell reference that points to a cell containing text) instead of a number. Edit the formula or cell to fix the problem.

#DIV./0!
You have tried to divide a number by zero, or by a cell reference that points to a cell containing a zero.

You will see the same error message if you try to divide a number by a cell reference that points to an empty cell. Excel interprets a blank cell as containing a zero.

#REF!
Typically, your formula contains a cell reference that points to a cell that has been deleted.

Excel's Zoom views

Excel's zoom feature enables you to magnify or reduce the worksheet display. You can use zoom in either of two ways:

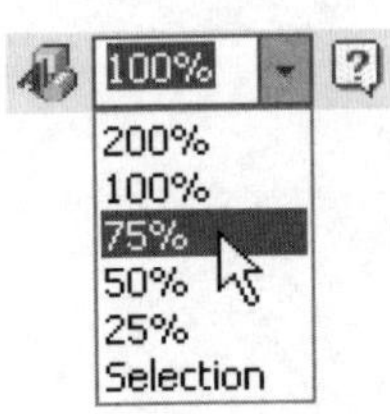

- Click in the *Zoom* box on the *Standard* toolbar, choose one of the listed magnification options or enter any number between 10 and 400, and press **Enter**. (You need not type the per cent (%) symbol.)
- Choose the **View | Zoom** command, and select a magnification option from the *Zoom* dialog box.

You can choose a preset option (*25-200%*), or select *Custom* and enter a number from 10 to 400. Alternatively, select the *Fit selection* option. This magnifies the area surrounding the active cell, or a range of selected cells, so that the cell or cells occupy the full screen. (You will learn about ranges of selected cells in Chapter 21.)

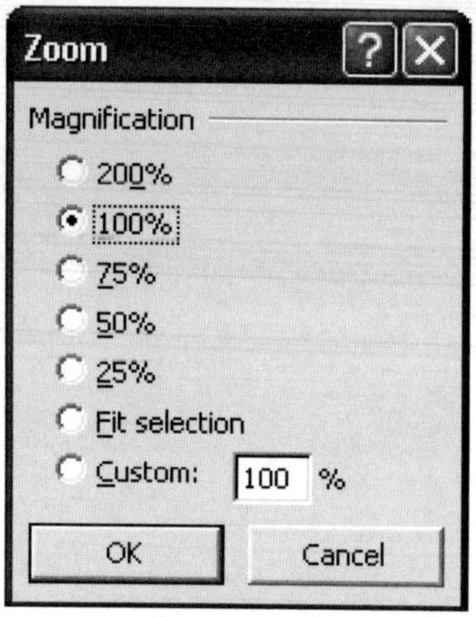

To return from an enlarged or reduced view to normal view, select a magnification of 100% or click the **Undo** button on the *Standard* toolbar.

Zoom and printing

The **Zoom** feature affects only the way that Excel displays a worksheet on-screen and not how Excel prints a worksheet. You will learn how to print a worksheet at a size other than 100% in Chapter 21.

Saving to a floppy disk

Have you been saving your workbook as you go along? You should. It is also a good idea to save a copy of your workbook to a floppy disk. Follow the steps in Exercise 20.15 to learn how.

Exercise 20.15: Saving an Excel workbook to a floppy disk

1) Insert a floppy disk in the floppy disk drive of your computer:
   - If it is a new floppy disk, ensure that it is formatted.
   - If it is a previously used one, ensure that there is sufficient space on it to hold the Excel workbook file. Your workbook should be about 16 KB in size.
2) Choose **File | Save As**, and locate the A: drive.

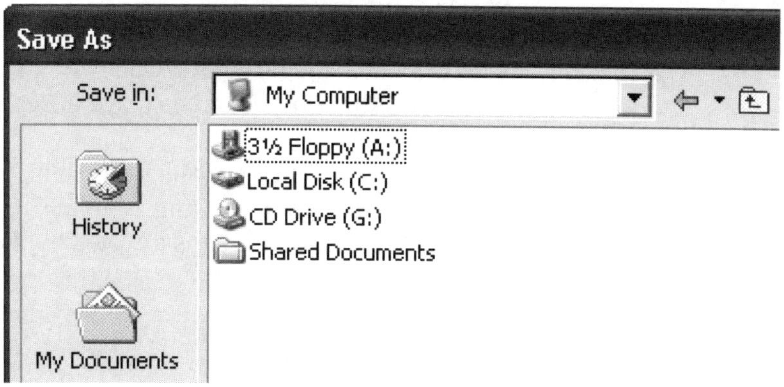

3) Excel suggests the current file name (for example, KenBloggs.xls) for you to accept or amend. Click **Save** to save the file and close the dialog box.
4) When finished, use **File | Save As** again to resave the workbook to its original location on your computer. (You will be asked if you want to replace the original file: click **Yes**.)

   If you do not resave your workbook at its original location, saving the file in future (by clicking the **Save** button on the *Standard* toolbar or choosing **File | Save**) will save the workbook to the floppy disk and not to your computer's hard disk.

You have now completed the second chapter of the ECDL spreadsheets module. You can close your workbook and Excel.

Chapter summary: so now you know

You can perform calculations on worksheet cells in two ways: using *formulas* and using *functions*. A formula begins with an 'equals' symbol (=) and contains one or more operators, for example addition (+), subtraction (-), multiplication (*) or division (/).

The components or *arguments* of a formula can be cell references, numbers or both. A sample formula would be:

=A12+B12+3

A single formula may contain *operators* of different types – addition and multiplication, for example. Excel follows the rules of arithmetic in calculating formulas: multiplication and division are done first, addition and subtraction second. You can use parentheses (brackets) to force Excel to calculate your formula in a particular order. The following two formulas, for example, give different results:

=(A1+A2)*B1

=A1+(A2*B1)

Excel stores the result of a calculation in a *calculated cell*, which contains the formula but displays the calculation result.

Excel's *zoom* feature enables you to magnify or reduce the worksheet display. Options range from 10 to 400% of normal size. Only screen display and not printing is affected by the zooming.

If a formula cannot calculate a result properly, Excel displays an *error message* in the calculated cell indicating the type of error that has taken place.

Quick quiz: arithmetic with Excel

Circle the correct answer to each of the following multiple-choice questions about arithmetic in Excel.

Q1	When making calculations, in the absence of brackets Excel performs:
A.	Subtraction first, followed by multiplication, then addition, and finally division.
B.	Division first, followed by multiplication, then subtraction, and finally addition.
C.	Division first, followed by multiplication, then addition, and finally subtraction.
D.	Multiplication first, followed by division, then addition, and finally subtraction.

Q2	If you change the value in a cell, you must re-enter formulas that make reference to that cell to recalculate them.
A.	True.
B.	False.

Q3	The division character in Excel is:
A.	:
B.	!
C.	~
D.	/

Q4	All formulas must begin with an equals (=) sign.
A.	True.
B.	False.

Q5	You can only use one operator in a formula.
A.	True.
B.	False.

Answers

1: C; **2:** B, **3:** D, **4:** A, **5:** B.

Chapter 21: Functions, formatting and printing

In this chapter

Formulas, as you learnt in Chapter 20, enable you to perform calculations on numbers. In this chapter you will discover a second type of calculation method, based on functions. You will also meet the very useful **AutoSum** button.

When you work with numbers, it's important to get the right answers. But it's also important that your answers look good. Excel provides a wide range of formatting, alignment, border and colour features to help you give your worksheets a professional appearance. You will also learn how to change the width of columns and the height of rows.

Other topics in this chapter include adjacent and non-adjacent cell ranges, find-and-replace, headers and footers, and worksheet printing.

New skills

At the end of this chapter you should be able to:

- Use Excel's SUM and Average functions to perform calculations on cells, and use the **AutoSum** button on Excel's *Standard* toolbar.
- Use the MIN/MAX, COUNT and IF functions.
- Select ranges of adjacent and non-adjacent cells.
- Adjust column width and row height.
- Change font, font style (bold and italic), and font size.
- Align cells horizontally and vertically, and rotate cells.
- Apply borders and fills (coloured backgrounds to cells).
- Find, replace and spellcheck items on a worksheet.
- Change page setup and insert headers and footers.
- Print from Excel.

New words

At the end of this chapter you should be able to explain the following terms:

- Function
- Adjacent cell range
- Non-adjacent cell range

Excel functions

You have learnt how Excel's formulas can add, subtract, multiply and divide numbers.

Excel offers a second way to perform calculations: functions.

Function
A predefined formula built in to Excel and used for a specific purpose.

Most Excel functions are of interest only if you are using a spreadsheet for specialized purposes, such as statistical analysis. But the most widely used – SUM, AVERAGE, MIN, MAX and COUNT – are useful to almost everyone.

Upper- or lower-case?

As with row and column letters, you can type function names in upper- or lower-case letters. In the same way that Excel accepts *A4* or *a4*, it accepts SUM or sum, Average or average.

In Excel's online help (and in this book), function names are written in upper case. When entering functions on a worksheet, however, you will find it quicker to type their names in lower-case, because you need not use the **Shift** key.

The SUM function

In Chapter 20, you learnt how to add numbers by using such formulas as:

=B3+B4+B5

You can imagine that addition formulas can become very awkward – and prone to typing errors – when they contain large numbers of arguments; for example, if there were 100 cells to add rather than just three.

Excel's SUM function allows you to calculate the total of a vertical or horizontal list of numbers by entering just three items:

- The name of the function (in this case, SUM).
- The reference of the first cell.
- The reference of the last cell.

The following exercise shows the SUM function in action.

Exercise 21.1: Using the SUM function

1) Open the workbook that you saved in Chapter 20.
2) Click the *Sheet2* tab to display the second worksheet of the workbook.

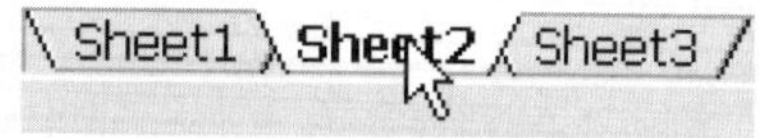

3) In cells *B3*, *B4* and *B5*, enter the numbers 2356, 4921 and 2903.
4) In cells *A3*, *A4* and *A5*, enter the words Conway, Murphy and Smith to label the entered numbers.
5) Type the following function in *B6* and press **Enter**:
   =SUM(B3:B5)

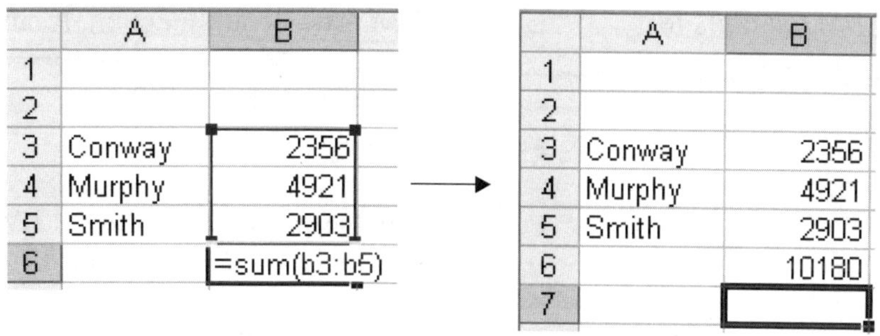

Well done! You have used Excel's SUM function to add numbers.

The AutoSum button

Because SUM is such a commonly used function, Microsoft put a button for it on the *Standard* toolbar.

Exercise 21.2: Using the AutoSum button

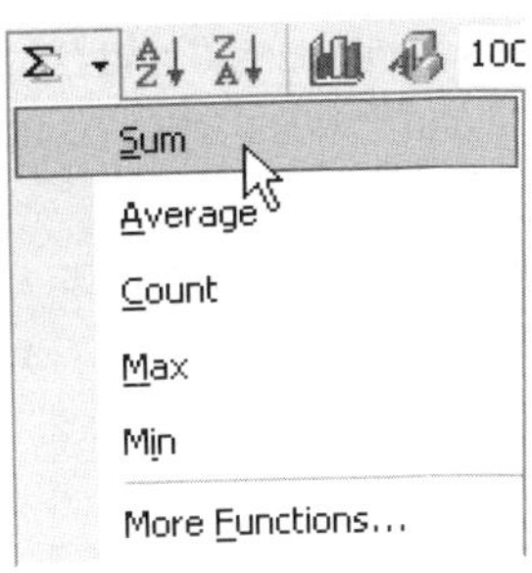

1) Delete the SUM function, entered in Exercise 21.1, from cell *B6*.
2) With *B6* as the active cell, click the down-arrow on the **AutoSum** button on the *Standard* toolbar and choose the *Sum* option.
   Excel tries to 'guess' which cells you want to add together. In this example, it assumes (correctly) that the cells start at *B3* and end at *B5*.
3) Press **Enter** to confirm that *B3*, *B4* and *B5* are the cells for adding.

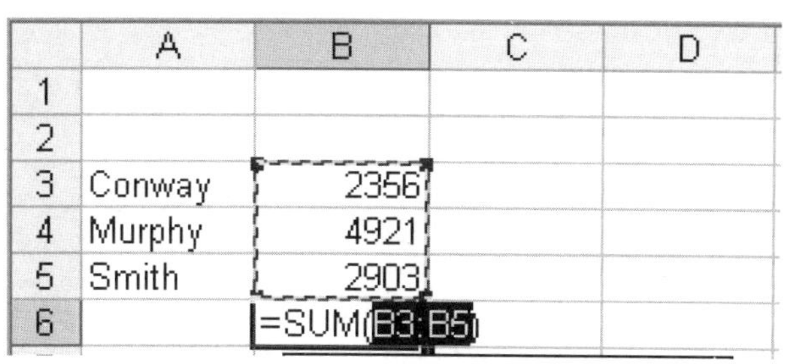

The total is displayed in cell *B6*.

	A	B
1		
2		
3	Conway	2356
4	Murphy	4921
5	Smith	2903
6		10180
7		

SUM tolerates text and spaces

Excel's SUM is a tolerant function. It ignores:

- Cells containing text.
- Empty cells.

For example, the function =SUM(W12:W16) adds whatever numbers it finds in the cells *W12*, *W13*, *W14*, *W15* and *W16*.

If any cell contains text instead of a number, or is empty, the SUM function does not display an error message. It just ignores the non-numeric cells and continues adding up the numeric ones.

In the next exercise you will enter more numbers and text to your worksheet.

Exercise 21.3: Entering more numbers and text

1) On *Sheet2*, enter two further columns of numbers in columns *C* and *D*, as shown below. Across the top of columns *B*, *C*, *D* and *E*, enter a row of labels (text), also as shown below.

   (The month of March is omitted deliberately. You will insert a new column for March in Exercise 22.2 of Chapter 22.)

	A	B	C	D	E
1					
2		January	February	April	Total
3	Conway	2356	3621	4560	
4	Murphy	4921	4055	3542	
5	Smith	2903	3308	3622	

2) Use the **AutoSum** button to total the numbers in rows *3*, *4* and *5*.

   AutoSum enters =SUM(B3:D3) in *E3*, and =SUM(B4:D4) in *E4*.

But, when you click *E5* and then click **AutoSum**, Excel 'guesses' (incorrectly) that you want to add the values in the two cells immediately above it, *E3* and *E4*, as shown on the right.

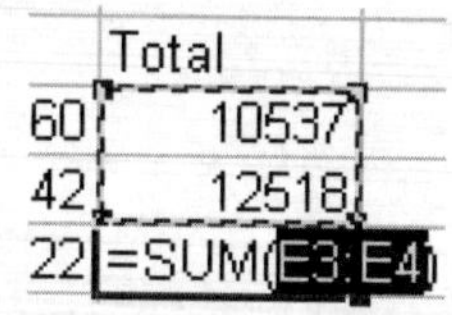

When this happens, double-click *E5* (or press **F2**) to make the cell editable. Next, change the SUM function to =SUM(B5:D5).

3) Use the **AutoSum** button to total, in row *6*, the numbers in each of the columns *C*, *D* and *E*. **AutoSum** enters =SUM(C3:C5) in *C6*, =SUM(D3:D5) in *D6*, and =SUM(E3:E5) in *E6*.

Your worksheet should now look as shown below.

	A	B	C	D	E
1					
2		January	February	April	Total
3	Conway	2356	3621	4560	10537
4	Murphy	4921	4055	3542	12518
5	Smith	2903	3308	3622	9833
6		10180	10984	11724	32888

The Average function

This Excel function – you guessed it – finds the average of a group of numbers.

As with the SUM function, the Average function begins with the = sign. Then follow the function name and finally the arguments within parentheses. You can select the Average function from the menu opened by clicking the down-arrow on the **AutoSum** button on the *Standard* toolbar. Exercise 21.4 provides an example of the Average function in use.

Exercise 21.4: Using the Average function

1) Click the *Sheet1* tab to display the first worksheet in your workbook.

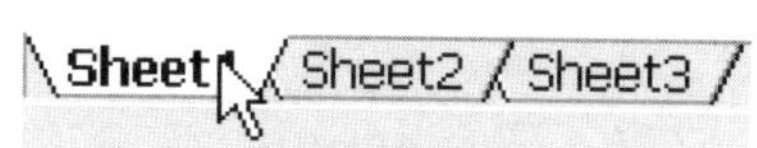

2) In cell *B44*, enter the word: Average
3) With *C44* as the active cell, click the down-arrow on the **AutoSum** button on the *Standard* toolbar and choose the *Average* option.

   Excel 'guesses' (correctly) that it should average the values in cells *C40*, *C41*, *C42* and *C43*, and enters the formula =Average(C40:C43) in *C44*.

   C44 now displays the average value of the contents of cells *C40*, *C41*, *C42* and *C43*.
4) Repeat step 3 for columns *D*, *E*, *F*, *G* and *H* to average the cells immediately above them.

Row 44 should now look as shown.

44	Average	1450	3350	670	2120	318	1802

The MIN and MAX functions

Use the MIN and MAX functions, respectively, to find the smallest and the largest values in a range of cells. This is particularly useful if you have a large range.

Function	Description
=MIN(A1:A80)	Finds the value of the cell with the smallest value in the range A1 to A80.
=MIN(A1:A80, 4)	Finds the value of the cell with the smallest value in the range A1 to A80. If no cell is found with a value less than 4, the value returned is 4.
=MAX(A1:A80)	Finds the value of the cell with the largest value in the range A1 to A80.
=MAX(A1:A80, 555)	Finds the value of the cell with the largest value in the range A1 to A80. If no cell is found with a value above 555, the value returned is 555.

The COUNT function

Use the COUNT function to count the number of rows or columns in a range that contain numbers. For example, if you had a column of purchase order numbers, you could use this function to find out how many purchase orders you had.

Function	Description
=COUNT(A1:A80)	Tells you how many of the cells in the range A1 to A80 contain numeric values.

The IF function

Use the IF function to check if the value in a cell or range of cells satisfies criteria you specify. You can also specify what values are returned if the criteria are met (*TRUE*) or not met (*FALSE*).

The format to use with the IF function is as follows:

=IF(logical_test, value_if_true, value_if_false)

Let's look at some examples of IF statements:

Function	*Description*
=IF(A1>=40%, "PASS", "FAIL")	*Logical test:* A1>=40% *Value if true:* PASS *Value if false:* FAIL Checks the value of the cell A1: if this is greater than 40%, displays the word PASS; otherwise it displays the word FAIL.
=IF(SUM(G44:G53)>=200, "PASS", "FAIL")	*Logical test:* (SUM(G44:G53)>=200 *Value if true:* PASS *Value if false:* FAIL Sums the values of fields G44 to G53. If this is greater than 200, displays the word PASS; otherwise it displays the word FAIL.
=IF(A5>A4, "Trend up", "Trend down")	*Logical test:* A5>A4 *Value if true:* Trend up *Value if false:* Trend down Checks if the value of A5 is greater than that of A4. If it is, displays the words 'Trend up'; if it is not, displays the words 'Trend down'.

Formatting and aligning single cells

Formatting refers to the *appearance* of numbers and text in cells. It includes such actions as making cell content bolder (heavier) and putting it in italics.

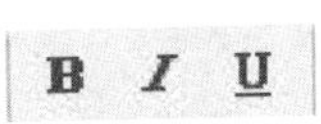

Format buttons

Alignment buttons

The *position* of numbers and text within cells is called alignment. Three common options are left, centred and right. The quickest way to apply a formatting or alignment option to a cell is to select it and then click the relevant button on Excel's *Formatting* toolbar.

You will now learn how to format and align cells on a worksheet – in this case, *Sheet2* of your workbook.

Exercise 21.5: Formatting and aligning cells

1) On *Sheet2* of your workbook, click cell *B2*.
2) Click the **Bold** button on the *Formatting* toolbar. Excel displays the word 'January' in bold.

3) Click the **Center-align** button on the *Formatting* toolbar. Excel centre-aligns the word 'January'.
4) Click cell *A3*, and then click the **Italic** button on the *Formatting* toolbar. Excel displays the word 'Conway' in italics.

Wrapping cell content

You can ensure that a cell expands in size to fit all of its content, and that it does not encroach upon its neighbouring cells.

Select the cells whose content you want to wrap, and choose **Format | Cells.** Then on the **Alignment** tab check the *Wrap text* box.

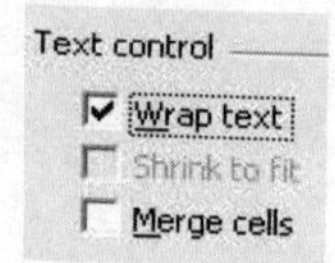

Before wrapping

Stephen M	Andy O'Ro	Johnny Ma	Mike Joyce

After wrapping

Stephen Morrissey	Andy O'Rourke	Johnny Marr	Mike Joyce

Merging cells and centring content

You can merge a number of cells and then centre their content over a range of columns. This is useful when you want to put a text heading on your worksheet.

Select the cells whose content you want to merge, and choose **Format | Cells.** Then on the **Alignment** tab check the *Merge cells* box.

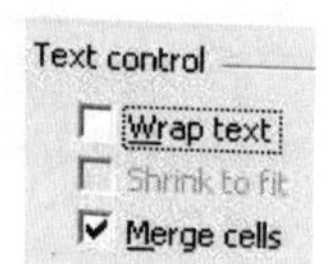

Before merging and centring

Sales Commission and Tax					
Person	Basic	Sales	Comm.	Gross	Tax
edgar	1200	3000			
Sheila	1300	3100			
Wallace	1600	3500			
Deirdre	1700	3800			

After merging and centring

Sales Commission and Tax					
Person	Basic	Sales	Comm.	Gross	Tax
edgar	1200	3000			
Sheila	1300	3100			
Wallace	1600	3500			
Deirdre	1700	3800			

Formatting and aligning cell groups

You can save time and mouse-clicks by formatting or aligning a group of cells in one, single operation. Before you can do so, you must first select the group of cells.

You can select a group of cells by clicking the top-left cell in the group, and then dragging the mouse across the other cells. Exercise 21.6 shows you how.

Exercise 21.6: Formatting and aligning a cell range

1) Click cell *C2*.

2		**January**	February	April	Total
3	*Conway*	2356	3621	4560	10537

2) Drag the mouse across to cell *E2*.

2		**January**	February	April	Total

3) Click the **Bold** button on the *Formatting* toolbar.
4) Click the **Center-align** button on the *Formatting* toolbar.
5) Select cell *A4*.
6) Drag the mouse down to cell *A5*.
7) Click the **Italic** button on the *Formatting* toolbar.

   Click anywhere on the worksheet outside the selected cells *A4* and *A5* to deselect the two cells.

   Sheet2 should now look as shown.

	A	B	C	D	E
1					
2		**January**	**February**	**April**	**Total**
3	*Conway*	2356	3621	4560	10537
4	*Murphy*	4921	4055	3542	12518
5	*Smith*	2903	3308	3622	9833
6		10180	10984	11724	32888

Cancelling a selection

Finished formatting your selected cells? Or selected the wrong cells? To cancel a selection, click anywhere outside the selected cell or range.

Cancelling a selection does not delete the cell or range from the worksheet. It just deselects the selected cells.

Cell ranges

In Excel, a group of cells in a worksheet is known as a cell range.

Cell range
A group of cells in a worksheet.

Cell ranges are of two kinds: adjacent and non-adjacent.

Adjacent cell range
A group of cells that are directly beside, above or below one another. Adjacent cells are sometimes called contiguous cells.

You identify an adjacent cell range by:

- The cell reference of the top-left cell.
- A colon (:).
- The cell reference of the bottom-right cell.

For example, the adjacent cell range *A1:B2* includes the following four cells: *A1*, *A2*, *B1* and *B2*.

Adjacent cell ranges may also include cells in one column only (for example, *B2:B5*) or in one row only (for example, *D9:F9*).

Non-adjacent cell range

Can you select cells that are located on different parts of a worksheet as a single range? Yes. This is what Excel calls a non-adjacent cell range.

Non-adjacent cell range
A group of cells that are not directly beside, above or below one another. Also called non-contiguous cells.

A non-adjacent cell range can consist of individual cells dotted around the worksheet. Or, as in Exercise 21.7, it can contain a number of smaller sub-groups of adjacent cells.

You select a non-adjacent cell range by selecting the first cell (or first sub-group of adjacent cells), holding down the **Ctrl** key, and then selecting further cells (or adjacent ranges).

A non-adjacent cell range is written with commas to separate the individual cells (for example, *A2,B3,C4*) or the smaller sub-groups of adjacent cells (for example, *A2:A6,H4:H8*).

Exercise 21.7: Selecting a non-adjacent cell range

1) Select the first cell or sub-group of adjacent cells. For example, *B2:B6* (that is, cells *B2*, *B3*, *B4*, *B5* and *B6*).

	A	B	C	D	E
1					
2		**January**	**February**	**April**	**Total**
3	*Conway*	2356	3621	4560	10537
4	*Murphy*	4921	4055	3542	12518
5	*Smith*	2903	3308	3622	9833
6		10180	10984	11724	32888

2) Hold down the **Ctrl** key.

3) Select the next cell or next sub-group of adjacent cells. For example, cell range *E2:E6*.

	A	B	C	D	E
1					
2		**January**	**February**	**April**	**Total**
3	*Conway*	2356	3621	4560	10537
4	*Murphy*	4921	4055	3542	12518
5	*Smith*	2903	3308	3622	9833
6		10180	10984	11724	32888

You can continue this process until you have selected all the cells in the non-adjacent range that you want to select.

Click anywhere outside the cell range to cancel the selection.

Selected cells and the active cell

In Chapter 19 you learnt how to select a single cell – by clicking it with the mouse, moving the cursor to it with the arrow keys, or entering its cell reference in the *Name Box*. That cell is then the active cell.

So, for a single cell, the terms 'active cell' and 'selected cell' mean the same thing. And 'select a cell' is simply another way of saying 'make a cell the active cell'.

While you can select any number of cells at one time, only one cell can be the active cell. Excel displays selected cells in reverse (white text on dark background). The active cell in a set of selected cells is shown as black text on a white background.

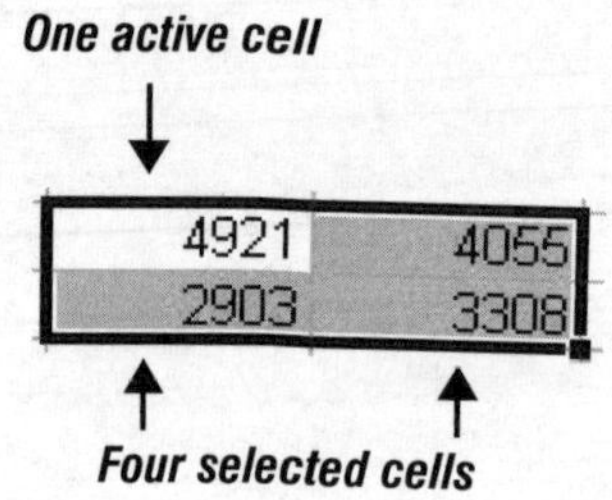

F8: Excel's Select key

In Exercise 21.6 you selected an adjacent cell range by selecting the first cell, and then dragging the mouse across the other cells in the range.

An alternative method is to select the first cell, press **F8**, and then press the arrow keys to extend the selected area over the other cells. **F8** is Excel's **Select** key. You may find this method faster than using the mouse, but you can use it only for selecting adjacent cell ranges.

Selecting columns and rows

Excel offers quick ways of selecting one or more rows or columns.

- To select an entire row, click the row heading.

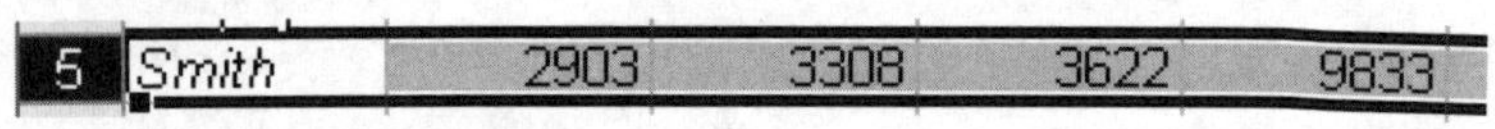

- To select several adjacent rows, click the top or bottom one, and hold down the mouse button as you drag down or up.
- To select several non-adjacent rows, click the first, hold down the **Ctrl** key, and click the others.
- To select an entire column, click the column heading.
- To select several adjacent columns, click one and then drag with the mouse to the right or left.
- To select several non-adjacent columns, click the heading of the first, hold down the **Ctrl** key, and click the headings of the others.

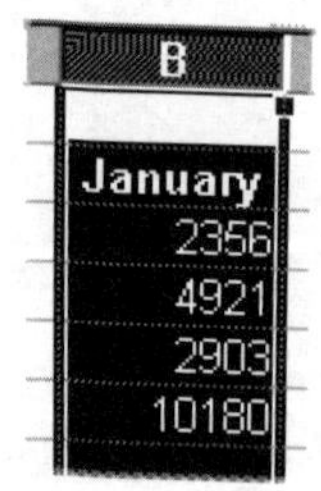

Deleting row and column contents

To delete the contents of one or a selection of rows or columns, select the rows or columns, and press the **Delete** key.

This operation removes only the row or column cell contents, leaving behind empty rows or columns. It does not delete the actual rows or columns. You will learn how to remove rows and columns from worksheets in Chapter 22.

Hiding rows and columns

You can hide rows and columns in an Excel worksheet. Data contained in hidden cells is still available for and included in calculations.

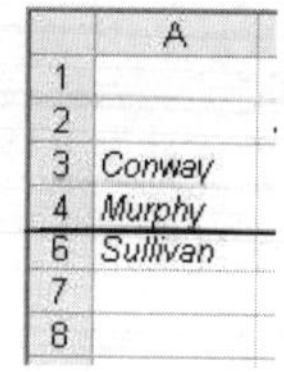

- To hide a row, click on a cell in the row, and choose **Format | Row | Hide**. In the example on the right, row *5* is hidden.
- To hide a column, click on a cell in the column, and choose **Format | Column | Hide**.
- To unhide a row, select cells in the rows on either side of the row you want to unhide, and choose **Format | Row | Unhide**.
- To unhide a column, select cells in the columns on either side of the row you want to unhide, and choose **Format | Column | Unhide**.

Freezing row and column titles

If your worksheet extends beyond one screen in length, you won't be able to see the column headings when you scroll down. Similarly, if your worksheet is wider than the screen, you won't be able to see row headings. To overcome this problem, Excel enables you to *freeze* the row and column titles so that they are always visible when you scroll.

Exercise 21.8: Freezing column titles

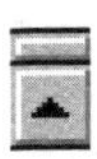

Vertical split box

1) Open the worksheet you've been working on.
2) Click and drag the vertical split box, located at the top of the vertical scroll bar to just below row 1.
3) Choose **Window | Freeze Panes**. The split divider is now replaced by a line.

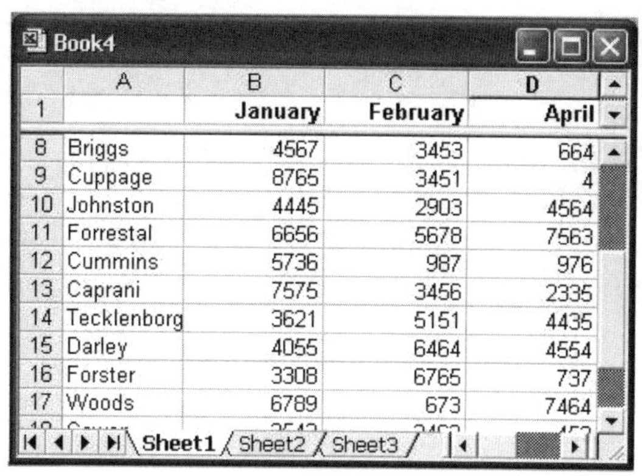

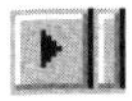

Horizontal split box

To freeze row titles, follow the same procedure using the horizontal split box.

To unfreeze the panes, choose **Window | Unfreeze Panes.**

Selecting an entire worksheet

To select a whole worksheet, click the top-left of the worksheet, where the row heading meets the column heading.

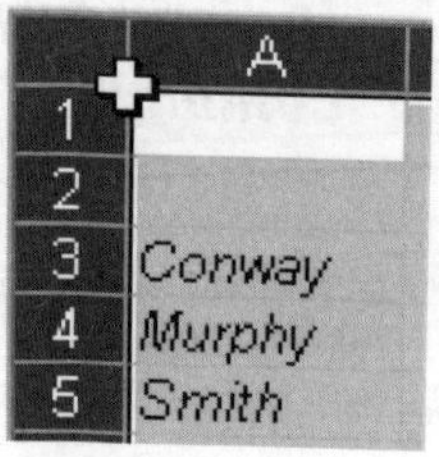

A fast way to delete the contents of all cells on a worksheet is to select the entire worksheet, and then press **Delete**.

Adjusting column width and row height

You can change the appearance of your worksheet by adjusting the width of one or more columns, or the height of one or more rows.

- **Column width:** To change the width of a column, move the mouse to the column heading, and then drag the boundary on the right side of the column heading until the column is the width you want. See Exercise 21.9.
- **Row height:** To change the row height, move the mouse to the row heading, and then drag the boundary below the row heading until the row is the height you want. See Exercise 21.10.

Exercise 21.9: Adjusting column width

1) In the column heading of *Sheet2*, click the boundary line between columns *A* and *B*.

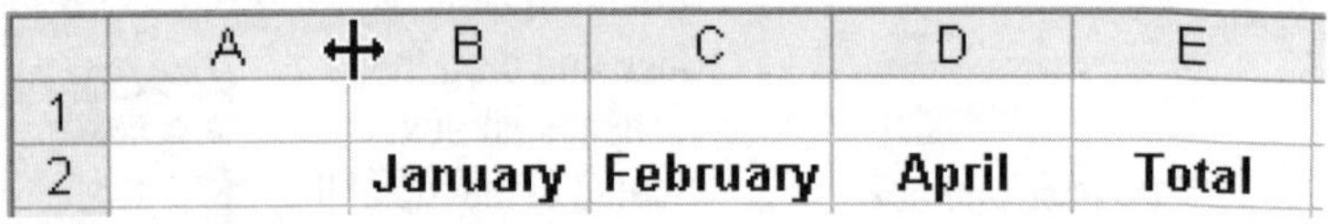

2) Drag the boundary to the left, making column *A* narrower.

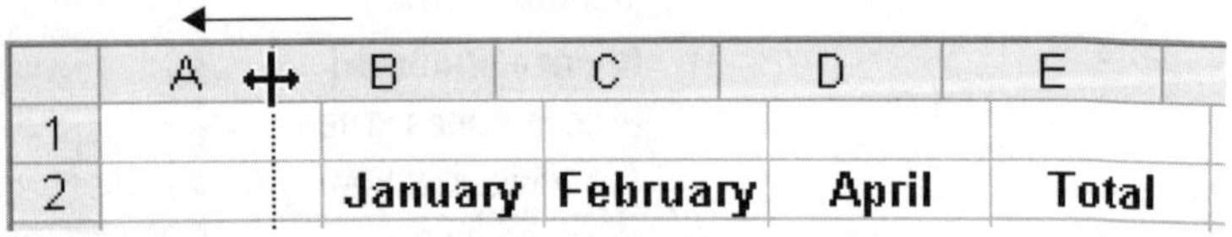

3) Reverse the effect of step 2 by dragging the column *A* boundary to the right, so restoring column *A* to its original width.

Exercise 21.10: Adjusting row height

1) In the row heading, click the boundary between rows *2* and *3*.

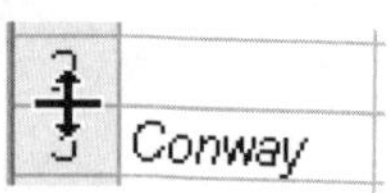

2) Drag the line down about one centimetre until it looks like that shown below.

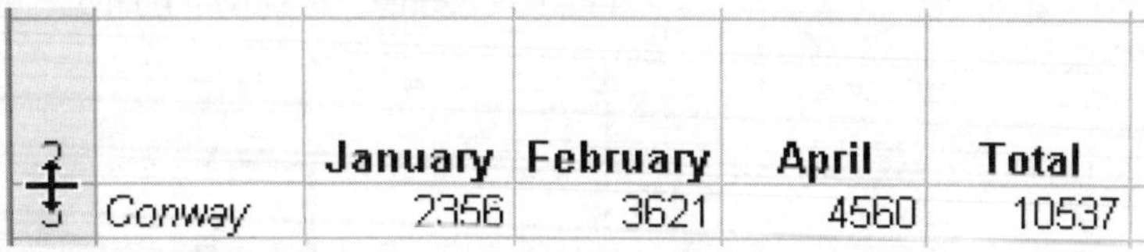

Well done. You have changed the height of a row on your worksheet. Leave the row at its increased height for Exercise 21.11.

Vertical alignment

The three alignment buttons (left, centre and right) on the *Formatting* toolbar enable you to position cell contents horizontally (left to right). Excel also allows you to align cell contents vertically (top to bottom). Exercise 21.11 provides an example of vertical alignment.

Exercise 21.11: Changing vertical alignment

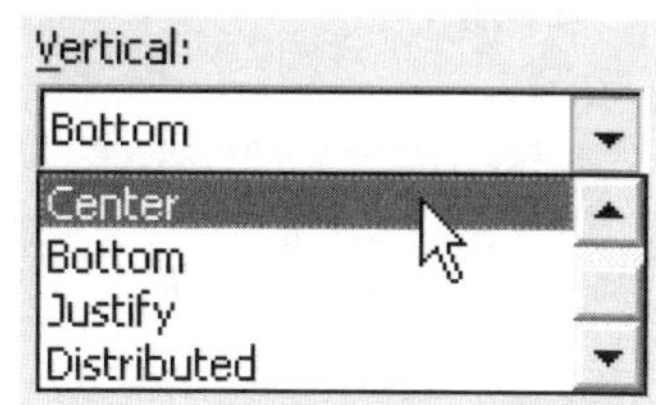

1) Select cell range *B2:E2* in row *2*, whose height you increased in Exercise 21.10.
2) Choose **Format | Cells**, select the *Alignment* tab, and select the alignment option you want from the *Vertical* list – in this case the *Center* option , and click **OK**.

   Excel now aligns the cells' content vertically so that it is centred between the top and bottom of the cells' boundaries.

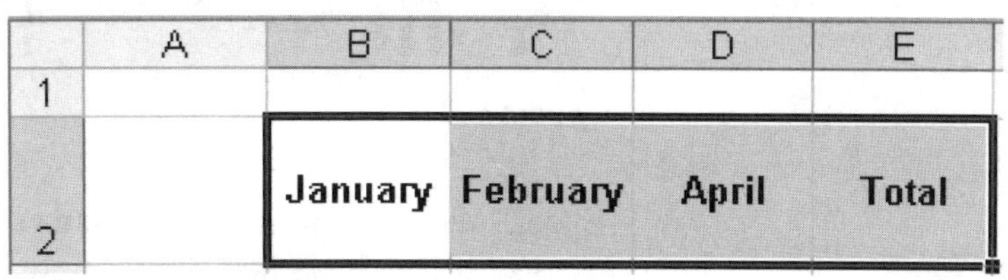

3) Click once on the **Undo** button on the *Standard* toolbar to return the cells to the default vertical alignment of *Bottom*, and then click a second time to return the row to its original, normal height.

Orientation

Another Excel formatting feature is the ability to rotate or orient the text or numbers at a specified angle within a cell. See Exercise 21.12.

Exercise 21.12: Rotating cell content

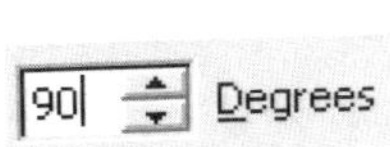

1) Select cell range *B2:E2*, choose **Format | Cells**, select the **Alignment** tab, type 90 in the *Degrees* box, and click **OK**.

Excel now rotates the cells' content so that it is positioned at ninety degrees to the horizontal, as shown below.

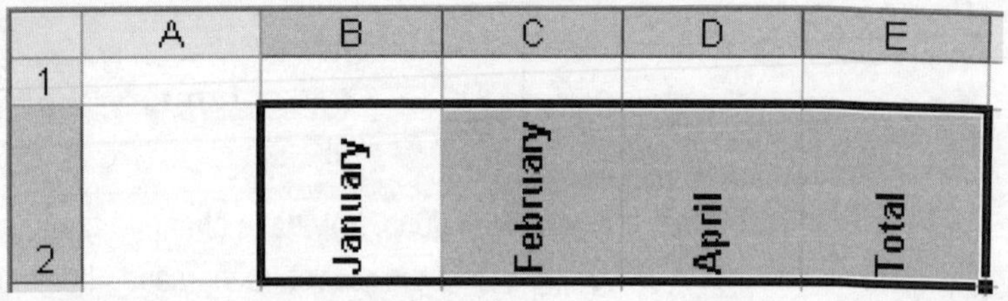

2) Click the **Undo** button on the *Standard* toolbar to return the cells' orientation to the default value of zero degrees.

Entering a positive number in the *Degree* box rotates the cell content from lower left to upper right. A negative number of degrees rotates the cell content from upper left to lower right.

Fonts

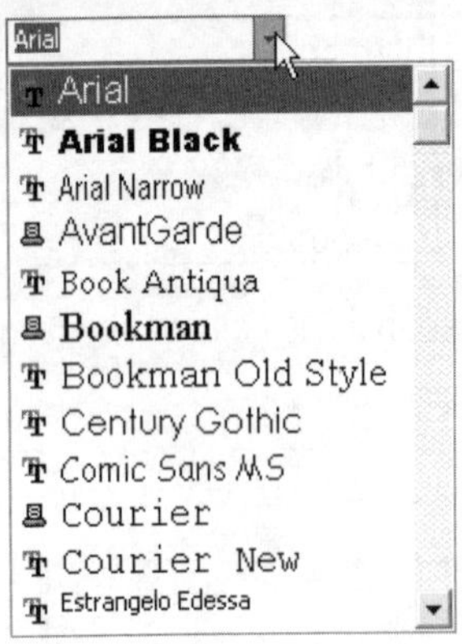

A font (also called a typeface) is a particular style of text. What fonts are installed on your computer? Click the arrow on the drop-down *Font* box on Excel's *Formatting* toolbar to see.

There are really just two kinds (families) of fonts: serif and sans serif. Sans serif just means without serifs. You can recognize which family a font belongs to by asking: Do its characters have serifs (tails or squiggles) at their edges?

Profit	**Profit**
A serif font	***A sans serif font***

Excel's default font is Arial, a sans serif font. The most commonly used serif font is named Times New Roman. Arial and other sans serif fonts are usually better for displaying numbers. You may want to use a serif font for worksheet labels.

Font
A typeface: a particular style of text. The two main font families are serif and sans serif.

You can change the font of any cell or cell range by first selecting the cells and then choosing a new font from the drop-down list on the *Formatting* toolbar.

Font sizes

Font size is measured in a non-metric unit called the point, with approximately 72 points equal to one inch. Excel's default font is 10 point.

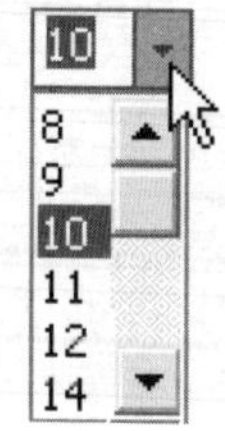

You can change the font size of any cell or cell range by first selecting the cells, and then choosing a new font size from the drop-down list on the *Formatting* toolbar.

Font colours

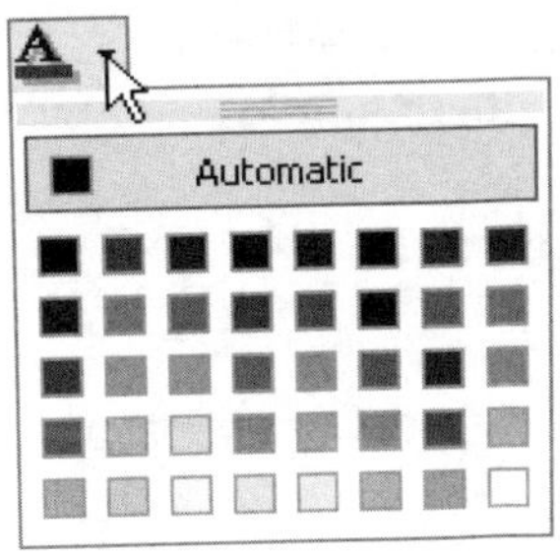

You can change the colour of cell contents from Excel's default of Automatic. What colour is Automatic? Automatic is black, unless the cell background is black or a dark grey, in which case Automatic switches to white.

You can change the colour of the text or numbers displayed in any cell or cell range by first selecting the cells, clicking the arrow on the right of the **Font Color** button on the *Formatting* toolbar, and then clicking a colour.

In the next exercise you will practise changing the fonts, font sizes and colours of the labels in *Sheet1* of your workbook.

Exercise 21.13: Changing fonts, font sizes and colours

1) Click the *Sheet1* tab to display the first worksheet of your workbook.
2) Click cell *B2*. Hold down the **Ctrl** key and click also on the following cells: *D2*, *F2* and *H2*.
3) From the *Formatting* toolbar, change the font to Times New Roman, the font size to 12 point, and the font colour to dark blue. Next, click the **Bold** and **Center-align** buttons.

   Your worksheet should now look as follows.

Add	Subtract	Multiply	Divide
1275	1275	1275	1275
52	25	25	25
1327	1250	31875	51

Underlining

You can also underline text in cells. Select the cells you want to underline, and choose **Format | Cells**. Then select the type of underlining you want: single, double, single accounting or double accounting. The accounting underlining adds extra space above the underlines.

Cell borders

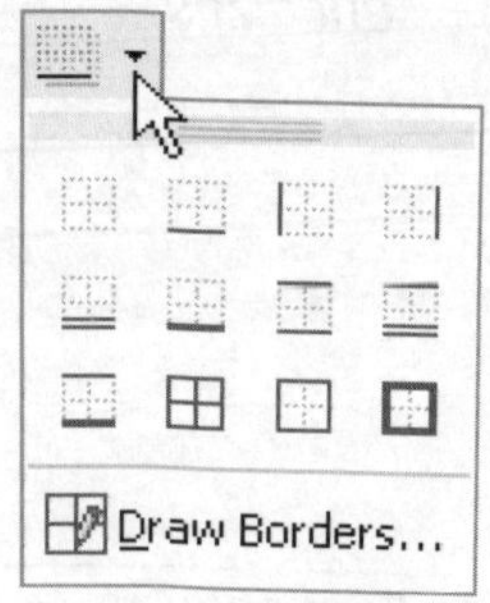

Excel provides a wide choice of borders that you can use to highlight a particular cell or cell range – such as cells containing sub- and final totals on a worksheet. You can access these options by clicking the arrow on the right of the **Borders** button on the *Formatting* toolbar.

The most commonly used cell border options are the single bottom line (the default), the double and heavier bottom lines, and the outline. The last places a border on all four sides of the selected cells. Exercise 21.14 provides an example.

Exercise 21.14: Placing a bottom border on cells

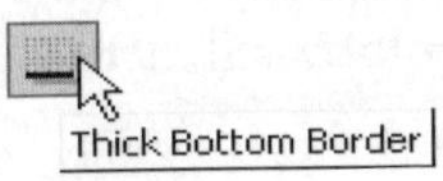

1) Select the non-adjacent cells *B4*, *D4*, *F4* and *H4*.
2) Click the arrow on the right of the **Borders** button, and, from the list of options displayed, select *Thick Bottom Border.*
   Your worksheet should now look as shown.

Add	Subtract	Multiply	Divide
1275	1275	1275	1275
52	25	25	25
1327	1250	31875	51

Cell colour backgrounds

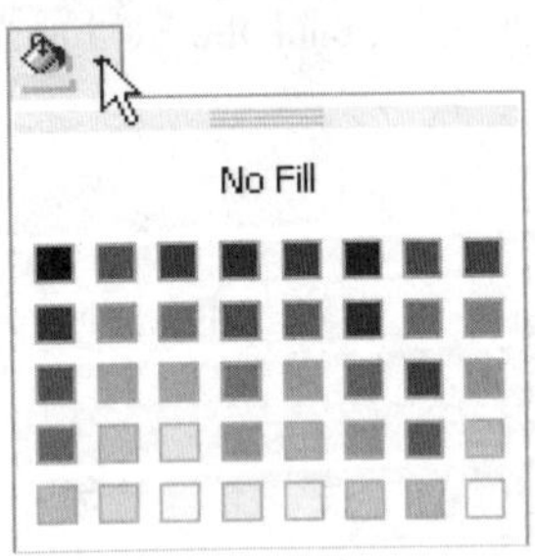

As with cell borders, Excel allows you to change the background colour of a cell – what Excel calls the Fill Color.

You access this option by clicking the arrow on the right of the **Fill Color** button on the *Formatting* toolbar.

Exercise 21.15 provides an example.

Exercise 21.15: Changing the fill colour

1) Select the adjacent cell range *B25:H25*.
2) Click the arrow on the right of the **Fill Color** button, and click the **Yellow** button.
   The background of the selected cells turns yellow.

In Exercise 21.16 you will practise your cell border and fill colour skills further.

Exercise 21.16: Further cell border and colour practice

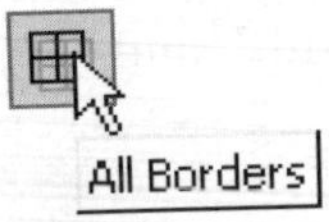

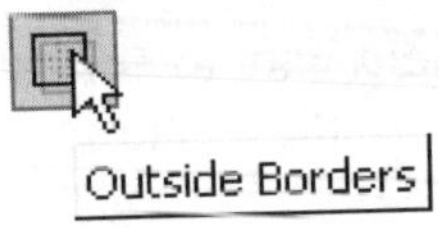

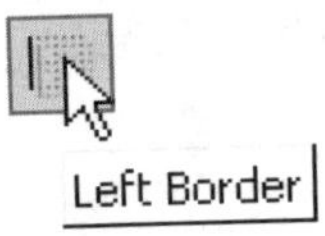

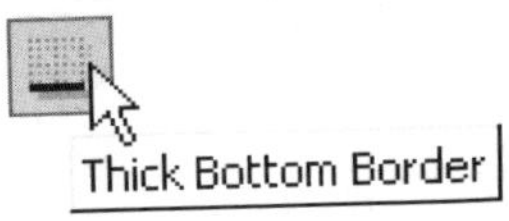

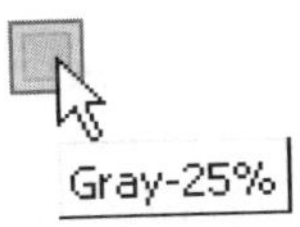

1) Select the adjacent cell range *A25:G29*.
2) Click the arrow on the right of the **Borders** button, and select *All Borders*.
3) Select cell range *B35:D36*.
4) Click the arrow on the right of the **Borders** button, and select *Outside Borders*.
5) Select cell range *D35:D36*.
6) Click the arrow on the right of the **Borders** button, and select *Left Border*.
7) Select cell range *B43:H43*.
8) Click the arrow on the right of the **Borders** button, and select *Thick Bottom Border*.
9) Select non-adjacent cell range *B46:C47,B49:D54*.
10) Click the arrow on the right of the **Borders** button, and select *Outside Borders*.
11) With the non-adjacent cell range still selected, click the arrow on the right of the **Fill Colors** button, and select *Gray (25%)*.

Finding cell content

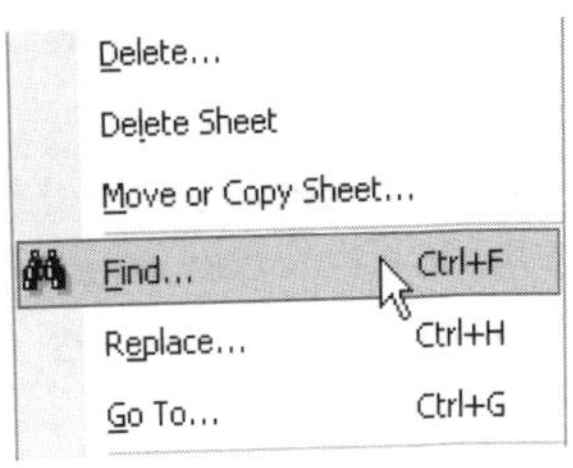

You can search a worksheet for label text, numbers that were entered directly, numbers resulting from calculations, and calculation components (function names, cell references, arithmetic operators and constants) as follows:

- Select the range of cells you want to search. (To search the whole worksheet, click any cell.)
- Choose **Edit | Find**.
- In the *Find what* box, enter the item you want to find, and click **Find Next**.

You can cancel a Find operation in progress by pressing the **Esc** key.

Find options

Excel's Find feature offers the following options:

- **Within:** Select whether to search in the current worksheet only, or in the whole workbook.
- **Search:** Select the direction you want to search in: down through columns, or rightwards across rows.
- **Look in:** The type of cells you want to search through.
- **Match case:** Searches only for characters that match the case of the entered search text. For example, a search for 'smith' does not find 'Smith'.

- **Match entire cell contents:** Searches only for complete matches. For example, a search for 'Sm' does not find 'Smith', and '330' does not find '3308'.

Format Painter

Excel's Format Painter provides a quick, convenient way to copy formatting from one piece of text to another. Follow these steps:

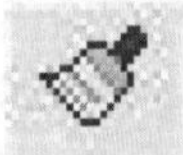

Format Painter button

- Select the cell or range of cells that have the formatting you want to copy.
- Click the **Format Painter** button on the *Standard* toolbar.
- Select the cell or cells to which you want to apply the formatting.

Replacing cell content

Anything that you can search for in a worksheet with **Edit | Find**, you can replace with a specified alternative. For example, you could replace occurrences of cell reference *F34* with *F36*. The procedure is as follows:

- Select the relevant range of cells. (To perform the find-and-replace operation on the whole worksheet, click any cell.)
- Choose **Edit | Replace**.
- In the *Find what* box, enter the item you want to replace. In the *Replace with* box, enter the replacement item. (You can delete from the selected cells the characters in the *Find what* box by leaving the *Replace with* box blank.)
- Select **Find Next**. To replace only the highlighted occurrence of the found characters, select **Replace**.
- To replace all occurrences of the found characters in the selected cells, click **Replace All**.

Exercise 21.17 provides an example of Excel's find-and-replace feature.

Exercise 21.17: Finding and replacing text on a worksheet

1) Click the *Sheet2* tab to display the second worksheet of your workbook.
2) Select the cell range *A2:E6*.
3) Choose **Edit | Replace**. In the *Find what* box, type 'Smith'. In the *Replace with* box, type 'Sullivan'.

4) Select the *Match case* and *Match entire cell contents* options. Select **Replace All**.

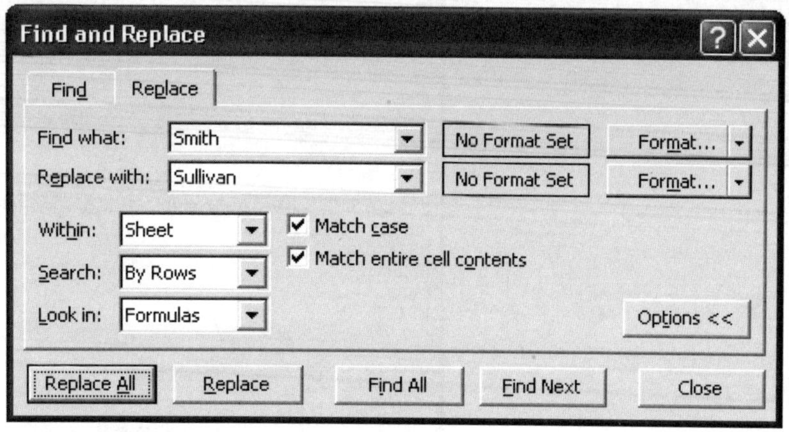

5) *Sheet2* should now look as shown below.

	A	B	C	D	E
1					
2		**January**	**February**	**April**	**Total**
3	*Conway*	2356	3621	4560	10537
4	*Murphy*	4921	4055	3542	12518
5	*Sullivan*	2903	3308	3622	9833
6		10180	10984	11724	32888

Spellchecking

Excel can check the spelling of text on all or part of a worksheet.

To check your spelling, follow this procedure:

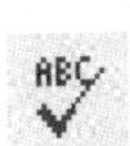

Spelling button

- Select the range of cells whose spelling you want to check. To check the whole worksheet, click any cell.
- Click the **Spelling** button on Excel's *Standard* toolbar.

When Excel meets a word that it does not recognize from its spelling dictionary (the same dictionary used by Microsoft Word), it displays the *Spelling* dialog box, as shown below.

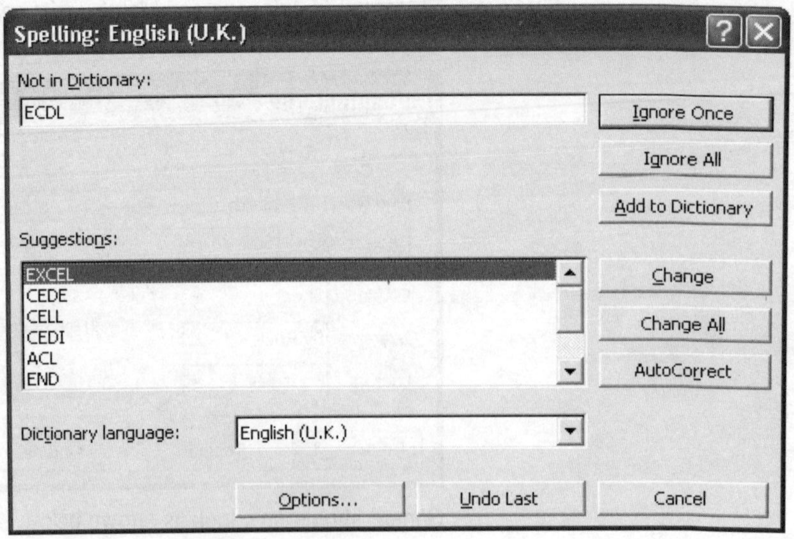

The following are your main options:

- **Ignore Once:** Leave this occurrence of the word unchanged.
- **Ignore All:** Leave this and all other occurrences of the word in the selected cells unchanged.
- **Add to Dictionary:** Add the word to the custom (your personal) dictionary. Use this option for the names of people or places, or abbreviations or acronyms, that you type regularly. Excel will recognize such added words during future spellchecks of any worksheet.
- **Change:** Correct this occurrence of the word, but prompt again on further occurrences.
- **Change All:** Correct this occurrence of the word – and all other occurrences without further prompting.

Practise by spellchecking *Sheet1* and *Sheet2* of your workbook.

Page setup

In the remainder of this chapter you will learn about Excel's various printing options, beginning with those available on the four tabs of the *Page Setup* dialog box (opened by selecting **File | Page Setup**): the **Page**, **Margins**, **Header/Footer** and **Sheet** tabs.

Orientation

Located on the **Page** tab of the *Page Setup* dialog box, orientation is the direction in which the page is printed. Your options are *Portrait* ('standing up') and *Landscape* ('on its side').

First page number

Use the *First page number* box to change the page number of the first page in your worksheet. The default is Auto.

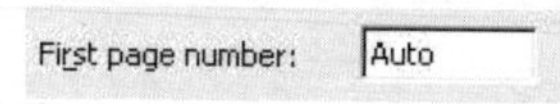

Scaling

Two scaling options on the **Page** tab enable you to reduce or enlarge the worksheet printout:

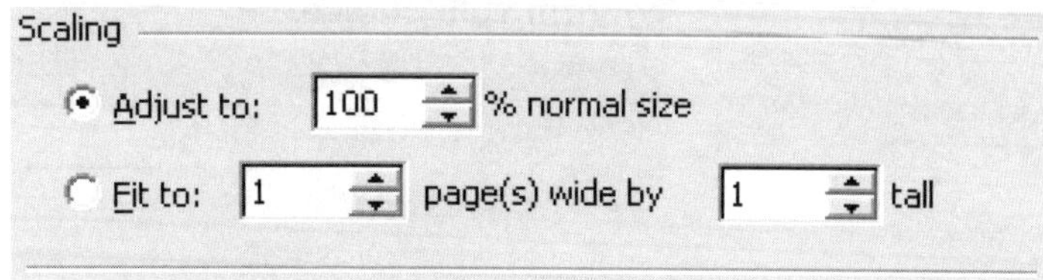

- **Adjust to:** You can enter a number in the range 10–400% of normal size. (You need not type the % symbol.)
- **Fit to:** Reduces the worksheet (or selected cells) so that it fits on the specified number of pages. You can specify the number of pages vertically (tall), horizontally (wide) or both.

Paper size

Also on the **Page** tab of the *Page Setup* dialog box, this option allows you to select the size of the paper you want to print on.

Margins

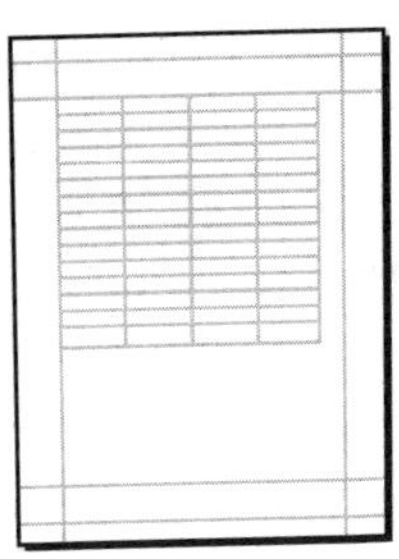

The margins are the distance that the printed worksheet or selected cells are positioned in from the four edges of the printed page. You set this on the **Margins** tab of the *Page Setup* dialog box. You can specify top, bottom, left and right margins and separate margins for headers and footers, which are covered in the next topic.

It is unlikely that you will need to change Excel's default margin values – top and bottom, 2.5 cm, left and right, 1.9 cm.

The **Margins** tab also allows you to centre your worksheet or selected cells horizontally (positioned evenly between the left and right margins of the printed page), vertically (between the top and bottom margins), or both.

Gridlines and headings

By default, Excel does not include cell boundary lines (gridlines) or row and

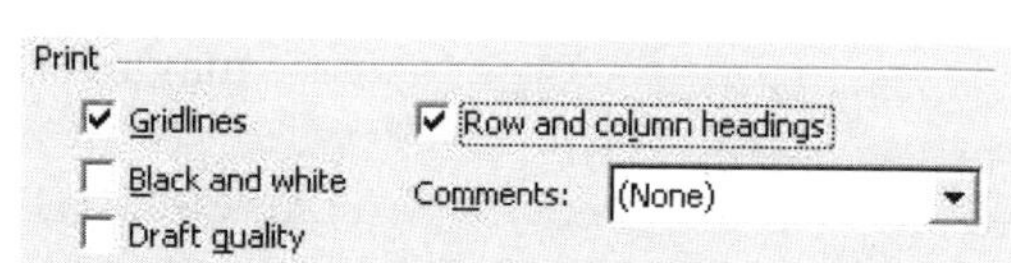

column headings on printouts. You can change either or both of these settings on the **Sheet** tab of the *Page Setup* dialog box.

Print titles

You can print row headings at the top of every printed page. You do this at the **Sheet** tab of the *Page Setup* dialog box. Place the cursor in the *Rows to repeat at top* box, then click on the row you want as the heading. Click **Print Preview** to check the effect. Click **OK** to confirm your choice.

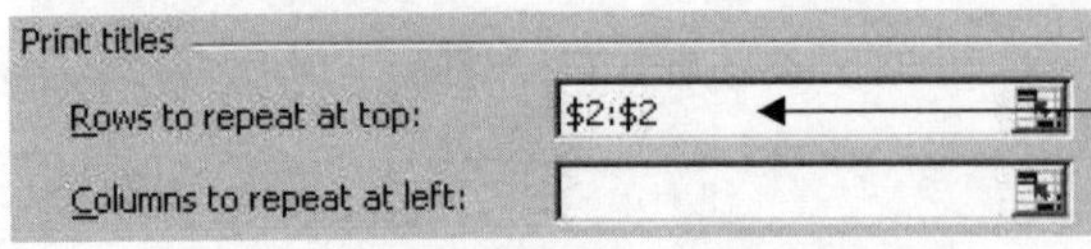

Row 2 specified as the title row

Headers and footers

These are pieces of text that appear at the top and bottom of every page of a printed worksheet. Typically, they contain such details as file name, author name, date and page number.

With Excel, you need only type in header and/or footer text once, and the program repeats the text on every page. You can apply formatting – font, bold and italics – to text in the headers and footers.

Here are a few facts about headers and footers in Excel:

- You insert them with the **Header/Footer** tab of the *Page Setup* dialog box.
- The **Header/Footer** tab offers a drop-down list of suggested header and footer texts, from which you can choose the one that best suits your needs.
- You can edit and/or format your chosen header or footer text by clicking the **Custom Header** or **Custom Footer** button on the **Header/Footer** tab, and then selecting the required options.
- The **Custom** buttons enable you to format the header or footer text, and to insert any or all of the following items: page number, total number of pages, date, time, Excel file name and worksheet name.
- When setting header and footer margins on the **Margins** tab of the *Page Setup* dialog box, ensure that the values are less than the top and bottom page margins – otherwise, the header and footer text may overlap the cells on the printout.

Exercise 21.18 provides an example of Excel's header and footer feature in action.

Exercise 21.18: Inserting a header and footer

1) With *Sheet1* of your workbook selected, choose **File | Page Setup** and select the **Header/Footer** tab.
2) On the *Header* drop-down list, select the Excel workbook file name – in this case, *KenBloggs.xls*.
3) On the *Footer* drop-down list, select *Page 1 of ?* to include page numbers in the footer.

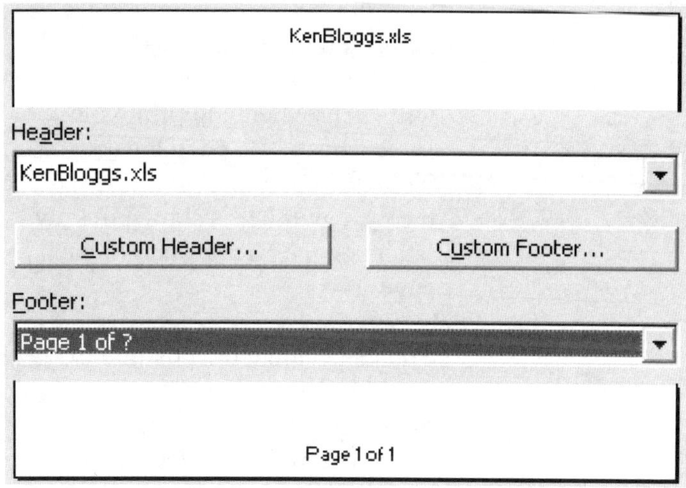

Text Formatting button

4) Click the **Custom Header** button, select *&[File]* in the *Center section*, click the **Text Formatting** button, and make the file name bold.
5) In the *Left section*, type My First Workbook. In the *Right section*, type ECDL Module 4.

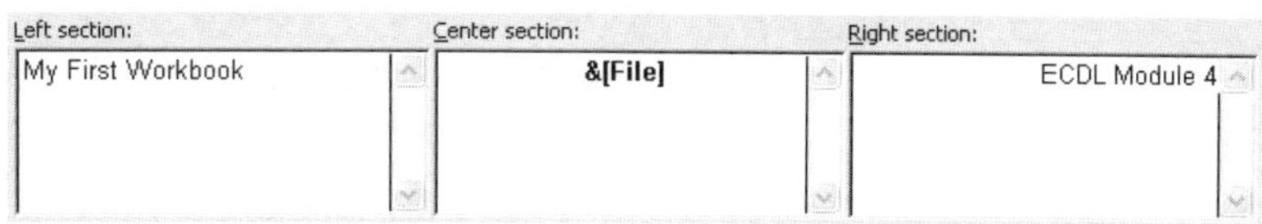

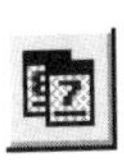

Date button

Time button

6) Click **OK** to return to the **Header/Footer** tab of the *Page Setup* dialog box.
7) Click the **Custom Footer** button, click in the *Left section*, and then click the **Date** button.
8) Click in the *Right section*, and then click the **Time** button.

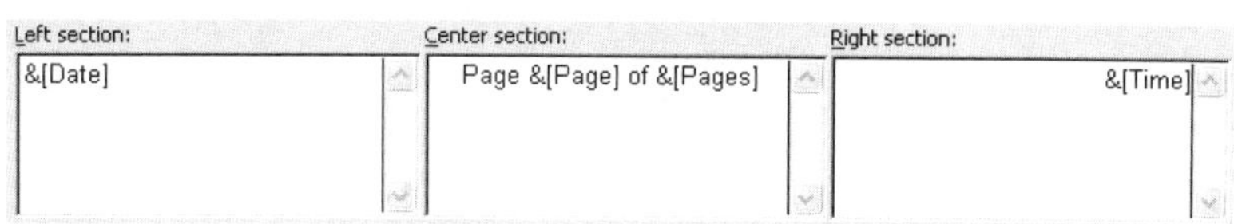

9) Click **OK** to return to the **Header/Footer** tab of the *Page Setup* dialog box. Click **OK** again to close the dialog box.

   Well done. You have inserted a header and footer in your workbook. You cannot see headers and footers on screen; they appear on printouts only.

Printing options

Excel offers a wide range of printing options. These include the ability to preview a worksheet on your screen before you print it, and the choice of printing all your worksheet, selected cells or pages, or your entire workbook.

Before you print or distribute your spreadsheet, it is a good idea to proof your spreadsheet and check all your calculations.

Select **View | Page Break Preview** to see where page breaks will occur when you print your spreadsheet. The page breaks are indicated by dark blue lines, and the page number is shown in grey letters on the background of each page.

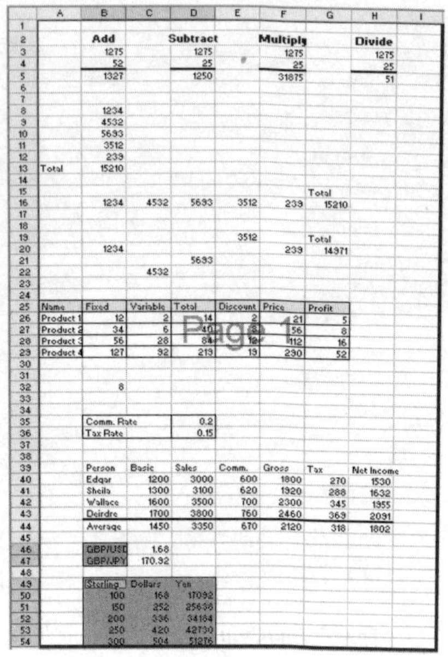

You can change the position of page breaks by dragging these dividing lines to new positions. Excel will resize the data in the worksheet to fit on the page. To return to the normal workbook view, select **View | Normal**.

Print preview

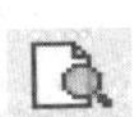

Print Preview button

This displays each page as it will appear when it is printed on paper. To preview your worksheet:

- Choose **File | Print Preview**.

  -or-

- Click the **Print Preview** button on the *Standard* toolbar.

Click **Close** to return to your worksheet.

Print range options

When you choose **File | Print**, you have a range of options regarding which parts of your workbook you may print.

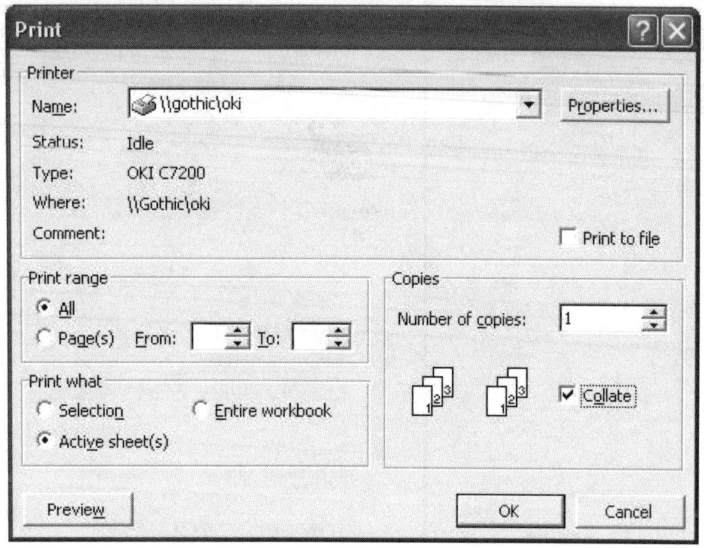

- **Print to file:** Sends the output to a file, such as a PostScript file.
- **All:** The current worksheet.
- **Page(s):** To print one or a range of pages from the current worksheet, enter the page number(s) here.
- **Selection:** Prints only the currently selected cells on the current worksheet.
- **Entire workbook:** All worksheets that contain data in the workbook.
- **Active Sheet(s):** Prints only the active worksheets in a workbook. To make a subset of the worksheets in a workbook active, click the tab for the first worksheet, then hold down the **Ctrl** key and click the tabs for all of the other worksheets you want to print.
- **Number of copies:** Specify the number of copies you want to print. For multiple copies you can also specify whether or not you want to collate them.

Exercise 21.19: Printing a worksheet

1) Click the *Sheet1* tab to select the first worksheet of your workbook.
2) Choose **File | Print**, accept the default options, and click **OK**.

3) Your printout should look like that shown.

My First Workbook **KenBloggs.xls** ECDL Module 4

Add	**Subtract**	**Multiply**	**Divide**
1275	1275	1275	1275
52	25	25	25
1327	1250	31875	51

1234
4532
5693
3512
239
Total 15210

					Total
1234	4532	5693	3512	239	15210

3512 Total
1234 239 14971
5693
4532

Name	Fixed	Variable	Total	Discount	Price	Profit
Product 1	12	2	14	2	21	5
Product 2	34	6	40	8	56	8
Product 3	56	28	84	12	112	16
Product 4	127	92	219	19	290	52

8

Comm. Rate	0.2
Tax Rate	0.15

Person	Basic	Sales	Comm.	Gross	Tax	Net Income
Edgar	1200	3000	600	1800	270	1530
Sheila	1300	3100	620	1920	288	1632
Wallace	1600	3500	700	2300	345	1955
Deirdre	1700	3800	760	2460	369	2091
Average	1450	3350	670	2120	318	1802

GBP/USD	1.68
GBP/JPY	170.92

Sterling	Dollars	Yen
100	168	17092
150	252	25638
200	336	34184
250	420	42730
300	504	51276

20/01/00 Page 1 of 1 22:27

Save and close your workbook and Excel. You have now completed the third chapter of the ECDL Spreadsheets module.

Chapter summary: so now you know

Functions are predefined formulas built in to Excel that allow you to perform specific calculations. As with formulas, functions always begin with an equals (=) symbol.

With the *SUM* function, you need enter only two arguments when totalling a vertical or horizontal list of cells: the first and last cell references. See Exercise 21.1 for an example of this. An example of a SUM function would be:

=SUM(A2:A6)

A fast way to total a vertical or horizontal list of cells is to select them and click the **AutoSum** button. Excel tries to 'guess' which cells you want to add. If Excel has guessed correctly, just press **Enter** to confirm the suggested arguments. If not, edit the arguments of the SUM function. See Exercise 21.2 for an example of this.

The *Average* function, as its name suggests, calculates the average of a vertical or horizontal list of numbers – for example:

=Average(D5:F5)

See Exercise 21.4 for an example of the Average function in use.

Use the *MIN* and *MAX* functions, respectively, to find the smallest and the largest value in a range of cells.

Use the *COUNT* function to count the number of rows or columns in a range that contain numbers.

Use the *IF* function to check if the value in a cell or range of cells satisfies criteria you specify.

A *cell range* is a group of cells on a worksheet. You can select an adjacent cell range by dragging the mouse across it. You can select a non-adjacent cell range by selecting the first cell (or the first sub-group of adjacent cells) and then holding down the **Ctrl** key when selecting further cells (or adjacent ranges). See Exercise 21.7 for an example of selecting non-adjacent cell ranges.

Selected cells can be *formatted* (bold or italic), *aligned* (horizontally or vertically) and *rotated*. You can also add borders and fills (coloured backgrounds), and change fonts and sizes. For examples of formatting and aligning text in cells, see Exercises 21.5, 21.6 and 21.13. For an example of applying borders and fill colours, see Exercise 21.16.

You can adjust column width and row height by dragging the cell boundaries in the row and column headings. For examples, see Exercises 21.9 and 21.10.

You can search all or part of a worksheet for label text, entered numbers, numbers resulting from calculations, and calculation components (function names, cell references, arithmetic operators and constants). And you can replace found items with alternatives. For an example, see Exercise 21.17. You can also spellcheck all or part of a worksheet.

Pages can be oriented in *portrait* or *landscape*. A *margin* is the distance of the cells from a particular edge of the page.

Headers and *footers* are small text items that recur on every printed page, and typically contain such details as the workbook name, author name and date. They can also contain automatically generated page numbers. For an example of adding headers and footers to a document, see Exercise 21.18.

Excel's *print options* include a print preview feature and the ability to print selected cells only.

Quick quiz: functions, formatting and printing

Circle the correct answer to each of the following multiple-choice questions about functions, formatting and printing in Excel.

Q1	The SUM function will generate an error if any of its arguments are not numbers.
A.	True.
B.	False.

Q2	To select non-adjacent cells you:
A.	Select the first cell, then hold down the **Shift** key and select the others.
B.	Select the first cell, then hold down the **Alt** key and select the others.
C.	Select the first cell, then hold down the **Ctrl** key and select the others.
D.	Select the first cell, then hold down the **F2** key and select the others.

Q3	When you use the Find command to search for content in a workbook, you can:
A.	Search in a single worksheet.
B.	Search in selected cells only.
C.	Search the whole workbook at once.
D.	All of the above.

Q4	When you print your workbook, headers and footers appear:
A.	On the first page only.
B.	On the first page of each worksheet.
C.	On odd numbered pages only.
D.	On all pages.

Q5	When you print from Excel, you must print the whole workbook.
A.	True.
B.	False.

Answers

1: B, **2:** C, **3:** D, **4:** D, **5:** B.

Chapter 22: Inserting, sorting and moving cells

In this chapter

Excel users spend only part of their time creating new workbooks and entering and formatting data in the worksheet cells. The remainder is spent reopening existing workbooks and amending previously entered data.

In this chapter you will learn how to perform three types of maintenance tasks.

Row and column insertion allows you to position new cells within a worksheet area that already contains cells with data in them. Insertion (or deletion) means that surrounding cells must adjust their position to make way for the new data (or fill the spaces previously occupied by the deleted data).

Copying, cutting and pasting enable you to reproduce or move cells within the same worksheet, between worksheets in the same workbook, or between different workbooks. Copying and cutting of calculations introduce the idea of relative and absolute cell references.

Finally, sorting allows you to rearrange selected cells in a sequence different from that in which they were entered to the worksheet.

New skills

At the end of this chapter you should be able to:

- Insert and delete rows, columns and cells.
- Copy, cut and paste the contents of cells.
- Explain the difference between relative and absolute cell references, and identify calculations in which absolute cell references are appropriate.
- Sort cells according to one or two criteria.
- Insert symbols and special characters in Excel.

New words

At the end of this chapter you should be able to explain the following terms:

- Marquee
- Sort
- Relative cell reference
- Sort order
- Absolute cell reference

Inserting and deleting rows

With over sixteen million cells on a single worksheet, why would you want to add some more? Answer: Sometimes you need to insert a row or column to hold new data *within* a range of cells that already contain text and numbers.

Exercises 22.1 and 22.2 take you through the steps of inserting new rows and columns.

Exercise 22.1: Inserting a new row

1) Open the second worksheet of your workbook, *Sheet2*.
2) Select the heading of the row immediately below where you want to insert the new row. For example, to insert a new row below row *4*, click the heading of row *5*.

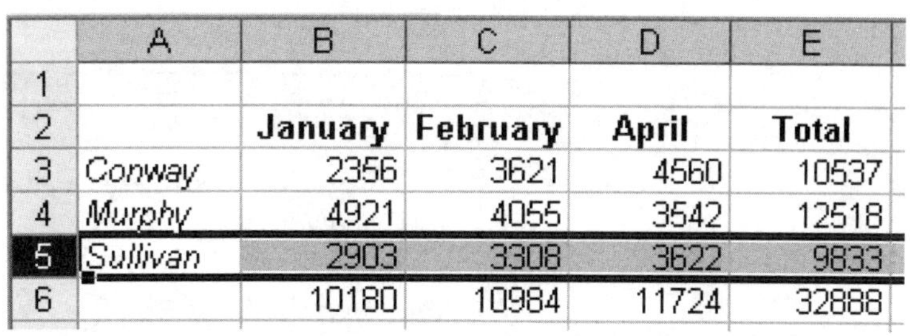

	A	B	C	D	E
1					
2		January	February	April	Total
3	Conway	2356	3621	4560	10537
4	Murphy	4921	4055	3542	12518
5	Sullivan	2903	3308	3622	9833
6		10180	10984	11724	32888

3) Choose **Insert | Rows**. Excel inserts a new row of blank cells.

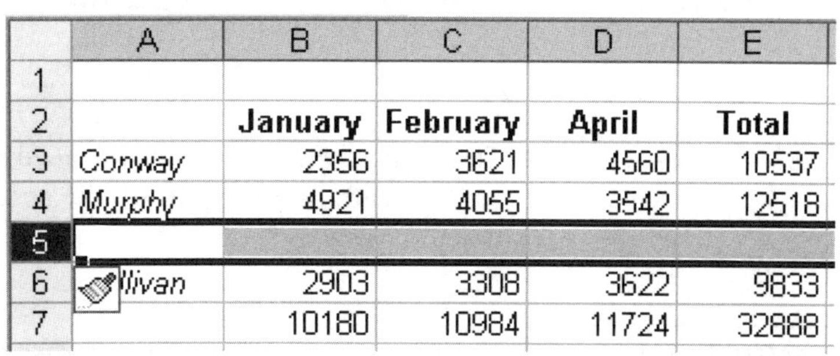

	A	B	C	D	E
1					
2		January	February	April	Total
3	Conway	2356	3621	4560	10537
4	Murphy	4921	4055	3542	12518
5					
6	llivan	2903	3308	3622	9833
7		10180	10984	11724	32888

4) An **Insert Options** button appears below the inserted row. Click the down-arrow which appears at the right of the button when you hover your mouse over it to see the formatting options you can apply to cells in the new row.

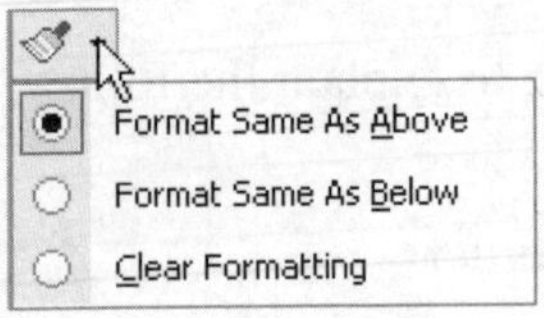

Click *Format Same As Above* to apply the same formatting to each cell in the new row as the cell directly above it in row *4*.

5) Enter new text and numbers in cells *A5*, *B5*, *C5* and *D5*, as shown below. Excel recalculates the totals on row 7 automatically as you add the new numbers.

6) If Excel does not automatically enter a new SUM function in *E5* to calculate the row total, do so yourself now by entering the following SUM function:

=SUM(B5:D5)

Excel recalculates *E7*, the total of the Totals column, to include *E5*, the sum of the numbers that you have entered in row *5*. Your worksheet should look as shown.

	A	B	C	D	E
1					
2		**January**	**February**	**April**	**Total**
3	*Conway*	2356	3621	4560	10537
4	*Murphy*	4921	4055	3542	12518
5	*Smith*	3872	2441	4949	11262
6	*Sullivan*	2903	3308	3622	9833
7		14052	13425	16673	44150
8					

7) To make your worksheet more readable, insert a blank row above the column totals, as shown.

	A	B	C	D	E
1					
2		**January**	**February**	**April**	**Total**
3	*Conway*	2356	3621	4560	10537
4	*Murphy*	4921	4055	3542	12518
5	*Smith*	3872	2441	4949	11262
6	*Sullivan*	2903	3308	3622	9833
7					
8		14052	13425	16673	44150

Deleting rows

To delete a row, select the row heading and choose **Edit | Delete**. The row beneath moves up to fill the space previously occupied by the deleted row.

Inserting and deleting columns

Inserting a new column in a worksheet is similar to inserting a new row. Exercise 22.2 shows you how.

Exercise 22.2: Inserting a new column

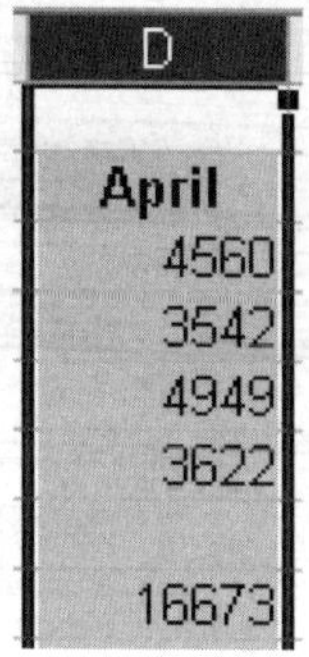

1) Select the heading of the column immediately to the right of where you want to insert the new column.
   For example, to insert a new column to the right of column *C*, click the heading of column *D*.
2) Choose **Insert | Columns**. Excel inserts a new column of blank cells.

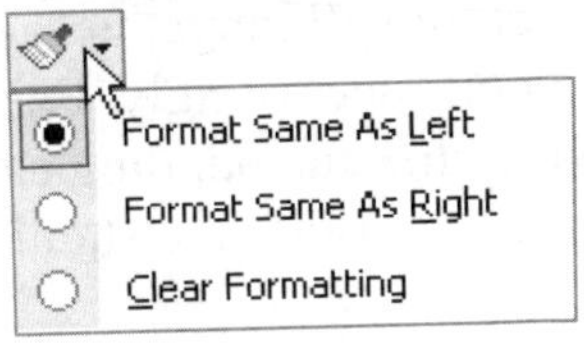

3) As with inserting a row, an **Insert Options** button appears. Click the down-arrow to the right of the button and select *Format Same As Left* to apply the same formatting to every cell in the new column as the cell immediately to its left.
4) Enter new text and numbers in *D2:D6* as shown below.
   Excel recalculates the totals in column *F* automatically as you add the new numbers in column *D*.
5) To total the new numbers in column *D*, enter the following function in cell *D8*:
   =SUM(D3:D6)

	A	B	C	D	E	F
1						
2		**January**	**February**	**March**	**April**	**Total**
3	*Conway*	2356	3621	4185	4560	14722
4	*Murphy*	4921	4055	3814	3542	16332
5	*Smith*	3872	2441	2888	4949	14150
6	*Sullivan*	2903	3308	3487	3622	13320
7						
8		14052	13425	14374	16673	58524

6) To make your worksheet more readable, insert a column to the right of the 'April' column.
7) This blank column is wider than it needs to be. In the column heading, click the boundary between columns *F* and *G*, and then drag the boundary to the left.

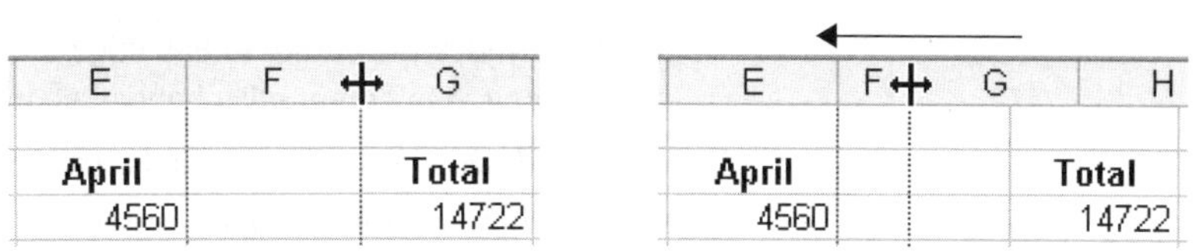

Deleting columns

To delete a column, select its heading and choose **Edit | Delete**. The column to the right moves left and fills the space previously occupied by the deleted column.

Inserting and deleting cells

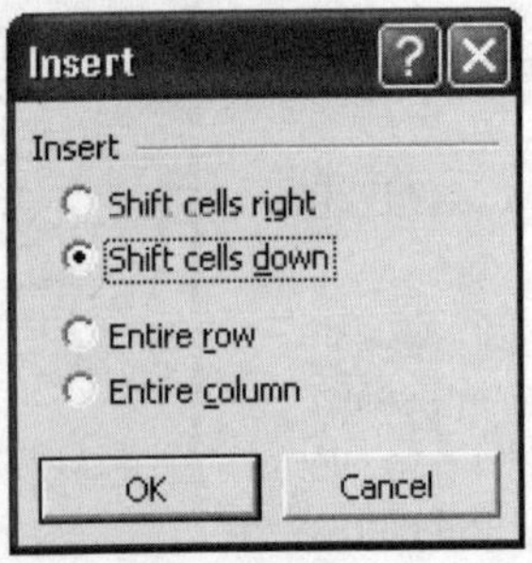

You can insert individual cells on a worksheet by first selecting a cell immediately below or to the right of where you want to insert the new cell, and then choosing **Insert | Cells**.

To delete a cell, select it and choose **Edit | Delete**.

Be careful about inserting or deleting a new cell or cell range, because Excel adjusts the position of the surrounding cells accordingly. Excel prompts you, when inserting, to choose whether the surrounding cells should move right or down, and when deleting, whether they should move left or up.

Copying and pasting cell contents

Suppose you have text or a number in one cell, and you want to copy it to another cell. How do you do it? Of the many ways of copying and pasting a cell or cells on a worksheet, here are the two most convenient:

- Drag-and-drop.
- Right-clicking.

You will learn about these in Exercises 22.3 and 22.4.

Exercise 22.3: Copy and paste with drag-and-drop

1) Select the cell you want to copy from. For example, click the *Sheet1* tab to display your first worksheet. Type 1234 in cell *B57* and press **Enter**. Next, click *B57* to select it.

   See how the cursor is shaped like a plus sign (+).

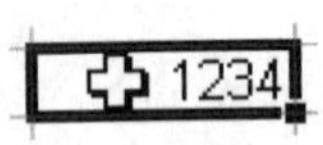

2) Move the cursor to the bottom edge of the selected cell and hold down the **Ctrl** key. Excel changes the cursor from a plus sign to an arrow with a smaller plus sign.

   (You can move the cursor to any edge of the selected cell – it doesn't matter which edge. The cursor still changes shape.)

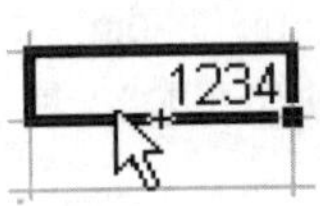

3) Holding down the **Ctrl** key, drag the cell to the destination cell that you want to paste to – for example, *D57*.
4) Release the mouse button first, and then the **Ctrl** key.

   (If you release **Ctrl** first, Excel cuts rather than copies the cell contents.)

   If there is already something in cell *D57*, Excel overwrites it with the pasted data.

   Well done. You have copied a number from one cell of a worksheet to another – without clicking a toolbar button or choosing a menu command!

Exercise 22.4: Copy and paste by right-clicking

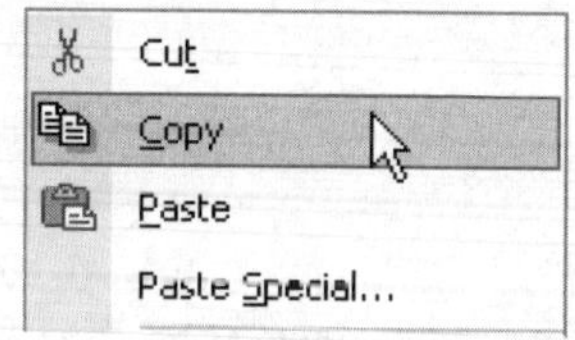

1) Select the cell whose contents you want to copy. As in Exercise 22.3, select *B57*.
2) Right-click with the mouse.
3) Choose **Copy** from the pop-up menu. Excel places the contents of *B57* in the clipboard.
4) Click cell *F57*.
5) Right-click with the mouse.
6) Choose **Paste**.

   If there is already something in cell *F57*, Excel overwrites it with the pasted data.

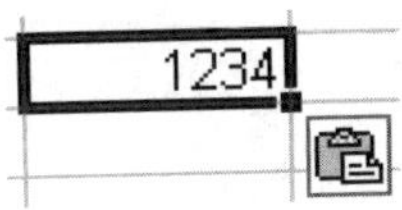

   A **Paste Options** button appears below the cell with the pasted content. Click the down-arrow which appears at the right of the button when you hover your mouse over it to see the formatting options you can apply to the pasted information.

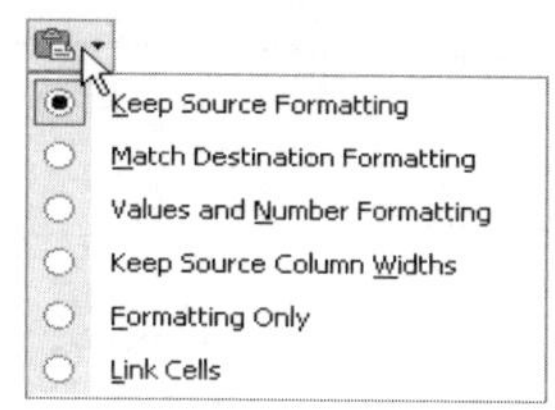

   Select **Keep Source Formatting** to format the pasted data in the same way as the data in the copied cell.

You are not limited to using drag-and-drop and right-clicking with single cells only. You can use both methods with selected ranges of cells.

About the clipboard

Points you should remember about the clipboard:

Clipboard
A temporary storage area to which you can copy text (or graphics). You can paste to any location within the same or different documents.

- The clipboard is temporary. Turn off your computer and the clipboard contents are deleted.
- The same clipboard is available to all Windows applications. For example, you can copy from Excel and paste into Word.
- The clipboard can hold up to twenty-four items at a time. When you copy or cut a twenty-fifth item, the first item in the clipboard is deleted.
- You can view the contents of the clipboard by opening the *Clipboard* task pane (choose **Edit | Office Clipboard**). This lists

all items in the clipboard, with the newest item at the top of the list.

Each item includes an icon representing the source Office program and a portion of copied text or a thumbnail of a copied graphic.

Clipboard ***task pane***

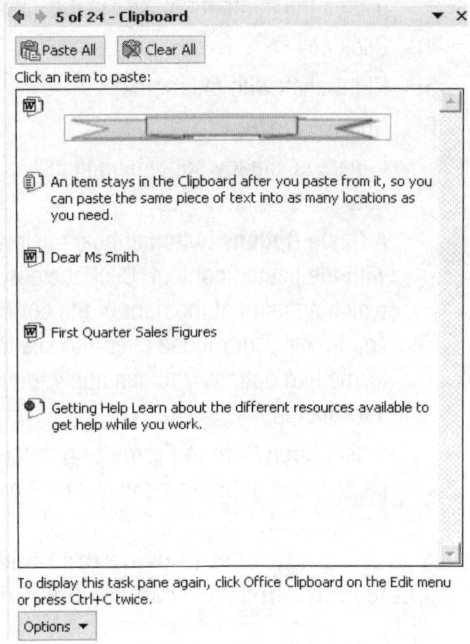

- To paste the most recently copied item from the clipboard, click the **Paste** button on the *Standard* toolbar, or choose **Edit | Paste**. To paste a different item, click its icon in the *Clipboard* task pane. To paste all previously copied/cut items, click the **Paste All** button in the task pane.
- An item stays in the clipboard after you paste from it, so you can paste the same piece of text into as many locations as you need.
- To delete an item from the clipboard, right-click on it in the *Clipboard* task pane and choose **Delete** from the pop-up menu. To delete all items from the clipboard, choose the **Clear All** button in the task pane.

The flashing marquee

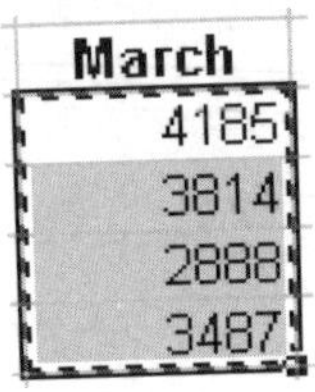

When you copy (or cut) a cell or cell range by any means other than drag-and-drop, Excel surrounds the selected cells with a flashing rectangle called a marquee.

Marquee
A flashing rectangle that Excel uses to surround a cell, or cell range, that you have copied to the clipboard.

You can remove a marquee at any stage by pressing the **Esc** key at the top-left of your keyboard.

If you remove a marquee, Excel removes the contents of the selected cell or cell range from the clipboard.

Exercise 22.5: Copy and paste a cell range

In this exercise you will copy and paste an adjacent cell range. You will use the keyboard shortcuts to perform the copy-and-paste actions.

1) Type 1234 in cells *C57* and *E57*.
2) Select the cell range *B57:F57*.
3) Press **Ctrl+c** to copy the cells to the clipboard.
4) Click cell *B59*, and press **Ctrl+v** to paste from the clipboard.

   Excel copies the cells to the new cell range *B59:F59*, as shown below.

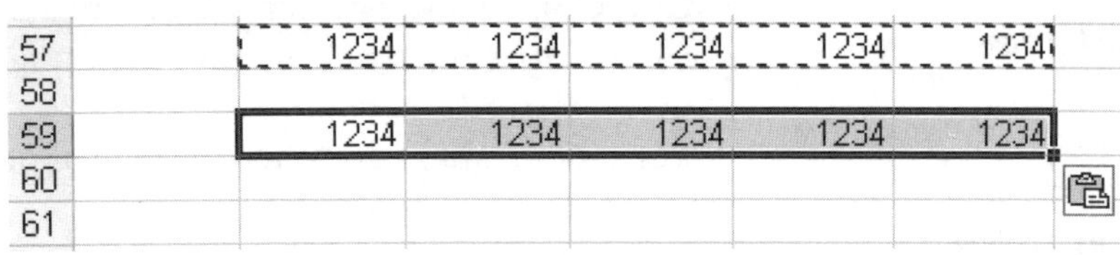

As before, the **Paste Options** button appears. Click the down-arrow to the right of the button and select *Keep Source Formatting*.

You can paste from the clipboard to several locations in a single action, as Exercise 22.6 demonstrates.

Exercise 22.6: Copy and paste to multiple locations

1) With cell range *B57:F57* still in the clipboard from Exercise 22.5, select the adjacent cell range *B61:F64*.
2) Press **Ctrl+v** to paste to the cells. All four adjacent rows of the destination cell range now contain the pasted cells.
3) Select the non-adjacent cell range *B66:F66*, *B68:F68*, *B70:F70*.

4) Press **Ctrl+v** to paste to the cells. The three non-adjacent rows of the destination cell range now contain the pasted cells.

   Your worksheet should look as shown.

Pasted to an adjacent cell range → rows 61 and 64

Pasted to a non-adjacent cell range → rows 66, 68 and 70

61		1234	1234	1234	1234	1234
62		1234	1234	1234	1234	1234
63		1234	1234	1234	1234	1234
64		1234	1234	1234	1234	1234
65						
66		1234	1234	1234	1234	1234
67						
68		1234	1234	1234	1234	1234
69						
70		1234	1234	1234	1234	1234

Cutting and pasting cell contents

Cut-and-paste differs from copy-and-paste in that Excel removes the original cell contents, whereas the contents of copied cells remain in their original location. Cutting does not remove the cell, in the way that the **Edit | Delete** command does. It just removes their contents, leaving behind empty cells.

Copy button

To cut and paste using drag-and-drop, do not hold down the **Ctrl** key while dragging the cell contents to their new location.

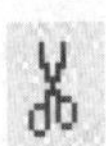

Cut button

To cut and paste using the pop-up menu, choose **Cut** rather than **Copy**. **Cut**, **Copy** and **Paste** commands are also available on Excel's **Edit** menu. The keyboard shortcut for cutting a cell or cell range is **Ctrl+x**.

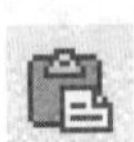

Paste button

Yet another cut or copy and paste method is to use the relevant buttons on Excel's *Standard* toolbar.

Copying between worksheets and workbooks

You are not limited to copying or cutting and pasting cells within the same worksheet (such as *Sheet1*). You can also copy or cut and paste between different worksheets of the same workbook (such as *Sheet1* and *Sheet2* of your workbook), and even between different workbooks.

Exercise 22.7: Copying and pasting between workbooks

1) On *Sheet2*, select cell range *A2:G8*.
2) Choose **Edit | Copy** to copy the cells to the clipboard.
3) Click the **New** button on the *Standard* toolbar to open a new workbook. The new workbook opens with *Sheet1* displayed.

4) In the *Name Box* of the new workbook, type A100 and press **Enter**. This moves the cursor to cell *A100*, making it the active cell.
5) Choose **Edit | Paste** to paste the cell range from the clipboard.

   You have completed the exercise. Close the new workbook without saving it.

Moving calculations

Numbers and text can be copied or cut and pasted without problems. But what about calculations? Can errors arise when moving formulas or functions?

Yes – but only when fixed-factor calculations are involved. As you learnt in Chapter 20, these are calculations where a common cell reference, indicating the fixed factor, is used in formulas or functions on different rows or columns. Common examples of fixed factors are currency exchange rates, and tax and sales commission rates.

Exercise 22.8 demonstrates a problem that can arise when copying fixed factor calculations.

Exercise 22.8: Copying fixed-factor calculations

1) On *Sheet1*, select the cell range *B46:D54*, and press **Ctrl+c** to copy it to the clipboard.
2) Click cell *F46*, and press **Ctrl+v**. Excel copies the cells to their new location without error.

   For example, *C50* contains the formula =B50*C46. The corresponding cell in the pasted data, *G50*, contains the formula =F50*G46.

   If you click any calculated cell you can see that Excel has automatically adjusted the formula arguments to reflect the new cell references.
3) Select the cell range *B49:D54*, and press **Ctrl+c** to copy it to the clipboard.
4) Select cell *J49*, and press **Ctrl+v** to paste from the clipboard.

   This time the pasting of the cells does produce calculation errors. Excel has changed the cell references of the two fixed factors (the dollar and yen conversion rates) so that the formula cells now point to the new cell locations *K46* and *K47* – but these cells are empty.

	J	K	L
46			
47			
48			
49	Sterling	Dollars	Yen
50	100	=J50*K46	=J50*K47
51	150	=J51*K46	=J51*K47
52	200	=J52*K46	=J52*K47
53	250	=J53*K46	=J53*K47
54	300	=J54*K46	=J54*K47

There is a way to remedy this problem. First, select the pasted cell range *J49:L54*, and delete it with the **Edit | Clear | All** command. This removes both the cell content and the cell formatting.

5) Double-click *C50*, and change the formula to the following: B50*C46. Similarly, in *C51:C54*, change all references from C46 to C46.

   Next, in cells *D50:D54*, change all cell references from C47 to the new format of C47. Your worksheet formulas should now look as shown below.

49	Sterling	Dollars	Yen
50	100	=B50*C46	=B50*C47
51	150	=B51*C46	=B51*C47
52	200	=B52*C46	=B52*C47
53	250	=B53*C46	=B53*C47
54	300	=B54*C46	=B54*C47

6) Select cells *B49:D54*, and press **Ctrl+c** to copy them.

7) Select cell *J49*, and press **Ctrl+v** to paste from the clipboard. No errors! If you click any of the formula cells, you can see that Excel has not adjusted the cell references that contained the $ symbol. Although pasted to a new location, the calculations continue to point to the original cell references of the two currency conversion rates.

   In this exercise you have learnt the difference between relative and absolute cell addresses. The next topic provides further details.

Cell references: the two kinds

In Chapter 19, you learnt that each cell on a worksheet has a unique reference, written in the form *A1* – column letter first, row number second.

In fact, Excel supports two kinds of cell references: relative (the *A1* type you know already) and absolute (the *A1* type you met in Exercise 22.8).

Why is one type of cell reference not enough? The answer, as you discovered in Exercise 22.8, lies in the way that Excel copies and pastes calculations that contain cell references.

A cell reference that Excel adjusts automatically when the calculation cell containing it is moved to a new location is called a relative cell reference.

Relative cell reference
A reference to a cell or cell range in the format A1. Excel changes a relative cell reference when you copy a formula or function containing such a reference.

An absolute cell reference, however, does not change when the calculation containing it is moved to a new location. Accordingly, you should use absolute cell references when entering fixed-factor-type calculations. You can make part of a cell reference absolute and part relative – for example, *G$13* or *$D17*.

Absolute cell reference
A reference to a cell or cell range in the format A1. Excel does not adjust an absolute cell reference when you copy a calculation containing such a reference.

Exercise 22.9: Working with absolute cell references

In this exercise, you will use the find and replace feature to convert relative cell references to absolute ones, and then copy the related calculations to a new location.

1) On *Sheet1*, select cell range *E40:E43*.
2) Choose **Edit | Replace**. Type the values shown below, and select **Replace All**.

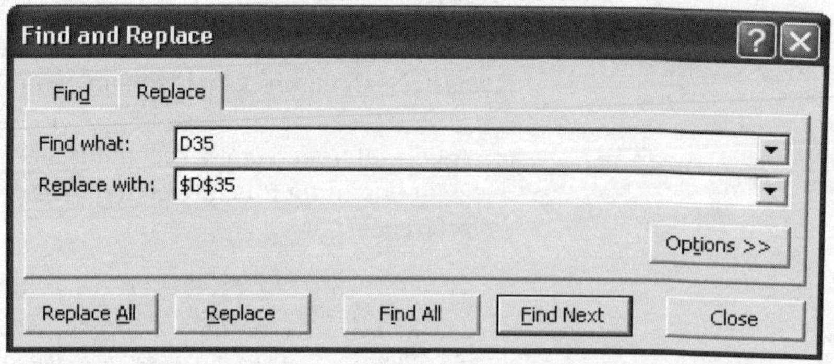

3) Select cell range *G40:G43*, and repeat step 2. This time, replace all occurrences of D36 with D36.
   You are now ready to copy the cells that point to the two fixed factors, sales commission and taxation rate.
4) Select cell range *B39:H44*, and press **Ctrl+c** to copy them to the clipboard.
5) Click cell *J39*, and press **Ctrl+v**. The calculations copy without error.

Sorting: reordering cells by content

The order in which you typed entries in a worksheet may not be the order in which, later on, you would prefer to display or print that information. Suppose, for example, that you have entered a list of numbers in a column of a worksheet.

By selecting the cell range and choosing the **Sort Ascending** (or **Sort Descending**) button, you can rearrange the cells so that Excel displays them in order of increasing (or decreasing) value. The reordered list may now be easier to read than the original, unsorted one.

Sorting
Rearranging columns of cells based on the values in the cells. Sorting does not change the content of cells, only their location.

Excel offers a number of sequencing options, called sort orders.

Sort order
A particular way of ordering cells based on value. A sort order can be alphabetical or numerical, and can be in ascending (0 to 9, A to Z) or descending (9 to 0, Z to A) sequence.

Exercise 22.10: A simple sort

1) On *Sheet1*, click *B73* and enter the word: Original

2) In the six cells immediately below *B73*, type the following vertical list of numbers: 453, 123, 340, 683, 987 and 213.
3) In cells *C73* and *D73*, enter the words: Ascending and Descending
4) Select the cell range *B74:B79*, and press **Ctrl+c**.
5) Select the cell range *C74:D79*, and press **Ctrl+v**.

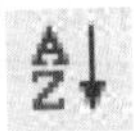

Sort Ascending button

6) Select the cell range *C74:C79*, and click the **Sort Ascending** button on the *Standard* toolbar.

   A *Sort Warning* dialog box appears to check if you want to sort the selected data only, or if the data in the cells beside the selected cells should also be sorted. Because this is a simple sort, select *Continue with the current selection* and click **Sort**. In Exercise 22.11 you will perform a multiple sort where you will sort the data in several columns at once.

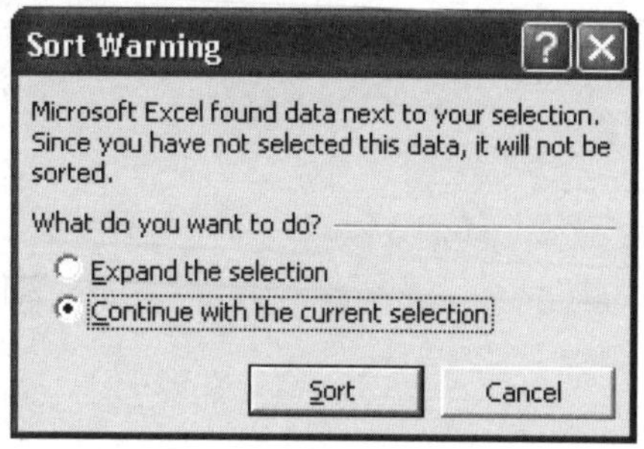

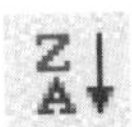

Sort Descending button

7) Select the cell range *D74:D79*, and click the **Sort Descending** button on the *Standard* toolbar.

   As before, when the *Sort Warning* dialog box appears, select *Continue with the current selection* and click **Sort**.

   Your worksheet should look as shown.

	B	C	D
72			
73	Original	Ascending	Descending
74	453	123	987
75	123	213	683
76	340	340	453
77	683	453	340
78	987	683	213
79	213	987	123

The two sort buttons give you a quick, one-click way of reordering a cell range. As you will discover in Exercise 22.11, Excel's **Data | Sort** menu command provides an additional option: you can sort a cell range based on the values in more than a single column. This is called a multiple sort.

Exercise 22.11: A complex sort

The rows of *Sheet2* are currently arranged in alphabetical sort order according to surname: Conway first, then Murphy, Smith and, lastly, Sullivan.

	A	B	C	D	E	F
1						
2		**January**	**February**	**March**	**April**	**Total**
3	*Conway*	2356	3621	4185	4560	14722
4	*Murphy*	4921	4055	3814	3542	16332
5	*Smith*	3872	2441	2888	4949	14150
6	*Sullivan*	2903	3308	3487	3622	13320
7						
8		14052	13425	14374	16673	58524

1) Select row *7* by clicking its row heading, and choose **Insert | Rows**. Next, press **Ctrl+y** twice. This is the keyboard shortcut for Excel's **Repeat** command. Excel inserts three new, blank rows under row *6*.

6	*Sullivan*	2903	3308	3487	3622	13320
7						
8						
9						
10						
11		14052	13425	14374	16673	58524

2) In rows *7*, *8* and *9* enter the text and numbers as shown below.

	A	B	C	D	E	F	G
1							
2		**January**	**February**	**March**	**April**		**Total**
3	*Conway*	2356	3621	4185	4560		14722
4	*Murphy*	4921	4055	3814	3542		16332
5	*Smith*	3872	2441	2888	4949		14150
6	*Sullivan*	2903	3308	3487	3622		13320
7	*Rafferty*	2512	2864	3290	3741		12407
8	*Higgins*	3463	3981	4210	4974		16628
9	*Smith*	5951	6226	6481	6852		25510
10							
11		25978	26496	28355	32240		113069

If Excel does not automatically enter new SUM functions in *G7*, *G8* and *G9* to calculate the row totals, do so yourself now. For example, in *G8* enter =SUM(B8:E8).

3) Select column *B* by clicking its column heading, and choose the **Insert | Columns** command. In the new column, enter the first names as shown.

	A	B	C	D	E	F	G	H
1								
2			**January**	**February**	**March**	**April**		**Total**
3	*Conway*	*John*	2356	3621	4185	4560		14722
4	*Murphy*	*Robert*	4921	4055	3814	3542		16332
5	*Smith*	*Zowie*	3872	2441	2888	4949		14150
6	*Sullivan*	*Andrew*	2903	3308	3487	3622		13320
7	*Rafferty*	*Aidan*	2512	2864	3290	3741		12407
8	*Higgins*	*Tracey*	3463	3981	4210	4974		16628
9	*Smith*	*Catherine*	5951	6226	6481	6852		25510
10								
11			25978	26496	28355	32240		113069

4) Select cell range *A3:H9*, and choose **Data | Sort**.

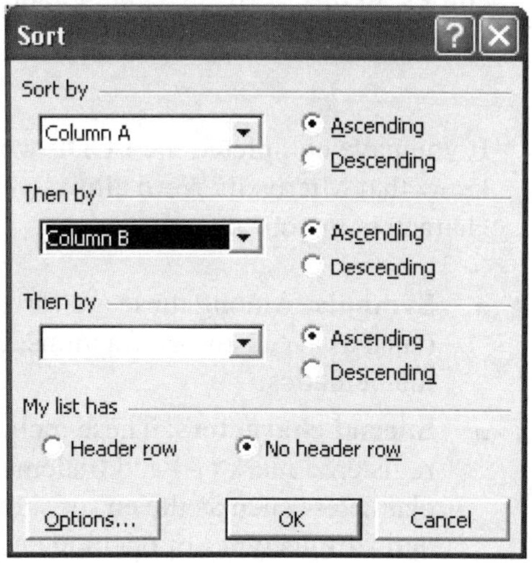

By default, Excel shows the first column in the selected range, *Column A*, in the *Sort by* drop-down box.

In the *Then by* drop-down box, select *Column B*.

Next, select the sort order of *Ascending* for both columns *A* and *B*, and click **OK**.

Your worksheet should now resemble that shown.

	A	B	C	D	E	F	G	H
1								
2			January	February	March	April		Total
3	Conway	John	2356	3621	4185	4560		14722
4	Higgins	Tracey	3463	3981	4210	4974		16628
5	Murphy	Robert	4921	4055	3814	3542		16332
6	Rafferty	Aidan	2512	2864	3290	3741		12407
7	Smith	Catherine	5951	6226	6481	6852		25510
8	Smith	Zowie	3872	2441	2888	4949		14150
9	Sullivan	Andrew	2903	3308	3487	3622		13320
10								
11			25978	26496	28355	32240		113069

The multiple-column sort is useful where one column has duplicate entries. In this exercise, cells *A5* and *A9* both initially contained the same text entry of 'Smith'.

Symbols and special characters

If you have completed the ECDL word processing module, you will know that Microsoft Word allows you to insert symbols and special characters in your documents.

- **Symbols:** Among these are foreign-language letters with accents (such as á, é, ä and ë), fractions, and characters used in science and mathematics.
- **Special characters:** These include the copyright sign (©), registered mark (®) and trademark (TM), plus typographic characters such as the en (or short) dash, the em (or long) dash, and various types of opening and closing quotes.

Like Word, Excel allows you to insert symbols or special characters using the **Insert | Symbol** command. To insert a symbol or special character:

- Click where you want to insert the symbol.
- Choose **Insert | Symbol**, and then click the **Symbols** or **Special Characters** tab.
- Double-click the symbol or character you want to insert.
- Click **Close** to close the dialog box.

Chapter summary: so now you know

A common maintenance task in Excel is *row and column insertion*. Insertion results in the surrounding cells adjusting their positions to make way for the new data. For examples of inserting rows and columns, see Exercises 22.1 and 22.2.

Conversely, *row and column deletion* causes the surrounding cells to move up or to the left, to fill the spaces previously occupied by the deleted data. You can also insert and delete individual cells and cell ranges.

You can reproduce (copy) or move (cut) a selected cell or cell range within the same worksheet, between worksheets in the same workbook, or between different workbooks. A wide variety of *copy, cut and paste methods* are provided by Excel, including drag-and-drop, commands on a pop-up menu activated by right-clicking, menu-bar commands, keyboard shortcuts, and buttons on the *Standard* toolbar. Exercises 22.3 to 22.8 give examples of different ways information can be copied and pasted.

Excel automatically adjusts the *cell references* in calculations whenever the calculations are pasted to a new location. To prevent Excel from adjusting a cell reference in this way, specify the cell address as an *absolute cell reference* in the format (*A1*). Absolute cell references are most commonly used with fixed-factor-type calculations.

Sorting allows you to rearrange selected cells on the basis of the values they contain. Sorting changes only the location of cells, and not their content. The *sort order*, the particular way in which cells are arranged by value, can be alphabetical or numerical, and can be in *ascending* (0–9, A–Z) or *descending* sequence (9–0, Z–A). For examples of simple and complex sorting of cells, see Exercises 22.10 and 22.11.

You can insert symbols and special characters in Excel using the **Insert | Symbol** command.

Quick quiz: inserting, sorting and moving cells

Circle the correct answer to each of the following multiple-choice questions about inserting, sorting and moving cells.

Q1	When you insert a new row or column in a worksheet:
A.	It replaces the selected row or column.
B.	It is inserted below the selected row, or to the right of the selected column.
C.	It is inserted above the selected row, or to the left of the selected column.
D.	It is always inserted at the top of the current worksheet.

Q2	To prevent information being accidentally lost, rows and columns can only be inserted, never deleted.
A.	True.
B.	False.

Q3	The clipboard can hold only one copied item at a time.
A.	True.
B.	False.

Q4	An absolute cell reference, which will not break when a formula is copied and pasted to another location, looks like:
A.	*$(F28)*
B.	*$F28*
C.	*F28$*
D.	*F28*

Q5	When performing a complex sort on several columns of data:
A.	Either all columns must be sorted in ascending order, or all columns must be sorted in descending order.
B.	Each column can be sorted in a different order.
C.	A sort order must be specified for every column selected.
D.	The first column must be sorted before the others.

Answers

1: C, **2:** B, **3:** B, **4:** D, **5:** B.

Chapter 23: More about numbers, text and calculations

In this chapter

In Chapters 19 and 20 you learnt the basics of working with numbers, cell references and text. Now it's time to build on what you know.

Here you will discover that there are really four types of number and two types of cell reference, and that Excel treats the different types in different ways.

You will also learn more about entering text, and meet **AutoFill**, a convenient, time-saving feature for entering data in cells.

New skills

At the end of this chapter you should be able to:

- Choose the appropriate number format for the type of numbers that you want to enter and store in your worksheet.
- Enter text across multiple columns.
- Enter numbers as text.
- Recognize the type of numbers that should be entered in calculations as absolute rather than relative cell references.
- Use **AutoFill** to copy numbers and text, and to increment number series and special entries (dates, days, months and years).
- Use **AutoFill** to copy calculations that apply to multiple rows or columns.

New words

At the end of this chapter you should be able to explain the following terms:

- Number format
- General format
- Comma style
- Currency style
- Percent style
- Relative cell reference
- Absolute cell reference
- Increment
- AutoFill

Numbers: the different formats

In Chapter 19 you learnt that a number was one of the four kinds of entries you could type in a worksheet cell – the others were text, cell references and calculations (formulas and functions).

In fact, Excel recognizes many types of numbers, and calls each a number format. Do not confuse this term with the use of the word 'format' for stylistic items such as bold and italic.

Number format affects only the way that a number looks on screen and on printouts – and not its value. Consider the following example:

- A cell contains the number 1.2345.
- The same cell has a number format of one decimal place.

The number will display as 1.2. But when its cell is used in calculations, the value used will be 1.2345. This can lead to surprising results!

In the example on the right, cell *A1* is multiplied by *B1*, and cell *A2* by *B2*. The results are shown in *C1* and *C2*. *A1* contains the same value as *A2*, but is formatted with only one number after the decimal point.

	A	B	C
1	1.2345	2	2.469
2	1.2	2	2.469

Number format
The way in which Excel displays a number on screen and on printouts. Number format affects only the appearance and not the value of numbers.

The General format

Excel's default number format is called the General format. Unless you change to a different number format, Excel applies this format to every number you enter.

123.4
345.75
9383.5
45

The General format, however, is unsuitable for displaying amounts of money on a worksheet, as you can see from the following points.

Trailing zeros after the decimal point

A zero you entered as the last digit after a decimal point is called a trailing zero. The General format does not display trailing zeros.

Enter 123.00, for example, and Excel's General format displays 123. Enter 123.40, and Excel's General format displays 123.4.

Thousands separators

The General format does not automatically insert the comma symbol (,) to separate thousands.

Enter 2500, for example, and Excel displays it as 2500, not 2,500.

All the above points make the General format unsuitable for displaying amounts of money on a worksheet.

Currency symbols

If you type a currency symbol (such as £) before a number (such as 123), Excel may treat your entry as text rather than a number. As a result, using the entry of £123 in a calculation may generate Excel's #VALUE! error message. Alternatively, Excel may simply ignore your entry when performing the calculation.

The Comma style

Change to the Comma style for Excel to insert a comma to separate thousands. Excel also displays all numbers to two decimal places. Exercise 23.1 demonstrates the Comma style.

Exercise 23.1: Changing number format to the Comma style

Comma Style button

1) Open *Sheet2* of your workbook and select cell range *C3:C9*.
2) Click the **Comma Style** button on the *Formatting* toolbar.

   Excel inserts commas and two decimal places in the selected cell range, as shown on the right.
3) Choose **Edit | Undo Style** (or press **Ctrl+z**) to revert to General format.

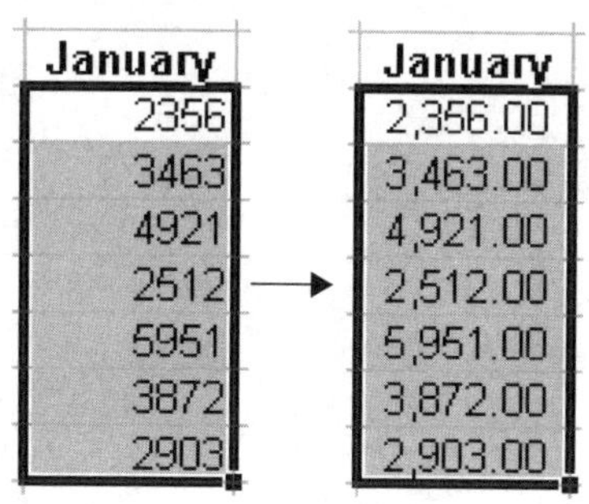

The Currency style

Change to the Currency style when your numbers represent amounts of money. Exercise 23.2 demonstrates the currency format.

Exercise 23.2: Changing number format to the Currency style

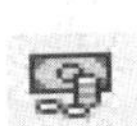

Currency Style button

1) On your worksheet select cell range *C3:H11*.
2) Click the **Currency Style** button on the *Formatting* toolbar.

Excel inserts the currency symbol (£), the thousands separator (,) and trailing zeros.

	A	B	C	D	E	F	G	H
1								
2			**January**	**February**	**March**	**April**		**Total**
3	*Conway*	*John*	£2,356.00	£3,621.00	£4,185.00	£4,560.00		£14,722.00
4	*Higgins*	*Tracey*	£3,463.00	£3,981.00	£4,210.00	£4,974.00		£16,628.00
5	*Murphy*	*Robert*	£4,921.00	£4,055.00	£3,814.00	£3,542.00		£16,332.00
6	*Rafferty*	*Aidan*	£2,512.00	£2,864.00	£3,290.00	£3,741.00		£12,407.00
7	*Smith*	*Catherine*	£5,951.00	£6,226.00	£6,481.00	£6,852.00		£25,510.00
8	*Smith*	*Zowie*	£3,872.00	£2,441.00	£2,888.00	£4,949.00		£14,150.00
9	*Sullivan*	*Andrew*	£2,903.00	£3,308.00	£3,487.00	£3,622.00		£13,320.00
10								
11			£25,978.00	£26,496.00	£28,355.00	£32,240.00		£113,069.00

3) Choose **Edit | Undo Style** (or press **Ctrl+z**) to revert to General format.

The Percent style

This number format performs two actions:

- It multiplies the selected cell or range by 100.
- It places the per cent sign (%) after each selected number.

Use it to display decimal fractions (such as 0.0525) as more readable percentages (such as 5.25%).

In Exercise 23.3, you will generate some decimal fractions suitable for expression as percentages. In Exercise 23.4, you will then change the numbers to the Percent style.

Exercise 23.3: Creating decimal fractions

In this exercise you will add two new items to *Sheet2*:

- A new column to show each person's total as a proportion of the overall total.
- A new row to show each month's total as a proportion of the overall.

1) Enter the per cent symbol (%) in cells *I2* and *B13*, make the symbols bold, and centre-align them.
2) In *I3*, enter the formula =H3/H11 to calculate the percentage of the total contributed by John Conway.
   Enter similar formulas for cells *I4:I9*.
   For example, in *I5* enter = H5/H11 and in *I6* enter =H6/H11.
   Column *I* should look as shown.

I
%
0.130204
0.147061
0.144443
0.109729
0.225614
0.125145
0.117804

3) In *C13*, enter the formula =C11/H11 to calculate the percentage of the total contributed in January.
   Enter similar formulas for cells *D13:F13*. For example, in *D13* enter = D11/H11. Row *13* should look as shown below.

13		%	0.229754	0.234335	0.250776	0.285136

Exercise 23.4: Applying the Percent style

Now you will display the calculation results from Exercise 23.3 as percentages, using the Percent style. You will also apply a fill (coloured background) to the percentage cells.

%

Percent style button

1) Select range *I3:I9* and click the **Percent Style** button on the *Formatting* toolbar. Also centre-align the cells.
2) With range *I3:I9* still selected, click the drop-down arrow to the right of the **Fill Color** button on the *Formatting* toolbar.
3) From the colour palette, choose *Gray-25%*.
4) Repeat steps 1, 2, and 3 for *C13:F13*.

	A	B	C	D	E	F	G	H	I
1									
2			**January**	**February**	**March**	**April**		**Total**	%
3	*Conway*	*John*	2356	3621	4185	4560		14722	13%
4	*Higgins*	*Tracey*	3463	3981	4210	4974		16628	15%
5	*Murphy*	*Robert*	4921	4055	3814	3542		16332	14%
6	*Rafferty*	*Aidan*	2512	2864	3290	3741		12407	11%
7	*Smith*	*Catherine*	5951	6226	6481	6852		25510	23%
8	*Smith*	*Zowie*	3872	2441	2888	4949		14150	13%
9	*Sullivan*	*Andrew*	2903	3308	3487	3622		13320	12%
10									
11			25978	26496	28355	32240		113069	
12									
13		%	23%	23%	25%	29%			

Well done. You have finished this exercise. Your worksheet should now look as shown above.

Changing from the General format

There are two ways that you can change Excel's number format:

- First, enter the numbers, and then change the number format.
- Change the number format of the blank cells first, and then enter the numbers.

The second method is better. If you are creating a new worksheet to enter financial amounts, select the whole worksheet and change the number format to Currency style before entering any numbers. The Currency style will affect only the entered numbers and not any text entries.

The Number format

Spreadsheets are often used to record physical measurements and the results of laboratory experiments. Such numbers do not represent financial amounts, so the Currency style is inappropriate. Moreover, such numbers typically require a number of decimal places greater than two or three. The number format to apply in such situations is called – guess what – Number format. Exercise 23.5 provides an example.

Exercise 23.5: Specifying the number of decimal places

Your task is to record the following numbers to four places of decimals: 3.4512, 5.13, 9.59383 and 4.531.

1) Click the *Sheet1* tab to display the first worksheet of your workbook.
2) Select cell range *B84:B88* and choose **Format | Cells**.
3) On the **Number** tab, select the *Category* of *Number*, and select 4 for *Decimal places*. Click **OK**.

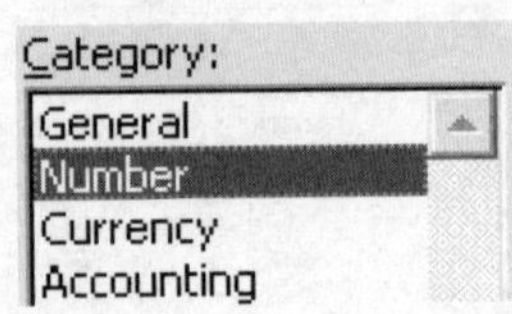

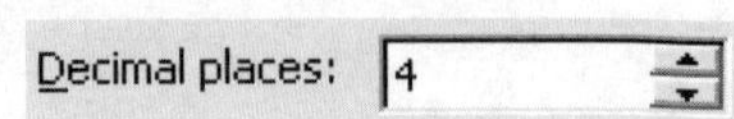

4) Click *B84*, and enter the first number. Next, enter the remaining numbers in the other three cells in the range.
5) As shown here, Excel displays your cell entries to the specified number of decimal places.
   - Where an entered number had more than four decimal places, Excel displayed only the first four.
   - Where the number had less, Excel added trailing zeros.

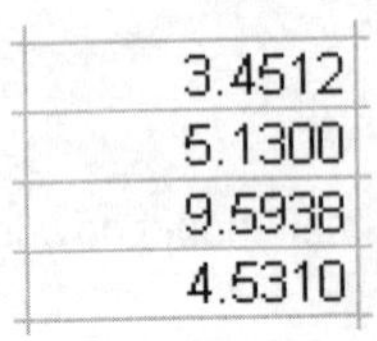

Also available when you select *Number* on the **Number** tab of the *Format Cells* dialog box is an option to specify the thousands separator (,).

Toolbar buttons

Two buttons on Excel's *Formatting* toolbar offer quick ways of increasing or reducing the number of decimal places displayed in a selected cell or range. Each time you click a button, the number of decimal places in the selected cells is increased or decreased by one.

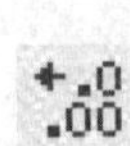

Increase Decimal button

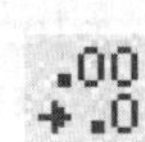

Decrease Decimal button

The buttons work with numbers in the General, Currency and Number formats.

Excel and dates

Whether entered with financial transactions or results of experiments, dates can be very important in a worksheet. Excel treats dates as numbers, with the serial number 1 corresponding to the date

1 January 1900. In this way Excel can add and subtract dates, and include them in other calculations.

Entering dates

Use a slash or a hyphen to separate the parts of a date. For example:

- 17/10/99
- 26-Nov-01

If you just type in the day and the month, for example 13/02 or 19-11, Excel assumes the current year.

When you type a date that Microsoft Excel recognizes, it applies one of its built-in date formats to the cell, and right-aligns it.

If Microsoft Excel cannot recognize the date, the date is recorded as text, and is left-aligned in the cell.

Formatting dates

The way that Excel displays entered dates depends on the number format applied to the cell containing the dates.

To view a list of possible date options, choose **Format | Cells**, select the **Number** tab, and select *Date* in the *Category* list. You can then see the date format options in the *Type* list.

Become familiar with how Excel handles dates by entering a number of dates in different formats in your worksheet. Then, select the cells and apply to your entries some of the formats listed in the *Format Cells* dialog box (see opposite).

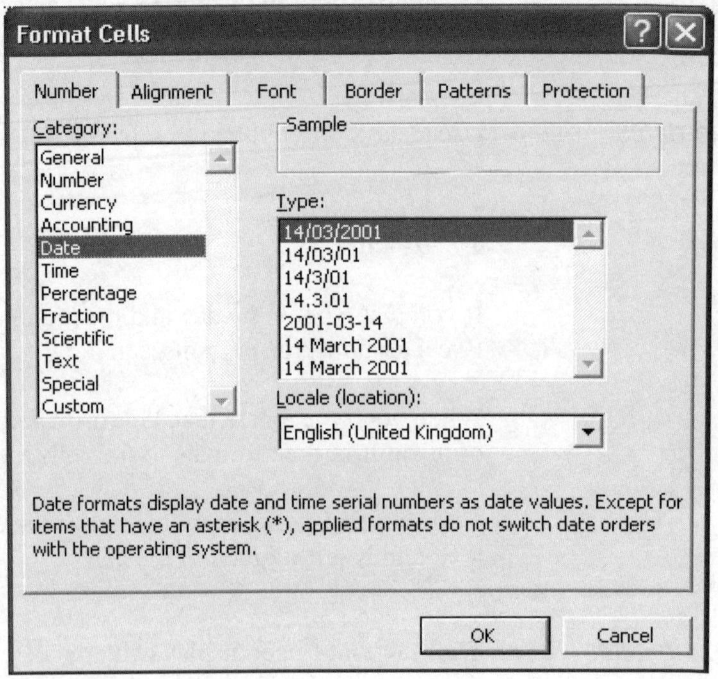

Regional settings

Options that you select in the **Regional Settings** of the Windows *Control Panel* affect the default currency and date conventions applied by Excel to your cell entries:

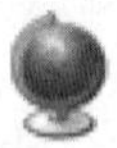

- **Changing currency:** To use a different currency on your workbooks, choose **Start | Control Panel**, and double-click the **Regional and Language Options** icon. On the **Regional Options** tab, select the required country and click **Customize**. On the **Currency** tab of the *Customize Regional Options* dialog box, accept or amend the currency conventions, such as symbol, number of decimal places and digit-grouping symbol.
- **Changing date:** To change the date conventions used in your workbooks, select the required country on the **Regional Options** tab, click **Customize**, and on the **Date** tab of the *Customize Regional Options* dialog box, accept or amend the calendar conventions.

Excel and text

Two further items you need to know about Excel and text: you can enter text that displays across several columns of a worksheet, and you can enter numbers as text.

Text across multiple columns

Sometimes you may want to enter a line of text that is longer than the width of a single cell. Excel allows you to do this – provided that the text does not run into any cell that has data in it.

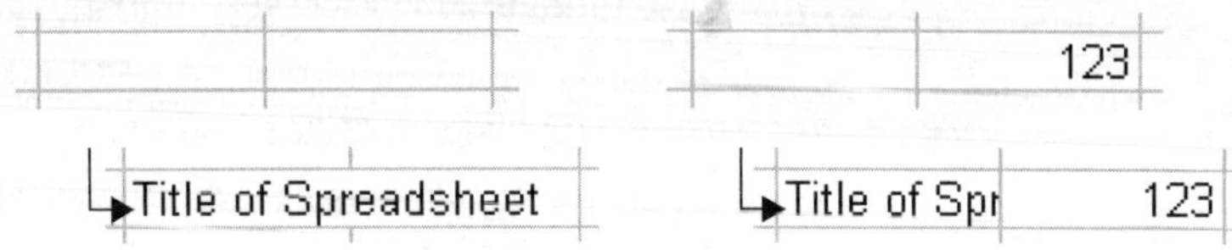

Exercise 23.6 provides an example of entering and displaying text that stretches across several columns.

Exercise 23.6: Entering text across multiple columns

1) Select row *1* of *Sheet2* by clicking the row heading.
2) Choose **Insert | Rows**.
3) Press **Ctrl+y** to repeat the row insertion. You now have two new, blank rows at the top of the worksheet.
4) In *C2*, enter the following text:
   First Quarter Sales Figures
5) Select *C2*, click the *Font Size* drop-down box, and select 14 point.
   With *C2* still selected, click the **Bold** and **Italic** buttons on the *Formatting* toolbar.
   The top rows of *Sheet2* should now look as shown.

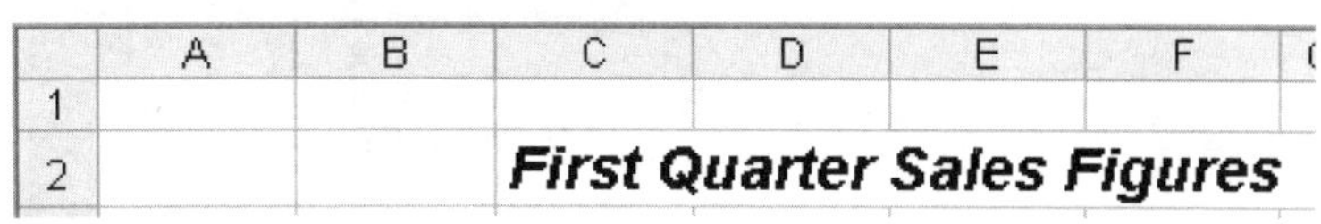

Entering numbers as text

Why would you ever want Excel to treat a number as anything other than a number? The answer is when the number is not an amount but an identifier of some kind. Examples include part and model numbers (such as 010-34 or M5339), ID numbers (such as 99-10837), and telephone and fax numbers.

If you find it hard to think of a telephone number as anything other than a number, imagine how ridiculous it would be to add together two telephone numbers!

To enter a number as text, you must first apply the Text format to the empty cells, and then enter the numbers, as shown in Exercise 23.7. If you enter the numbers first, Excel will not apply the Text format to them – you will need to re-enter all the numbers.

Exercise 23.7: Formatting numbers as text

1) On *Sheet2*, select cells *B20:B23*.
2) Choose **Format | Cells**.
3) On the **Number** tab, select *Text* from the *Category* list, and click **OK**.
4) Enter the numbers in cells *B20:B23* as shown here.

010-56
M56-47N
091-10000
W1-S9

Excel treats the numbers as text. You can now delete the four entries from the worksheet.

Excel's AutoFill feature

Excel provides a very convenient feature called AutoFill for copying or incrementing (increasing in a defined sequence) the entries in a cell or range.

Exercise 23.8: Using AutoFill to copy and increment numbers and text

1) In *Sheet1*, enter the following in cell range *M19:Q19,N20*.

19	12	12	Hello	Jan	Mon
20		13			

2) Click cell *M19* and position the cursor over the fill handle – the black square at the bottom-right of the selected cell.

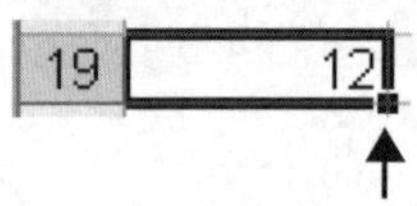

The fill handle

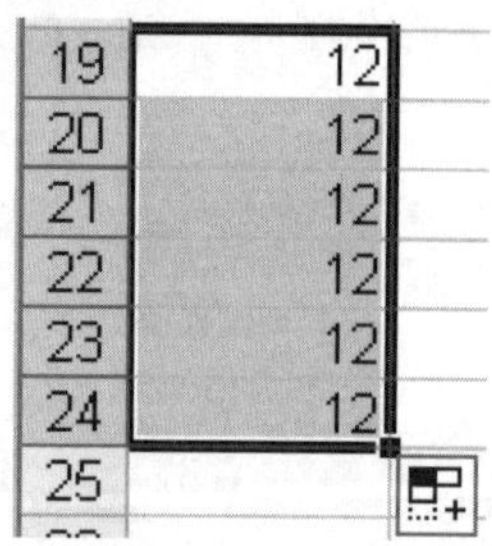

3) Drag the fill handle down to cell *M24*. Excel copies the contents of cell *M19* to the other selected cells.

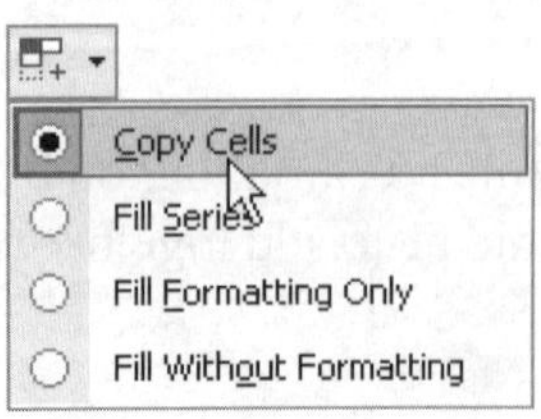

An **AutoFill Options** button appears below the cell range. Click the down-arrow which appears at the right of the button when you hover your mouse over it to see the options you can apply to the filled cells. Excel has automatically 'guessed' that you want to use the *Copy Cells* option to copy the contents of *M19* to the other selected cells.

4) Select cell range *N19:N20* and drag the fill handle down to *N24*. This time Excel uses the *Fill Series* option to continue incrementing by 1 the numbers it fills into subsequent cells.

5) Select *O19* and drag the fill handle down to *O24*. Excel uses the *Copy Cells* option to copy the contents of *O19* to the other selected cells.
6) Select *P19* and drag the fill handle down to *P24*. Excel uses the *Fill Series* option to increment the months of the year as it fills in subsequent cells.
7) Select *Q19* and drag the fill handle down to *Q24*. Excel uses the *Fill Series* option to increment the days of the week as it fills in subsequent cells.

Your worksheet should now look as shown.

	M	N	O	P	Q
18					
19	12	12	Hello	Jan	Mon
20	12	13	Hello	Feb	Tue
21	12	14	Hello	Mar	Wed
22	12	15	Hello	Apr	Thu
23	12	16	Hello	May	Fri
24	12	17	Hello	Jun	Sat

AutoFill and single numbers

For cell ranges *M19:M24* and *O19:O24*, you began by selecting a single cell containing a number (12) and text item (Hello). As you dragged the fill handle, Excel copied the number and text into the cells that you dragged over.

AutoFill and number series

For cell range *N19:N24*, you began by selecting two cells. Excel recognized that they contained two numbers in an increasing series (12 and 13). As you dragged the fill handle, Excel placed increments of the series (14, 15, and so on) into the cells that you dragged over.

AutoFill and months, days, times and years

For cell ranges *P19:P24* and *Q19:Q24*, Excel recognized that the single cell you selected contained the name of a month and a day. As you dragged the fill handle, Excel placed increments of the series (Feb, Mar ... and Tue, Wed ...).

Excel also recognizes times (such as 9:00 or 12:30), years (such as 1998 or 2003) and dates (such as 1-May or 10-April).

AutoFill and calculations

Columns or rows of a worksheet often need the same action applied to them; for example, summing or averaging. Use AutoFill in a two-step process to avoid entering calculations (formulas and functions) individually to sum or average each row or column:

- Enter the calculation for one row or column.
- Use AutoFill to copy the formula or function to the adjacent cells.

AutoFill and cell references

AutoFill adjusts the cell references as it copies the calculation to the selected cells.

Where a calculation contains a fixed factor – such as a tax, currency conversion or sales commission rate – you will not want Excel to adjust the fixed factor's cell reference as it autofills the selected cells. In such cases, first change the fixed factor's cell reference to an absolute cell reference. Exercise 23.9 shows AutoFill used with relative and absolute cell references.

Exercise 23.9: Using AutoFill to copy calculations

1) On *Sheet2*, select cell range *H6:I11*, and press **Delete** to delete its contents.

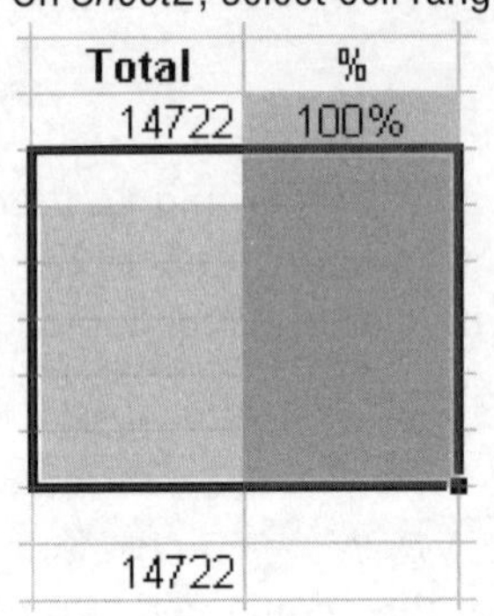

Cell *I5* now shows 100%, and the total cell *H13* shows 14722.

2) Select cell *H5* and drag the fill handle down to cell *H11*.

AutoFill extends the calculation in *H5* to the cells in the range *H6:H11*.

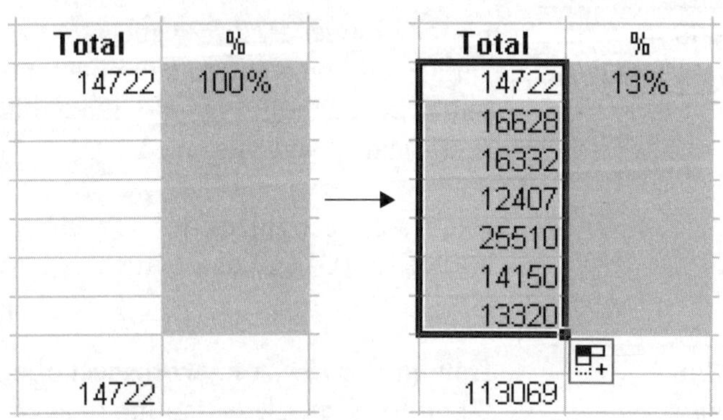

In each case, AutoFill adjusts the cell reference. For example, cell *H5* contains the function =SUM(C5:F5) but cell *H9* contains the function =SUM(C9:F9).

3) Select cell *I5*, and edit the function to change relative cell reference H13 to absolute cell reference HI3.

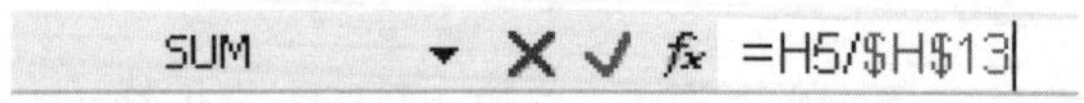

4) With *I5* still selected, drag the fill handle down to cell *I11*.
AutoFill extends the calculation in *I5* to the cells in the range *I6:I11*. As it does, AutoFill adjusts the relative cell reference *H5* but not the absolute cell reference *HI3*.

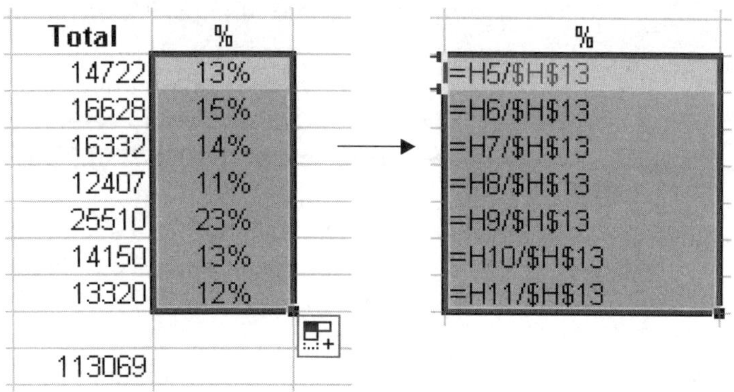

AutoFill works across rows as well as down columns, as you will learn in steps 5 and 6 of this exercise.

5) Select cell range *D13:F13*, and press **Delete** to delete their contents.

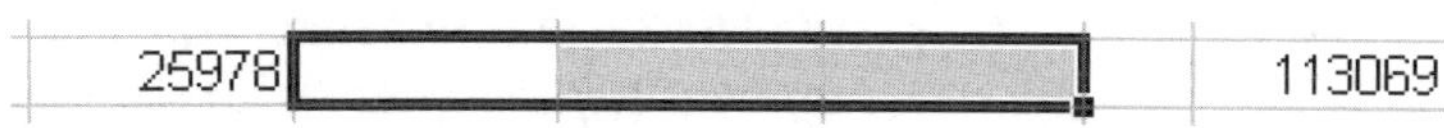

6) Select *C13* and drag the fill handle to the right as far as cell *F13*.

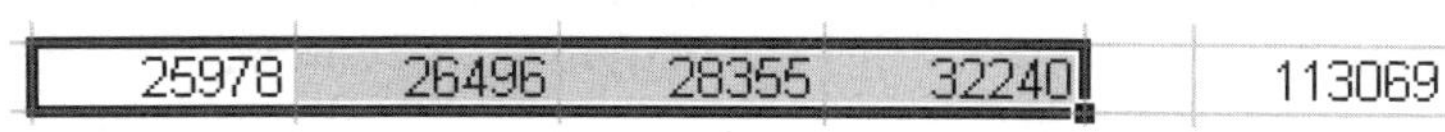

AutoFill keyboard shortcuts

You may find it quicker to apply AutoFill using the keyboard shortcuts rather than dragging the fill handle with the mouse. Follow these steps:

- Select the cells you want to fill from.
- Drag the mouse down (or right) to select the cells you want to fill.
- Press **Ctrl+d** to fill down or **Ctrl+r** to fill right.

AutoFill
An Excel tool for quickly copying or incrementing (increasing in a defined sequence) the entries in a cell or range.

You have now finished the fifth chapter of the ECDL spreadsheets module. You may save and close your workbook, and close Excel.

Chapter summary: so now you know

Excel's default number format, the *General format*, does not display trailing zeros, does not automatically insert commas to separate thousands, and is unsuitable for entering financial amounts. The *Comma style* automatically inserts a comma to separate thousands, and displays all numbers to two places of decimals. See Exercise 23.1 for an example of applying the Comma style.

The *Currency style* automatically inserts your national currency symbol, and follows your currency's convention for decimal places. See Exercise 23.2 for an example of applying the Currency style.

The *Percent style* multiplies numbers by 100, and places the per cent sign (%) after each one. See Exercise 23.4 for an example of applying the Percent style.

When changing to a non-default number format, it is better to do so before you enter your numbers. Only numbers, not text, are affected by number formatting.

You can enter multi-column text (provided the other, over-typed cells are blank) and format text as numbers. This can be useful when the numbers are *identifiers* (part numbers, phone numbers and so on) rather than amounts.

In calculations, cells can have *relative references* or *absolute references*. Excel changes relative cell references when you copy the calculation to another cell; absolute references are unchanged by copying. Use absolute cell references for cells containing fixed factors such as tax rates.

AutoFill copies the contents of a cell to other, selected cells in the same row or column. AutoFill can also increment a series of numbers, times, dates, days, months and years. See Exercises 23.8 and 23.9 for examples of using AutoFill.

Quick quiz: more about numbers, text and calculations

Circle the correct answer to each of the following multiple-choice questions about numbers, text and calculations.

Q1	Which of the following statements about the Comma style is not true?
A.	The Comma style shows numbers to two decimal places.
B.	The Comma style changes the decimal separator from a full stop to a comma.
C.	The Comma style uses a comma as a thousands separator.
D.	The Comma style can be applied using a button on the *Formatting* toolbar.

Q2	The number format of a cell can be set before entering a number in it.
A.	True.
B.	False.

Q3	Excel never allows text to span multiple columns.
A.	True.
B.	False.

Q4	Relative cell references may change when a formula is copied to another cell.
A.	True.
B.	False.

Q5	You can use AutoFill to:
A.	Copy numbers and text to subsequent cells.
B.	Increment months of the year and days of the week in subsequent cells.
C.	Copy formulas to subsequent cells.
D.	All of the above.

Answers

1: C, **2:** A, **3:** B, **4:** A, **5:** D.

Chapter 24: Charting with Excel

In this chapter

So far you have used Excel to enter, edit, calculate, format and reposition cells on your worksheets.

In this chapter you will learn how to present the contents of your worksheet cells in what Excel – an American product – calls a chart. On this side of the Atlantic, we would use the term 'graph' or 'diagram' rather than chart.

New skills

At the end of this chapter you should be able to:

- Use Excel's *Chart Wizard* to create charts that are based on the numbers, text and calculations in your worksheet.
- Choose the appropriate options from the dialog boxes of Excel's *Chart Wizard.*
- Create column, bar and pie charts.
- Format chart text and change chart colours.
- Add and edit data labels.
- Move and resize charts.
- Change the scale of chart axes.

New words

At the end of this chapter you should be able to explain the following terms:

- Chart
- Chart area
- Plot area
- Data point
- Data series
- Data label

Charting: the two steps

You follow two main steps to creating a chart in Excel:

- Select the cells whose contents you want to chart.

- Select and run Excel's *Chart Wizard*.

Excel chart
A graphic or diagram based on the numbers, text and calculations that are located in the rows and columns of an Excel worksheet.

The four dialog boxes to an Excel chart

When you run the *Chart Wizard*, Excel presents you with a series of four dialog boxes. These are:

- **Chart Type:** Excel offers lots of different chart types. You decide which is best for your data.
- **Chart Source Data:** What data do you want to chart – all the cells on your worksheet, or just a selected cell range?
- **Chart Options:** How do you want your chart to look? Excel offers a variety of options.
- **Chart Location:** Where do you want the chart stored – on your current worksheet, on a different worksheet, or in a new workbook? You decide.

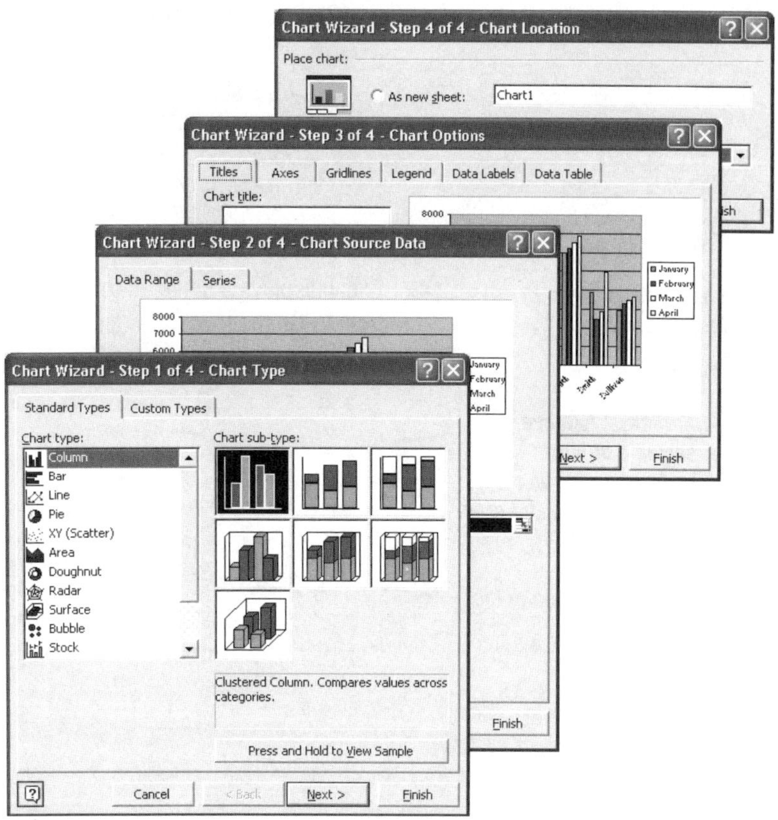

Does this seem like a lot of dialog boxes to learn about? Don't worry. All four dialogs offer a default option that in most cases will create an impressive-looking, ECDL-test-passing chart. So, when in doubt, just click the **Next** button on the first three dialog boxes, and the **Finish** button on the fourth.

Perform Exercise 24.1 to make yourself familiar with charting in Excel.

Exercise 24.1: Creating a simple Excel chart

1) Open the workbook that you saved in Chapter 23 and click *Sheet2* to display its second worksheet.
2) Select the non-adjacent cell range *A4:A11,C4:C11*.

   Do this by clicking in *A4*, dragging the mouse down to *A11*, and releasing the mouse button. Next, hold down the **Ctrl** key, click in cell *C4* and drag down to *C11*.

	A	B	C
4			**January**
5	*Conway*	*John*	2356
6	*Higgins*	*Tracey*	3463
7	*Murphy*	*Robert*	4921
8	*Rafferty*	*Aidan*	2512
9	*Smith*	*Catherine*	5951
10	*Smith*	*Zowie*	3872
11	*Sullivan*	*Andrew*	2903

Chart Wizard button

3) Click the **Chart Wizard** button on the *Standard* toolbar.
4) Excel displays a series of four dialog boxes. On the first three, click the **Next** button. On the fourth and last, click **Finish**.

   Congratulations. You have drawn your first chart in Excel!

Chart area: to move your chart to a different position on your worksheet, click here and drag with the mouse

Plot area: the area of the plotted chart

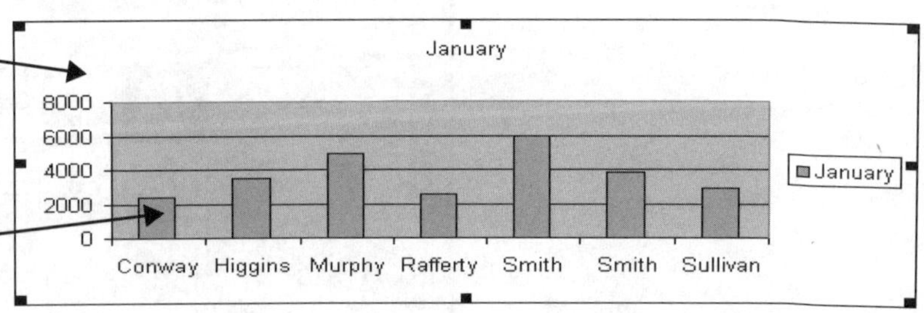

5) Unfortunately, Excel positions your chart on top of your data, so you cannot see both at the same time.

   Move the chart by clicking any blank part of the chart margin – Excel calls this the chart area – and then dragging the chart down until its top-left corner is positioned over the cell *B19*.

Chart area
The margin area inside the chart boundaries but outside the actual plotted chart. It typically holds labels identifying the chart axes.

To move your chart to a different position on the worksheet, click anywhere on the chart area and drag with the mouse. To delete a chart, click anywhere on the chart area and press the **Delete** key.

Plot area
The area containing the actual plot. It is bounded by the two chart axes and enclosed within the chart area.

Charts: two ideas you need to know

All charting – in Excel or with pen and paper – is based on two very basic ideas: the *data point* and the *data series*. You will see these two terms a lot on Excel's charting dialog boxes and online help screens. Understand these two ideas and you will be able to exploit fully Excel's charting possibilities.

About data points

Data point: the idea is so simple that you will wonder why anyone bothered even to give it a name. Consider the four examples below.

Item	Value		Item	Value
Apples	4		January	£1,965.34
Pears	3		February	£2,451.50
Bananas	6		March	£8,301.49
Item	**Value**		**Item**	**Value**
Mary	15%		Sales	£4,954,032.00
Catherine	50%		Costs	£394,823.00
Margaret	35%		Overheads	£25,068.00

Each example consists of individual items being measured. They are types of fruit, months of the year, people and amounts of money.

Each item has a number that is its measured value. A data point is a single item and its numerical value.

In the first example, the three data points are: Apples and 4, Pears and 3 and Bananas and 6. Other data points from the above examples are February and £2,451.50, Catherine and 50%, and Overheads and £25,068.00.

A data point always has two parts: the item and the value. On its own, a number is not a data point, nor is an item. You need both for a data point.

Data point
An item being measured and its measured value.

About data series

A single data point does not tell us very much. A chart is useful only if there is more than one data point. A collection of data points is called a data series.

For instance, you may want to create a chart that shows the company's sales figures for different months, or a chart that compares one month's sales figures for different departments.

Data series
A group of related data points. For example, your data series may compare different items measured at the same time, or single items measured at different times.

Single data series charts

We used the word 'simple' to describe the chart that you created in Exercise 24.1. More precisely, it is an example of a single data series chart.

Exercise 24.2: Creating more single data series charts

1) Practise your charting skills using the data on *Sheet2* of your workbook to create the four charts below, using the indicated non-adjacent cell ranges.

Data Series: A4:A11,F4:F1

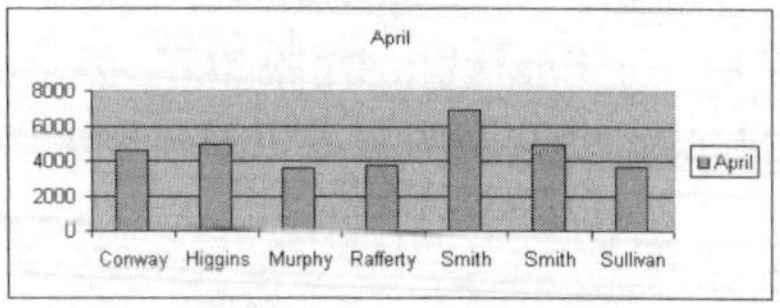

Data Series: A4:A11,I4:I11

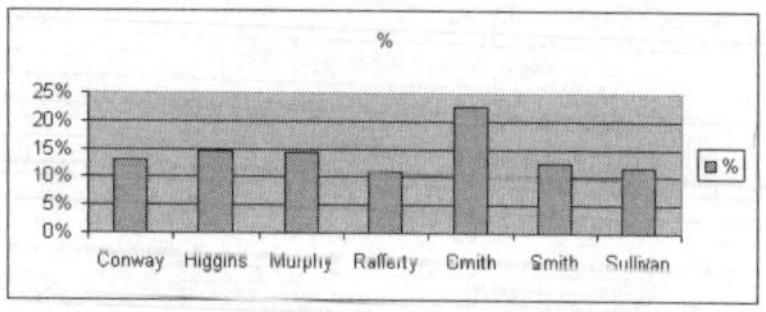

Data Series: C4:F4,C15:F15

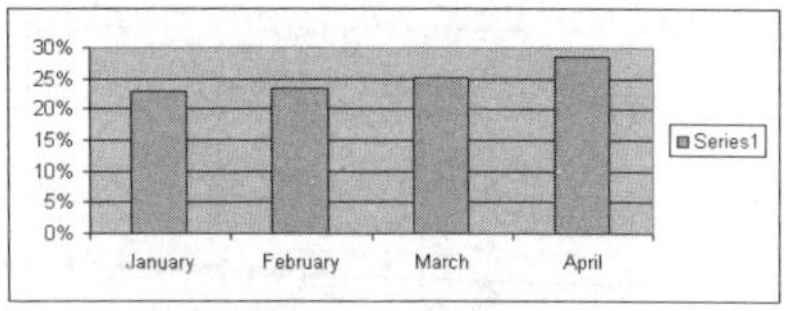

Data Series: B4:B11,H4:H11

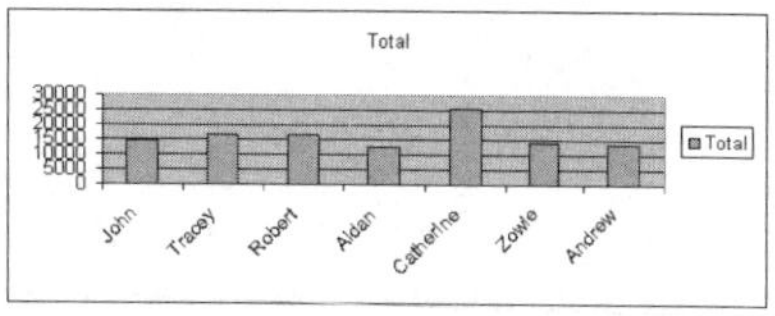

2) Drag the first chart down beneath the chart from Exercise 24.1. Then drag the other three down *Sheet2* so that each is positioned beneath the previous one.

Creating a multiple data series chart

You can have more than one data series in a collection of related information.

Consider the part of your worksheet shown on the right. How many data series can you see? Answer: two.

	January	February
Conway	2356	3621
Higgins	3463	3981
Murphy	4921	4055
Rafferty	2512	2864
Smith	5951	6226
Smith	3872	2441
Sullivan	2903	3308

There is one data series for January, and a second for February.

	January
Conway	2356
Higgins	3463
Murphy	4921
Rafferty	2512
Smith	5951
Smith	3872
Sullivan	2903

	February
Conway	3621
Higgins	3981
Murphy	4055
Rafferty	2864
Smith	6226
Smith	2441
Sullivan	3308

Two data series, one for each of the two months

In Exercises 24.3 and 24.4 you will create a two-data series and a three-data series chart.

Exercise 24.3: Creating a two-data series chart in Excel

1) Select the cell range *A4:A8,C4:D8*.
2) Click the **Chart Wizard** button and accept the default options in the sequence of four dialog boxes. Your chart should look as shown below.

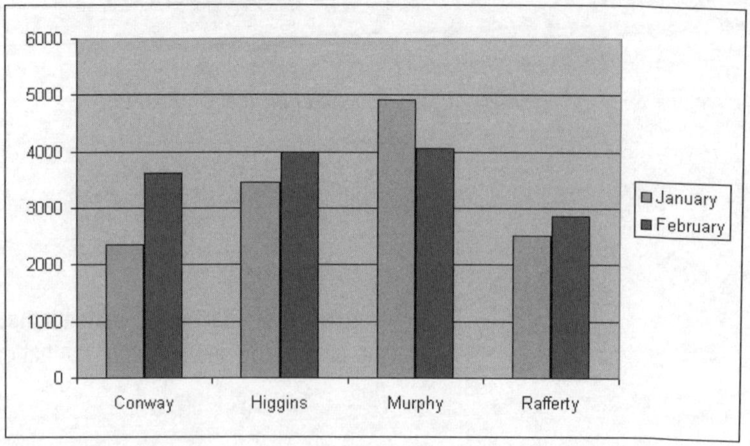

3) Drag your chart down the worksheet to beneath the last of the four charts that you created in Exercise 24.2.

When Excel draws a chart with more than a single data series, it uses a different colour to represent different items.

Exercise 24.4: Creating a three-data series chart in Excel

1) Select the cell range *A4:A8,C4:E8*.
2) Click the **Chart Wizard** button and accept the default options in the sequence of four dialog boxes. Your chart should look as shown.

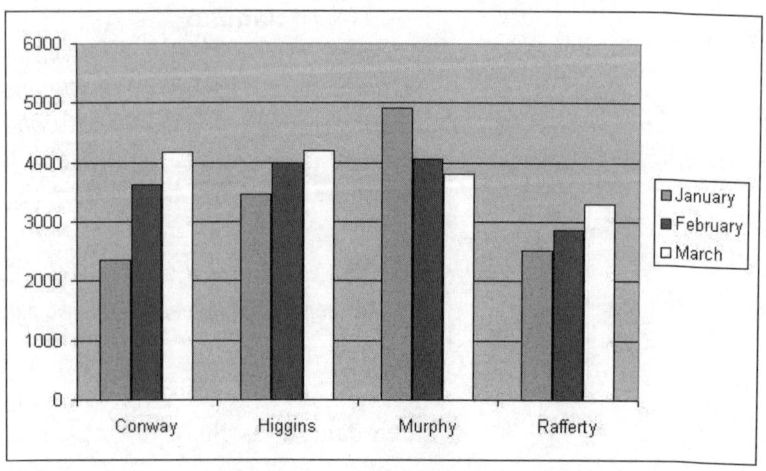

3) Drag the chart down the worksheet to beneath the chart that you created in Exercise 24.3.

Editing your chart

When you create a chart, don't think of it as fixed forever. You can change just about every aspect of a chart.

Changing chart data

You can amend the content of worksheet cells on which your chart is based: as soon as you change the cells in your worksheet, Excel updates the chart to reflect your changes.

Resizing the chart

Changing your chart's size can affect its appearance dramatically. To resize a chart:

- Click once on the chart area. Handles (small black squares) appear around the chart's edges.
- Click any handle and hold down the mouse button as you drag the chart to a different shape.

If you drag on a corner handle, the chart expands and contracts proportionately to its current size; if you drag on an edge handle, the chart expands or contracts in that direction only. Excel automatically adjusts the font of chart text as you resize.

Changing the chart title

To edit the chart title, click anywhere on it, and then click anywhere within the title text. You can now edit the text.

Removing the chart title

To remove the chart title, click it once and press **Delete**.

Reformatting the chart title

To reformat the chart title, double-click anywhere on it to display the *Format Chart Title* dialog box. Select the options you require from the three tabs of the dialog box: **Patterns**, **Font** and **Alignment**.

Adding a chart title

If your chart does not have a title, you can add one as follows:

- Right-click the chart area.
- From the pop-up menu displayed, choose **Chart Options**, select the **Titles** tab, type the new title in the *Chart title* box, and click **OK**.

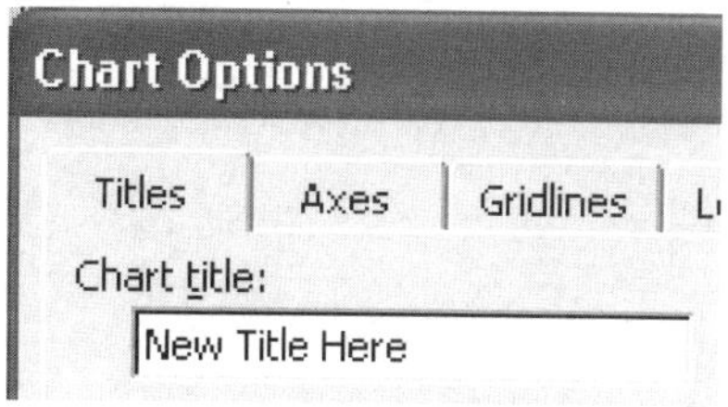

Chart title

Text describing the chart. By default, Excel centres the chart title in the chart area over the plot area.

Adding data labels

In an Excel chart, a data label is an item showing the name (such as Conway) or value (such as £2,356.00) of a data point in a plotted data series. By default, Excel does not display labels.

You can add two kinds of data labels to a chart:

- **Value labels:** These indicate the numerical values of the individual data points. See Exercise 24.5.
- **Text labels:** These display the names of the data points. By default, Excel already displays these names on an axis. See Exercise 24.6.

Exercise 24.5: Adding data labels

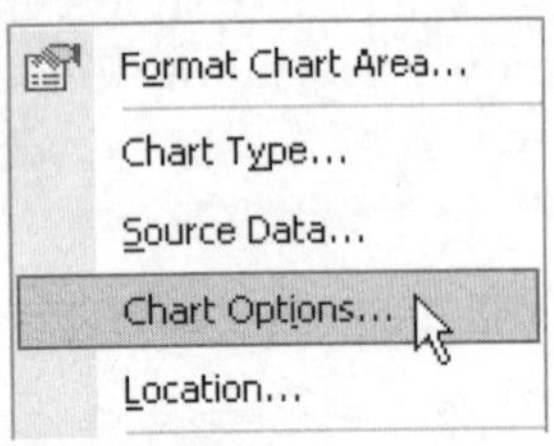

1) On *Sheet2*, click the chart area of the first chart you created, the one in Exercise 24.1, and press **Ctrl+c** to copy it to the clipboard.
2) Click the *Sheet3* tab to display the third worksheet of your workbook. Click cell *B3* and press **Ctrl+v** to paste the chart from the clipboard.
3) Right-click the chart area, choose **Chart Options** from the pop-up menu, and select the **Data Labels** tab of the dialog box.
4) Select the *Value* option, and click **OK**.

   Adding data labels to your chart provides more information to the reader, but has the disadvantage of making your chart more cluttered. You can remedy this by stretching the chart horizontally.
5) Click the chart, and then click the middle handle on the right edge of the chart area.
6) Drag with the mouse until the chart's right boundary ends in column *K*. The axes and plot area of your chart should look as shown below.

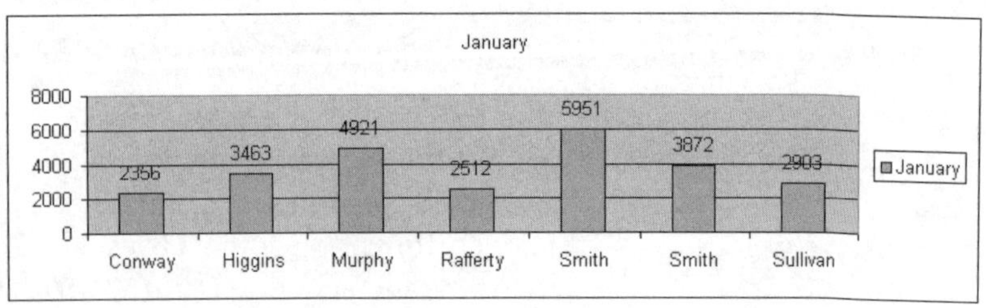

Exercise 24.6: Adding data name labels

1) Is the first chart you created, the one in Exercise 24.1, still in the clipboard? If not, copy it to the clipboard now.
2) Click a cell beneath the chart pasted in Exercise 24.5, and press **Ctrl+v**. Right-click the chart area, choose **Chart Options** from the pop-up menu, and select the **Data Labels** tab of the dialog box.

3) Select the *Category name* option, and click **OK**.
4) As in Exercise 24.5, drag the chart's right boundary to column *K*. The axes and plot area of your chart should look as shown below.

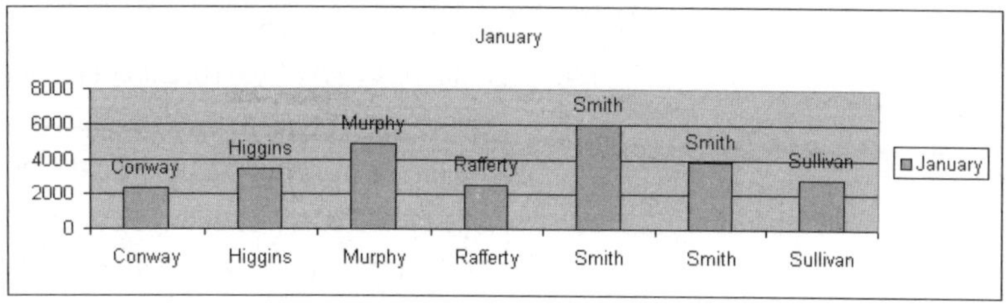

Formatting data labels

To format data labels, right-click a label, choose **Format Data Labels** from the pop-up menu, and select your required options from the following four dialog box tabs: **Patterns**, **Font**, **Number** and **Alignment**.

Data label
The name or numerical value of a data point in a plotted data series.

Removing labels

To remove labels, right-click the chart area, and choose **Chart Options**. Select the **Data Labels** tab, and choose the *None* option.

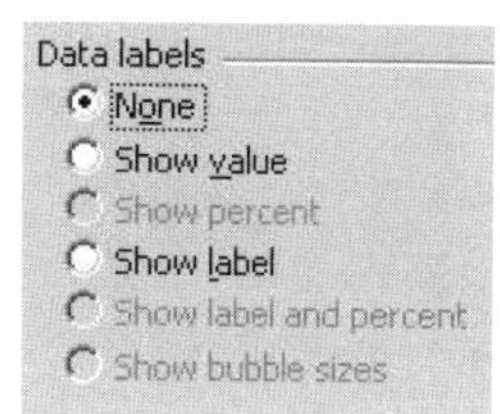

Changing the scale

To change the scale of an axis, double-click anywhere along the axis and choose **Format Axis** from the pop-up menu.

Excel allows you to change the minimum, maximum and increment values displayed for each axis, and the point at which the two axes cross. In Exercise 24.7 you will change the scale of a chart's vertical (or *y*) axis.

Exercise 24.7: Changing the scale of the vertical axis

1) Is the first chart you created, the one in Exercise 24.1, still in the clipboard? If not, copy it to the clipboard now.
2) Click the *Sheet3* tab to display the third worksheet of your workbook. Click a cell beneath the chart pasted in Exercise 24.6, and press **Ctrl+v**.
3) Click the chart, and then click the middle handle on its lower edge. Drag down the mouse until the chart is about twice its original height.
4) Double-click anywhere on the chart's vertical axis and, on the *Format Axis* dialog box, select the **Scale** tab.
5) Change the value in the *Minimum* box from 0 to 2000. And change the value in the *Major unit* box from its default to 500. Click **OK** to close the dialog box.
6) Double-click again anywhere on the chart's vertical axis, and, in the *Format Axis* dialog box, reselect the **Scale** tab.

   Notice that Excel has changed the *Category (X) axis Crosses at* box from 0 to 2000. This is because you changed the *Minimum* box from 0 to 2000.

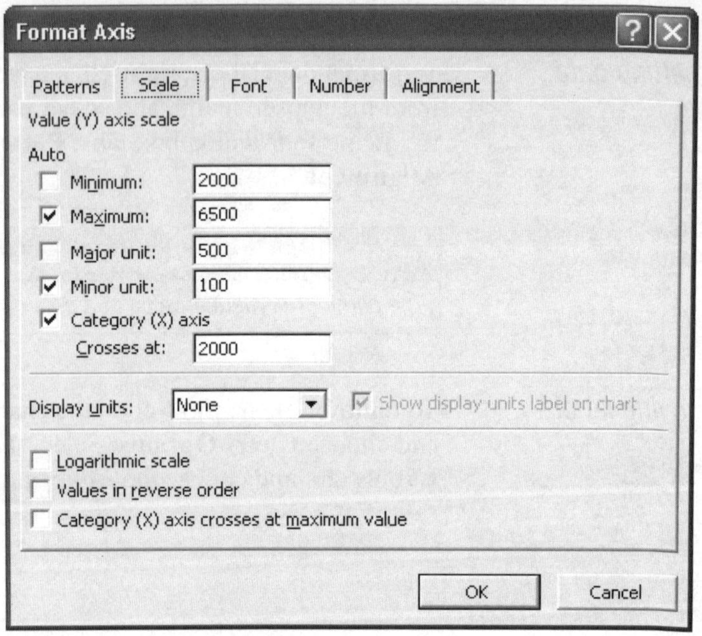

To make the chart easier to read, resize it, stretching it vertically. The rescaled and vertically stretched chart should now look as shown.

Rescaled chart: vertical axis values begin at £2,000 rather than at £0. Also, vertical axis is expressed in units of £500 rather than £2000

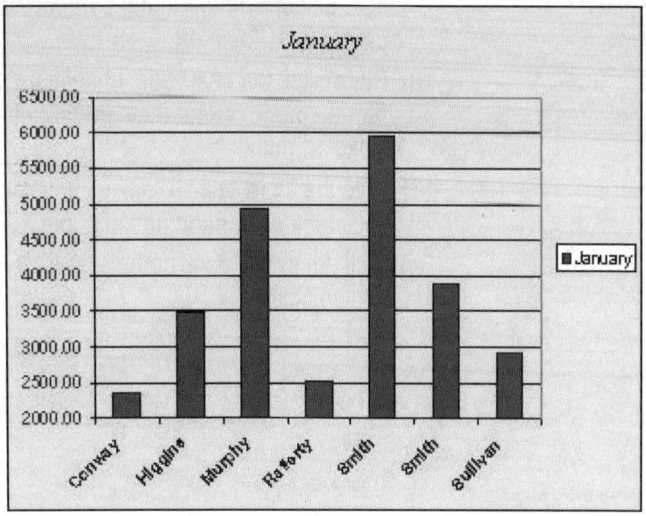

Changing chart colours

Excel enables you to change the colours of three parts of a chart: the chart area, the plot area and the data series. In each case, you right-click the relevant element, choose the appropriate **Format** command from the pop-up menu, and select the required fill colour. See Exercise 24.8.

Exercise 24.8: Changing a chart's colours

1) Right-click the chart area of the chart you created in Exercise 24.7. (The chart area is the blank margin surrounding the actual plotted chart.)
2) Choose the **Format Chart Area** command from the pop-up menu, select the **Patterns** tab, click the colour yellow in the *Area* section of the dialog box, and click **OK**.
3) Right-click the plot area of the chart. (This is the actual plotted chart, bounded by the two chart axes.)
4) Choose the **Format Plot Area** command from the pop-up menu, click the colour yellow in the *Area* section of the dialog box, and click **OK**.
5) Right-click any of the chart columns. (The columns represent the data series of this chart . For pie charts or line charts, click on the slice or line whose colour you want to change.)
6) Choose the **Format Data Series** command from the pop-up menu, select the **Patterns** tab, click the colour red in the *Area* section of the dialog box, and click **OK**.

In the second part of this exercise, you will reformat the text elements of the chart.

7) Double-click the *X-axis* (horizontal), select the **Font** tab, change the font style to Bold and the font colour to dark blue, and click **OK**.

8) Repeat step 7 for the *Y-axis* (vertical), but do not close the dialog box.

9) With the *Y-axis* still selected, select the **Number** tab on the *Format Axis* dialog box. Select *Number* in the *Category* area, and set the number of decimal places to 2. Click **OK**.

10) Right-click the chart title, choose the **Format Chart Title** command from the pop-up menu, select the **Font** tab, change the font to Times New Roman, italic, 14 point.

11) With the chart title still selected, select the **Patterns** tab of the dialog box, select the **Automatic** option in the *Border* section, and click **OK**.

Well done. You have completed the exercise. Your chart should now look as shown below.

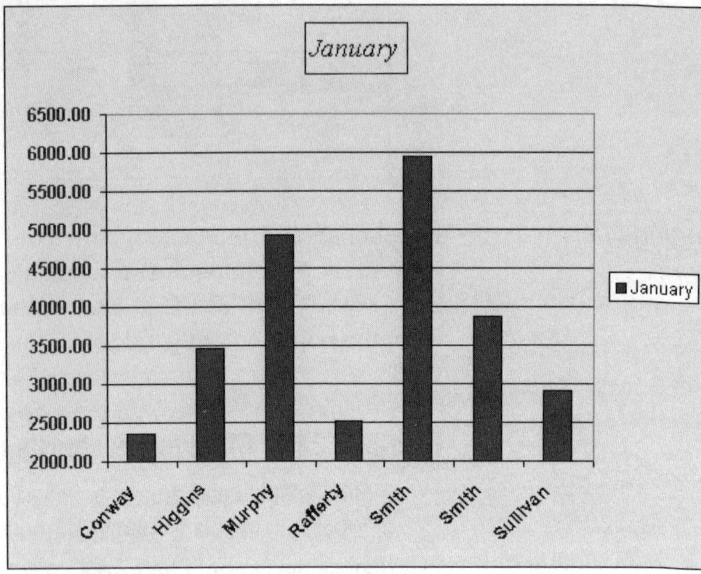

Chart types

Excel offers over a dozen chart types, but you need know only the following four:

- **Column chart:** Items are shown horizontally and values vertically. This is Excel's default chart type, and the only one you have used in your charting exercises so far.

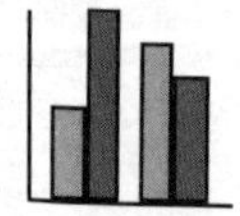

- **Pie chart:** Shows the proportion of each item that makes up the total. Unlike column, bar and most other chart types, you can use pie charts for a single data series only.

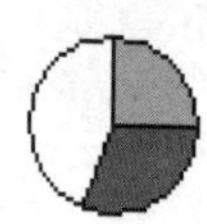

- **Line chart:** Shows value changes over time. A line chart would be a good choice for a report that dealt with annual levels of power consumption – peaking in winter and declining in summer.

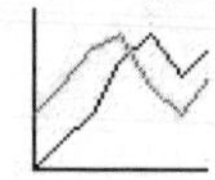

- **Bar chart:** A 'sideways' column chart that shows items horizontally and values vertically.

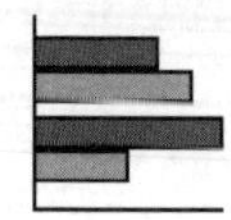

Setting the chart type

When you select a cell range and choose the *Chart Wizard*, you decide which chart type you want to use in the first of the four dialog boxes displayed by the Wizard, the *Chart Type* box. As you can see, most chart types offer sub-types or variations.

You can preview how your data will look in a chart by selecting a Chart type option and clicking the Press and hold to view sample button

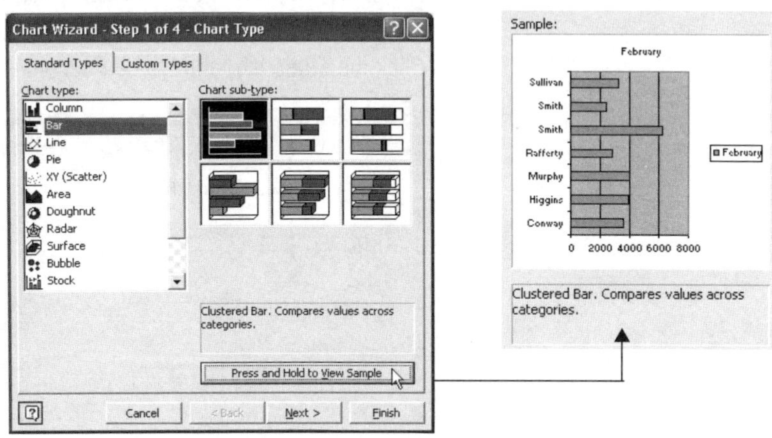

Changing the chart type

To change the current type of a chart, right-click anywhere within the chart (chart area, plot area or data series – it does not matter), choose the **Chart Type** command from the pop-up menu, and select a different type (or sub-type) from the *Chart Type* dialog box.

In Exercise 24.9 you will create a new chart of the bar chart type. In Exercise 24.10, you will change a bar chart to a column chart.

Exercise 24.9: Creating a bar chart

1) On *Sheet3*, click a cell beneath the chart you worked on in Exercise 24.8. This will be the location at which the chart you create in this exercise will begin.
2) Click the *Sheet1* tab to display the first worksheet of your workbook.
3) Select non-adjacent cell range *B25:C26,E25:F26*, and click the **Chart Wizard** button.

4) Excel now displays the **Standard Types** tab of the *Chart Wizard – Step 1 of 4 – Chart Type* dialog box. Select the *Bar* chart type and click **Next**.

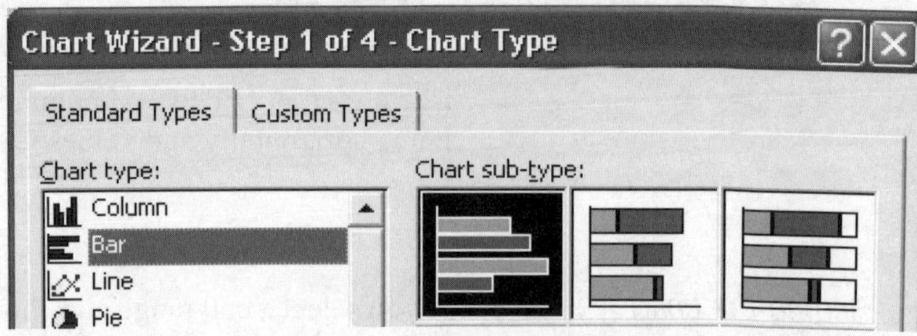

5) Excel now displays the **Data Range** tab of the *Chart Wizard – Step 2 of 4 – Chart Source Data* dialog box. Click **Next**.

6) Excel now displays the **Data Labels** tab of the *Chart Wizard – Step 3 of 4 – Chart Options* dialog box.

Click the **Titles** tab, and type a *Chart title* of Product 1 and click **Next**.

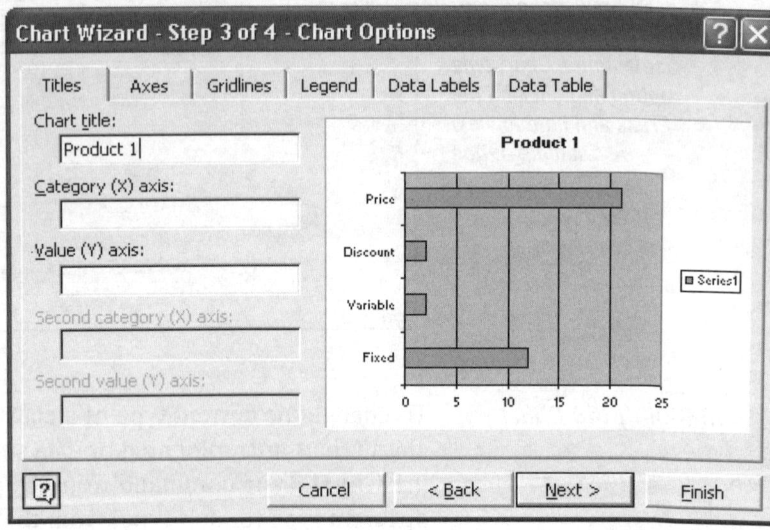

7) Excel now displays the *Chart Wizard – Step 4 of 4 – Chart Location* dialog box.

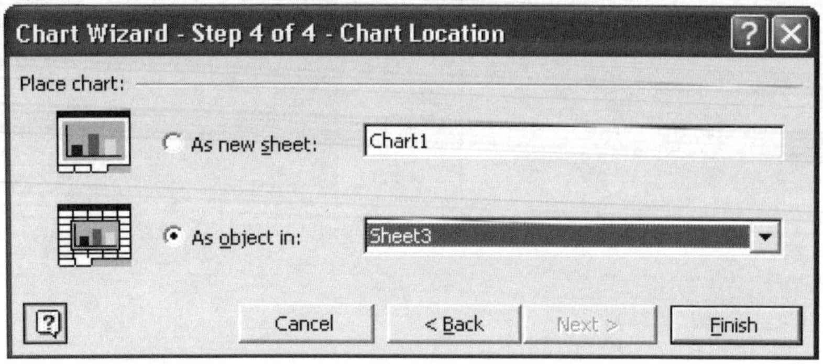

Change the *As object in* box to *Sheet3* and click **Finish**.

Excel positions the chart on your third worksheet, *Sheet3*. It positions the chart so that its top-left corner is at the cell you clicked most recently in that worksheet. Your bar chart should look like that shown.

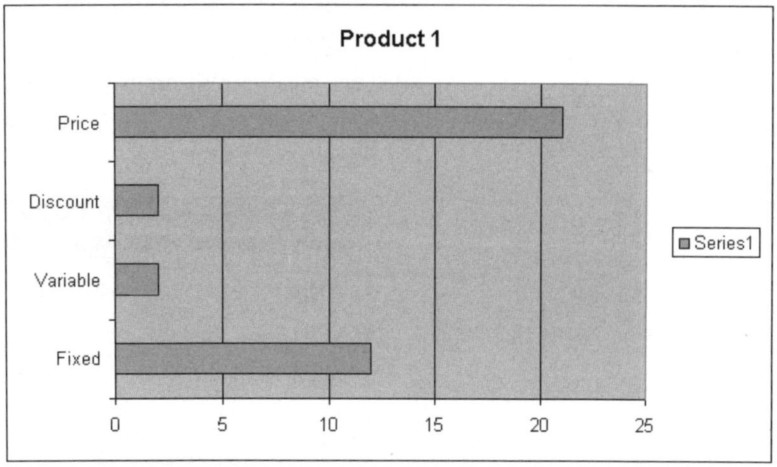

Exercise 24.10: Changing a column to a bar chart

1) On *Sheet2*, click the third chart you created in Exercise 24.2. It is based on the cell range *C4:F4,C15:F15* and shows percentage values for January, February, March and April. Copy it to the clipboard.
2) Click the *Sheet3* tab to display your third worksheet. Paste the chart from the clipboard to a cell beneath the chart from Exercise 24.9.
3) Right-click the chart area, choose **Chart Type** from the pop-up menu, select *Bar* chart from the dialog box, and click **OK**.

Your bar chart should look like that shown.

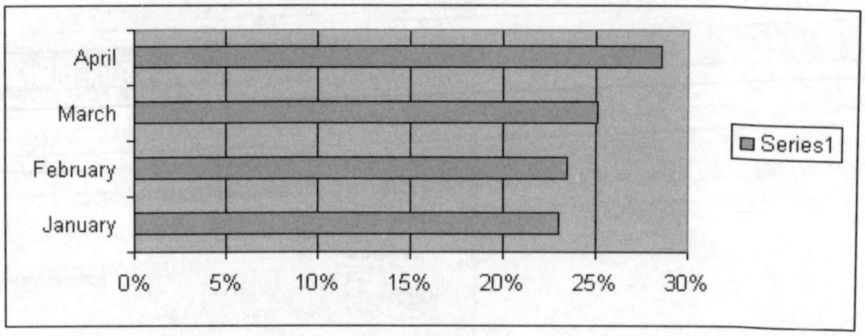

Working with pie charts

In Exercise 24.11 you will create a pie chart based on a single data series. You will then format the pie chart, and 'explode' a slice of the pie to draw particular attention to the contribution it represents to the total.

Exercise 24.11: Creating and formatting a pie chart

1) On *Sheet2*, select the cell range *A4:A11,C4:C11*.
2) Click the **Chart Wizard** button.
3) In the *Chart Type* dialog box, select *Pie* as the *Chart type*, and *Pie with a 3-D visual effect* as the *Chart sub-type*. Click **Next**.

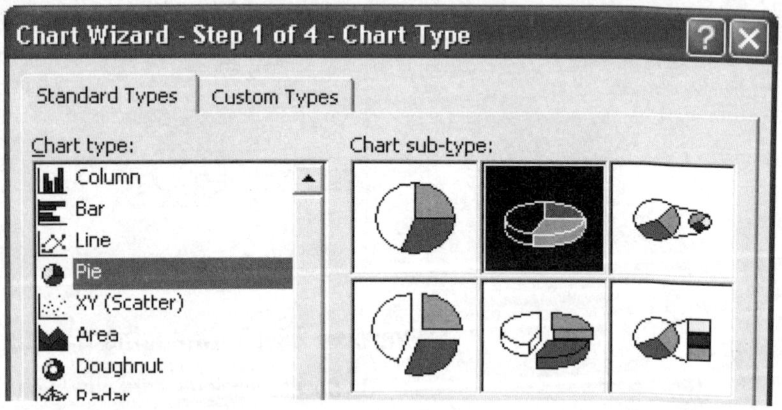

4) On the remaining *Chart Wizard* dialog boxes, click **Next** and, finally, **Finish**.

Drag the pie chart down *Sheet2* to beneath the chart you created in Exercise 24.4. Your chart should look as shown.

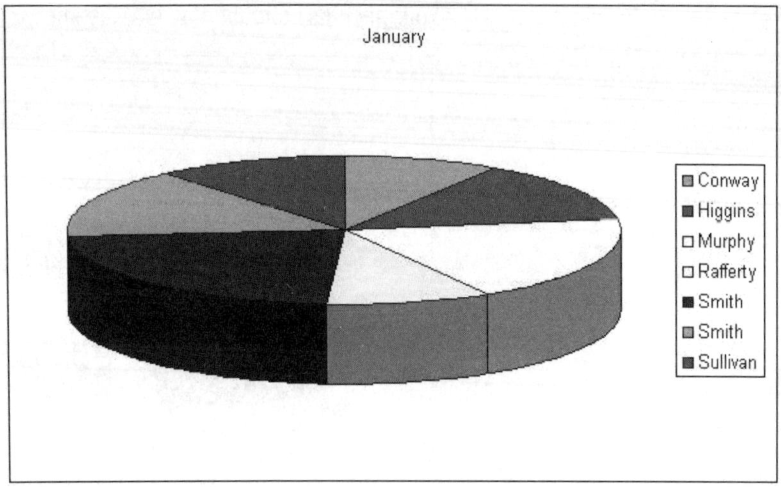

Because pie charts do not have axes to indicate data point names and values, the various slices are typically accompanied by data labels. You will add these in the next step of this exercise.

5) Double-click the pie chart plot area (and not the surrounding chart area) to display the *Format Data Series* dialog box.

6) Select the **Data Labels** tab, select the *Percentage* option, and click **OK**. Your pie chart should now look as shown below. Notice how the plot area shrank in size to make room for the percentage data labels.

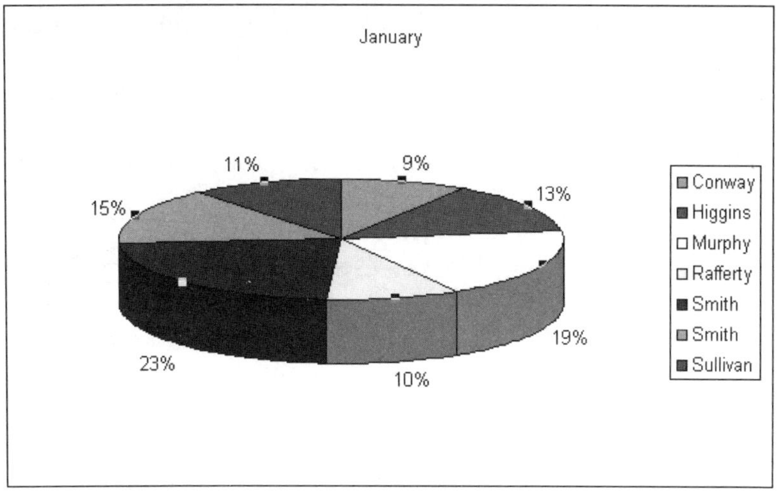

In the final step of this exercise, you will 'explode' one slice of the pie chart.

7) Click once on the plot area of the pie chart. Next, click the slice you want to explode and drag it out of the pie.

For example, click the largest slice, the one with the 23% data label, and drag it down and to the left.

Your pie chart should now look as shown.

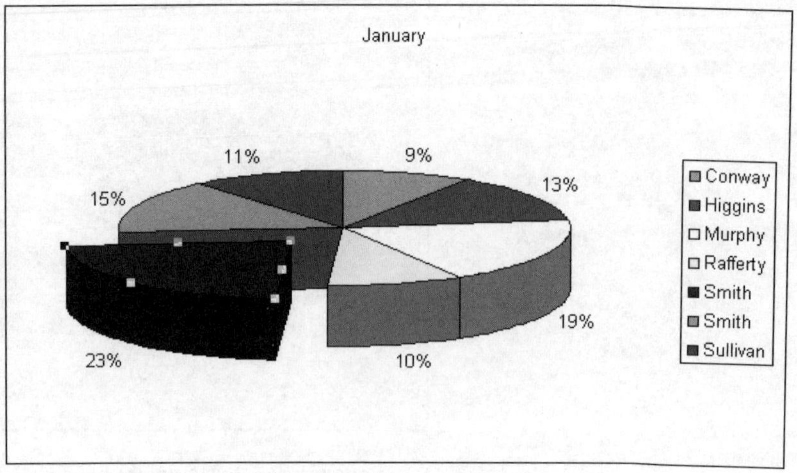

Managing charts

You can perform all of the standard management functions on charts: copy and move them, delete them and resize them.

Copying, moving and deleting charts

You can copy and move charts within the current worksheet or workbook or within any currently open workbook.

Highlight the chart and choose **Edit | Copy** to copy the chart or **Edit | Cut** to remove the chart from its current location. Go to the location where you want to place the chart and choose **Edit | Paste**. You can paste the copy of the chart in another place in the same worksheet, in a different worksheet or in a different workbook.

Note that removing a chart does not affect the underlying data source you used to create it.

Resizing charts

You can change the size of a chart by clicking and dragging on one of the sizing handles. The screentip displays the text *Chart Area*.

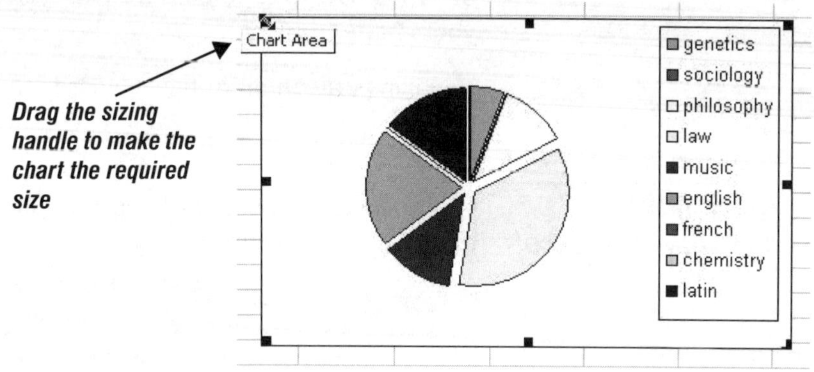

Printing charts

You can print charts independently of the worksheet they belong to.

Select the chart you want to print, and choose **File | Print**. In the *Print* dialog box, the option *Selected Chart* is selected. Click **Preview** to check what the chart will look like when printed, or click **OK** to print.

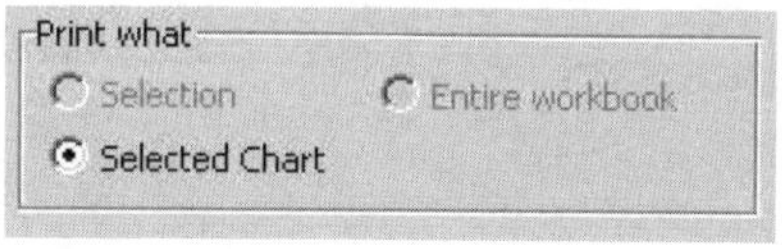

Chapter summary: so now you know

To draw a chart in Excel, first select the cells with the numbers and text that you want to chart, and then run Excel's *Chart Wizard*. The Wizard's default options on its four dialog boxes are acceptable in most cases. If you change any of the data on which a chart is based, Excel updates the chart to reflect the changes. See Exercise 24.1 for an example of creating a simple chart.

By default, Excel positions your chart on top of your worksheet data. You can move the chart by clicking any blank part of the chart margin, and then dragging the chart to a new position.

Charting is based on the ideas of *data points* and *data series*. A data point is a single item and its related value (for example, the sales figure in January), while a data series is a group of related data points (for example, monthly sales figures over a year). You can chart more than one data series at one time. See Exercises 24.3 and 24.4 for examples of creating charts with more than one data series.

Excel offers a wide range of *chart types*, with column, bar, line and pie charts being the most commonly used. You can format your chart in a variety of ways by adding data labels, colours and borders.
See Exercises 24.5 to 24.8 for examples of how you can customize your charts.

You can perform all of the standard management functions on charts: copy and move them, delete them and resize them.

Quick quiz: charting with Excel

Circle the correct answer to each of the following multiple-choice questions about charting with Excel.

Q1	The plot area is:
A.	The cell range used as source data for a chart.
B.	The area of the chart containing the actual plot.
C.	The margin area inside the chart boundary.
D.	An area on one of the *Chart Wizard* dialog boxes.

Q2	A bar chart can contain:
A.	Only one data point.
B.	Only one data series.
C.	Many data series.
D.	Many plot areas.

Q3	If your source data changes after you have created a chart, you must recreate the chart to update it.
A.	True.
B.	False.

Q4	A pie chart can contain:
A.	Only one data point.
B.	Only one data series.
C.	Many data series.
D.	Many plot areas.

Answers

1: B, **2:** C, **3:** B, **4:** B.

Chapter 25: File formats and data importing

In this chapter

In this chapter you will learn how Excel uses a particular file format. You will also discover how to convert your documents into other, non-Excel file formats, so that they can be opened and read by people who work with applications other than Excel.

You will also discover how files containing images, graphs and text may be inserted into Excel worksheets.

New skills

At the end of this chapter you should be able to:

- Save Excel files in the following file formats: Excel template, earlier versions of Excel, non-Excel spreadsheets, databases, HTML (web format), and text-only.
- Explain the difference between character-delimited and column-delimited text files.
- Explain the difference between two types of character-delimited text files: tab-delimited and comma-separated.
- Insert image files in an Excel worksheet, and files containing graphs created in applications other than Excel.
- Import text files using Excel's *Text Import Wizard.*

New words

At the end of this chapter you should be able to explain the following terms:

- File format
- Tab-delimited text file
- Comma-separated values (csv) text file
- Column-delimited text file

File formats

In ECDL Module 1, you learnt how all information stored on a computer consists ultimately of just two characters: 1 and 0. This raises two, related questions:

- When you open an Excel workbook file, how are these 1s and 0s translated into the text, numbers and charts you see on your computer screen?
- And, when you save a file, how are the text, numbers and charts converted back to 1s and 0s on your computer?

The answer is that the application developers apply a set of rules that translate between the 1s and 0s and the displayed text, numbers and charts. Such a set of rules is called a file format.

File format
A set of rules that translates 1s and 0s into text and graphics on computers screens and printouts, and vice versa.

An Excel file, for example, is said to be in Excel file format; an Access file in Access file format, and so on.

Different applications, different file formats

Different software companies, however, use different sets of rules for translating 1s and 0s into the text and graphics on screens and printouts.

Moreover, different versions of the one application often use different file formats. The Microsoft Excel XP file format, for example, is different from the file formats of previous versions of Excel.

These different file formats, as you can imagine, can create problems:

- In one file format, for example, the characters 10101010 might translate as the number '12' positioned in cell *A4*.
- In another, the same characters of 10101010 might convert to the label 'Annual Profit' in cell *Z54*.

File name extensions

The format of a file is revealed by its three-letter file name extension, which the software application adds to the file name when the user saves the file.

The file name extension of .xls, for example, indicates an Excel workbook, while .mdb indicates an Access database.

The file format used in pages on the World Wide Web is HTML, which stands for HyperText Markup Language. HTML file names typically end in .htm or .html.

Excel's file format options

Excel offers you the ability to save your documents in a format other than its own. This feature is very useful when you want to provide a file you have created to someone who uses an application other than Excel.

To view the file formats in which you can save your Excel documents:

- Open a document.
- Choose **File | Save As**.
- Click the arrow to the right of the *Save as type* box.

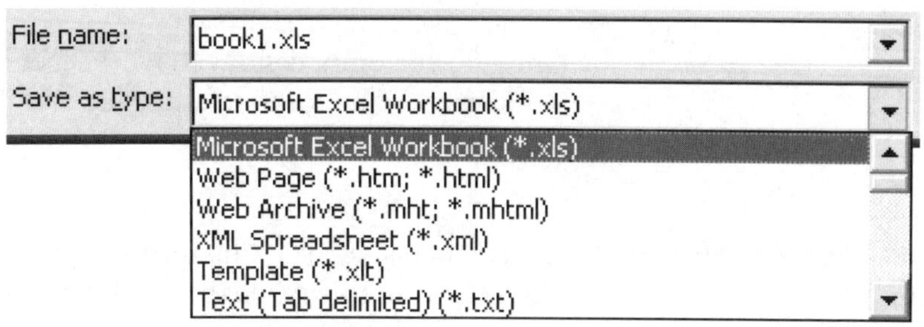

Only some of the listed options are relevant to this ECDL spreadsheets module. Note that the features and formatting of a Microsoft Excel XP workbook might not be available if you save the workbook in the file format of a previous version of Microsoft Excel or of another application.

Excel templates

Excel offers you the ability to save a workbook as a template, and then to use the saved template as a basis for quickly creating other, similar workbooks.

For example, you could create a workbook for use as an expense form, enter and format relevant text labels, place borders around certain cells, and enter the function =SUM(C2:C22) in cell *C23* so that whatever numbers were typed in the range *C2:C22* are totalled and displayed in *C23*.

By saving such a workbook as a template, you speed up the process of creating further expense forms because the text, formatting and addition calculation need not be re-entered.

To save a workbook as a template, choose **File | Save As** and select the *Template (*.xlt)* option.

Previous Excel versions

You can save your Excel XP workbook in the file formats of previous versions of Microsoft Excel. You have two main options:

- A format that can be read by Excel 5.0 and Excel 95.
- A format that can be read by Excel 5.0, Excel 95 and Excel 97–2002.

dBASE, Lotus 1-2-3 and Quattro Pro formats

Select from these options to save your work so that it can be opened and read by users with versions of Lotus 1-2-3 or Quattro Pro (two other spreadsheet applications) or dBASE (a database application).

Only the currently displayed worksheet is converted. To convert other worksheets of a workbook, display and then save each one individually.

Text-only format

As its name suggests, this format saves only the text of a file. The word 'text' in this context includes numbers as well as alphabetic characters. All formatting is lost. This format is also called plain-text or ASCII format.

Two of the more commonly used plain-text options are as follows:

- **Text (tab-delimited):** This saves only the currently displayed worksheet. To convert other worksheets of a workbook, switch to each sheet and save it separately. The file name extension added is .txt.

  In this format, cell entries in the same row but in different columns are separated from each other by tabs. Different rows are separated by paragraph breaks. As you can see in the example below, text in the tab-delimited format does not necessarily line up vertically in neat columns.

Original data in Excel file

	A	B	C	D	E	F
1						
2		January	February	March	April	M
3		12	45	35	41	
4		11	42	34	39	

Excel worksheet saved in tab-delimited format, and viewed in Notepad text editor

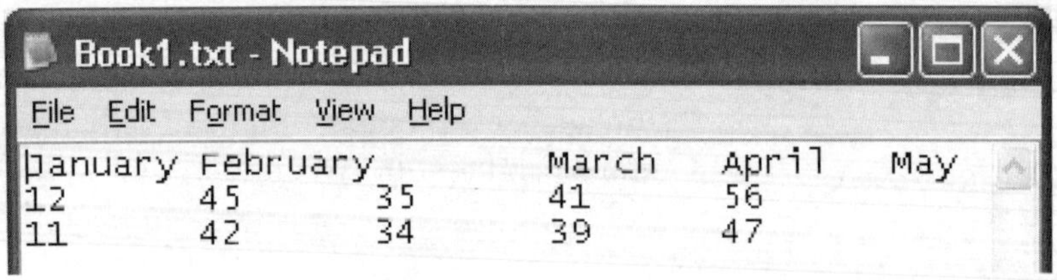

- **CSV (comma-delimited):** As tab-delimited above, but with a comma separating cells on the same row. The file name extension added is .csv, meaning comma-separated values.

Excel worksheet in CSV format, and viewed in Notepad text editor

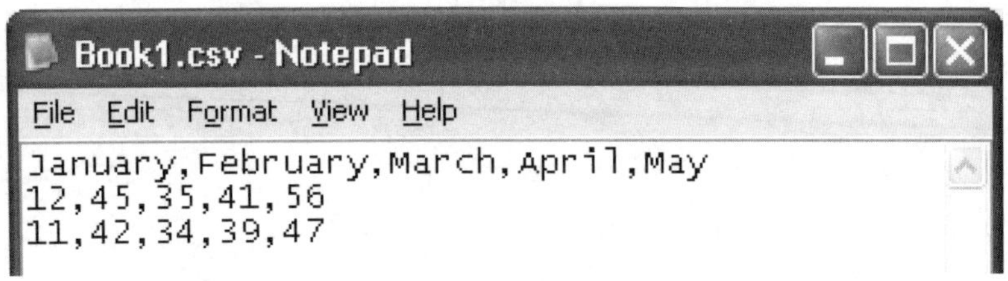

Tab-delimited text file

A text format file in which data items are separated horizontally by tabs and vertically by paragraph breaks.

Comma-separated values (CSV) text file

A text format file in which data items are separated horizontally by commas and vertically by paragraph breaks.

HTML (web) format

Web pages are created using the HTML file format. The file name extension of this format is .htm (or, sometimes, .html).

You can save an Excel file in HTML format in either of two ways:

- Choose **File | Save As Web Page**.

  -or-

- Choose **File | Save As**, and select the *Web Page* option.

The worksheet cells are converted to table cells in the HTML file. You can display and print HTML format files with a web browser application such as Microsoft Internet Explorer or Netscape Navigator.

Inserting from other applications

Microsoft Office applications (and most other Windows applications) allow you to transfer information between them. For this ECDL spreadsheets module, you need only know how to insert images, graphs and text in Excel.

Inserting images

To insert an image, choose **Insert | Picture**, and then select the relevant option. The range of options available to you depends on whether you have installed the Microsoft Office Clip Art Gallery and whether a scanner is attached to your computer.

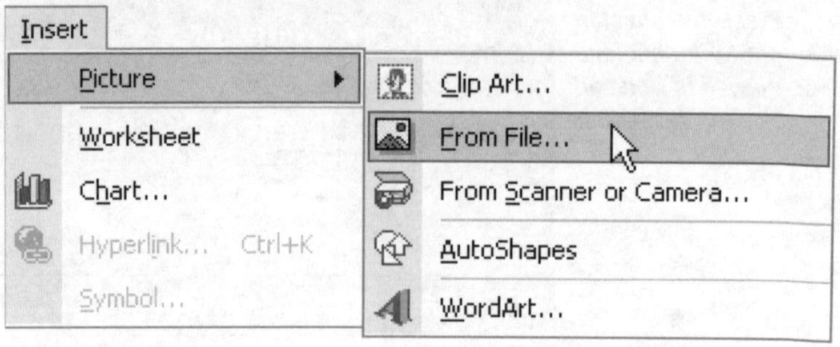

- To *reposition* an inserted image, click it to select it, and then drag the image to a different part of your worksheet.
- To *resize* an inserted image, click it to select it, then click any handle and drag the image to a different shape.

If you drag on a corner handle, the image expands and contracts proportionately to its current size; if you drag on an edge handle, the image expands or contracts in that direction only. Other inserted objects can be repositioned and resized in the same way.

Exercise 25.1: Inserting an image file in Excel

To insert an image in a worksheet, you need an image to work with. If you do not have one to hand, follow steps 1 and 2 of this exercise to obtain one from the author's website.

1) Connect to the Internet, start Microsoft Internet Explorer or Netscape Navigator, and visit the author's website at www.munnelly.com.
2) Right-click the image at the top-right of the first page to display a pop-up menu, choose **Save Picture As** (or, in Netscape, **Save Image As**), and save the image file to your computer as munnelly_com.jpeg.

3) Display an Excel worksheet, click a cell, choose **Insert | Picture | From File**, locate the munnelly_com.jpg image file (or any other image file), and click **Insert**. Excel inserts the image as shown.

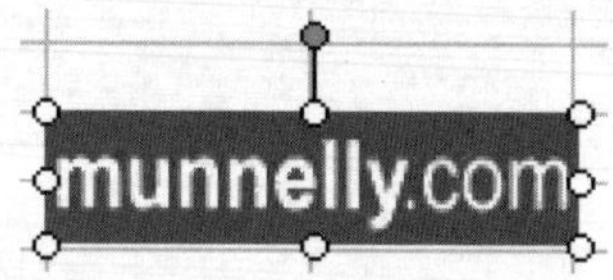

Inserting graphs

Graphs can be created in applications other than Excel – for example, in Microsoft PowerPoint or in non-Microsoft applications. To insert such a graph, select it in the application in which it was created, copy it to the clipboard, open the Excel worksheet, and choose the **Edit | Paste** command.

As with inserted images, you can reposition an inserted graph by selecting it, and then dragging it to a different part of your worksheet, and you can resize it by selecting it, then clicking any handle and dragging it to a different shape.

Inserting text

You may want to insert two types of text into an Excel worksheet:

- **Small amounts of text:** You may want to select one or a few words from a text file for use in Excel as worksheet headings, for example, or labels for individual cells.

  To insert text in a single cell of a worksheet, open the application in which the text was created, copy the text to the clipboard, switch to Excel, and then use Excel's **Edit | Paste** command to insert it in a selected Excel cell.
- **An entire text file:** This may contain numbers as well as text characters, which you want Excel to 'interpret' and arrange correctly across rows and down columns.

  To help you insert a text file in this way, Excel provides a *Text Import Wizard.*

Text Import Wizard

Earlier in this chapter you learnt about tab-delimited and comma-separated text files in which the tab and comma characters are positioned within the file to indicate where one column of data ends and the next begins. These are called *character-delimited* files, because a specific character consistently indicates column endings.

In other text files, a column ending may be indicated not by a single occurrence of a specific character but by a series of blank spaces. These are called *column-delimited* files, because the blank spaces cause the data to line up vertically. In both types of text files, row endings are indicated by paragraph breaks.

In Exercise 25.2, you will create a tab-delimited file, and in Exercise 25.3 you will import that file using Excel's *Text Import Wizard*.

Column-delimited text file
A text format file in which data items are separated horizontally by a series of spaces and vertically by paragraph breaks. The blank spaces cause the data to line up vertically.

Exercise 25.2: Creating a tab-delimited text file

1) Using Notepad or other text editor, create a new file.
2) Type the following five words, pressing the **Tab** key after each word except the last (do not type spaces between the words):
   January February March April May
3) Press **Enter** to move the cursor to a new line.
4) Type the following five numbers, pressing the **Tab** key after each one except the last (do not type spaces between the numbers):
   12 45 35 41 56
5) Press **Enter** to move the cursor to a new line.
6) Type the following five numbers, pressing the **Tab** key after each one except the last (again, do not type spaces between the numbers):
   11 42 34 39 47

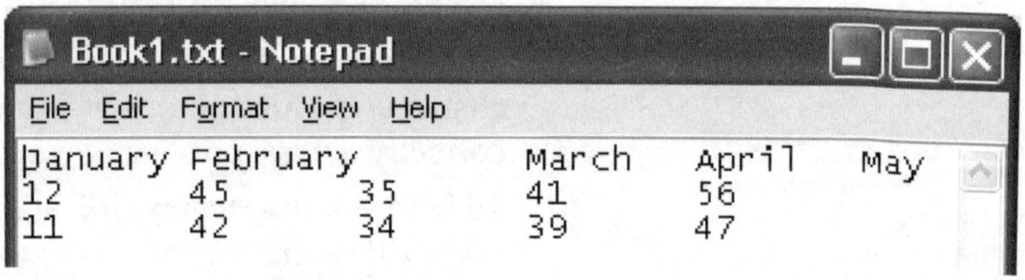

   Your file should look as shown. (The columns may not always line up vertically.)
7) Save, name and close the file.

Exercise 25.3: Importing a tab-delimited text file

1) In Excel, choose **File | Open**, and select the text file saved in Exercise 25.2.

2) Excel displays the first of three *Text Import Wizard* dialog boxes. Ensure that the field values in the top part of the dialog box are as shown. Click **Next**.

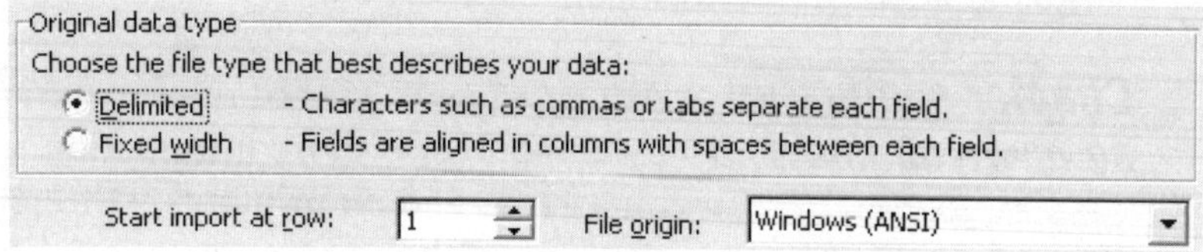

3) Excel displays the second *Text Import Wizard* dialog box. Ensure that the field values in the top part of the dialog box are as shown. Click **Next**.

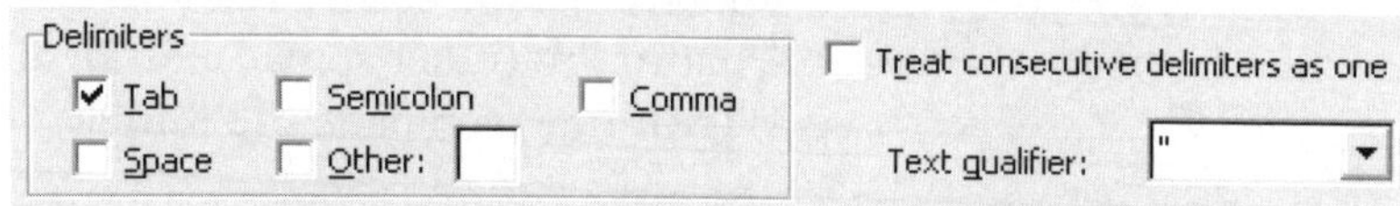

4) Excel displays the third *Text Import Wizard* dialog box. Ensure that the field values look as shown. Click **Finish**.

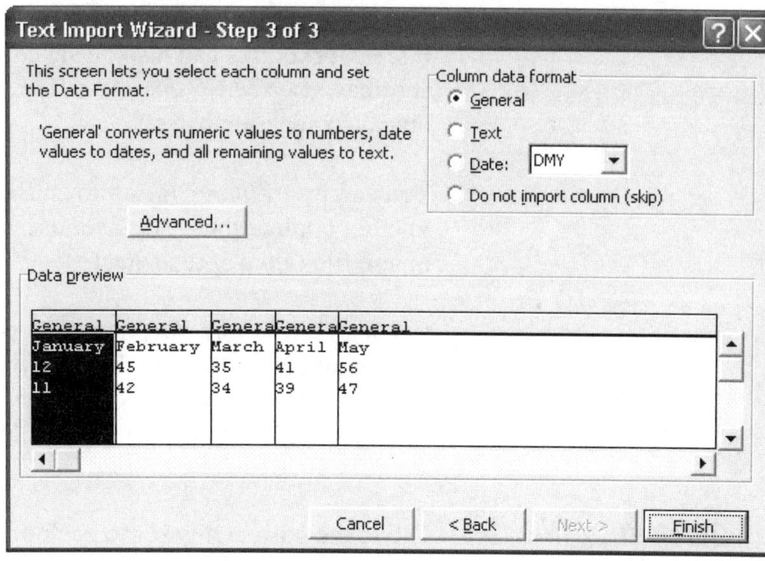

5) Excel closes the *Text Import* wizard and displays a worksheet that should look similar to that shown. The workbook file name will be the same as that of the text file.

6) Your worksheet cells should now look as shown below.

	A	B	C	D	E
1	January	February	March	April	May
2	12	45	35	41	56
3	11	42	34	39	47

You can save and close your workbook, and close Excel.

You have now completed the final chapter of the ECDL spreadsheets module. Congratulations!

Chapter summary: so now you know

A *file format* is a set of rules that translates between the 1s and 0s used by computers to store information and the text and graphics displayed on screens and on printouts. Different applications – even different versions of the same application – can use different and incompatible file formats. To help you share your files with others, Excel XP allows you to save your workbooks in a file format other than its own. The options include earlier versions of Microsoft Excel, Lotus 1-2-3 and Quattro Pro (other spreadsheets), dBASE (a database application) and HTML (the web page file format).

Another option is to save an Excel XP workbook as an *Excel template*, and reuse any text, numbers, formatting and calculations in the template as a basis for creating further workbooks.

Excel workbooks can also be saved as *text-only files*, with tabs or commas inserted to separate different columns, and with paragraph breaks to separate rows.

You can insert *image files* into an Excel worksheet, and graphs created in other applications. See Exercise 25.1 for an example of inserting an image file into a spreadsheet.

Excel's *Text Import Wizard* assists you in opening text files because it can recognize characters that have been inserted in the text files to separate different columns and rows. See Exercise 25.3 for an example of importing a tab-delimited text file.

Quick quiz: file formats and data importing

Circle the correct answer to each of the following multiple-choice questions about file formats and data importing.

Q1	Excel can import data from files saved in:
A.	Earlier versions of Excel.
B.	dBase, Lotus 1-2-3 and Quattro Pro formats.
C.	Plain text format.
D.	All of the above.

Q2	The file extension CSV stands for:
A.	Common sharing version.
B.	Current section values.
C.	Comma separated values.
D.	Consecutive serial values.

Q3	Excel can save files as:
A.	Earlier Excel versions.
B.	Web pages.
C.	Text files.
D.	All of the above.

Q4	Images and graphs created using other software cannot be included in an Excel spreadsheet.
A.	True.
B.	False.

Q5	File format refers to:
A.	The formatting used on the text in a file.
B.	A set of rules that translates 1s and 0s into text and graphics, and vice versa.
C.	Whether a file is on a floppy disk, hard disk or CD.
D.	The page size and layout of a document.

Answers

1: D, **2:** C, **3:** D, **4:** B, **5:** B.

5 Databases

You can never be too rich, too healthy, or too informed. And the best kind of information to have is that which is organized in such a way that you can find the facts you need quickly and easily. It's also important to be able to store new items that you come across.

Databases – structured collections of facts about a particular topic – existed long before computers. Address books, card indexes and telephone directories are all examples of databases. But by storing your facts in a database file on a computer, you gain the power to manage and manipulate that information – even very large amounts of information – in a variety of ways.

You will discover how to view information in your database file from different perspectives, sort and select particular pieces you are interested in, and produce printed reports.

Think of this module as your chance to file rather than be filed. Good luck with it.

Chapter 26: What is a database?

In this chapter

A database, as you will learn in this chapter, is an organized collection of information relating to the same topic or subject matter. By 'organized' we mean that it should be easy to find a particular item of information, and to add new items to the database.

By considering some examples of practical, everyday databases, you will gain an insight into the kind of decisions that designers need to make before they begin constructing their databases.

New skills

At the end of this chapter you should be able to:

- Explain what a database is.
- List some common examples of databases.
- Understand the advantages of computer databases over paper-based ones.
- Understand tables, records and fields.
- Explain the purpose of primary keys and indexes.
- Explain the advantages of relating tables in a database.

New words

At the end of this chapter you should be able to explain the following terms:

- Database
- Table
- Relational database
- Database management system
- Field
- Field data types
- Record
- Index
- Primary key

An organized collection of information

A database is a collection of information relating to the same topic or subject matter. It is usually organized in such a way that you can easily:

- find the items of information you are interested in, and
- file away the new items that you come across.

Database
An organized collection of related information.

A database does not have to be kept on a computer. For example, address books, card indexes and telephone directories are all databases (even though very few people would call them that).

Storing a database on a computer, however, enables you to manipulate the information easily and quickly. For example, using a paper-based telephone directory, it is relatively easy to find a person's telephone number, but it is very difficult (but not impossible) to find the person's name if you only have their telephone number.

Data and information
Typically, the term 'data' is used for what is in a database, and the term 'information' is used for data that is retrieved in a meaningful way.

A computer-based directory enables you to find that information quickly and easily. You could also find the names of everyone who lives on a particular road, or everyone whose first name is Paul. Or you could print a report showing the five most common surnames.

Computer-based databases are flexible: they enable you to deal with information – even very large quantities of information – in a variety of ways. Microsoft Access is an example of a database management system – an application that enables you to create and manage a database on a computer.

Database management system (DBMS)
An application such as Microsoft Access that enables you to collect information on a computer, organize it in different ways, sort and select pieces of information of interest to you, and produce reports.

Records and fields

In a database, information is typically broken down into its smallest parts. For example, if you were entering names and addresses into a database, you would not only create an entry for each individual, but you would also break each entry down into its smallest logical parts, such as First Name, Last Name, Address Line 1 and Address Line 2. The following is an example of how entries in an address book database might be broken down.

FirstName:	James
MiddleName:	Coogan
LastName:	Sweeney
FirstAddress:	10744 South Hoyne
SecondAddress:	
City:	Chicago
State:	Illinois
Zipcode:	60643
Country:	USA

In a database, individual pieces of information (such as first name, last name and telephone number) are called *fields*, and the set of information relating to one individual is called a *record*.

Field

A single piece of information about an item. More precisely, it is the space where that information is held.

Record

One complete set of fields relating to the same item.

Tables and databases

A collection of records with the same fields is called a *table* – for example, a table could contain information about suppliers or customers. If a database contains just a single table, the table is, in effect, the database. It is more usual to have more than one table in a database, as we will see later.

When there are thousands or hundreds of thousands of records, a computer-based database comes into its own. A computer asked to extract and show only records of surnames that begin with 'S' and of postcodes that begin with '60' responds at breathtaking speed, far beyond the capacity of human sorters.

Table

A collection of records that contain the same fields. A database may contain one or more tables.

This example shows a suppliers table with fields for:

- ***Supplier ID***
- ***Company Name***
- ***Contact Name***
- ***Contact Title***

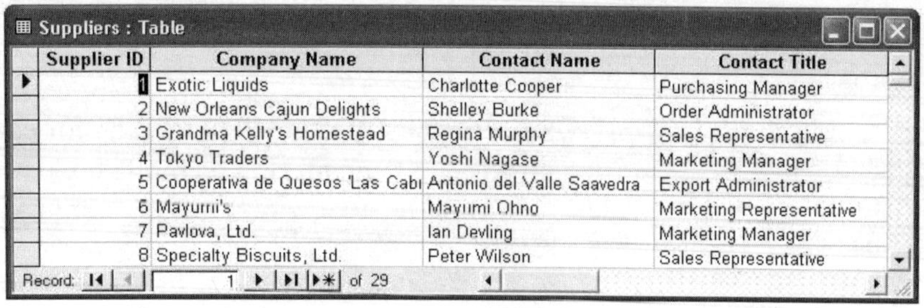

Suppliers : Table

Supplier ID	Company Name	Contact Name	Contact Title
1	Exotic Liquids	Charlotte Cooper	Purchasing Manager
2	New Orleans Cajun Delights	Shelley Burke	Order Administrator
3	Grandma Kelly's Homestead	Regina Murphy	Sales Representative
4	Tokyo Traders	Yoshi Nagase	Marketing Manager
5	Cooperativa de Quesos 'Las Cabı	Antonio del Valle Saavedra	Export Administrator
6	Mayumi's	Mayumi Ohno	Marketing Representative
7	Pavlova, Ltd.	Ian Devling	Marketing Manager
8	Specialty Biscuits, Ltd.	Peter Wilson	Sales Representative

Record: 1 of 29

Primary keys

In the telephone directory, there are many people listed with the surname Smith; a number of them share the first name John. To find the one you want, you need some more information: for example, where do they live? Even that might not be enough – father and son might have the same name – and you might have to ask them some further questions to confirm that you are talking to the right one.

Well, in a computer system, that is obviously not satisfactory. Access needs to know which John Smith you mean. And you don't want to send a bill or, worse still, a cheque to the wrong John Smith. So you give each record an identifier, called a *primary key*, which is unique to that record – it is not shared with any other.

In a customer database, you could use a CustomerID as the primary key – this type of key is an *artificial* key because it gives no real information about the customer, and its only purpose is to provide a unique identifier for the customer. By contrast, in a books database, you could use the ISBN as the primary key – the ISBN is unique for every book, and a book's ISBN is useful information in its own right.

Primary key

A field (or combination of fields) in a database record that is used to identify that record uniquely.

Field data types

A field's *data type* determines the kind of data that you can store in a field and how Access handles that data. For example, you can set a field's data type so that it accepts only numbers, or dates and times, or Yes and No values.

Fields with Text and Memo data types can store both text and numbers, but fields with a Number data type will accept only numbers. Similarly, fields with a Date/Time data type will accept only dates and times, and fields with a Currency data type will accept only currency values.

Selecting an appropriate data type for each field helps to prevent mistakes when entering data in a table.

Field data type
Controls the kind of data that may be entered into fields.

Indexes

Looking up a name in the index of a book is an easier way of finding a reference than scanning through hundreds of pages of text. When Access responds to a query on a database, it uses indexes to help it find information more quickly.

You can base the indexes that Access uses on a single field or on multiple fields. Multiple-field indexes enable Access to distinguish between records in which the first field may have the same value. A multiple-field index might, for example, be based on surname, first name and city, since searches are often based on these criteria.

When you create a database, Access automatically creates an index based on the primary key.

Database index
A list of one or more fields that a database can use to find and sort records. Indexes make such operations faster, as the database needs to examine only the index fields rather than entire records.

Table relationships

A database consisting of just one table may be called 'flat'. A single table contains all of the required information. In certain cases, this is fine. However, when a flat database needs to be updated you might be faced with duplicated (redundant) data and lots of unnecessary work.

For instance, imagine a situation where a company wants to keep records of customer orders. In a flat database, full customer details, including the customer name, address and phone number, must be entered into the database each time an order is received. When thousands of orders come in from a regular base of customers, their details are duplicated unnecessarily many times in the database.

Now imagine what happens when we need to update the addresses and phone numbers of regular customers. In a flat database, we must update them in every record where they occur.

A database that separates its data into two or more related tables – a 'relational database' can cut out all this extra work and duplication very easily. For example, in the case of our imaginary company we can create separate, but related, Customers and Orders tables.

In the Customers table, we store customer names, addresses, and so on, with each customer identified by a unique customer ID. In the Orders table we store order numbers, dates, product IDs, and so on. And instead of including full customer details for each order, we include just the customer ID.

Full customer details in the Customers table

Customers : Table

	CustID	CompanyName	Address	City
▶	ALFKI	Alfreds Futterkiste	Obere Str. 57	Berlin
	BERGS	Berglunds snabbköp	Berguvsvägen 8	Luleå
*				

Record: 1 of 2

Orders : Table

	OrderID	OrderDate	ProductID	Qty	CustID
▶	10643	25/08/2002	28	11	ALFKI
	10692	03/10/2002	63	4	ALFKI
	10952	16/03/2003	3	5	ALFKI
	10953	17/03/2003	2	3	BERGS
*	ɔNumber)				

Record: 1 of 4

Customer ID field in the Orders table

Now whenever we enter a new order in the Orders table, the only customer detail we enter is the customer ID. And when we need to update a customer's address or phone number, we do so just once, in the Customers table. This greatly minimizes the size of our database and the work involved in entering and editing records.

We can then define a relationship between the two tables based on their common CustID fields. This means that Access can bring information from the two tables back together again by matching values in those fields. For example, for invoicing purposes we might want to display order details and customer details at the same time. Provided that a relationship has been defined between the two tables, we can do this easily. Access retrieves the order details from the Orders table. And to retrieve the customer details, it checks the CustID value for each order in the Orders table and then searches the Customers table for the record with the matching CustID value.

Orders table

	OrderID	OrderDate	ProductID	Qty	CustID
▶	10643	25/08/2002	28	11	ALFKI
	10692	03/10/2002	63	4	ALFKI
	10952	16/03/2003	3	5	ALFKI
	10953	17/03/2003	2	3	BERGS

Customers table

	CustID	CompanyName	Address	City
▶	ALFKI	Alfreds Futterkiste	Obere Str. 57	Berlin
	BERGS	Berglunds snabbköp	Berguvsvägen 8	Luleå
*				

Data combined from Customers table and Orders table

	OrderID	OrderDate	ProductID	Qty	CustID	CompanyName	Address
▶	10643	25/08/2002	28	11	ALFKI	Alfreds Futterkiste	Obere Str. 57
	10692	03/10/2002	63	4	ALFKI	Alfreds Futterkiste	Obere Str. 57
	10952	16/03/2003	3	5	ALFKI	Alfreds Futterkiste	Obere Str. 57
	10953	17/03/2003	2	3	BERGS	Berglunds snabbköp	Berguvsvägen 8
*	ɔNumber)						

So, dividing our data into logical, separate tables and relating them helps us to avoid data duplication and saves on data entry time, while allowing us to combine information from the two tables in many different ways, whenever we want.

Database design considerations

In Chapter 28 you will create a database of your very own. But before using Access to build *any* database, take some time to think about the kind of information that you want to put into your database, and how you want to use it.

The following four examples demonstrate the kind of decisions that database designers need to make before they begin constructing their databases.

Example 1: The wine connoisseur's database

Henry is interested in wine. He reads the wine column in the newspapers and notes the recommendations. When he goes to the supermarket, he brings a list with him, so that he can select wine based on the recommendations. When he buys wine, he might have it in the house for some time before he tastes it, and he likes to record his impressions and compare notes with the original review.

Henry might include the following fields in his database:

- Wine style (red/white)
- Name
- Country/region
- Grower
- grape varieties
- Vintage
- Recommended by
- Available from (shop)
- Price
- Number bought
- Date bought
- Date tasted
- Tasting notes
- Buy again?

With such a database, Henry could print out a separate list for each shop, he could list all the red wines, he could list all the white wines that cost less than £10, he could find where the wines by a particular grower are available, he could view all the comments on different vintages of the same wine, and so on.

Example 2: The CD collector's database

Michelle plays the piano and has a large collection of CDs. When she is learning a new piece, she likes to listen to other people playing it. She has built a database with the following fields:

- CD title
- Artist
- Track number
- Name of tune
- Composer
- Date recorded

By sorting the database on the *Name of Tune* field, she can quickly identify the particular CDs that include the tune she is working on.

Example 3: The household manager's database

Oscar started his database for insurance purposes: it enabled him to build up a detailed record of his house contents. It included the following fields:

- Room
- Item
- Category
- Date purchased
- Price paid

With this database, he was able to provide an accurate inventory to the insurance company to support a claim. He could provide the original cost, along with the depreciated value and the replacement value, based on the original cost and the elapsed time since the purchase. He could also quickly give a value for all the paintings in the house, the value of all the clothes in the upstairs rooms, or all the contents of a particular room.

Example 4: The bookworm's database

Declan is an avid reader and book lover. Over the years he has built up a large collection of books of all sorts, and now he wants to sort and catalogue them. He decides to build a database in Access with the following fields:

- Author
- Title
- ISBN
- Date purchased
- Price
- Category
- Copyright year
- Number of Pages
- Notes
- Publisher
- Recommended?

Because he has over two thousand books, Declan is looking at quite a sizable data entry task, but he plans to make the job easier by creating separate tables for authors and books, and then creating a relationship between them.

Over the next few chapters, we will build a bookworm database, much the same as Declan's.

Thinking hard about fields

When you are deciding on the fields in the database, think carefully about how they are to be used. If, for example, you want to sort or select wines by country of origin, you should have a column for country: while you might know that Bordeaux is in France, Access doesn't. If you want to find all the albums produced by Nick Lowe, you have to record that information, and preferably in a consistent way (for example, last name followed by first name).

Chapter summary: so now you know

A *database* is a collection of information, typically held on a computer, and organized in such a way that you can find what you are looking for quickly and easily, and add new data as you need.

Microsoft Access is an example of a *database management system* – an application that stores information on a computer, organizes it in different ways, sorts and selects pieces of information of interest to you, and produces reports.

A database holds at least one *table* of information; each table has a number of records, and each record has a number of *fields*. A field is a single piece of information about an item. And a field's *data type* determines the kind of data that you can store in a field and how Access handles that data.

A *record* is one complete set of fields relating to the same item and a table is a collection of records. Each record has an identifier known as its *primary key*, which is unique to that record. In single-table databases, the table *is* the database. However, most databases are made up of a number of *related* tables.

Access uses *indexes* to help it respond to queries more quickly and efficiently.

Quick quiz: what is a database?

Circle the correct answer to each of the following multiple-choice questions about databases.

Q1	A single piece of information about an item is ...
A.	A record.
B.	A field.
C.	A table.

Q2	A record is a complete set of fields for an item; and a table is a collection of records for items of the same type and with the same fields.
A.	True.
B.	False.

Q3	The primary key of a database table is a field or combination of fields that uniquely identifies each record in the table.
A.	True.
B.	False.

Q4	Specifying a field data type enables you to ...
A.	Set limits to the values entered in a field.
B.	Control the type of information the field contains.
C.	Speed up data entry.

Q5	An index is a feature that a database uses to find and sort records more quickly.
A.	True.
B.	False.

Answers

1: B, **2:** A, **3:** A, **4:** B, **5:** A.

Chapter 27: Exploring Access

In this chapter

Microsoft Access is an application that enables you to create and work with databases. To give you an idea of what a computer database looks like, this chapter will take you on a tour of one of the sample databases provided with Access.

New skills

At the end of this chapter you should be able to:

- Start and quit Access.
- Open and close database objects.
- Explore the sample database provided with Access.
- Understand and switch between different database viewing modes.
- Use Access online help.

New words

At the end of this chapter you should be able to explain the following terms:

- Reports
- Forms
- Queries
- Datasheet view
- Form view
- Design view

Starting Access

Microsoft Access

To start Access, either:

- Double-click the **Microsoft Access** icon.

  -or-

- Choose **Start | All Programs | Microsoft Access**.

Access starts and displays the application window.

Access application window

The Access application window displays a menu bar, a toolbar and, on the right, the *New File* task pane. This task pane collects in one place the various commands you need for creating new databases and opening existing ones.

If the task pane is not open, choose **View | Toolbars | Task Pane** to open it.

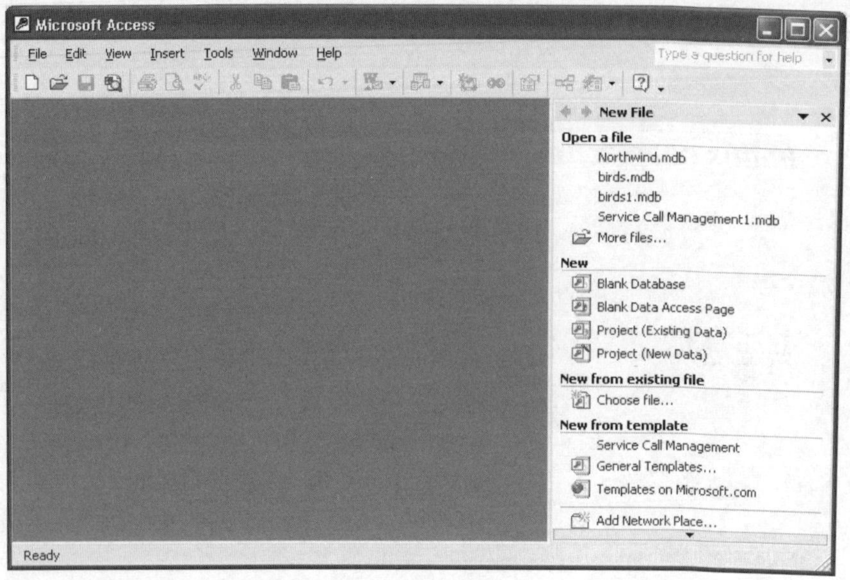

Opening a database

Now let's take a tour of a database that Microsoft prepared earlier – the Northwind sample database.

Exercise 27.1: Opening the Northwind database

You can open an existing database by choosing **File | Open**, by clicking the **Open** button on the *Database* toolbar, or by using the *New File* task pane. In this exercise, you will use the task pane.

1) If you have previously opened the Northwind database, it will be listed under *Open a file* in the *New File* task pane, and you can open it simply by clicking it.

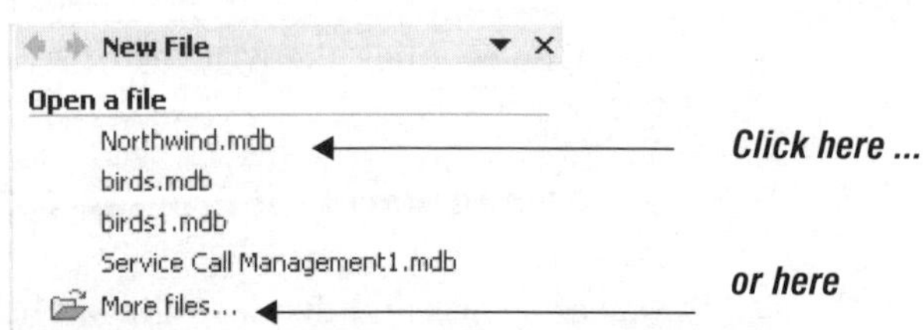

If the database is not listed, select the *More files...* option. In the *Open* dialog box, you can then navigate through the folders on your PC to find the database. It is most likely to be in the following location:

C:\Program Files\Microsoft Office\Office10\Samples

Use Windows Explorer or My Computer to find it if necessary.

2) When you find Northwind.mdb, select it and click **Open**.

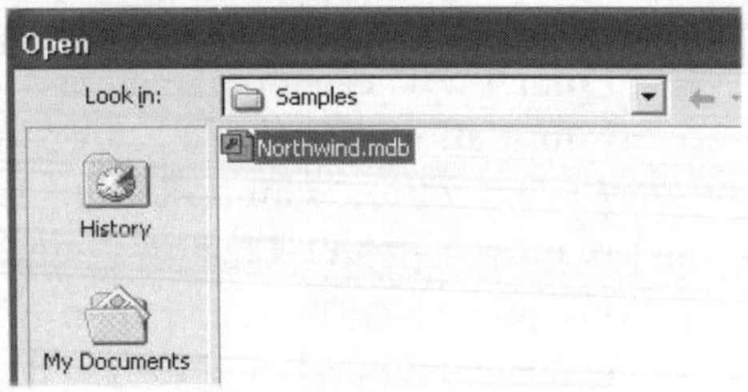

3) If you are presented with a welcome screen, click **OK** to close it.

Access now displays both the *Main Switchboard* window and the *Database* window. The *Database* window is the control centre of Access. The *Main Switchboard* provides a simpler interface for people who are using the database rather than working on its design.

Throughout this module you will use the *Database* window and not the *Main Switchboard*. Close the *Main Switchboard* by clicking **Display Database Window**.

The Database window – the control centre of Access

From here you can work with the various database objects

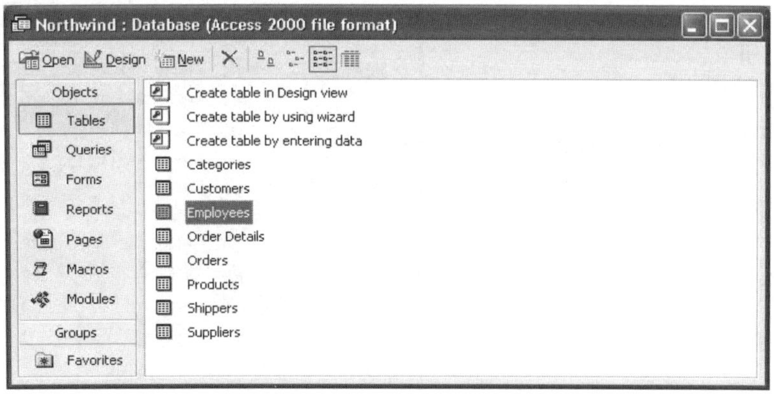

Access file name extension

The file names of Access databases end in .mdb (Microsoft database). This helps you to distinguish Access files from other file types such as Excel spreadsheets (.xls) or Word documents (.doc).

The Database window

In the *Objects* area of the *Database* window, the following are listed: Tables, Queries, Forms, Reports, Pages, Macros and Modules. These are all sets of items – Access calls them *objects* – that are associated with the database in some way. In this book, you will learn about the first four: you don't need to worry about the ones named Pages, Macros and Modules.

- **Tables:** You will learn how to create a table in Chapter 28, and how to modify it in Chapter 29.
- **Queries:** These are named and saved requests for specific information from one or more tables. Each time you run a query, Access retrieves an up-to-date set of records that match the request. Chapter 32 shows you how to create queries.
- **Forms:** These are like paper forms, and are used primarily for entering and updating data. Chapter 33 shows you how to create and format the appearance of forms, and how to use them to enter and modify records.
- **Reports:** These are used to display, format, summarize and print selected information. You will learn about reports in Chapter 34.

When you select an option in the *Objects* area you see a list of existing objects of that type and options for creating new objects.

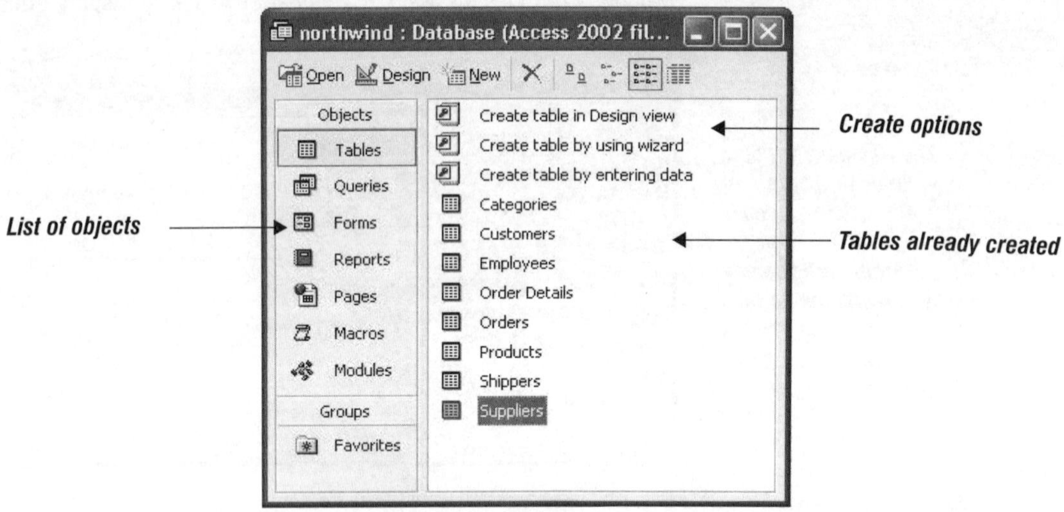

You will see the *Database* window a lot when you are working with Access. From here, you can open any of the database objects – to work with them or to change them – and when you are finished with that object, Access returns you to this *Database* window. You can also return to the *Database* window by choosing the database from the **Window** menu.

Viewing tables

When you first open a database, the Table objects are normally displayed by default. If not, simply click the **Tables** button in the *Objects* list.

Notice that the Northwind database contains several tables. Open the Employees table, either by right-clicking it and choosing **Open** from the pop-up menu, or by double-clicking its name or icon. Have a look at the type of information it contains. This will give you a good idea of how databases are actually used.

- When a table, such as Employees, contains more fields than can be shown on a single screen, use the horizontal scroll bar to move right and left.

  If your horizontal scroll bar is not visible, you will have to click the **Maximize** button on the Table window, after which the scroll bar becomes visible.

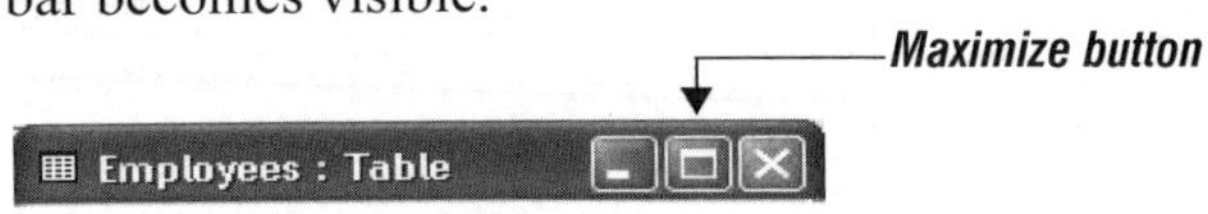

- When a table contains more records than can be shown on a single screen, use the vertical scroll bar to move up and down the range of records. Or use the navigation buttons displayed along the bottom of the table.

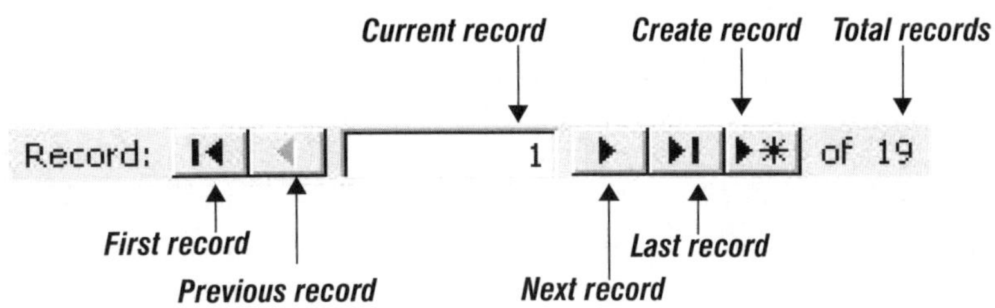

Viewing forms

Click **Forms** in the *Objects* list to see a list of forms that have already been created. The example below shows a record from the Employees form.

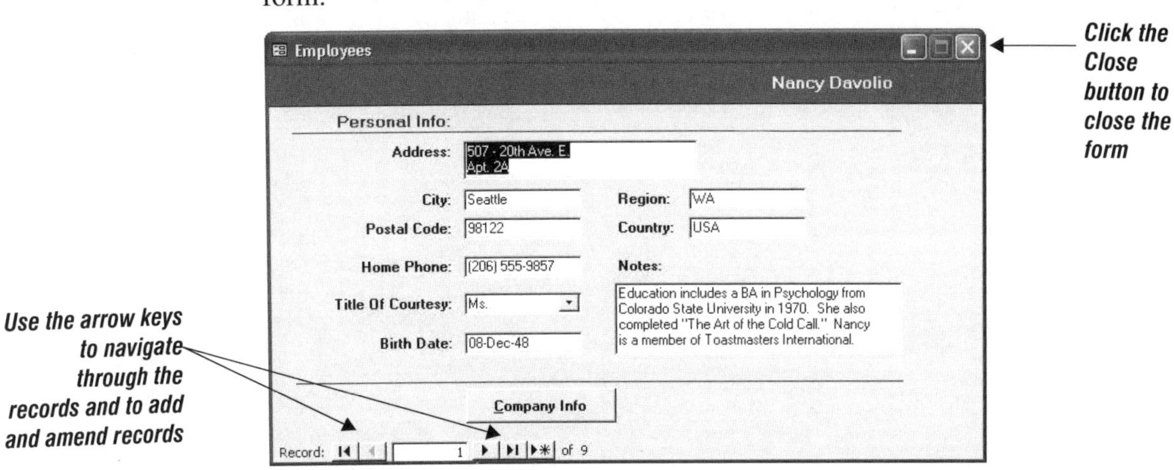

Viewing queries

Click **Queries** in the *Objects* list to see a list of queries that have already been created. The example below shows the information retrieved by the Sales by Category query. This combines data from a number of different tables in order to show the total sales figure for each product within the different categories. In Chapter 32 you will learn how to construct queries.

Use the arrow keys to navigate through the records and to add and amend records

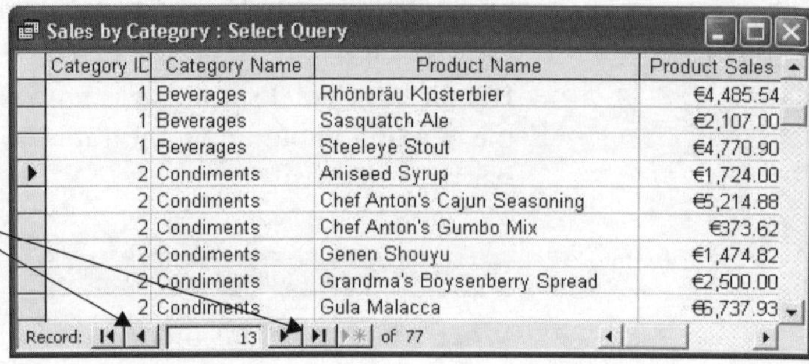

Click the Close button to close the query

Viewing reports

Click **Reports** in the *Objects* list to see a list of reports that have already been created – have a look at some of the sample reports of the Northwind database.

Datasheet, Forms and Design views

Access provides a number of different viewing modes for tables, forms, queries and reports. This table lists the most commonly used view modes and the database objects to which they apply. They can be selected from the **View** menu, or by clicking the **View** button.

View	Used for
Datasheet	Tables, forms and queries
Design	Forms
Form	Tables, forms, queries, reports
Print Preview	Reports

Datasheet view

In Datasheet view, you see the information arranged in columns (one for each field) and rows (one for each record); it is similar in appearance to a spreadsheet.

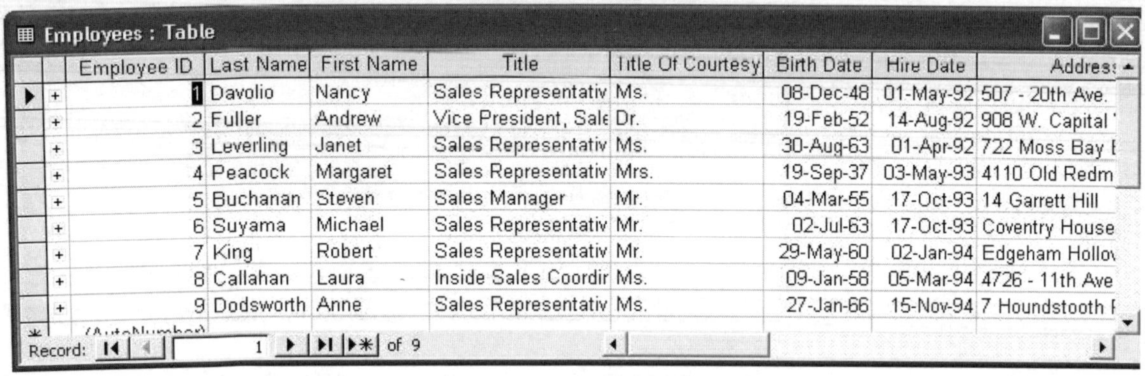

Employees : Table

Employee ID	Last Name	First Name	Title	Title Of Courtesy	Birth Date	Hire Date	Address
1	Davolio	Nancy	Sales Representativ	Ms.	08-Dec-48	01-May-92	507 - 20th Ave.
2	Fuller	Andrew	Vice President, Sale	Dr.	19-Feb-52	14-Aug-92	908 W. Capital
3	Leverling	Janet	Sales Representativ	Ms.	30-Aug-63	01-Apr-92	722 Moss Bay
4	Peacock	Margaret	Sales Representativ	Mrs.	19-Sep-37	03-May-93	4110 Old Redm
5	Buchanan	Steven	Sales Manager	Mr.	04-Mar-55	17-Oct-93	14 Garrett Hill
6	Suyama	Michael	Sales Representativ	Mr.	02-Jul-63	17-Oct-93	Coventry House
7	King	Robert	Sales Representativ	Mr.	29-May-60	02-Jan-94	Edgeham Hollo
8	Callahan	Laura	Inside Sales Coordir	Ms.	09-Jan-58	05-Mar-94	4726 - 11th Ave
9	Dodsworth	Anne	Sales Representativ	Ms.	27-Jan-66	15-Nov-94	7 Houndstooth

Record: 1 of 9

An example of Datasheet view, where you see several records at once

> **Datasheet view**
>
> *A view of database records where you see information presented in rows and columns, with several records visible at the same time.*

Form view

Form view typically presents all or selected information for a single record at a time. The form can be laid out in a format that is easier to read, perhaps with explanatory text. You can structure the form in such a way that it looks like a paper form, with the fields in the corresponding place on the screen.

An example of Form view, where you see details from a single record only

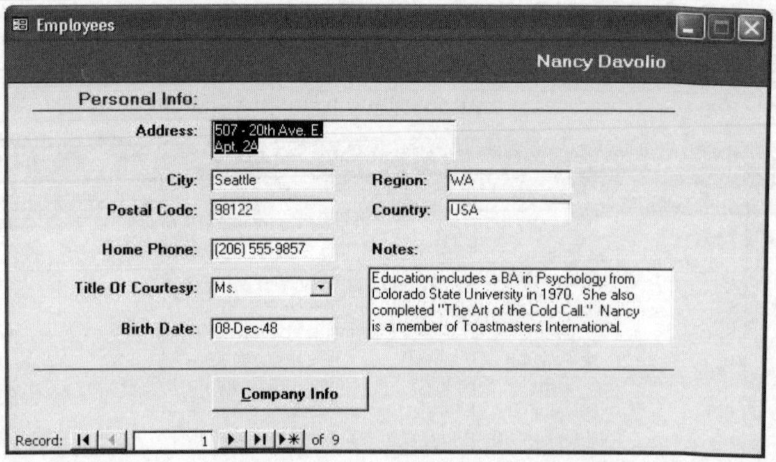

> ***Form view***
>
> *A view that typically presents all or selected information for a single record, suitably laid out and in an easy-to-read format.*

Design view

The third view you need to know about is Design view. Design view relates to all database objects, and its contents differ depending on each object type. What it has in common for all objects is that it is the view in which you can create objects from scratch and change the design of existing objects. Design view provides all the tools and options for designing and creating an object.

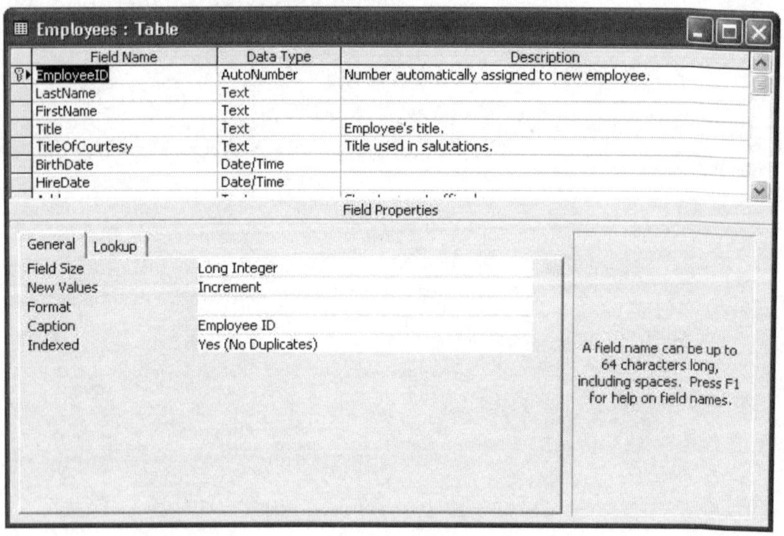

The previous example shows a table in Design view. In this case, all the fields in the table are listed together with their data types (you will learn about data types in Chapter 28) and it also displays the properties of each field.

Print Preview

Print Preview is the view you use to look at reports to check what they look like before you print them.

CustomerOrders

ProductID	*OrderID*	*OrderDate*	*Qty*	*CustID*	*Company*
3	10952	16/03/1998	16	ALFKI	Alfreds Futterkiste
28	10951	16/03/1998	2	ALFKI	Alfreds Futterkiste
28	10643	25/08/1997	15	ALFKI	Alfreds Futterkiste
39	10644	25/08/1997	21	ALFKI	Alfreds Futterkiste
46	10645	25/08/1997	2	ALFKI	Alfreds Futterkiste
63	10692	03/10/1997	20	ALFKI	Alfreds Futterkiste

Switching views

To switch between views of an object, use the **View** menu options or click the **View** button. The options available depend on the object type (as outlined in the table on page 434). Here are some examples of how to switch view:

Design View button

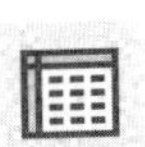

Datasheet View button

- If your table is open in Datasheet view, switch to Design view by choosing **View | Design View** or by clicking the **Design View** button on the toolbar.
- If your table is open in Design view, you can return from Design view to Datasheet view by choosing **View | Datasheet View** or by clicking the **Datasheet View** button on the toolbar.

The toolbar buttons enable you to switch quickly between the two views, so that when you make any design changes you can see their effect immediately.

If your table is not open, you can open it in Design view by selecting Design View in the *Database* window, and clicking the **Design** button on the Database window toolbar.

Design view

A view in which you can change the organizational structure of your table. You create an index in Design view.

Access toolbars

The most frequently used Access functions are available by clicking a button on one of the Access toolbars. Normally, Access displays the most suitable toolbar for your current task – the one containing the buttons for the functions that you are most likely to use.

If you want to hide the toolbar (and choose all your options from the menus), or if you want to display other toolbars, choose **View | Toolbars**. Then, in the list of toolbars displayed, select the ones you want to view and deselect the ones you want to hide.

If a particular toolbar is not listed, choose *Customize* to display a full list of available toolbars. Then select or deselect the toolbar, as appropriate. Click **Close** when you have finished.

The *Database* window has its own toolbar, which is always displayed. The options on this toolbar vary depending on the object type that is currently selected.

Online help

Like Excel, Word, PowerPoint and other Microsoft applications, Access offers a searchable online help system.

- The word 'help' means that the information is there to assist you understand and use the application.
- The word 'online' means that the material is presented on the computer screen rather than as a traditional printed manual.

You can search through and read online help in various ways: from the Help Window, from dialog boxes, and by using the Office Assistant.

Using the Office Assistant

The Office Assistant is a friendly, animated tool that allows you to type a topic or question about what you are looking for. It then presents a list of relevant help topics for you to choose from, as Exercise 27.2 demonstrates.

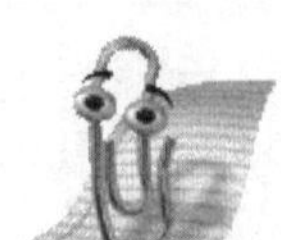

Office Assistant

Exercise 27.2: Using the Office Assistant to get help

1) Click the Office Assistant.

   If the Office Assistant is not visible on your screen, choose **Help | Show the Office Assistant**.

2) In the search balloon displayed, type: help

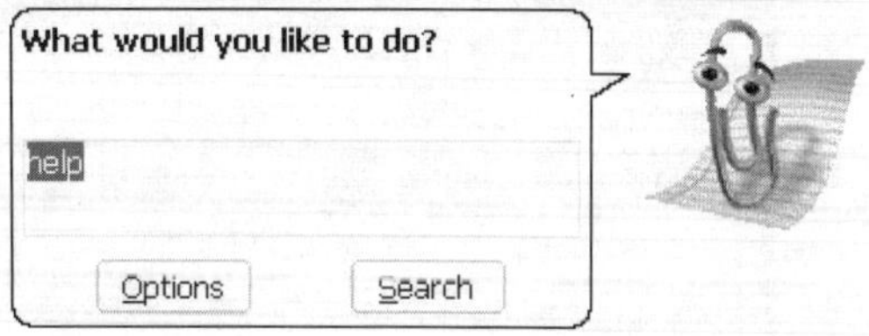

3) Click the **Search** button.
4) Click any topic in the list retrieved by the search. That topic is then displayed in the Microsoft Access Help window.
5) Close the window by clicking the **Close** button in its top right corner.

Close button

Using Ask a Question to get help

The *Ask a Question* box on the right side of the Access menu bar allows you to type a topic or question to get help without using the Office Assistant.

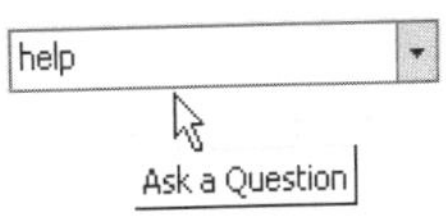

- Type your topic or question in the box and press **Enter**. Access displays a list of topics that you can choose from in the same way as you do when using the Office Assistant.

Using the Help window to get help

To open the Microsoft Access Help window, choose **Help | Microsoft Access Help**, or press **F1**.

If these actions open the Office Assistant instead of the Help Window, turn off the Office Assistant as follows:

- Right-click the Office Assistant and choose **Options** from the drop-down menu.
- Deselect the *Use the Office Assistant* option and click **OK**.

The Help window presents three tabs that allow you to search for help in different ways.

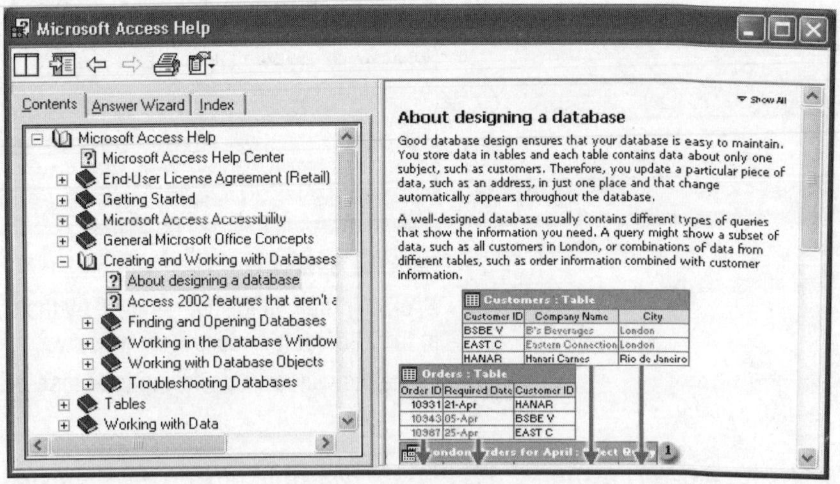

- **Contents tab:** This provides a table of contents for Access help.

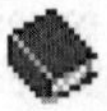

Where you see a heading with a book symbol, double-click to view the related sub-headings.

Double-click a question mark symbol to read the help text.

- **Answer Wizard tab:** Type your question in the *What would you like to do?* box, and click **Search**. Access displays all matches from the online help.

  Click a topic to display the associated text in the right-hand pane.

- **Index tab:** Type the word you are interested in, or choose a keyword from the list displayed. Then click **Search**. Access displays a list of suggested help topics in the lower-left of the window.

  When you find the topic that you are looking for, click it to display the associated text in the right-hand pane.

As you search through and read online help topics, you will see the following buttons at the top of the online help window:

- **Hide/Show:** Hides or displays the left pane of the Help window.

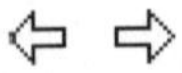

- **Back/Forward:** Moves you backwards and forwards through previously visited help topics.

- **Print:** Prints the currently displayed help topic.

- **Options:** Offers a number of display options.

Take a few minutes to look through the online help system.

Using help from dialog boxes

You can also access online help directly from a dialog box, as Exercise 27.3 demonstrates.

Exercise 27.3: Using online help in a dialog box

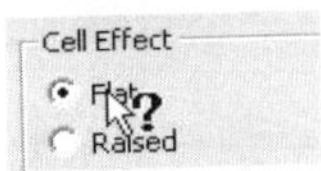

1) With the Northwind database open in Datasheet view, choose **Format | Datasheet** to display the *Datasheet Formatting* dialog box.
2) Click the **Help** button near the top-right of the dialog box. Word displays a question mark to the right of the mouse pointer.
3) Select the *Flat* option in *Cell Effect* section of the dialog box.
4) Access displays online help text telling you about the purpose of the selected element.

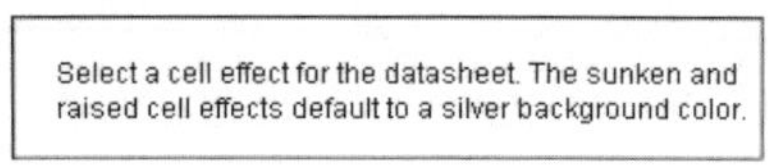

5) Click anywhere else on the Access screen to remove the online help text, and click **Cancel** to close the dialog box.

   Practise this exercise with other dialog boxes in Access.

Closing the database and quitting Access

To close an Access database, choose **File | Close**, or click the **Close** button on the *Database* window.

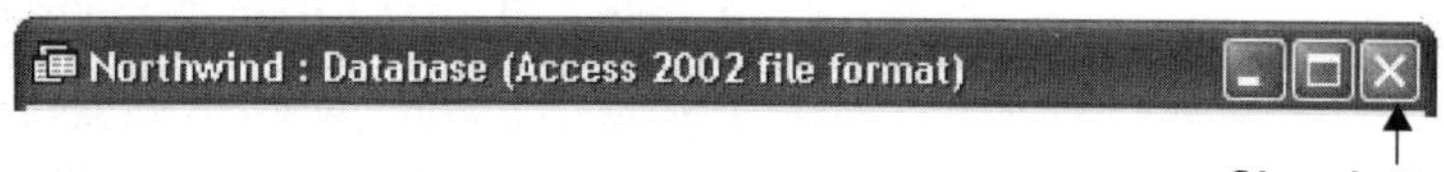

Close button

To leave Access, choose **File | Exit**, or click the **Close** button on the Access window.

Chapter summary: so now you know

The *Database window* is the control centre of Access. Using its options, you can open and work with any of the application's *objects* including *Tables*, *Queries*, *Forms* and *Reports*.

Forms are used primarily for data entry and typically show a single record at a time. *Queries* are named and saved requests for specific information from one or more tables and each time you run a query, Access retrieves an up-to-date set of records that match the request. *Reports* are used to display, format, summarize and print selected information.

Access provides a number of different viewing modes for tables, forms, queries and reports; these are *Datasheet view, Form view, Design View* and *Print Preview.*

Access offers a searchable *online help* system that you can access in various ways: from the Help window, from dialog boxes, and by using the Office Assistant. See Exercises 27.1, 27.2 and 27.3.

Quick quiz: exploring Access

Circle the correct answer to each of the following multiple-choice questions about exploring Access.

Q1	In Datasheet view, records in a table are displayed one at a time, with fields selected by the database designer.
A.	True.
B.	False.

Q2	You can return to the Database window at any time by ...
A.	Choosing **View | Database window**.
B.	Choosing **View | Datasheet view**.
C.	Choosing **Window | <database name>**.

Q3	Which of the following procedures can you use to open an existing database?
A.	Click the database name in the *Open a file* area of the *New File* task pane.
B.	Choose **File | Open**, locate the database, select it and click **Open**.
C.	Click the **Open** button on the *Database* toolbar, locate the database, select it and click **Open**.
D.	Select the *More files* option in the *Open a database* area of the *New File* task pane, locate the database, select it and click **Open**.

Q4	What is the file name extension for Access database files?
A	.doc
B	.adb
C	.mdb

Q5	In which view would you see data laid out in columns (one for each field) and rows (one for each record)?
A.	Form view.
B.	Datasheet view.
C.	Design view.

Answers

1: B, **2:** C, **3:** A, B, C, D, **4:** C, **5:** B.

Chapter 28: Building your Access database

In this chapter

Get ready to build your first database in Access. This is not as an intimidating as it may sound. Access comes with a number of samples that you can use as a basis for just about any new database that you might want to create. A lot of the work is already done for you.

The decisions you need to make are: Which sample table is closest to the one I want? Which of its fields will I use? And what new names will I give to the fields that I select?

One aspect of database creation that Access cannot help you with is data entry; only you can do that.

New skills

At the end of this chapter you should be able to:

- Create a new database.
- Use the *Table Wizard* to create a table.
- Create a table in Design view.
- Enter records in a table.
- Edit records in a table.
- Delete records from a table.
- Save and copy a table.
- Save a database to a new location.

Overview of database creation

In this chapter you will create your first Access database. It will be a Bookworm database, cataloguing a personal library.

Access includes a *Table Wizard* to simplify the process of creating a database. You will use this automated feature to do some of the work, and you will do some of it the hard way, so that you will learn more about how the application works. The steps involved in creating a database are:

- Create a blank database.
- Create a table either with the *Table Wizard* or in Design view.
- Enter your database records.

Creating a new, blank database

The first step is to create a new blank database, and to name and save it.

Exercise 28.1: Creating a new, blank database

1) Start Access.
2) In the *New File* task pane, under *New*, click the *Blank Database* option. Access displays the *File New Database* dialog box.

   If the task pane is not open in the Access window, click the **New** button on the toolbar to display it.

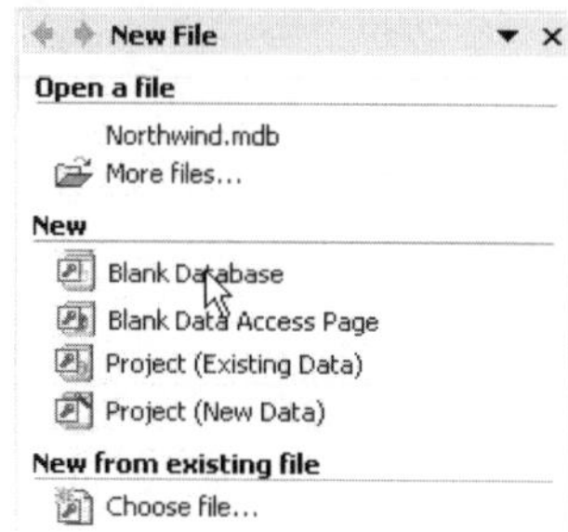

3) In the *File New Database* dialog box, give your new database a name – Bookworm – and indicate the folder in which you want to store it. Access automatically adds the file name extension .mdb.

   By default, Access suggests that you save your databases in the My Documents folder. Accept or amend this location, as required.
4) Click the **Create** button.

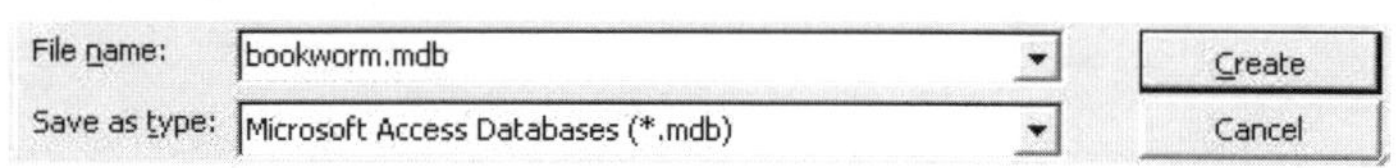

   Access now displays the *Database* window for the new Bookworm database.
5) Normally when you create a database, the Table objects are displayed by default in the Database window. If they are not, click the **Tables** button in the *Objects* list.

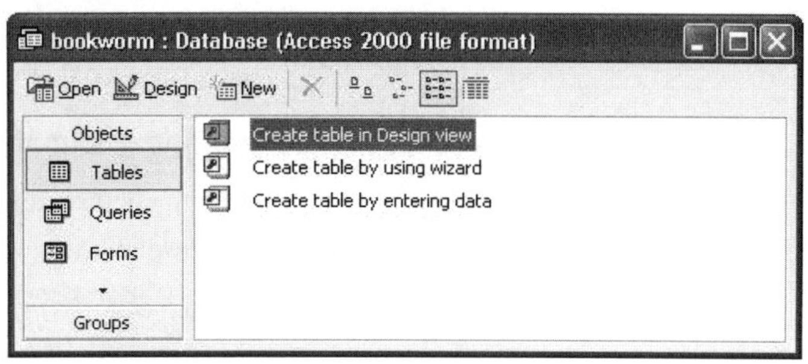

Notice that, unlike the Northwind sample database, each of the object sets (tables, queries, forms, and so on) in the database you just created is empty. In this chapter you will create two table objects; in Chapter 32, query objects; in Chapter 33, form objects; and in Chapter 34, a report object.

Creating a table with the Table Wizard

With the *Table Wizard*, creating a table involves the following steps:

Step one	**Starting the wizard and selecting a sample table:** Rather than create a new table from scratch, it is easier and faster to base it on one provided by Access. See Exercise 28.2.
Step two	**Selecting your fields:** You probably won't want every field from the sample table included in your table, so you must specify which ones you need. See Exercise 28.3.
Step three	**Renaming your fields:** Typically, you will need to rename at least some of the fields that you have selected from the sample table. This is the step at which you also name your table. See Exercise 28.4.
Step four	**Setting your primary key**: You need to tell Access which of your fields will act as the primary key field – the one that uniquely distinguishes each record from all the others. See Exercise 28.5.
Step five	**Entering data into your table**: You will enter data into your new table in Datasheet view. See Exercise 28.6.

Step one: starting the wizard and selecting a sample table

It would be impossible for anyone to anticipate precisely what you want to do with your database, so the Access *Table Wizard* offers you a wide range of choices.

In the next few exercises you will pick the options that come closest to matching your needs, and you will modify them until they are exactly what you want.

Exercise 28.2: Selecting a sample table

1) Start the *Table Wizard* by double-clicking the *Create table by using wizard* option in the *Database* window.

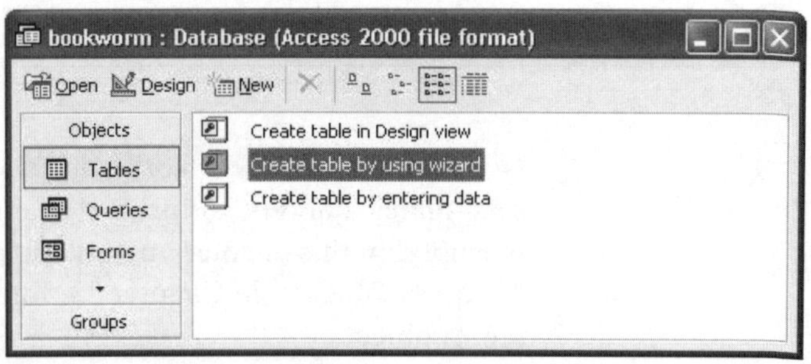

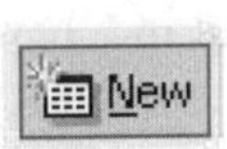

New Table button

Alternatively, click the **New** button on the *Database* window toolbar, select the *Table Wizard* option in the *New Table* dialog box, and click **OK.**

2) In the *Table Wizard* dialog box now displayed, you can see two option buttons – *Business* and *Personal*. Depending on which of these options you select, Access displays a different list of sample tables.

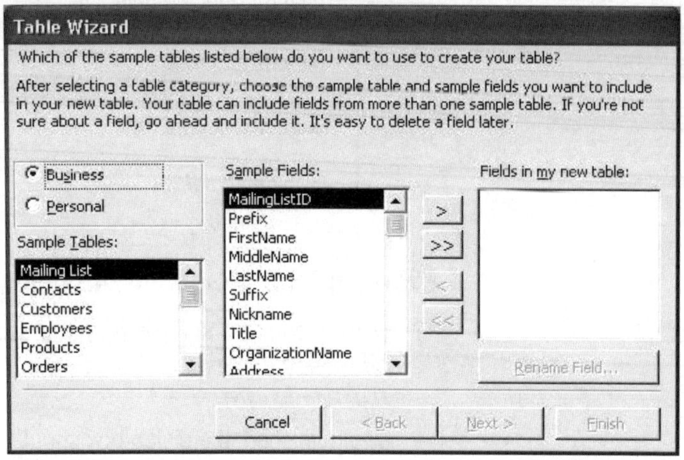

3) Select the *Business* option and browse through the *Sample Tables* list. For each table in the first list box, scroll through the sample fields in the second list box. None of the tables seems to be particularly appropriate for your needs.
4) Select the *Personal* option. Again, look through the sample tables. Luckily for us there is a sample table for books.

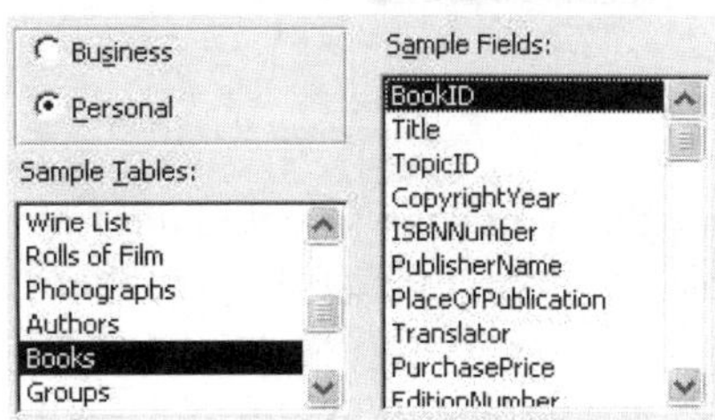

5) Select the *Books* table – you will work with it in Exercise 28.3.

Step two: selecting your fields

The first screen of the *Table Wizard* shows three list boxes. The first displays Access's sample tables. (You selected the Books table from this list in Exercise 28.2.) The second list shows all the fields supplied with the selected sample table. The third list shows the fields that you have decided to include in your new table. Initially, the third list is empty.

To move a field from the *Sample Fields* box to the *Fields in my new table* box, click on it to select it, and then click the **>** button. If you change your mind about a particular field, select it in the right-hand box and click the **<** button. You can include all the sample fields by clicking the **>>** button. Or you can remove all the fields from the right-hand box by clicking the **<<** button.

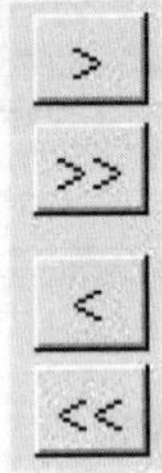

Include selected field

Include all fields

Exclude selected field

Exclude all fields

Exercise 28.3: Selecting the fields you need

1) Move the following fields from the *Sample Fields* list to the *Fields in my new table* list: *ISBNNumber*, *Title*, *Pages*, *CopyrightYear*, *PurchasePrice*, *DatePurchased*.

   When finished, the dialog box should look as shown.

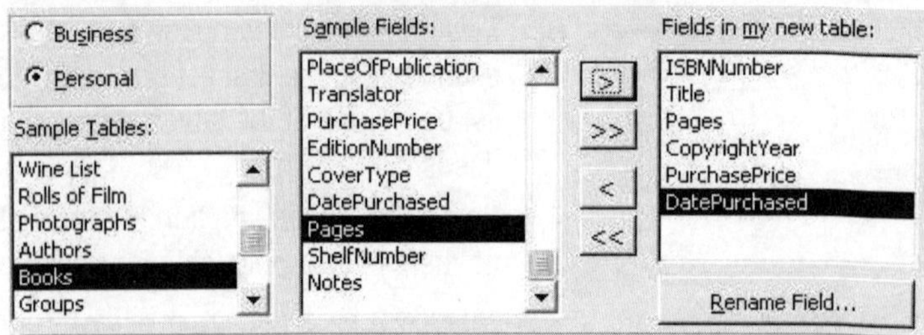

Step three: renaming your fields

Now that you have selected the fields you want to use from the sample table, your next task is to give them suitable names. To rename a field, click it in the *Fields in my new table* list and click the **Rename Field** button. You then type the new name for the field in the *Rename Field* dialog box. Rename your fields as shown in Exercise 28.4.

Exercise 28.4: Renaming your fields

1) In the *Fields in my new table* list, select *ISBNNumber*. Click the **Rename Field** button.
2) In the *Rename Field* dialog box, type the new name for the field: *ISBN*. Click **OK**.
3) Repeat for the other fields in your new table, as follows:

Old name	New name
ISBNNumber	ISBN
PurchasePrice	Cost
DatePurchased	PurchaseDate

4) Click the **Next** button in the *Table Wizard* dialog box.

   Congratulations! You have just created your first Access table.

5) Now you have to give it a name.

   Call your table Books – the same name as the database that contains it.

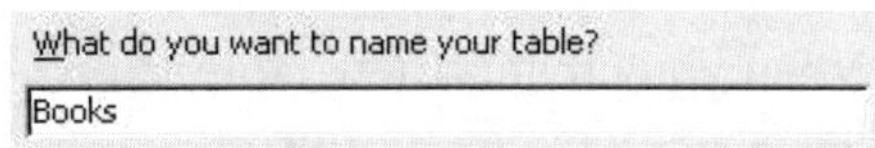

In the same dialog box, Access asks you whether you want the *Table Wizard* to set a primary key, or whether you want to do it yourself – this takes us on to step four.

Step four: setting your primary key

The primary key is a field that is used to identify each record in the database uniquely. We will use the ISBN as the primary key for our Books database.

Exercise 28.5: Setting a primary key

1) On the second *Table Wizard* screen, having specified a name for your new table (in Exercise 28.4), select the *No, I'll set the primary key* option and click the **Next** button.

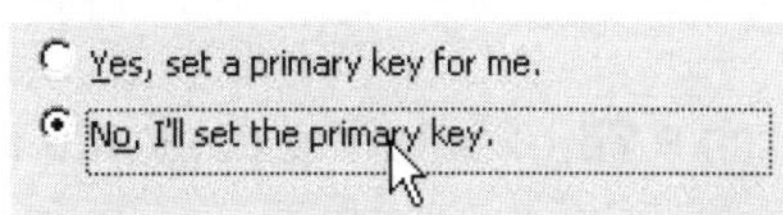

2) In answer to the question *What field will hold data that is unique for each record?*, select *ISBN*. (It should already be selected as the default.)

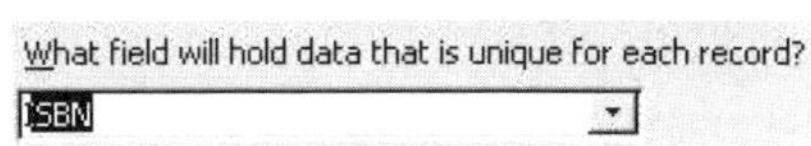

   In answer to the question *What type of data do you want the primary key field to contain?*, select *Numbers and/or letters I enter when I add new records*.

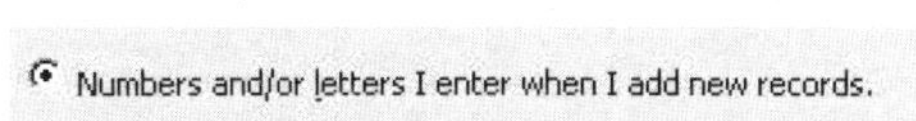

3) Click the **Next** button.

   You have now defined your own primary key for your table.

4) Access then asks you what you want to do next – modify the table design, enter data directly into the table, or enter data into a table using a form that the wizard creates?

   Well, a table with no data is rather boring, so you probably want to enter data directly into the table without further delay. Choose that option.

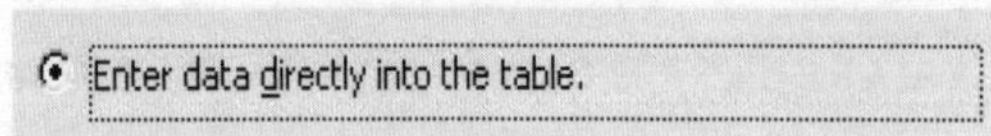

5) Click the **Finish** button. Access now displays your table in Datasheet view.

Step five: entering data into your table

When you create a new table, Access displays the table initially in Datasheet view as follows:

- Along the top are column headings that show your field names.
- Underneath the column headings is a single, blank row.

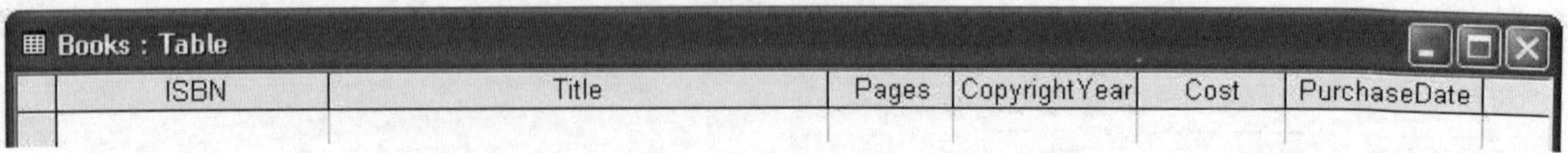

Click in any field: you can then enter data in that field. You can move from field to field using the **Tab** key or the arrow keys. As soon as you start entering data for a record, a new line opens up underneath. No matter how many records you enter, there is always a blank record at the end where you can enter the next one.

At this stage you have created a blank table with all the fields you need. You can now begin to enter data into the table.

Exercise 28.6: Entering data into the table

1) In the Books table, fill in the details of the books shown here. Don't worry too much about getting the ISBN number exactly right, but *do copy the other fields exactly* – later on in the book, we'll use the data shown here for queries and reports.

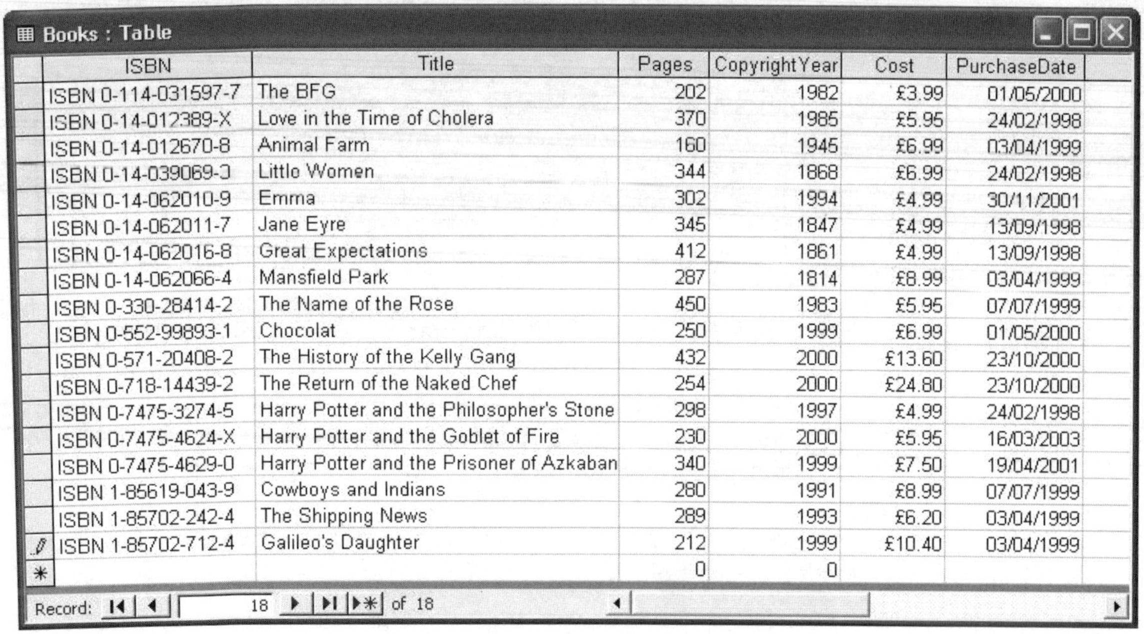

Books : Table

ISBN	Title	Pages	CopyrightYear	Cost	PurchaseDate
ISBN 0-114-031597-7	The BFG	202	1982	£3.99	01/05/2000
ISBN 0-14-012389-X	Love in the Time of Cholera	370	1985	£5.95	24/02/1998
ISBN 0-14-012670-8	Animal Farm	160	1945	£6.99	03/04/1999
ISBN 0-14-039069-3	Little Women	344	1868	£6.99	24/02/1998
ISBN 0-14-062010-9	Emma	302	1994	£4.99	30/11/2001
ISBN 0-14-062011-7	Jane Eyre	345	1847	£4.99	13/09/1998
ISBN 0-14-062016-8	Great Expectations	412	1861	£4.99	13/09/1998
ISBN 0-14-062066-4	Mansfield Park	287	1814	£8.99	03/04/1999
ISBN 0-330-28414-2	The Name of the Rose	450	1983	£5.95	07/07/1999
ISBN 0-552-99893-1	Chocolat	250	1999	£6.99	01/05/2000
ISBN 0-571-20408-2	The History of the Kelly Gang	432	2000	£13.60	23/10/2000
ISBN 0-718-14439-2	The Return of the Naked Chef	254	2000	£24.80	23/10/2000
ISBN 0-7475-3274-5	Harry Potter and the Philosopher's Stone	298	1997	£4.99	24/02/1998
ISBN 0-7475-4624-X	Harry Potter and the Goblet of Fire	230	2000	£5.95	16/03/2003
ISBN 0-7475-4629-0	Harry Potter and the Prisoner of Azkaban	340	1999	£7.50	19/04/2001
ISBN 1-85619-043-9	Cowboys and Indians	280	1991	£8.99	07/07/1999
ISBN 1-85702-242-4	The Shipping News	289	1993	£6.20	03/04/1999
ISBN 1-85702-712-4	Galileo's Daughter	212	1999	£10.40	03/04/1999
		0	0		

Record: 18 of 18

2) At this stage, some fields may be too small to display all the information you enter: don't worry – you'll learn how to adjust column width in Chapter 29.

3) Close your table by clicking the **Close** button in the Table window (not the one in the Access window). Access may ask you if you want to save changes to the design of the table. Click **Yes**.

4) Access returns you to the Database window, this time with one important difference: the new table you created – Books – is listed with the Table objects.

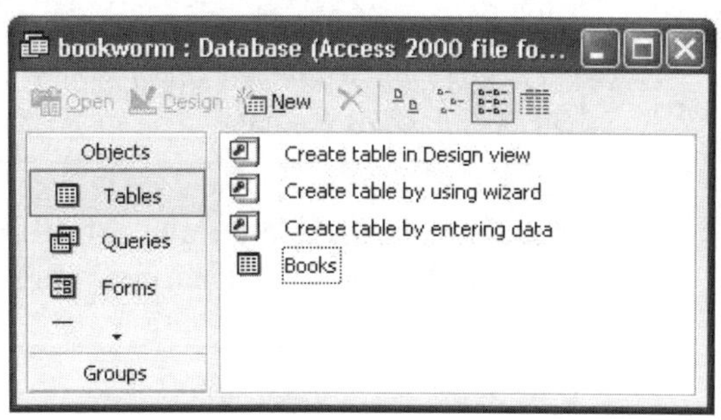

That's it. Now you know how to create a table in Access, and how to enter data into it in Datasheet view.

The different data types

As you were building the Bookworm database, you might have noticed that the *PurchaseDate* field accepts only dates, and that the *Pages* field accepts only numbers. Try entering text into the

PurchaseDate field and see what happens. You probably get a message something like this:

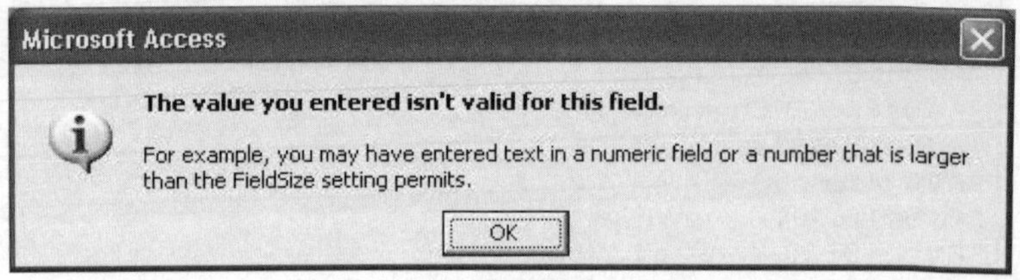

Click **OK** and undo the text entry. You probably think that Access is reading your mind. How does it know that the *PurchaseDate* column should contain only dates? And how does it know that *Pages* accepts only numbers? Well, the answer is in the table design, and, to be honest, we cheated a bit.

When you set up a table in Access, there are two things you have to do for each field:

- You have to give the field a *name*.
- You have to give the field a *data type*.

When you used the *Table Wizard* to set up the Books table, you changed the names of some fields, but otherwise the fields you selected from the sample table more or less matched your requirements, and you didn't need to change the data types.

Data type

The data type determines the kind of data that you can store in a field and how Access handles the data.

Access recognizes a number of different data types. The most important ones for our purposes are as follows:

Data type	Used for	Examples
Text	Any sort of alphabetic or numeric data. Typically used where there is a limit on the amount of data. No more than 255 characters may be input. (If the data is numeric, it cannot be used in calculations.)	Surname, Colour, Postal Code, Telephone Number

Memo	Any sort of alphabetic or numeric data. Typically used for free-form input. Up to 65,535 characters may be input. (Again, if the data is numeric, it cannot be used in calculations.)	Description, Notes
Number	Numeric data that may be used in calculations.	Quantity in Stock, Number Sold
Date/Time	Date or time data.	Date Bought, Arrival Time, Departure Time
Currency	Money values or other numeric data used in calculations involving data with one to four decimal places.	Price, Current Value
AutoNumber	A number assigned to each new record automatically. Access assigns the numbers in sequence, starting with 1.	Sequence, Number
Yes/No	Fields that can have simple yes/no, true/false, or on/off values only.	Second Hand Goods

Creating a table in Design view

You might have noticed that the Books table we have created contains no field for *Author* – a rather serious omission you might think. The problem is, though, that if we did have an author field in the Books table, we could end up entering the same author's details many times over. To get around duplication of this kind, we create a separate table for authors and link it to the Books table. Later on, you will learn how to link tables so that Access can retrieve data from both of them at the same time.

In Exercise 28.7 you will create a new Authors table in Design view. The steps you follow are much the same as those you followed when using the *Table Wizard* in the earlier exercises in this chapter:

Step one	Open the Books database.
Step two	Create the table in Design view.
Step three	Add fields and data types.
Step four	Set the primary key.
Step five	Save and name the table.
Step six	Add records to the table.

Exercise 28.7: Creating a table in Design view

1) Open the Bookworm database that you created in Exercise 28.1.

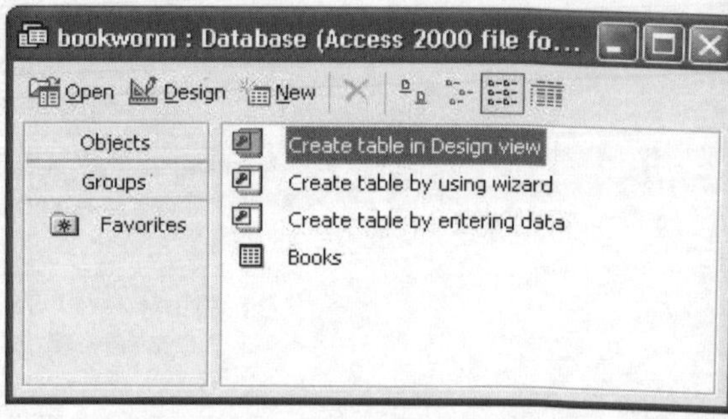

2) Choose *Create table in Design view.*
3) Add the following four fields:
   - AuthID
   - AuthLastName
   - AuthFirstName
   - Nationality

   Enter the field name in the *Field Name* column and select the data type from the drop-down list in the *Data Type* column. Use the *Description* column to enter a brief description of each field. Give *AuthID* the datatype *AutoNumber* and give the other fields the data type *Text* (default). *AutoNumber* is an automatically assigned sequence number, and you cannot have more than one field with this data type in a table. Use the Description field to enter a brief description of each field. Your screen should now look like this:

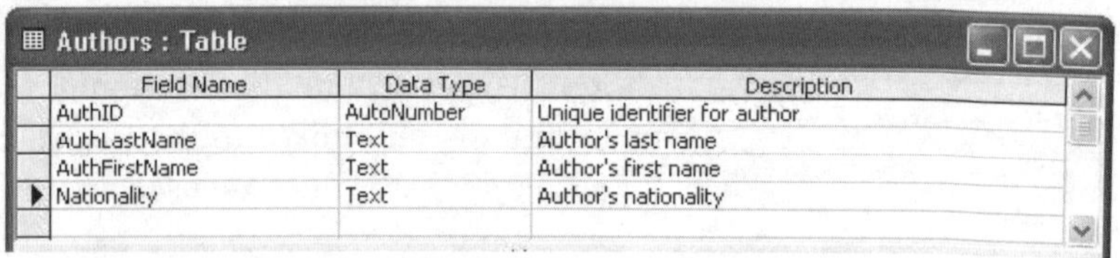

4) Now you need to set the AuthID as the primary key for the table. Right-click the AuthID field and then click *Primary Key*. A key symbol appears to the left of the field name.

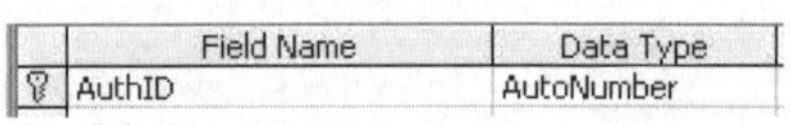

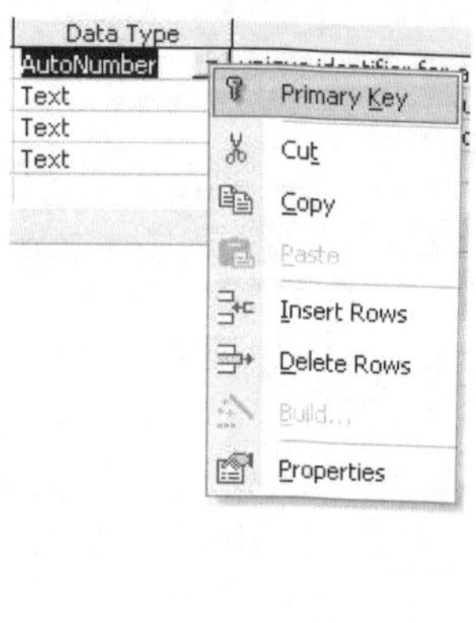

5) Choose **File | Save** to save the table, and give it the name *Authors*.

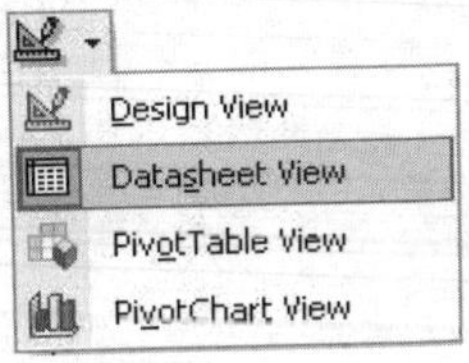

6) Now switch to Datasheet view where you can begin to enter records. Copy the details from the example on the right. Note that the AuthID value is added automatically. We have included some deliberate mistakes that we will correct later.

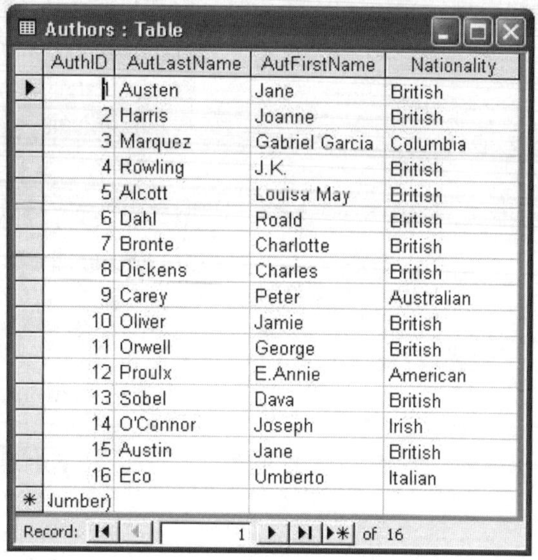

Authors : Table

AuthID	AutLastName	AutFirstName	Nationality
1	Austen	Jane	British
2	Harris	Joanne	British
3	Marquez	Gabriel Garcia	Columbia
4	Rowling	J.K.	British
5	Alcott	Louisa May	British
6	Dahl	Roald	British
7	Bronte	Charlotte	British
8	Dickens	Charles	British
9	Carey	Peter	Australian
10	Oliver	Jamie	British
11	Orwell	George	British
12	Proulx	E.Annie	American
13	Sobel	Dava	British
14	O'Connor	Joseph	Irish
15	Austin	Jane	British
16	Eco	Umberto	Italian
Jumber)			

Record: 1 of 16

Editing, saving, copying and deleting records

Earlier in this chapter, you learned how to create database tables in Access. Now that you have entered records in your tables, it's time to learn how to modify tables in various ways. To change or delete a record in your Bookworm database, open Access, open the Bookworm database, and then open the Authors table. By default, your table opens in Datasheet view.

Editing a field

To change data in a field, begin by clicking on that field.

- If you click anywhere a field, you can use the **Backspace** or **Delete** keys to delete characters one by one, or you can insert new characters. In Exercise 28.8 you will correct the errors in the Authors table.

- If you click the extreme left of the field, or click in the field and press **F2**, the entire field is selected and anything you type immediately overwrites the whole field. Or press **Delete** to delete the contents of the field.

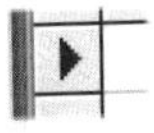

Arrow indicates current record

Notice that when you click in a field, an arrow appears in the box on the extreme left of the record. This box is called the *record selector* box, and an arrow in the box indicates the current record (that is, the record you are currently working on).

Remember that you cannot change the *AuthID* field – it is assigned automatically by Access.

Exercise 28.8: Editing fields

1) Open the Authors table in Datasheet view.
2) Click the Nationality field for Louisa May Alcott, and change the entry to **American**.

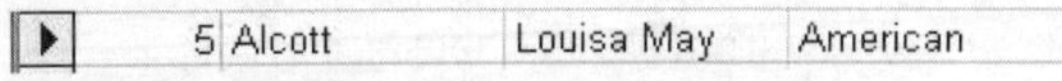

3) Open the Books table in Datasheet view.
4) Change the CopyrightYear for *Emma* to 1816.

Saving records

You don't have to *explicitly* save records as you enter or modify them – Access automatically saves a record when you move the insertion point to another record. If you do wish to explicitly save a record, choose **Records | Save Record**.

Copying and pasting records

Where most of the details you want to enter in a record are much the same as in a record you have already entered, you can copy the content of the original and paste it into the new record.

To copy an entire record, click the *Record Selector*, right-click and then choose **Copy**.

Record selector

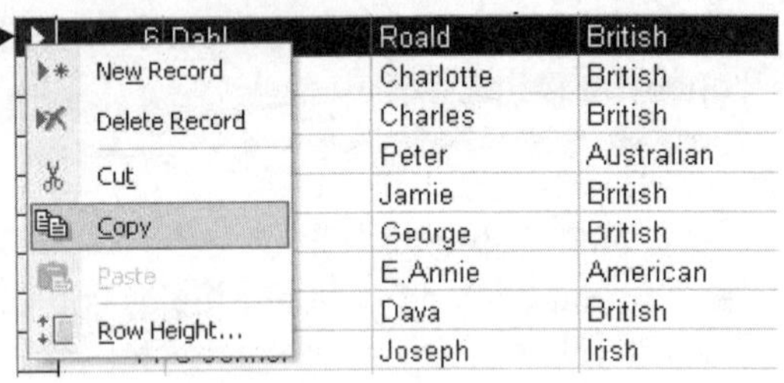

You can then paste the record to a new location. Remember, the primary key must be unique, so if you are pasting into the same table, you will need to update this. If the primary key is an AutoNumber, Access updates it automatically.

Deleting a record

To delete a record, first make it the current record by clicking anywhere in it. Then click the **Delete Record** button on the toolbar. Alternatively, right-click the *Record Selector* and then choose **Delete Record**.

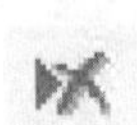

Delete Record button

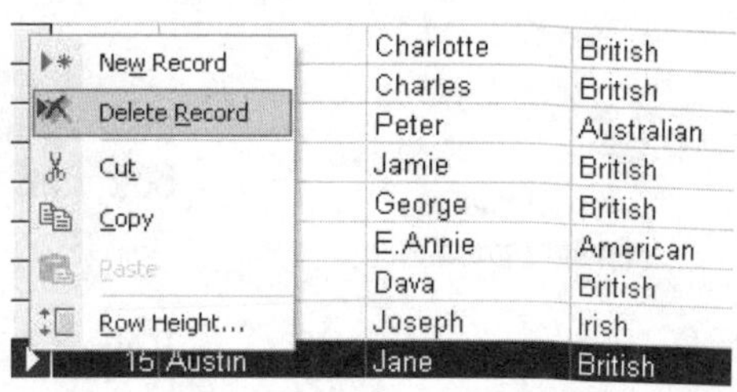

You can then confirm that you want to delete the record, or change your mind and leave it alone.

Exercise 28.9: Deleting a record

In our Authors table, there is an incorrect entry for Jane Austin (AuthID 15). The correct entry is Jane Austen (AuthID 1), and in this exercise you will delete the incorrect entry.

1) Open the Authors table.
2) Right-click the record selector for Jane Austin (AuthID 15) and choose **Delete Record**.

If your table has an AutoNumber field (as in our Authors table), and you delete a record, Access does *not* reassign the number of the deleted record to another record. Access ensures that records keep the numbers initially assigned to them, and it always assigns higher numbers to later additions than to earlier ones.

The Undo command

If you make an error when editing database records, choose **Edit | Undo**.

Saving, copying and deleting tables

Access saves changes and additions to the records in a table automatically. What it does not save, however, are changes to the structure or layout of a table. For example, if you swap the order of columns in Datasheet view, you need to save this explicitly – choose **File | Save**. You are also prompted to save any changes to the layout or design when you close a table.

Copying tables

You can also make copies of a table, within the current database or in a different database. To copy a table, highlight it in the *Database* window, right-click it and choose **Copy**. Then choose **Edit | Paste**. You are prompted to give a name to the copy, and you are offered a choice of what you want to copy.

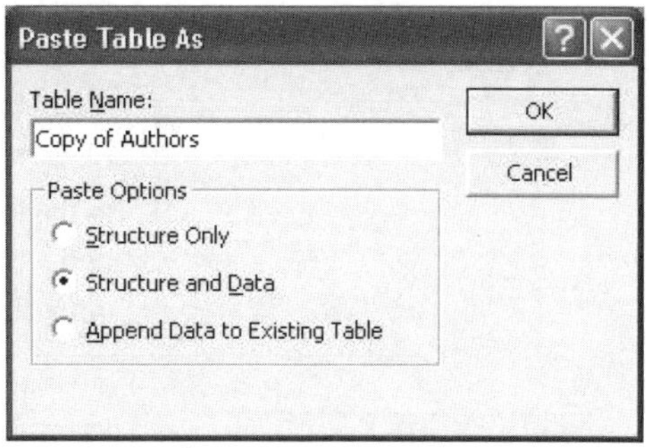

Paste option	Description
Structure Only	Copies the structure of the table only, without any of the data.
Structure and Data	Copies both the structure of the table and all the data.
Append Data to Existing Table	Enter the name of the table you want to append the data to in the *Table Name* field. The destination table must have the same structure as the table you are copying from.

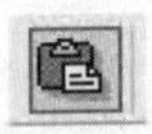

Paste button

To copy a table to another database, you must first close the current database and then open the database you want to copy it to. Then click the **Paste** button on the toolbar. In the *Paste Table As* dialog box, give the new table a name, and specify what you want to copy as above.

Deleting tables

To delete a table, right-click it in Objects view and choose **Delete**. You are asked to confirm that you want to delete the table.

Saving, copying and deleting a database

Strictly speaking, there is no such thing as saving a database in Access. As you work with a database, the database objects are saved individually as you proceed, so there is no need to save the database itself. However, you might want to make a security copy of a database as a backup.

Exercise 28.10: Saving your Access database to a different location

1) Close the Bookworm Database window and open Windows Explorer.
2) In the left-hand pane, navigate to the folder that contains your Bookworm database: for example, the My Documents folder. The folder contents appear in the right-hand pane.
3) Click the Bookworm database file once to select it, and choose **Edit | Copy**.
4) In the left-hand pane, navigate to the location where you want to make the copy, click on it and choose **Edit | Paste**. For example, you could make a copy to a floppy disk on drive A: in this way.

Deleting a database

Use Windows Explorer to delete a database you no longer need. See Exercise 11.13 for details of how to delete a file with Windows Explorer.

Chapter summary: so now you know

Access offers a *Table Wizard* that simplifies the process of creating a new database by providing a number of *sample tables*. Choose one that resembles the table that you want to create. You can customize your chosen sample table by selecting which of its fields you want to use, and then renaming the selected fields as required. See Exercises 28.2, 28.3, 28.4 and 28.5 for examples of how to do these tasks.

When you create a new table, Access displays it in Datasheet view, with *column headings* that show your selected field names above a single, blank row. You can type record data into the blank row. As soon as you enter one record, Access opens up a new line underneath, so that there is always a blank record at the end where you can enter the next one. See Exercise 28.6 for an example of how to do this.

The *primary key* is a field (or combination of fields) in a table that uniquely identifies each record.

Access allows you to assign a *data type* to each field, so that you can specify the kind of data that the field contains: for example, Text, DateTime, Currency, AutoNumber, and so on. See Exercise 28.8 for an example of how to do this.

You can also create tables in *Design view.* The steps you follow are much the same as those you use when creating a table with the wizard. See Exercise 28.7 for an example of how to do this.

Access *saves* the data you enter into a table as you proceed, so there is no need to save explicitly (as in other applications). You do, however, need to save any changes you make to the structure or layout of database objects.

Use the *Record Selector* to highlight individual records that you want to copy or delete. See Exercise 28.9 for an example of how to do this. If you make an error when entering or modifying data, use the **Undo** command to undo the error. You can copy records, tables or entire databases.

You can make a copy of a table within the current database or in a different database. You can choose to copy the structure and the data, or just the structure, or you can append the data to a different table with the same structure.

You must *save* and *name* both the database and the tables that the database contains. See Exercise 28.10 for an example of how to do this.

Quick quiz: building your Access database

Circle the correct answer to each of the following multiple-choice questions about building your Access database.

Q1	To create a new database, you ...
A.	Click the **New** button in the Database window for an existing database. Enter a name and location for the new database and click **Create**.
B.	Open the *New File* task pane, choose the *Blank Database* option under *New*, enter a name and location for the new database and click **Create**.
C.	Choose **Insert | Database**, enter a name and location for the new database and click **Create**.

Q2	The primary key of a database table is a field or combination of fields that uniquely identifies each record in the table.
A.	True.
B.	False.

Q3	To start the Table Wizard, you ...
A.	Choose **File | New**, and then select the *Table Wizard* option in the *New File* task pane.
B.	Choose **Insert | Table**, select the *Datasheet View* option and click **OK**.
C.	In the Database window, click the *Tables* option in the *Objects* list and then click the *Create table by using wizard* option.

Q4	To switch from Datasheet view to Design view, you ...
A.	Click the **View** button on the toolbar.
B.	Choose **Window | <database name>: Design View**.
C.	Choose **File | Open | Design View.**

Q5	Which data type would you choose for free-form text comments?
A.	Text.
B.	Memo.
C.	Yes/No.

Answers

1: B, **2:** A, **3:** C, **4:** A, **5:** B.

Chapter 29: Modifying your database design

In this chapter

In Chapter 28 you learned how to create a database and to add and modify its content. In this chapter we move on to learn about how to modify the design, or structure and layout, of a database.

New skills

At the end of this chapter you should be able to:

- Change column widths.
- Hide columns.
- Freeze columns.
- Move columns.
- Add a field to a table.
- Delete a field from a table.
- Change data types.
- Change field sizes and display formats.
- Create validation rules.

New words

At the end of this chapter you should be able to explain the following terms:

- Field size
- Display format
- Validation rule

Adjusting the layout of a table

There are a number of ways in which you can adjust the layout of a table in Access. You can:

- Change column widths.
- Freeze and unfreeze columns.
- Hide and unhide columns.
- Reorder fields in a table (move columns).

Changing column widths

When you create your tables, you will notice that Access starts off by making all the columns the same width. Some of them are too narrow for their contents to be displayed in full (as, for example, in some of the book titles).

And some columns are too wide: the datasheet takes up more space than necessary, with the result that some of your data may be pushed off the screen, and you have to use the left–right scroll bar to see it.

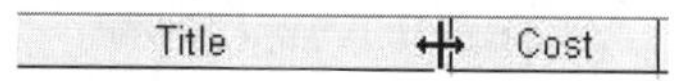

Drag left or right to adjust the width of columns

To change the width of a column, click on the dividing line (known as the *field delimiter*) between the column title and the one to its right. Notice that the shape of the mouse pointer changes. Then drag the pointer left or right until the column is the right size.

You can make the column width adjust automatically to fit the longest entry in the column by double-clicking the field delimiter.

Exercise 29.1: Changing column width

1) In the Database window, double-click the Books table to open it.
2) Change the width of the *Title* column to make the longer titles fully visible.

Before

Title
Harry Potter and the Philos
Harry Potter and the Goble
Harry Potter and the Prisor
Made in America
From Potter's Field
The New Guide to Cat Care
December Bride
A Children's Treasure of Mi
Cowboys and Indians
The Shipping News

After

Title
Harry Potter and the Philosopher's Stone
Harry Potter and the Goblet of Fire
Harry Potter and the Prisoner of Azkaban
Made in America
From Potter's Field
The New Guide to Cat Care
December Bride
A Children's Treasure of Milligan
Cowboys and Indians
The Shipping News

Freezing and unfreezing columns

If you want to ensure a particular column is always visible even when you scroll, you can *freeze* it. Right-click the column header and click **Freeze**. Access moves the column to the left side of the datasheet and it remains visible no matter where you scroll.

You cannot unfreeze individual columns, but you can unfreeze all columns by choosing **Format | Unfreeze All Columns**.

Hiding and unhiding columns

You can hide individual columns in a table – for example, this might be useful if you are not using all the columns in a table, or if there is some data that you don't want other people to see.

Right-click the column header, and then choose **Hide Columns**. To unhide columns, choose **Format | Unhide Columns** and select the columns you want to unhide.

The columns that are checked are not hidden

To unhide a column, select its check box and then click Close

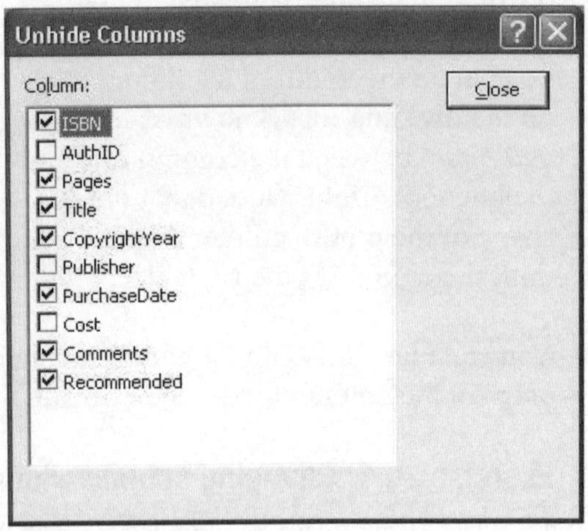

Reordering the fields in a table (moving columns)

To change the order of fields in the table, click the header of the one you want to move. Then click it again, but this time hold down the mouse button: note that a box appears on the tail of the mouse pointer.

Now drag it left or right to the new location. When you arrive at your chosen destination, note how a bold line has appeared, indicating Access's understanding of where you want to place your moving column: if this is correct, release the mouse button, and the column moves. Try this a number of times until you are confident about it.

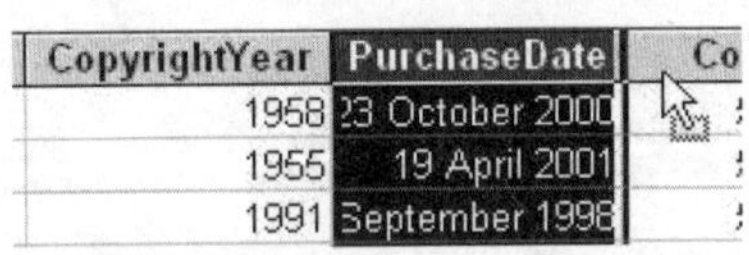

PurchaseDate column selected for moving

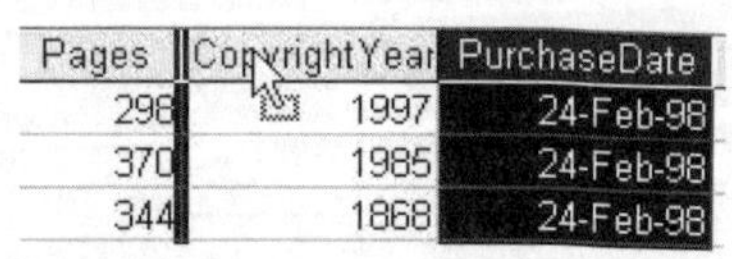

PurchaseDate column about to be placed between Pages and CopyrightYear columns

Adding new fields to a table

Can you add new fields to your database tables at any time? Yes. And you can use either Datasheet view or Design view to do this.

A danger of adding new fields is that you may have to go back and edit all records you have already entered. This applies particularly to numeric fields (where a blank field may be interpreted as 0), and Yes/No fields (where a blank field may be interpreted as No), but it is also important for any field that you use for sorting or filtering data.

However, it is better if you think about the fields you want to add when you are setting up the database, and modify the design as little as possible after that.

- Exercise 29.2 shows how to use Datasheet view to insert a Comments field into our Books table.
- Exercise 29.3 shows how to use Design view to insert a Recommended field into our Books table.

Exercise 29.2: Adding a new field in Datasheet view

1) Display your Books table in Datasheet view.
2) Click anywhere in the column to the right of where you want to place the new field column – let's put it to the left of CopyrightYear.
3) Choose **Insert | Column**. The new column is inserted with the title *Field1*.
4) Right-click the column header, choose **Rename Column** and type *Comments.* If you wish, enter comments on the books.
5) Choose **File | Save** to save the change to the table.

You cannot set the data type for a field in Datasheet view. But Access applies a data type of Text by default and this is suitable for your Comments field. If you think you will want to enter comments longer than 255 characters, change the data type to Memo – you can do this in Design view.

Exercise 29.3: Adding a new field in Design view

1) Display your Books table in Design view.
2) Where do you want to add a new field: at the end of a record or somewhere in the middle?
   - To add a new field between two existing fields, click in the row above which you want to add the field and choose **Insert | Rows**.
   - To add a new field at the end of the record, click in the next unused *Field Name* box. For this exercise, use this option.
3) Enter the name of the new field: Recommended. Then select a data type of Text.
4) Choose **File | Save** to save the change to the table.

Deleting a field from a table

You can delete a field in either Datasheet view or Design view:

- **Datasheet view:** right-click on the column header and choose **Delete Column**.
- **Design view:** click anywhere in the row you want to delete and choose **Edit | Delete Rows**.

Changing data types

It is easy to change the data type of a field, but ideally you should get it right at the design stage. If you try to change the data type after you have input a lot of data, you can confuse Access and may lose some of your data.

In Exercise 29.4 you will change the data type of the Recommended field to Yes/No.

Exercise 29.4: Changing data types

1) Display your Books table in Design view. You can see that the window is divided into two main panes.
   At the top is the list of fields with their names and data types. An arrow in the row selector at the left of a field indicates the current field. A key icon in the row selector of a field indicates a primary key field.
2) Click the data type for the *Recommended* field and choose *Yes/No.* This data type accepts only Yes/No, True/False or On/Off values. By default, Access uses a check box to represent these values: selected means Yes and unselected means No.
3) Save the changes you have made (choose **File | Save**) and switch to Datasheet view to see the impact on the *Recommended* field. As you can see, the field now contains a check box that you can select to indicate a book that you would recommend. Initially, the field is set to *No* for all records.

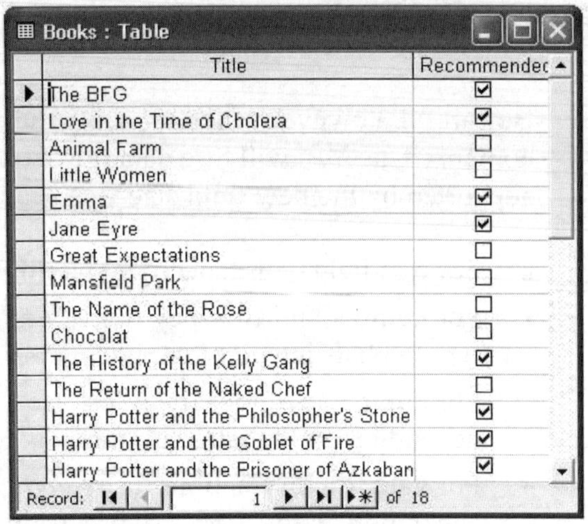

Note: In this screen we have hidden some of the fields so that the Title and Recommended fields are side by side.

Changing field properties

All database fields have properties that determine how Access handles, displays and stores their data. These specify characteristics such as the maximum size of the field, the format for displaying data, and the way in which AutoNumber fields are incremented. Field properties are displayed at the lower part of a table's Design view window. To view the properties of a particular field, click anywhere on the row for that field in the upper part of the window.

Properties for the ISBN field

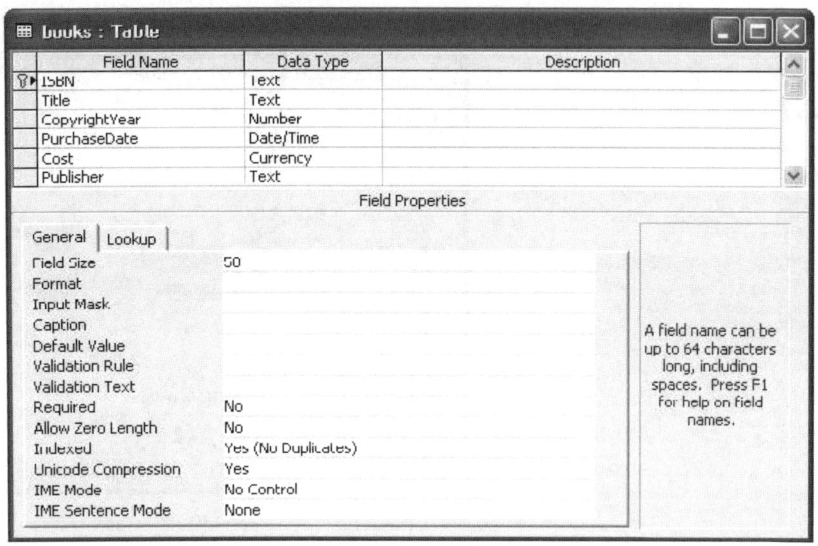

Changing field size

Some fields have a *Field Size* property that you can use to set the maximum size for data in a field. You should use the smallest possible setting, as smaller data sizes can be processed faster and require less memory than larger ones. You will not be able to enter values larger than the specified field size.

Be careful, however, when reducing the size of a field that already contains data. You will lose data if existing values are larger than those supported by the new field size.

- For text fields, just specify a maximum number of characters.
- For number and currency fields, *Field Size* sets a specific number type such as integer, long integer and so on.
- For numbers without fractions, use *Byte*, *Integer* or *Long Integer*, depending on the range of numbers required.
- For values with fractions, use *Single*, *Double* or *Decimal*, depending on the degree of precision required – *Single* is adequate for most numbers with fractions.

Exercise 29.5: Changing field size

1) Open the Books table in Design view – in this exercise you will reduce the field size of the *ISBN* field, which will never be more than 20.
2) In the upper part of the window, click on the *ISBN* field.
3) Then go to *Field Properties* in the lower part of the window, and change the *Field Size* value from 50 to 20.

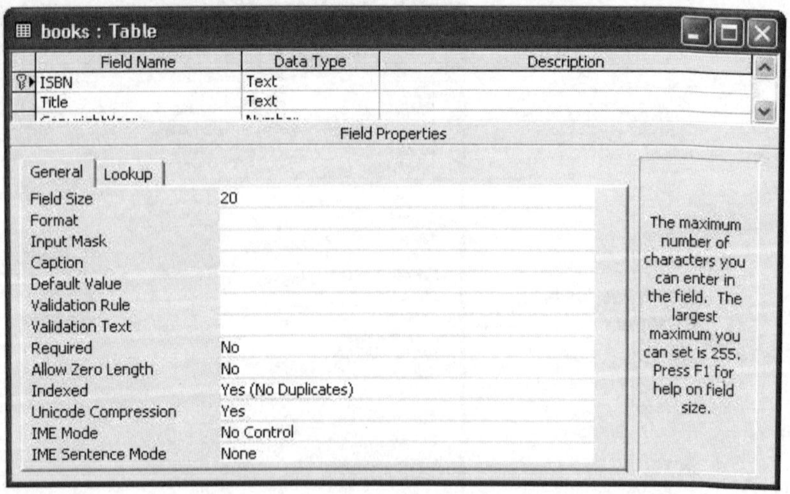

Note that to the right of the *Field Properties* list, Access displays a brief description of the property you are currently working with. You can press **F1** for more detailed information.

Changing field format

Many Access data types have a *Format* property that you can use to specify how data is displayed and printed. This does not affect how data is stored in a field. For example, you can choose to display dates in any of the following formats:

- 23/5/03
- 23-May-02
- Wednesday, May 23, 2003

For each data type, you can select from a list of predefined formats.

For some predefined number, currency and date/time formats, Access uses the regional settings specified in the Windows Control Panel. The examples used in this book assume that your regional settings are set to English (United Kingdom). So the default currency symbol is £, the default sequence in dates is day, month, year, and commas are used as the thousands separator.

Be aware that if you are using a different country setting, dates and numbers may display differently on your screen than in the images in this book.

Exercise 29.6: Changing the format of a date field.

1) Open the Books table in Design view – in this exercise you will change the *PurchaseDate* format.
2) In the upper part of the window, click the *PurchaseDate* field.
3) Then go to *Field Properties* in the lower part of the window, and click the arrow to the right of the *Format* field to display the range of date format options.
4) Choose *Medium Date.*

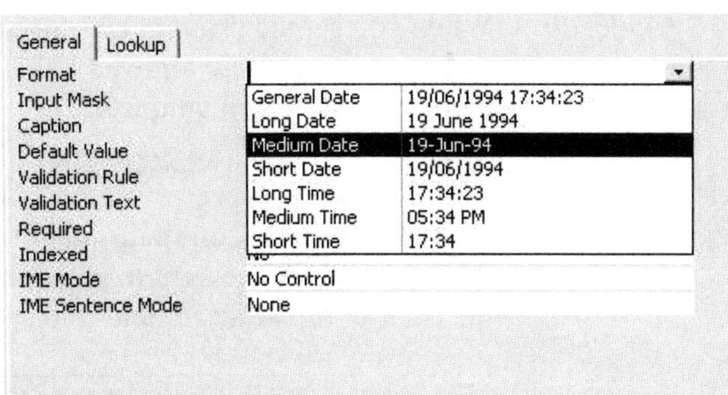

5) Choose **File | Save** to save the change, and change to Datasheet view to see the impact of the change you have made.

Title	CopyrightYear	PurchaseDate
The BFG	1982	01-May-00
Love in the Time of Cholera	1985	24-Feb-98
Animal Farm	1945	03-Apr-99
Little Women	1868	24-Feb-98
Emma	1994	30-Nov-01

Medium date format

Don't forget that the dates displayed here are in *Medium Date* format. You can also enter the date in *Short Date* format (this is the preferred format in the *PurchaseDate* field).

Exercise 29.7: Changing the format of a number field

In this exercise you will explore the range of formats available for a number field – Pages. The current format is *General Number* and this is the most appropriate for a field indicating the number of pages in a book. Have a look at the various number formats available, and see the impact of changes you make.When you have finished, reset the format to *General Number.*

1) Open the Books table in Design view.
2) Click the *Pages* field.
3) Go to the *Format Properties* field in the lower part of the window, and change the *Format* value to *Fixed*.
4) Choose **File | Save** to save the change and switch to Datasheet view to see the impact of the change you have made.
5) Try out the other format options and view them in Datasheet view.
6) When you have finished experimenting, change the *Format* value back to *General Number* and save the table.

Changing the Indexed field

When you set the primary key for a table, it is indexed automatically and no duplicates are allowed – this is because the primary key must identify each record uniquely.

Indexed	Yes (No Duplicates)

You can also index on fields other than the primary key, and you can decide whether you want to allow duplicate values. Click the arrow to the right of the *Indexed* field to display the range of options:

No	Field is not indexed.
Yes (Duplicates OK)	Field is indexed, and duplicates are allowed.
Yes (No Duplicates)	Field is indexed, and duplicates are not allowed.

Summary of the Books table and the Authors table

The following two tables summarize the fields and data types of the two tables we have created and modified: the Books table and the Authors table. For later exercises in this book, it is best that your tables are as similar as possible to those we have created.

The easiest way for you to compare your table against the summary is to open each table in Design view. In Design view you can compare the *Field Name* and *Data Type* columns in the upper part of the window.

Summary of fields in the Books table

Field	Data Type
ISBN	Text
Title	Text
Pages	Number
CopyrightYear	Number
Cost	Currency
PurchaseDate	Date/Time
Comments	Memo
Recommended	Yes/No

Summary of fields in the Authors table

Field	Data Type
AuthID	AutoNumber
AuthLastName	Text
AuthFirstName	Text
Nationality	Text

Validation rules

A database is only going to work if data is entered correctly and in a consistent format. This can be difficult to achieve, particularly where different people are responsible for data entry over time.

To help minimize data entry errors, we use validation rules that set limits or conditions on the actual values that may be entered in the fields. These work in addition to the data type settings. For example, you could set the data type for a field to *numeric* to allow only numbers, and you could then use a validation rule to limit the allowed numbers to 0 to 9.

> ***Validation rule***
>
> *Sets limits or conditions on the values that may be entered into a field. When a user enters data into a field, the data is checked to ensure that it complies with the validation rule.*

Operators

A validation rule is written as an expression consisting of a combination of operators (for example, +, >, =), literal values (for example, 123.5, 23/1/03, 'Hello').

Operator	**Meaning**
=	Equals
<>	Not equal to
<	Less than
<=	Less than or equal to
>	Greater than
>=	Greater than or equal to
IN	Introduces a list of values to which input is confined
BETWEEN ... AND	Introduces a list of set values
OR	Introduces a different value
AND	Introduces another value to be used

You specify validation rules in Design view when using two field properties.

Field Property	**Description**
Validation rule	Specifying the rule itself
Validation text	Specifying the text that appears when the wrong data is entered

Here are some examples of validation rules:

To specify that a date must be post-1950:

Validation Rule	>1950
Validation Text	Publication date must be post-1950

To specify that a price must be less than £99:

Validation Rule	<99
Validation Text	Must be less than £99.

To specify that a date must not be before today – in this case **Date()** means 'today':

Validation Rule	>=Date()
Validation Text	Date must be in the future.

To specify a valid date range (always enclose dates within hash symbols):

Validation Rule	>=#01/01/2003# And <=#31/12/2003#
Validation Text	Date must be in 2003

To specify that only certain text values (in this case the countries England, Wales, Scotland and Ireland) are allowed in a *Text* field (always use double quotes to enclose individual text values):

Validation Rule	In ("England","Wales","Ireland","Scotland")
Validation Text	You may only enter one of these countries.

To specify that a value must be within a certain range:

Validation Rule	Between 10 And 100
Validation Text	Price must be between £10 and £100

Exercise 29.8: Creating a validation rule – price range

In this exercise we impose a price restriction on the books that can be entered in the database – only books in the price range £4–£100 may be included in the Books table.

1) Display your Books table in Design view.
2) Click in the *Cost* field. You can then move to the lower part of the screen to modify the *Field Properties* for *Cost*.
3) In the *Validation Rule* field, enter >=4 AND <=100
4) For *Validation Text*, enter the following:
   Only books costing between £4 and £100 can be entered.

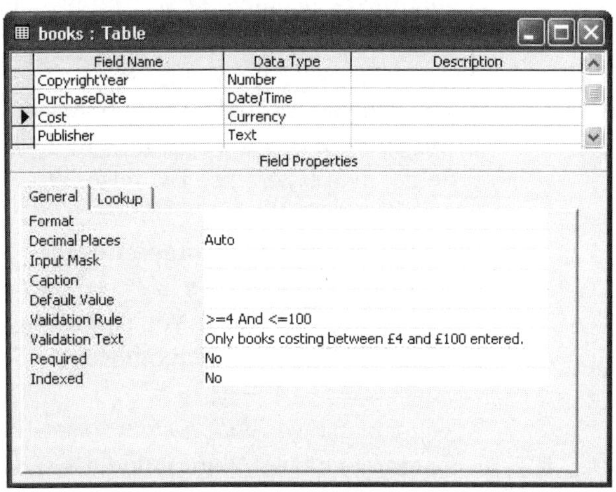

5) Save the Books table.

Exercise 29.9: Creating a validation rule – date range

In this exercise we require a purchase date to be on or before the current date.

1) Display your Books table in Design view.
2) Click in the *PurchaseDate* field. You can then move to the lower part of the screen to modify the *Field Properties* for that field.
3) Then click in the *Validation Rule* of *Field Properties* and enter: < =Date()
4) In the *Validation Text* field, type:
   You cannot enter a date after today's date.

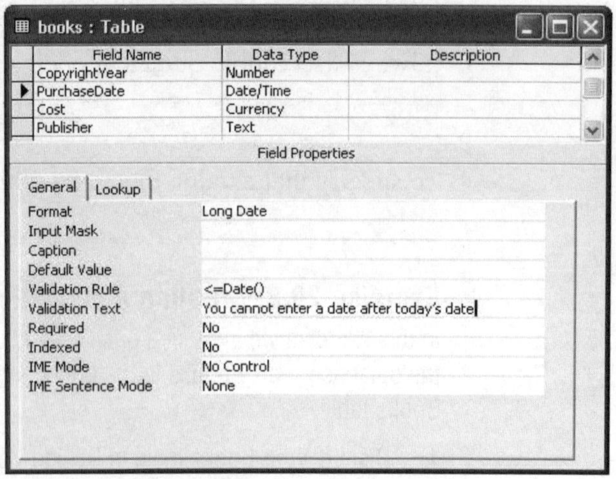

5) Save and close the table.

Chapter summary: so now you know

There are a number of ways in which you can adjust the layout of a table in Access. You can change column widths, *freeze* and *unfreeze* columns, *hide* and *unhide* columns, and reorder fields in a table (move columns). See Exercise 29.1 for an example of how to do this.

You can add and delete new fields and add records. See Exercises 29.2 and 29.3 for examples of how to do these tasks. You can also change a field's data type – see Exercise 29.4.

Database fields have properties that determine how data in the field is stored or displayed. *Field Properties* are displayed at the bottom of the Design view window. You can change properties, such as field size and field format – see Exercises 29.5, 29.6 and 29.7.

You can use *validation rules* to sets limits or conditions on the values that may be entered into a field – see Exercises 29.8 and 29.9.

Quick quiz: modifying your database design

Circle the correct answer to each of the following multiple-choice questions about modifying your database design.

Q1	To delete a field from a table, you ...
A.	Display the table in Design view, click anywhere in the field you want to delete, and choose **Edit | Delete Record**.
B.	Display the table in Design view, click anywhere in the field you want to delete, and click the **Delete Record** button on the toolbar.
C.	Display the table in Design view, click anywhere in the field you want to delete, and choose **Edit | Delete Rows**.

Q2	You can change a field's data type in both Datasheet view and Design view.
A.	True.
B.	False.

Q3	Which of the following procedures can you use to add a new field to a table?
A.	Display the table in Datasheet view, click on the column to the left of which you want to add the new column, and choose **Insert | Column**.
B.	Display the table in Design view, click on the row above which you want to add the new row, and choose **Insert | Column**.
C.	Display the table in Datasheet view, right-click on the title of column to the left of which you want to add the new column, and choose **Insert Column** from the pop-up menu.

Q4	To change the position of a field in a table, you ...
A.	Click the title of the field you want to move and drag the field to its new position.
B.	Click anywhere in the field you want to move and drag the field to its new position.
C.	Click the title of the field you want to move. Click it again and hold down the mouse button while moving the pointer to the new position for the field. Finally, release the mouse button.

Q5	Validation rules concern ...
A.	Whether you can eat chocolate and drink coffee while stressing about databases.
B.	Specifically the values that you may enter into a database.
C.	The layout and precise formatting of the data entered into a database, so that it all looks pretty cool.

Answers

1: C, **2:** B, **3:** A, B, C, **4:** C, **5:** B.

Chapter 30: Table relationships

In this chapter

In the earlier chapters of this module you created a database with two tables (Books and Authors), and you learned how to manipulate and view data in these tables individually. In this chapter you will discover how to relate, or link, tables so that you can manipulate and view information from more than one table at a time.

New skills

At the end of this chapter you should be able to:

- Explain the different types of relationships.
- Create a one-to-one relationship.
- Create a one-to-many relationship.
- Delete a relationship.
- Explain referential integrity.
- Prevent deletion of records if there are related records in a linked table.

New words

At the end of this chapter you should be able to explain the following terms:

- One-to-one relationship
- One-to-many relationship
- Many-to-many relationship
- Referential integrity
- Foreign key

Relationship types

The following table summarizes the relationship types that you need to know about, taking examples from our Books and Authors tables.

Relationship type	Description
One-to-one relationship	In a one-to-one relationship, a record in either table can have only one matching record in the other table. Typically, the two tables have the same primary key. One-to-one relationships are fairly rare in relational databases.
One-to-many relationship	In a one-to-many relationship, a record in the first table can have many matching records in the second table, but a record in the second table can have only one matching record in the first table. In our database, the Authors and Books tables have this type of relationship, as some authors have written more than one book but no book has more than one author.

If any books in our database had more than one author, then our Authors and Books tables would have a *many-to-many* relationship. That is, each Author record could have many related Books records and each Books record could have many related Authors records. However, for ECDL 4 you don't need to know about this type of relationship, so we include only books with a single author in the database.

Creating relationships: overview

You use the *Relationships* window to create, modify and view the relationships between tables.

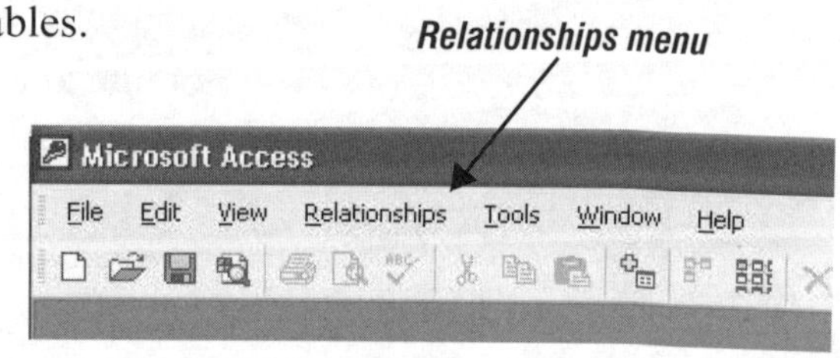

Step 1: Choose **Tools | Relationships** to view the *Relationships* window. Once you do this, a **Relationships** menu is added to the Access menu.

Step 2: The first time you do this, the window will be empty and you need to display the tables you want to relate. Choose **Relationships | Show Table**. This displays the *Show Table* dialog box where you select the tables you want to display in the Relationships window. For the moment, select the Books and Authors tables and click **Add**. Click **Close** to close the *Show Table* dialog box.

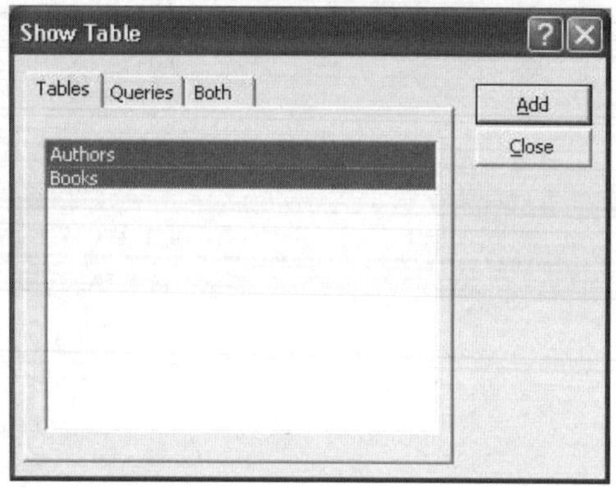

Step 3: You can now use the *Relationships* window and the commands on the **Relationships** menu to create and modify relationships between the tables.

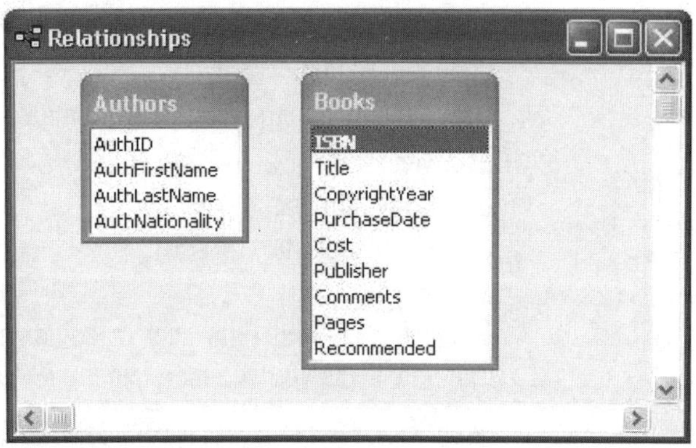

Relationships window
The Relationships window enables you to create, modify and view relationships between tables in your database.

Creating a one-to-one relationship

One-to-one relationships are often used where sensitive or private data is being stored and it is necessary to keep it separate from the records to which it refers. For example, user passwords, salary information, exam grades or disciplinary records might be stored in this way. In our Bookworm database, let's imagine that you want your comments and recommendations kept private, and don't want them to be part of the Books table itself.

In Exercise 30.1 you will create a new BookComments table to hold the *Comments* and *Recommended* fields from the Books table. Then in Exercise 30.2 you will make a one-to-one relationship between the Books table and the new BookComments table.

Exercise 30.1: Creating a BookComments table

1) Make a copy of the Books table and call it BookComments. To do this, right-click on *Books* in the *Database* window and choose **Copy**. Then choose **Edit | Paste**. You are prompted to give the copy a name – call it BookComments.

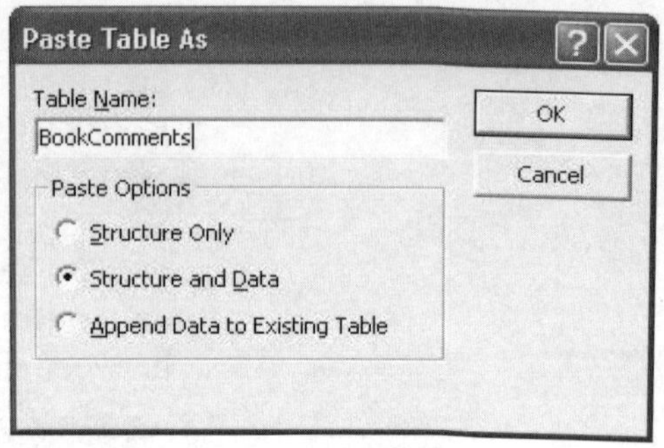

Select the *Structure and Data* option so that Access copies both the table structure and its records – later on you can remove the data you don't want. Click **OK** to close the dialog box.

2) The BookComments table is now listed in the *Database* window: double-click on it to open it in Datasheet view.

3) Delete the following columns from the BookComments table:

- Title
- CopyrightYear
- PurchaseDate
- Cost

To delete a column, right-click its column header and choose **Delete Column**. The only fields you should retain are *ISBN*, *Comments* and *Recommended*.

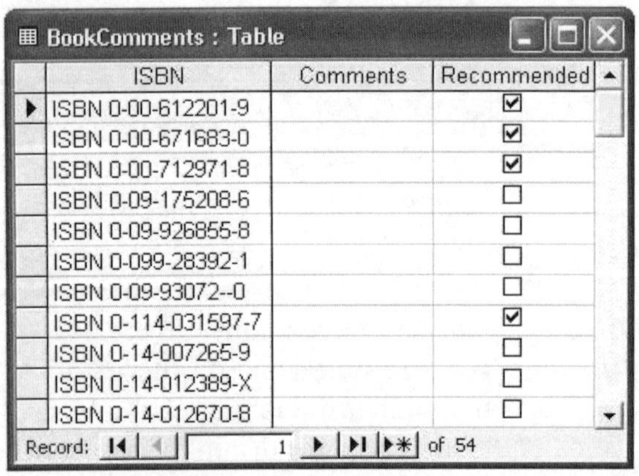

4) Choose **File | Save** to save the BookComments table and then close it. Note that you cannot define a relationship for a table that is currently open.

Exercise 30.2: Creating a one-to-one relationship between Books and BookComments

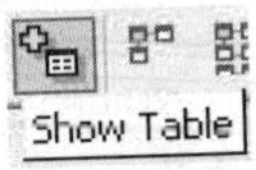

1) Choose **Tools | Relationships**. You should see the three tables you have created in the *Relationships* window. If you don't, just click the **Show Table** button and add any missing table.

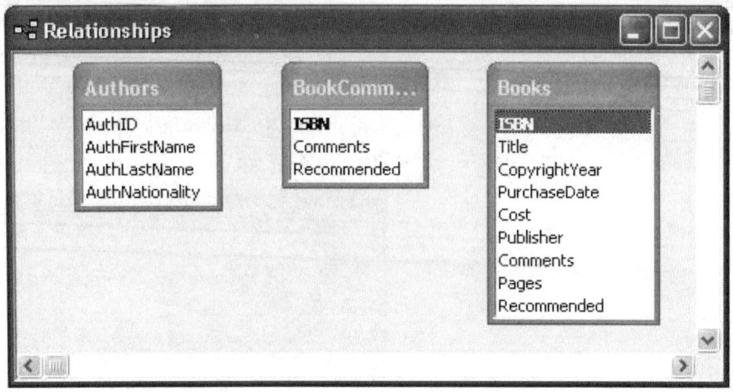

2) Drag the *ISBN* field from the Books table to the *ISBN* field in the BookComments table. To do this, click the *ISBN* field in the Books table and hold down the mouse button (notice how the mouse pointer changes). Then drag the pointer over to the *ISBN* field in the BookComments table and release the mouse button. The *Edit Relationships* dialog box now appears.

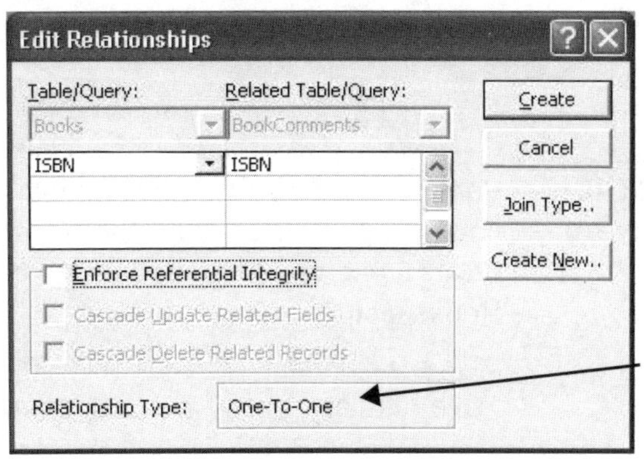

Access has recognized our intention to create a one-to-one relationship between the tables

3) Select the *Enforce Referential Integrity* box and click the **Create** button. (We will deal with referential integrity very shortly.) A join line now links the *ISBN* fields in the two tables – this represents the relationship you have just created.

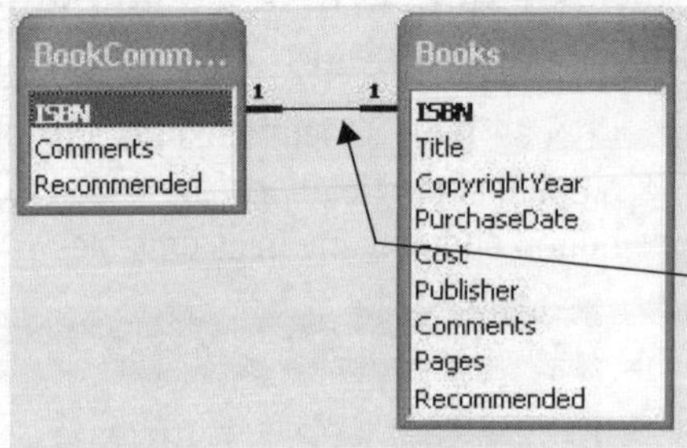

Represents the one-to-one relationship between the tables

4) Close the *Relationships* window and save the Relationships layout when prompted.

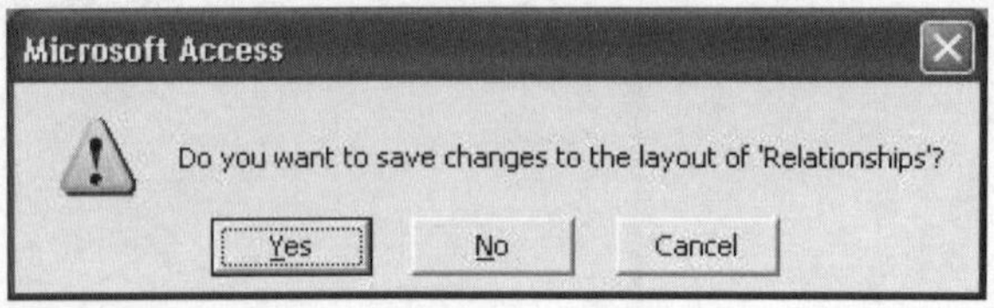

5) If you open the Books table now, you will notice that there is a series of + signs in a column to the left of the *ISBN* column When you click the + sign beside an ISBN name, you see the matching record from the related table.

Click on the minus sign to close the record from the related table

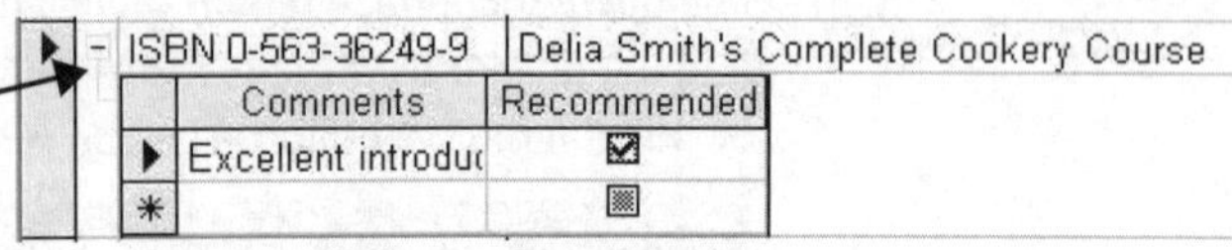

Creating a one-to-many relationship

Some of the authors in the Authors table wrote more than one of the books in the Books table (for example, Jane Austen). So, we need to create a one-to-many relationship between the Authors table and the Books table.

One (author) ...	... to many (books)
	Pride and Prejudice
Jane Austen	Sense and Sensibility
	Emma

The primary key of the Authors table is *AuthID*; so, if we add that field to the Books table, then we can relate books to their authors and vice versa.

In Exercise 30.3 we add the *AuthID* field to the Books table, and in Exercise 30.4 we create the relationship between the two tables.

A word of caution: in general, the fields that you use to define relationships must have the same data type in each table. AutoNumber fields, however, are an exception. In the Authors table, *AuthID* is the primary key and has an AutoNumber data type. In the Books table, however, it should have a *Number* data type and a field size of *Long Integer*.

Exercise 30.3: Adding the *AuthID* field to the Books table

1) Display the Books table in Design view.
2) Click in the second row and choose **Insert | Rows**.
3) Enter *AuthID* as the field name, and choose *Number* as the data type.
4) Make sure the field size is *Long Integer*.

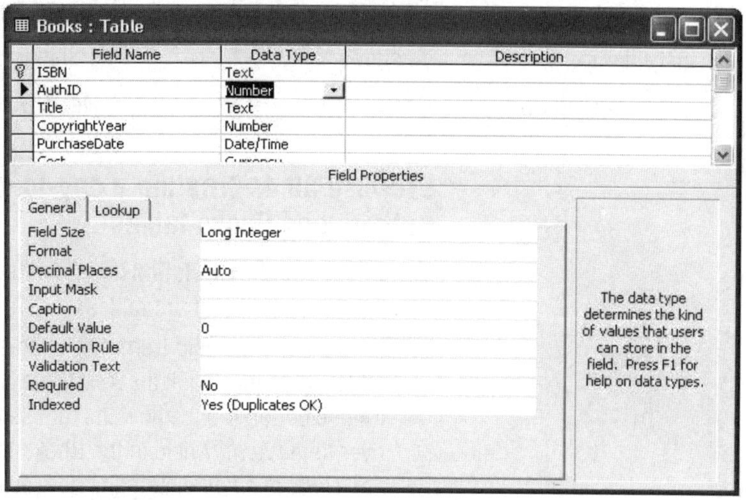

5) Save the table and switch to Datasheet view to enter the AuthID for each of the books. Copy the AuthID information from these tables:

Book	Author	AuthID	Book	Author	AuthID
The BFG	Dahl	**6**	Chocolat	Harris	**2**
Love in the Time of Cholera	Marquez	**3**	The History of the Kelly Gang	Carey	**9**
Animal Farm	Orwell	**11**	The Return of the Naked Chef	Oliver	**10**
Little Women	Alcott	**5**	Harry Potter and the Philosopher's Stone	Rowling	**4**
Emma	Austen	**1**	Harry Potter and the Goblet of Fire	Rowling	**4**
Jane Eyre	Bronte	**7**	Harry Potter and the Prisoner of Azkaban	Rowling	**4**
Great Expectations	Dickens	**8**	Cowboys and Indians	O'Connor	**14**
Mansfield Park	Austen	**1**	The Shipping News	Proulx	**12**
The Name of the Rose	Eco	**16**	Galileo's Daughter	Sobel	**13**

Exercise 30.4: Creating a one-to-many relationship between the Authors and Books tables

1) Choose **Tools | Relationships** and then click the **Show Table** button to add the Books and Authors tables.
2) Drag the *AuthID* field from the Authors table to the *AuthID* field in the Books table. To do this, click the *AuthID* field in the Authors table and hold down the mouse button (notice how the mouse pointer changes). Then drag the pointer over to the *AuthID* field in the Books table and release the mouse button. The *Edit Relationships* dialog box now appears.

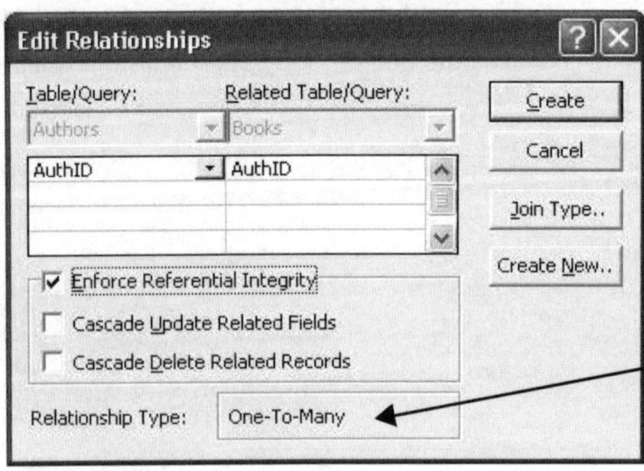

Access has recognized our intention to create a one-to-many relationship between the tables

3) Check the *Enforce Referential Integrity* box and click the **Create** button. A black line appears confirming the relationship between the tables.

The one-to-many symbol represents the one-to-many relationship between the tables

4) Close the *Relationships* window and save the relationships layout when prompted.

The primary key and the foreign key

The *AuthID* field is the primary key for the Authors Table. Within the Books table, however, it is a *foreign key* – this is the term we use to describe a field in one table that refers to the primary key in another table.

Similarly, *ISBN* is the primary key in the Books table, but it is a foreign key in the BooksComments table.

Referential integrity

In Exercises 30.2 and 30.4 you selected the *Enforce Referential Integrity* check box. Let's look at what this means.

To ensure consistency between the two related tables, each AuthID value in the Books table must have a matching value in the Authors table. In other words, the AuthID must be that of an author listed in the Authors table – and that is what we mean by referential integrity.

If in the Books table you enter an AuthID that is not in the Authors table, then your database will not have referential integrity.

Enforcing referential integrity prevents you from entering an AuthID in the Books table if it is not in the Authors table and also protects you from accidentally deleting records from the Authors table if they are referenced in the Books table. For example, if you did not enforce referential integrity and deleted Jane Austen from the Authors table, then all the references to Jane Austen's AuthID in the Books table would be invalid.

Referential integrity
Referential integrity is a set of rules that ensures that the relationships between records in related tables are valid, and that you do not accidentally delete or change related data.

Restrictions imposed by referential integrity

When referential integrity is enforced, Access applies the following restrictions to relationships:·

- You cannot enter a value in a foreign key field if that value doesn't exist in the primary key field of the related table.

  ***Example**: In the Books table, you cannot point to an author who is not listed in the Authors table.*
- You cannot delete a record from a table if foreign key values in a related table point to that record.

  ***Example**: You cannot delete an author from the Authors table if that author is referenced in the Books table.*
- You cannot change a primary key value if there are matching values in foreign key fields of a related table.

  ***Example**: You cannot change an AuthID value in the Authors table if that value is referenced in the Books table.*

To enforce referential integrity in Access, you select the *Enforce Referential Integrity* check box when creating relationships between tables. You did this when you created the relationships between the Books and Authors tables and the Books and BooksComments tables in previous exercises.

You may have noticed that when you selected this option, two further options became available:

- *Cascade Update Related Fields.*
- *Cascade Delete Related Records.*

These allow you to perform the actions restricted by referential integrity but ensure that Access automatically takes action to prevent inconsistencies. So, if you change a primary key in one table, Access automatically changes all matching values in related tables. And, if you delete a record whose primary key is referenced by records in other tables, Access automatically deletes those records as well.

It is a good idea to enforce referential integrity for all relationships. However, selecting the *Cascade* options may result in Access automatically deleting or changing many records, so you should do so only after careful thought. In the previous exercises, you left these options unselected, and you can continue to do so now.

Deleting a relationship

To delete a relationship, right-click on the relationship symbol and choose **Delete**.

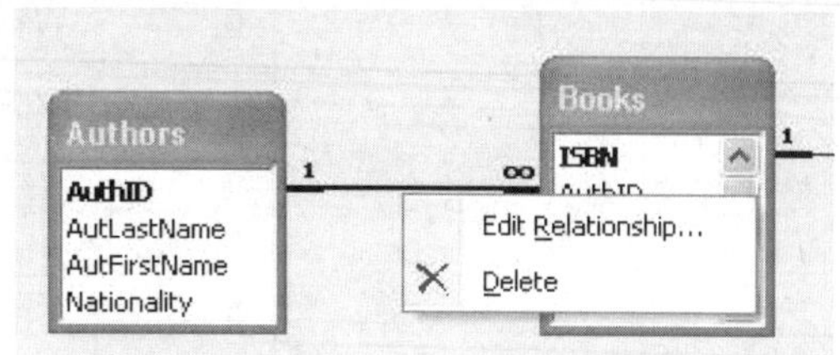

Chapter summary: so now you know

Organizing data logically into separate tables helps us to avoid data duplication and saves on data entry time. Defining relationships between the tables then allows us to manipulate and view information from more than one table at a time.

A *one-to-one relationship* is where a single record in one table relates to a single record in another table. Typically, this type of relationship is used to ensure privacy of certain data. In Exercise 30.2 we made a one-to-one relationship between the Books table and the BooksComments table.

A *one-to-many relationship* is where a single record in one table (such as a customer record) relates to more than one record (such as more than one customer order) in another table. You made a one-to-many relationship between the Authors table and the Books table using the *AuthID* field as the link. See Exercises 30.3 and 30.4 for examples of how to do these tasks.

Referential integrity is an automatic device in Access which, when you choose to enforce it, uses a set of rules to automatically check that relationships between tables (and between records in tables) are valid. It will act to prevent you creating, deleting or changing data in such a way that you threaten or break a relationship. You simply select a check box to enforce it, and Access does the rest.

Quick quiz: table relationships

Circle the correct answer to each of the following multiple-choice questions about table relationships.

Q1	A flat database ...
A.	Was not formatted to have 3D characteristics.
B.	Was not saved properly and so lost data.
C.	Stands alone and does not relate to any other table.

Q2	Referential integrity is ...
A.	A guarantee of the quality of the data in a table.
B.	A set of rules that ensures that the relationships between records in related tables is valid.
C.	A means of referring from one table to another.

Q3	To set rules governing the relationships between tables you ...
A.	Check the *Enforce Referential Integrity* option in the Edit *Relationships* dialog box.
B.	Click, drag and drop one table on another in the Database window.
C.	Right-click each table, click **Properties**, and click to select the *Relate My Table Please* check box.

Q4	We relate databases to ...
A.	Keep them from getting lonely on the computer hard disk.
B.	Create more work and therefore more money for database planners.
C.	Avoid having lots of redundant information in a single table, and to minimize the work involved in data entry and data updating.

Q5	A key in one table that refers to a primary key in another table is:
A.	A foreign key.
B.	A primary key.

Answers

1: C, **2:** B, **3:** A, **4:** C, **5:** A.

Chapter 31: Finding, sorting and filtering records

In this chapter

After the preceding chapters you might still be asking: why bother? You can use a word processor to keep lists of things, and if you want to put them in neat columns you can use a spreadsheet. Well, this chapter should convince you that a database is a very useful tool for managing your information and for quickly finding the particular items of interest.

For example, the order in which you originally entered records in your table may not be the order in which, later on, you would prefer to display those records. You could reorder – *sort* – a table of customers, for instance, so that the biggest spenders appear at the top of the list.

Another very useful feature is *filtering* – the ability to reduce the amount of information displayed by showing only those records that match certain criteria.

Finally, as with other Microsoft Office applications, Access includes a *Find* feature that enables you to locate a particular item quickly.

New skills

At the end of this chapter you should be able to:

- Find a particular record in the database.
- Sort the database records.
- Use filters to find particular records and to restrict the fields displayed.

New words

At the end of this chapter you should be able to explain the following terms:

- Sort
- Sort order
- Filter
- Find

Finding data in a table

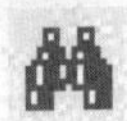

Find button

Is there a quick way of finding a particular record among hundreds or thousands? Yes. Use the Access **Find** feature. You can search an entire table, or just a single field.

You can run Find in any of the following ways: choose **Edit | Find**, click the **Find** button on the toolbar, or use the keyboard shortcut **Ctrl+f**. You are then presented with the *Find and Replace* dialog box.

Enter the string you want to find

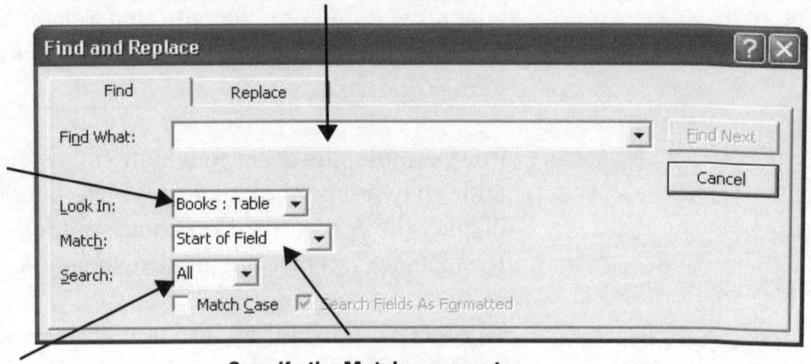

Specify where you want to look: in the whole table or in one field only – the default is the field where the cursor currently is

Specify the direction of the search

Specify the* Match *you want:
- **Any Part of Field** – ***search for the string in any part of the field***
- **Whole Field** – ***search for exact matches with the string***
- **Start of Field** – ***search for fields that start with the string***

Exercise 31.1: Finding a specific record in the Books table

1) Display the Books table in Datasheet view. Click the **Find** button on the toolbar.
2) In the *Find What* field, type the following:
   Galileo
3) In the *Look In* box, select *Books : Table* so that the search will include the whole table. In the *Match* box, select *Any Part of Field* so that the search will look for the string in any part of the field.

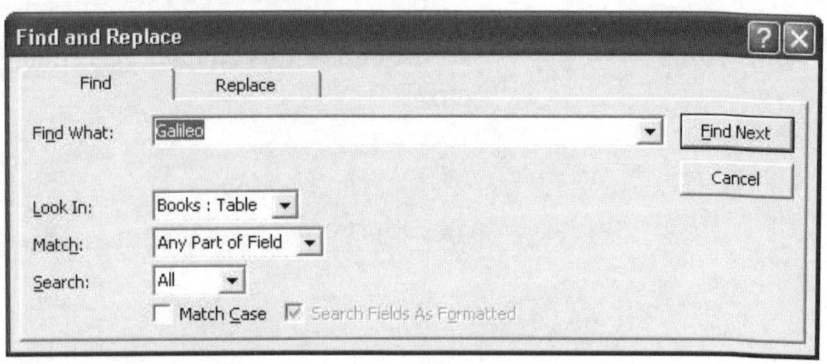

4) Click the **Find Next** button.

5) Access now highlights *Galileo* in the *Galileo's Daughter* field.

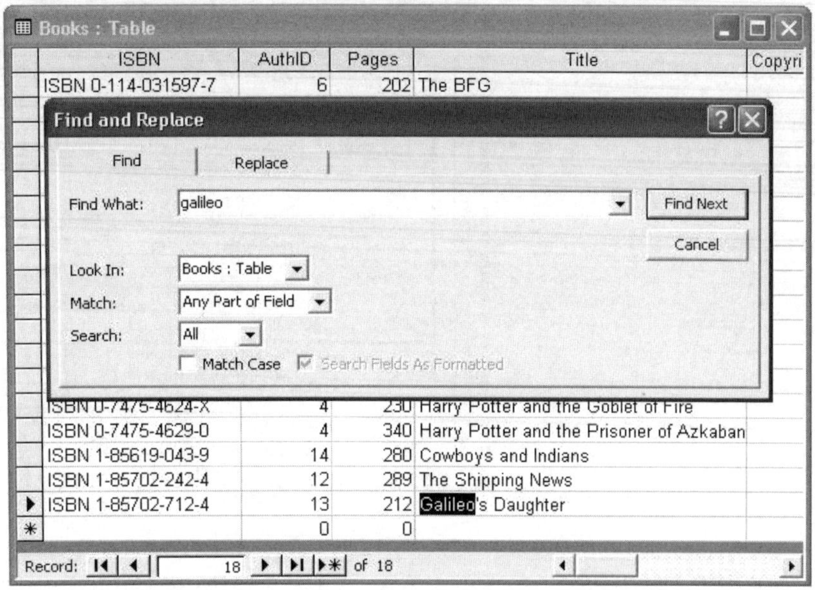

6) Click the **Find Next** button. Access indicates that there are no further records that match the criterion. Click **OK**.

7) In the *Find and Replace* dialog box, click the **Cancel** button.

Exercise 31.2: Finding a specific value in a field

1) Display the Books table in Datasheet view and click anywhere in the column you want to search – in this case *CopyrightYear.*

2) Click the **Find** button on the toolbar.

3) We want to find books with the copyright year 2000, so enter the following in the *Find What* field:

   2000

4) In the *Look In* box, select *CopyrightYear* so that we search in that field only. In the *Match* box, select *Whole Field*.

5) Click the **Find Next** button.

6) Access now highlights the first book with the copyright year 2000. Click **Find Next** to find the next, and so on.

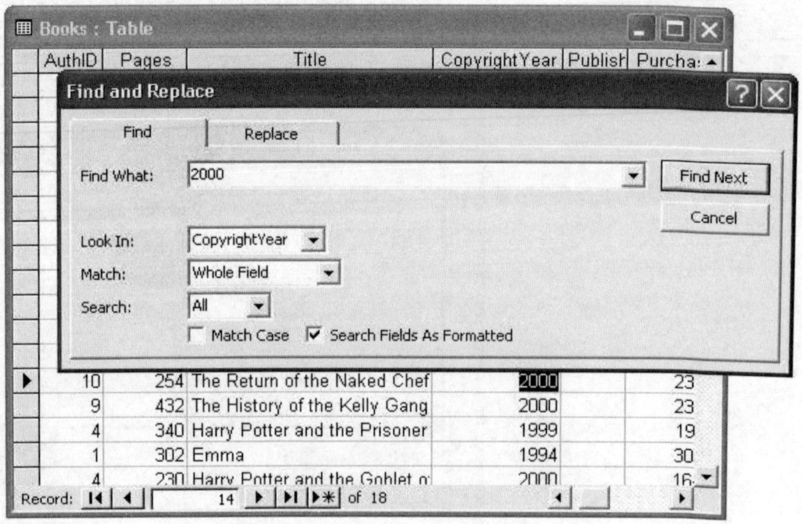

Sorting records in a table

Open Access and open your Bookworm database and the Books table. The records are displayed in the order of the primary key. If you have no primary key, they are sorted by default in the order they were entered.

However, you can choose to display the records in a different order by *sorting* them.

Sort
An operation that you carry out on a table to change the order in which the records are displayed. Sorting does not change the content of records, only the order in which they are displayed.

Access offers two sequencing options, called sort orders. These determine whether records are sorted in ascending (1 to 9, A to Z) or descending (9 to 1, Z to A) order.

Sort order
A way of ordering records based on field values. A sort order can be in ascending (1 to 9, A to Z) or descending (9 to 1, Z to A) sequence.

Simple sorts

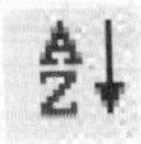

Sort Ascending button

Suppose you want the records to be displayed in order of the number of pages – how would you go about it? Easy. Click any *Pages* field. Then click the **Sort Ascending** button on the toolbar.

Pages	Title
160	Animal Farm
202	The BFG
212	Galileo's Daughter
230	Harry Potter and the Goblet of Fire
250	Chocolat
254	The Return of the Naked Chef
280	Cowboys and Indians
287	Mansfield Park
289	The Shipping News
298	Harry Potter and the Philosopher's Stone
302	Emma
340	Harry Potter and the Prisoner of Azkaban
344	Little Women
345	Jane Eyre
370	Love in the Time of Cholera
412	Great Expectations
432	The History of the Kelly Gang
450	The Name of the Rose

Sorted by Pages, ascending

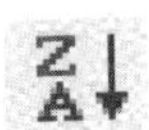

Sort Descending button

Now click the *CopyrightYear* field and click the **Sort Descending** button to sort the books in order of copyright year.

If you have sorted a table to view records in a particular order, you can return to an unsorted view by choosing **Records | Remove Filter/ Sort**.

Multiple-criteria sorts

Now imagine that you have more complex requirements: you want to sort all the books by their author ID, and for each author to show them in order of their copyright year. This type of sort is called a *multiple-criteria sort*, and you use Access's Advanced Filter/Sort feature to perform them. Exercise 31.3 shows you how.

Exercise 31.3: Sorting records using a number of criteria

1) Open the Books table in Datasheet view. Choose **Records | Filter | Advanced Filter/Sort**. This displays the *Filter* dialog box, with a field list in the upper pane and a design grid in the lower pane.

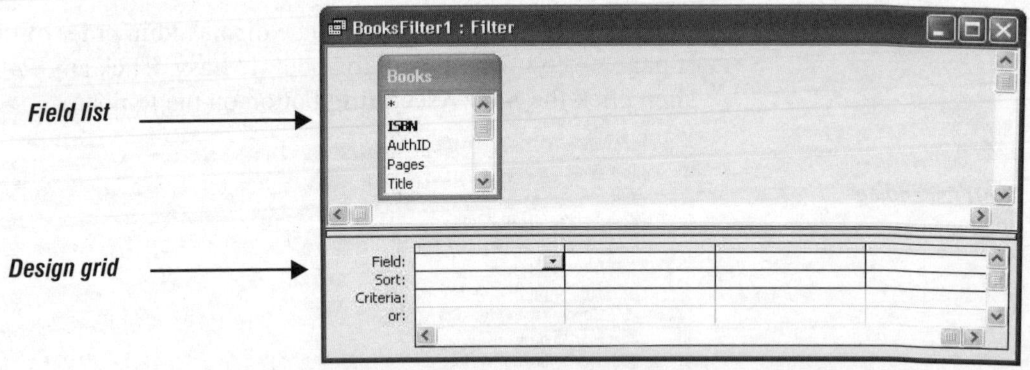

- In the *Field* row in the design grid, you specify the fields by which you want to sort your table, in the order you want the sorts performed. Access sorts on the left-most field first, then on the next field to the right, and so on.
- In the *Sort* row in the design grid, you specify the sort order for each field.
- The *Criteria* row is not used for sorting records; it is relevant only for filtering records.

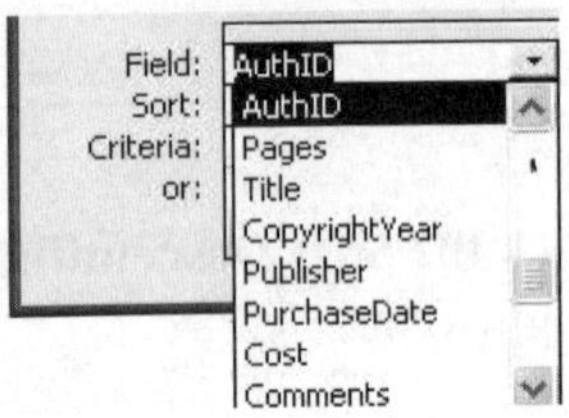

2) Click the arrow in the first column of the *Field* row. Access shows a list of all the fields in your table. Select *AuthID*.
3) Click in the *Sort* row below *AuthID*. Access displays an arrow at the right of the field. Click this to select a sort order. Select *Descending*.
4) Click in the second column of the *Field* row: an arrow is displayed. Click it, and select *CopyrightYear* from the list.
5) Click in the *Sort* row below *CopyrightYear*: an arrow is displayed. Click it and select *Ascending*.

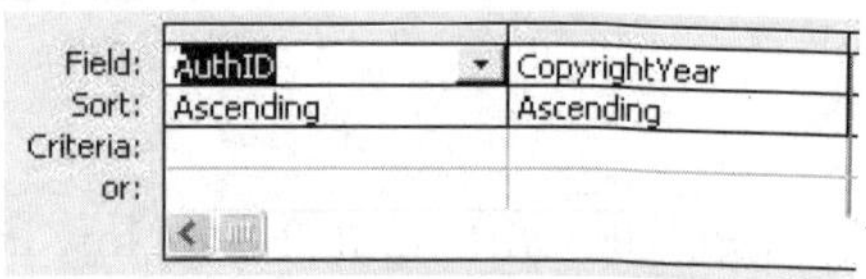

6) Click the **Apply Filter** button in the toolbar, and the datasheet is shown, this time listing the books in order of their AuthorID, and then in order of copyright year.

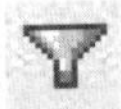

Apply Filter button

Books : Table

AuthID	Title	CopyrightYear	PurchaseDate
1	Mansfield Park	1814	03-Apr-9
1	Emma	1994	30-Nov-0
2	Chocolat	1999	01-May-0
3	Love in the Time of Cholera	1985	24-Feb-9
4	Harry Potter and the Philosopher's Stc	1997	24-Feb-9
4	Harry Potter and the Prisoner of Azkat	1999	19-Apr-0
4	Harry Potter and the Goblet of Fire	2000	16-Mar-0
5	Little Women	1868	24-Feb-9
6	The BFG	1982	01-May-0
7	Jane Eyre	1847	13-Sep-9
8	Great Expectations	1861	13-Sep-9
9	The History of the Kelly Gang	2000	23-Oct-0
10	The Return of the Naked Chef	2000	23-Oct-0
11	Animal Farm	1945	03-Apr-9
12	The Shipping News	1993	03-Apr-9
13	Galileo's Daughter	1999	03-Apr-9
14	Cowboys and Indians	1991	07-Jul-9
16	The Name of the Rose	1983	07-Jul-9

Record: 1 of 18

7) Save and close your table.

Why is the button called **Apply Filter**? Well, Access regards this kind of sort as a particular example of a filter. What's a filter? Don't worry about that for now: we'll be looking at filters a little later.

It's quite likely that you will want to repeat some of these sorts regularly. For example, if you have several hundred books in your database, sorting them by physical location might help you find them more easily in your library. You can enter the sort criteria each time you want to sort the table in this way, or you can make life easy for yourself by saving the sort criteria as a query – see Chapter 32 for more information about queries.

Filtering records in a table

So far, we are still viewing all records and all fields in a table. What if we want to view specific records or specific fields only? Then we use filters or queries.

- **Filters:** Allow you to restrict the display of a table to records that match certain criteria.
- **Queries:** Give you greater filtering possibilities. For example, you might want to display only certain fields, to combine data from multiple tables, or to perform calculations on field values. Chapter 32 deals with queries.

> **Filter**
>
> *A filter restricts the display of your database to records that match criteria that you specify.*

Filtering by selection

The simplest way to filter records is to use the **Filter by Selection** feature – this allows you to select a value in a field, and to display only those records that have the same value. Suppose, for example, you want to concentrate on books with the copyright year 2000. Simply find one book with that value, click the value, and then click the **Filter by Selection** button in the toolbar.

Filter by Selection button

The display is immediately restricted to records with the copyright year 2000.

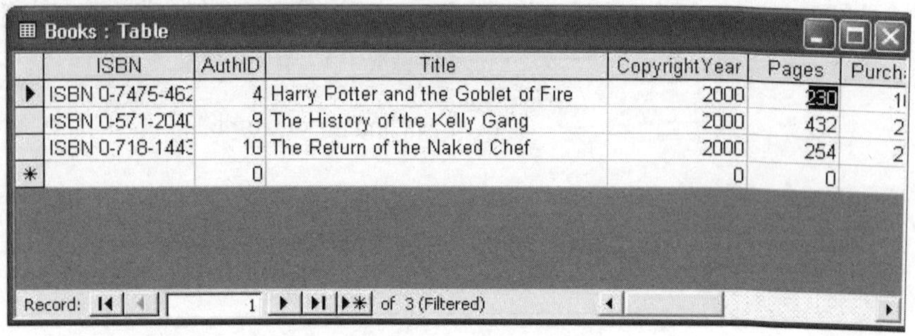

	ISBN	AuthID	Title	CopyrightYear	Pages	Purch
▶	ISBN 0-7475-462	4	Harry Potter and the Goblet of Fire	2000	230	1
	ISBN 0-571-2040	9	The History of the Kelly Gang	2000	432	2
	ISBN 0-718-1443	10	The Return of the Naked Chef	2000	254	2
*		0		0	0	

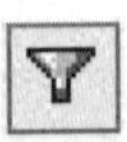

Remove Filter button

Don't panic: the rest of your records are still in the database. The filter just limits the amount of information in the display. To see all your records again, you remove the filter: click the **Remove Filter** button on the toolbar.

Note that you don't have to select a whole field when filtering by selection. For example, if your table contained a large number of cookery books, you might want to display only those with the word 'Italian' in their title.

Which records are displayed by the filter by selection operation depends on how you selected the word on which you based the filter. Filtering by selection includes the ideas 'Beginning with ...' and 'Ending with ...'. If you select the first letters or numbers in a field and filter by selection, Access displays all records in which the field *begins with* those letters or numbers. Similarly, if you select the last letters or numbers in the field, Access displays the records in which the field *ends with* those letters or numbers.

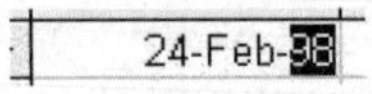

Finds records that end with '98'.

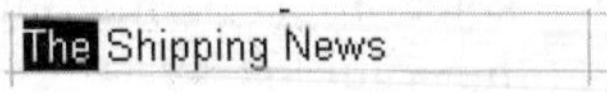

Finds records that begin with 'The'.

If you want to filter based on the first word or the last word in a field, include the first letter or the last letter only if you want to restrict the display to records that begin with or end with the selection. If you want all records that include the word anywhere in the field, select only *part* of the word.

In Exercise 31.4 you create a filter that displays only books that you bought in 1998. You can also experiment with other partial filters in the Books table – remember to remove the filter when you have finished.

A word of caution: Remember that you can change the information in the database at any time. And remember that you change a Yes/No check box field by clicking on it. If you are filtering based on a Yes/No check box field, you will change the information when you select it. So in the case of a Yes/No check box field, you will have to click the field twice before you click on the **Filter by Selection** button.

Exercise 31.4: Filtering on part of a field

1) Open the Books table and find a book with the purchase date 1998.
2) Highlight '98' (last two digits of the date) and click the **Filter by Selection** button. The display is now restricted to books with a 1998 date in their PurchaseDate field.

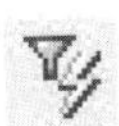

Filter by Selection button

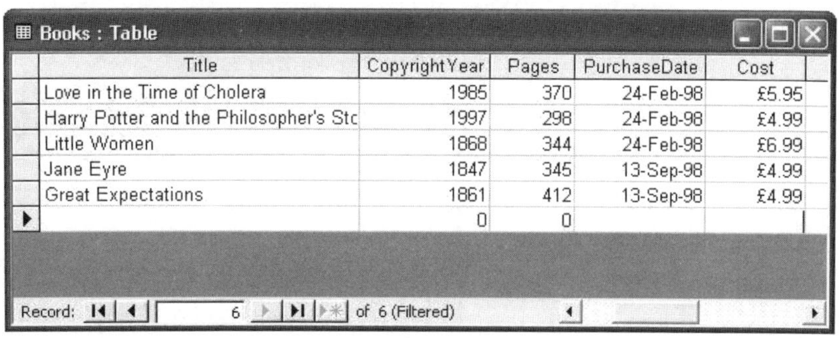
Books : Table

Title	CopyrightYear	Pages	PurchaseDate	Cost
Love in the Time of Cholera	1985	370	24-Feb-98	£5.95
Harry Potter and the Philosopher's Stc	1997	298	24-Feb-98	£4.99
Little Women	1868	344	24-Feb-98	£6.99
Jane Eyre	1847	345	13-Sep-98	£4.99
Great Expectations	1861	412	13-Sep-98	£4.99
	0	0		

Record: 6 of 6 (Filtered)

Filtering by selection on multiple fields

When you are filtering by selection, you can base the filter on data in several fields. A word of caution: there are two conditions that you must observe:

- The data you select must be in contiguous columns – if necessary move one of the columns.
- You must use the entire values in both fields – you cannot use partial values as we did in Exercise 31.4.

Click the value in the first field, hold down the **Shift** key, and click the value in the second field.

Click in the first field

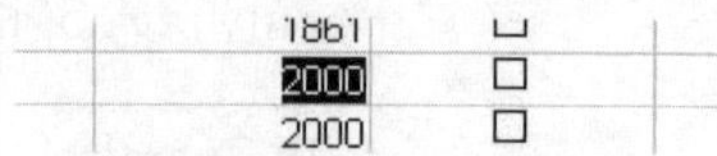

Hold Shift and then click in the second field

Filtering filtered records

In Exercise 31.4 you created a filter to display only books you bought in 1998. If you wanted to further restrict the records displayed – say to books with a copyright year in the nineteenth century – you simply perform a second filter by selection.

Apply the filter with '18' highlighted to display only books whose copyright year begins with '18'

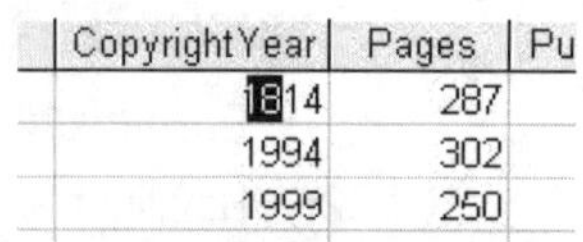

CopyrightYear	Pages	Pu
1814	287	
1994	302	
1999	250	

Of course, you could perform the two filters in reverse order and achieve the same results.

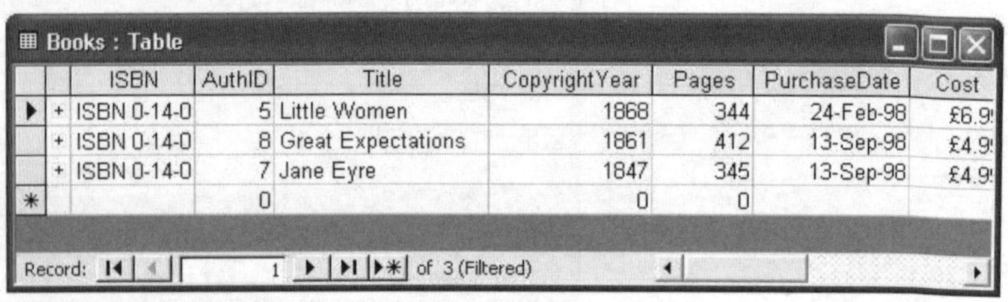

Books : Table

	ISBN	AuthID	Title	CopyrightYear	Pages	PurchaseDate	Cost
▶	+ ISBN 0-14-0	5	Little Women	1868	344	24-Feb-98	£6.9
	+ ISBN 0-14-0	8	Great Expectations	1861	412	13-Sep-98	£4.9
	+ ISBN 0-14-0	7	Jane Eyre	1847	345	13-Sep-98	£4.9
*		0		0	0		

Record: 1 of 3 (Filtered)

When you are finished, remove the filter.

Chapter summary: so now you know

Access's *Find* feature provides a quick way of locating a particular record or records based on their field values. See Exercises 31.1 and 31.2 for examples of how to do this.

A *sort* is an operation that you carry out on a table to change the order in which the records are displayed. Access allows you to perform single criterion and multiple criteria sort operations. See Exercise 31.3 for an example of how to do this.

Filtering is the process of reducing the amount of information displayed by Access by showing only those records that match certain criteria. To view all your records again, remove the filter.

You can filter a table by clicking on a particular field, or by dragging the mouse over the word (or part of a word) that you want to match, and then clicking the **Filter by Selection** button on the toolbar. See Exercise 31.4 for an example of a filter on part of a field.

Note that if you are filtering based on a Yes/No field, you need to click on the field twice before you click the **Filter by Selection** button. A single click on a Yes/No field will change the information in that field.

You can filter the result of a filter operation to further restrict the information displayed.

Quick quiz: finding, sorting and filtering records

Circle the correct answer to each of the following multiple-choice questions about finding, sorting and filtering records.

Q1	To sort records by multiple criteria ...
A.	In Datasheet view, choose **Records | Filter | Advanced Filter/ Sort**, and then specify your sort fields and their sort order in the design grid.
B.	In Datasheet view, apply the **Sort Ascending** or **Sort Descending** button to each sort field in turn.
C.	In Datasheet view, select each sort field in turn and choose **Records | Sort | Sort Ascending** or **Sort Descending**.

Q2	Use the *Look In* field in the Find and Replace dialog box to...
A.	Specify the table or field you want to look in.
B.	Specify what database you want to search in.

Q3	With the Filter by Selection feature you can restrict the display to specific fields only.
A.	True.
B.	False.

Q4	To remove a filter from a table ...
A.	Choose **Edit | Delete Filter**.
B.	Choose **Records | Filter | Remove Filter**.
C.	Click the **Remove Filter** button on the toolbar.

Answers

1: A, **2:** A, **3:** B, **4:** C.

Chapter 32: Creating and using queries

In this chapter

In Chapter 31 you learnt how to sort and filter data. In this chapter we move on to describe how to create and use queries. You can use queries to retrieve database records based on criteria you specify. And you can name and save queries for later use, even after you have changed the content of the database.

New skills

At the end of this chapter you should be able to:

- Save a sort as a query.
- Save a filter as a query.
- Create a query using the *Query Wizard*.
- Create a query in Design view.
- Create single-table and two-table queries.
- Copy and delete a query.

New word

At the end of this chapter you should be able to explain the following term:

- Design grid

What is a query?

A query is a database operation that retrieves specific information from the database, based on criteria and sort orders that you specify. You can name and save queries and reuse them later on after you have added, modified or deleted records. You simply open the query, and the records are presented in the manner defined by the query. Using queries, you can:

- Sort on one or more fields.
- Display selected fields only.
- Retrieve related data from multiple tables.
- Display only records that match specified criteria.

Note that queries do not make any permanent change to the data in your database – they simply extract the information and present it in a certain way.

Saving a sort as a query

In Chapter 31 you learnt about sorting and filtering, and we told you that you could save sort criteria as a query. This is particularly useful if you want to repeat a sort regularly.

For example, if you have several hundred books in your database, you might want to sort them by date or by cost or by category. You can enter the sort criteria each time you want to sort the table in this way, or you can make life easy for yourself by saving the sort criteria as a query.

> **Query**
>
> *Queries are used to repeatedly retrieve database records that match specific criteria and to display them in a specific order.*

Exercise 32.1 shows you how to save a simple sort as a query.

Exercise 32.1: Saving a simple sort as a query

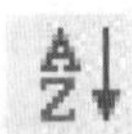

Sort Ascending button

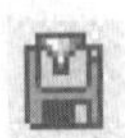

Save as Query button

1) Display your Books table in Datasheet view.
2) Click on any *CopyrightYear* field, and then click on the **Sort Ascending** button. The table is then displayed in the order of the books' copyright years.
3) Choose **Records | Filter| Advanced Filter/Sort** to display the *Filter* dialog box.
4) Choose **File | Save as Query** or click the **Save As Query** button on the toolbar.
5) In the *Save As Query* dialog box, enter a name for the query: say 'books in copyright year order'. Then click **OK**.

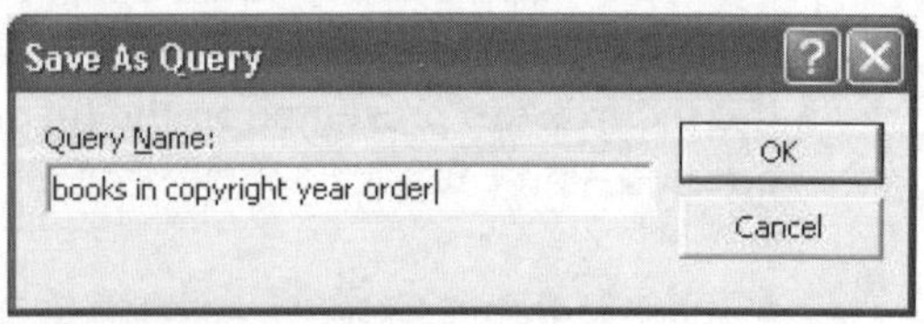

6) Close the *Filter* dialog box. Close your table. Access displays the Database window.

And that's it! Notice that the query is now listed in the Database window when you select the *Queries* option in the *Objects* list. From now on, even after you have added more records to the database, or changed the ones that are already there, you simply open this query and the records in the table will be presented in the manner defined by the query.

For practice, why not save the multiple criteria sort you did in Exercise 31.3.

Saving a filter as a query

As with sorts, you will probably want to repeat some filter operations regularly. You can perform the filter operation each time you want to filter a table in a particular way, or you can make life easy for yourself by saving the filter criteria as a query.

Exercise 32.2: Saving filter criteria as a query

1) Display the Books table in Datasheet view.
2) First you are going to filter for books published in the twentieth century. Select the initial digits 19 in any *CopyrightYear* field and click the **Filter by Selection** button.
3) In the *Recommended* column, select a recommended book (that is, one with the check mark). Click it twice and then click the **Filter by Selection** button again. (You need to click the field twice, because the first click unchecks it.)

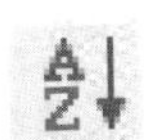

Sort Ascending button

4) Now sort the books in the order of their purchase date: click in the *PurchaseDate* field and click **Sort Ascending.**
5) Choose **Records | Filter | Advanced Filter/Sort** to display the *Filter* dialog box. This displays your filter criteria in the design grid.

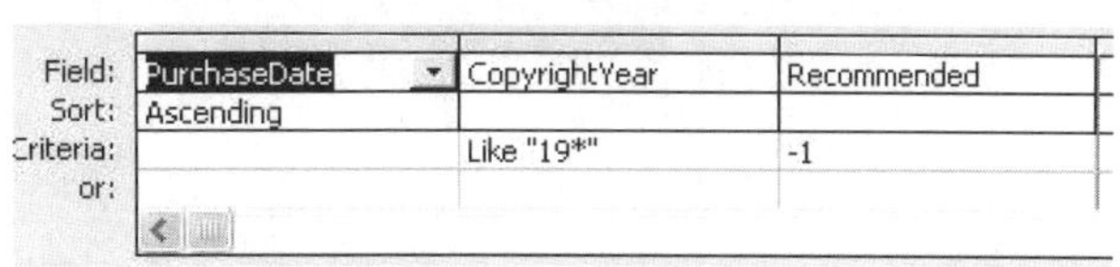

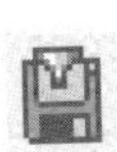

Save as Query button

6) Choose **File | Save As Query**, or click the **Save as Query** button on the toolbar.
7) Give the query a name: Recommended 20th century books.

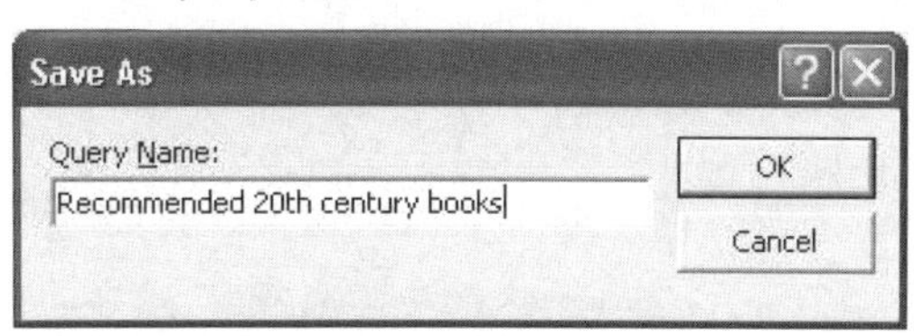

8) Click **OK**, and close the *Filter* dialog box. Close your table.

You can now reapply the filter at any time by opening the Filtered Records query from the Database window. To do this you click on the *Queries* option in the *Objects* list and double-click on the query name.

Using the Simple Query Wizard

In Exercises 32.1 and 32.3 you learnt how to save sort and filter criteria as a query. In Exercise 32.3 you will learn how to create a query from scratch with the *Simple Query Wizard*.

Exercise 32.3: Creating a query with the Simple Query Wizard

1) In the Database window, click the *Queries* option in the *Objects* list.
2) Double-click on the *Create query by using wizard* option. This starts the *Simple Query Wizard*.
3) The first page of the wizard asks you to select the table or query on which you want to base your query and the fields you want to include in the query.
   - Select your Books table in the *Table/Queries* listbox.
   - Move the fields you want to include in your query from the *Available Fields* box to the *Selected Fields* box by using the arrow buttons. For this exercise, move the fields shown. When finished, click the **Next** button.

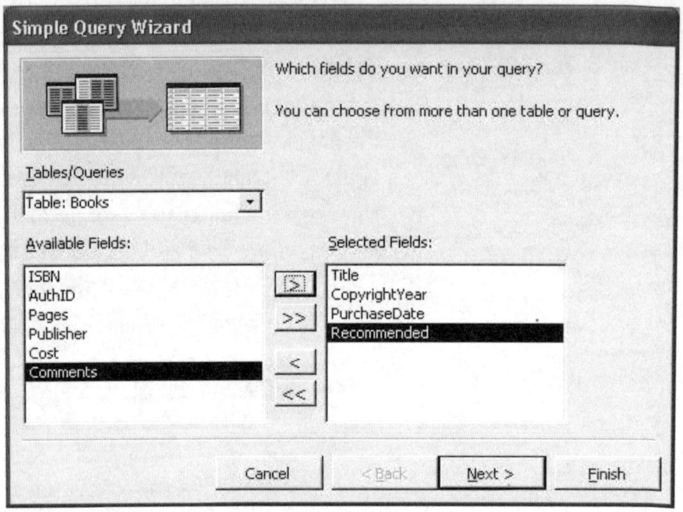

4) Choose *Detail* at the next dialog box and click **Next**.

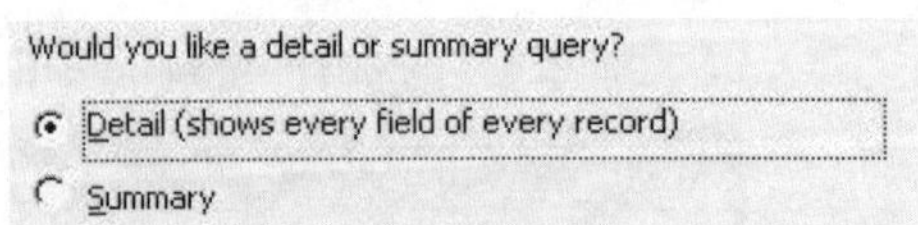

5) You must now give your query a name: Simple query.

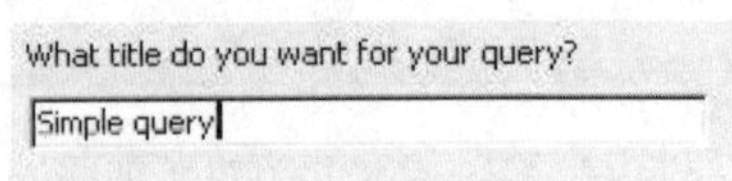

6) You can then either view the query results immediately, or go back and modify the query. Select the option *Open the query to view information* and click the **Finish** button.

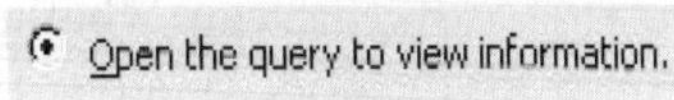

Your query displays the Books table with only the selected fields, and cuts out unnecessary or unwanted information in adjacent fields. You can now close the *Query* window.

Creating a query in Design view

The *Simple Query Wizard* allowed you to restrict the display to selected fields only. However, it did not offer options for sorting the records or retrieving only records that match certain criteria.

For these you must create your query in Design view. Open the simple query you created in Exercise 32.3 in Design view – in the Database window, click the *Queries* option in the *Objects* list and choose the query. You now see the *Select Query* dialog box.

The upper pane displays the tables on which the query is based – in this case the Books table

The lower pane displays the details of the query in a design grid

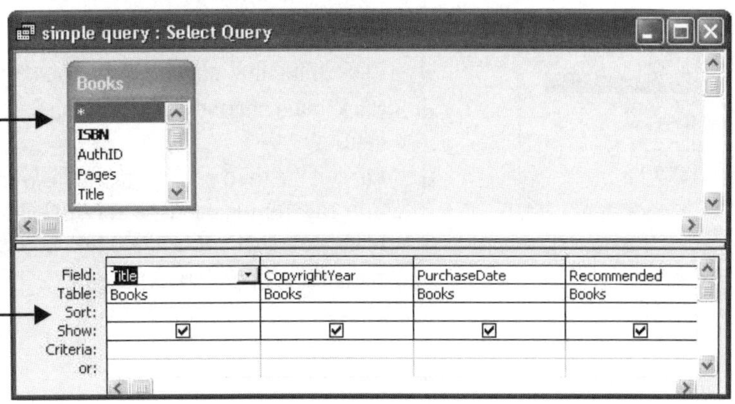

- In the *Field* row, you specify the fields you want to include in your query, in the order in which you want them displayed. There are a number of ways in which you can add a field:
  - Select the field from the list in the field row.
  - Drag the field from the field list to a column in the design grid.
  - Double-click the field in the field list – it is then added to the next free column.
- In the *Table* row, choose the table to which each field you choose belongs – in this case only the Books table is available. Choose **Query | Show Table** if you want to add other tables to the query.

- In the *Sort* row, you specify the sort order for each field. Access sorts on the left-most field first, then on the next field to the right, and so on.

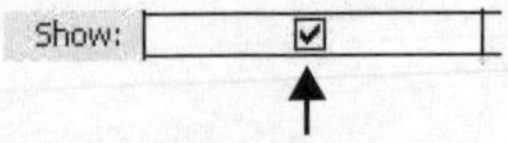

Select to show the column in the query results

- In the *Show* row, indicate whether you want to show or hide the column from the query results. By default, this box is checked.
- In the *Criteria* row, you specify criteria that restrict the records that are retrieved by the query.

In Exercise 32.4 you create a query that retrieves only books that cost more than £7.

Exercise 32.4: Creating a query in Design view

1) In the *Database* window, click the *Queries* option in the *Objects* area, and then double-click the *Create query in Design View* option.
2) In the *Show Table* dialog box, select the Books table, click **Add**, and then click **Close**.
3) Access displays the *Select Query* dialog box, with the Books field list in the upper pane and a design grid in the lower pane.

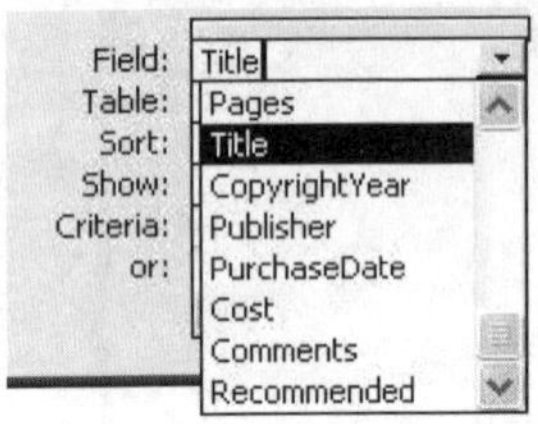

4) Enter the query details as follows:
   - Click in the first column of the *Field* row and select the *Title* field.
   - Click in the second column of the *Field* row and select the *PurchaseDate* field.
   - Click in the third column of the *Field* row and select the *Cost* field. In the *Sort* row for this field, select *Descending*. In the *Criteria* row, enter **>7** to indicate that you want to find books with a cost greater than £7.

   See the table of operators on page 472 for details of the operators you can use when specifying your criteria.

Field:	Title	PurchaseDate	Cost
Table:	Books	Books	Books
Sort:			Descending
Show:	☑	☑	☑
Criteria:			>7
or:			

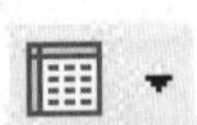

Datasheet View button

5) Switch to Datasheet view to see the results of your query. To do this, click the **Datasheet View** button on the toolbar.

   Your query returns only the fields you selected in Design view. The books are listed in ascending alphabetical order by book title. Only books that cost more than £7 are displayed.

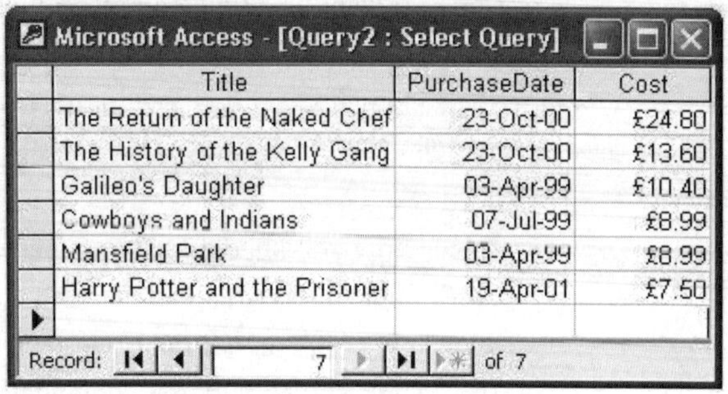

Microsoft Access - [Query2 : Select Query]

Title	PurchaseDate	Cost
The Return of the Naked Chef	23-Oct-00	£24.80
The History of the Kelly Gang	23-Oct-00	£13.60
Galileo's Daughter	03-Apr-99	£10.40
Cowboys and Indians	07-Jul-99	£8.99
Mansfield Park	03-Apr-99	£8.99
Harry Potter and the Prisoner	19-Apr-01	£7.50

Record: 7 of 7

6) Close the query window. You are prompted to save the query – click **Yes**. Give the query a name you will remember, such as Books over £7. Click **OK**, and it's saved.

You can subsequently view the selected fields in the order you specified, simply by opening the query from the *Queries* area of the *Database* window.

Specifying multiple criteria

In Exercise 32.5 you build a new query based on the query you created in Exercise 32.4. In doing this, you edit and remove fields, add new fields, and enter multiple criteria. The query will display books with a copyright year between 1950 and 2000 and that cost more than £20 or less than £5. The display will be sorted by purchase date.

Exercise 32.5: Specifying multiple criteria in a query

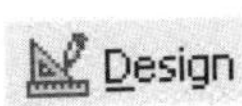

Design button

1) Display the query you created in Exercise 32.4 in Design view. To do this, select the query in the *Database* window and click the **Design** button on the *Database* window toolbar.
2) Delete the *PurchaseDate* column. To do this, click anywhere in the column and choose **Edit | Delete Columns**. This deletes the field from the query.
3) Add a new column to the left of the *Cost* column. To do this, click anywhere in the *Cost* column and choose **Insert | Column**. This inserts a blank column to the left of the *Cost* column.
4) Click in the *Field* row of the new column, click the arrow that appears at the right of the field, and select *CopyrightYear* from the field list displayed.

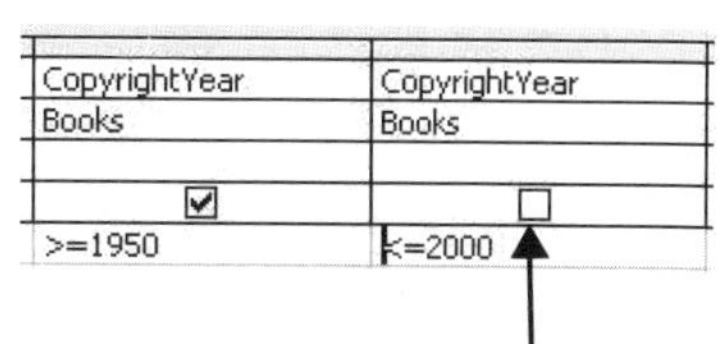

We want only one CopyrightYear field in the query output, so this box is not selected

5) In the first *Criteria* row for the field, enter >=1950.
6) Repeat steps 3 to 5. This time enter the criteria <=2000. Unselect the *Show* box. You've now included the

CopyrightYear field twice so that you can apply two different criteria for this field.

7) Click in the first *Criteria* row for the *Cost* field and enter the following:

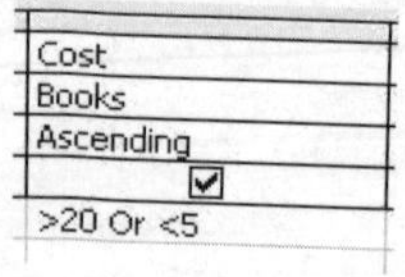

>20 or<5.

This is how you specify that you want books that cost over £20 or books that cost less than £5.

Click in the *Sort* row of the *Cost* field and select *Ascending*.

8) The design grid should now look as shown:

Field:	Title	CopyrightYear	CopyrightYear	Cost
Table:	Books	Books	Books	Books
Sort:				Ascending
Show:	☑	☑	☐	☑
Criteria:		>=1950	<=2000	>20 Or <5
or:				

9) Switch to the Datasheet view of your query to review the results – this includes only books with a copyright year between 1950 and 2000 and that cost either over £20 or under £5.

Books over £7 : Select Query

Title	Expr1001	CopyrightYear	Cost
The BFG	1982	1982	£3.99
Harry Potter and the Philosopher's Stone	1997	1997	£4.99
The Return of the Naked Chef	2000	2000	£24.80
	0	0	

Record: 4 of 4

10) Save and close the query.

Moving fields in a query

To change the order of fields in the query, place the cursor just above the column (the cursor becomes a downward arrow) and click to select the entire column.

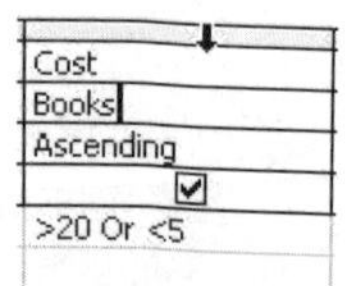

Then drag the column to the position you want it.

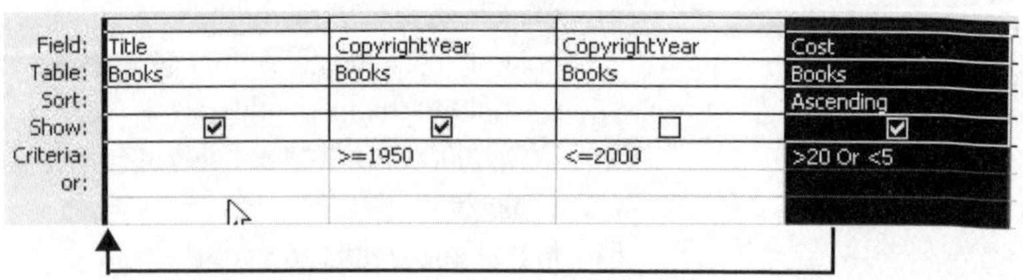

The Cost column being moved to the left of the Title column

Then click it again, but this time hold down the mouse button: note that a box appears on the tail of the mouse pointer. Now drag it left or right to the new location. When you arrive at your chosen destination, note how a bold line has appeared, indicating Access's understanding of where you want to place your moving column: if this is correct, release the mouse button, and the column moves. Try this a number of times until you are confident about it.

Specifying AND and OR criteria

In Exercise 32.5 you specified multiple criteria in a query, and you used both AND and OR operators. Did you know that?

Criteria that are entered on the same *Criteria* row in the design grid are combined using the logical operator AND: a record will be displayed only if it satisfies *all* criteria.

CopyrightYear	CopyrightYear
Books	Books
☑	☑
>=1950	<=2000

In the example in Exercise 32.5, the query displays only books with a copyright year after 1950 *and* before 2000. You could have specified the same criteria by using just one *CopyrightYear* field. In this case, you would enter the following expression in the *Criteria* row for the field:

=>1950 AND <=2000

Criteria that are entered on different *Criteria* rows are combined using the logical operator OR: a record will be displayed if it satisfies *any* of the criteria.

Creating a multi-table query

You can use multi-table queries to bring together data from different tables. In Exercise 32.6 you build a query that outputs recommended books with a copyright year before 1950. This query draws data from both the Books table and the Authors table.

Exercise 32.6: Creating a multi-table query

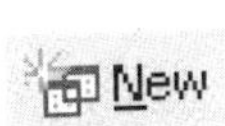

New Query button

1) In the *Database* window, click the *Queries* option in the *Objects* area, and then click the **Create query in Design View** option.
2) In the *Show Table* dialog box, add the Books and Authors tables and then click **Close**.
3) Access displays the *Select Query* dialog box, with field lists for both of the tables in the upper pane and a design grid in the lower pane.
4) Specify the query as follows:

Double-click to run the recommended books query

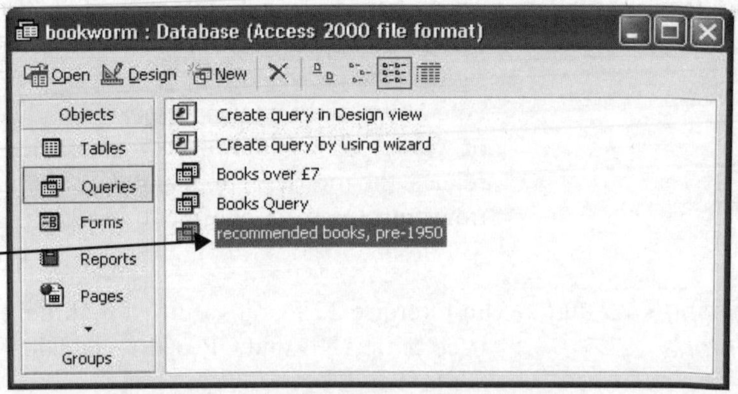

- AutLastName from the Authors table, sorted in ascending order.
- Title from the Books table.
- Recommended =Yes from the Books table. Uncheck the *Show* check box for this field – all the books are recommended.
- CopyrightYear <1950 from the Books table.

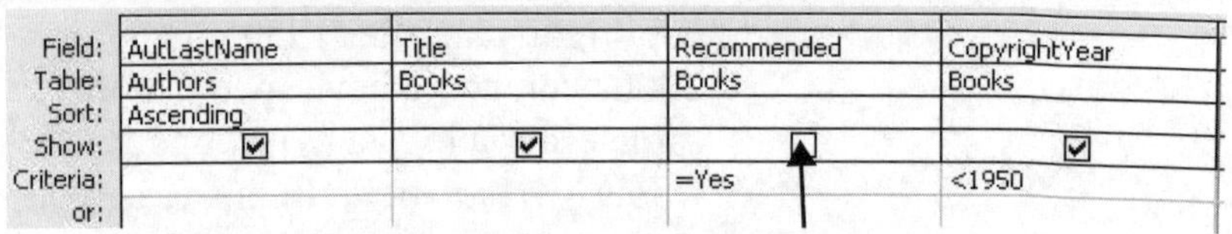

All the books output by the query will be recommended books, so you do not need to display the Recommended column

5) Switch to the Datasheet view of your query to review the results. (Alternatively, click the **Run** button in the *Query* toolbar.) Records matching the query specification are displayed in alphabetical order of the Authors' last names.

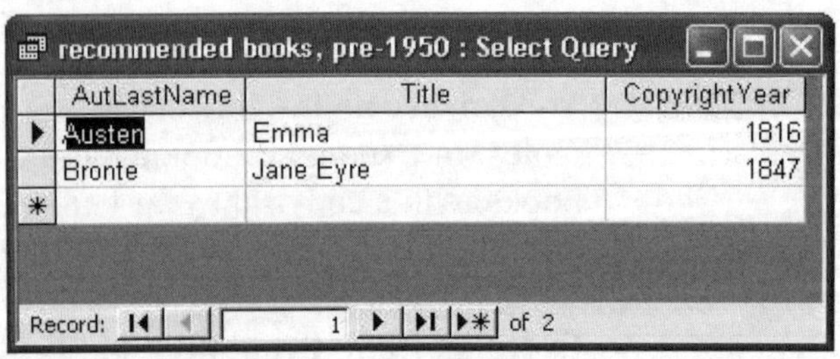

6) Save and close the query.

Running a query

To run a query you created previously, double-click on it in the *Queries* area of the *Database* window.

Each time you run the query it will be updated to reflect any changes you have made to the database since the last time you ran it.

Updating records in a query

In certain circumstances you can add, modify and delete the records in a query (in Datasheet view) so that the changes you make are implemented on the query's underlying table. The query must be based on a single table or on tables that are linked by a one-to-one relationship.

The procedures for doing this are the same as for updating records in a table – see page 455.

Copying a query

You might find it convenient to save a copy of the query for practising changes in the query. Right-click the query in the *Objects* area and click **Copy**. Right-click in the white space in the middle of the screen, and click **Paste**. You are now prompted to give the query a different name. Click **OK** when you have finished.

Deleting a query

To delete a query, right-click it in Objects view and choose **Delete**. You are asked to confirm that you want to delete the query.

Chapter summary: so now you know

A query is a database operation that you use to repeatedly retrieve database records that match specific criteria and you can display records in a specified order.

You can save both simple sorts and filters as queries – see Exercises 32.1 and 32.2. There are two other ways of creating queries: you can use the *Simple Query Wizard* or you can use Design view – see Exercises 32.3 and 32.4.

You can specify multiple criteria for a query, and you can combine these using logical operators such as AND and OR – see Exercise 32.5. You can create a query using multiple tables – see Exercise 32.6.

Quick quiz: creating and using queries

Circle the correct answer to each of the following multiple-choice questions about creating and using queries.

Q1	Criteria that you enter on the same *Criteria* row are combined by the logical operator AND.
A.	True.
B.	False.

Q2	**When you combine two sets of criteria with the OR operator, records that satisfy either criteria are displayed.**
A.	True.
B.	False.

Q3	**To retrieve all records where the cost is over £20 or under £5, you ...**
A.	Create a query in Design view. In the first *Criteria* row of the *Cost* field enter 1>20’, and in the second *Criteria* row of the field enter ‘<5’.
B.	Create a query in Design view. In the first *Criteria* row of the Cost field enter: ‘>20’ And ‘<5’.
C.	In Datasheet view, select any Cost, and click **Filter by Selection**. Then delete records that fall outside the cost range you want.

Q4	**To add a field to a query in the design grid, you ...**
A.	Select the field from the list in the field row.
B.	Drag the field from the field list to a column in the design grid.
C.	Double-click the field in the field list – it is then added to the next free column.

Answers

1: A, **2:** A, **3:** A, **4:** C.

Chapter 33: Working with forms

In this chapter

Until now, you have been looking at your database records in Datasheet view – they have been shown in rows, with a column for each field. Datasheet view can make reading the information difficult, and it's annoying if the fields and records extend beyond the edges of your screen so that you have to scroll left and right and up and down to see the items of interest.

Forms are better for those times when all you really want is to see information relating to a single record at one time, laid out in an attractive manner. Forms have the added advantage of being much easier to read, and you can design different, eye-pleasing forms for different purposes. Forms are also more convenient for data entry.

As you will learn in this chapter, everything you can do in a datasheet you can also do in a form. You can input new records and change existing records, you can sort the records into a different order, and you can filter the records so that only the ones that match your criteria are displayed.

New skills

At the end of this chapter you should be able to:

- Create a form using AutoForm.
- Create a form using the *Form Wizard.*
- Navigate in Form view.
- Use a form to add new records to your database.
- Use a form to search for and update a record.
- Sort records in a form.
- Filter records in a form.
- Modify the layout and content of a form.
- Copy and delete a form.

New words

At the end of this chapter you should be able to explain the following terms:

- Header
- Footer

About forms

The primary use of forms is for displaying and editing records and for entering records. Forms are based either on tables or on queries. In forms based on tables, you can view all records; in forms based on queries, you can view all records retrieved by the query. In both cases, you can include fields from different tables. There are a number of ways that you can create a form:

- **AutoForm options:** Access automatically creates your form with a predefined layout and style. You can select only a single table or query as the basis for the form, and Access automatically includes all fields from that table or query.
- **Form Wizard:** Access automatically creates your form with a layout and style you select in the wizard. You can base the form on more than one table or query, and you can select which fields are included in the form.
- **Design view:** In Design view you create and edit your form manually. You decide what fields to include, where they are positioned, what they look like, what the field labels are, and so on.

Creating a form using AutoForm

The easiest way to create a form is to use Access's AutoForm feature. You have the option of creating the form with a columnar layout, a tabular layout, or a datasheet layout. A columnar (top-to-bottom) layout is usually the best layout for data entry forms.

Exercise 33.1: Creating a form using AutoForm

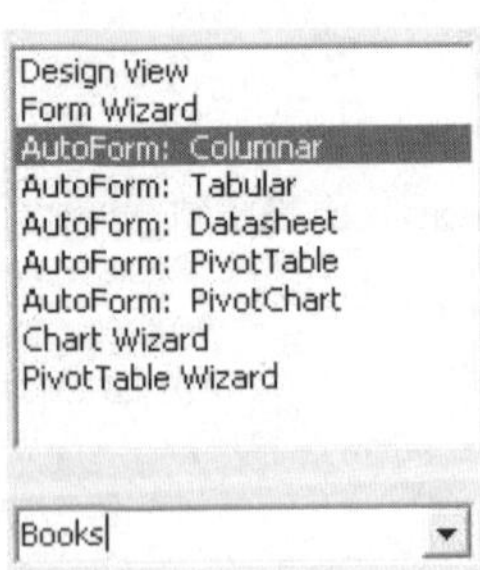

1) In the Database window, click the *Forms* option in the *Objects* list. Click the **New** button on the *Database* window toolbar.
2) Select *AutoForm: Columnar*, and specify the Books table.
3) Click **OK**.
   And that's it. Access now presents a new form, ready for use.
4) Close your form, and save it with the name BooksAllFields.
5) Now create another form for the Authors table. Repeat steps 1) to 4), but this time select the Authors table as the basis for the form, and save the form with the name AuthorsAllFields.

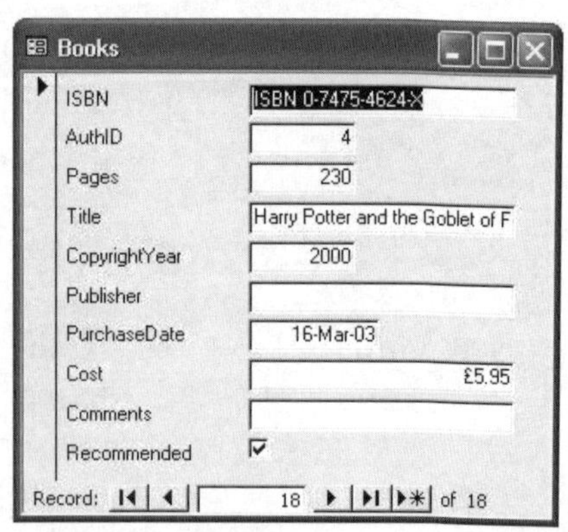

You can subsequently access the two forms at any time from the *Forms* section of the *Database* window, and use it to view the records in your table, to change them, or to create new records.

Using your form to view records

To view one of the forms you created in Exercise 33.1 (BooksAllFields or AuthorsAllFields), you start from the *Database* window, click the *Forms* option in the *Objects* list, and double-click the form you want.

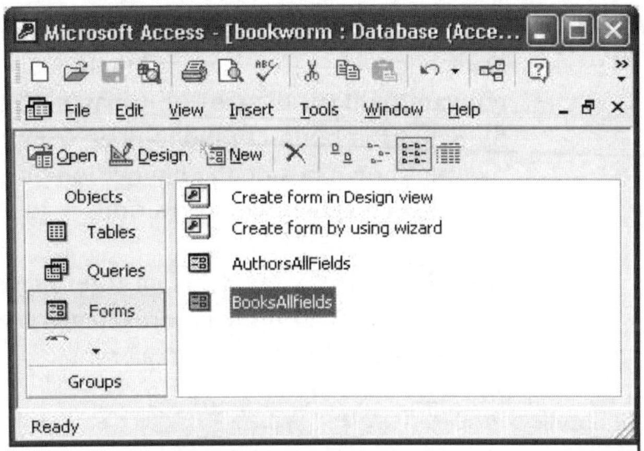

Switching views

Use the **View** menu options or the **View** button to switch between views of a form – between Design view, Datasheet view and Form view.

Navigating in Form view

Once the form is displayed, you can step through the different records one at a time by using the navigation buttons displayed along the bottom of the form.

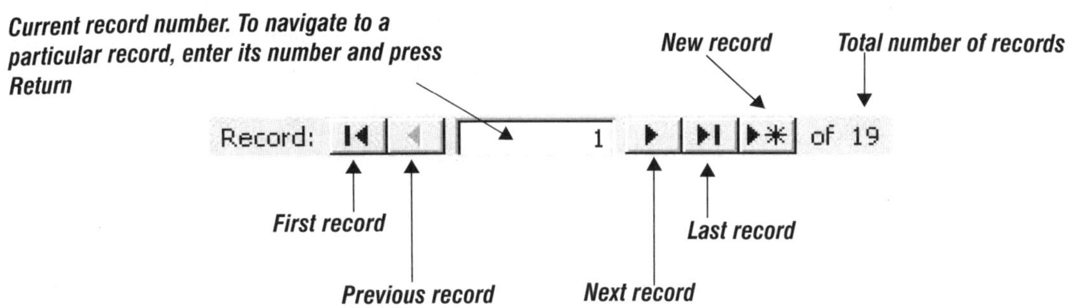

Sorting in Form view

As in Datasheet view, you can sort the records by selection: click on the field that you want to use as the basis for the sort, and click the **Sort Ascending** or **Sort Descending** button in the toolbar.

Sort Ascending and Sort Descending buttons

You can also perform a multiple-criteria sort, in exactly the same way as in Datasheet view: choose **Records | Filter | Advanced Filter/Sort**. And you can save your sort criteria as a query.

Filtering by selection in Form view

In Form view, you can filter records by selection, exactly as you did in Datasheet view: find a record that meets your criterion, select the relevant field (or the part of it that is of interest), and click the **Filter by Selection** button in the toolbar. You will see that the number of records shown beside the navigation buttons reflects the number of records that satisfy your criterion.

Filter by Selection button

As in Datasheet view, you can filter these records again to further refine the search for the records that you are interested in. And you can save your filter criteria as a query.

Advanced filter/sort

In Exercise 31.3 you learned how to perform an advanced filter/sort, using the design grid. This option is also available for forms. Choose **Records | Filter | Advanced Filter/Sort** and specify the criteria for the filter.

Filtering by form

Another filtering option is Filter by Form. For example, Exercise 33.2 shows you how to restrict the records displayed to those with a copyright year later than 1950.

Exercise 33.2: Using filtering by form to filter records

Filter By Form button

1) Open the BooksAllFields form. Click the **Filter by Form** button in the toolbar or choose **Records | Filter | Filter By Form**.

   Access displays a form, into which you can enter your filter criteria. In this case, the copyright date is the criterion of interest – we want to filter for books with a copyright year later than 1950. (If there are default entries in any of the fields, delete them now.)
2) Click in the *CopyrightYear* field. Notice the arrow that appears to the right of the field. Click the arrow to view a drop-down list of all the years represented in the table.
3) Enter the following in the *CopyrightYear* field: >1950.

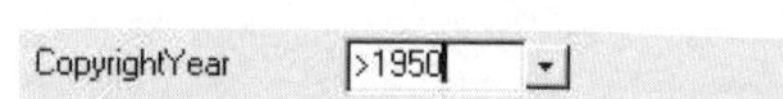

4) Click the **Apply Filter** button in the toolbar: the first record with a post-1950 copyright year is shown, and the record count shows the number of such records in the table.

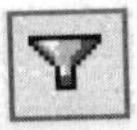

Apply Filter button

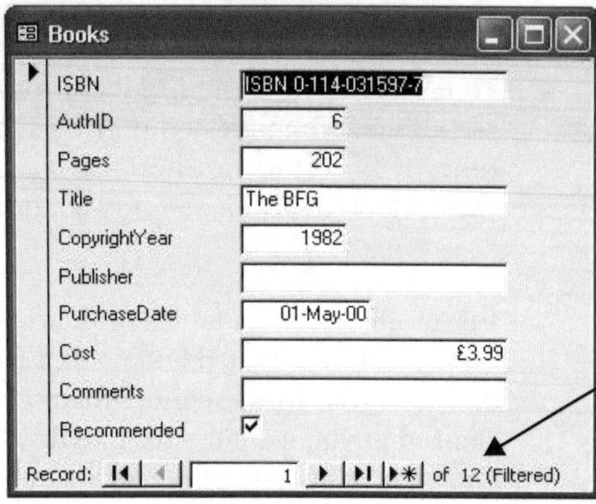

Number of records matching criteria

5) Click the **Remove Filter** button in the toolbar, and all the records in the table are again viewable.

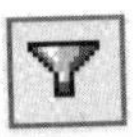

Remove Filter button

Using your form to enter new records

To add a new record, click the **Create New Record** button in the navigation bar at the bottom of the form. Access presents a new, blank form. Fill it in.

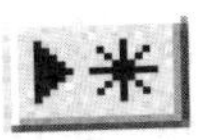

Create New Record button

You can complete the fields in any order by clicking in the field and entering the information. The easiest way to complete the form, however, is to fill in the first field (Access automatically positions the cursor there when you open the form) and then proceed in order through the fields either by pressing **Tab** or by pressing **Enter**. When you have filled in the last field in the form, press **Tab** or **Enter** to open up a new, blank form.

Exercise 33.3: Using a form to enter a new record

1) Open the AuthorAllFields form in the Database window.
2) Click the **Create New Record** button and enter the details of the Australian author Murray Bail – the *AuthID* field is filled in automatically by Access.

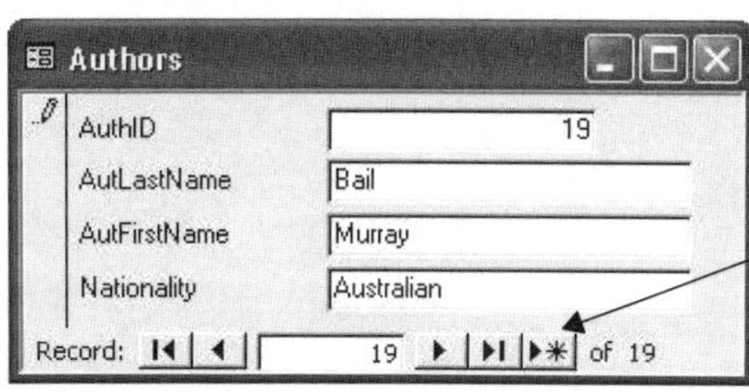

New Record

3) When finished, close the form.

Using your form to update existing records

Any changes you make to the information in a form are reflected immediately in the table. Remember that the datasheet and the form are just two ways of looking at the same information.

To use the form to modify the information in your table, locate the record you are interested in (by paging through the records one at a time, or by sorting or filtering), click the field you want to change, and then delete, overwrite, or add a value.

Creating a form with the Form Wizard

Forms are based on tables or queries, so you can create a form only after you have created a table or a form. With the *Form Wizard* you can base your form on more than one table or query, you can select the fields that you want the form to display, and you select the form layout and style from lists of predefined options. In Exercise 33.4, you will use the Access *Form Wizard* to create a new form based on the Authors table.

Exercise 33.4: Creating a form using the Form Wizard

1) Open Access, open your Bookworm database, and click the *Forms* option in the *Objects* list.
2) Choose the *Create form by using wizard* option.

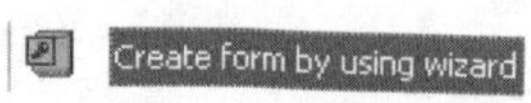

3) Select the table on which the form is based (Authors) and then specify which fields you want to include in the form. This dialog box is very similar to the one you used to create the Books table in Exercises 28.2 and 28.3:
   - On the left you can see all the fields in the table.
   - On the right you can see the fields that you have chosen to include in the form. Initially, this list is empty.

   Use the arrow buttons to move the fields you need from the *Available Fields* list to the *Selected Fields* list.

   For this exercise, move the fields shown. When finished, click the **Next** button.

Specify the table or query you want to use

Specify the fields you want to include

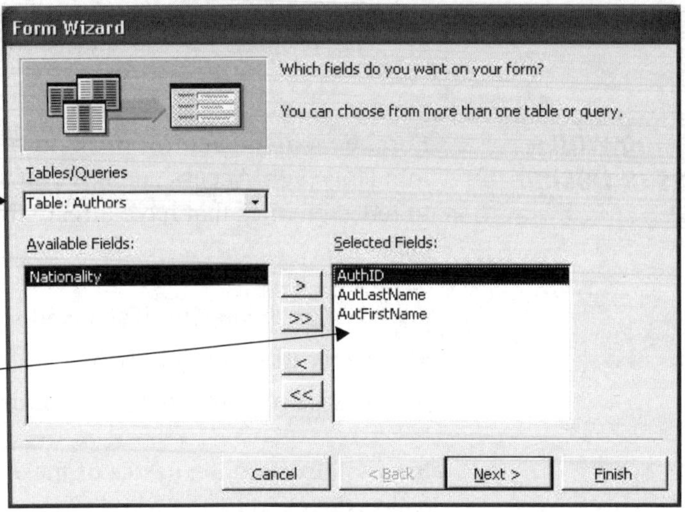

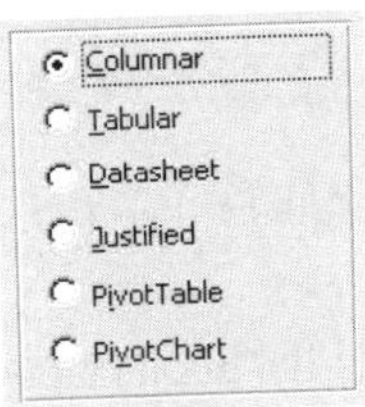

4) The *Form Wizard* then presents you with several possible layouts for the form. You can get an idea of what each is like by selecting them in turn. The best for your purposes is *Columnar*. Select this one, and click the **Next** button.

5) The *Form Wizard* then offers you a choice of styles for the form. Again, you can preview styles by selecting them in turn.

Select *Standard* and click the **Next** button.

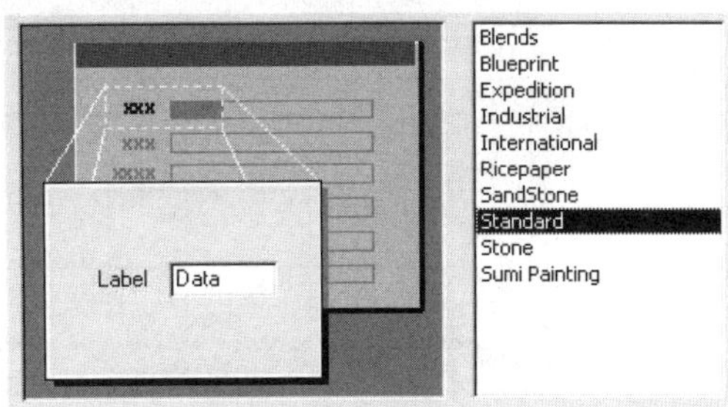

6) Access suggests a name for the form: change this to 'Authors Form' to make it easier to identify later.

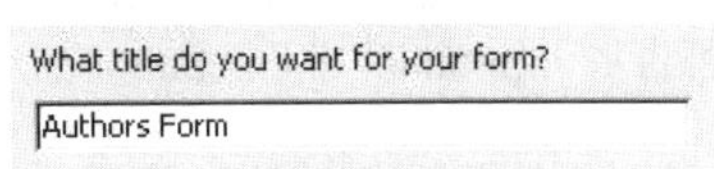

7) You can then either use the form immediately, or go back and modify it. Select *Open the form to view or enter information*, and click the **Finish** button.

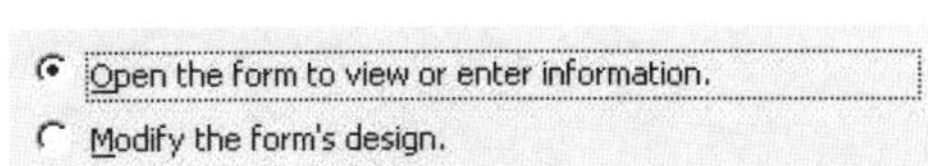

You can now use the form to browse through the records in the Authors table, to update those records, and to add new records.

Working with forms in Design view

For the moment, and for most purposes, the *Form Wizard* does a fine job. However, Access enables you to design forms from scratch, and to redesign ones that have already been designed. For example, you can:

- Change the position, size and shape of fields.
- Apply formatting to fields and field labels.
- Insert a picture (such as a company logo) on to a form.

You will explore the basics of these form design features in the following exercises.

Creating a form in Design view

Exercise 33.5: Creating a form in Design view

1) In the Database window, click the *Forms* option in the *Objects* list. Click the **New** button on the *Database* window toolbar.
2) In the *New Form* dialog box, select *Design View*, specify the Books table, and click **OK**. Your screen should look as shown.

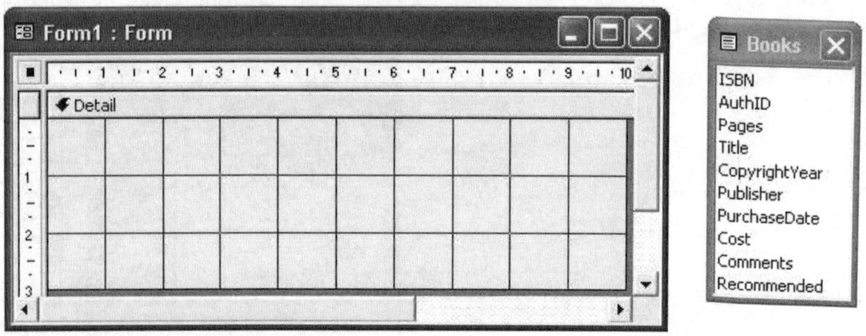

Form **Field list**

3) To add a new field to your form, you need the *Field List* (that is, the list of fields in your table). If it is not already displayed, choose **View | Field List**.

4) Drag the following fields from the *Field List* to the form: *ISBN*, *AuthID* and *Title*.

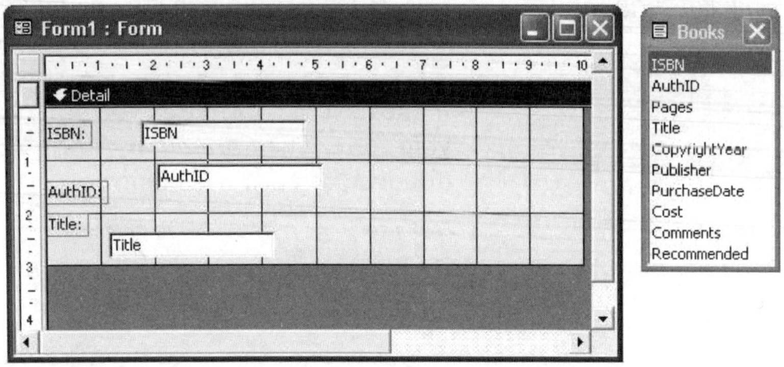

Notice how each field has a label and a text box. By default, the label is the same as the name you gave the field.

5) You need to tidy up your form by repositioning the titles and text boxes. You can use the grid structure to help you position the fields neatly. To move a field's text box and label together:

- Click either the text box or the label. Move handles appear at the top left corner of both elements, and sizing handles are displayed on the element on which you clicked.

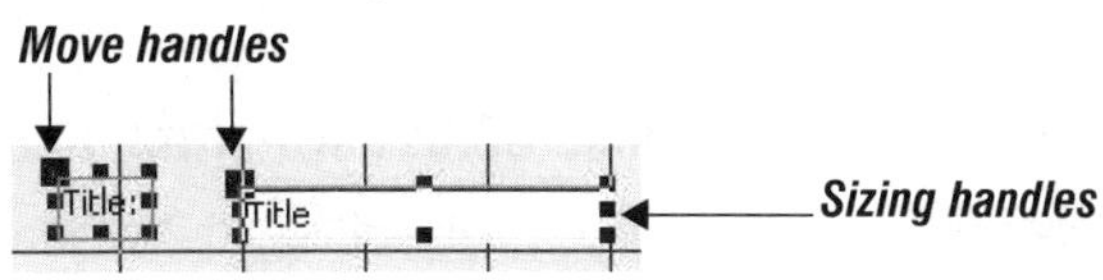

- Move the mouse pointer over a border of the element with the sizing handles. It changes to an open hand shape.
- Click and drag the field to its new location.

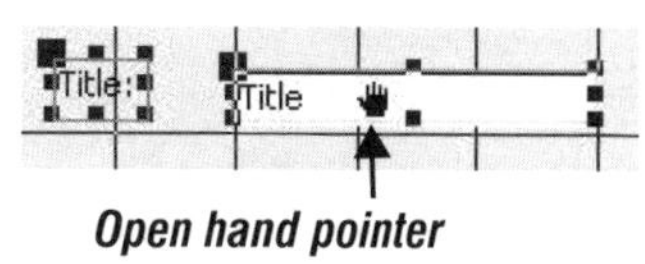

For small adjustments, click either the text box or label and then use the arrow keys to move the field right, left, up and down. For smaller adjustments again, press and hold down the **Ctrl** key while pressing the arrow keys.

Reposition your three field labels and text boxes until they are aligned neatly along the grid.

6) To move the label or text box independently of each other, click the element you want to move and then click its move handle. The mouse pointer changes to a pointing hand. You can then drag the label or text box to its new location.

7) Click the **Form View** button on the toolbar and admire your handiwork. Switch back to Design view by clicking the same button again.

8) Close your form and save it as ISBN-Auth-Title.

Form View button

Resizing the form background

You can change the size of the background area of a form in Design view by clicking the boundary (the pointer changes to a double-headed arrow) and then dragging with the mouse.

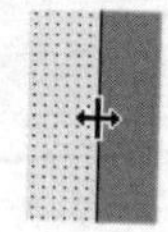

In the next two exercises you will change the appearance of your form. The *Formatting (Form/Report)* toolbar, as you will discover, offers a wide range of formatting possibilities.

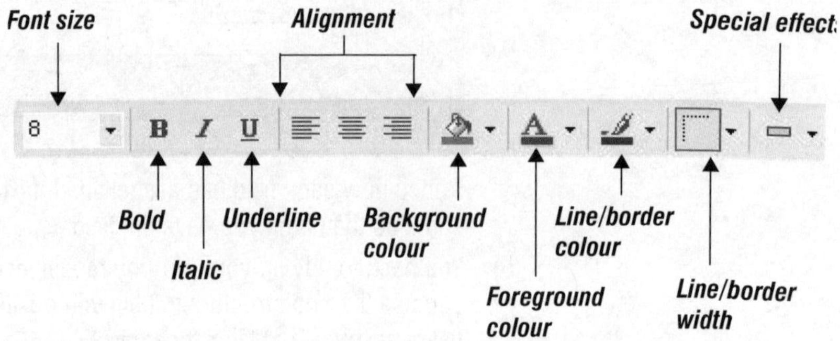

Remember, however, that the best forms are simple, are laid out clearly, and use colour and graphics sparingly.

Formatting and resizing labels and text boxes

Exercise 33.6: Formatting and resizing labels and text boxes

1) Display your ISBN-Auth-Title form in Design view.

   (To do this, display the *Database* window, click the *Forms* option in the *Objects* list; select the ISBN-Auth-Title form, and click the **Design** button on the *Database* window toolbar.)

2) Click the *ISBN* label and click the **Bold** button on the toolbar. Repeat this action for the other two labels.

3) Click the *ISBN* text box and click the **Italic** button on the toolbar. Repeat this action for the other two text boxes. Your fields should look as shown.

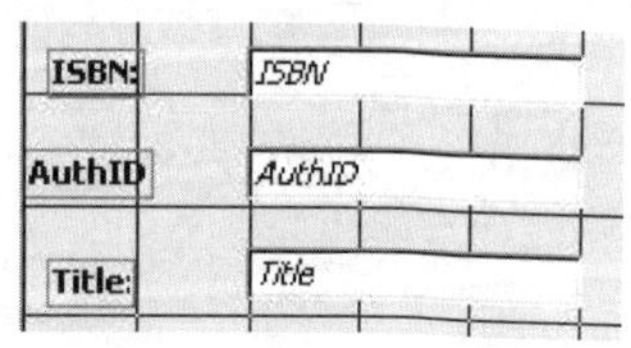

4) Your next step is to change the size of the text boxes. To do this:

   - Click a text box to select it.
   - Hold the mouse pointer over a sizing handle. It changes shape to a double-headed arrow.

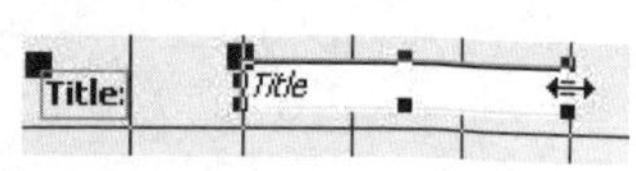

   - Drag the sizing handle in the required direction.

   Increase the size of your three text boxes by dragging their right borders about two centimetres further to the right.

   Save and close your form.

Feeling adventurous? There are other changes that you can try out – for example, you could change the font or font colour of the field labels or text boxes.

Creating headers and footers

In Exercise 33.7 you insert headers and footers on your form. These help you to personalize a form and to make its purpose clearer to users.

Exercise 33.7: Inserting headers and footers into a form in Design view

1) Display your ISBN-Auth-Title form in Design view.
2) Choose **View | Form Header/Footer**. This adds a form header and form footer section to the form. You use these sections to display information that is the same for all records. For example, you could display a title for the form in the form header.

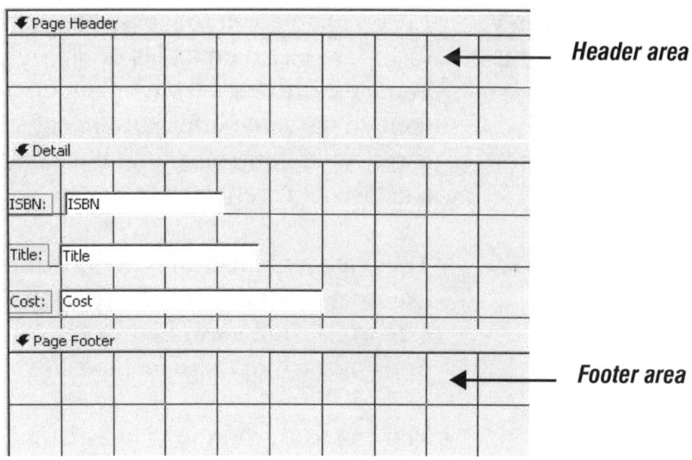

3) You are now going to insert a title for the form in the header area. To do this, you need to use the **Label** button, which is available in the *Toolbox*. To access the *Toolbox,* choose **View | Toolbox**.

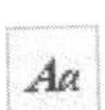

Label button

Click the **Label** button in the *Toolbox*. The mouse pointer now changes to a crosshairs that you use to draw the box for the header and footer text.

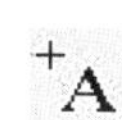

4) Click and drag to create a form header box in the form header section. Enter the following text:

   My Library
5) Click and drag to create a form footer box in the form footer section. Enter an apt quotation in the footer.

   Books do furnish a room – Anthony Powell
6) Save your form.

Modifying headers and footers

To modify a form's header or footer, open the form in Design view and make any changes you require, as above.

Copying a form

You might find it convenient to save a copy of the form for practising redesigning the form without affecting the original. Right-click the form in the Database window and click **Copy**. Then right-click again and click **Paste**. You are now prompted to give the form a different name. Click **OK** to save the form with the name you have specified.

Deleting a form

You can subsequently delete the form. Right-click the form in the *Database* window and click **Delete**. If you do this by mistake, choose **Edit | Undo.**

Chapter summary: so now you know

Forms enable you to view your database records one at a time. As forms are based on tables or queries, you can create a form only after you have created a table or a query. Both forms and the datasheet contain the same information: any change you make to data in a form is reflected immediately in the datasheet, and any change you make in a datasheet is reflected in the associated forms.

There are a number of ways in which you can create forms: you can use Access's *AutoForm* feature, you can use the *Form Wizard*, and you can use Design view. See Exercises 33.1, 33.4 and 33.5 for examples of using each of these methods.

You can use a form to view existing records in your database. A series of *navigation buttons* along the bottom of the form enable you to step through different records one at a time. Within Form view you can also sort and filter records – see Exercise 33.2. You can use a form to enter data into a table – see Exercise 33.3.

In Design view you can change the formatting of both field labels and text boxes, adjust the shape and size of any field, add new fields and add headers and footers – see Exercises 33.6 and 33.7.

Quick quiz: working with forms

Circle the correct answer to each of the following multiple-choice questions about working with forms.

Q1	To open a form in Design view, you ...
A.	Choose **File | Open**, select the form you want to view, and click **Open**.
B.	In the *Database* window, click the *Forms* option in the *Objects* list, and then double-click the form you want to view.
C.	In the *Database* window, click the *Forms* option in the *Objects* list, click the form you want to display, and then click the **Design** button on the *Database* window toolbar.

Q2	Which is the fastest and easiest method for creating an 'All Fields' form?
A.	Create a new form in Design view and add each field in turn from the *Field List*.
B.	Create a form using the *Form Wizard* and select all the fields when prompted to specify which fields you want to include in the form.
C.	Create a form using any of the *AutoForm* options listed in the *New Form* dialog box.

Q3	To sort records in a form, you ....
A.	Click the field you want to use as the basis for the sort, and click the **Sort Ascending** or **Sort Descending** button.
B.	Click the field you want to use as the basis for the sort, and click the **Filter By Selection** button.
C.	Click the field you want to use as the basis for the sort, and click the **Filter By Form** button.

Q4	To add a new record by means of a form, you ...
A.	Open the form, click the **Create New Record** button in the form's navigation bar, fill in the record details, and close the form.
B.	Open the form in Design view, fill in the record details, and close the form.
C.	In the *Database* window, click the form you want to use to add the record, choose **Insert | New Record**, fill in the record details, and close the form.

Q5	When designing a form, you can reposition a field's label and text box both together and independently of each other.
A.	True.
B.	False.

Answers

1: C, **2:** C, **3:** A, **4:** A, **5:** A.

Chapter 34: Working with reports

In this chapter

In the earlier chapters of this module you learnt how to put information into your database, and how to manipulate it and view it on screen. In this chapter you will discover how to produce reports to present data in useful and accessible ways.

New skills

At the end of this chapter you should be able to:

- Create a report using AutoReport.
- Create a report using the *Report Wizard.*
- Modify the layout of a report.
- Group records in a report.
- Summarize fields in grouped reports.
- Sort records in a report.
- Copy and delete a report.

New words

At the end of this chapter you should be able to explain the following terms:

- Report
- Report sections
- Grouped report

About reports

Generally speaking, a report is a way of presenting information in printed form. However, the word is used increasingly to describe information in a form suitable for printing – even if it is only displayed on screen.

Report
A document (printed or on screen) that presents information in a structured way.

You can, of course, print out any Access screen – such as the result of sorting or filtering records in Datasheet view. If these are adequate for

Print button

your purposes, simply click the **Print** button on the toolbar, or choose **File | Print**.

Access's reporting options give you a great deal of control over how your information is presented. You can highlight important information, group data into categories, and give totals for each category and subcategory and for the entire report.

A report can be based on tables or on queries. And you can choose what records and fields you want to include in the report.

There are three ways that you can create reports:

AutoReport options	Use these options to include all fields from a table in a predefined columnar or tabular layout.
Reports Wizard	You can select fields from different tables/queries, choose from a wide range of predefined layouts and styles, and sort, group and calculate totals, averages, and so on.
Design view	You can create reports from scratch, deciding what fields to include, where they are positioned, what they look like, what the field labels are, and so on.

Creating a report using AutoReport

The simplest way to produce a report is to use the AutoReport feature. Its two options are:

- **AutoReport: Columnar:** Access prints each field on a separate line with the field name to its left.
- **AutoReport: Tabular:** Access prints the fields of each record on a single line. Field names are printed once at the top of each page of the report.

Columnar report

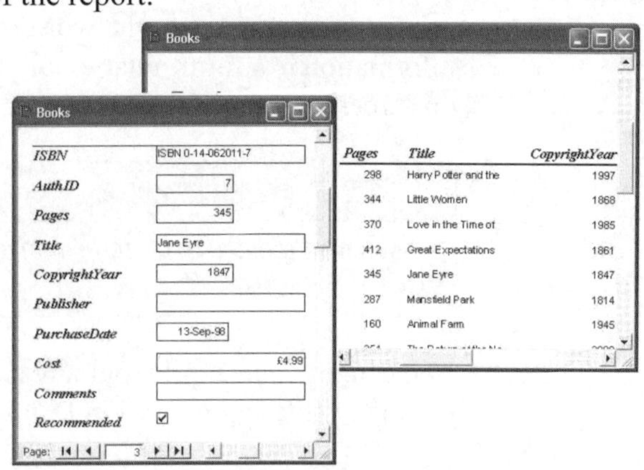

Tabular report

Let's begin by creating a report based on the Books table.

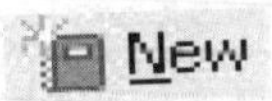

New button

Exercise 34.1: Creating a report with AutoReport

1) Open Access and open the Bookworm database. In the *Database* window, click the *Reports* option in the *Objects* list, and click the **New** button on the *Database* window toolbar.
2) Select *AutoReport: Columnar.* In the drop-down list of tables and queries, select the Books table.

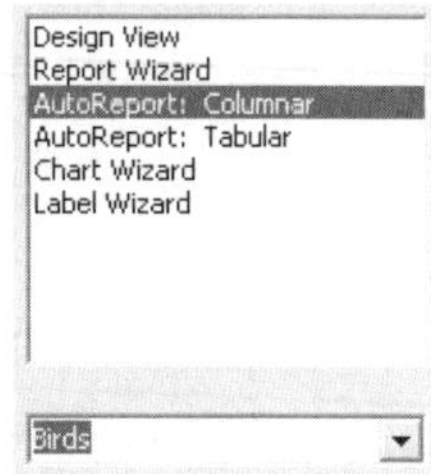

3) Click **OK** and examine the report on screen. To view the various pages of your report, click the navigation buttons at the bottom of the *Report* window.

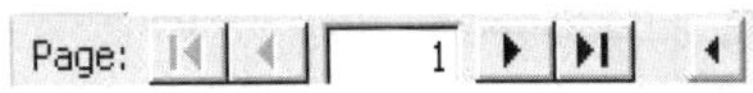

4) If you have a printer, click the **Print** button on the toolbar, or choose **File | Print**.
5) Close the *Report* window. You are prompted to save the report. Name it 'My First Report' and click **Save**.

Report Wizard

While AutoReports makes it very easy to produce good-looking reports, you can take greater control of the content and layout of your report by using the *Report Wizard.* The wizard provides the following report options:

- **Sorting:** You can apply single or multiple criteria sorts to the information that you want to include in your reports.

  For example, if a business wanted to print a report on its customers, it could sort the information in order of (descending) sales value within (ascending) region name.
- **Grouping:** An elegant way of producing reports is to group the records based on values in one or more fields.

  In the example of the customer report, you could group the records by region. Access will print each region name only once and will list under it the records for the customers in that region.

  When you group your data in this way, you can tell Access to perform calculations on the data within each group.
- **Layout:** Your options include columnar and tabular layouts, and you can also decide whether you want the report to be in landscape or portrait orientation.

- **Style:** There are different styling options to suit different types of report – these include formal, casual and compact styles.

Grouped report
A report in which information is grouped by the values in one or more fields. Calculations may be performed on the data within each group.

The best way to learn about the Access *Report Wizard* is to use it. Exercise 34.2 takes you through the steps.

Exercise 34.2: Creating a report using the Report Wizard

1) In the Database window, click the *Reports* option in the *Objects* list, and then click the **New** button.
2) In the *New Report* dialog box, select the *Report Wizard* option and click **OK** – don't select a table or query at this stage.
3) When the *Report Wizard* dialog box is displayed, you can select the fields you want to include in the report.
   - Select *AuthLastName* from the Authors table.
   - Select *Title*, *PurchaseDate*, *Cost* and *Pages* from the Books table. Click the **Next** button.
4) How do you want to view your data? The wizard checks for any natural relationships between the fields you have selected. For example, because the Authors table has a one-to-many relationship with the Books table, it suggests grouping records by author. For the moment, however, choose *Books* and click **Next** – we will group records manually at the next dialog box.
5) Do you want to add any grouping levels? Grouping is a way of refining the way your report data is presented. We want to group records by author, so double-click *AuthLastName* and click **Next**.

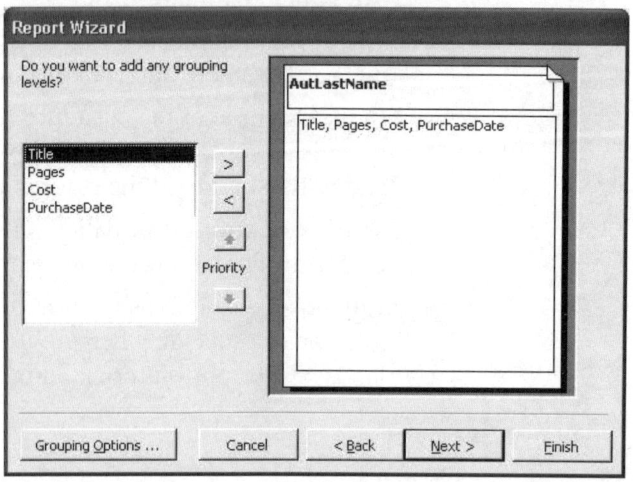

6) You are now asked how you want to sort the records in the report. Sort on:

- Title, Ascending.
- Cost, Ascending.
- Pages, Descending.

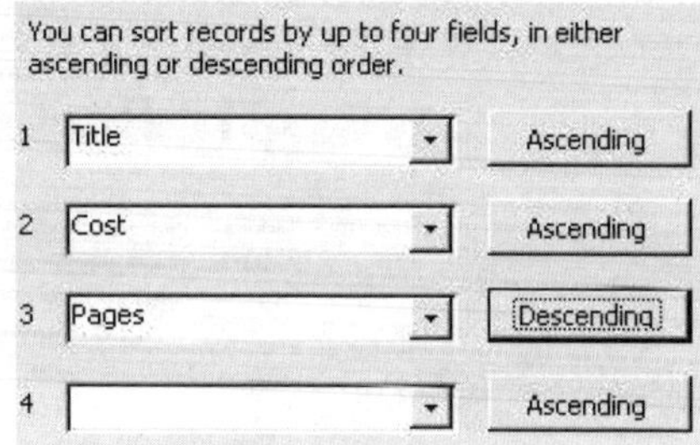

Now specify the summary options you want to apply for the numeric fields – click **Summary Options**. These enable you to calculate the sum, average, minimum and maximum values for a field in each group. Choose the *Sum* option for *Cost* – this will include the total cost of books by each author, and the total cost of all the books. Select the *Detail and Summary* option in the *Show* area to include the cost details of each book. (If you select *Summary Only,* only the total cost for each author will be included.) Click **OK** to close the *Summary Options* dialog box, and then click **Next**.

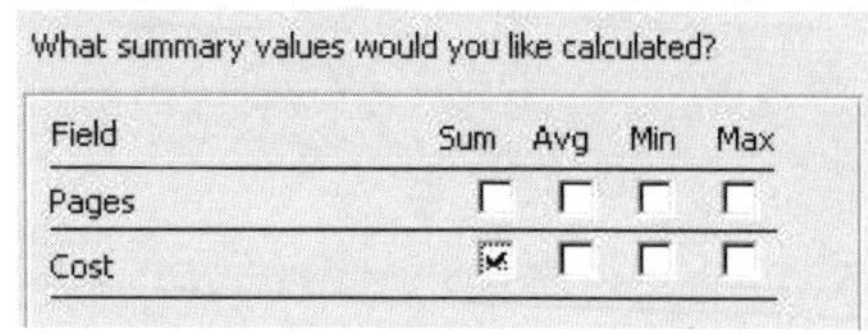

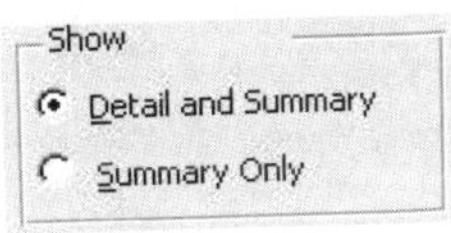

7) Now select the layout for the report. As in previous wizard exercises, you can get a good idea of what the final result will look like by selecting each in turn. For this exercise, select the *Stepped* layout, and click **Next**.

8) Now specify the style for the report. Again, see what the styles look like by selecting them in turn. For this exercise, select *Bold*, and click **Next**.

9) Finally, give the report a title: My Books. Select the *Preview the report* option, and click **Finish**.

After a few seconds, you see your report on screen.

My Books

AutLastName	Title	Cost	Pages	PurchaseDate
Alcott				
	Little Women	£6.99	344	24-Feb-98
Summary for 'AutLastName' = Alcott (1 detail record)				
Sum		**6.99**		
Austen				
	Emma	£4.99	302	30-Nov-01
	Mansfield Park	£8.99	287	03-Apr-99
Summary for 'AutLastName' = Austen (2 detail records)				
Sum		**13.98**		
Bronte				
	Jane Eyre	£4.99	345	13-Sep-98
Summary for 'AutLastName' = Bronte (1 detail record)				
Sum		**4.99**		

Example of a report produced by the Report Wizard

Report sections

An Access report can contain five main sections, four of which are headers and footers; the fifth is the actual body of the report itself. Let's look at each in turn:

- **Report header and footer:** Access prints these only once: at the start and at the end of the report, respectively. Typically, a report header is used for items such as the report title, a company logo, and so on. You can use the report footer for items such as report totals.
- **Page header and footer:** Access prints these at the top and at the bottom of every page.

  If a report includes a report header, Access prints the page header after it on the first page. If a report includes a report footer, Access prints the page footer after it at the bottom of the last page of the report.
- **Group header and footer:** User-defined groups can have their own headers and footers, which appear before and after the grouped data.

  Typically, the group header displays the value of the field that the group is defined on and the field labels. The group footer is used to create sub-totals of values within the group.

- **Report details:** This is the part of the report that contains the information, drawn from a table or query, that you are reporting on. The number of lines in this section depends on the number of records in the table or query.

  In grouped reports, there is a *Detail* section for each group, the number of lines depending on the number of records in the group.

Take a good look at the report you created in Exercise 34.2 to see its elements and how the records have been grouped and sorted. You can see that the wizard has included a report title, group headers, and a footer on each page displaying the page number. Notice that the field labels are included at the top of each page (page header). The wizard has also added lines and borders to make the report easier to read. When finished, you can close the report.

Modifying the report

If the report produced by the *Report Wizard* does not meet your requirements exactly, you may want to fine-tune it. For example, the report you created in Exercise 34.2 needs to be tidied up a little. The range of possibilities in Access is very wide.

Report Design view

To make modifications to a report's content, layout and formatting, you open it in Design view: select the report in the *Database* window and click the **Design View** button on the *Database* window toolbar.

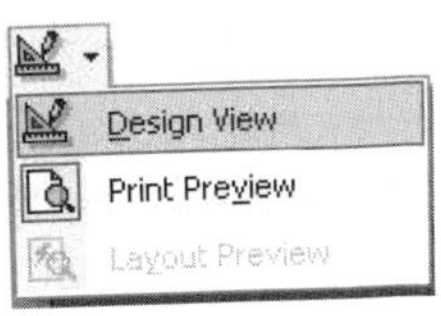

The report elements are shown against a grid.

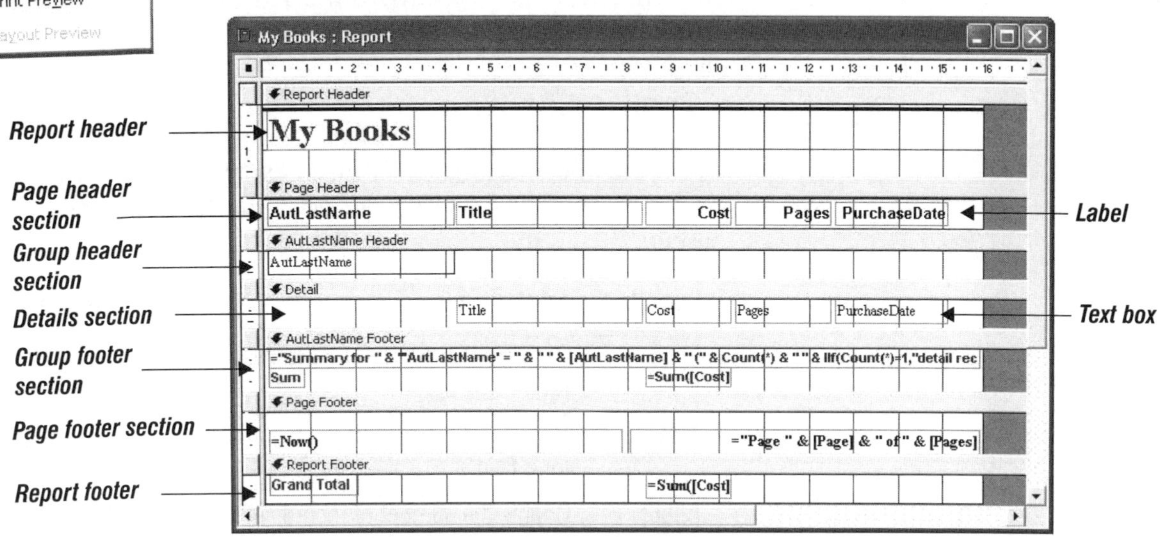

As you see, the report sections are represented as bands, and each section that the report contains is shown once. On the printed report, however, some sections may be repeated many times.

Each report field (*AuthLastName*, *Title*, *Cost*, *Pages* and *PurchaseDate*) is represented by a label and a text box. The labels are positioned in the *Page Header* section so that they are displayed only once at the top of each page when you print the report. The field text boxes are positioned in the *Detail* section.

The report title is positioned in the *Report Header* section, and the Access codes for today's date and for the page numbering are positioned in the *Page Footer* section. The *Report Footer* contains the grand total for all the records.

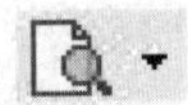

View Print Preview button

When a report is open in Design view, you can switch to Print Preview view by choosing **View | Print Preview** or by clicking the **View Print Preview** button on the toolbar.

When a report is open in Print Preview view, you can switch to Design view by choosing **View | Design View**.

Sum, Min, Max and Count functions

In the report you created in Exercise 34.2, the cost of all books by each author and the total cost of all books were included in the report. This was a consequence of you selecting the *Sum* option for *Cost* in the *Summary Options* dialog box. In effect, the *Report Wizard* inserts the following expression into the group footer and in the report footer:

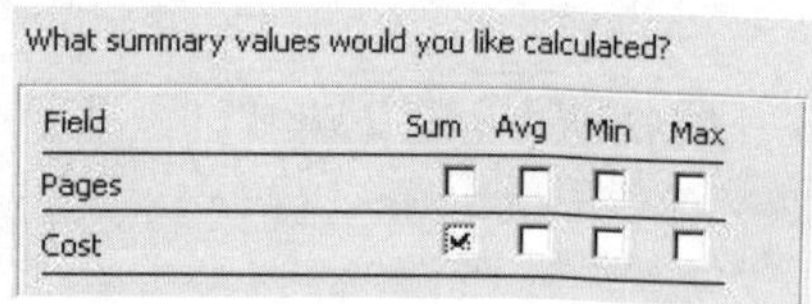

=Sum([Cost])

You can, of course, manually insert expressions such as this into a report in Design view. Here are some functions that you will find useful:

Function	Description	Example
Min	Displays the minimum (or lowest) value for a field.	=Min([Cost])
Max	Displays the maximum (or highest) value for a field.	=Min([Cost])
Count	Counts the number of records in a group or in the overall report.	=Count([Title])

These functions operate on the section into which you place them.

Report properties

You can change the content, formatting, size, position and so on of any element in a report in the same way as you did when you were designing a form (Exercise 33.5).

Some of these properties you can change using buttons on the *Formatting* toolbar. Some you can change using the mouse. Another way is to use the element's properties sheet. To access this, double-click the element, or right-click it and choose **Properties** from the pop-up menu.

Have a look at the properties for various report elements and close the properties sheet each time by clicking its **Close** button.

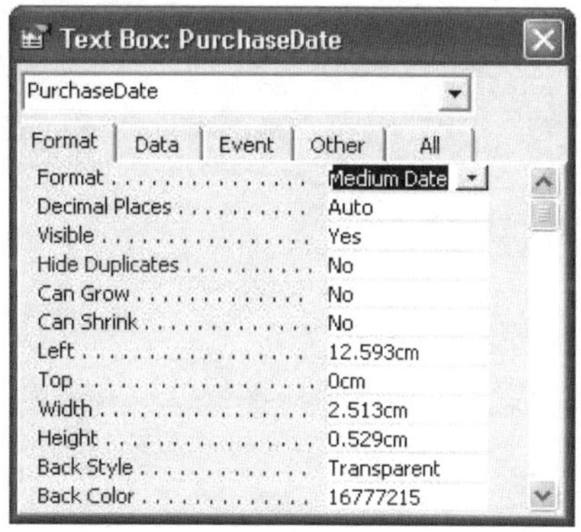

This is the properties sheet for the text box of the *PurchaseDate* field.

In Exercise 34.3 you will make three changes to the layout and properties of the report you created in Exercise 34.2.

- Change the text and font characteristics of two labels.
- Change the border style of a text box.
- Swap the position of two labels/text boxes.

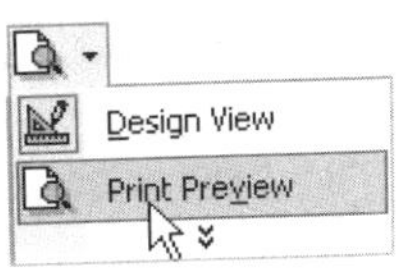

You can check the effect of changes you make as you go along – click the arrow to the right of the **View** button on the toolbar, and choose **Print Preview**.

Exercise 34.3: Changing report properties and layout

1) Open your My Books report in Design view.

2) Change the following labels as shown. Do not, however, change the text boxes that correspond to these labels:

Before	**After**
AuthLastName	*Author*
PurchaseDate	*Date Bought*

In the labels' properties sheets, the property to change is the *Caption* property on the *Format* tab.

Alternatively, you can edit a label in place by clicking it and then editing and deleting the text as required.

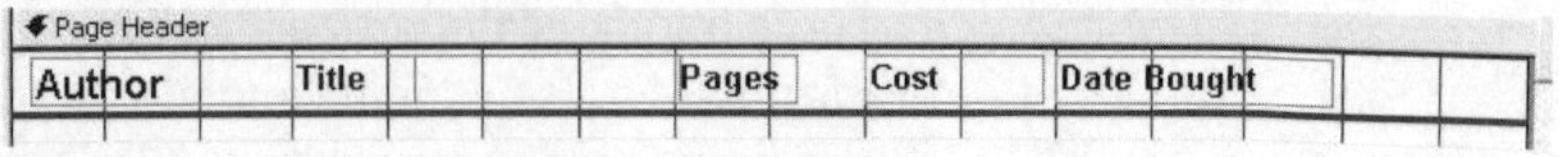

3) Now you want to display each author's name in bold and each book title in italic.

- Select the *AuthLastName* text box (not the Author label) by clicking it, and then click the **Bold** button on the toolbar.
- Select the *Title* text box (not the Title label) by clicking it, and then click the **Italic** button on the toolbar.

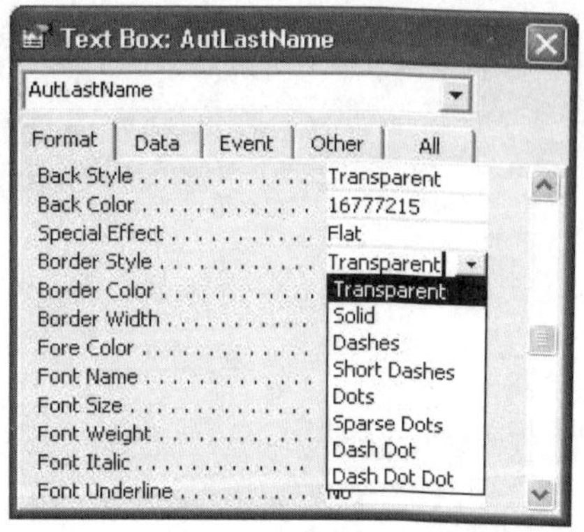

4) Your next step is to remove the box around the authors' names. Right-click the *AuthLastName* text box and choose **Properties**. Then scroll down to the *Border Style* entry, and change it to *Transparent*.

5) Now swap the position of the *Pages* and *Date Bought* (*PurchaseDate*) fields. Note that you need to swap both the labels and the text boxes. Click each field in turn and move it to the position you want it – you might have to do this in stages, so that one field does not temporarily obscure another.

When you want to move a label or text box, click it, and then move the mouse pointer over the top left-hand corner until it changes to a hand shape – you can then drag the field to the position you want. Use the grid lines to help you position fields neatly.

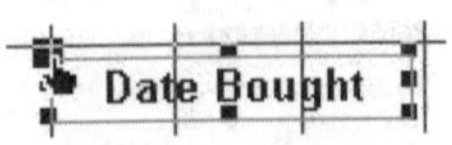

Selected label, with cursor over top left-hand corner

Your report design should look similar to this.

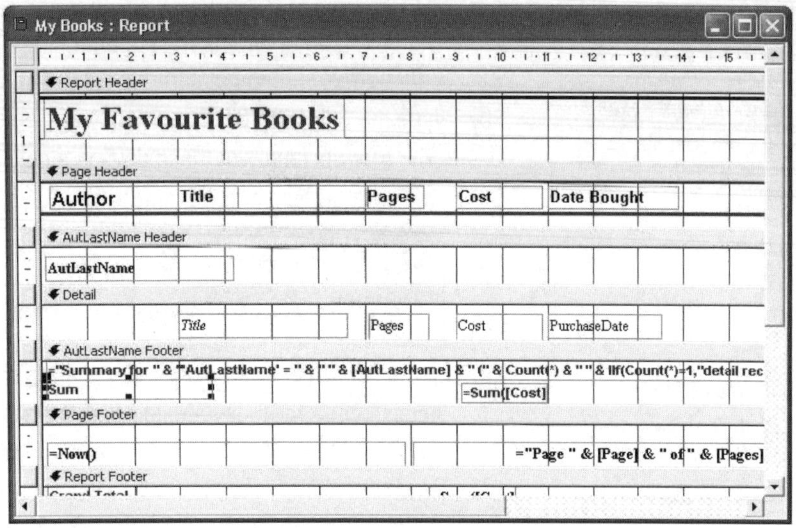

6) Make any other changes that you want to your report. For example, you could use different colours for different fields, or you could change the alignment of text within fields. Take a look at the report in Print Preview. When finished, save and close your report.

Exercise 34.4: Working with the Report Header

1) Open your My Books report in Design view.

   In the *Report Header* section, click the *My Books* label. You can now edit or delete the text.

   Change the text to 'My Favourite Books'. If necessary, enlarge the text box to accommodate the text.

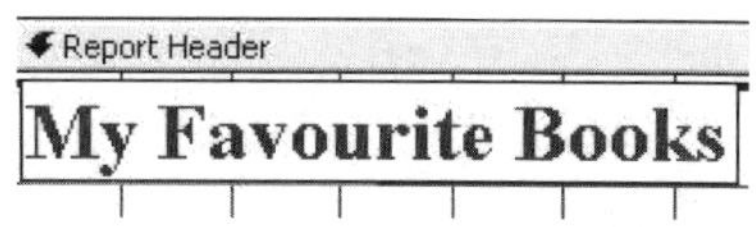

2) Now add a subtitle to the report header. Move the mouse pointer over the line dividing the *Report Header* and the *Page Header* sections – it becomes a moving tool. Click and drag the *Page Header* bar down to make the Report Header bigger.

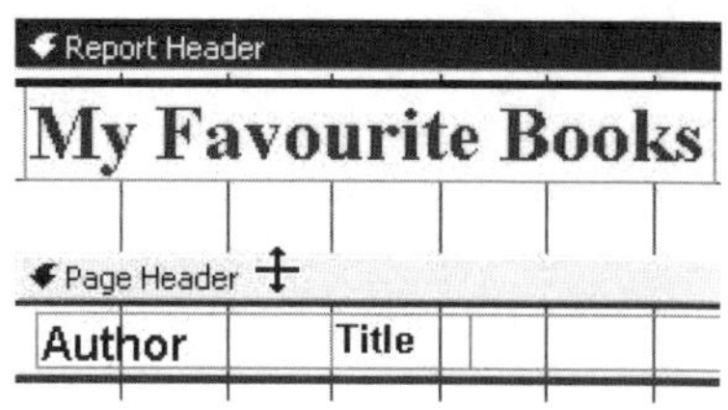

3) Click the **Toolbox** button on the toolbar to display the Access *Toolbox*. This provides tools for adding labels, text boxes and other controls to Access forms and reports. In the *Toolbox*, click the **Label** button.

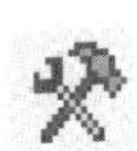

Toolbox button

Label button

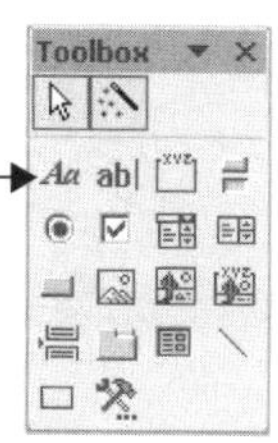

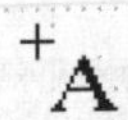

Pointer shape for drawing label boxes

4) Move the mouse pointer over the *Report Header* area. Notice how the pointer changes shape. Click where you want to position the top-left corner of the text box, hold down the mouse button, drag the pointer to where the bottom-right corner should be, and release the mouse button.
5) Type the following text into the newly created text box:
   'The true university of these days is a collection of books' – Carlyle.
   Or, if you prefer, enter a motto of your own choice.

Fill/Back Color

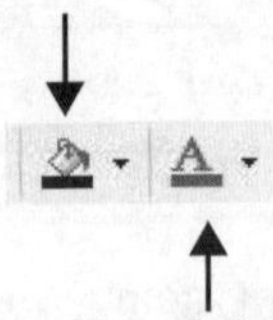

Font/Fore Color

6) In the *Page Footer* area, click the text box that contains 'Now()'. This is the Access code for today's date. Click the arrow to the right of the **Font/Fore Color** button on the toolbar, and select a red colour.
7) Again in the *Page Footer* area, click the rightmost text box; this contains Access codes for page numbering. Click the arrow to the right of the **Fill/ Back Color** button on the toolbar, and select a colour of yellow.
8) Switch to Print Preview view to inspect your work.
9) Not happy with your colour choices? Return to Design view (choose **View | Design View**) and make some further changes. When finished, save and close your report.

Copying a report

You might find it convenient to save a copy of the report for practising redesigning the report without affecting the original. Right-click the report in the *Database* window and click **Copy**. Then right-click again and click **Paste**. You are now prompted to give the report a different name. Click **OK** to save the report with the name you have specified.

Deleting a report

You can subsequently delete the report. Right-click the report in the *Database* window and click **Delete**. If you do this by mistake, choose **Edit | Undo**.

Chapter summary: so now you know

A *database report* is a document (printed or on screen) that presents information in a structured way. Access provides two automated solutions – *AutoReport* and the *Report Wizard* – that will satisfy most reporting requirements. See Exercises 34.1 and 34.2 for examples of how to use these features.

AutoReports offers two reporting options: *columnar*, in which Access prints each field on a separate line with the field name to its left, and *tabular*, where the fields of each record are printed on a single line and field names are printed once at the top of each page of the report.

To use the *Report Wizard*, choose the relevant table/query, select the fields you want to include, and specify the *grouping*, the *sort order*, the *layout* option and the presentation *style*.

Grouping is an elegant way of producing sorted reports, as information is divided into easy-to-read blocks, with data sorted within each block. Within a grouped report, you can calculate minimum, maximum, sum and average values for specified fields.

An Access report can contain five main sections, four of which are headers and footers; the fifth is the actual body of the report itself. The report header and report footer are each printed only once, at the start and at the end of the report, respectively. At the top and bottom of every page Access can print a page header and page footer. Any user-defined groups can have their own group header and group footer. Finally, the *Report Detail* section contains the information, drawn from a table or query, that you are reporting on.

You can modify a report by changing the content of each field's label and text box, by adjusting their size and position, by applying formatting such as font, font colour and background colour, by adding and removing fields, and by creating group and report totals. See Exercise 34.3.

You can insert or amend any of a report's headers and footers to the report as a whole or to each page. See Exercise 34.2.

You can create a grouped report that calculates minimum, maximum, sum and average values for a field or fields.

Quick quiz: working with reports

Circle the correct answer to each of the following multiple-choice questions about working with reports.

Q1	Access's AutoReport feature allows you to select which fields you want to include in an AutoReport.
A.	True.
B.	False.

Q2	A Group Header section in a report is ...
A.	Displayed at the start of the report only.
B.	Displayed at the start of each page in the report.
C.	Displayed at the start of each group in the report.

Q3	Group Footer sections are typically used to ...
A.	Display the page numbers.
B.	Display the group title.
C.	Display subtotals of values within the group.

Q4	To open a report in Design view, you ...
A.	Double-click on the report name in the *Database* window.
B.	Select the report in the *Database* window, click the **New** button, and select the *Design View* option.
C.	Select the report in the *Database* window and click the **Design** button on the *Database* window toolbar.

Q5	Which of the following actions displays the properties sheet for a report element?
A.	Display the report in Design view, click on the element whose properties you want to view, and choose **View | Properties**.
B.	Display the report in Design view, right-click on the element whose properties you want to view, and choose **Properties** from the pop-up menu.
C.	Display the report in Design view, click on the element whose properties you want to view, and click the **Properties** button on the *Report Design* toolbar.
D.	Display the report in Design view and double-click on the element whose properties you want to view.

Answers

1: B, **2:** C, **3:** C, **4:** C, **5:** A, B, C, D.

Chapter 35: Printing database information

In this chapter

To print any database object, you choose **File | Print** while the object is open – just as you would in Word or Excel. There are, however, a number of print-related issues that you need to be aware of when you are printing from Access, and these are described in this chapter.

For example, with databases, you are probably less likely to want to print an entire database than the results of a query, or a report, or a single table. For this reason, the Print Preview function is particularly useful in Access.

New skills

At the end of this chapter you should be able to:

- Preview database objects before you print them.
- Set margins and page setup.
- Print a complete table or selected records.
- Print the results of a query.
- Print a report.

Preparing to print

Access offers you a range of options that help you control the appearance of printed material. But what about the page on which the text appears?

Choose **File | Page Setup** to view the two tabs of page setup options: **Margins** and **Page**.

- **Margins:** Specify the width of the margins you want to use.
- **Page:** Specify the paper size and orientation you want: *Portrait* ('standing up') or *Landscape* ('on its side').

Previewing tables, forms and reports

Before you print any database object, you can preview it to see what it will look like when it is printed. To do this, choose **File | Print Preview** while the object is open. The example below shows a print preview of the Books table.

Use **Print Preview** with any of the objects you have created in earlier chapters in this module.

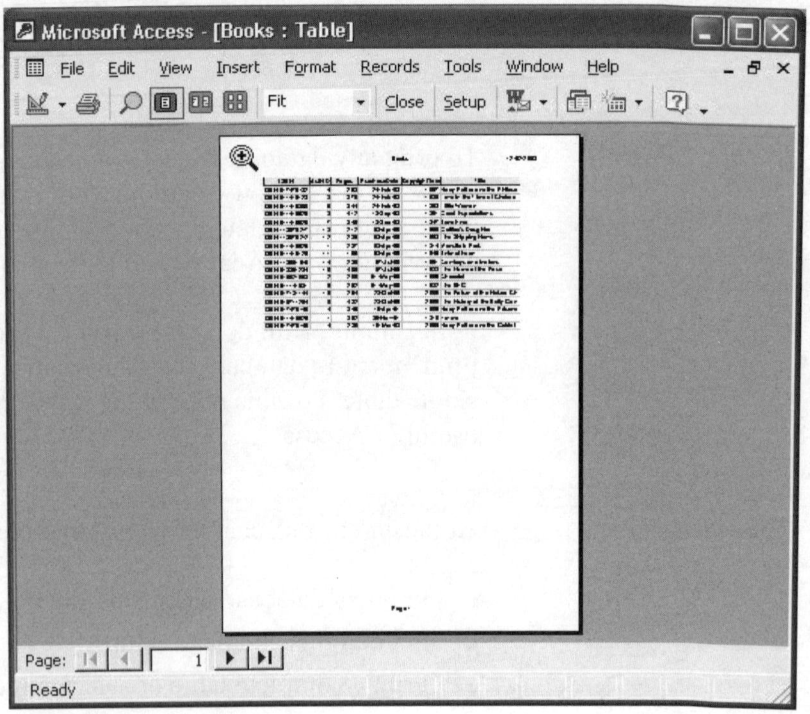

The Preview window has a number of tools that you can use to change your view of the previewed object.

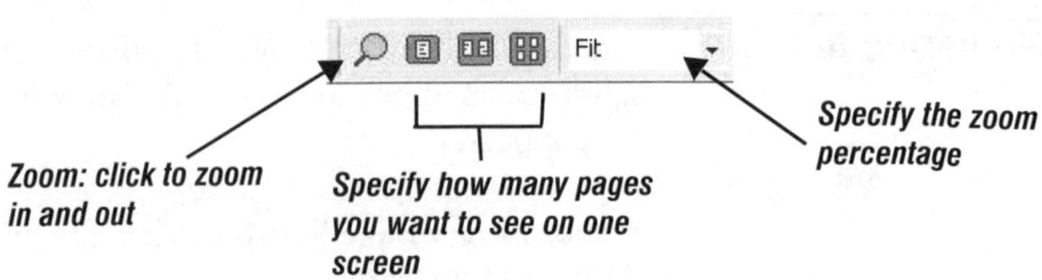

Printing a table

Choose **File | Print** to print the currently open table. Before you print, make sure that you set the margins and page setup to suit your requirements.

In the *Print* dialog box, you can specify that you want to print the whole table (the *All* option), a range of pages (the *Pages* option) or selected records (the *Selected Record(s)* option). The next exercise prints selected records.

Exercise 35.1: Printing selected records from the Books table

1) Open the Books table in the Database window.
2) Sort the table by *CopyrightYear* in ascending order.
3) Select all the books with a copyright year of 1990 or later.

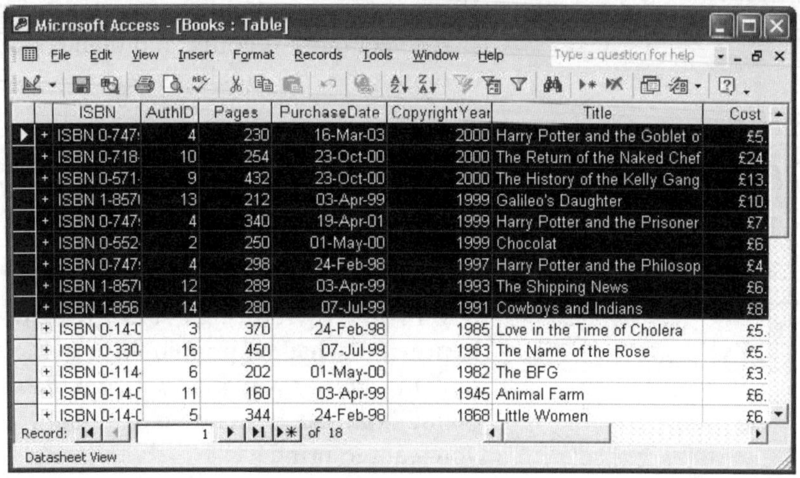

4) Choose **File | Print**, and then choose the *Selected Record(s)* option in the *Print* dialog box.

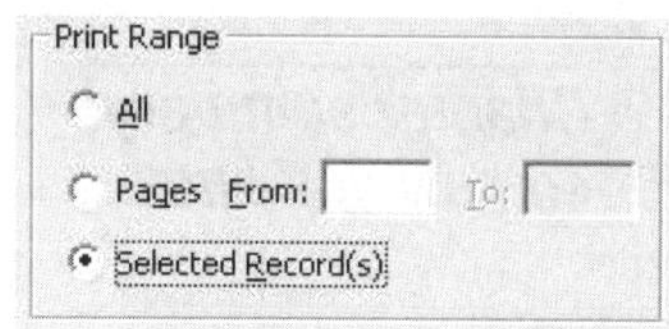

Printing a form

Choose **File | Print** to print the currently open form. Before you print, make sure that you set the margins and page setup to suit your requirements.

You can print a form in either Form view or Datasheet view:

- If you print in Datasheet view, you can choose the range of pages you want to print, and you can choose to print only currently selected records.
- If you print in Form view, you can select the range of pages you want to print.

Use **Print Preview** to preview what the printed form will look like before you print it.

Printing the results of a query

Choose **File | Print** to print the currently open query results. Before you print, make sure that you set the margins and page setup to suit your requirements.

If you want to print only a selection of records from a query result, first select those records, and then choose the *Selected Record(s)* option in the *Print* dialog box.

Printing a report

Choose **File | Print** to print the currently open report. Before you print, make sure that you set the margins and page setup to suit your requirements.

Use **Print Preview** or **Layout Preview** to preview what the printed form will look like before you print it. In the *Print* dialog box, specify the range of pages you want to print.

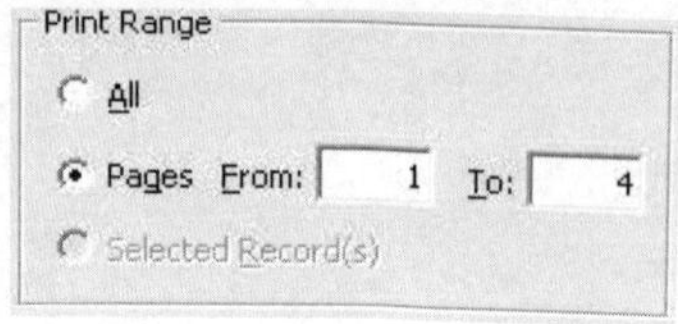

Chapter summary: so now you know

To print any database object, you choose **File | Print** while the object is open – just as you would in Word or Excel.

You can choose the range of pages you want to print. To print currently selected records, you can select the *Selected Record(s)* option in the *Print* dialog box – see Exercise 35.1.

Use *Print Preview* for an on-screen preview of what your printout will look like.

Quick quiz: printing database information

Circle the correct answer to each of the following multiple-choice questions about printing database information.

Q1	To set the margin widths on a printed database object, you ...
A.	Set the margins you want in Design view.
B.	Choose **Margins** from the **Print** menu.
C.	Choose **File | Setup** and set the margins on the **Margins** tab.

Q2	Print preview enables you to ...
A.	Change your default printer.
B.	Check what a database object will look like when it's printed.
C.	Specify parameters before you print a database object.

Answers

1: C, **2:** B.

6 Presentations

Tomorrow you have two appointments: a visit to the dentist and a presentation to an audience of strangers and friends.

Which one fills you with greater terror?

Whether it's to a group of potential customers, a national conference of fellow workers, or a local community group, delivering an address can be an intimidating prospect.

Faced with these situations, you'll want to learn about any tools that will help you to feel less pressurized and more organized – tools that will make you more confident and help you make your points more effectively. This is where presentation software comes in.

In this module you will discover how to create support materials that will reinforce your message, both textually and graphically. You will also find out how to design your materials – both on-screen slides and paper handouts – so as to maximize their audience impact.

Software won't turn a bad presentation into a good one. But it can help a good presentation succeed in its aim: better communication of your bright ideas.

Think of this module as your chance to speak rather than be spoken to. Good luck with it.

Chapter 36: Presentation basics

In this chapter

Slides are the building blocks of a visual presentation. In this chapter you will learn how to use Microsoft PowerPoint to create simple slides, enter text in them, and save your work.

New skills

At the end of this chapter you should be able to:

- Explain what presentation software is used for.
- Start and quit PowerPoint.
- Create and close a presentation.
- Insert slides in a presentation.
- Type, edit and delete text in a slide.
- Save a presentation to hard disk or floppy disk.
- Use PowerPoint's online help facilities.
- Modify PowerPoint's toolbar and menu display.

New words

At the end of this chapter you should be able to explain the following terms:

- Presentation software
- Slide
- Title slide
- Placeholder
- Slide layout
- Normal view
- Outline view
- Note view

Presentations and presentation software

When you demonstrate a new product, describe the results of your research, or announce a new organizational structure, you typically make a speech. Two things can help your speech to have a greater impact:

- **Visual aids:** To grab your audience's attention, and reinforce your messages, you show them a variety of visual aids while you are talking.

- **Handouts:** To ensure that your audience retains key information, you give them handouts to take away and study afterwards.

How do you create your visual aids? You have four main options:

- **OHP foils:** You could print out your visual aids on transparent plastic sheets (known as foils or acetates), and display them using an overhead projector (OHP).
- **35-mm slides:** You could create 35-mm slides, similar to photographic slides, and display them with a slide projector.
- **Computer screen:** For presentations to individuals or small groups, you could show your presentation on the screen of a portable computer.
- **Digital projector:** You could connect your desktop or portable computer to a digital projector, and display your presentation on a large screen or even a suitable wall.

The choice of output depends on the number of people in your audience, the size of the room in which you are making the presentation, the technology available, and your budget.

Your visual aids should reinforce and complement what you say – they shouldn't duplicate it. Text should be kept to a minimum, using headline style and bullet points. Where possible, include images (pictures, graphs, charts, maps, cartoons, diagrams).

Presentation software such as Microsoft PowerPoint can help you to design and to produce the visual aids and the printed handouts. Unfortunately, it doesn't help you with the speech. For the ECDL, you need to know how to produce the visual aids and handouts; you don't have to make a speech. Phew!

Presentation software
Applications such as Microsoft PowerPoint that create visual aids and printed handouts for use when addressing an audience.

Slide
The basic building block of a visual presentation. It is equivalent to a page in a printed document. A slide typically contains text and graphics, and possibly sound, animations and video.

Starting PowerPoint

Double-click the **PowerPoint** icon.

PowerPoint icon

-or-

Choose **Start | All Programs | Microsoft PowerPoint**.

PowerPoint creates a new, blank presentation when you start the application.

Creating a presentation

In this first exercise you will work with a slide called the title slide. The first slide in any PowerPoint presentation is *always* the title slide. It introduces your presentation to the audience. Like the first page of a book, it usually has a different layout from the rest of the presentation.

Title slide
The first slide in a presentation. Typically, it has a different layout from the rest of the presentation.

Exercise 36.1: Working with the title slide of a presentation

1) If PowerPoint is not already open, choose **Start | All Programs | Microsoft PowerPoint**.
2) PowerPoint displays a screen that contains two boxes surrounded by dotted lines. PowerPoint calls these boxes *placeholders*.

   Click anywhere in the top placeholder.

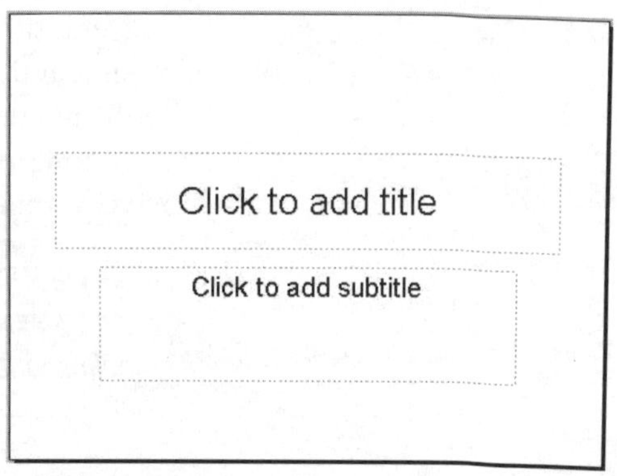

3) The border of the placeholder changes and a blinking text cursor appears inside it. You can now type text in the placeholder.

   Type the following text in the top placeholder:
   Product Launch
4) Click in the lower placeholder and type the following text:
   Round Wheels

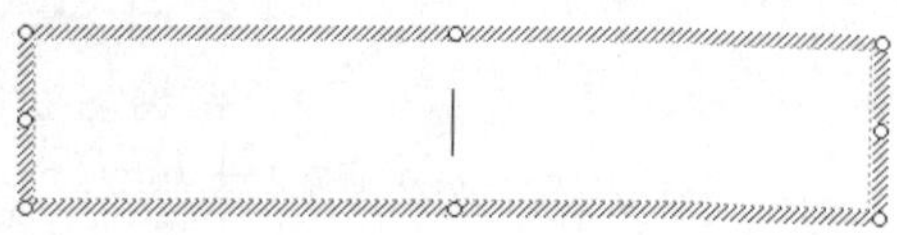

5) Your screen should look as shown.

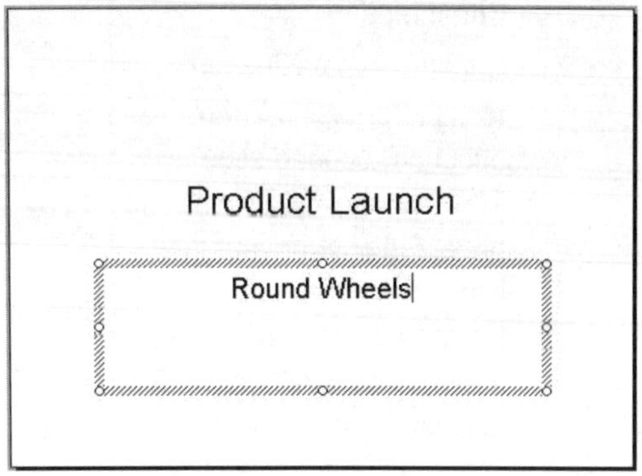

Congratulations. You have created the first slide of your first presentation in PowerPoint. You have also met an important term in PowerPoint: *placeholder*.

Placeholder
A frame or box within a slide for holding text or graphics.

Remember:

- Click on a placeholder to select it so that you can type or edit text.
- Click anywhere outside a placeholder to deselect it.

Adding slides to your presentation

After the title slide, you will want to create further slides to hold the main body of your presentation. Exercise 36.2 shows you how.

Exercise 36.2: Adding a second slide

1) Choose **Insert | New Slide** or click the **New Slide** button on the *Standard* toolbar.
2) Click the arrow to the right of the *New Presentation* task pane. Select the *Slide Layout* option from the drop-down list. Choose *Text Layouts* and select the slide layout that you want to use. For this exercise, select the *Title and Text* option, and then click **OK**.
3) Click in the top placeholder and type the following:
   Amazing Features
4) Click in the lower placeholder, type the following and press **Enter**:
   Smooth Travelling for Passenger Comfort
   Note that PowerPoint places a bullet character (•) in front of your line of text.
5) Type the following and press **Enter**:

6) Reduced Fuel Consumption

7) Continue typing lines of text and pressing **Enter** until your second slide looks as shown.(Do not press **Enter** after your final line of text. If you do, PowerPoint displays another line beginning with a bullet. You can delete such an unnecessary line and bullet by pressing the **Backspace** key twice.)

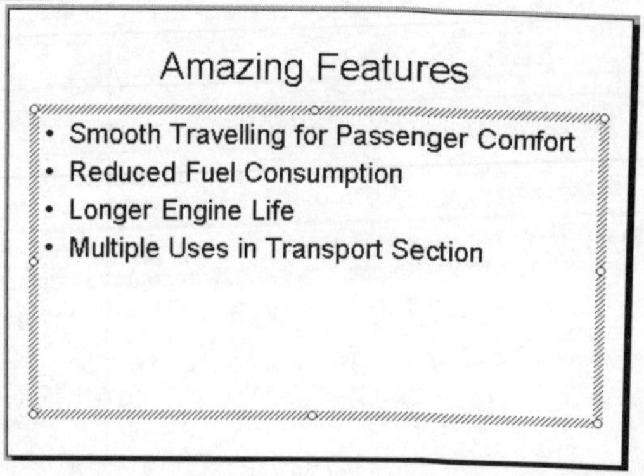

Well done! That's two slides created already.

Slide layout

One of 27 ready-made slide layouts found in the Slide Layout task pane. They typically include placeholders for text and other objects, such as images and charts.

At step 2 in Exercise 36.2 you applied the *Title and Text* layout. If you subsequently change your mind and want to use a different layout, select the slide, choose **Format | Slide Layout**, and then select the layout you want.

Editing your text

If you make a typing error in PowerPoint, you can quickly correct your mistake using either of the following two keys:

- **Backspace:** Deletes the character to the *left* of the cursor. You will find the **Backspace** key at the top-right of the keyboard, just above the **Enter** key.
- **Delete:** Deletes the character to the right of the cursor. You will find the **Delete** key in a group of six keys to the right of the **Enter** key.

Moving between slides

When you have more than a single slide in your presentation, you will want to be able to view and work with each particular one:

- Press the **Page Down** key to move forward, one slide at a time.
- Press the **Page Up** key to move backwards, through your presentation, one slide at a time.

- Press **Home** to go to the very first slide.
- Press **End** to go to the very last slide.

On a desktop PC, you will find these four keys in a group of six keys to the right of the **Enter** key.

In the next exercise, you will add a third slide.

Exercise 36.3: Adding a third slide

1) Is your second slide currently displayed? If not, press **Page Down** to view it.

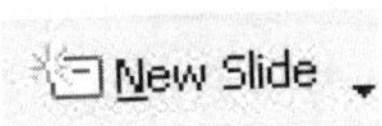

2) Choose **Insert | New Slide** or click **New Slide** on the *Standard* toolbar.
3) Choose *Text Layouts* in the *Slide Layout* task pane. Select the *Title and 2-Column Text* option.

   Your screen should look as shown.

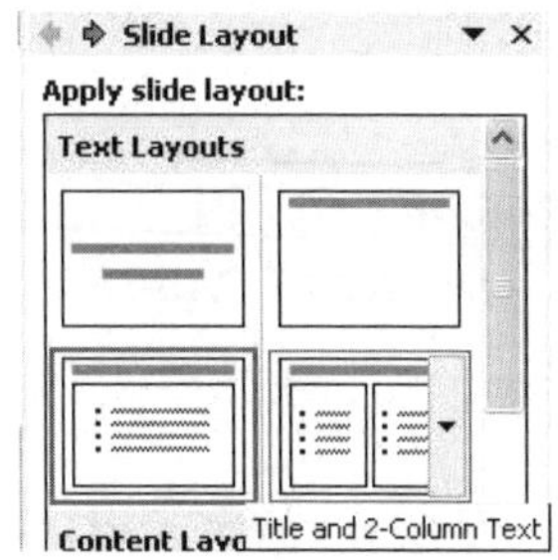

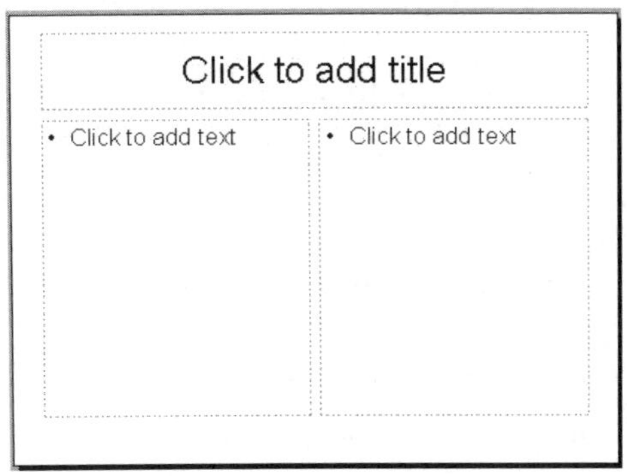

4) Click in the top placeholder and type the following:

   Choice of Colours
5) Click in the left placeholder, and type the following two lines of text, pressing **Enter** after the first line only:

   Red

   Green
6) Click in the right placeholder, and type the following two lines of text, pressing **Enter** after the first line only:

   Blue

   Grey

Your slide should look as shown.

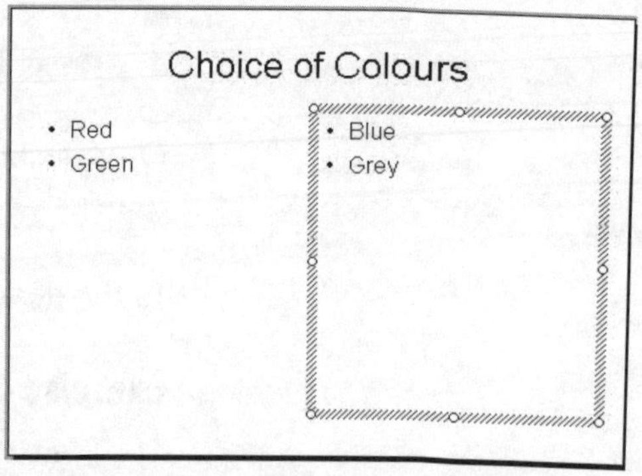

You have now created a three-slide presentation.

Location of inserted slides

PowerPoint always inserts a new slide after a slide that is displayed when you choose the **Insert | New Slide** command or click the **New Slide** button on the *Standard* toolbar.

New slide at end of presentation

To insert a new slide *at the end* of your presentation (as in Exercises 36.2 and 36.2):

- Display the final slide.
- Insert the new slide.

New slide within a presentation

To insert a new slide anywhere *within* your presentation:

- Display the slide that will be located *before* your new slide.
- Insert the new slide.

Saving your presentation

Although your presentation contains only three slides, you should save it now. As with other applications, the first time you save a file in PowerPoint you are asked to specify:

- The location on your PC where you want your file saved.
- The name of your new file.

PowerPoint file name extension

The file names of PowerPoint presentations end in .ppt. This helps you to distinguish PowerPoint files from other file types, such as Word documents (which end in .doc) and Excel spreadsheets (which end in .xls).

Exercise 36.4: Saving and naming your presentation

1) Choose **File | Save** or click the **Save** button.

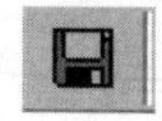

2) The first time that you save a presentation, PowerPoint prompts you to select a location. By default, PowerPoint suggests that you save your presentations in the My Documents folder. Accept or amend this location as required.
3) PowerPoint prompts you to give a name to your new file. Type a name that you will find easy to remember and recognize. If your initials are KB, for example, call it KBpres1.

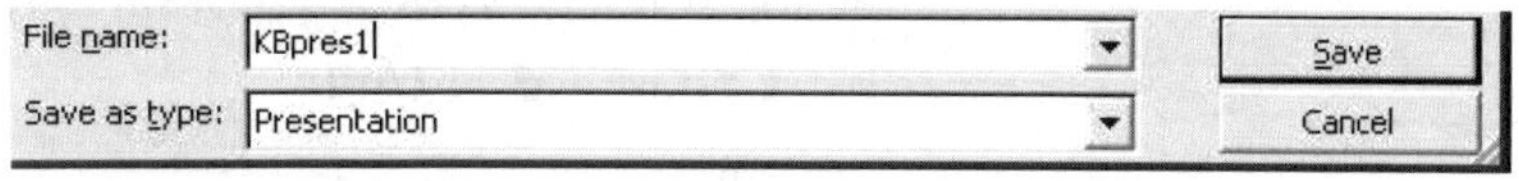

You need not type .ppt after your file name when saving a file. PowerPoint adds the three-letter file name extension automatically.

4) Click the **Save** button to save the file and close the dialog box.

Saving to a floppy disk

In the next exercise you will save your presentation again, this time on a floppy disk.

Exercise 36.5: Saving your presentation to a floppy disk

1) Insert a floppy disk in the disk drive of your computer.
   - If it is a new floppy disk, ensure that it is formatted.
   - If it is a previously used one, ensure that there is sufficient space on it to hold the presentation file. Your file should be about 12 KB in size.
2) Choose **File | Save As** and locate the A: drive.
3) PowerPoint suggests the current file name (for example, KBpres1.ppt) for you to accept or amend – use a different file name if you wish. Click the **Save** button to save the file and close the dialog box.

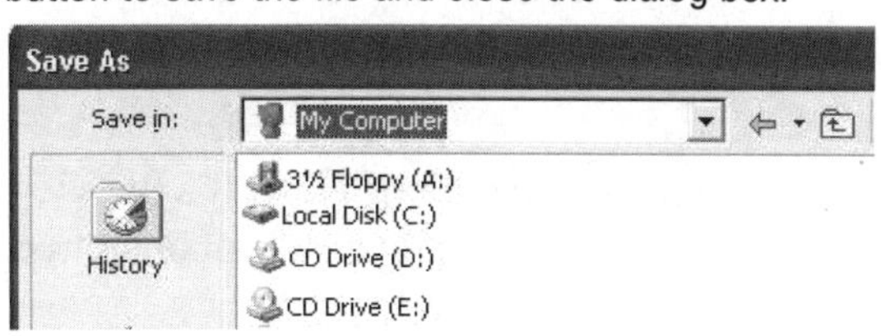

4) When finished, use **File | Save As** again to resave the file to its original location on your computer. (You will be asked if you want to replace the original file: click **OK**.)

   If you do not resave your presentation at its original location, saving the file in the future (by clicking **Save** on the *Standard* toolbar or by choosing **File |**

Save) will save the presentation to the floppy disk and not to your computer's hard disk.

PowerPoint presentation
A file containing one or more slides. Presentation files end in .ppt.

Undo and Redo

Entered the wrong text? Pressed the wrong key? Don't panic. PowerPoint allows you to undo the most recent text entry or editing action if it has produced unwanted results. To undo an action:

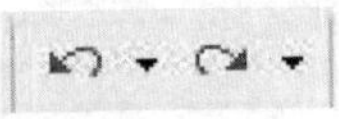

Undo and Redo buttons

- Choose **Edit | Undo.**

-or-

- Click **Undo** on the *Standard* toolbar. Repeatedly pressing the **Undo** button repeatedly reverses your last series of actions.

To view a list of recent actions that you can undo, click the arrow at the right of the **Undo** button. If you undo an action and then change your mind, click the **Redo** button (to the right of the **Undo** button).

Practise using the Undo and Redo options by deleting characters from the text on your slides and then reversing your deletions.

Repeat

To repeat the last action or command you used, choose **Edit | Repeat** (or press **Ctrl+y**).

Views of your presentation

PowerPoint enables you to look at your presentation in four main ways or views: Normal view, Slide Sorter view, Notes view and Slideshow view. Let's look in detail at Normal view. You will learn about the other three views in Chapter 37.

Working in Normal view

This is the default view. It's the view you have been using in this chapter. Normal view contains three sub-windows or panes:

- **Slide pane:** This is where you work on a single slide – you can add and amend text, graphics and multimedia elements.
- **Outline pane:** Here you can work with the text of all slides in your presentation in a structured way. You will learn more about outlines in Chapter 37.

- **Notes pane:** This lets you add and edit speaker notes. You will learn more about speaker notes in Chapter 38.

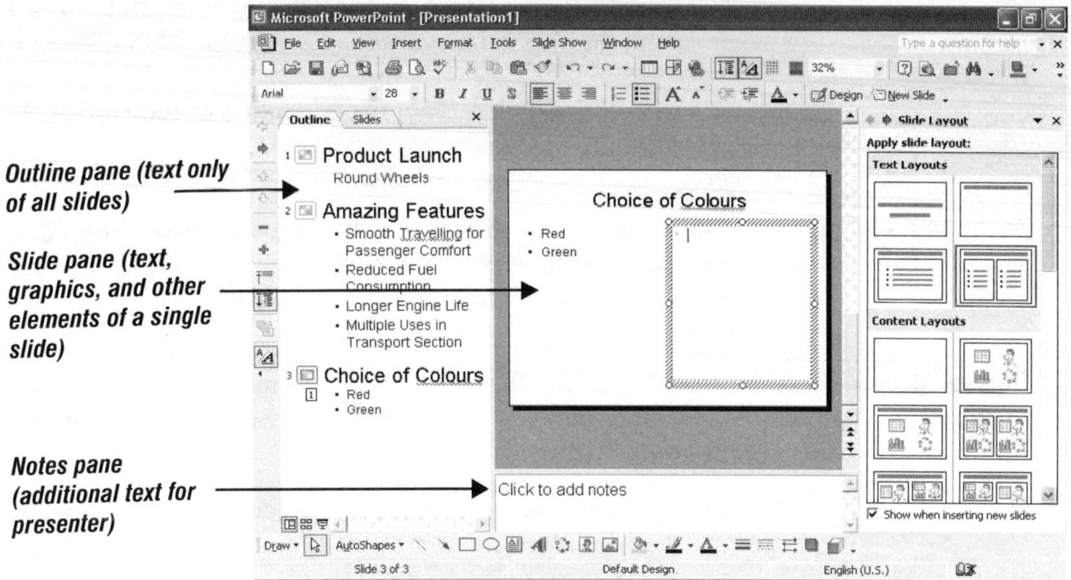

Changing the pane size

You can adjust the size of different panes by clicking on and then dragging the pane borders. Try it and see.

- Move your cursor over a pane border. Notice how the cursor changes shape.

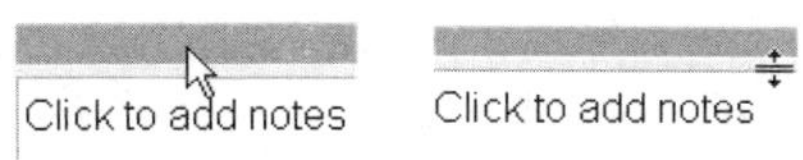

- Hold down the left mouse button and move the mouse in any direction.

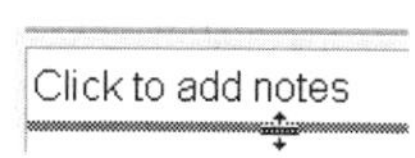

- Finally, release the mouse button.

You can reverse your pane resizing action by dragging the pane border back to its original location.

Normal view
A PowerPoint view composed of a Slide pane (where you work with one slide at a time), an Outline pane (where you can work with the text of all slides), and a Notes pane (where you can work with additional text for the presenter).

Zoom view

PowerPoint's zoom feature enables you to magnify or reduce the screen display. You can use Zoom in either of two ways:

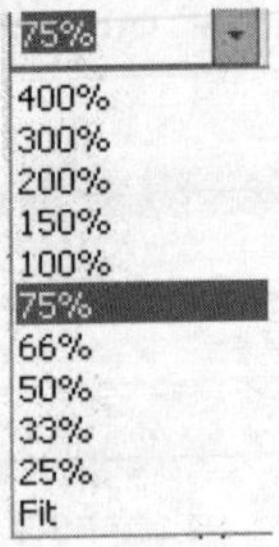

- Click in the *Zoom* box on the *Standard* toolbar, enter a number between 10% and 400%, and press **Enter**.
- Choose **View | Enter**, and select a magnification or reduction from the *Zoom* dialog box.

When in Normal view, your magnification or reduction affects *only* the pane in which the cursor is located.

Zoom and printing

The Zoom feature affects only the way that PowerPoint displays a presentation on-screen – *not* how a presentation is printed. (You will learn about printing presentations in Chapter 38.)

PowerPoint's toolbars

PowerPoint's toolbars give you convenient, one-click access to the commands that you use most often. By default, PowerPoint displays just three toolbars:

- The *Standard* and *Formatting* toolbars located on two rows across the top of the screen.
- The *Drawing* toolbar, located along the bottom of the screen. You will learn more about the *Drawing* toolbar in Chapter 38.

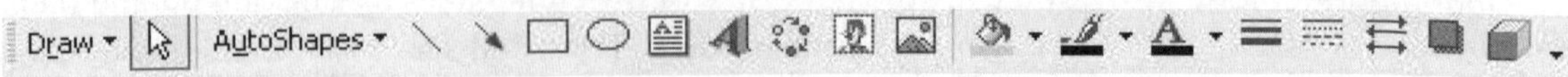

Powerpoint's Drawing toolbar

Standard and Formatting toolbars

The toolbar buttons that you will need most frequently are located on just two toolbars – the *Standard* and *Formatting* toolbars.

The *Standard* toolbar includes buttons for managing files – that is, PowerPoint presentations – and for inserting new slides. You have already used three of these buttons (**File New**, **File Save** and **New Slide**) in this chapter.

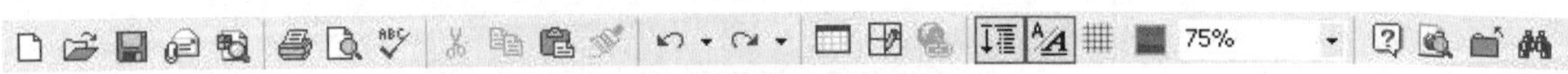

Powerpoint's Standard toolbar

The *Formatting* toolbar includes buttons for changing the appearance and position of text, and for working with bullets. Rather than introduce all these buttons at once, we will explain each one as it becomes relevant through this ECDL Presentations module. .

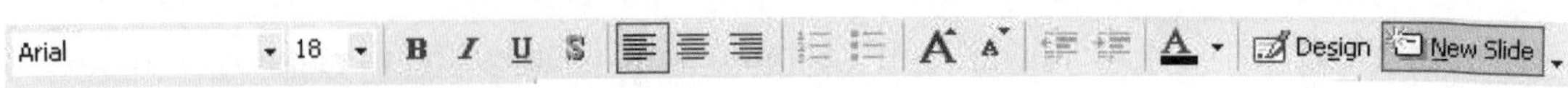

Powerpoint's Formatting toolbar

Hiding and displaying toolbars

You can hide or display any of PowerPoint's toolbars, according to your personal preferences.

- To display a particular toolbar, choose **View | Toolbars** and select the toolbar that you want to display. On the toolbar sub-menu, PowerPoint displays a check mark against the toolbar(s) that you have selected.

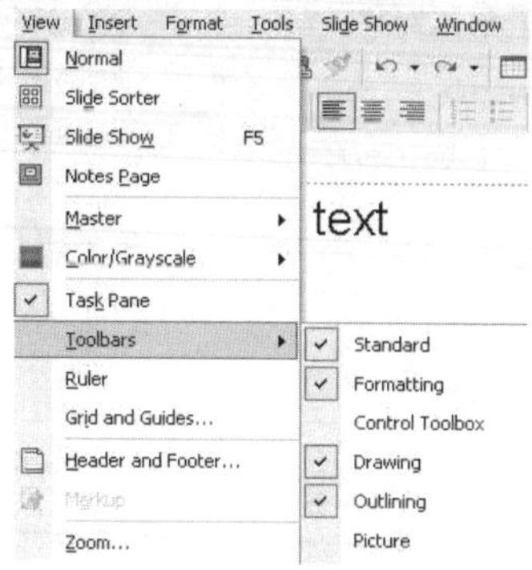

- To hide a particular toolbar, choose **View | Toolbars** and select the toolbar that you want to hide. On the toolbar sub-menu, PowerPoint removes the check mark from the toolbar.

The check marks beside the *Standard* and *Formatting* toolbars indicate that they are already selected for display on-screen.

Hiding and displaying toolbar buttons

You can remove one or more buttons from a toolbar. Follow these steps:

- Display the toolbar that you want to change.
- Hold down the **Alt** key and drag the button off the toolbar. PowerPoint removes the selected button from the toolbar.

Want the button back again? Follow these steps:

- Display the toolbar. Click the arrow to the right of the **New Slide** button. From the drop-down list displayed, select *Add or Remove Buttons*. Choose the *Formatting/Standard* option.
- Click the button that you want to display again.

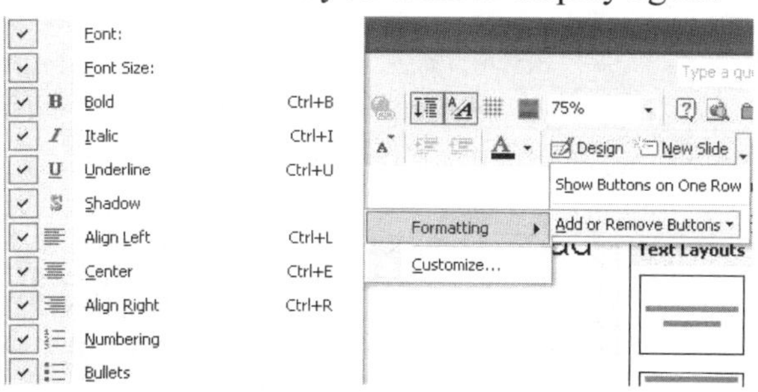

- Click anywhere outside the menu to close it.

PowerPoint redisplays the button on the toolbar.

PowerPoint's personalized menus

By default, when you first choose a menu, PowerPoint displays only *some* of the commands on that menu. To view a complete list, click the double-arrow at the bottom of the menu.

If you choose a command that is not displayed by default, PowerPoint adds it to the displayed list the next time you choose the menu.

To view all commands each time you choose a menu, follow these steps:

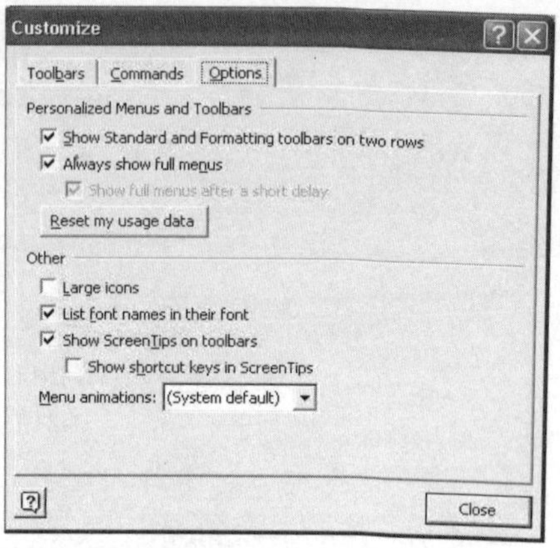

- Choose **Tools | Customize** and click the **Options** tab.
- Select the *Always show full menus* option, and click **Close**.

Modifying basic options

You can customize the way PowerPoint works and set your own personal preferences. Choose **Tools | Options** to see the range of options available.

For example, to change the name that appears on document property sheets and for tracking changes and comments, choose the **General** tab and enter your name.

To change the default folder that PowerPoint uses when you open and save files, choose the **Save** tab and specify the folder you want to use.

Online help

PowerPoint offers a searchable online help system. You can search through and read online help in different ways: from the dialog boxes or from the Help menu.

- The word 'help' means that the information is there to assist you to understand and use the application.
- The word 'online' means that the material is presented on the computer screen rather than as a traditional printed manual.

Using help from dialog boxes

Exercise 36.6: Using online help in a dialog box

1) Choose **File | Print** to display the *Print* dialog box.

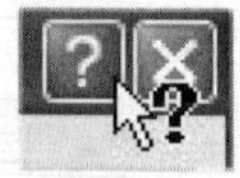

2) Click the question mark symbol near the top-right of the dialog box. PowerPoint displays a question mark to the right of the cursor.

3) Drag the mouse down and right, and click anywhere in the *Name* box.

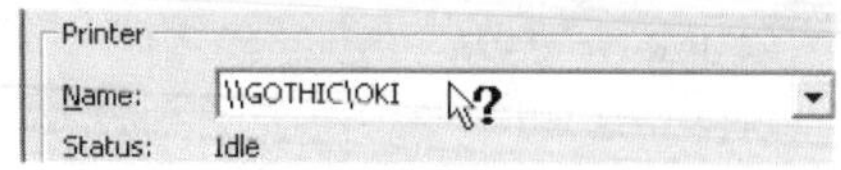

4) PowerPoint now displays help text telling you about the selected box.

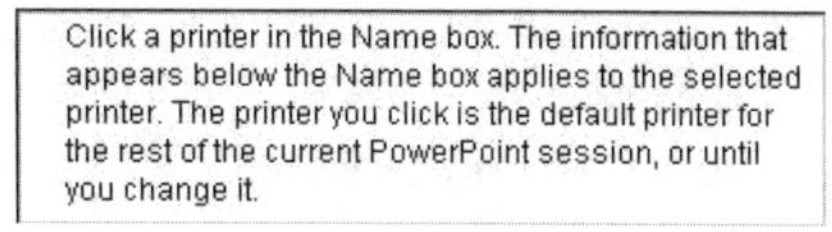

Practise this exercise with other dialog boxes in PowerPoint.

Using Help menu options

Contents tab

This offers short descriptions of PowerPoint's main features. Where you see a heading with a book symbol, double-click it to view the related sub-headings. Double-click on a question mark symbol to read the online help text.

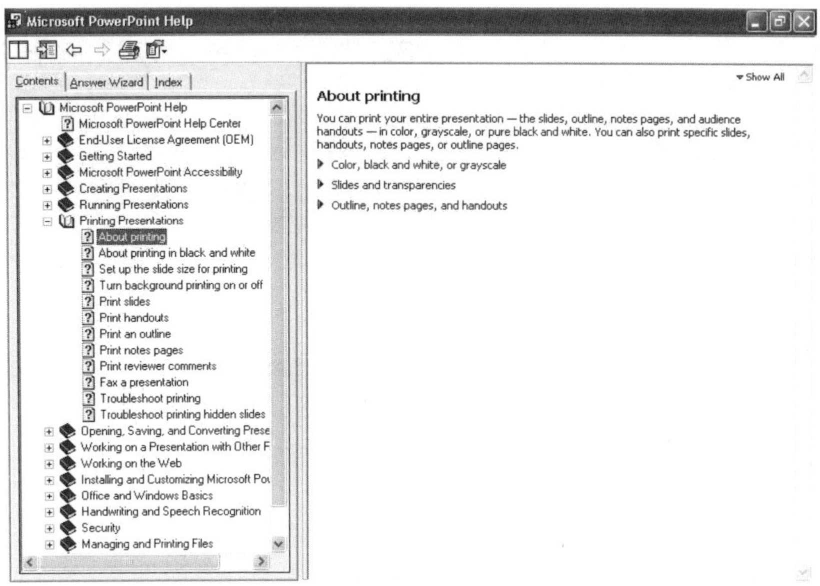

Answer Wizard tab

Type your question in the box at the top-left of the dialog box, and click **Search**. PowerPoint displays a list of suggested help topics in the lower-left. Click on a topic to display the associated text in the right pane.

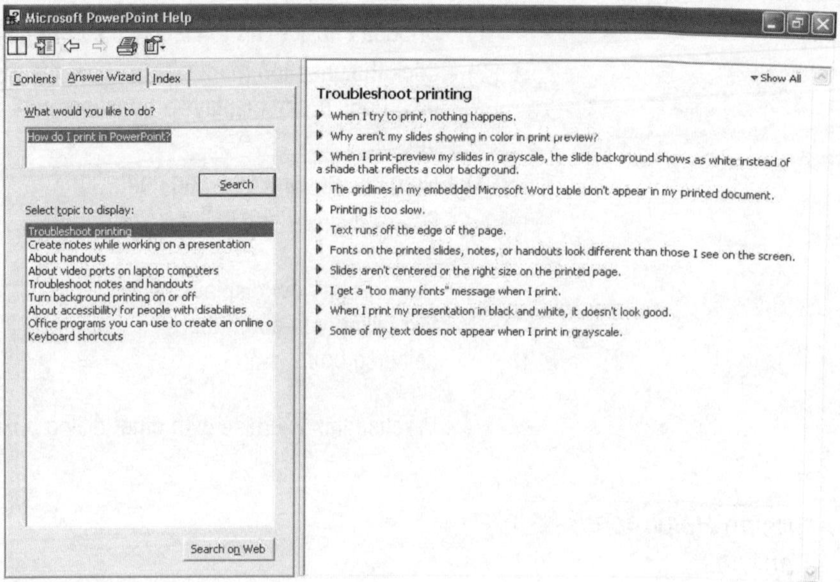

Index tab

Select the word or phrase that you are interested in and click **Search**. PowerPoint displays all matches from the online help in the lower-left dialog box. When you find the index entry you are looking for, click it to display the associated text in the right pane.

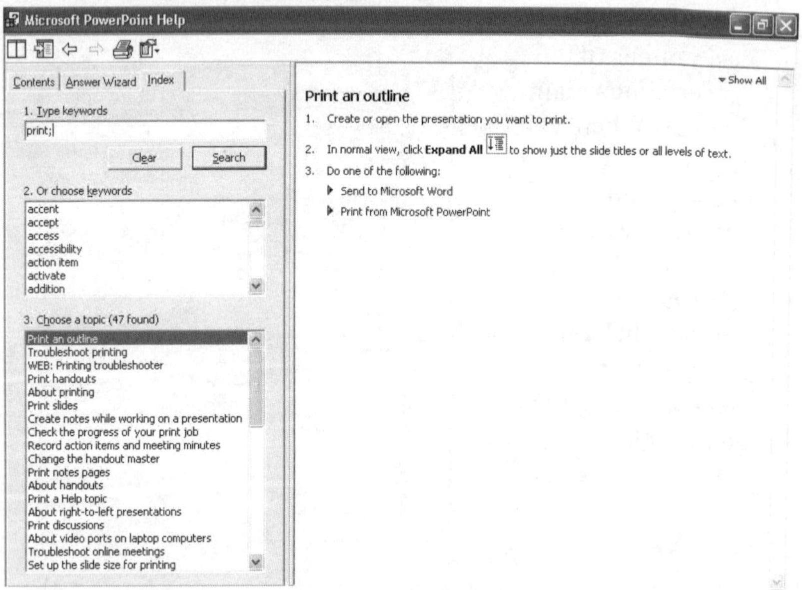

You can access online help from the **Help** menu. Choose **Help | Microsoft PowerPoint Help** or click **Online Help** on the *Standard* toolbar to display the three-tab dialog box. You can also access the **Help** menu by typing your question into the *Type a question for help* dialog box. This is located on the top-right of your screen, above the *Standard* toolbar.

As you search through and read online help topics, you will see the following buttons at the top of the online help window:

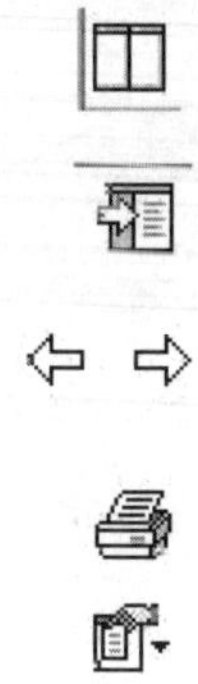

- **Auto Tile:** Enables you to view both the online help dialog box and the document that you were working on.
- **Hide/Show:** Hides or displays the left pane of the online help dialog box.
- **Back/Forward:** Moves you backwards and forwards through previously visited help topics.
- **Print:** Prints the currently displayed help topic.
- **Options:** Offers a number of display choices.

Take a few minutes to look through PowerPoint's online help system.

Closing a presentation

To close a PowerPoint presentation:

- Choose **File | Close**

  -or-

- Click the **Close** button on the presentation window.

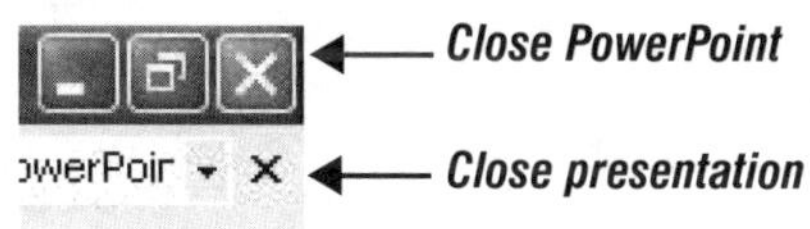

If you have made changes to the presentation since you last saved it, PowerPoint prompts you to save the changes before it closes the file.

Quitting PowerPoint

To leave PowerPoint:

- Choose **File | Exit**.

  -or-

- Click the **Close** button on the PowerPoint window.

If you have left open any files containing unsaved work, PowerPoint prompts you to save them.

You can close your presentation and PowerPoint. You have now completed the first chapter of the ECDL presentations module.

Chapter summary: so now you know

A *presentation* is an address to an audience, accompanied by visual aids, such as slides or overhead projection foils (OHPs), and possibly handouts for the audience. *Presentation software*, such as PowerPoint, helps you prepare visual aids and printed handouts. PowerPoint file names end in .ppt.

The basic building blocks of a presentation are called *slides*. When you create a new presentation, PowerPoint automatically creates a single new slide. You insert further slides individually. PowerPoint always inserts a new slide *after* the one currently displayed. See Exercises 36.1 and 36.2 for examples of how to do this.

When you create a new slide, you can choose from 27 ready-made slide layouts. For example, one layout, called *Title and Text*, is designed for the first or *title slide* of a presentation. Each slide layout contains one or more boxes called *placeholders*, within which you type and edit. See Exercise 36.3 for an example of how to do this.

PowerPoint offers a number of *views* – ways of looking at your slides. In the default Normal view, the screen is split into three panes: a *Slide pane* (where you work with one slide at a time), an *Outline pane* (where you work with the text of all slides), and a *Notes pane* (where you can work with additional text for the presenter). You can adjust the size of the different panes by clicking on and then dragging the pane borders.

You can move forward and backward through a presentation, one slide at a time, by pressing the **Page Down** and **Page Up** keys. Press the **Home** key to go to the very first slide, and press the **End** key to go to the very last slide.

You can modify the toolbar display so that the features you use most often are readily available.

PowerPoint includes a built-in help facility that contains reference material on all the software's functions and many useful tips for creating convincing presentations.

Quick quiz: presentation basics

Circle the correct answer to each of the following multiple-choice questions about presentation basics in PowerPoint.

Q1	PowerPoint always inserts a new slide ...
A.	Before the one currently displayed.
B.	At the start of a sequence of slides.
C.	After the one currently displayed.
D.	At the end of a sequence of slides.

Q2	**Where can you choose ready-made slide layouts for new slides?**
A.	From the *Formatting* toolbar.
B.	From the *Slide Layout* task pane.
C.	From the *Drawing* toolbar.
D.	From the *Standard* toolbar.

Q3	**What can you do in the Outline pane?**
A.	You can work with the text of one slide only.
B.	You can work with the additional text for the presenter.
C.	You can change the outline of all slides.
D.	You can work with the text of all slides.

Q4	**PowerPoint file names end in ...**
A.	.ppt
B.	.doc
C.	.ptt
D.	.xls

Q5	**How do you add a slide to your PowerPoint presentation?**
A.	Choose **File | New**, and select **Blank Presentation** from the *New Presentation* task pane.
B.	Choose **View | Toolbars**, and select *Standard* from the drop-down list displayed.
C.	Choose **File | New**. Click the arrow at the right of the *New Presentation* task pane and select *Slide Layout* from the drop-down list. Select the slide layout that you want to use.
D.	Choose **Insert | New Slide** or click **New Slide** on the *Standard* toolbar.

Answers

1: C, **2:** B, **3:** D, **4:** A, **5:** D.

Chapter 37: Working with views and bullet points

In this chapter

In Chapter 36 you learnt how to create a presentation by inserting a series of individual slides and typing text on each one. Now you will discover a second method: entering the text of all slides in the Outline pane, thus avoiding the need to switch forward and backward through individual slides.

Also in this chapter you will learn about Slide Sorter view, which enables you to display all slides in a presentation at once and to check that the appearance of slides is consistent.

You can use the Outline pane and Slide Sorter view for changing the order of the slides in your presentation, and for copying slides within and between presentations.

New skills

At the end of this chapter you should be able to:

- Open a saved presentation.
- Promote or demote the level of a bullet point.
- Increase or decrease the spacing between bullet points.
- Copy or cut and paste text within a slide or presentation and between presentations.
- Copy slides within and between presentations.
- Import text from Microsoft Word or another non-PowerPoint source.
- Change the bullet character.
- Apply and change numbered bullets.
- Run a PowerPoint presentation on your computer.
- Hide and unhide individual slides.

New words

At the end of this chapter you should be able to explain the following terms:

- Bullet point
- Outline pane
- Slide Sorter view

Opening a presentation

In this chapter you will work with the three-slide presentation that you created in Chapter 36. You begin by opening your saved presentation.

Exercise 37.1: Opening a presentation

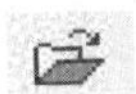

File Open button

1) How you open a saved presentation depends on whether PowerPoint is already open on your PC: if PowerPoint is not already open, open it now.
2) If PowerPoint is already open, choose **File | Open** or click **File Open** on the *Standard* toolbar. You can also open your presentation from the *New Presentation* task pane.
3) Locate and select the three-slide presentation that you saved in Chapter 36 (we called it KBpres1). Click **OK**. Your presentation now opens on the screen.

Different levels of bullet points

Except for the title slide, the text on PowerPoint slides typically consists of *bullet points* – a bullet character (•) followed by one or by a few words of text.

Different bullet points may contain different categories or levels of information. Consider the following sample slide:

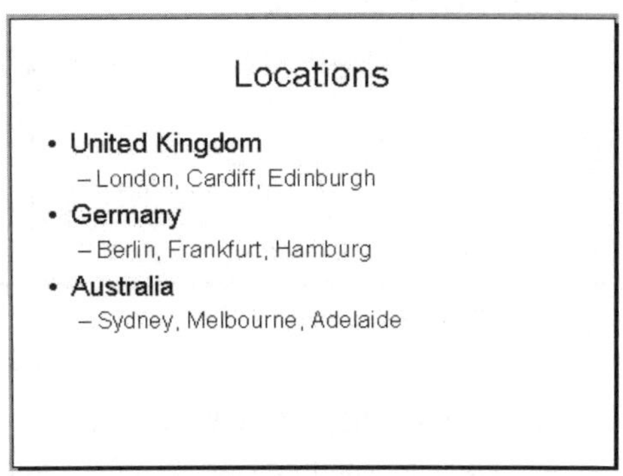

The slide has two levels of bullet points: three *main* bullet points, each of which contains three minor points. The two different levels of bullet points are distinguished by:

- Different indents (the distance from the left edge of the slide).
- Different font size (the minor bullet points are in smaller text).
- Different bullet characters.

PowerPoint enables you to change bullet point levels with a single mouse click; it alters the indents, font size and bullet characters for you. Follow Exercise 37.2 to discover how.

Bullet point
A bullet character (such as •) followed by one or more words of text. Bullet points may be at different levels, indicated by their indentation, bullet character and font size.

Exercise 37.2: Promoting and demoting bullets

1) Use the **Page Down** or **Page Up** keys to display the second slide of your presentation.
2) Click at the end of the fourth bullet point.

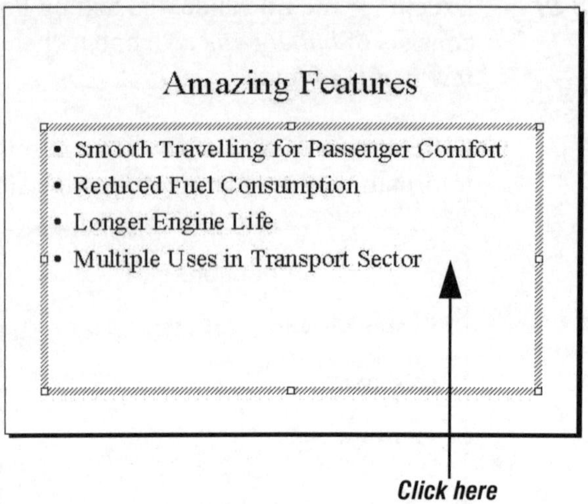

3) Press **Enter** to begin a new bullet point.
4) Type the following three words, pressing **Enter** after the first and second words only:

   Cars

   Bicycles

   Trucks

   Your new bullet points should look as shown.
5) Click at the start of the word 'Cars'. Then drag down and to the right with the mouse until you have selected all three new bullet points.

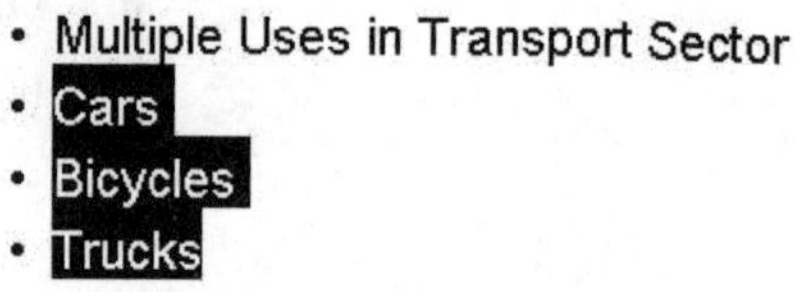

6) Click the **Demote** button (on the *Outlining* toolbar at the left of the screen). Notice how PowerPoint changes the display of the selected bullet points. Click anywhere else on the slide to deselect the three bullet points.

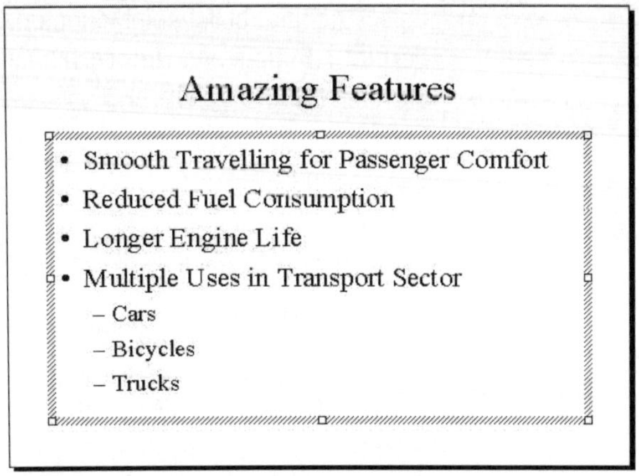

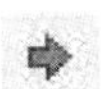
Demote button

Promote button

7) As practice, select the three bullet points again, click the **Promote** button, and view the effect on the bullet points. When finished, and with the bullet points selected, click **Demote**. The bullet points are again demoted.

The three demoted bullet points are variously known as minor bullets, sub-bullets or level-two bullets. You are advised not to use more than two levels of bullets on a slide. Otherwise, you risk confusing your audience.

Changing the bullet character

By default, PowerPoint uses the filled circle (•) and the dash (–) as the bullet characters for the first two levels of bullet points.

As Exercise 37.3 shows, you can choose from a range of other bullet character and colour options.

Exercise 37.3: Changing the bullet character

1) Display the second slide of your presentation, and select the first bullet point.

• Smooth Travelling for Passenger Comfort

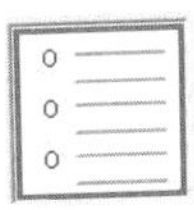
Hollow circle bullet

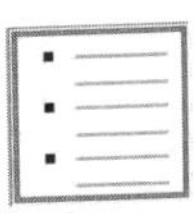
Filled square bullet

2) Choose **Format | Bullets and Numbering**. On the **Bulleted** tab of the dialog box, select the hollow circle bullet and click **OK**.

3) Select the second bullet point, choose **Format | Bullets and Numbering**, and on the **Bulleted** tab select the filled square bullet.

Click the arrow to the right of the **Color** drop-down list and select the colour blue. When finished, click **OK**.

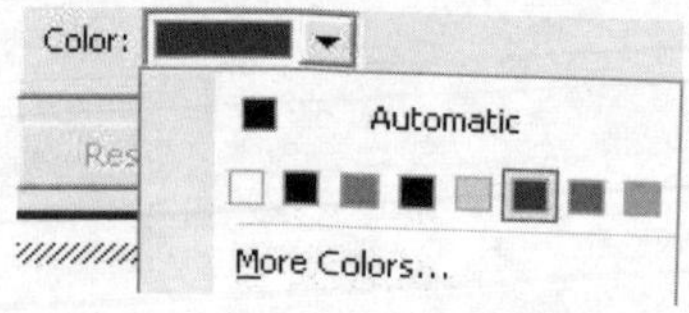

4) Select the third bullet point, choose **Format | Bullets and Numbering**, and click the **Picture** button.

You are now shown PowerPoint's *Picture Bullet* gallery.

Select a bullet by clicking on it, and then click **OK** to close the *Picture Bullet* gallery.

PowerPoint replaces the default bullet character with the bullet you selected from its *Picture Bullet* gallery.

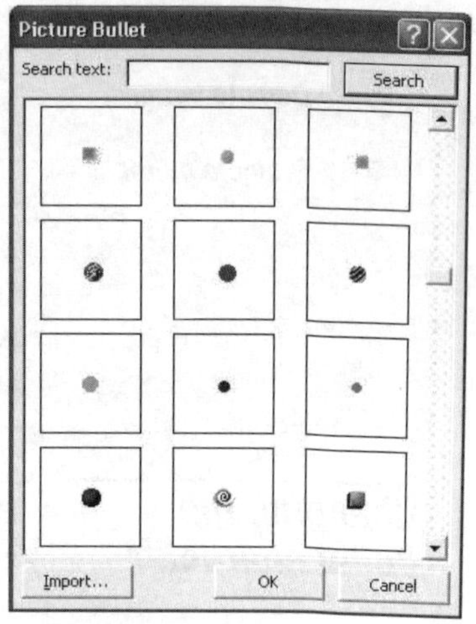

5) Select the three minor bullet points on the slide, choose **Format | Bullets and Numbering**, and on the **Bulleted** tab click the **Customize** button.

In the *Symbol* dialog box, select Wingdings in the *Font* drop-down list, click on any displayed character to select it, and then click **OK** twice.

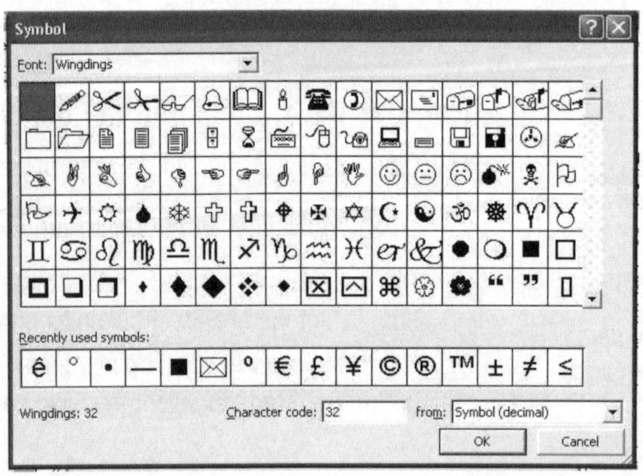

Your selected bullet character is now applied to the three minor bullet points.

6) The purpose of this exercise is not to change your slide but to show you the choices available for selecting bullet characters.

As the final step, press the **Undo** button repeatedly to return your slide to what it was at the beginning of this exercise.

Numbering bullet points

You can use sequentially increasing numbers (1, 2, 3, ...) or letters (a, b, c, ...) as bullet characters on your slides. Numbered lists are an appropriate choice when the order of reading is important, such as in directions and instructions.

To apply a numbered list to selected text:

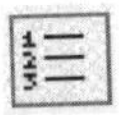

Numbering button

- Click **Numbering** on the *Formatting* toolbar.

  -or-

- Choose **Format | Bullets and Numbering**, click the **Numbered** tab, select your numbering option, and click **OK**.

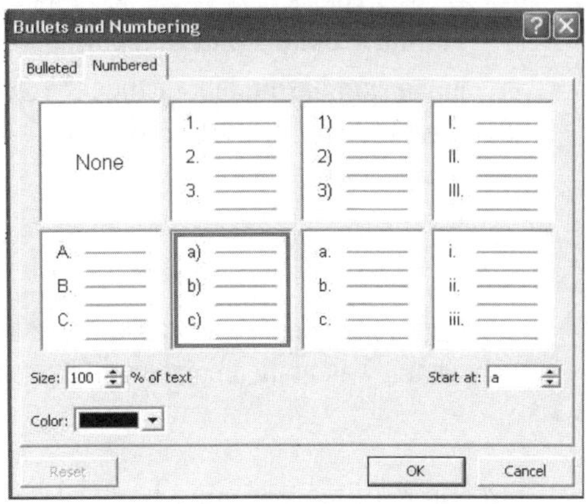

You can accept or change the default colour and starting value of the number or letter, and its size relative to the text of the line.

Exercise 37.4: Creating a slide with numbered bullets

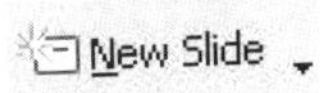

1) You are about to add a fourth slide at the end of your presentation. So, display your third slide, entitled 'Choice of Colours', and click **New Slide** on the *Standard* toolbar.
2) In the *New Presentation* task pane, select **Slide Layout** from the drop-down list. Under **Text Layouts**, select the *Title and Text* option.

   Type the following text in the top placeholder of your new slide:

   Marketing Plan
3) In the lower placeholder of your new slide, type the following bullet points:

   Develop pricing plan

Build distribution network

National launch

International launch

4) Select the four bullet points that you typed in step 3, and click **Numbering** on the *Formatting* toolbar.

   PowerPoint applies its default numbering style to your bullet points.

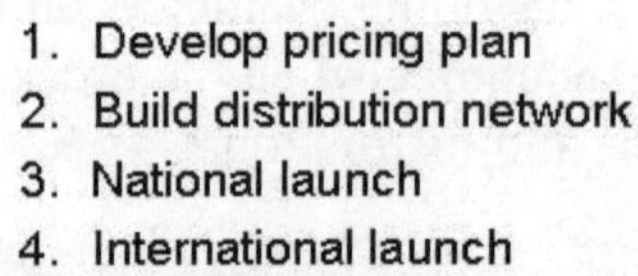

In the next exercise you will change the numbering style.

Exercise 37.5: Changing the numbering style

1) Display your fourth slide, select the four numbered bullet points, and choose **Format | Bullets and Numbering**.
2) In the **Numbering** tab, change the *Size* to 120, the *Color* to green, and the *Start at* value to 2. Click **OK**.

   Notice the effect on your slide. Use the **Undo** button to return your slide to what it was at the beginning of this exercise.

Line spacing

On some slides you may have very few lines of text. On others you may have quite a lot. PowerPoint allows you to space out or squeeze lines of text so that they fit the area of a single slide. Exercise 37.6 provides an example.

Exercise 37.6: Changing the line spacing

1) Display the third slide of your presentation.
2) Select the two bullet points in the left placeholder.

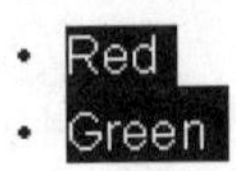

   Choose **Format | Line Spacing**, change the *Line spacing* value from 1 to 2 lines, and click **OK**.

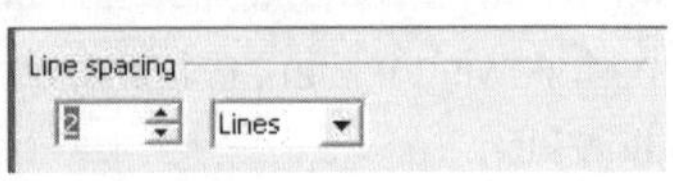

3) Repeat step 2 for the two bullet points in the right placeholder.

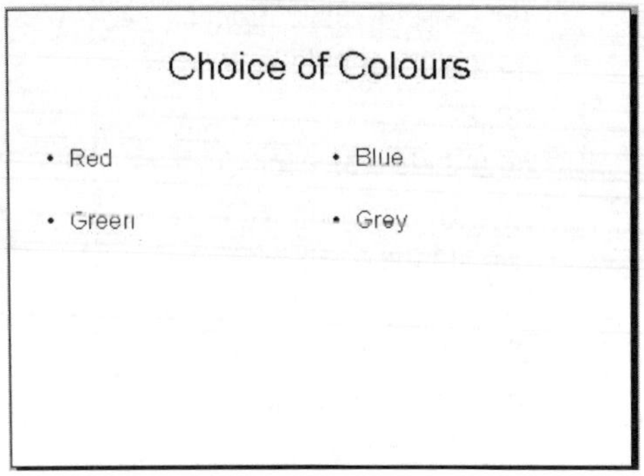

Your slide should now look as shown.

Save your presentation.

The *Line Spacing* dialog box also allows you to alter the spacing before and after one or more selected lines.

Text alignment

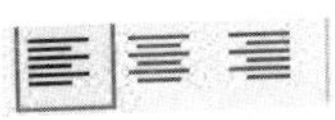

Alignment buttons: left, centre and right

Alignment refers to the *position* of the text on a slide. Each of the three common options (left, right and centre-aligned) can be applied by clicking the associated button on the *Formatting* toolbar or by choosing **Format | Alignment**.

By default, PowerPoint applies the following text alignment to slides:

- **Title slide:** All text is centre-aligned.
- **Other slides:** Title text is centred; bullet points are left-aligned.

As with other Microsoft Office applications, aligning text in PowerPoint is a two-step process: first select, then align. Exercise 37.7 shows you how.

Exercise 37.7: Changing text alignment

1) Display your second slide and select all the bullet points in the lower placeholder.
2) Choose **Format | Alignment | Center** or click the **Center-align** button.

Click anywhere else to deselect the bullet points. Your slide should look as shown.

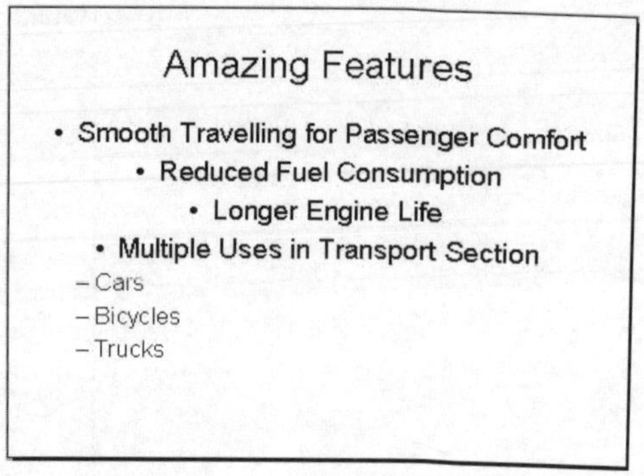

3) Your slide was easier to read before you centre-aligned the text. Select all the bullet points again, and click the **Left-align** button. Your slide should look as it was at the start of this exercise. Save your presentation.

A fourth alignment option of justified text is available only with the **Format | Alignment** command and not on the *Formatting* toolbar. Avoid justifying text on slides: it can be difficult for your audience to read.

About outlines

In PowerPoint, an outline is the text of all slides in a presentation, with the text positioned in such a way that you can identify:

- Text that is the *title* of a slide.
- Text that is a *bullet point* within a slide.

Consider the following presentation about ECDL, written as an outline:

ECDL: An Overview
Benefits for Schools
    Computer literacy for pupils
    Modular, practical syllabus
    Not tied to one IT supplier
Benefits for Colleges
Benefits for Training Providers
Benefits for Employers
    Skills benchmark for new employees
    Organization-wide competence
    Reduction in IT support costs

As you can see, there are five slide titles. Of these, only slide 2 (Benefits for Schools) and slide 5 (Benefits for Employers) currently contain bullet points. Notice that the text of the bullet points is indented further than the text of the slide titles. (The term indented means moved in from the left margin.)

Working in the Outline pane

The Outline pane in Normal view enables you to enter and edit text throughout your presentation without the need to switch forward and backward through individual slides. You can also use the Outline pane to change the levels of text and to change the order of the slides.

Outline pane
In Normal view, this shows the text of all your slides, so that you can judge how well your ideas and text flow from one slide to the next.

In Exercise 37.8 you will create a new presentation, and type and structure its text in the Outline pane.

Exercise 37.8: Creating a presentation in the Outline pane

File New button

1) Click **File New** on the *Standard* toolbar.
2) In the *New Presentation* task pane, select **Slide Layout** from the drop-down list. Under *Text Layouts*, select the *Title Slide* option.
3) Click on the Outline pane (the tab located on the left of the screen).

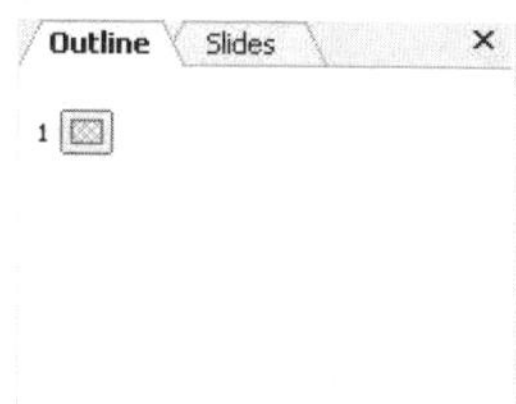

4) Click anywhere in the Outline pane to select it. Type the following two lines, pressing **Enter** after the first line only:

   ECDL: An Overview
   ABC Training Corporation

   Your text should look as shown.

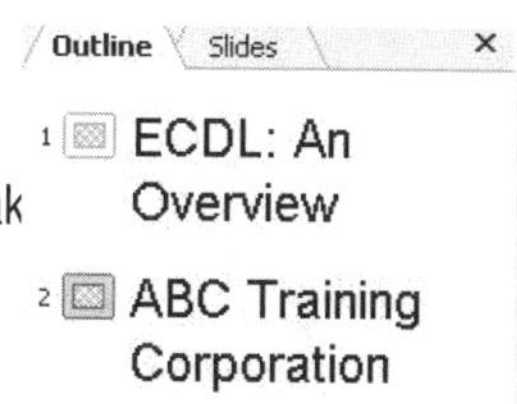

   Notice that the second line of text automatically tak
   previous one: it appears as a slide title.

Demote button

5) Click anywhere in your second line of text, and then click **Demote** on the *Formatting* toolbar.

   Your second line is now bullet-point text within the first slide rather than a slide title.

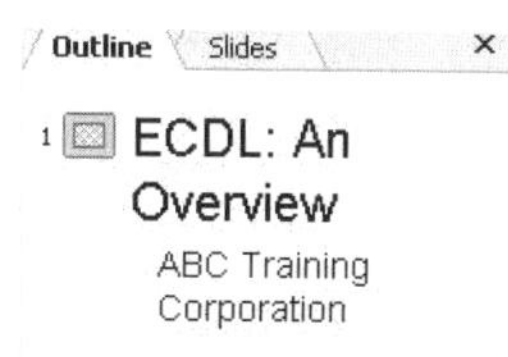

6) Press **Enter** at the end of your second text line and type the following four lines, pressing **Enter** after the first three:

    Benefits for Schools
    Benefits for Colleges
    Benefits for Training Providers
    Benefits for Employers

    Your typed text should look as shown.

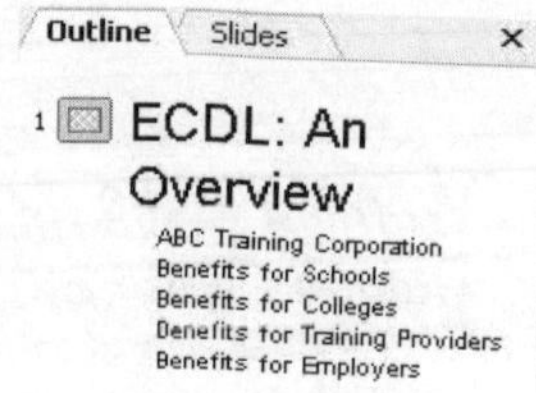

7) Select the four lines that you have just typed and click **Promote** on the *Formatting* toolbar. PowerPoint changes the level of the selected lines so that they are now slide titles.

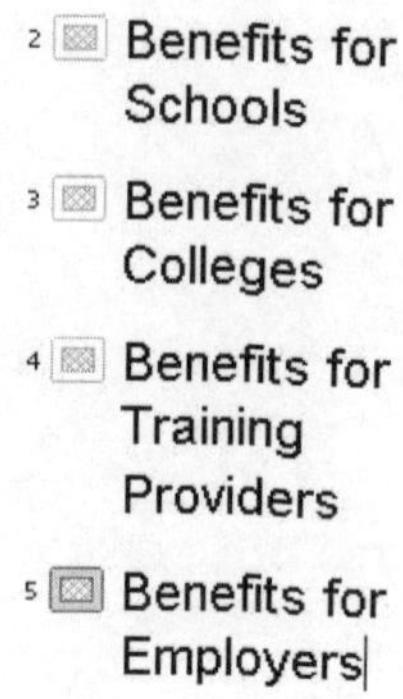

8) Click at the end of the line that contains the title of slide 2, 'Benefits for Colleges', press **Enter**, click **Demote**, and type the following lines of text:

    Computer literacy for pupils
    Modular, practical syllabus
    Not tied to one IT supplier

9) Click at the end of the line that contains the title of slide 3, 'Benefits for Colleges', press **Enter**, click **Demote**, and type the following lines of text:

    Increased staff efficiency
    Students better able to use IT facilities
    Internationally recognized qualification

10) Click at the end of the line that contains the title of slide 4, 'Benefits for Training Providers', press **Enter**, click **Demote**, and type the following lines of text:

    Capacity to offer valued qualification
    Easy-to-deliver syllabus
    Option to offer walk-in tests

11) Click at the end of the line that contains the title of slide 5, 'Benefits for Employers', press **Enter**, click **Demote**, and type the following lines of text:

    Skills benchmark for new employees
    Organization-wide competence
    Reduction in IT support costs

    Your complete outline should look as shown.

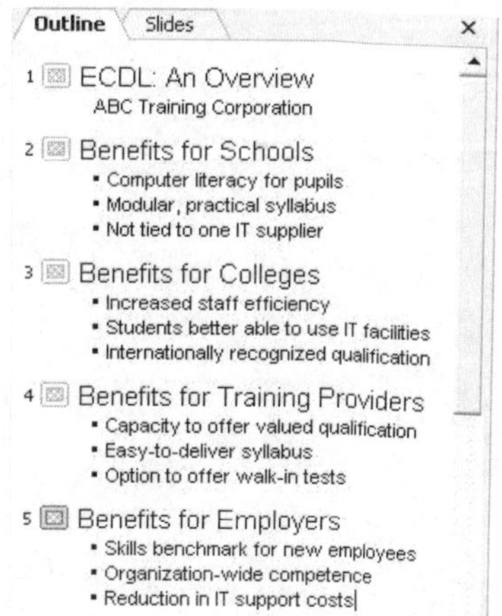

12) Well done! You have created a second presentation. Save your presentation. If your initials are KB, for example, name it KBpres2.

Outline text and individual slides

What is the relationship between the outline text and the content of individual slides?

- **Slides:** PowerPoint creates a new slide for each slide title that you type in the **Outline** pane.
- **Bullet points:** PowerPoint inserts the demoted text lines in the **Outline** pane as bullet points on the associated slide.

Any text change you make in the **Outline** pane affects the individual slide, and any text change to a slide affects the **Outline** pane.

Switching between presentations

You now have two presentation files open at the same time in PowerPoint. To switch between presentations:

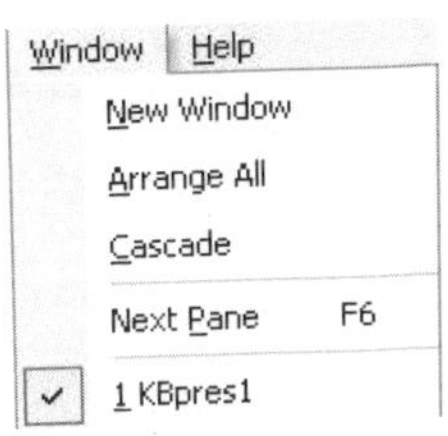

- Click the **Windows** menu, and then choose the file you want to work with.

  -or-
- Click the file name in the *New Presentation* task pane under the heading **New Presentation**.

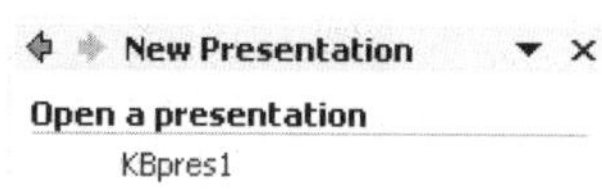

  -or-
- Click the file name on the Windows taskbar.

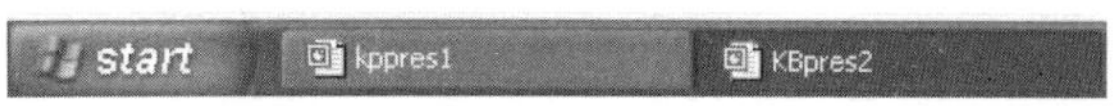

When you have more than one slide in your presentation, you will want to display different slides at different times on your screen. You have two main options:

- Press the **Page Down** or **Page Up** keys to move forward or backward through your presentation, one slide at a time.
- Switch to Slide Sorter view to display all your slides at once, and then double-click on the slide that you want to display.

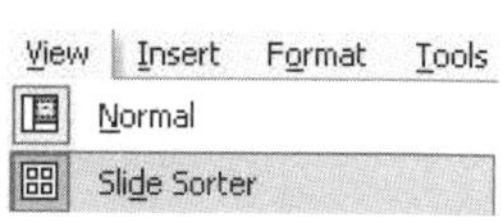

To display your presentation in Slide Sorter view, choose the **View | Slide Sorter** command. You can return from Slide Sorter view to Normal view by choosing **View | Normal**.

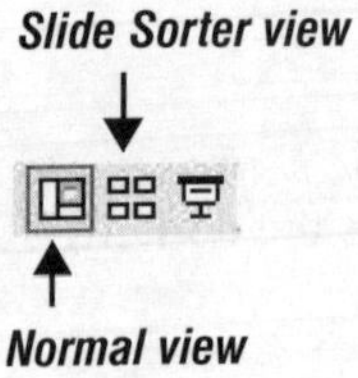

Another way of switching between views is to click on the small buttons at the lower-left of your PowerPoint screen.

Slide Sorter view is also useful for:

- Checking that the appearance of slides is consistent.
- Changing the order of the slides in your presentation.
- Copying slides within and between presentations.

Slide Sorter view
A view where you can see all slides of a presentation at once.

Switch to your first presentation and display it in Slide Sorter view. It should look as shown.

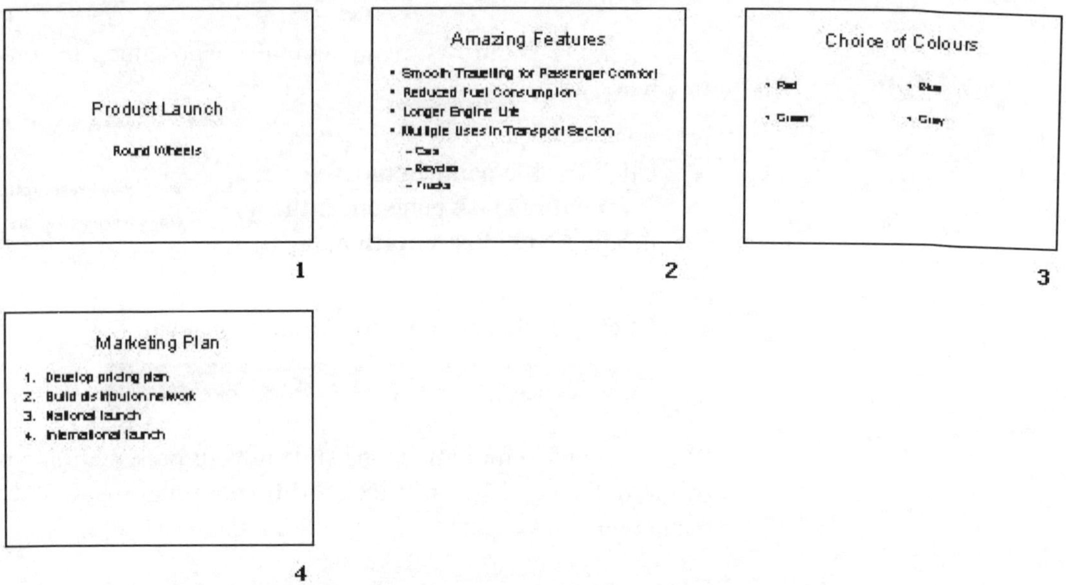

To see the result of the outline that you typed in Exercise 37.8, switch to your second presentation, and display it in Slide Sorter view. It should look as shown.

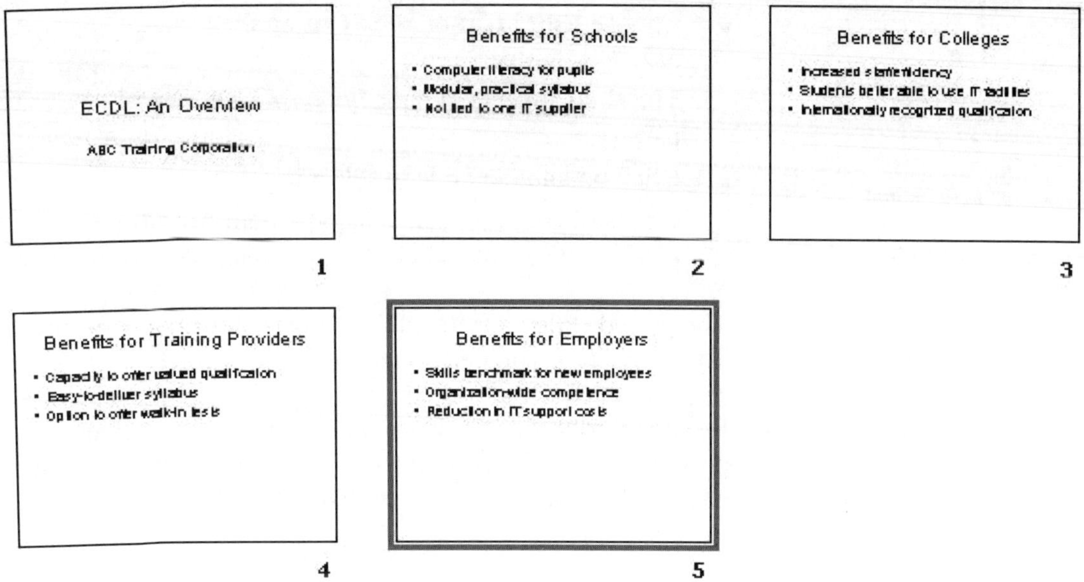

Slide Sorter view and zoom

You can use PowerPoint's Zoom feature to reduce or enlarge the display of Slide Sorter view. The default is 66%, allowing up to four slides to be displayed on a single row.

Reordering slides in Slide Sorter view

When you look at your slides in Slide Sorter view, you may decide to change the order in which they appear. You can do this in two ways:

- By dragging them with the mouse (better for small presentations).
- By using cut-and-paste (better for larger presentations).

Reordering by dragging

Follow these steps:

- In Slide Sorter view, click on the slide that you want to move to select it. Notice that PowerPoint displays a thicker border around your selected slide.
- Drag it with the mouse so that a vertical line appears to the left of where you want to position the slide.
- Release the mouse button.

Reordering by cut and paste

You can cut, copy and paste slides in PowerPoint as you would text in a Word document. Follow these steps:

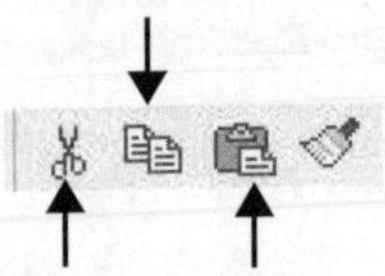

- In Slide Sorter view, click the slide to select it.
- Choose **Edit | Cut** or click **Cut** on the *Standard* toolbar.

  The slide appears in the *Clipboard* task pane.

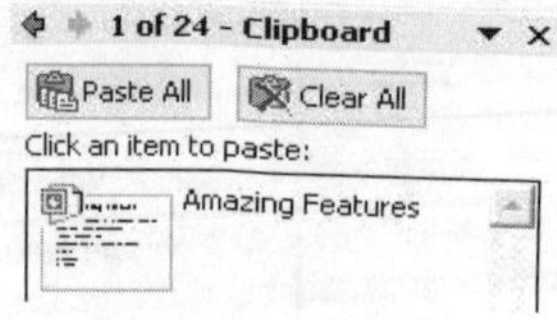

- Click on another slide to select it.
- Choose **Edit | Paste** or select the item from the *Clipboard* task pane. You can also click **Paste** on the *Standard* toolbar.

The pasted slide appears after (to the right or beneath) the slide you selected before you performed the paste action.

In Slide Sorter view, practise reordering the five slides in your presentation by dragging them to a new location, and then cutting and pasting them back to their original location.

Keyboard shortcuts

A fast way to perform copy, cut and paste actions is to use the relevant shortcut keys. To copy a selected item, for example, hold down the **Ctrl** key and press the letter 'c'.

Action	Keyboard shortcut
Copy	**Ctrl+c**
Cut	**Ctrl+x**
Paste	**Ctrl+v**

Copying and moving slides

You can copy and move slides within a presentation, and between different presentations. Exercises 37.9 and 37.10 provide examples.

Exercise 37.9: Copying a slide within a presentation

1) Display your second presentation, entitled 'ECDL: An Overview'. In Slide Sorter view, click on your title (first) slide to select it.

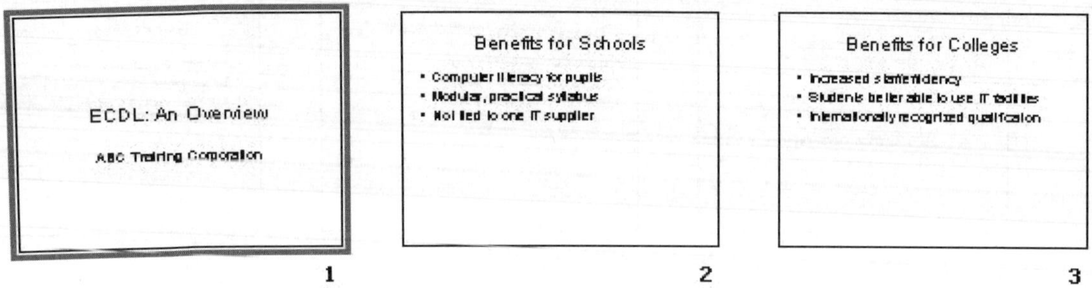

2) Press **Ctrl+c** to copy your title slide.
3) Click on your fifth slide to select it.

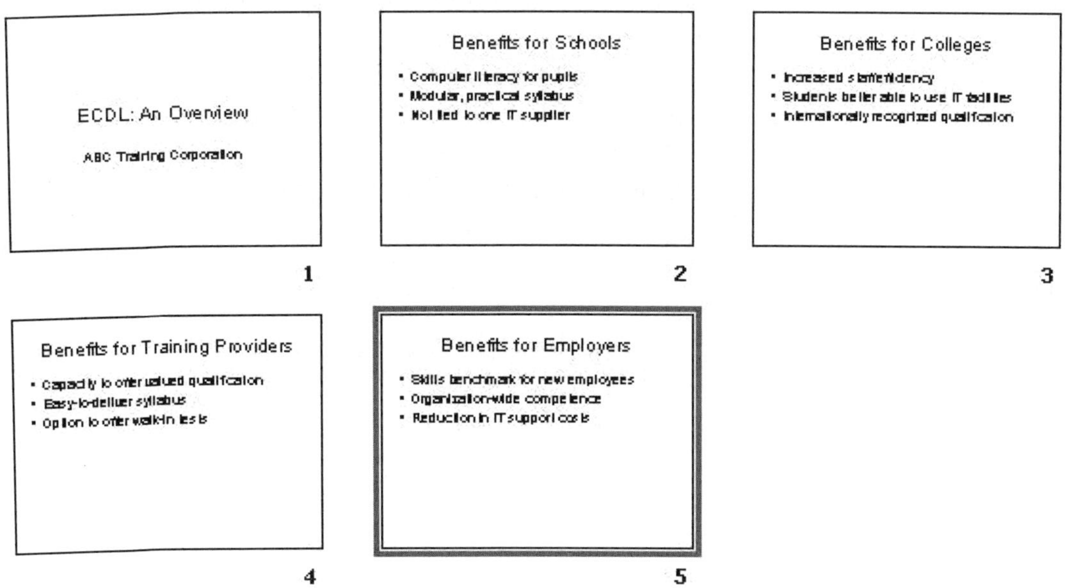

4) Press **Ctrl+v** to paste the title slide at the end of your presentation.
Your presentation now has six slides. In the final step, you will delete slide 6.

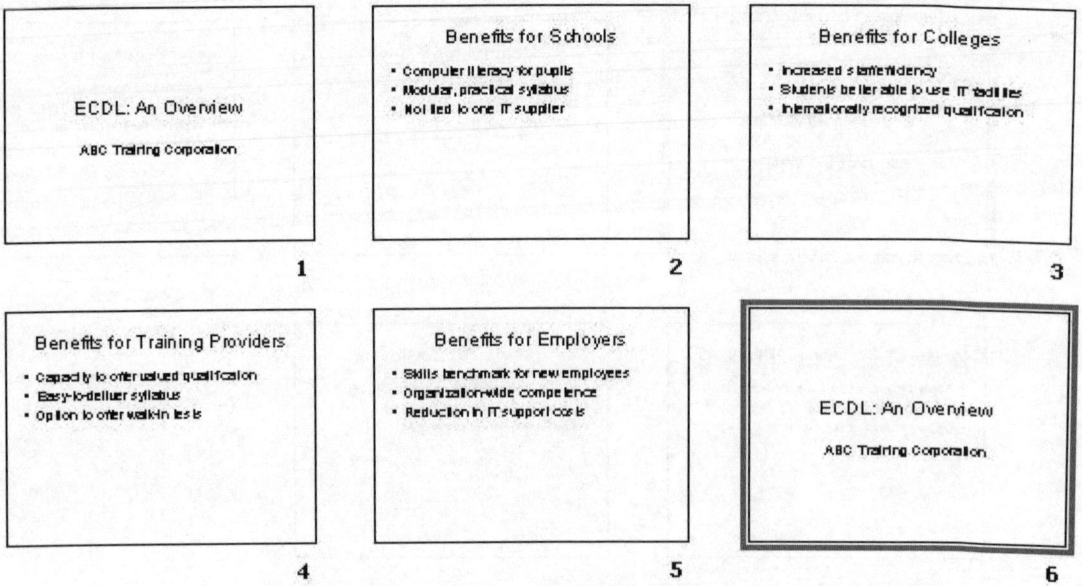

5) Select slide 6 and press the **Delete** key.

Exercise 37.10: Copying a slide between presentations

1) Display your second presentation in Slide Sorter view. We called it KBpres2.ppt.
2) Click the title slide, and press **Ctrl+c**.
3) Switch to your first presentation, entitled 'Product Launch', and display it in Slide Sorter view.
4) Click the second slide, entitled 'Amazing Features', to select it.

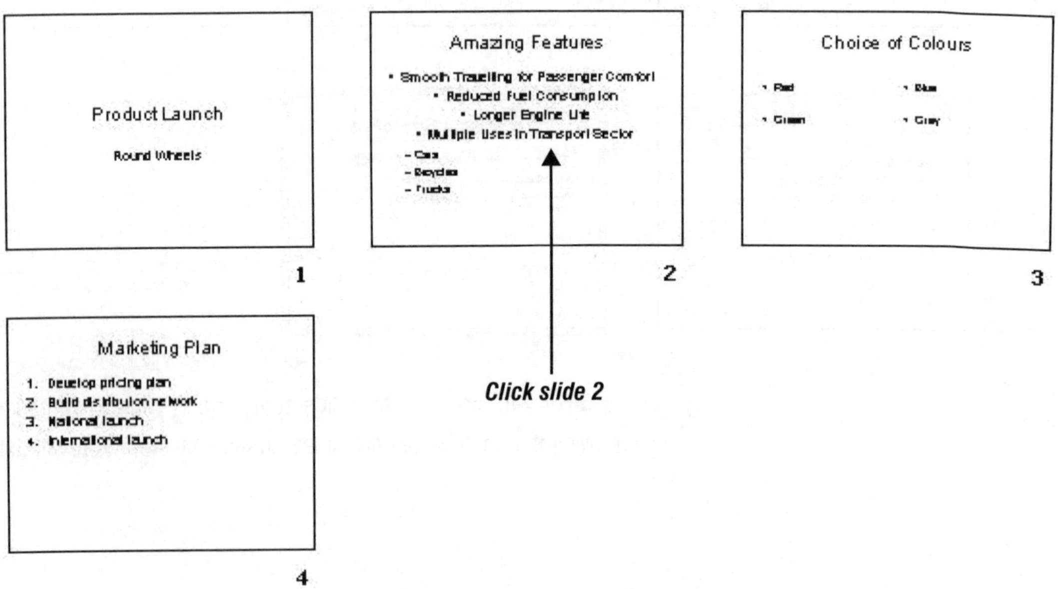

5) Press **Ctrl+v**. PowerPoint pastes the slide as the new third slide of your 'Product Launch' presentation.

6) With the pasted slide selected, press the **Delete** key.

Copying and moving text

To copy or move text from one slide to another, or between different slides of the same or different presentations:

- Select the text by clicking and dragging.
- Copy or cut the text.
- Position your cursor where you want the text to appear.
- Paste the text.

Exercise 37.11 provides an example of cut-and-paste.

Exercise 37.11: Moving text within a slide

1) In Normal view, display the third slide of your first presentation, entitled 'Choice of Colours'.

2) Select the two bulleted points in the right placeholder, and press **Ctrl+x**. The selected text is removed from the right placeholder.

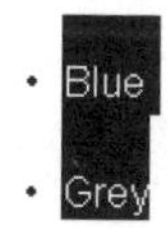

3) Click in the left placeholder at the end of the second bullet point.

4) Press **Enter**. PowerPoint creates a new line beginning with a bullet character.

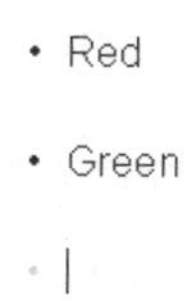

5) Press **Ctrl+v** to paste the two bullet points.

   If PowerPoint adds an additional bullet character on a new line after the two bullet points that you pasted, click the **Backspace** key twice – once to remove the bullet character and a second time to remove the new line.

6) Click anywhere in the right placeholder, and then click on its border. Press the **Delete** key to remove the right placeholder.

7) Choose **Format | Slide Layout** to display a list of slide layouts in the *Slide Layout* task pane. Under **Text Layouts**, select *Title and Text*.

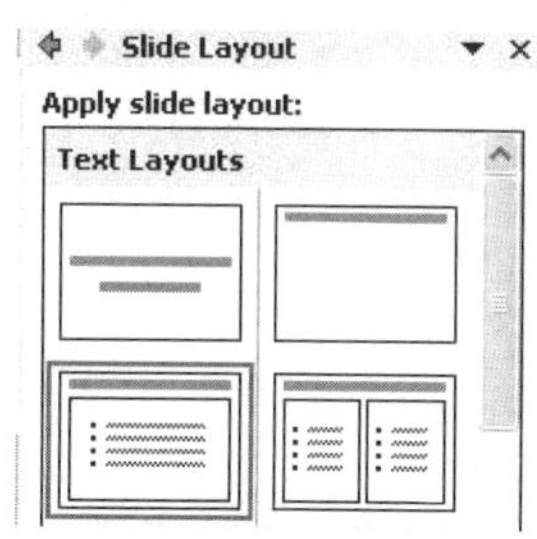

Your third slide should look as shown.

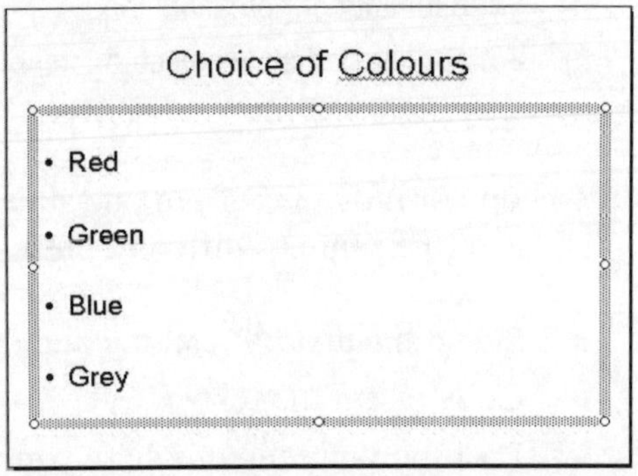

Importing text from another application

If you have text in another application, such as Microsoft Word, you can use that text in PowerPoint without having to retype it. The simplest way is as follows:

- In the other application, select the text.
- Copy it.
- In PowerPoint, position your cursor where you want the text to appear.
- Paste the text.

Follow the steps in Exercise 37.12 to discover how.

Exercise 37.12: Importing non-PowerPoint text

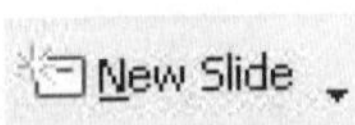

New Slide button

1) Display the second slide, entitled 'Amazing Features', of your first presentation. In Normal view, click the **New Slide** button on the *Standard* toolbar.
   The new slide becomes the third slide of your presentation; the former third and fourth slides are now your fourth and fifth slides.
2) In the *Slide Layout* task pane, choose the *Title and Text* slide layout under **Text Layouts**.
3) Click in the top placeholder and type the text:
   Online Help Text
4) Choose **Help | Microsoft PowerPoint Help**. If this is not already displayed, click the **Contents** tab.
5) Click the heading '*What's New*', in the right pane of the online help window. Select the heading '*Key new features in Microsoft PowerPoint*', and press **Ctrl+c** to copy it.

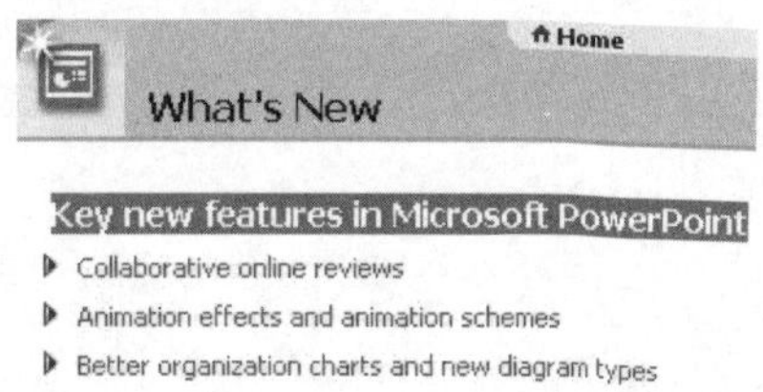

6) Switch back to PowerPoint. Ensure that the new slide that you created in step 1 is displayed.

Click at the first bullet character, and press **Ctrl+v** to paste the selected text. Put the cursor at the end of the text and press **Enter**. Your slide should look as shown.

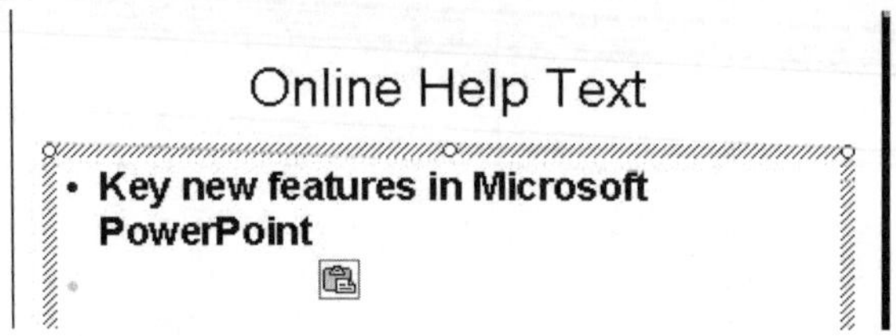

7) Repeats steps 5 and 6 for the following other headings from PowerPoint online help:

More new features in PowerPoint

New Microsoft Office features

(Don't select from the list of hyperlinked headings near the top of the online help right-hand pane. Instead, select the headings as they appear down through the body of the text.)

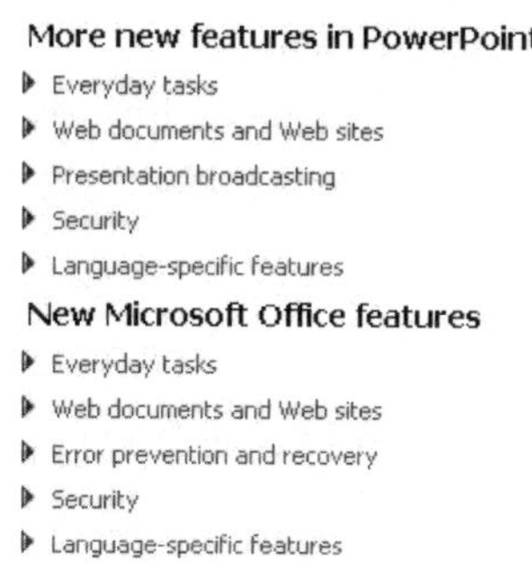

8) The inserted text on your slide is in bold – as it was in the online help.

Select the three bullet points and click **Bold** on the *Formatting* toolbar to remove the bold effect.

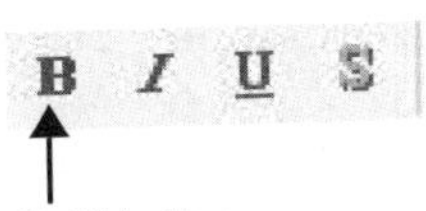

Bold button

Your slide should look as shown. Save your presentation.

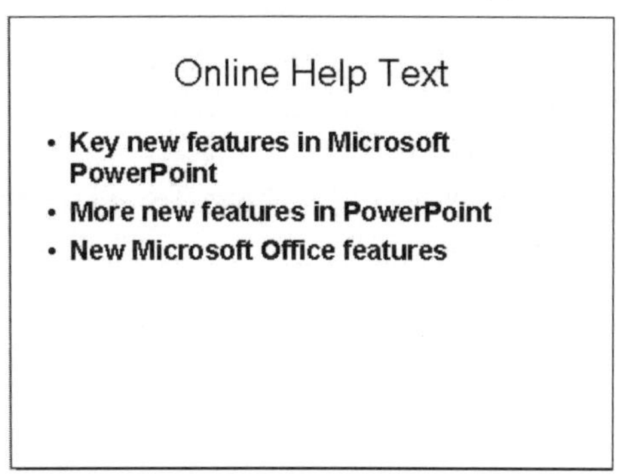

9) Close the **Online Help** window.

10) Display your presentation in Slide Sorter view. It should look as shown.

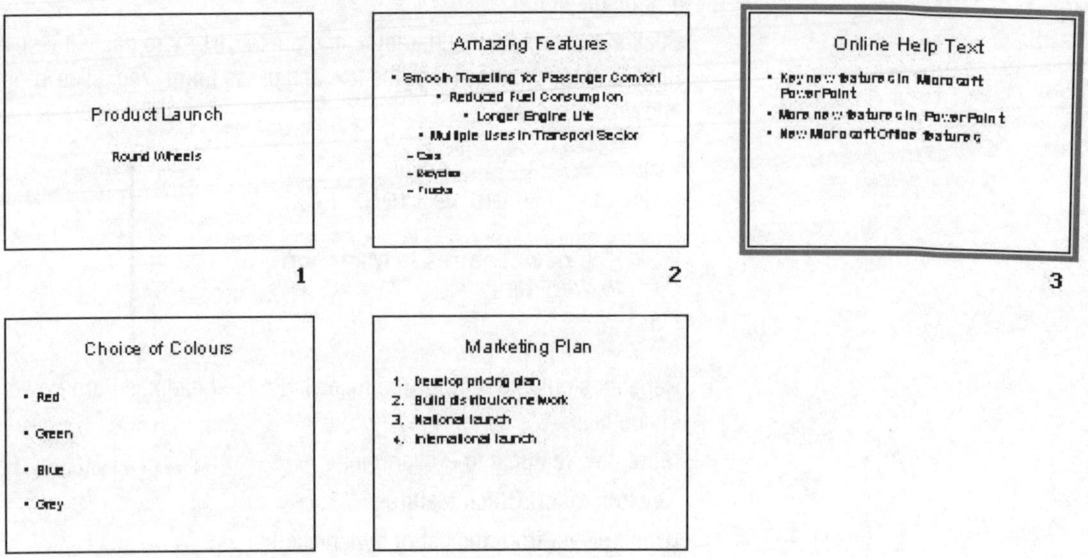

You can use the same method for copying the following to PowerPoint:

- Text from a Word document.
- A cell, cell range or chart from an Excel worksheet.
- A picture (such as a scanned photograph) from a graphics application.

Running your presentation

When you have created a number of slides, you can preview how they will look to your audience by choosing **View | Slide Show**. This will start the display at your first slide. To start the display at the current slide, click **Slide Show** (from current slide) at the bottom of the screen.

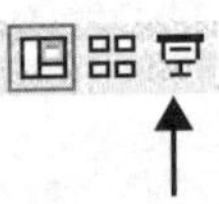

Slide Show button

You can also start a slide show on any slide. Choose **Slide Show | Set Up Show** and then specify the range of slides you want to present.

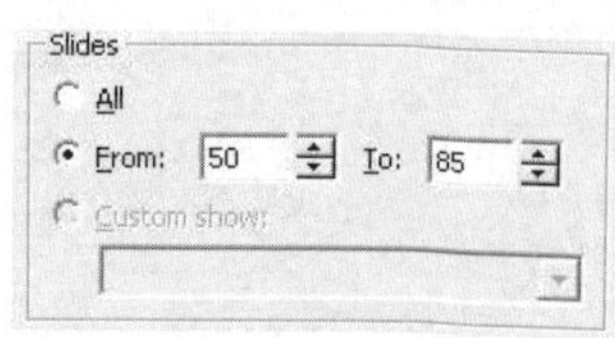

Your slides are shown without any PowerPoint menus, toolbars or other screen elements that are displayed when you are creating or editing slides. To move between slides:

- Press the **Page Down**, **Page Up**, **Home** or **End keys**, as you would in Normal view.

  -or-

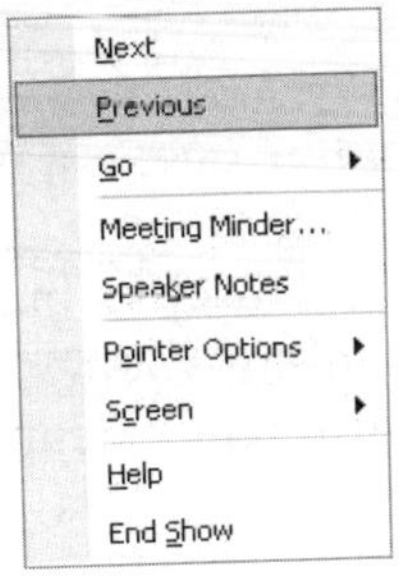

- Right-click anywhere on the screen with the mouse, and choose a navigation option from the pop-up menu displayed.

  -or-

- Click anywhere on the screen to move forward to the next slide.

To exit the slide show and return to your previous view, press the **Esc** key.

Slide Show view
A view you use for presenting your slides to your audience. PowerPoint's various menus and toolbars are not displayed in Slide Show view.

Deleting and hiding slides

In Exercises 37.9 and 37.10, you deleted slides in Slide Sorter view by selecting them and then pressing the **Delete** key. To delete a slide in Normal view, display the slide and choose **Edit | Delete Slide**.

Practise this command by deleting any of your slides. After deleting the slide, click **Undo** on the *Standard* toolbar to restore it to your presentation. There may be times when you do not want to show a certain slide or slides in a presentation to a particular audience. PowerPoint allows you to hide such slides, so that they remain part of your presentation but are not displayed.

To hide a slide:

- In Normal view, display the slide and choose **Slide Show | Hide Slide**.

  -or-

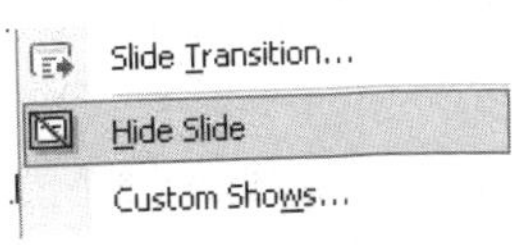

- In Slide Sorter view, click the slide to select it before choosing **Slide Show | Hide Slide**.

To unhide a hidden slide, select it and choose **Slide Show | Hide Slide** again.

Practise this option by hiding a slide, running your presentation again in Slide Show view, and then revealing the slide.

You can now save and close your presentations and close PowerPoint.

You have now completed the second chapter of the ECDL presentations module.

Chapter summary: so now you know

Except for the title slide, the text on PowerPoint slides typically consists of *bullet points* – a bullet character followed by one or a few words of text. *Bullet characters* can be symbols, sequentially increasing numbers (1, 2, 3, ...), or letters (a, b, c, ...). Different bullet points may contain different categories or levels of information. Different *bullet levels*, which are distinguished by different indents, font sizes and bullet characters, may be *demoted* or *promoted*, as required. See Exercises 37.2, 37.3, 37.4 and 37.5.

PowerPoint's *line spacing* feature allows you to space out or squeeze lines of text so that they fit into a single slide. See Exercise 37.6.

By default, PowerPoint centre-aligns text on title slides, and left-aligns text on all other slides. You can override these defaults on individual slides by using the *alignment* options. See Exercise 37.7.

The *Outline pane* of Normal view offers a fast way to enter and edit text, and to change the level of text and the order of slides. See Exercise 37.8.

PowerPoint's *Slide Sorter* allows you to display all slides in a presentation at once. It is useful for checking that the appearance of slides is consistent, changing the order of the slides in your presentation, and copying slides within and between presentations.

You can *copy-and-paste* text and other items from other applications into PowerPoint.

Quick quiz: working with views and bullet points

Circle the correct answer to each of the following multiple-choice questions about working with views and bullet points in PowerPoint.

Q1	The Outline pane of Normal view enables you to ...
A.	Enter and edit text, change the level of the text, and change the order of the slides.
B.	View all slides at once.
C.	Enter and edit text only.
D.	Enter and edit text, and change the order of the slides.

Q2	You access Slide Sorter view by ...
A.	Clicking **View | Slide Sorter**.
B.	Clicking **Slide Show | View Show**.
C.	Clicking **View | Normal**.
D.	Clicking **View | Task Pane | Slide Layout**.

Q3	How do you change the line spacing in a presentation?
A.	Choose **Format | Font**, select the font type required, and click **OK**.
B.	Choose **Format | Line Spacing,** change the line spacing value in the dialog box, and click **OK**.
C.	Choose **Format | Alignment**. Select the alignment option required, for example, **Justify.**
D.	Choose **Format | Slide Layout**. In the *Slide Layout* task pane, select the slide layout required.

Q4	You can't copy-and-paste from an Excel spreadsheet into PowerPoint.
A.	True.
B.	False.

Q5	How do you change a bullet character?
A.	Select the bullet. Click **Demote**. PowerPoint changes the display of the selected bullet.
B.	Choose **Format | Slide Layout**. In the *Slide Layout* task pane, select the slide layout *Title and Text.*
C.	Select the bullet. Choose **Format | Bullets and Numbering**. On the **Numbering** tab, select the required bullet character, and click **OK**.
D.	Select the bullet. Choose **Format | Bullets and Numbering**. On the **Bulleted** tab, select the required bullet character, and click **OK**.

Answers

1: A, **2:** A, **3:** B, **4:** B, **5:** D.

Chapter 38: Formatting your presentation

In this chapter

The presentations that you created in Chapters 36 and 37 contained black text against a plain white background. PowerPoint offers two main ways of formatting your slides to make them more attractive.

The first is to change the appearance of your presentation one slide at a time. The second is to reformat your entire presentation in a single action. The second, global approach is better: it saves you effort and time, and your slides benefit from having a consistent appearance.

New skills

At the end of this chapter, you should be able to:

- Apply text and background effects to individual slides.
- Apply text and background effects to a presentation using the slide master.
- Apply and customize a presentation colour scheme.
- Prepare speaker notes.
- Prepare handouts for your audience.
- Print slides, handouts and speaker notes.

New words

At the end of this chapter you should be able to explain the following terms:

- Slide master
- Colour scheme
- Handout

Presentation format

Slide formatting refers to the appearance of slides in your presentation. It includes:

- **Text format:** The font, size and colour of text on slides, and any text effects such as bold, italics and shadows.
- **Background colour or pattern:** The solid (plain) colour or decorative pattern behind the text of your slides.

One way to format your slides is to change them one slide at a time. That is, display your first slide, reformat the text and background, and repeat this action for all slides in your presentation. Is there a faster way? Yes – in fact there are two.

Making global changes

PowerPoint offers two main methods of reformatting all slides in your presentation in a single operation:

- **Colour schemes:** These are combinations of text and background colours. You simply select the colour scheme you require, and PowerPoint applies it to all your slides. You can even change any of the built-in colour schemes to suit your needs or taste.
- **Slide master:** Every slide in a presentation is based on what PowerPoint calls a slide master. When you change the background or text format on the slide master, all slides on your presentation are updated accordingly.

(A third formatting option, called design templates, is explained in Chapter 39.)

What choices do I have?

As you experiment with PowerPoint's reformatting features, you may be overwhelmed by the number of options available. But really you have only three choices:

- **Dark text, light background:** In a lit room, this is the preferred option.

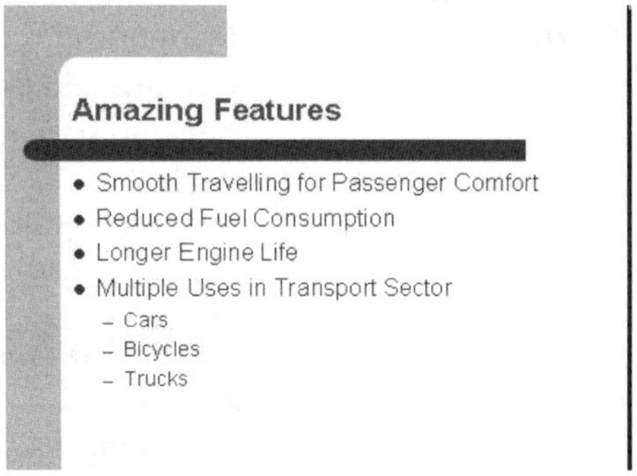

- **Light text, dark background:** In a darkened room, reversed type (text in a light colour, background in a dark colour) is easier for your audience to read.

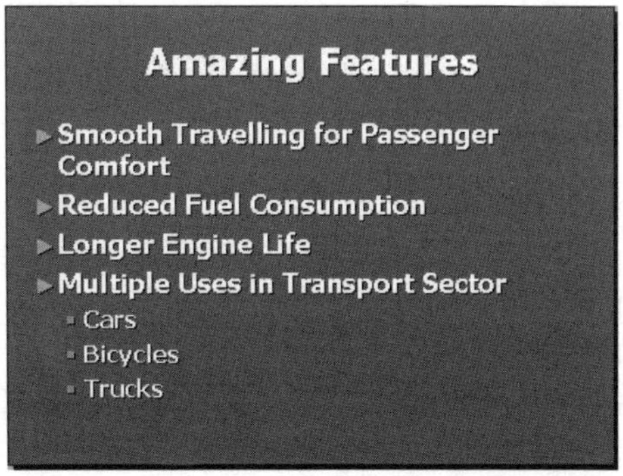

Whichever choice you make, ensure that the colours you choose for text and background are sharply contrasting.

- **Solid or decorative background:** You are not limited to using a solid (single-colour) background in your slides. You can also specify gradients, textures, patterns or pictures.

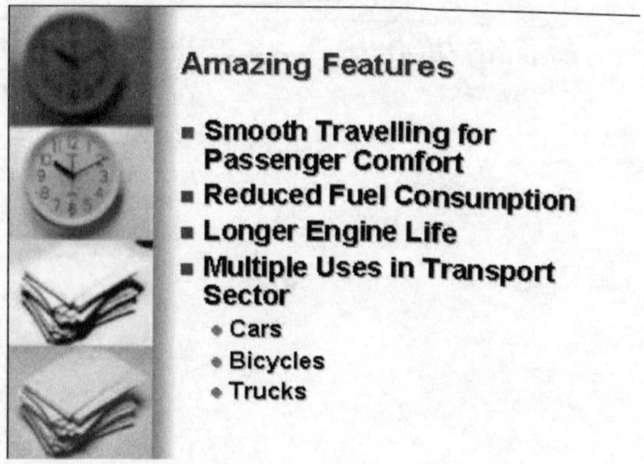

  A word of caution: these decorative background options are intended to make your slides more exciting; however, if you do not use them carefully, they can make your slides illegible.
  A plain slide that can be read easily is much more valuable (to you and your audience) than a fancy one that nobody can read.

Before working with colour schemes and the slide master, you need to be familiar with the text formatting options in PowerPoint.

Text format

Formatting refers to the appearance of text. It includes actions such as making text bolder (heavier), putting it in italics, or placing a shadow beneath it. You may also change the text font, size and colour.

You can apply text formatting by selecting your text, choosing **Format | Font**, selecting your required options, and clicking **OK**.

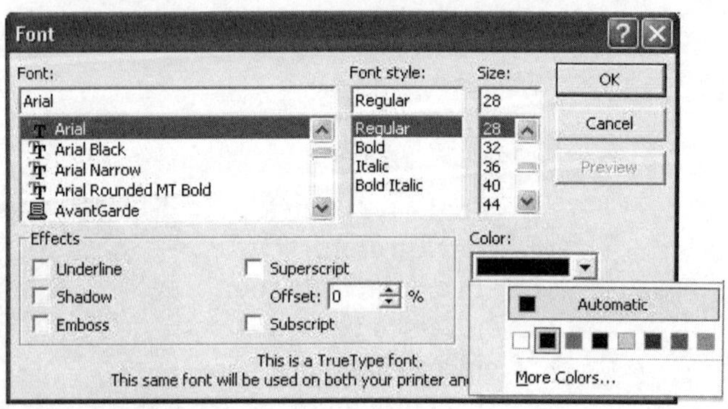

You can also apply most formatting to selected text by clicking the relevant buttons on the *Formatting* and *Drawing* toolbars.

Let's look at PowerPoint's font options in more detail.

About fonts

You can see what fonts are installed on your computer by clicking the arrow on the drop-down *Font* box on the left of the *Formatting* toolbar. Most fonts fall into two categories (families):

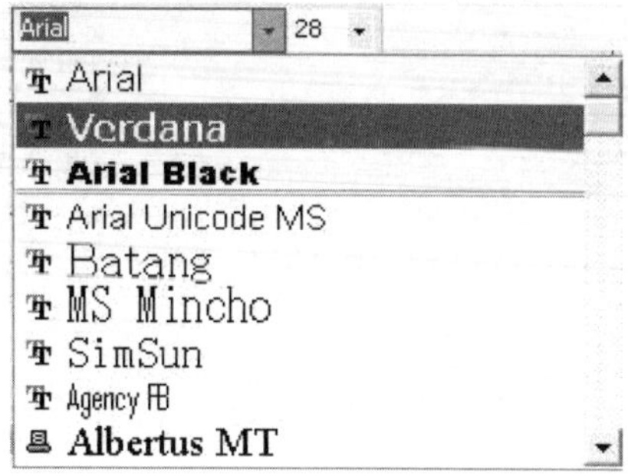

- **Serif fonts:** So-called because of their serifs (tails or squiggles). Common examples are Times New Roman and Garamond.
- **San serif fonts:** Sans serif means without serif. Common examples include Arial, Arial Narrow and Gill.

In printed text, serif fonts are generally easier to read. For slides, however, sans serif fonts are a better choice.

Changing font

To change the font of selected text:

- Click the arrow to the right of the *Font* drop-down list box on the *Formatting* toolbar.
- Click the font you require from the list displayed.

Changing font on every slide

Want to replace the font on every slide? Just choose the **Format | Replace Fonts** command, select the current and replacement fonts, and click **Replace**.

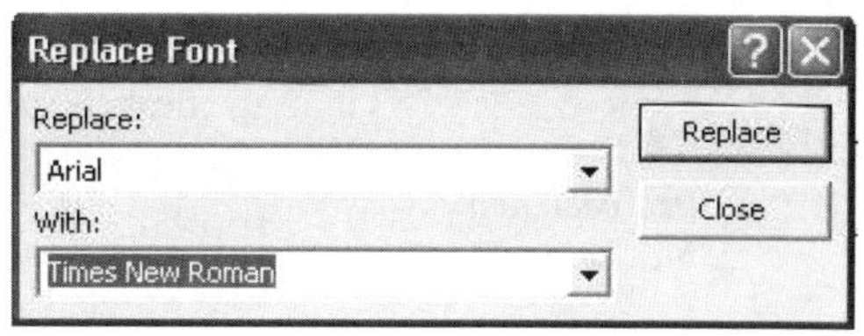

Changing font case

You can change the case – for example, from lower-case to upper-case – of a selected letter, word, or group of words using the options on the **Format | Change Case** command.

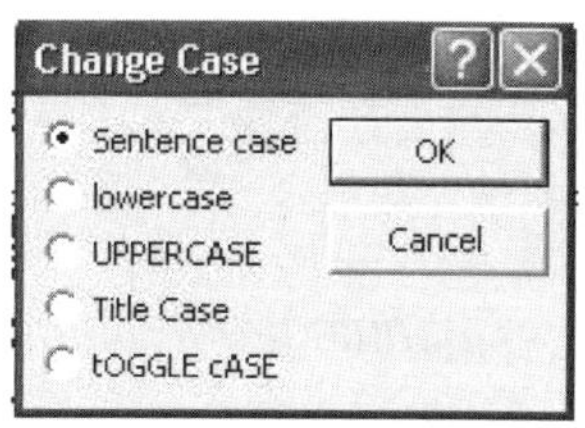

Your options are as follows:

- **Sentence case:** Capitalizes the first letter of the first word in the selected sentence(s). All other letters are in lower-case.
- **lowercase:** Changes all text to lower-case.
- **UPPER CASE:** Changes all text to upper-case (capitals).
- **Title Case:** Makes the first letter of every word in the selected text upper-case. All other letters are in lower-case.
- **tOGGLE cASE:** Changes the current case of all letters: upper-case becomes lower, and lower-case becomes upper.

Changing font size

Font size is developed in a non-metric unit called the point, with approximately 72 points equal to one inch.

To help you choose suitable font sizes, the placeholders in PowerPoint's **Slide Layouts** include built-in size values.

If you select the **Slide Layout** of *Title and Text,* for example, text you type in the top placeholder defaults to 18 points, and in the bottom placeholder to 32 points.

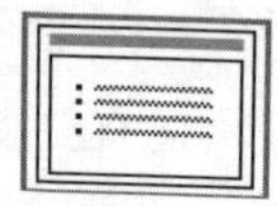

Fonts vary in their legibility, and you might need to choose a bigger point size for certain fonts.

To change the font size of selected text:

- Click the arrow to the right of the *Font Size* drop-down list box on the *Formatting* toolbar.
- Click the font size you require from the list displayed.

Increase font Size button

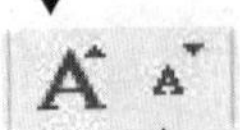

Decrease font Size button

If your required value is not listed, you can type the font size directly in the box. Alternatively, you can increase or decrease font size, in four-point steps, by clicking the appropriate button on the *Formatting* toolbar.

Changing font colour

You can change the colour of the selected text by clicking the arrow to the right of **Font Color** on the *Drawing* toolbar. Don't see the colour you need? Click **More Colors** and select from the range available.

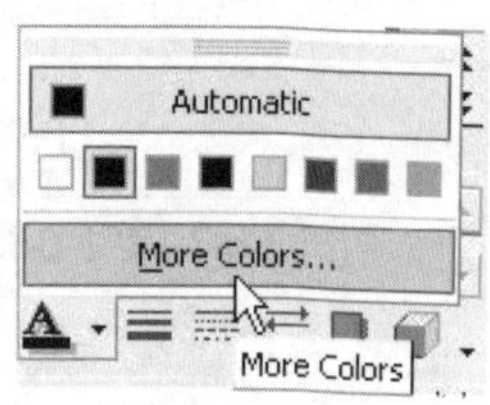

Changing font effects

You can apply bold, italics, underline and shadow effects to selected text by clicking the relevant buttons on the *Formatting* toolbar.

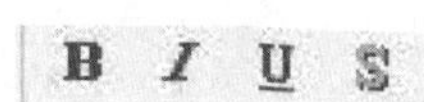

Two font effects that are not available from any toolbar are *superscript* and *subscript.* To apply either effect to selected text, you need to display the **Format | Font** dialog box.

- **Superscript:** This raises the selected text above the other text on the same line, and reduces font size. Superscript is used most commonly for mathematical notation.

  For example: 2^2, x^8, 10^3
- **Subscript:** This is the opposite of superscript. Subscript is text that is lowered beneath other text on the same line and is reduced in font size. Subscripts are commonly used in chemical texts for formulas.

  For example: H_2SO_4

Exercise 38.1 demonstrates PowerPoint's text formatting options in action.

Exercise 38.1: Changing text format on a single slide

1) Open your first presentation (we called it KBpres1) in Normal view. Display the second slide, entitled 'Amazing Features'.

   Save your presentation before continuing further.

2) Select the slide title text 'Amazing Features'. Using the *Font* box at the left of the *Formatting* toolbar, change the font to Verdana.

Shadow button

3) With the title text still selected, click **Shadow** on the *Formatting* toolbar. PowerPoint applies a shadow effect to your title slide.
4) Click the arrow to the right of **Font Color** on the *Drawing* toolbar and click **More Colors**. From the colours displayed, select a medium green, and click **OK**.

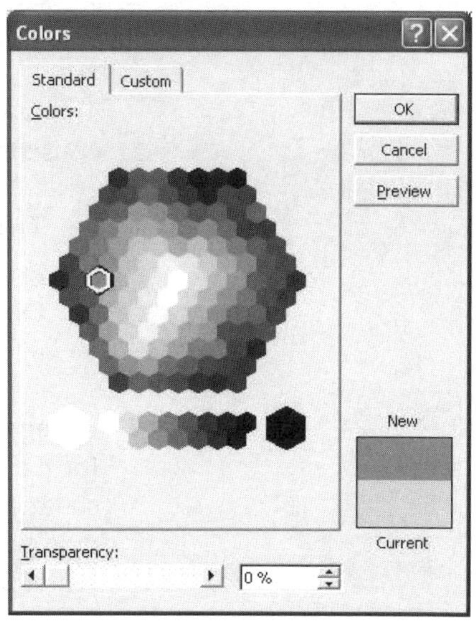

5) Select all the major and minor bullet points, change the font to Verdana, and change the text colour to the medium green that you selected in step 4) above.

   Click anywhere else on the slide to deselect the text.

Your slide should now look as shown.

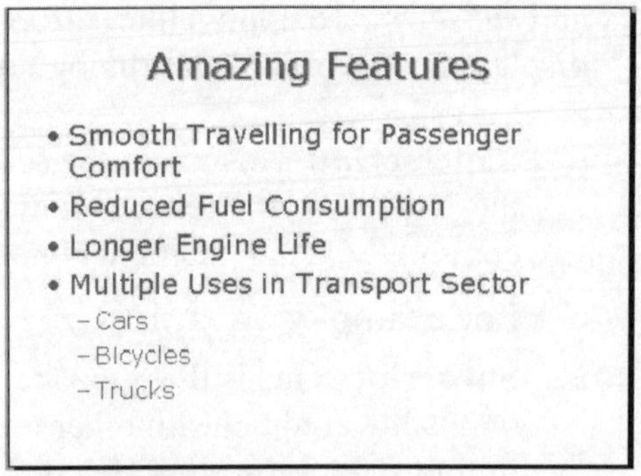

Don't save your presentation yet.

You can imagine that for a presentation containing a large number of slides, changing the font on each slide individually would take a lot of time and effort. In the next topic you will learn about the slide master and how to use it to apply text effects to an entire presentation.

Working with the slide master

Whether you know it or not, every slide you insert in a PowerPoint presentation is based on a slide master.

- It is from the slide master that all slides take their default text formatting and positioning.
- Anything that you insert on the slide master appears automatically on every slide of your presentation. As you will discover in Chapter 39, this is useful for company logos or for recurring graphics such as lines and borders.

To view the slide master, choose **View | Master | Slide Master**. It consists of two main placeholders:

- **Title placeholder:** Controls the format and positioning of text in every title placeholder in your presentation.
- **Object placeholder:** Controls the format and positioning of text in every non-title placeholder.

Along the bottom of the slide master you can see three placeholders for the date/time, footer text and slide numbering. If you prefer, you can move these to other positions on the master slide – just select and drag with the mouse. See Exercise 38.8 to see how to insert the date, footer text and slide numbers.

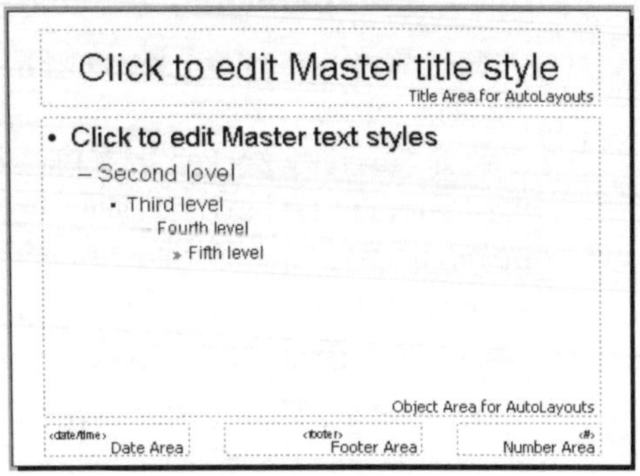

Your audience never sees the slide master; they see only its effects on the slides in your presentation. You can override the defaults supplied by the slide master on any individual slide.

Slide master
This stores all the default attributes that you wish to apply to slides, including text formatting and positioning, background, and standard graphics, such as your company logo.

In the next exercise you will change the text format of your presentation by changing the slide master.

Exercise 38.2: Formatting text in the slide master

1) Choose **View | Slide Master** and select the title text in the top placeholder.
2) Change its font to Arial, apply a shadow effect, and change its colour to the medium green that you selected in Exercise 38.1.
3) Select the first- and second-level bullet points in the lower placeholder.

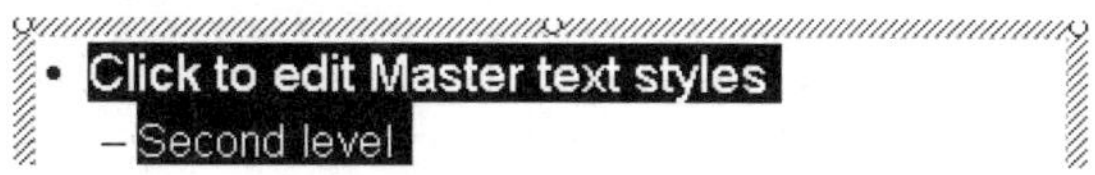

Change the font to Verdana, and change the colour to medium green.
4) When finished, switch to Slide Sorter view. Notice that PowerPoint has reformatted the text of all your slides. Don't save your presentation yet.

Working with backgrounds

You can transform the appearance of your slides by changing their background. Follow Exercise 38.3 to discover how.

Exercise 38.3: Changing the background in the slide master

1) Choose **View | Master | Master Slide** to display your presentation's slide master.
2) Choose **Format | Background**. Click on the drop-down list box, and select the *More Colors* option.

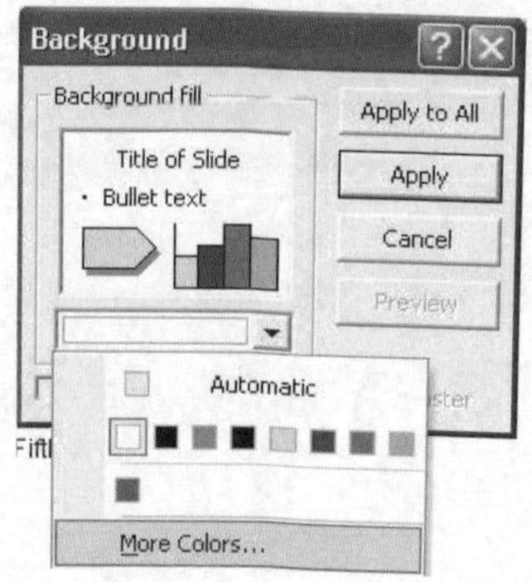

3) From the colour displayed, select a light yellow. Click **OK** and then **Apply to All**.
4) Choose **View | Slide Sorter** to verify that all slides in your presentation now have the yellow background.
5) How will your reformatted presentation appear to your audience? To find out, switch to Slide Show view and page through your slides.
6) Choose **File | Save As**, and save the presentation with a name that indicates its colour. If your initials are KB, for example, save it as KBpres1_green_on_yellow.ppt.

   In Slide Sorter view, your presentation should look as shown.

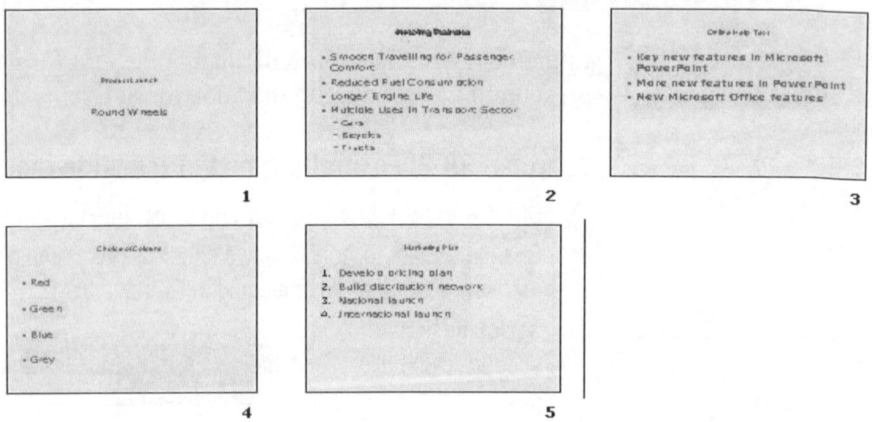

You now have two versions of your first presentation: one with black text against a white background, and a second with green text against a yellow background.

Slide master and backgrounds

You don't need to display your presentation's slide master in order to apply a background to all slides. When you choose **Format | Background**, the dialog box gives you two options: **Apply** (to this slide only), and **Apply to All** (the entire presentation). In the next exercise you will apply a decorative background to your presentation, and change the font to suit the new background.

Exercise 38.4: Applying a decorative background

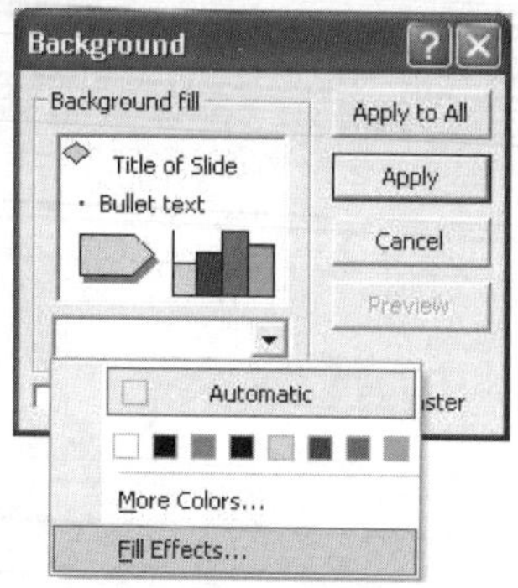

1) In Normal view, choose **Format | Background**, click on the drop-down list near the bottom of the dialog box, and click *Fill Effects*.
2) On the **Gradient** tab, select **Preset**. In the *Preset colors* drop-down list, select *Daybreak*. Click **OK** and then **Apply to All**.
3) Choose **View | Master | Slide Master** to display your presentation's slide master.

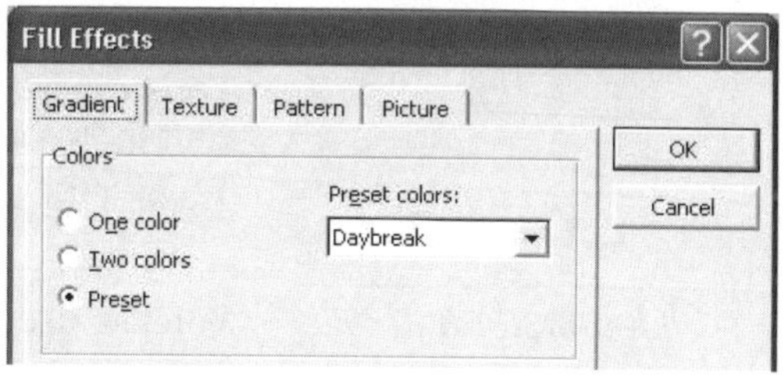

4) In the top placeholder, select the title text. On the *Drawing* toolbar, click the arrow to the right of **Font Color**, click *More Colors*, select a shade of dark green, and click **OK**.
5) In the lower placeholder, select the first- and second-level bullet points. Change their font colour to the darker green.

   The darker green gives a better contrast against the background pattern and is easier to read.
6) Switch to Slide Show view, and take a look at how your presentation would appear to the audience.

   Notice that all the text on your second slide, entitled 'Amazing Features', is still in the medium green that you applied to it in Exercise 38.1.

   Why? Because, where the slide has been formatted individually, the slide master does not override the individual settings.

   Display this second slide in Normal view, and change the colour of the slide title and bullet point text to the darker green. All your slides now have a common text colour.
7) When finished, choose **File | Save As**, and save the presentation with a name that indicates its background effect. If your initials are KB, for example, save it as KBpres1_daybreak.ppt.

In Slide Sorter view, your presentation should look as shown.

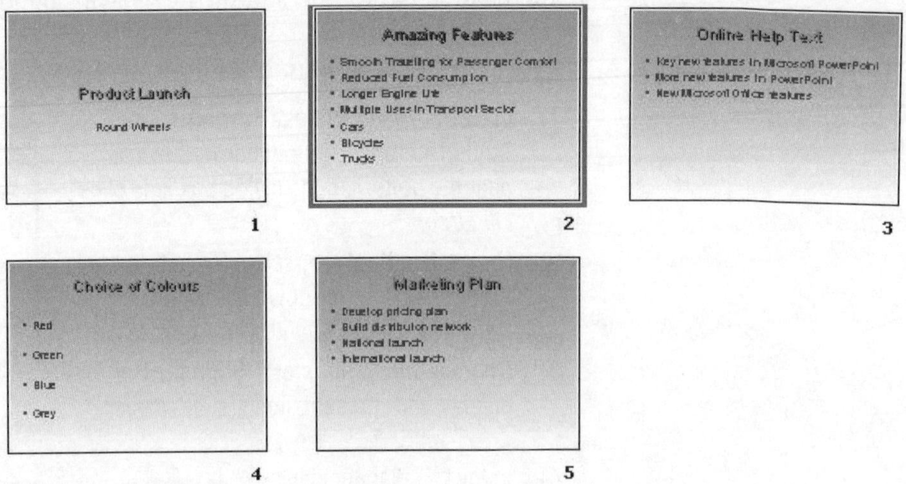

You now have three versions of your first presentation: black text with a white background, green text with a yellow background, and dark green with a decorative 'daybreak' background.

Slide master and text options

You can use the slide master to change default attributes of text in your presentation. For example, you might with to change the default font, bullet characters or alignment of text.

Slide master and graphics

If you want to place a graphic on every slide in your presentation, then insert it on the slide master.

Working with colour schemes

As you have seen, the slide master gives you total control over every aspect of your slides' text and background. Is there an even faster way to change your presentation's appearance?

Yes. PowerPoint comes supplied with a number of built-in colour schemes – professionally designed combinations of background and text colours.

In Exercise 38.5 you will apply a preset colour scheme to a presentation. In Exercise 38.6 you will learn how to customize a colour scheme.

Exercise 38.5: Applying a colour scheme

1) Open your saved presentation, entitled 'ECDL: An Overview', and display it in Slide Sorter view. In this view you will be better able to see how different colour schemes affect your presentation. Save your presentation before continuing.

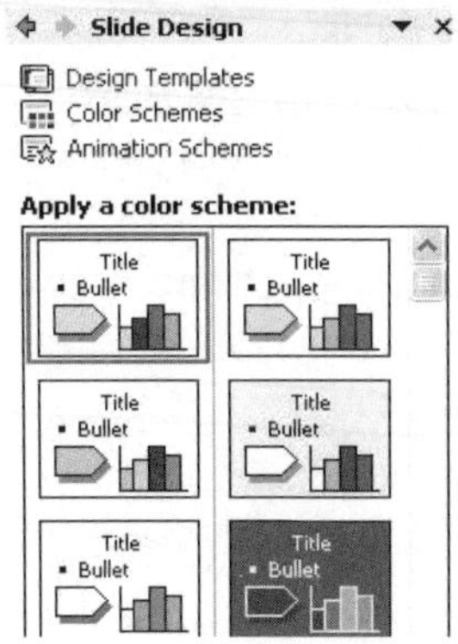

2) Choose **Format | Slide Design**. You can also click **Design** in the *Formatting* toolbar. In the *Slide Design* task pane, select **Color Schemes.**
3) Choose the slide with the yellow background. Click the arrow to the right of the slide. From the drop-down list that appears, select *Apply to All Slides.*
   In Slide Sorter view, you can immediately see the impact on your presentation.
4) You already have one presentation with dark text against a light background. So go to the *Slide Design* task pane again and choose **Color Schemes** if not already selected. This time, select the dark blue background, and click *Apply to All Slides.*

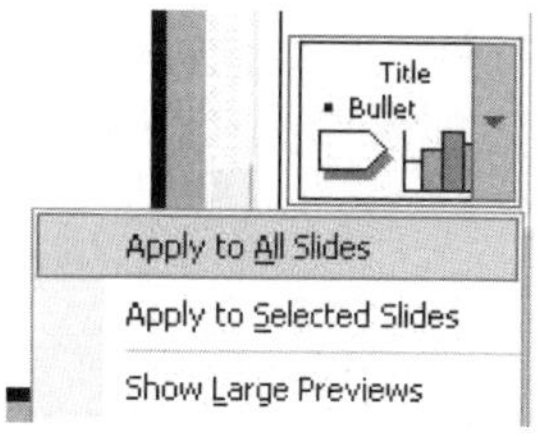

5) Choose **Format | Replace Fonts**. In the *Replace* box, select the Times New Roman font, and click **Replace**.When finished, click **Close** to close the *Replace Font* dialog box. Do not save your presentation.

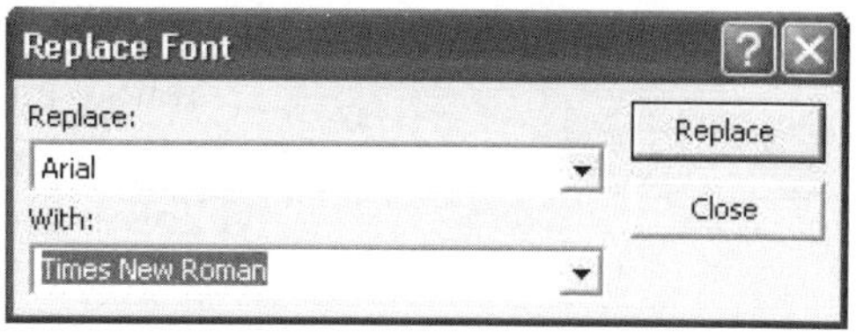

Customizing colour schemes

You don't have to accept the default options of PowerPoint's preset colour schemes. As the next exercise shows, you can customize a colour scheme to suit your tastes or needs.

Exercise 38.6: Customizing a colour scheme

1) Choose **Format | Slide Design**. In the *Slide Design* task pane, select **Color Schemes**. Click **Edit Color Schemes**, located at the end of the *Slide Design* task pane.
2) On the **Custom** tab, select *Title text*, and click **Change Color**.

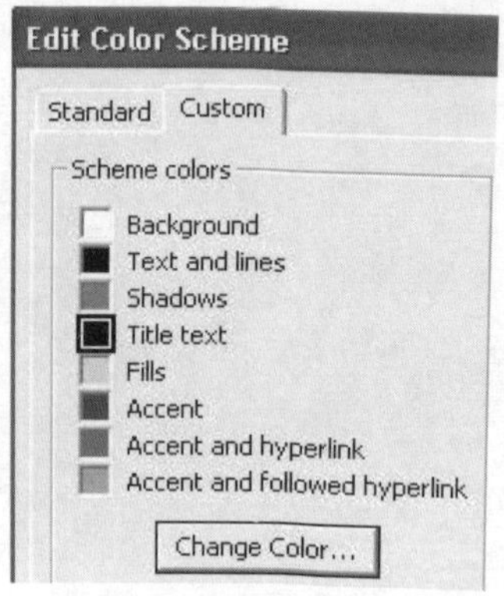

3) From the colours displayed, select a medium green, and click **OK**, and then **Apply**.
4) Go to the **Edit Color Schemes** again. On the **Custom** tab, select *Text and lines*, and click **Change Color**.
5) From the colours displayed, select a medium yellow colour, click **OK**, and then click **Apply**.
6) Switch to Slide Show view and inspect your work.
7) When finished, choose **File | Save As**, and save the presentation with a name that indicates its colour scheme effect. If your initials are KB, for example, save it as KBpres2_yellow_on_blue.ppt.

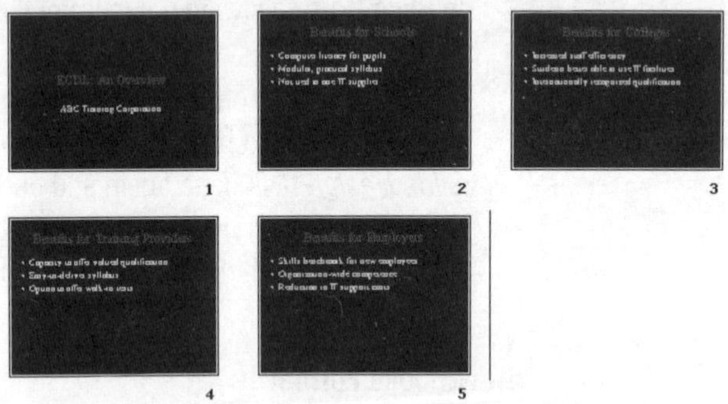

You now have two versions of your second presentation: one with black text on a white background, and a second with green titles and yellow bullet points on a blue background.

Color scheme
A collection of preset coordinated colours you can apply to a presentation to give it an attractive and consistent appearance.

Combining colour scheme and slide master effects

In any presentation, you are not faced with the choice of using the slide master *or* colour scheme; you can use both when formatting the same presentation. For example, you could:

- Begin by selecting a preset colour scheme.
- Next, customize some element(s) of the scheme.
- Then, use the slide master to apply various effects – such as font sizes, line spacing and special bullet characters – to your slides.

When all slides are not the same

Color Schemes in the *Slide Design* task pane has an *Apply to Selected Slides* option. This appears when you click the arrow to the right of a select slide in the *Slide Design* task pane.

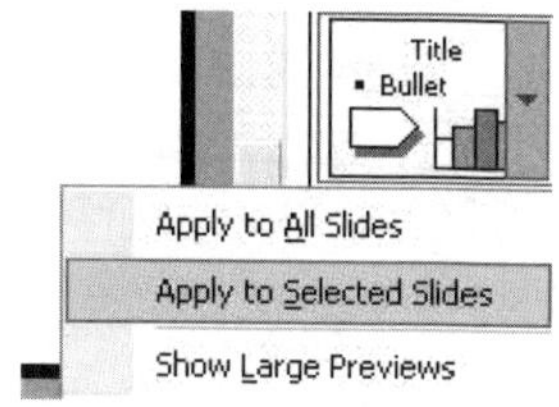

Typically, you use this option when:

- Your presentation deals with different topics, and the different sections would benefit from having different formatting.
- One or a few slides contain material that needs to stand out from the remainder of the presentation.

Even with the same colour scheme or background throughout a presentation, you can still emphasize particular slides by applying font effects to their text.

Speaker notes

For each slide that you create in a presentation, PowerPoint creates what it calls a speaker notes page. You can ignore or use these pages as you wish. Typically, you use speaker notes pages to remind you (or whoever is giving the presentation) of key points or background information.

You can enter or alter text in speaker notes pages at any stage when creating or editing your presentation

Speaker notes
A page created by PowerPoint to accompany each slide. You can use it to record key points or additional details about your presentation.

Speaker notes page view

You can access a speaker notes page in either of two ways:

- In Normal view, you can type or edit text in the Notes pane at the lower right of your screen. If required, you can enlarge the Notes pane by dragging its pane borders upwards or to the left. Just click in the Notes pane and begin typing or editing the text.
- Choose **View | Notes Page** to display a screen where you can type or edit text for the currently selected slide.

Each notes page contains a miniature view of the slide and an area for working with text.

By default, PowerPoint displays a speaker notes page at about 39% of its full size. You may wish to increase this to nearer 100% when typing or editing.

Exercise 38.7: Adding speaker notes

1) Open the green-on-yellow version of your first presentation. In Normal view, display its first slide, entitled 'Product Launch'.
2) Click in the Notes pane, and type the following text:
   Introduce myself
   Give special welcome to Anne
3) Click in the Slides pane, and use the **Page Down** key to display your fourth slide, entitled 'Choice of Colours'.
4) Change to Notes Page view, increase the Zoom magnification to 100%, and type the following text:
   New colours will be introduced shortly
5) Return to Normal view. Save your presentation.

Handout pages

As you will learn in the final part of this chapter, you can, if you wish, simply print out your slides and distribute them to your audience. However, this is somewhat inelegant: the size of type that is appropriate for a slide is much too big for normal reading.

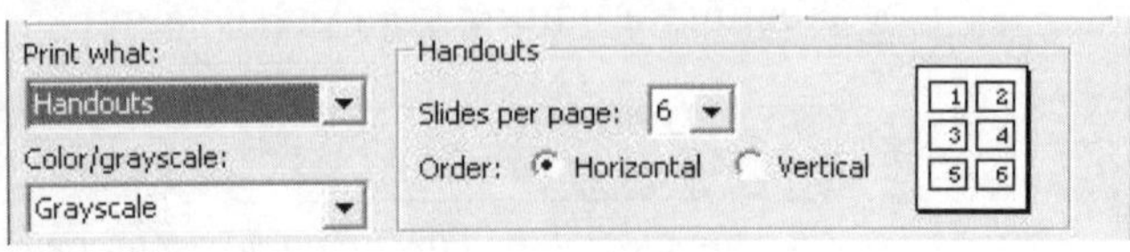

PowerPoint gives you the option of producing handouts in which two, three, four, six or nine slides are shown to a page. A drop-down list in the *Print* dialog box allows you to specify the format you want to use.

Headers and footers

As with Word documents and Excel worksheets, you can include headers and footers in your Powerpoint presentations. Typically, you can use headers and footers to include details such as the slide number, the date, and the title of the presentation.

Exercise 38.8: Adding the date, slide numbers and footer text

1) Display the yellow-on-blue version of your second presentation. In Normal view, choose **View | Header and Footer**.
2) In the **Slide** tab, check the *Date and time* check box.

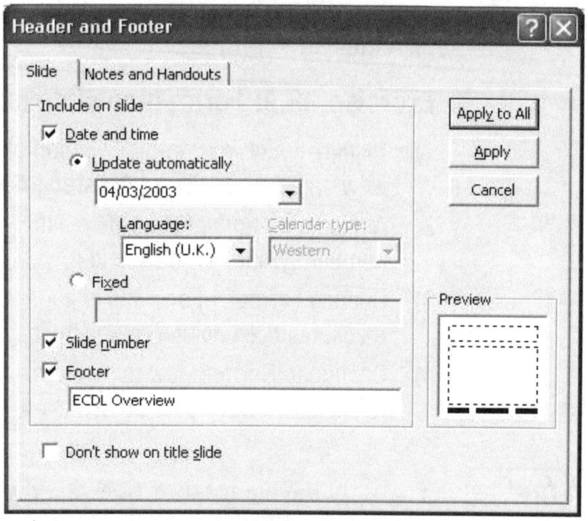

3) Then choose whether you want the date/time to be updated automatically or whether you want to insert a fixed or unchanging date/time. Select the date/time format that you want to use:
   - If you want the date to be updated automatically, select the *Update automatically* option button, and then specify the format you want to use.
   - If you want to use a fixed date, select the *Fixed* option button, and then enter the date.
4) Click the *Slide number* check box to number the slides in your presentation.
5) To insert footer text, select the *Footer* box and then enter the text you want to use – in the example above, the text 'ECDL Overview' is inserted.
6) Click **Apply to All** to apply the changes you have made to all slides.
   -or-
   Click **Apply** to apply the changes to the current slide only.
7) Switch to Slide Sorter view to confirm that PowerPoint has made the changes you wanted. Save your presentation.

You can use the **Notes and Handouts** tab of the same dialog box to include page numbers on your speaker notes and audience handouts.

If you change the order of slides that contain slide numbers, PowerPoint automatically updates the slide numbers to reflect their new sequence.

If you want to display a particular slide in Slide Show view, just type the slide number and press **Enter**.

Formatting slide numbers

To change the font, font size or font colour of your slide numbers, display the slide master and make your changes there. Exercise 38.9 provides an example.

Exercise 38.9: Formatting slide numbers

1) Display the yellow-on-blue version of your second presentation in Normal view and choose **View | Master | Slide Master** to display the slide master.
2) At the lower-right of the slide master, click the slide number symbol (#) to select it.

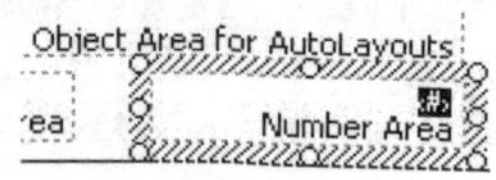

3) Choose **Format | Font**, and change the text to Arial Black, bold, 14 point. Change the colour to white. Click **OK**.
4) Change to Normal view to verify that your slide numbers have been reformatted. Save your presentation.

The story so far

You now have a total of five saved presentations, summarized in the following table.

Presentation topic	Presentation format	Suggested file name
Product Launch	Black text, white background	KBpres1.ppt
Product Launch	Medium green text, light yellow background	KBpres1_green_on_ yellow.ppt
Product Launch	Darker green text, preset decorative background of daybreak	KBpres1_daybreak.ppt
ECDL Overview	Black text, white background	KBpres2.ppt
ECDL Overview	Medium green title text, medium yellow bullet text, dark blue background	KBpres2_yellow_on_ blue.ppt

Page setup

Before you print a presentation, you need to check that the page setup suits your requirements – choose **File | Page Setup** to display the *Page Setup* dialog box.

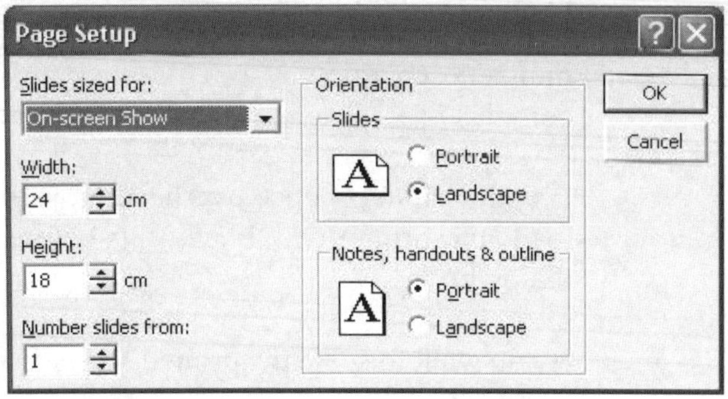

- **Slides sized for:** Select from the list. If you choose *Custom*, you can then specify the width and height settings.
- **Number slides from:** Indicate the number from which you want to number your slides – the default is *1*.
- **Orientation:** Select whether you want *portrait* or *landscape* for:
  - Slides.
  - Notes, handouts and outline.

Printing your presentation

Print button

You can print out a PowerPoint presentation in a variety of ways, depending on your requirements and on the hardware at your disposal. Printing in PowerPoint is similar to printing in other applications:

- First, choose **File | Print**, or click the **Print** button on the *Standard* toolbar.
- Then, in the *Print what* drop-down box, you can choose to print slides, handouts, speaker notes or the outline. If you choose handouts, you can choose the number of slides per handout.

Whichever option you select, you can then specify, in the *Print range* area of the dialog box, whether you want to print all slides (or handouts, notes or the outline view), the current slide, or a selected range of slides. You can also specify the number of copies you want to print.

To print a contiguous range, type the number of the first slide, a hyphen and the number of the last slide. To print non-contiguous slides, type the individual slide numbers separated by commas.

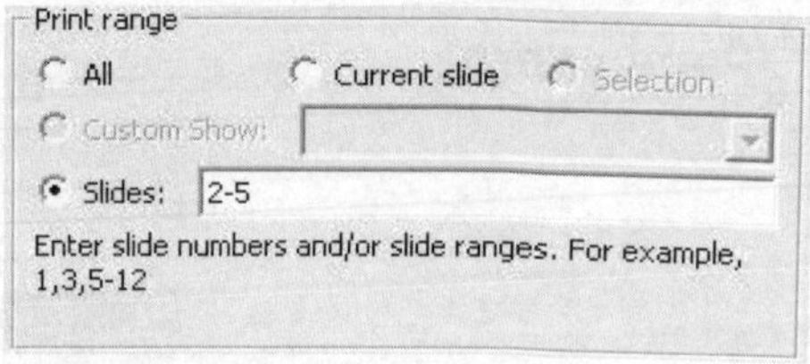

If you wish to produce overhead projection foils (OHPs), you need to load your printer with blank foils before clicking **OK** on the *Print* dialog box.

If you want to scale the printed slides to fit the paper, click on **Scale to fit paper.**

If you wish to produce 35-mm slides, you need to have a special desktop film recorder connected to your computer. Alternatively, you could take your presentation to a service bureau.

Exercise 38.10: Exercises in printing

1) Switch to the green-on-yellow version of your first 'Product Launch' presentation.
2) Print a set of handouts for the entire presentation with six slides on each page of the printout.

   (As your presentation contains only five slides, this step prints your entire presentation on a single page.)
3) Print the first and fourth slide of your presentation.
4) Print the speaker notes for your first slide.

You can save and close all your presentations and then close PowerPoint. You have now completed the third chapter of the ECDL presentations module.

Chapter summary: so now you know

Slide formatting refers to the appearance of slides and includes text formatting and background formatting behind the slide text.

Your text *formatting* options include making text bolder (heavier), putting it in italics, or placing a shadow behind it. You may also change the text font, size and colour. See Exercises 38.1 and 38.2 for examples of these tasks.

The two main *background formatting* options are dark text against a light background (good for lighted rooms) or light text against a dark background (good for darkened rooms). Backgrounds may consist of a solid, single-colour area or a decorative pattern. See Exercises 38.3 and 38.4 for examples of these tasks.

You can change the appearance of an entire presentation by changing the text or background formatting on its *slide master*. See Exercise 38.4 for an example of this.

A second method of reformatting a presentation is to apply one of PowerPoint's *colour schemes* – sets of preset text and background colours. You can customize colour schemes, combine colour schemes with slide master effects, and override colour scheme or master slide settings on any individual slide. See Exercises 38.5 and 38.6 for examples of these tasks.

You can insert *headers and footers* on slides – these include details such as the slide number, the date, and the title of the presentation. See Exercises 38.8 and 38.9 for examples of these tasks.

Speaker notes are pages that PowerPoint creates to accompany each slide. You can use them to record key points or additional details for the presenter. See Exercise 38.7 for an example of this task.

PowerPoint gives you the option of producing printed *handouts* for your audience, in which two, three, four, six or nine slides are shown to a page. See Exercise 38.10 for an example of this.

PowerPoint's *print options* enable you to print one, all or a range of slides, handouts, speaker notes or the outline. If you wish to produce overhead projection foils (OHPs), you need to load your printer with blank foils. To produce 35-mm slides, you need to have a special desktop film recorder connected to your computer or you can use a service bureau.

Quick quiz: formatting your presentation

Circle the correct answer to each of the following multiple-choice questions about formatting your presentation in PowerPoint.

Q2	Which command do you use to access the slide master?
A.	**Format | Slide Design**.
B.	**View | Master | Slide Master**.
C.	**View | Master | Handout Master**.
D.	**View | Slide Sorter**.

Q1	*How do you apply a colour scheme to one slide?*
A.	Choose **Format | Slide Design**. On the *Slide Design* task pane select **Color Schemes**. Select the slide required and click the arrow to the right of the slide. From the drop-down list that appears, select *Apply to All Slides*.
B.	Choose **Format | Slide Layout**. On the *Slide Layout* task pane select **Color Schemes**. Select the slide required and click the arrow to the right of the slide. From the drop-down list that appears, select *Apply to Selected Slides*.
C.	Choose **Format | Slide Design**. On the *Slide Design* task pane select **Color Schemes**. Select the slide required and click the arrow to the right of the slide. From the drop-down list that appears, select *Apply to Selected Slides.*
D.	Choose **Format | Slide Design**. On the *Slide Design* task pane select **Design Templates**. Select the slide required and click the arrow to the right of the slide. From the drop-down list that appears, select *Apply to All Slides*.

Q3	*How do you apply a decorative background to all slides in a presentation?*
A.	Choose **Format | Background**. Click **Fill Effects** from the drop-down list at the bottom of the dialog box. From the **Gradient** tab select **Preset**. Select a preset colour from the drop-down list, click **OK**, and then click **Apply to All**.
B.	Choose **Format | Background**. Click **Fill Effects** from the list at the bottom of the dialog box. From the **Gradient** tab select **More Colors**. Select a colour, click **OK**, and then click **Apply to All**.
C.	Click the arrow on the right of **Font Color** on the *Formatting* toolbar. From the drop-down list select **More Colors**. Select a colour, click **OK**, and then click **Apply to All**.
D.	Choose **Format | Background**. Click **Fill Effects** from the drop-down list at the bottom of the dialog box. From the **Gradient** tab select **Preset**. Select a preset colour from the drop-down list, click **OK**, and then click **Apply**.

Q4	*The audience can see what is written in the notes page of a presentation.*
A.	True.
B.	False.

Q5	***How do you print handouts?***
A.	Select **File | Print**. Select *Handouts* from the *Print what* box.
B.	Select **File | Print**. Select *Notes Page* from the *Print what* box.
C.	Select **File | Print**. Select *Outline View* from the *Print what* box.
D.	Select **File | Print**. Select *Slides* from the *Print what* box.

Answers

1: C, **2:** B, **3:** A, **4:** B, **5:** A.

Chapter 39: Working with graphics and pictures

In this chapter

It's time to inject some visual flair into your presentations by discovering how to insert graphics and pictures on slides. In this chapter you will learn how to include pictures and other graphics in your slides.

New skills

At the end of this chapter you should be able to:

- Draw simple graphics such as lines and boxes on a slide.
- Draw AutoShapes on a slide.
- Insert and use text boxes on a slide.
- Insert Clip Art and other pictures on a slide.
- Move, change the size and shape, rotate, group and flip objects in a slide.
- Apply line styles to lines and object borders, and fill colour and shadow effects on a slide.
- Copy objects between slides.

New words

At the end of this chapter you should be able to explain the following terms:

- AutoShapes
- Clip Art

About graphics

The term 'graphics' includes plain and decorative lines, squares and rectangles, circles and ovals, and a wide variety of symbolic shapes.

You have two main options for including graphics in your slides:

- **Draw your own graphics:** You can use PowerPoint's drawing tools to create your own graphics.
- **Use built-in graphics:** PowerPoint includes AutoShapes – ready-made shapes such as flowchart elements, stars and banners, and callouts. You can select and include AutoShapes as supplied, or you can modify them to your taste or needs.

Drawing toolbar

Displayed along the bottom of your screen, the *Drawing* toolbar includes a number of tools for drawing simple objects, including lines, arrows, rectangles and ellipses.

PowerPoint's Drawing toolbar

If the *Drawing* toolbar is not currently visible in Normal view, choose **View | Toolbars | Drawing** to display it.

Line and arrow tools

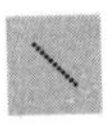

Line button

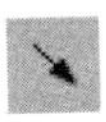

Arrow button

To draw a line, click the **Line** button, place the cursor where you want the line to begin, click and drag to where you want the line to end, and release the mouse button.

To draw an arrow, click the **Arrow** button and draw it in the same way.

To draw a freestyle line, choose **Lines** from the **AutoShapes** menu. You can then choose the particular type of freeform line you wish to draw.

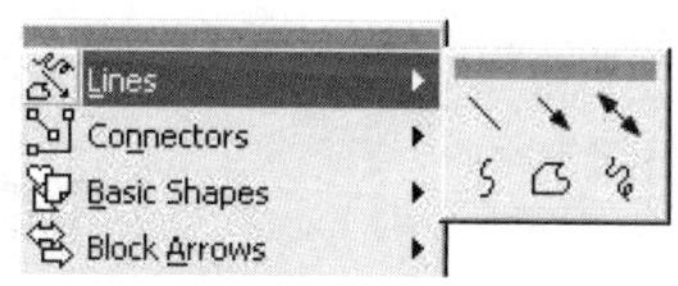

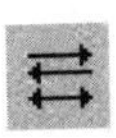

Arrow Style button

Change the style of arrowhead, or the direction of the arrow, by clicking the **Arrow Style** button.

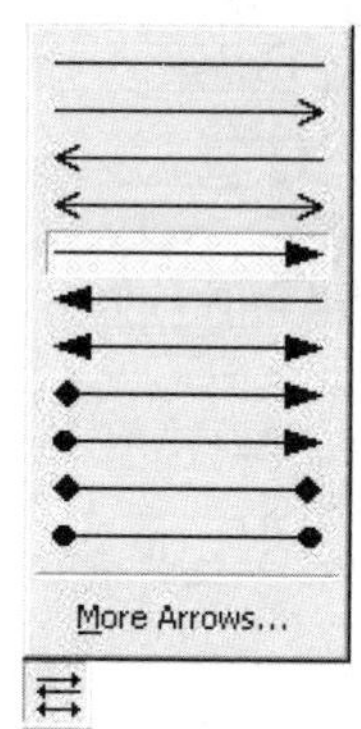

Rectangle and square tool

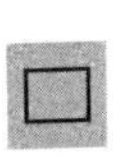

Rectangle and Square button

To draw a rectangle, click the **Rectangle** button, place the cursor where you want one corner of the rectangle, click and drag diagonally to where you want the opposite corner of the rectangle, and release the mouse button.

To draw a square, hold down the **Shift** key as you drag with the mouse.

Ellipse and circle tool

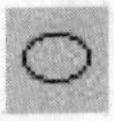

Ellipse button

To draw an ellipse, click on the **Ellipse** button, place the cursor where you want the shape to begin, click and drag until the shape it is the size you want, and release the mouse button.

To draw a circle, hold down the **Shift** key as you drag with the mouse.

Line colour and style

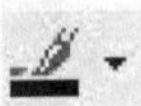

Line Color button

For lines, arrows and closed shapes (such as rectangles and circles), you can specify the colour and thickness of the line. Click the arrow to the right of the **Line Color** button and select a colour, either before you draw the line or closed shape, or, with the line or shape selected, after you have drawn it.

To delete a border around a closed shape, select **No Line** in the line colour pop-up menu.

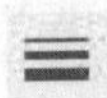

Line Style button

Change the thickness of a line or border by clicking the **Line Style** button.

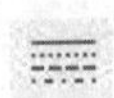

Dash Style button

Make the line a dashed line (in a choice of dash styles) by clicking the **Dash Style** button.

Fill Color

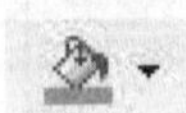

Fill Color button

Use the arrow to the right of the **Fill Color** button to select the background colour with which the inside of the selected closed shape (such as a square or ellipse) should be filled.

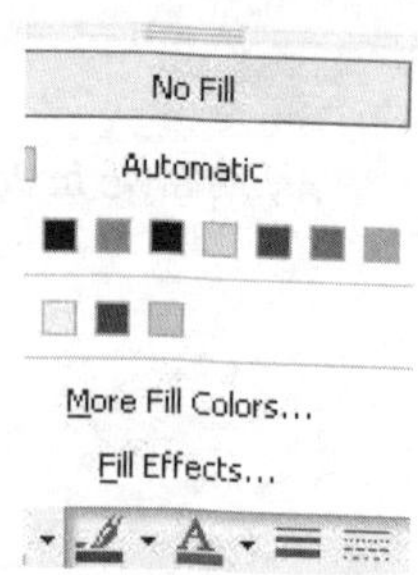

Working with AutoShapes

AutoShapes are commonly used, ready-made shapes that you can insert in your presentations. AutoShape categories include lines, basic shapes, flowchart elements, stars and banners, and callouts.

To select an AutoShape, click the **AutoShapes** button and choose from the options offered by the pop-up menu.

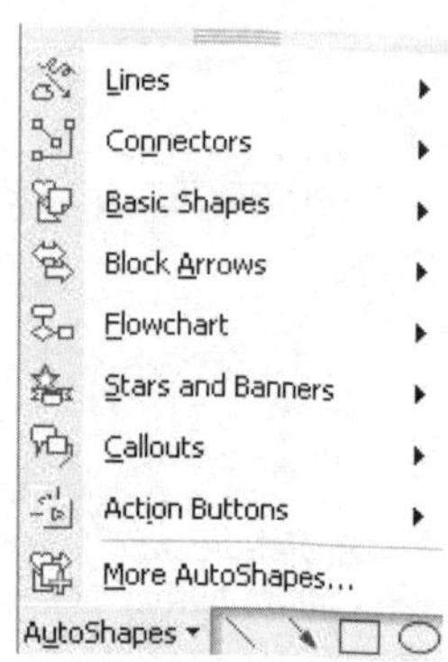

AutoShapes
Ready-made shapes, including lines, geometric shapes and flowchart elements, that you can use in your presentations.

Working with objects

Lines, rectangles, circles, text boxes, images and AutoShapes are all examples of what PowerPoint calls objects. So too are placeholders and inserted pictures, which you will meet later in this chapter.

There are a number of common operations that you can perform on objects, regardless of their type.

Moving and copying objects

To move an object within the same slide, first select it by clicking anywhere on it. A cross appears at the tip of the cursor arrow. Then drag the object to its new position.

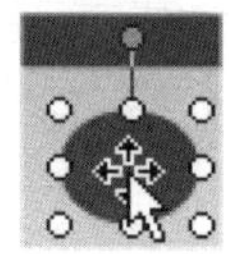

To move or copy an object between slides, select it, and then use the **Cut, Copy** and **Paste** commands. You can copy objects on the same slide, on another slide in the same presentation, or on a slide in another open presentation.

Changing object size and shape

You can change the size or shape of any object by selecting it and clicking on any of its sizing handles. A cursor appears as a double arrow. Next, drag a sizing handle until the object is the new shape that you require.

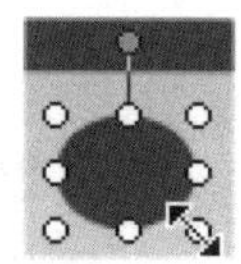

Aligning drawn objects

You can align drawn objects to suit your requirements. Select the object, and choose **Align or Distribute** from the **Draw** menu. You can then specify the horizontal and vertical alignment you want.

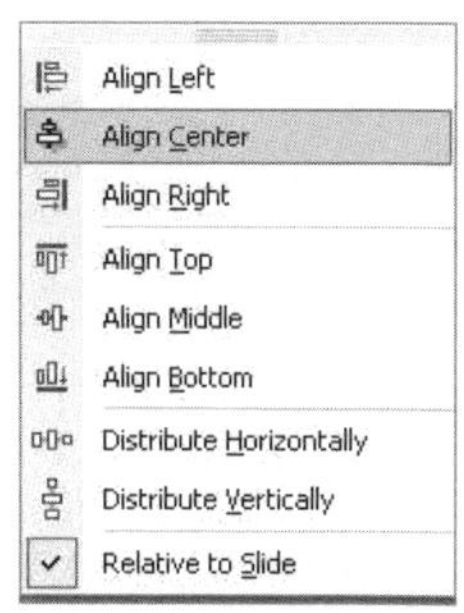

Make sure the Relative to Slide option is selected.

Shadow effects

To place a shadow behind a selected object, click **Shadow Style** on the *Drawing* toolbar, and choose from the shadow styles available on the pop-up menu.

Rotating and flipping objects

You can rotate a selected object through any angle to the left or right up through 360 degrees. You may only rotate objects created in PowerPoint, not images or other items imported from another application.

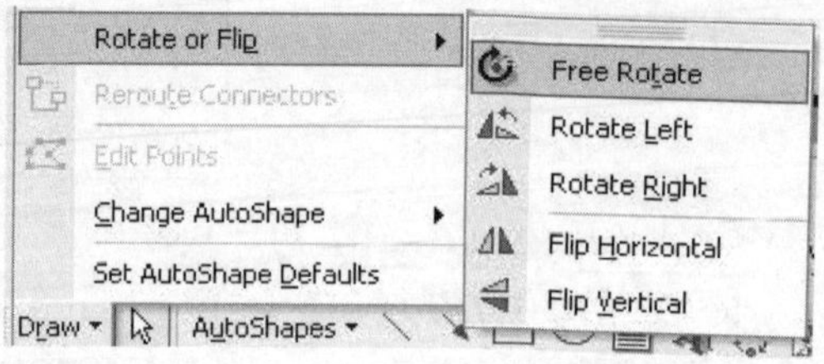

To rotate a selected object, click on the object to select it, and then click **Draw** on the *Drawing* toolbar and from the pop-up menu choose **Rotate or Flip**. Then choose **Free Rotate**. The border of the selected object disappears, and is replaced by four green dots, one at each corner.

Click any of these (the cursor changes to a shape), and drag the object to its new orientation. You can limit the object's rotation to 15-degree steps by holding down the **Shift** key as you drag with the mouse.

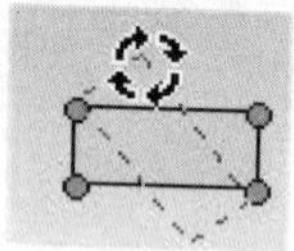

To flip (create a mirror image of) a selected object, click **Draw** on the *Drawing* toolbar and from the pop-up menu choose **Rotate or Flip**. Then choose **Flip Horizontal** or **Flip Vertical**.

Grouping and ungrouping objects

You can group objects so that you can work with them as if they were a single object. For example, you can move, rotate or format grouped objects in a single operation.

To group objects, hold down the **Shift** key and click each of the objects in turn. Next, click **Draw** on the *Drawing* toolbar and choose the **Group** command.

To ungroup a selected group of objects, click **Draw** on the *Drawing* toolbar and choose the **Ungroup** command.

Ordering objects

Objects that you place on a slide are stacked in layers, and you can choose which layer you want an object placed in. To change an object's layer, select it, choose **Draw | Order**, and then choose which of the order options you want. In this example, the black circle is placed behind the star.

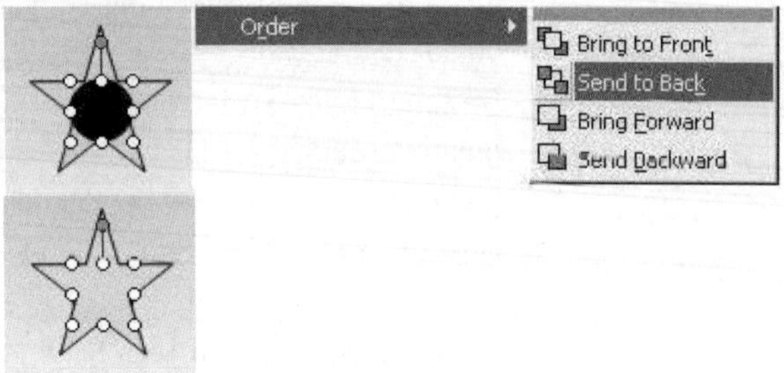

You could subsequently reverse this procedure and bring the circle forward.

Deleting objects

To delete any object or object group, click it and press the **Delete** key. You can always reverse a deletion by clicking the **Undo** button.

The following seven exercises provide examples of PowerPoint's graphic capabilities in action.

Exercise 39.1: Applying a border, fill and shadow to a placeholder in the slide master

1) If PowerPoint is not already open, open it now.

   Open the 'Product Launch' presentation, with medium green text against a plain yellow background, that you created in Chapter 38. We named it KBpres1_green_on_yellow.ppt.
2) Choose **View | Master | Slide Master** to display your presentation's slide master.
3) Click anywhere in the top placeholder to select it, and then click anywhere on the placeholder border.

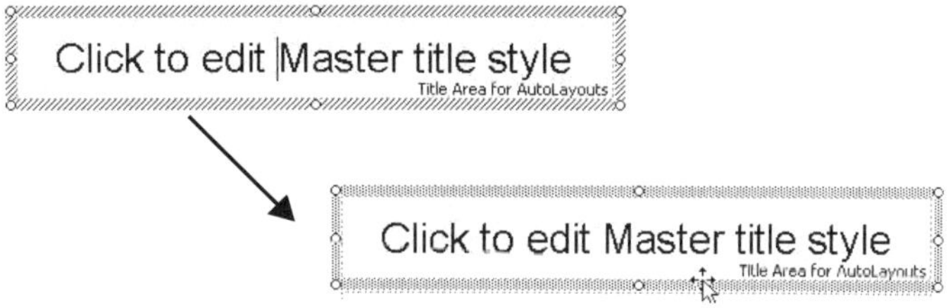

   Notice how the border pattern changes when you click it after selecting the placeholder.

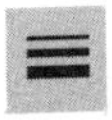

Line Style button

4) Click the **Line Style** button, and select a line width of 3 points.

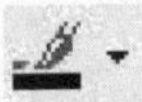

Line Color button

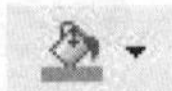

Fill Color button

Shadow Styles button

5) With the top placeholder selected, click the arrow to the right of **Line Color** on the *Drawing* toolbar. From the pop-up menu, select the same medium green colour as the text.

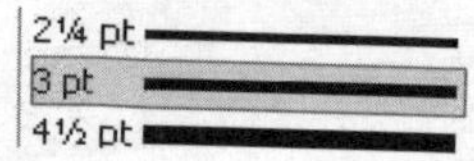

   Switch to Slide Sorter view. Notice that the titles of all slides have now got green borders.

6) Switch back to the slide master, click anywhere in the top placeholder, and click the arrow to the right of **Fill Color** on the *Drawing* toolbar.

   From the pop-up menu displayed, choose **More Fill Colors**, and select a darker yellow than the slide background colour.

7) Switch to Slide Show view. Notice that the titles of all slides now have the darker yellow fill colour.

   Finally, let's apply a shadow effect.

8) Switch back to the slide master, click anywhere in the top placeholder, and click **Shadow Styles** on the *Drawing* toolbar.

   From the pop-up menu displayed, select *Shadow Style 6* (shadow beneath and to the right).

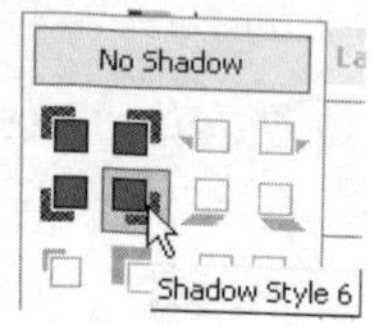

9) With the top placeholder selected, click **Shadow Styles** on the *Drawing* toolbar. From the pop-up menu displayed, choose **Shadow Settings**, and click the arrow to the right of **Shadow Color** on the *Shadow Settings* toolbar. (This toolbar appears on the top-right of the *Standard* toolbar.)

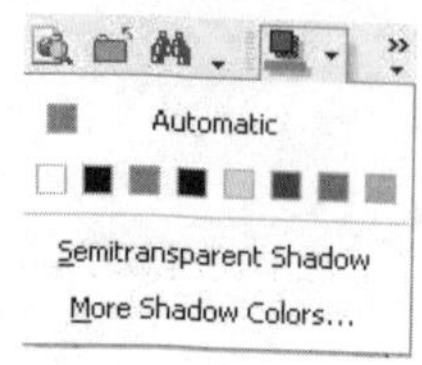

   From the colours displayed, select the same medium green colour as the text. Close the *Shadow Settings* toolbar.

10) Switch to Slide Show view. Notice that the titles of all slides now have a shadowed green border and a dark yellow fill colour.

11) Save your presentation.

Well done! In just a few steps, you have changed the appearance of your entire presentation. Next, let's apply some graphic effects to just a single slide.

Exercise 39.2: Applying graphics effects to a placeholder on a single slide

1) In Normal view, display the title slide of the presentation that you worked on in Exercise 39.1.

2) Click in the top placeholder to select it, click the arrow to the right of **Fill Color** on the *Drawing* toolbar, and select the same medium green colour as the text.

3) With the top placeholder selected, click **Shadow Styles** on the *Drawing* toolbar. From the pop-up menu displayed, choose **No Shadow**. (This removes the shadow from the placeholder – not from the title text.)

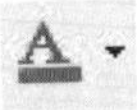

Font Color button

4) Select the text in the upper placeholder by dragging across it with the mouse, and click the arrow to the right of **Font Color** on the *Drawing* toolbar.

   From the pop-up menu displayed, select the same dark yellow that you applied to the title text placeholder in Exercise 39.1.

5) With the text still selected, click **Bold** on the *Formatting* toolbar. Your title should look as shown.

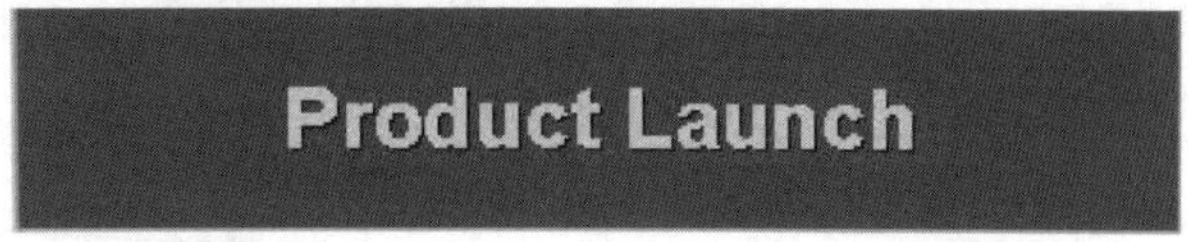

   Save your presentation.

In the next exercise you will draw, copy and group graphics, and then apply fills and borders to the grouped graphics.

Exercise 39.3: Drawing, copying and grouping circles on a single slide

1) In Normal view, display the title slide of the presentation that you worked on in Exercises 39.1 and 39.2. We named it KBpres1_green_on_yellow.ppt.

Ellipse button

2) Click **Ellipse** on the *Drawing* toolbar, and hold down the **Shift** key.

   This ensures that the shape you are about to draw will be a circle rather than an oval.

3) Move the cursor over the slide and draw a small circle to the left of the words 'Round Wheels'.

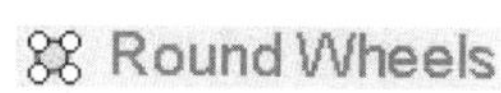

   If your circle is not positioned as shown, reposition it by dragging the green dot above the circle. (For small, precise movements, hold down the **Ctrl** key and use the arrow keys.)

4) With the circle selected, press **Ctrl+c** to copy it and then **Ctrl+v** to paste it.

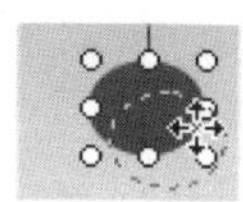

5) Drag your second circle over to the right of the words 'Round Wheels'.

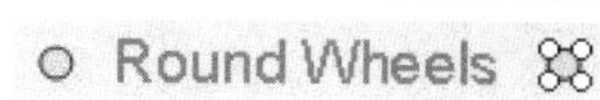

6) With your second circle selected, hold down the **Shift** key, and click on your first circle. Both circles are now selected.

7) Click **Draw** on the *Drawing* toolbar. From the pop-up menu displayed, choose **Group**.

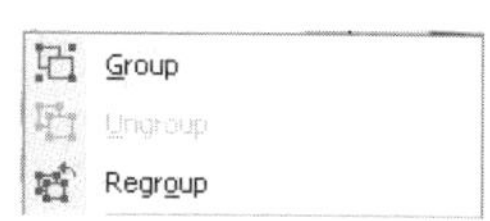

   You can now work with the two grouped graphics as if they were a single object.

8) Click the arrow to the right of **Fill Color** on the *Drawing* toolbar, and select the same medium green colour as the text.

9) Click the arrow to the right of **Line Color** on the *Drawing* toolbar, and select the **No Line** option. This removes any border from the two grouped graphics.

10) As a final step, click **Draw** to the left of the *Drawing* toolbar. From the pop-up menu displayed, choose **Ungroup**.

Well done! You have learnt how to draw and work with simple graphics on a slide. In the next exercise you will add a decorative line to all slides of your presentation.

Exercise 39.4: Inserting lines on all slides

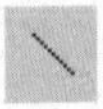

Line button

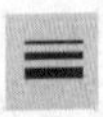

Line Style button

1) Display the slide master of the presentation that you worked on in Exercises 39.1, 39.2 and 39.3.
   We named it KBpres1_green_on_yellow.ppt.
2) Click **Line** on the *Drawing* toolbar. Move the cursor over the slide, and draw a line along the bottom of your slide master.
3) With the line selected, click **Line Style**, and change the line thickness to 3 points.

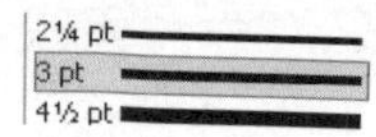

4) Click the arrow to the right of **Line Color** on the *Drawing* toolbar. From the pop-up menu, select the same medium green colour as the text.
5) Switch to Slide Sorter view.
   Notice that all your slides now have a line along their lower edge.
   In Normal view, your title slide should look as shown.

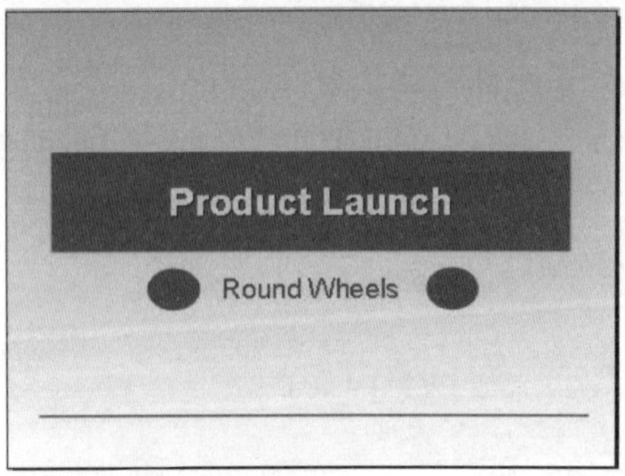

Save your presentation.

You have completed the exercises on your 'Product Launch' presentation. You can close this presentation if you wish.

In the remainder of this chapter, you will work with your 'ECDL: An Overview' presentation. You will begin by inserting one of PowerPoint's AutoShapes on the slide master.

Exercise 39.5: Inserting an AutoShape on every slide in a presentation

1) Open the ECDL presentation, with the yellow text against a dark blue background, that you created in Chapter 38.

   We named it KBpres2_yellow_on_blue.ppt.

2) Choose **View | Master | Slide Master** to display the slide master for your presentation.

3) Click **AutoShapes** on the *Drawing* toolbar. From the pop-up menu displayed, choose **Stars and Banners**, and select *5-Point Star.*

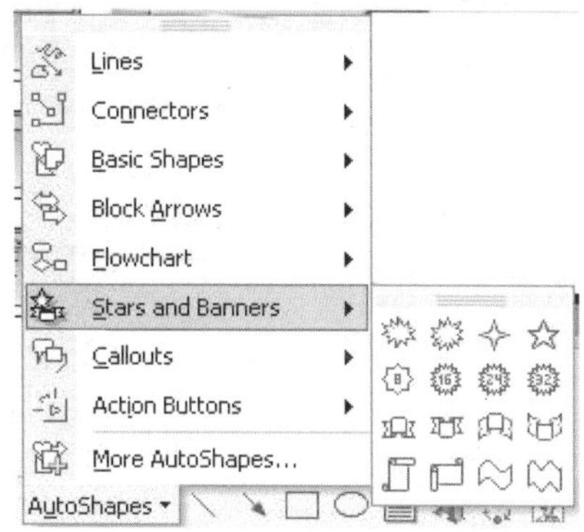

4) Draw the star in the lower-right of the *Object Area for AutoLayouts*.

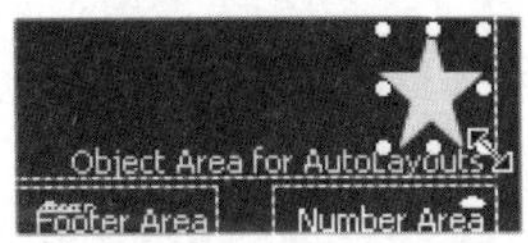

5) On the *Standard* toolbar, increase your Zoom magnification to 100%.

6) With the star selected, use **Fill Color** on the *Drawing* toolbar to change its fill colour to the same yellow as the text.

7) With the star selected, use the **Line Color** button to change the star's border to yellow also.

8) With the star selected, press **Ctrl+x** to cut it and then **Ctrl+v** to paste it. Press **Ctrl+v** twice again to paste the star a second and third time.

9) Reposition the three stars so that they are along a straight line in the bottom-right corner.

   (For small movements, hold down the **Ctrl** key and press the arrow keys.)

10) Using their corner sizing handles, change the size of the left and middle stars, so that the first one is bigger than the second, and the second smaller than the third.

11) Switch to Slide Sorter view. Notice that each slide now has three stars in its lower-right corner.

    In the same way, you can import any graphic image or other object directly into your slide master, or copy (or cut) and paste an object from another presentation or from another application program. You can then reposition and resize the object as above.

Text boxes

Up to now, you have entered text on slides by selecting a placeholder and typing text into it. You can also enter text by drawing a text box and then typing text into that.

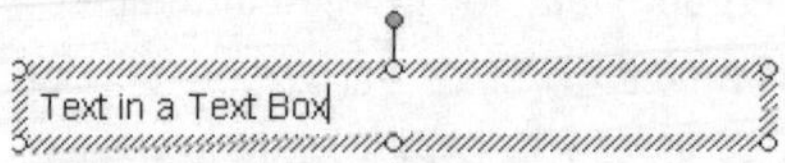

You can change the format and alignment of text in a text box in the same way as you would change text in a placeholder. You can place a text box on top of a graphic such as an AutoShape.

Note, however, that PowerPoint does not display text entered in a text box in Outline view.

Exercise 39.6: Inserting a text box

Text Box button

1) In Normal view, display the title (first) slide of the presentation that you worked on in Exercise 39.5. Change the Zoom setting so that you can see the whole slide on your screen.
2) Click **Text Box** on the *Drawing* toolbar, and draw a text box in the lower-left corner of the slide.

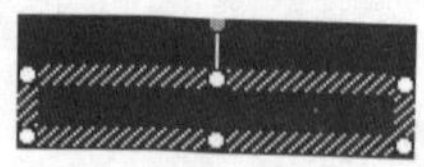

3) Select the text box and type the following:

   Best Results
4) Select the text, and change it to Verdana, bold, 24 point.

   If the text does not fit on a single line in your text box, click on a corner of the box and drag to make the box wider.
5) With the text selected, change its colour to the same medium green as the slide titles.

   Click anywhere else on the slide to deselect the text box.

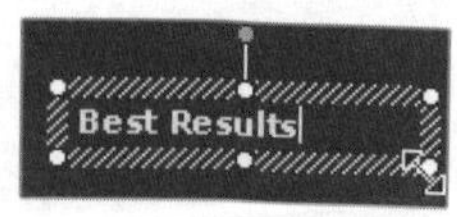

Exercise 39.7: Placing a text box on top of a graphic and rotating it

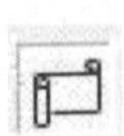

Horizontal Scroll button

1) Insert a horizontal scroll on the same slide that you created in Exercise 39.6. To do this, click the **AutoShapes** button, choose **Stars and Banners**, and select *Horizontal Scroll*. Make the scroll wide enough to hold the Best Results text box.

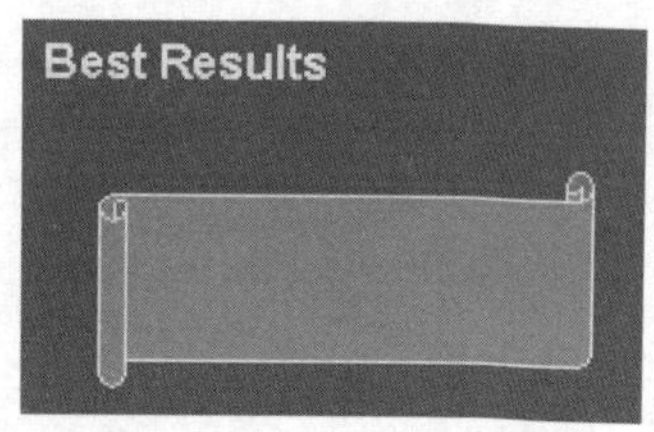

2) Select the Best Results text box, and choose **Order | Bring to Front** from the **Draw** menu.

3) Drag the text box into position over the scroll.

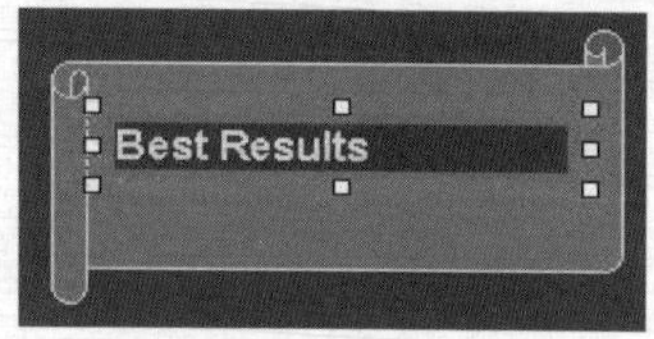

4) Group the text box and the horizontal scroll: to do this, select both of them and choose **Draw | Group**.

Free Rotate button

5) With the grouped objects selected, click on the **Free Rotate** button on the toolbar. Notice how Powerpoint replaces the border of the group with four green dots, one at each corner.

6) Click on the top left green dot, and rotate the group by about 45 degrees. Press the **Esc** key to switch off the rotation feature.

   Your scroll and text should look as shown.

   Save your presentation.

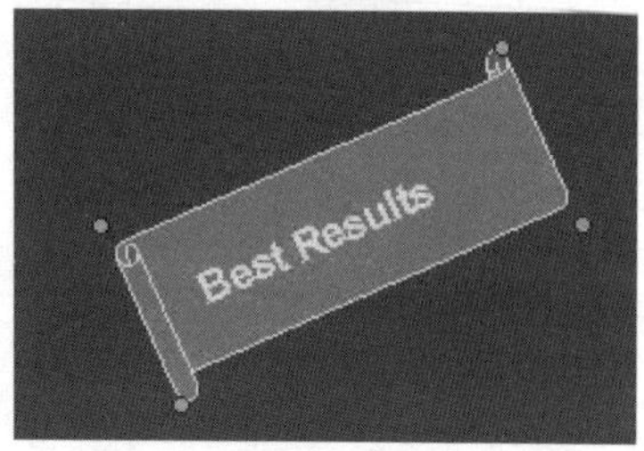

Well done. You have now finished your exercises in PowerPoint graphics. It's time to learn about importing pictures.

Importing pictures

You can also illustrate your slides by inserting pictures – drawings created in other software applications, scanned photographs or Clip Art.

PowerPoint includes a gallery of Clip Art images that you can use in different presentations. They are grouped in many different categories such as academic, business, food and travel to mention just a few. You can access this gallery from the *Insert Clip Art* task pane. Click the arrow to the right of the current task pane and select **Insert Clip Art**. The *Insert Clip Art* task pane is now displayed.

Clip Art
Standard or stock images that can be used and reused in presentations and other documents.

You can include a picture in a slide in any of the following ways:

- Create a new slide, and select either of the following two slide layouts from the *Slide Layout* task pane: Title, Text and Clip Art or Title, Clip Art and Text.

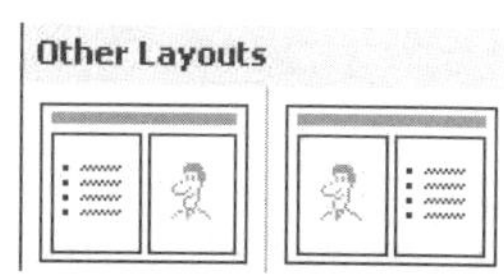

PowerPoint displays the Clip Art icon on your slide. Double-click the **Clip Art** icon, search for the picture you want, and click **OK**.

Clip Art icon

-or-

- Display an existing slide, and do either of the following:

  Choose **Insert | Picture | Clip Art**. The *Insert Clip Art* task pane is displayed. In the *Search text* box enter what type of picture you want. Select the picture required and from the drop-down list select **Insert**.

  -or-

  Choose **Format | Slide Layout**, and select either Title, Text and Clip Art or Title, Clip Art and Text. Click **Apply to Selected Slides**. Double-click the **Clip Art** icon, and select the picture that you require.

To insert a picture on every slide in a presentation, place it on the slide master.

You will practise working with pictures in the next two exercises.

Exercise 39.8: Inserting a Clip Art picture

1) In Normal view, display the presentation that you worked on in Exercise 39.7, and display the third slide entitled 'Benefits for Colleges'.
2) Choose **Format | Slide Layout**. In the *Slide Layout* task pane select the *Title, Clip Art and Text* layout in the **Other Layouts** section. Click **Apply to Selected Slides.**

   Your slide should now look as shown.

   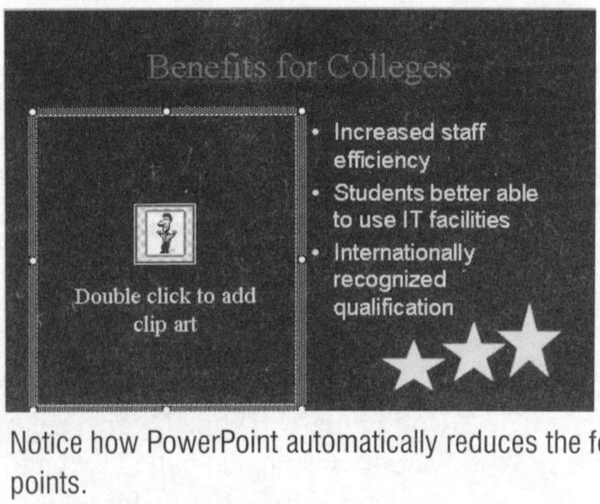

   Notice how PowerPoint automatically reduces the font size of the bullet points.
3) Double-click on the **Clip Art** icon to open the Clip Art gallery in the *Select Picture* dialog box.

4) Type 'Graduation' in the *Search text* box and click **Search**. Select the top-right image of the woman graduate and click **OK**.

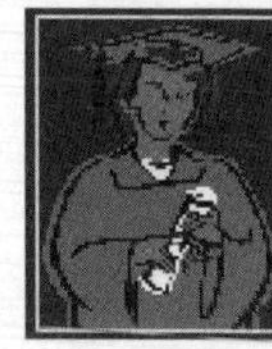

PowerPoint inserts the picture in your slide.

5) Click on the lower-right handle of the inserted picture and reduce it in size by about 20%.

Your slide should look as shown.

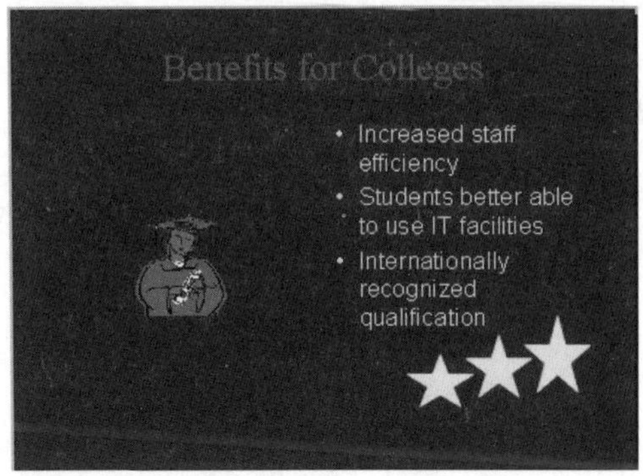

6) In Normal view, display your fifth slide, entitled 'Benefits for Employers'. Choose **Insert | Clip Art | Picture**. In the *Insert Clip Art* task pane, type 'business' in the *Search text* box and click **Search**.

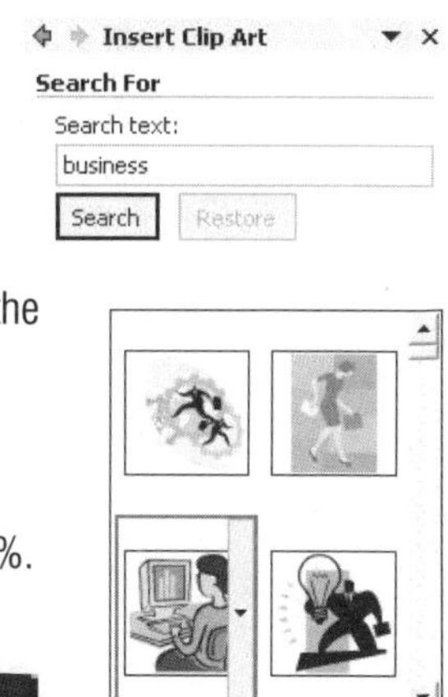

7) Select the bottom-left picture of the woman and the PC. Click the arrow to the right of the picture and select **Insert**.

PowerPoint inserts the picture in your slide.

8) Reduce your inserted picture in size by about 20%.

Your slide should look as shown.

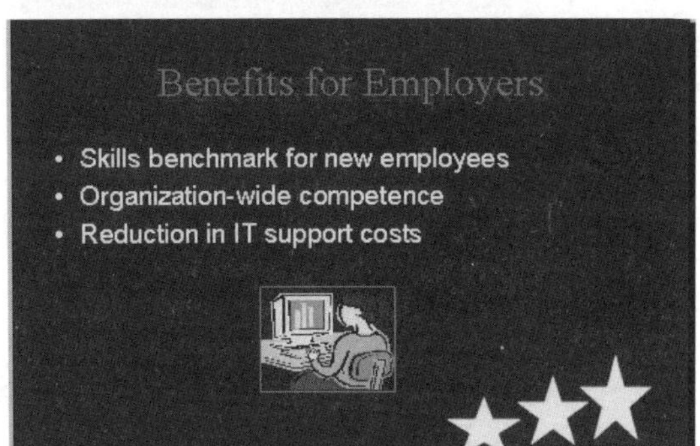

9) With your fifth slide still displayed in Normal view, click **New Slide** on the *Standard* toolbar.

10) In the *Slide Layout* task pane, select the *Title, Text and Clip Art* layout in the **Other Layouts** section. Click **Apply to Selected Slides**.

11) In the title placeholder of your new, sixth slide, type the following:

    Benefits for Society

    In the text placeholder, type the following:

    Participation for all in the Information Society

12) Double-click on the **Clip Art** icon to open the Clip Art gallery in the *Select Picture* dialog box.

13) Type 'Senior Citizens' in the *Search text* box and click **Search**. Select the top-right image of a couple and click **OK**.

    PowerPoint inserts the picture in your slide.

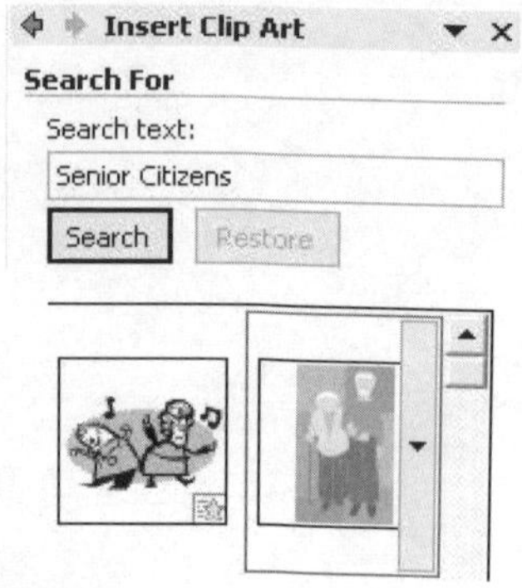

14) Click on the lower-right handle of the inserted picture and reduce it in size by about 20%.

    Drag the picture up until it is level with the bullet point text in the left placeholder.

    Your slide should look as shown.

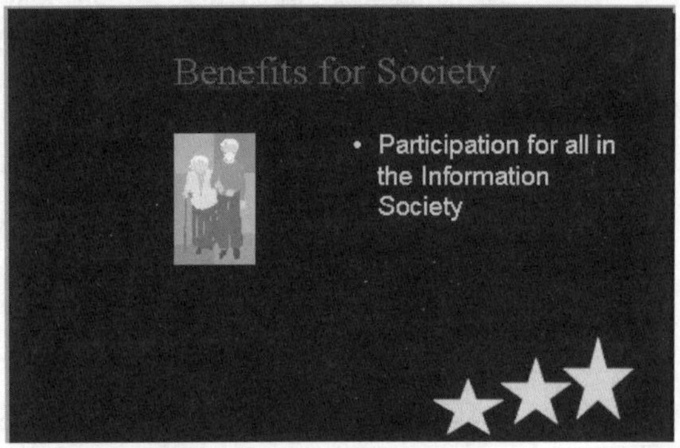

15) Choose **View | Slide Show**, or click the **Slide Show** button. Move forward and back through your presentation to see how it would look to an audience.

You can move, resize or delete an imported image as you would any other object. As the next exercise shows, you can also place borders and shadows around them.

Exercise 39.9: Placing borders and shadows around pictures

1) In Normal view, display the presentation that you worked on in Exercise 39.8, and display your third slide, entitled 'Benefits for Colleges'.

2) Click the inserted picture to select it.

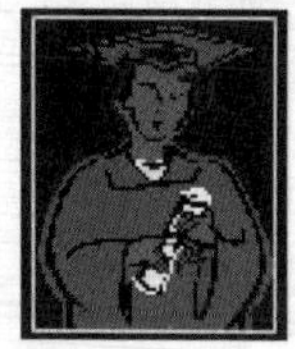

3) Click **Line Style** on the *Drawing* toolbar. From the menu displayed, select a line width of 1 point.

   PowerPoint places a 1-point solid border around your inserted picture.

4) With the picture selected, click the **Line Color** button, and change its colour to the same green as the slide title text.

5) Display your sixth slide, entitled 'Benefits for Society'. Click the inserted picture to select it.

6) Click **Shadow Style** on the *Drawing* toolbar. From the pop-up menu displayed, select the *Shadow Style 2* option.

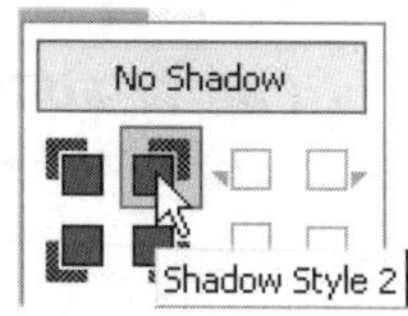

   PowerPoint places a shadow around your inserted picture.

7) With the inserted picture selected, click again on the **Shadow Style** button, and select **Shadow Settings** to view the *Shadow Settings* toolbar.

8) Click the arrow to the right of the **Shadow Color** button, and select a light blue from the colours available.

9) PowerPoint places a light blue shadow around your imported picture.

   Save your presentation.

Well done! You have completed the picture exercises in PowerPoint.

Non-Clip Art pictures

To insert an image of your own – your company logo, for example – on a slide, choose **Insert | Picture | From File**, select the required image file, and choose **Insert**. If you want the image on every slide in the presentation, do this from the slide master.

PowerPoint accepts images in most common image file formats.

The Picture toolbar

To change the colours, brightness or contrast of the picture, you can use the *Picture* toolbar. Either choose **View | Toolbars | Picture**, or right-click on the image and choose the *Show Picture Toolbar* option.

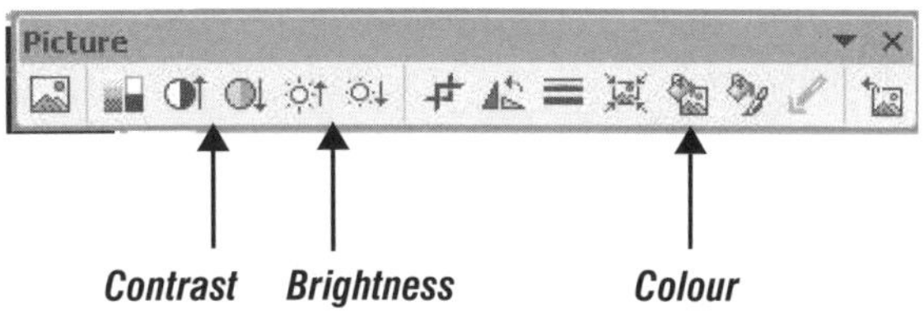

Any changes you make are shown on-screen. Click on the **Close** box at the top right of the *Picture* toolbar when you are finished.

Experiment on your three inserted pictures using the *Picture* toolbar. You can reverse any changes you make with the **Undo** button.

You may now save and close all open presentations, and close PowerPoint. You have completed the fourth chapter of the ECDL presentations module.

Chapter summary: so now you know

The *graphics* that you can draw on PowerPoint slides include simple shapes such as lines, arrows, rectangles, circles and ellipses. *AutoShapes* are commonly used, ready-made shapes that you can insert in your presentations.

You can change the shape, size, position and colour of simple graphics and AutoShapes. You can rotate them, flip them, and add shadows behind them. You can also group them so that you work with them as if they were single objects. See Exercises 39.1, 39.2, 39.3, 39.4 and 39.5 for examples of how to do these tasks.

A *text box* is a text placeholder that you insert directly on a slide. You can change the format and alignment of text in a text box in the same way as you would text in a placeholder that is part of an AutoLayout. See Exercises 39.6 and 39.7 for examples of how to do this.

You can illustrate your slides by *inserting* pictures – drawings created in other software applications or scanned photographs. PowerPoint includes a gallery of *Clip Art* pictures that you can use in different presentations. See Exercise 39.8 for an example of how to do this.

You can move, resize or delete imported pictures as you would any other object, and place borders and shadows around them. See Exercise 39.9 for an example of how to do this.

Quick quiz: working with graphics and pictures

Circle the correct answer to each of the following multiple-choice questions about working with graphics and pictures in PowerPoint.

Q1	How do you group two circles on a single slide?
A.	Select one circle. Click **Draw** on the *Drawing* toolbar, and choose **Group** from the pop-up menu displayed.
B.	Select both circles. Click **Draw** on the *Drawing* toolbar, and choose **Group** from the pop-up menu displayed.
C.	Select both circles. Click **Draw** on the *Drawing* toolbar, and choose **Rotate or Flip | Free Rotate** from the pop-up menu displayed.
D.	Select both circles. Click **Draw** on the *Drawing* toolbar, and choose **Order | Bring to Front** from the pop-up menu displayed.

Q2	How do you insert a text box?
A.	Click **Text Box** on the *Drawing* toolbar, and draw a box in the slide. Select the box and type the text you want. Click anywhere outside the box to deselect it.
B.	Click **Rectangle** on the *Drawing* toolbar, and draw a box in the slide. Select the box and type the text you want. Click anywhere outside the box to deselect it.
C.	Click **Line** on the *Drawing* toolbar, and draw a box in the slide. Select the box and type the text you want. Click anywhere outside the box to deselect it.
D.	Click **Arrow** on the *Drawing* toolbar, and draw a box in the slide. Select the box and type the text you want. Click anywhere outside the box to deselect it.

Q3	How do you insert an AutoShape on the slide master?
A.	Choose **View | Master | Notes Master**. Click **AutoShapes** on the *Drawing* toolbar, and choose the AutoShape required. Draw the object on the slide.
B.	Choose **View | Normal**. Click **AutoShapes** on the *Drawing* toolbar, and choose the AutoShape required. Draw the object on the slide.
C.	Choose **View | Slide Sorter**. Click **AutoShapes** on the *Drawing* toolbar, and choose the AutoShape required. Draw the object on the slide.
D.	Choose **View | Master | Slide Master**. Click **AutoShapes** on the *Drawing* toolbar, and choose the AutoShape required. Draw the object on the slide.

Q4	How do you rotate an object?
A.	Select the object, click **Draw** on the *Drawing* toolbar and from the pop-up menu choose **Rotate or Flip**. Then choose **Free Rotate**. Four green dots appear at each corner of the object. Click these and rotate the object.
B.	Select the object, click **Draw** on the *Drawing* toolbar and from the pop-up menu choose **Nudge**. Then choose **Up**. The object moves up the slide.
C.	Click **Draw** on the *Drawing* toolbar and from the pop-up menu choose **Rotate or Flip**. Then choose **Free Rotate**. Four green dots appear at each corner of the object. Click these and rotate the object.
D.	Select the object, click **Draw** on the *Drawing* toolbar and from the pop-up menu choose **Nudge**. Then choose **Down**. The object moves up the slide.

Answers

1: B, **2:** A, **3:** D, **4:** A.

Chapter 40: Working with tables and charts

In this chapter

You are not limited to creating slides with bullet points in PowerPoint. In this chapter you will learn about three other types of slides that are suited for presenting particular types of information: slides with *tables*, slides with *organization charts*, and slides with *quantitative* charts.

Tables consist of rectangular cells of text and numbers, arranged in rows and columns. Organizational charts are suitable for showing the roles of people in an organization (represented by boxes) and their relationships (represented by lines). Quantitative (number-based) charts include the bar, column and pie chart types.

New skills

At the end of this chapter you should be able to:

- Create, enter text on, and format a table on a slide.
- Create, enter text on, and format an organization chart on a slide.
- Modify the structure of an organization chart.
- Create bar, column, line and pie charts for presenting quantitative information.
- Reformat the appearance of a chart or selected chart elements.
- Change a chart's type.

New word

At the end of this chapter you should be able to explain the following term:

- Organization chart

Working with tables

You can create a table in PowerPoint in the following ways:

- On an existing slide, click **Insert Table** on the *Standard* toolbar. Next, drag to select the number of rows and columns that you want.

  -or-

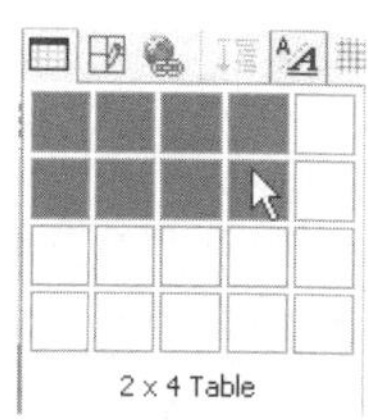

- On an existing slide, choose the **Insert | Table** command, select the number of rows and columns required, and click **OK**.

-or-

- Click **New Slide** on the *Formatting* toolbar. In the *Slide Layout* task pane select the *Title and Table* layout found under **Other Layouts**. Click the arrow to the right of the *Title and Table* layout and select *Apply to Selected Slides.*

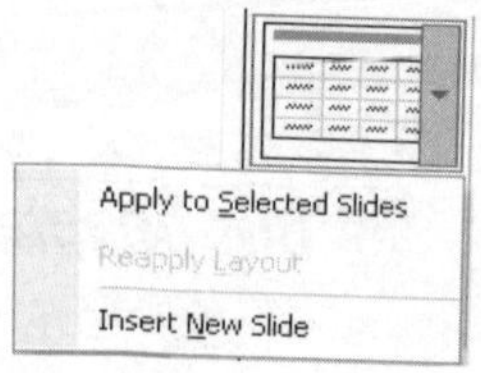

As with text in a text box, PowerPoint does not display text in a table in the Outline pane of Normal view.

Moving, copying and deleting tables

As with other graphic objects, you can move, copy and delete tables. Select the table and then use the **Cut, Copy** and **Paste** commands.

You can move and copy tables between slides, both in the current presentation and in other open presentations.

Exercise 40.1: Inserting a table

1) If PowerPoint is not already open, open it now. Open the ECDL presentation with yellow text against a dark blue background, which you worked with in Chapter 39. We called it KBpres2_yellow_on_blue.ppt.

2) Display your sixth slide, entitled 'Benefits for Society', and click **New Slide** on the *Formatting* toolbar. In the *Slide Layout* task pane, select the *Title and Table* layout found under **Other Layouts**. Click the arrow to the right of the *Title and Table* layout and select *Apply to Selected Slides*.

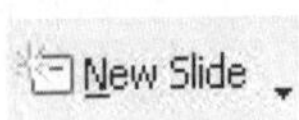

New Slide button

Double-click the **Table** icon. In the *Insert Table* dialog box, select two columns and four rows, and click **OK**. Type text in your slide until it looks as shown.

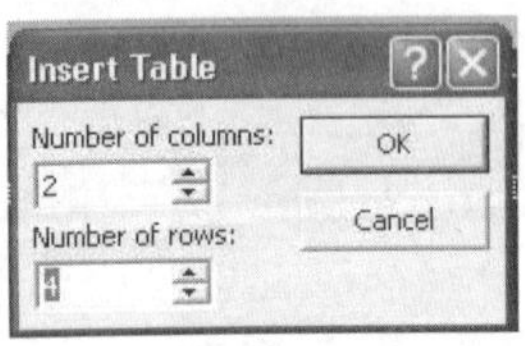

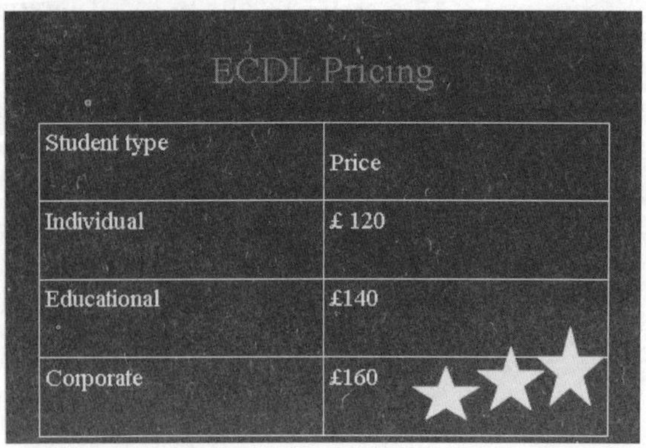

3) Select the top row of your table by dragging across the two top table cells with the mouse.

4) With the top row selected, click **Bold** and then **Center-align** on the *Formatting* toolbar.

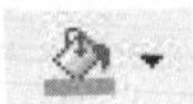

Fill Color button

5) With the top row still selected, use **Fill Color** on the *Drawing* toolbar, and change its colour to the same medium green as the slide title text.
6) With the top row still selected, choose **View | Toolbars | Tables and Borders**.

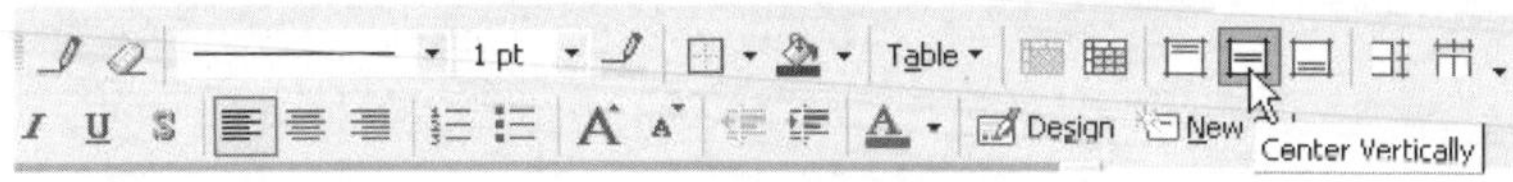

On the toolbar, select **Center Vertically**. Close the *Tables and Borders* toolbar.

7) Select the three cells containing prices, and click **Center-align** on the *Formatting* toolbar.
8) With the table placeholder selected, click the centre sizing handle on the lower placeholder border. Your cursor changes to a double-ended arrow.
9) Drag the sizing handle upwards until the table placeholder no longer overlaps the three stars.

Click anywhere else on the slide to deselect the table placeholder.

Your slide should look as shown.

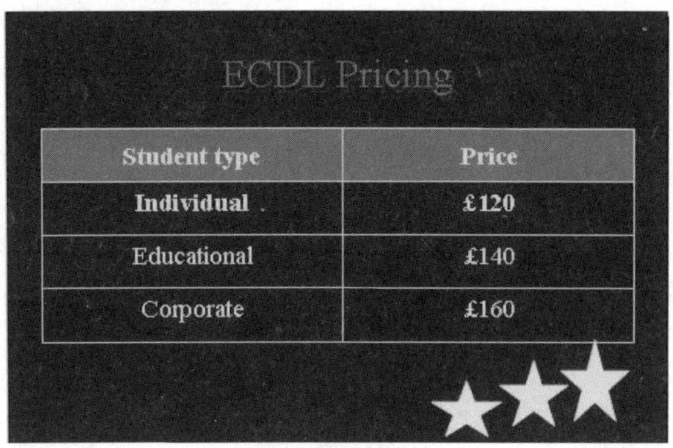

10) Save your presentation, which now has seven slides.

Organization charts

Organization charts are used to illustrate people's positions within an organization or the structure of components within a physical system or process. Such charts have two main components:

- **Boxes:** These represent people in the organization or components within the system or process.
- **Lines:** These represent relationships between people or units of the organization or system.

You could create organization charts using the drawing tools, but they are used so frequently that PowerPoint provides a tool especially for producing them.

Organization chart
A diagram used to illustrate the people or units in an organization (represented by boxes) and their relationships (represented by lines).

You can insert an organization chart in the following ways:

- Start with a blank slide, or one with only a title, and choose **Insert | Picture | Organization Chart**.

  -or-

- Choose **Insert | Diagram**. PowerPoint opens the *Diagram Gallery*, which displays an organization chart template and offers other diagram types.

  -or-

- Choose **Format | Slide Layout**. In the *Slide Layout* task pane select the *Title and Diagram or Organization Chart layout* found under *Other Layouts*. Click the arrow to the right of the slide layout and select **Apply to Selected Slides**. PowerPoint displays the Organization Chart icon on your slide. Double-click it.

  PowerPoint opens the *Diagram Gallery,* which displays an organization chart template and offers other diagram types.

Exercise 40.2: Inserting an organization chart in a new slide

1) In Normal view, display the slide entitled 'ECDL Pricing' that you created in Exercise 40.1.

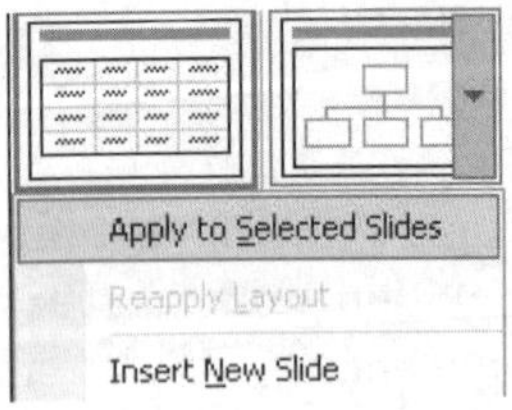

2) Click **New Slide** on the *Formatting* toolbar. In the *Slide Layout* task pane select the *Title and Diagram or Organization Chart* layout found under *Other Layouts*. Click the arrow to the right of the slide layout and select **Apply to Selected Slides**.

3) On the slide, double-click the **Organization Chart** icon to open the *Diagram Gallery* dialog box. Select *Organization Chart* and click **OK**. Type the text in the template as shown, and save your presentation.

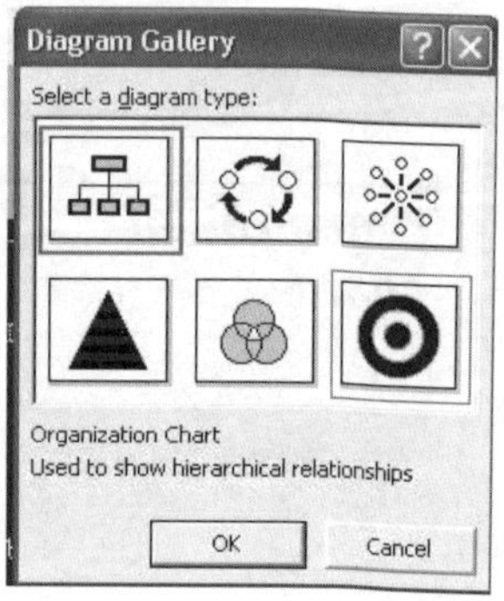

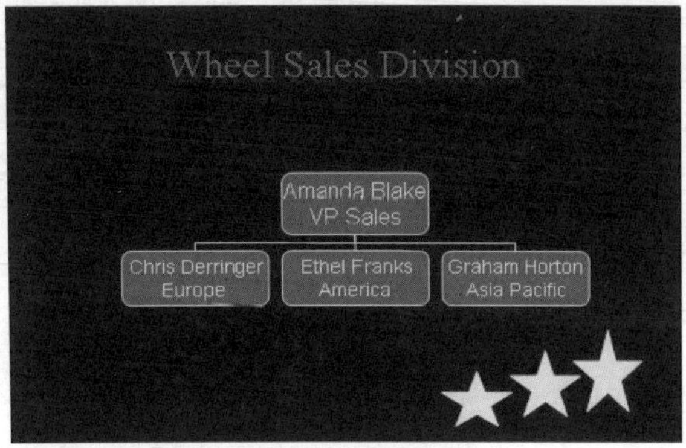

Within PowerPoint, you can move, resize, place borders or shadows around, or delete a chart as you would any other object.

Exercise 40.3: Reformatting an organization chart

1) Display your organization chart in Normal view, and select the chart by clicking anywhere on it.
2) As you learnt in Chapter 39, you can make text and graphics on your slides appear to stand out from the background by adding a shadow to them.

   Click **Shadow Style** on the *Drawing* toolbar. From the menu displayed, select *Shadow Style 5*.
3) With the chart still selected, click **Shadow Style** again. From the pop-up menu displayed, choose **Shadow Settings**. The *Shadow Settings* toolbar appears on the top-right of the *Standard* toolbar. Click the arrow to the right of **Shadow Color**, and select light blue as the shadow colour.

   Close the *Shadow Settings* toolbar.

   Be careful when choosing a colour for the shadow that you do not interfere with the legibility of your text. Save your presentation.

Exercise 40.4: Modifying the structure of an organization chart

1) In Normal view, display the organization chart slide that you created in Exercise 40.2. Click the organization chart.
2) The *Organization Chart* toolbar appears. The toolbar provides buttons for adding boxes (Subordinates, Coworkers, Assistants) and lines.
3) Click the box containing Graham Horton. Next, click the arrow to the right of **Insert Shape** on the *Organization Chart* toolbar.

   A new box is created, at the same level in the hierarchy, and the other chart elements are rearranged.

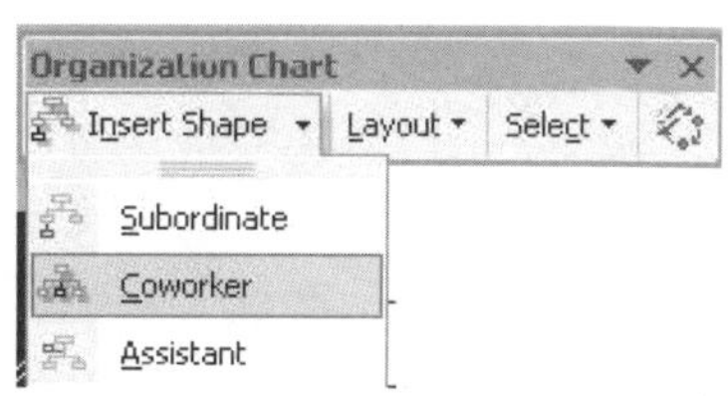

4) Click the new box, and enter text as shown below.

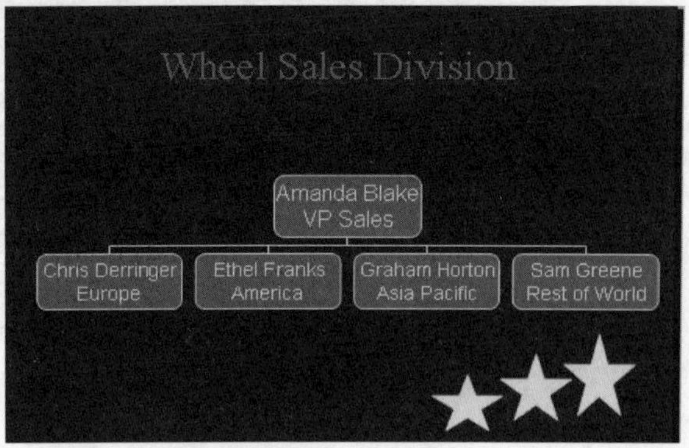

5) Save your presentation.

To remove an organization chart box, right-click it and choose **Cut** from the pop-up menu.

Charts

PowerPoint provides a variety of chart types (notably bar, column, line and pie) that are useful for presenting quantitative (number-based) information.

To include a chart in a slide:

- Choose **Insert | New Slide** or click **New Slide** on the *Formatting* toolbar.
- In the *Slide Layout* task pane, select the *Title and Chart* layout found under *Other Layouts*. Click the arrow to the right of the slide layout and select *Apply to Selected Slides*.
- Double-click the **Chart** icon on the slide.

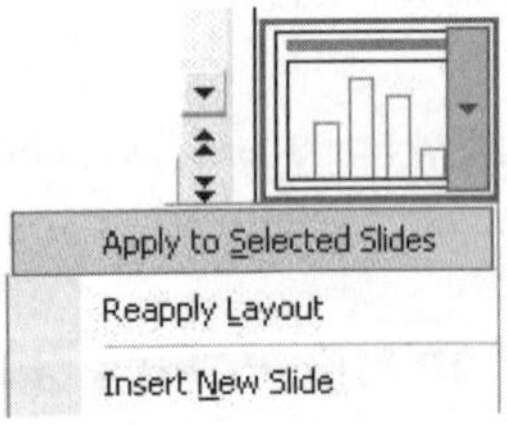

When you insert a chart, PowerPoint displays the following:

- **Datasheet:** A small spreadsheet that you can adapt by typing in your own text and numbers, overwriting those already present. You can add or delete rows or columns as necessary.

  You can move the datasheet to a different part of your screen by clicking and dragging its title bar.
- **Chart:** This changes as you drag the contents of the datasheet. You can change the colour or format of any element in the chart by double-clicking it: you are presented with options that are relevant to that element.

- **Chart menus:** Excel-like menus of charting commands appear at the top of the PowerPoint window.

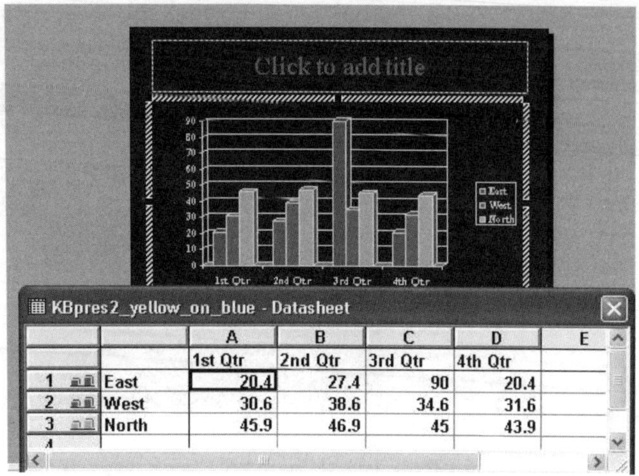

You can close the datasheet window by clicking anywhere else on the PowerPoint screen.

Moving, copying and deleting charts

As with other graphic objects, you can move, copy and delete charts. Select the chart and then use the **Cut, Copy** and **Paste** commands.

You can move and copy charts between slides, both in the current presentation and in other open presentations.

Chart type options

Perhaps your most important decision with a chart is the selection of the appropriate chart type. The most commonly used types are column, bar, line and pie.

- **Column charts:** These are typically used to show figures that are measured at a particular time.

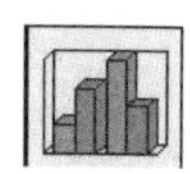

- **Bar column charts:** 'Sideways' column charts that show items vertically and values horizontally.

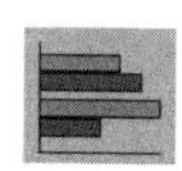

- **Line charts:** These are typically used to illustrate trends over time.

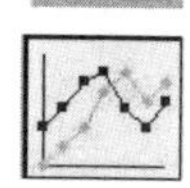

- **Pie charts:** These are typically used to illustrate the breakdown of figures in a total. A pie chart is always based on a *single* column of numbers.

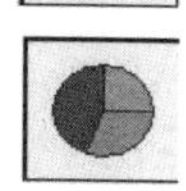

To change the chart type:

- If the Datasheet window is not already open, double-click the chart to open it.
- Right-click on the chart and, from the pop-up menu displayed, choose **Chart Type**.

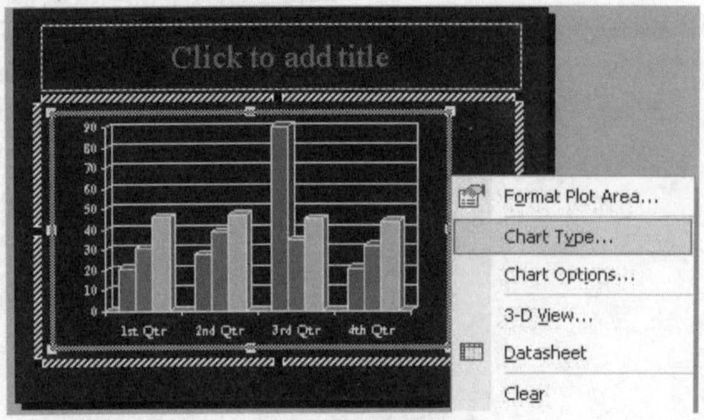

- Select the chart type and sub-type from the list in the **Standard Types** tab of the *Chart Types* dialog box, and then click **OK**.

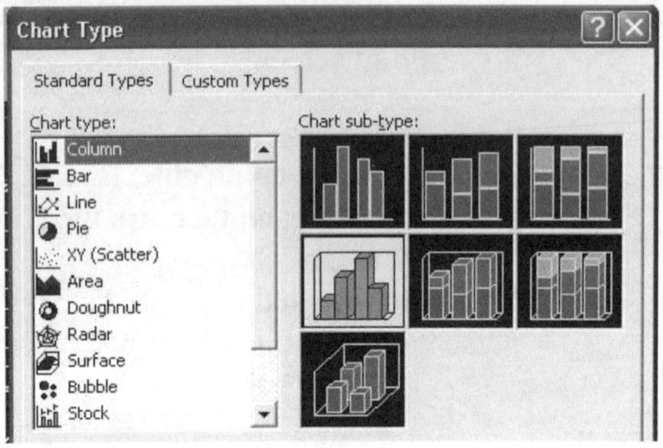

PowerPoint gives you a wide variety of presentation options for charts. Some of them, however, are more decorative than informative: be careful that your message is not obscured.

Exercise 40.5: Inserting a chart

1) In Normal view, display the organization chart that you worked on in Exercise 40.4.
2) Choose **New Slide** on the *Formatting* toolbar. In the *Slide Layout* task pane, select the *Title and Chart* layout found under *Other Layouts*. Click the arrow to the right of the slide layout and select *Apply to Selected Slides*.
3) Click in the title text placeholder and type the following text:

   Sales Projections
4) Double-click the **Chart** icon to open the datasheet window.

5) Edit the text in the datasheet as shown. You can resize the Datasheet window at any stage by clicking on its lower-right corner and dragging.

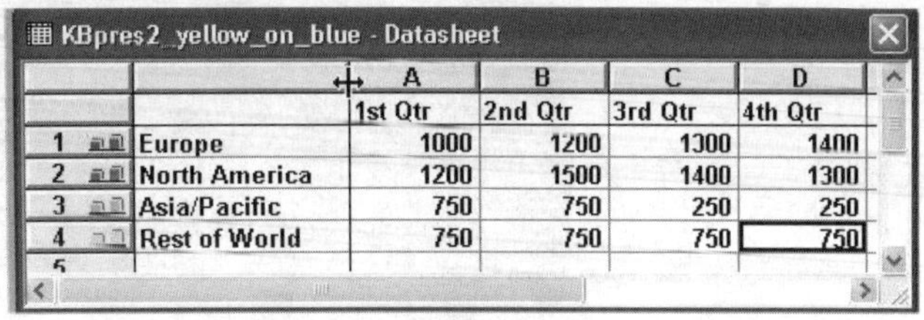
KBpres2_yellow_on_blue - Datasheet

		A	B	C	D
		1st Qtr	2nd Qtr	3rd Qtr	4th Qtr
1	Europe	1000	1200	1300	1400
2	North America	1200	1500	1400	1300
3	Asia/Pacific	750	750	250	250
4	Rest of World	750	750	750	750
5					

Notice how the chart changes as you edit and type text.

You will need to make the first column wider by clicking the boundary in the column header and then dragging the boundary to the right.

6) When you have finished working in the Datasheet window, close it. You are returned to your slide.

7) Save your presentation.

Click anywhere else on your slide to deselect the chart placeholder.

Your slide should look as shown.

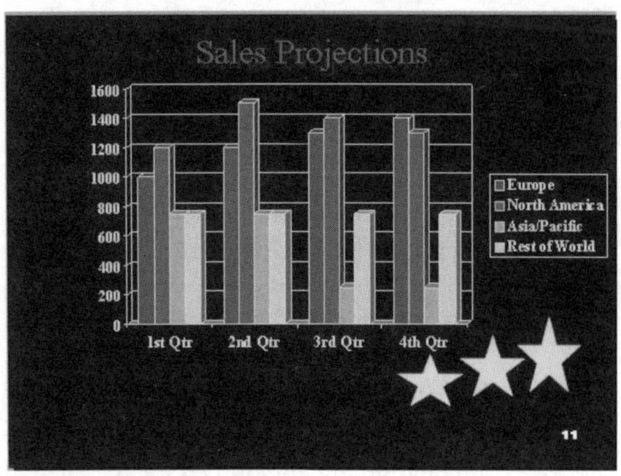

Sometimes, you may wish to change the colour of an element of a chart (such as a column in a column chart, a bar in a bar chart, or a slice in a pie chart). Perhaps the colour you want to change does not contrast sufficiently with your slide background colour – or maybe you just don't like the colour.

The next exercise shows you how to change the colour of a chart column, and the colours of the chart axes and chart legend.

Exercise 40.6: Reformatting a chart

1) In Normal view, display the chart slide that you created in Exercise 40.5.

Double-click on the chart, and then right-click on any column of the chart. From the pop-up menu displayed, choose **Format Data Series.**

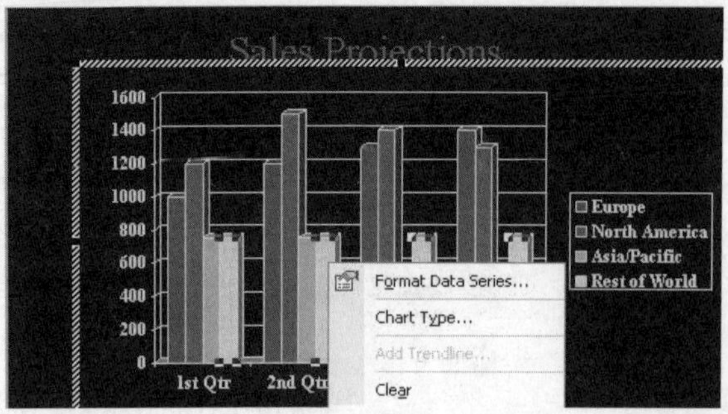

2) On the **Patterns** tab of the dialog box displayed, select white as the colour, and click **OK**.

PowerPoint changes the colour of the column to white.

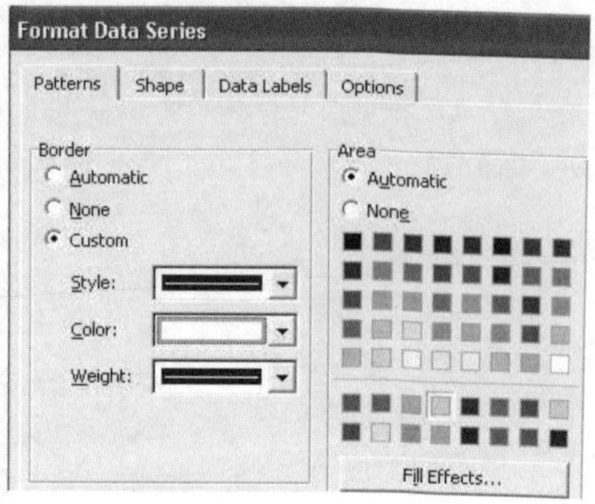

Next, let's change the colour of the axes, axes text and legend text.

3) With the chart selected, right-click on the vertical axis and choose **Format Axis** from the pop-up menu.
4) On the **Font** tab of the dialog box displayed, click the arrow to the right of the *Color* box, select white and click **OK**.
5) With the chart selected, repeat steps 3 and 4 for the chart's horizontal axis.
6) With the chart selected, right-click on the chart legend, choose **Format Legend** and, on the **Font** tab, change the legend text colour to white.

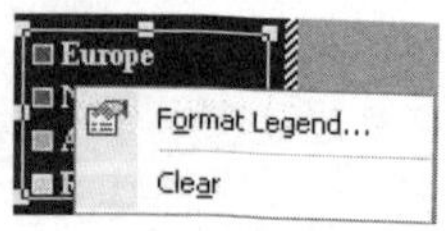

Within PowerPoint, you can move, resize or delete a chart as you would any other object. To make changes to the data in the chart, however, you have to double-click on the chart and make your changes in the Datasheet window

In the next exercise, you will change the chart type from a column chart (the PowerPoint default) to a bar chart.

Exercise 40.7: Changing chart type

1) In Normal view, display the chart that you worked on in Exercise 40.6. Double-click the chart to select it.

2) Right-click anywhere in the area surrounding the chart within the chart placeholder. From the pop-up menu displayed, choose **Chart Type**.

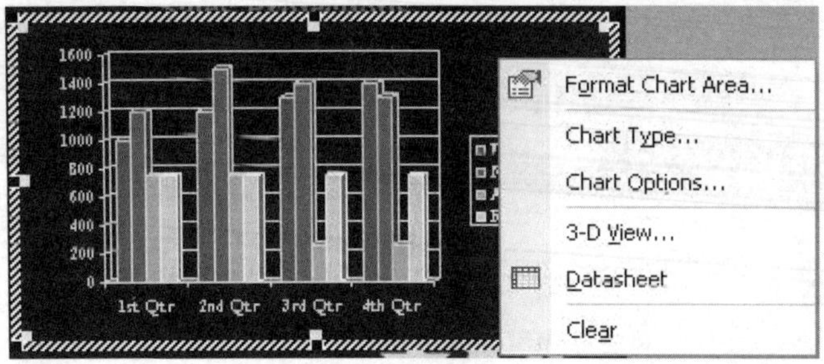

3) In the *Chart Type* dialog box, select *Bar* as the chart type, click the first chart sub-type, and click **OK**.

PowerPoint changes the chart type from column to bar.

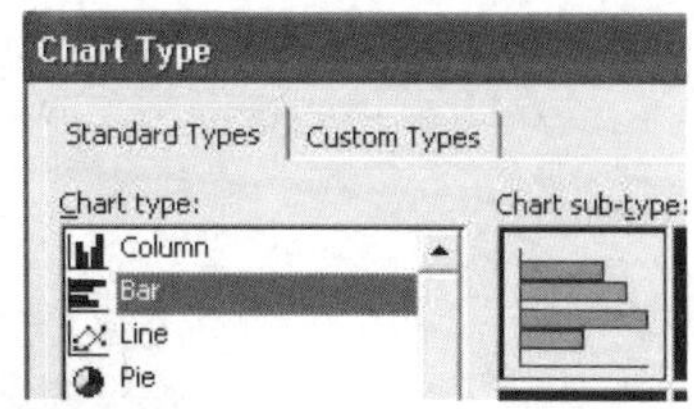

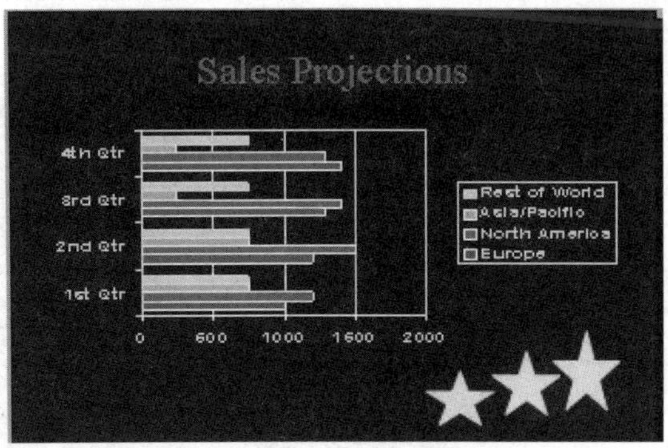

Exercise 40.8: Inserting a pie chart

1) In Normal view, display the chart slide that you worked on in Exercise 40.7.
2) Click **New Slide** on the *Formatting* toolbar. In the *Slide Layout* task pane, select the *Title and Chart* layout found under *Other Layouts*. Click the arrow to the right of the slide layout and select *Apply to Selected Slides*.
3) Click in the title text placeholder and type the following text:

   Annual Sales Growth
4) Double-click the **Chart** icon to open the Datasheet window.

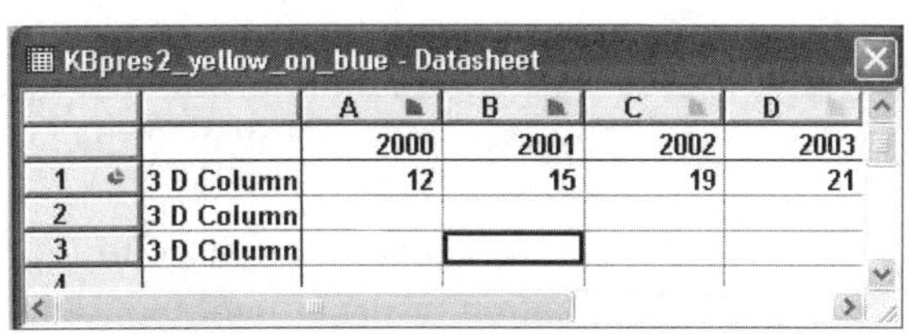

5) Edit the text as shown in the datasheet.

   To remove sample numbers and text that PowerPoint has placed in the cells, click in each cell and press the **Delete** key. When finished, close the datasheet and return to your slide.

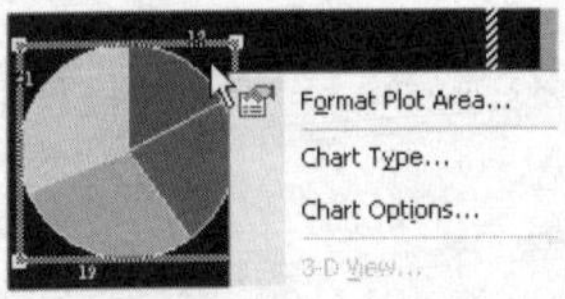

6) Right-click any column of your chart, choose **Chart Type** from the pop-up menu, select *Pie* as Chart Type, select the first chart sub-type, and click **OK**.
7) With the chart selected, right-click in the plot area – the area outside the pie shape but inside the chart area.
8) From the pop-up menu displayed, choose **Format Plot Area**.

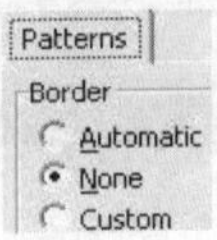

9) On the dialog box displayed, select *None* for *Border*, and click **OK**.
10) With the chart selected, right-click the chart legend, choose **Format Legend** and, on the **Font** tab, change the legend colour to white.

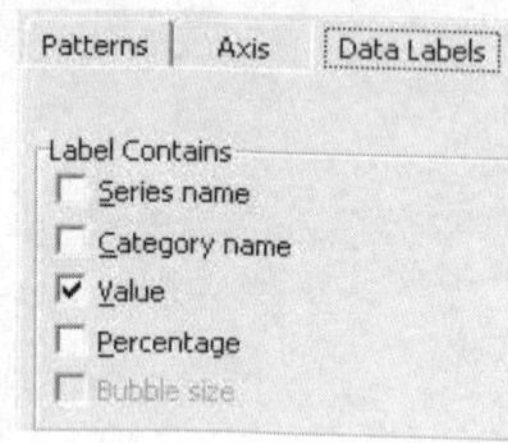

11) Right-click anywhere on the pie-chart and choose **Format Data Series**. On the **Data Labels** tab, select *Value* and click **OK**.
12) Click anywhere else on the slide to deselect the chart. Your slide should look as shown.

    Save your presentation.

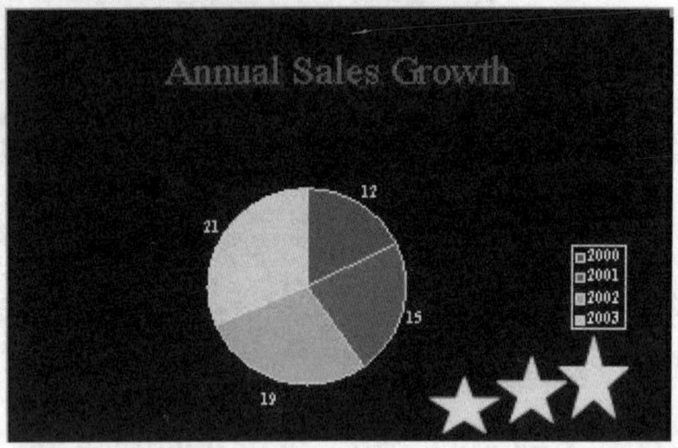

13) Switch to Slide Show view, and inspect your ten-slide presentation as it will be seen by your audience. Impressive, eh?

You may now save and close all open presentations, and close PowerPoint. You have completed the fifth chapter of the ECDL presentations module.

Chapter summary: so now you know

You can create a *table* on a slide with a selected number of rows and columns, enter numbers and text headings, and apply formatting to it. See Exercise 40.1 for an example of how to do this.

Organization charts are used to illustrate people's positions within an organization or the structure of components within a physical system or process. See Exercise 40.2 for an example of how to do this. Organization charts consist of boxes (for representing people or components) and lines (for representing their relationships). PowerPoint's organization chart tool provides a customizable chart template, with boxes arranged in a hierarchical structure. See Exercises 40.3 and 40.4 for examples of how to do these tasks.

You can present quantitative (number-based) information in a variety of *chart types*, such as bar, column and pie charts. PowerPoint's chart-creating tool includes a *datasheet* (a small spreadsheet into which you can type your own text and numbers) and chart menus with relevant spreadsheet-like commands. See Exercises 40.5 and 40.7 for examples of how to do these tasks.

Your chart changes as you modify the contents of the datasheet. You can change the colour or format of any element in the chart (such as a column in a column chart, the chart axes or the chart legend) by double-clicking it and choosing an option from the menu displayed. See Exercises 40.6 and 40.8 for examples of how to do these tasks.

You can move, resize and place borders or shadows around an organizational chart or quantitative data chart as you would any other slide object.

Quick quiz: working with tables and charts

Circle the correct answer to each of the following multiple-choice questions about working with tables and charts in PowerPoint.

Q1	How do you change the colour of a chart column?
A.	Double-click the chart, and then right-click on the vertical axis. Choose **Format Axis** from the pop-up menu displayed. On the **Patterns** tab, select the colour required, and click **OK**.
B.	Double-click the chart, and then right-click on the horizontal axis. Choose **Format Axis** from the pop-up menu displayed. On the **Patterns** tab, select the colour required, and click **OK**.
C.	Double-click the chart, and then right-click on any column. Choose **Format Data Series** from the pop-up menu displayed. On the **Patterns** tab, select the colour required, and click **OK**.
D.	Double-click the chart, and then right-click on the chart legend. Choose **Format Legend** from the pop-up menu displayed. On the **Patterns** tab, select the colour required, and click **OK**.

Q2	How do you change shadow colour in a chart?
A.	Select the chart, click **Shadow Style** on the *Drawing* toolbar. Click **Shadow Settings** on the pop-up menu displayed. The *Shadow Settings* toolbar appears on the top-right of the *Standard* toolbar. Click the arrow to the right of **Shadow Color**, and select the colour required.
B.	Select the chart, click **3-D Style** on the *Drawing* toolbar. Click **3-D Settings** on the pop-up menu displayed. The *3-D Settings* toolbar appears on the top-right of the *Standard* toolbar. Click the arrow to the right of **3-D Color**, and select the colour required.
C.	Select the chart, click the arrow to the right of **Font Color** on the *Drawing* toolbar. Click **More Colors** on the pop-up menu displayed. The *Colors* dialog box is displayed. Select the colour required, and click **OK**.
D.	Select the chart, click the arrow to the right of **Fill Color** on the *Drawing* toolbar. Click **More Fill Colors** on the pop-up menu displayed. The *Colors* dialog box is displayed. Select the colour required, and click **OK**.

Q3	How do you change a chart type?
A.	Right-click in the area surrounding the chart within the chart placeholder. From the pop-up menu displayed, choose **Datasheet**. In the datasheet, insert the information required and close the **Datasheet** box.
B.	Right-click in the area surrounding the chart within the chart placeholder. From the pop-up menu displayed, choose **Chart Options**. In the dialog box, select the **Title** tab, type a title in the *Chart title* box, and click **OK**.
C.	Right-click in the area surrounding the chart within the chart placeholder. From the pop-up menu displayed, choose **Chart Type**. In the dialog box, select the chart type required, such as *Bar*, click the first chart sub-type, and click **OK**.
D.	Right-click in the area surrounding the chart within the chart placeholder. From the pop-up menu displayed, choose **Format Chart Area**. In the dialog box, select the font type required, such as *Bold*, and click **OK**.

Q4	How do you add a colleague to an organization chart?
A.	Double-click the chart, and the *Format AutoShape* dialog box appears. On the **Text box** tab, change the value in the *Text anchor point* box to *Top*, and click **OK**.
B.	Click the chart, and the *Organization* toolbar appears. Click the arrow to the right of **Select**, and select the option required.
C.	Click the chart, and the *Organization* toolbar appears. Click the arrow to the right of **Layout**, and select the option required.
D.	Click the chart, and the *Organization* toolbar appears. Click the arrow to the right of **Insert Shape**, and select the option required.

Q5	How do you insert background colour in a table?
A.	Select the table. Click **Font Color** on the *Drawing* toolbar, and choose the colour required.
B.	Select the table. Click **Fill Color** on the *Drawing* toolbar, and choose the colour required.
C.	Select the table. Click **Line Color** on the *Drawing* toolbar, and choose the colour required.
D.	Select the table. Click **Line Style** on the *Drawing* toolbar, and choose the colour required.

Answers

1: C, **2:** A, **3:** C, **4:** D, **5:** B.

Chapter 41: Wowing your audience

In this chapter

Your slides may contain convincing content, attractive colours and backgrounds, and impressive charts, yet they may still lack something. That 'something' – call it *movement* – is what you learn about in this section.

You will discover how you can make your slides advance automatically after a specific time interval, insert visual transition effects between slides, and animate slide elements so that they appear progressively rather than all at once.

Animations, as you will learn, are more than a visual effect. By enabling the presenter to highlight each point on a slide in turn, they help to focus the audience's attention.

New skills

By the end of this chapter, you should be able to:

- Apply manual, time-automatic and 'whichever comes first' slide advance methods.
- Specify the nature and timing of transition effects.
- Apply preset animation.
- Customize animation effects so as to modify the order, direction, sound effect and dim effect of animations.
- Include graphics and pictures in animations.
- Animate elements within a chart.
- Check the spellings in your presentation.

New words

At the end of this chapter you should be able to explain the following terms:

- Advance method
- Slide transition
- Animated slide

Automatic or manual advance?

When presenting your slides to your audience, you don't need to press the **Page Down** key or click with the mouse each time you want to move from the current slide.

Here's another option: get PowerPoint to run the show for you, so that your presentation proceeds automatically. You are then free to stand back from your computer and interact more directly with your audience.

Automatic advance, available with the **Slide Show | Slide Transition** command, is often used in presentations that are left running in public areas, such as trade shows, where they are not accompanied by a speaker.

Whichever comes first

You can combine the manual and automatic advance methods so that the presenter can directly override the automatic, timed advance at any time.

To do so, apply a timed advance, but also select the *On mouse click* check box. (When *On mouse click* is selected, pressing the **Page Down** key or the **Enter** key will also display the next slide.)

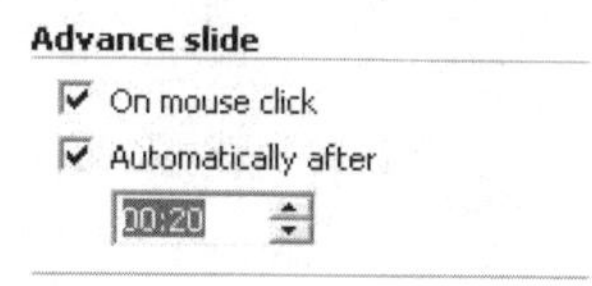

Exercise 41.1: Applying an advance method to a presentation

1) If PowerPoint is not already open, open it now.
2) Open the ECDL presentation with the yellow text against a dark blue background, which you worked on in Chapter 40. We called it KBpres2_yellow_on_blue.ppt.
3) With any slide open in Normal view, choose **Slide Show | Slide Transition**.
4) Choose **Modify transition** in the task pane, and select *Applause* from the *Sound* drop-down list.
5) In the **Advance slide** area, click *Automatically after*, and then type the number of seconds (for example, 15) that you want each slide to remain on-screen. Ensure that the *On mouse click* check box is selected.

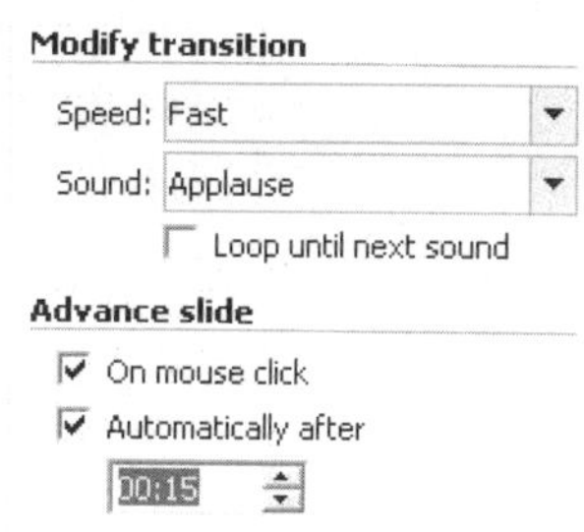

6) Click **Apply to All Slides** to apply the automatic slide advance to your entire presentation. Save your presentation.
7) Choose **View | Slide Show** and see how your selected advance methods affect the running of your presentation.

> ***Advance method***
>
> *The way that PowerPoint displays the slides of a presentation: manually, automatically, or automatically with manual override. Automatic advance is often used for unaccompanied presentations.*

Slide transitions

A transition is a graphic effect that controls how one slide replaces another – for example, the new slide could appear to drop down from the top of the screen, or the old slide could be made to dissolve, revealing the new slide.

PowerPoint lets you select two aspects of a transition – the style and the timing to apply to the transition.

- **Apply to selected slides:** The nature of the special effect with which PowerPoint introduces the slide.
- **Modify transition:** The speed at which PowerPoint runs the visual effect when introducing the slide.

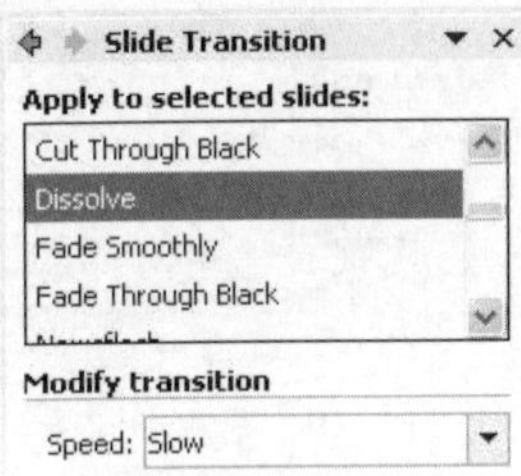

Some transition options

Optionally, for added impact, you can link a sound to the transition between slides. Exercise 41.2 provides an example.

> ***Transition***
>
> *A visual effect, such as a drop-down box, dissolve or fade, that controls how one slide in a presentation is replaced by another.*

Exercise 41.2: Applying a transition to a presentation

1) In Normal view, display any slide of the presentation that you worked on in Exercise 41.1. Choose **Slide Show | Slide Transition**.
2) First explore the transition options on offer:

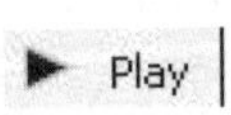

   - **Apply to selected slides:** Each time you click an option from the drop-down list, PowerPoint runs the effect in the slide. You can rerun the preview by clicking **Play.**
   - **Modify transition:** The options – *Slow, Medium* or *Fast* – set the speed at which the transition effect runs. Click an option and PowerPoint runs the effect with that timing in the slide.
   - For this exercise, select the effect *Dissolve*, with a speed of *Fast*.

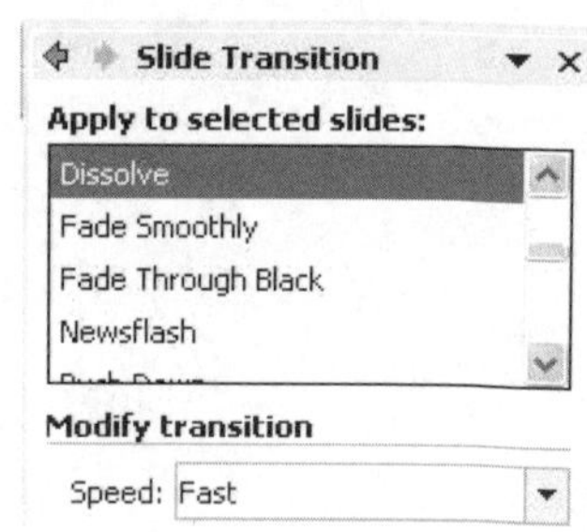

3) Click **Apply to All Slides**.

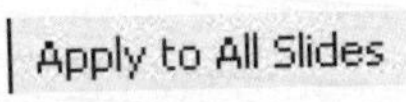

Notice that PowerPoint gives you the option of applying a different transition to each slide (by not clicking **Apply to All Slides**), but be careful: this option may have the effect of distracting or unsettling your audience.

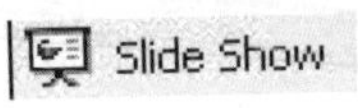

4) See how the transitions affect the presentation by clicking **Slide Show** and moving through the presentation. Save your presentation, and leave it open. You will use it again in Exercise 41.5.

Slide advance methods and transition effects

You specify the slide advance method and the slide transition effects in the **Slide Transition** task pane. The two effects are independent, however:

- You can automate the running of your slide show without applying a transition.
- You can apply a transition without automating your slide show.

Also, the timings have nothing to do with one another:

- **Modify transition** (slow, medium, fast) controls the speed of the transition from the previous slide.
- **Advance slide** specifies how long the slide is displayed for before being replaced.

Animated slides

Animated slides are slides on which the information – typically bullet points – is revealed gradually rather than all at once. When you first show the slide, the audience sees only the first bullet point. You then reveal the remaining bullets, one by one, as you continue to talk to your audience.

With an animated slide, you can highlight each point in turn to focus your audience's attention. When you are talking about your second point, for example, you can leave the first one on the screen, but dim it, so that it still serves as a context and reminder but doesn't distract.

Animated slide
A slide in which different elements are revealed at different times.

You can create animated slides using either of the following two methods:

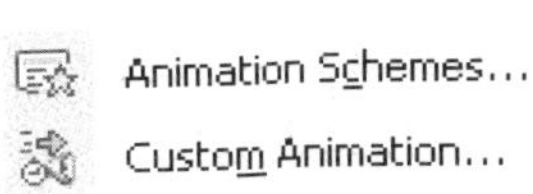

- **Animation schemes:** A series of ready-to-go animations, some with associated sound effects, which you can apply quickly to your slides.
- **Custom animations:** These offer a wide range of dynamic effects and options.

Animated slides enable you to keep your audience engaged with what you are saying, rather than having them read ahead while you are still talking about the first point.

Animations and the slide master

To apply an animation to an entire presentation, first display your slide master, and then apply an animation scheme or custom animation. Let's begin by applying an animation scheme to a slide master.

Exercise 41.3: Applying animation schemes to a presentation

1) Open the Product Launch presentation, with dark green text against a daybreak effect background, which you worked with in Chapter 38. We called it KBpres1_daybreak.ppt.
2) Choose **View | Master | Slide Master** to display your presentation's slide master.
3) Click anywhere in the lower placeholder, where the bulleted text is.
4) Choose **Slide Show | Animation Schemes**. In the task pane, select the option called *Faded Wipe* in the *Apply to selected slides* box. Click **Apply to All Slides**.

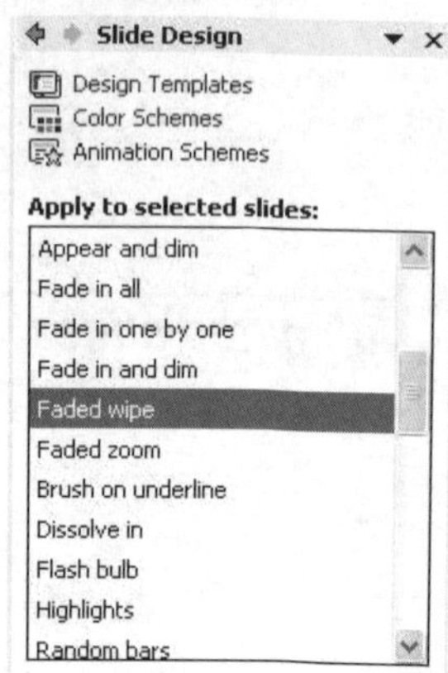

5) Choose **Slide Show** and move through your slides to view the animation effect.

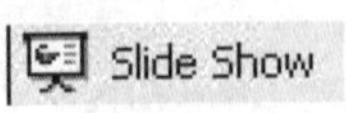

   Remember: you need to click the mouse (or press the **Page Down** key or the **Enter** key) for each bullet point to appear.
6) Save your presentation.

In the next exercise, you will change some settings applied by the animation schemes.

Exercise 41.4: Customizing an animation scheme

1) Display the Product Launch presentation that you worked on in Exercise 41.3. Choose **View | Master | Slide Master** and click anywhere in the lower placeholder.

2) Choose **Slide Show | Custom Animation**. The task pane displays the settings of the animation schemes, and gives you the ability to change them.

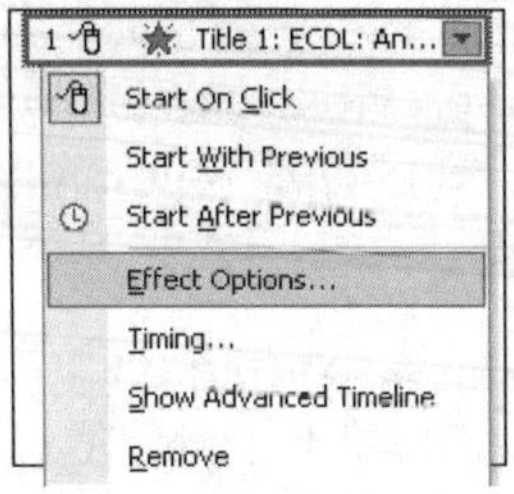

3) Click the arrow to the right of the first item on the Custom Animation List, *Title 1: Click to edit Master title style*. From the list displayed, select *Effect Options*.

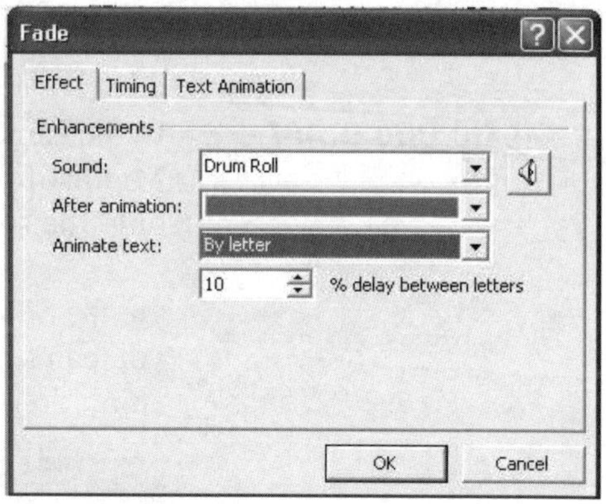

4) On the **Effect** tab, click the arrow to the right of the *Sound* box. Select *Drum Roll* from the drop-down list displayed. Next, in the *After animation* box, select a medium green colour.

5) Click on the **Timing** tab, and click the arrow to the right of the *Start* box. Select *On Click.* Click **OK**. Save your presentation.

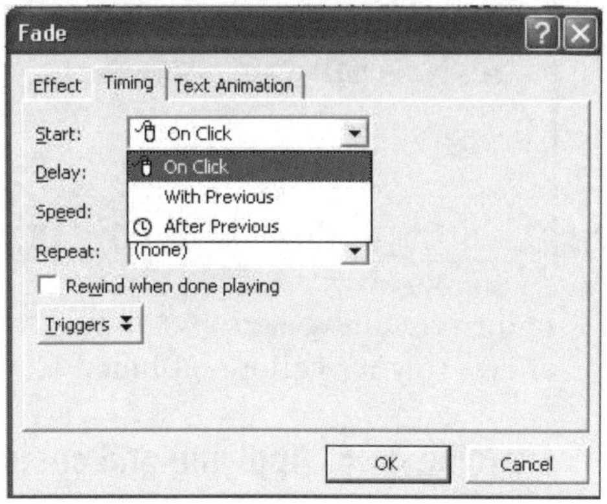

6) Choose **View | Slide Show** and move through your slides to view the animation effect. You can close your presentation when finished.

Customizing animation schemes

As you can see when you run your presentation, you have customized the animation effects in the following ways:

- **Sound:** You have changed the sound effect associated with the animation.
- **Dim effect:** As soon as a new bullet point appears, PowerPoint changes the previous one to a less prominent colour. This dimming effect helps your audience to focus on the flow of your presentation.

Many PowerPoint users find it best to follow the approach of Exercises 41.3 and 41.4. They first apply an animation scheme that is close to what they want, and then they use the custom animation command to make adjustments where necessary.

Music and other noises

In the same way that you insert pictures other than those in Microsoft's Clip Art Gallery into slides, you are not limited to using only the sound effects that are supplied with PowerPoint.

On the *Sound* drop-down list on the **Effect** tab of the *Fade* dialog box, you can see the *Other Sound* option. To associate a sound with an animation, click this option and select any sound file.

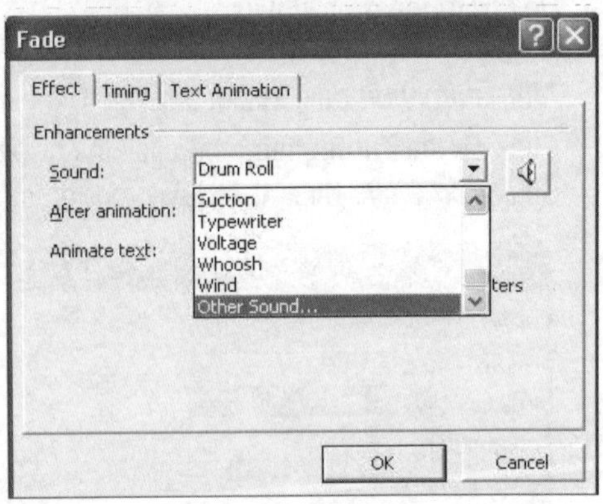

In the remaining exercises in this section, you will apply animation effects to your yellow-on-blue ECDL presentation.

Exercise 41.5: Applying and customizing animation effects

1) Display the yellow-on-blue ECDL presentation that you last worked on in Exercise 41.2.
2) Choose **View | Master | Slide Master** and click in the top (Title Area for AutoLayouts) placeholder.

3) Choose **Slide Show | Animation Schemes** and in the task pane, select the option named *Faded zoom.*

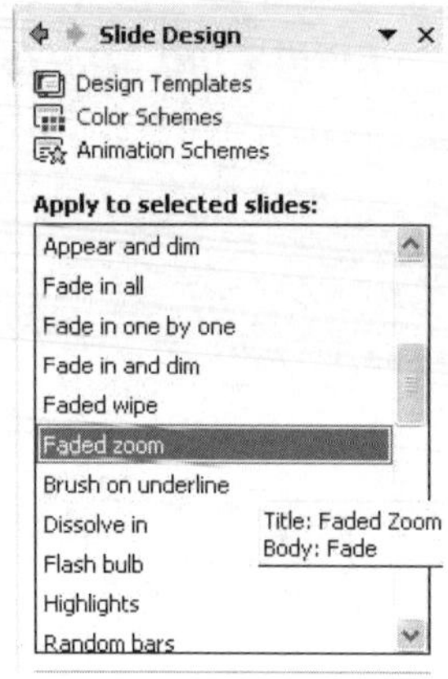

4) Click anywhere in the lower (Object Area for Autolayouts) placeholder, choose **Slide Show | Animation Schemes** and select the option In the task pane named *Faded zoom.*
5) With the lower placeholder still selected, choose **Slide Show | Custom Animation.** Click the arrow to the right of *Title 2: Click to edit Master text style*. From the pop-up menu displayed, select *Effect Options.* On the **Effect** tab, change the *After Animation* setting to a light blue colour, and click **OK**.
6) Save your presentation. Choose **View | Slide Show** and page through your presentation.

   Notice that the animations have no impact on your slide transitions – the two visual effects, and any associated sounds, are independent.

Including tables, pictures and charts in animations

The presentation that you worked on in Exercise 41.5 has one table, three inserted pictures, one organization chart, and two data charts.

As you ran the presentation, did you notice that the table on slide 7, 'ECDL Pricing' was not animated by PowerPoint?

That is, the table appeared as soon as the relevant slide was displayed. By default, PowerPoint does not animate tables. As you will discover in Exercise 41.6, PowerPoint gives you complete control over table, picture and chart animations.

Exercise 41.6: Including pictures and charts in animations

1) Display the yellow-on-blue presentation that you worked on in Exercise 41.5.
2) In Normal view, display the 'Benefits for Colleges' slide. Click anywhere on the slide and choose **Slide Show | Custom Animation**.
3) Select the table and then click **Add Effect** in the task pane. From the pop-up menu displayed, select **Entrance** and then **Box**. PowerPoint runs the effect with that timing in the slide.

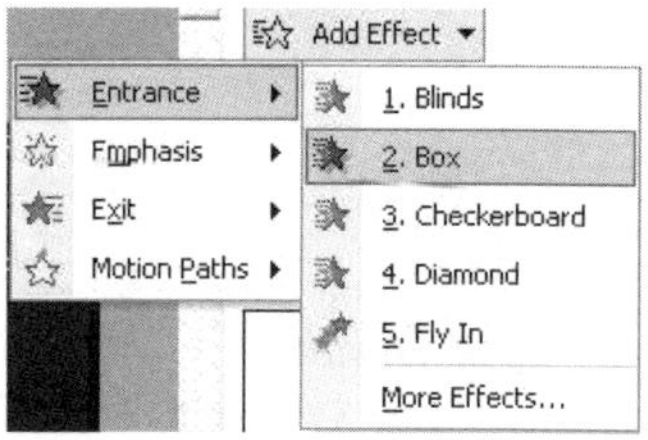

4) Save your presentation. Choose **View | Slide Show** and page through your presentation to see the effect on the 'ECDL Pricing' slide. Save your presentation.

Animating charts

As you have seen, you can include a chart in a slide animation, or exclude it if you prefer. But PowerPoint offers yet another animation feature regarding charts – it allows you to animate the elements *within* a chart, so that chart elements are displayed progressively rather than all at once.

Exercise 41.7: Animating the elements of a chart

1) Display the yellow-on-blue presentation that you worked on in Exercise 41.6. In Normal view, display the 'Sales Projections' slide.
2) Click once on the chart to select it, choose **Slide Show | Custom Animation**.
3) In the task pane, click **Add Effects | Entrance | Checkerboard**.

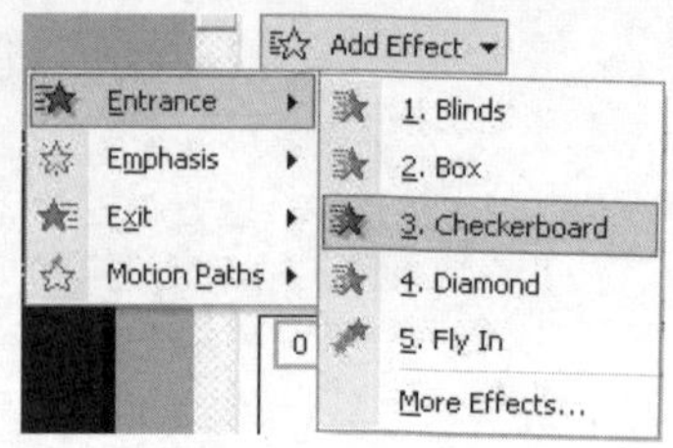

4) Click **Add Effects | Motion Paths | Right**.

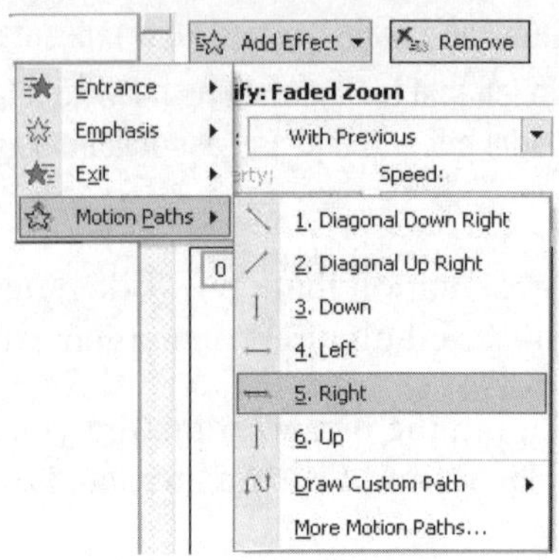

5) Save your presentation. Choose **Slide Show** and page through your presentation to see the effect on the 'Sales Projections' slide.

Check your spelling

Spelling mistakes really spoil a presentation: they make you look either careless or ignorant – and your effort to impress the audience may be wasted. While it is dangerous to rely totally on a spelling checker, it is foolish not to use one at all.

In PowerPoint, you can check your spelling in two ways:

- As you type and edit text on slide (the automatic option). Wavy underlines indicate words with possible spelling errors. To correct the spelling, right-click on the wavy line, and then choose the option you want from the pop-up menu displayed.
- Whenever you choose **Tools | Spelling**, press **F7** or click **Spelling** on the toolbar (the on-request option).

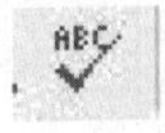

Spelling button

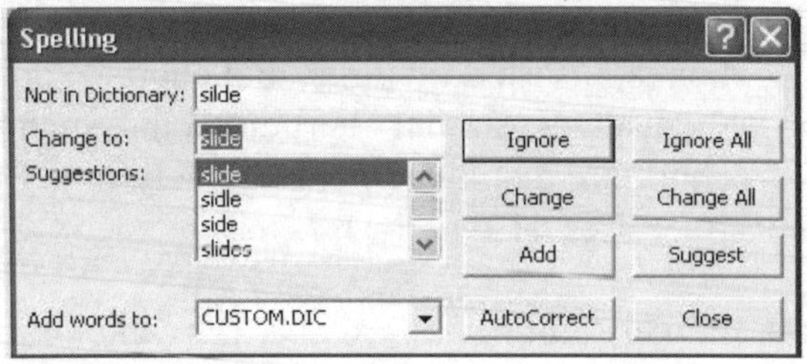

To turn automatic spelling on or off, choose **Tools | Options** and select or deselect the *Check spelling as you type* check box on the **Spelling and Style** tab.

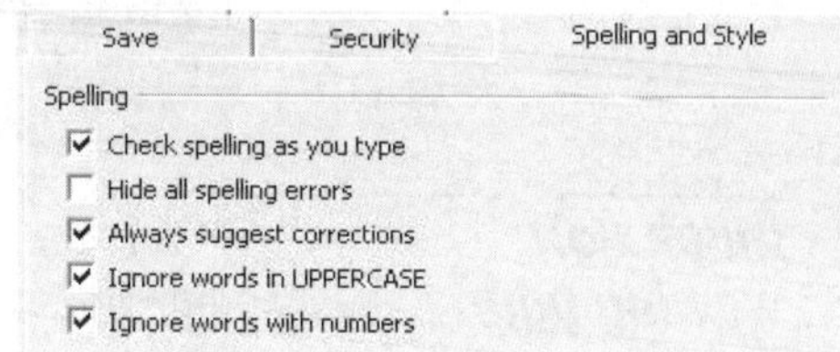

The spelling checker identifies suspect words, and shows suggested alternatives. You can accept one of the suggestions, edit the word yourself, or leave the original unchanged.

The spelling checker will not find incorrect spellings that are themselves valid words (such as 'form' instead of 'from').

Chapter summary: so now you know

PowerPoint offers three *slide advance* methods: manual (operated by the presenter), automatic (after a specified time interval), and 'whichever comes first' (automatic with manual override). See Exercise 41.1.

A *transition* is a graphic effect that controls how one slide replaces another – for example, the new slide could appear to drop down from the top of the screen. You can control the speed with which PowerPoint runs your selected transition effect, and link a sound to the transition between slides. See Exercise 41.2.

An *animated slide* is one on which elements are revealed gradually rather than all at once. These can help the presenter focus the audience's attention on each point in turn.

PowerPoint offers a set of ready-to-go preset animations, some with associated sound effects, which you can apply quickly to your slides. You can customize preset animations as required. Options that you can modify include the order in which a slide's elements appear, the direction from which they appear, and the way in which previous elements are dimmed. See Exercises 41.3, 41.4 and 41.5.

Animated elements can be bullet points, graphics such as lines or boxes, inserted pictures, and charts. You can also *animate charts* themselves, so that chart elements, such as the columns in a column chart, are displayed progressively rather than all at once. See Exercises 41.6 and 41.7.

PowerPoint's *spelling checker* can be run automatically so that it highlights suspect words as you type and edit slide text, or only as required.

Quick quiz: wowing your audience

Circle the correct answer to each of the following multiple-choice questions about wowing your audience in PowerPoint.

Q1	How do you apply a transition to a presentation?
A.	Choose **Slide Show | Slide Transition**. In the *Slide Transition* task pane, choose a transition such as *Dissolve* in the *Apply to selected slides* box. In the *Modify Transition* box, select a speed such as *Fast* and a sound such as *Applause*. Select an *Advance Slide* option. Click **Apply to All Slides**.
B.	Choose **Slide Show | Animation Schemes**. In the *Slide Design* task pane, choose an animation scheme such as *Fade in all,* found under *Subtle* in the *Apply to selected slides* box. Select an *Advance Slide* option and click **Apply to All Slides**.
C.	Choose **Slide Show | Slide Transition**. In the *Slide Transition* task pane, choose a transition such as *Dissolve* in the *Apply to selected slides* box. In the *Modify Transition* box, select a speed such as *Fast* and a sound such as *Applause*. Select an *Advance Slide* option.
D.	Choose **Slide Show | Animation Schemes**. In the *Slide Design* task pane, choose an animation scheme such as *Fade in all,* found under *Subtle* in the *Apply to selected slides* box.

Q2	To check your spelling you press F5.
A.	True.
B.	False.

Q3	How do you animate the elements of a chart?
A.	Choose **Slide Show | Slide Transition**. In the *Slide Design* task pane, choose an animation scheme such as *Fade in all,* found under *Subtle* in the *Apply to selected slides* box. Select an *Advance Slide* option and click **Apply to All Slides**.
B.	Choose **Slide Show | Custom Animation**. In the *Custom Animation* task pane, click **Add Effects**. From the pop-up menu displayed, select the option required – such as **Entrance | Checkerboard** or **Motion Paths | Right**. Click **Remove**.
C.	Choose **Slide Show | Slide Transition**. In the *Slide Design* task pane, choose an animation scheme such as *Fade in all,* found under *Subtle* in the *Apply to selected slides* box. Select an *Advance Slide* option.
D.	Choose **Slide Show | Custom Animation**. In the *Custom Animation* task pane, and click **Add Effects**. From the pop-up menu displayed, select the option required – such as **Entrance | Checkerboard** or **Motion Paths | Right**. Click **Play**.

Q4	How do you apply an advance method to a presentation?
A.	Choose **Slide Show | Slide Transition**. Choose **Advance Slide** in the *Slide Transition* task pane. Click *Automatically after*, and then type the number of seconds (for example, 15) that you want each slide to remain on-screen. Ensure that the *On mouse click* check box is selected. Click **Apply to All Slides**.
B.	Choose **Slide Show | Custom Animation**. In the *Custom Animation* task pane, click **Add Effects**. From the pop-up menu displayed, select the option required – such as **Entrance | Checkerboard** or **Motion Paths | Right**. Click **Remove**.
C.	Choose **Slide Show | Slide Transition**. Choose **Advance Slide** in the *Slide Transition* task pane. Click *Automatically after*, and then type the number of seconds (for example, 15) that you want each slide to remain on-screen. Ensure that the *On mouse click* check box is selected.
D.	Choose **Slide Show | Custom Animation**. In the *Custom Animation* task pane, click **Add Effects**. From the pop-up menu displayed, select the option required – such as **Entrance | Checkerboard** or **Motion Paths | Right**. Click **Apply Effect**.

Q5	How do you customize an animation scheme?
A.	Choose **Slide Show | Custom Animation**. In the *Custom Animation* task pane, click the arrow to the right of the first item in the corresponding Custom Animation List (example, *Title 1: Click to edit Master title style*). From the pop-up menu, select **Effect Options**. Select the effect required and click **OK**.
B	Choose **Slide Show | Custom Animation**. In the *Custom Animation* task pane, click the arrow to the right of the first item in the corresponding Custom Animation List (example, *Title 1: Click to edit Master title style*). From the pop-up menu, select **Remove**. Select the effect required and click **OK**.
C	Choose **Slide Show | Custom Animation**. In the *Custom Animation* task pane, click the arrow to the right of the first item in the corresponding Custom Animation List (example, *Title 1: Click to edit Master title style*). From the pop-up menu displayed, select **Show Advanced Timeline**, and click **Play**.
D	Choose **Slide Show | Custom Animation**. In the *Custom Animation* task pane, click the arrow to the right of the first item in the corresponding Custom Animation List (example, *Title 1: Click to edit Master title style*). From the pop-up menu displayed, select **Hide Advanced Timeline**, and click **Play**.

Answers

1: A, **2:** B, **3:** D, **4:** A, **5:** A.

Chapter 42: Presentations and file formats

In this chapter

How can you use information contained in PowerPoint presentations in files of other formats, such as web pages and graphics files? This section shows you how. You will also discover how to import spreadsheet data into PowerPoint slides.

PowerPoint comes with a range of design templates that you can use as a basis for quickly creating other, similar presentations. You will learn how to apply the presupplied templates, and how to create templates of your own.

New skills

At the end of this chapter you should be able to:

- Save PowerPoint presentation files in the following file formats: PowerPoint slideshows, earlier versions of PowerPoint, Excel, HTML (web format), graphics (GIF or JPEG), Rich Text Format (RTF), and PowerPoint design templates.
- Create a presentation based on a design template, and apply a design template to a new presentation.
- Import cells and charts from Microsoft Excel into PowerPoint slides.

New word

At the end of this chapter you should be able to explain the following term:

- Design template

Saving your presentation as a slide show

You already know how to use Slide Show view to preview how your presentation will look to your audience. Another option is to save the presentation as a slide show, so that it always opens as a slide show, whether you open it within PowerPoint or directly from the desktop.

To save an open presentation as a slide show:

- Choose **File | Save As**.

- Click on the arrow to the right of the *Save as type* box.

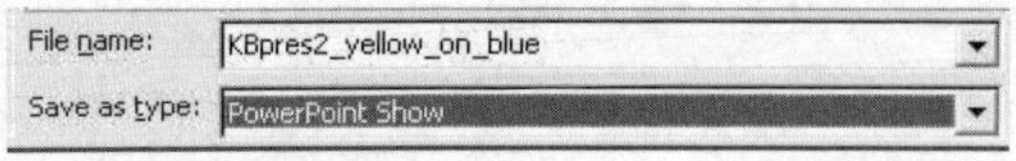

- Select PowerPoint Show.

PowerPoint saves the file with the extension .pps. Your original presentation file is unaffected. Exercise 42.1. provides an example.

Exercise 42.1: Saving a presentation as a slide show

1) If PowerPoint is not already open, open it now.
   Open the ECDL presentation with yellow text against a dark blue background, which you worked with in Chapter 41. We called it KBpres2_yellow_on_blue.ppt.
2) Choose **File | Save As**, and select the folder where you want to save the file.
3) In the *Save as type* box, select PowerPoint Show (*.pps), accept or change the current file name, and click **Save**.
4) Open My Computer and locate the folder where you saved your slide show.

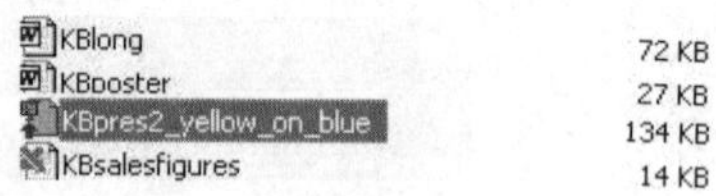

5) Double-click on the slide show.
   PowerPoint responds by running the slide show on your screen.
   When finished, close the slide show but leave the presentation open.

Working with earlier versions of PowerPoint

Each version of the Microsoft PowerPoint software includes features that were not available in earlier versions. This means that while you can generally use a later version of the software to open and work with a presentation that was created in an earlier version, the reverse is not necessarily true.

You can save your PowerPoint 2002 presentations in the file formats of previous versions of PowerPoint. You have three main options:

- PowerPoint 2000
- PowerPoint 97
- PowerPoint 95

HTML (web) format

Web pages are created using the HTML file format. The file name extension of this format is .htm (or, sometimes .html).

You can convert a complete PowerPoint presentation, a single slide or a range of slides into HTML format, so that they can be displayed in a web browser such as Microsoft Internet Explorer or Netscape Navigator. Follow Exercise 42.2 to discover how.

Exercise 42.2: Saving a presentation in web format

1) Display the presentation that you worked on in Exercise 42.1.
2) Choose **File | Save as Web Page** and select the folder where you want to save the file.

   To change the web page title (the text that appears in the title bar of the web browser), click **Change Title**, type the new title in the *Page title* box, and then click **OK**. When finished, click **Publish**.

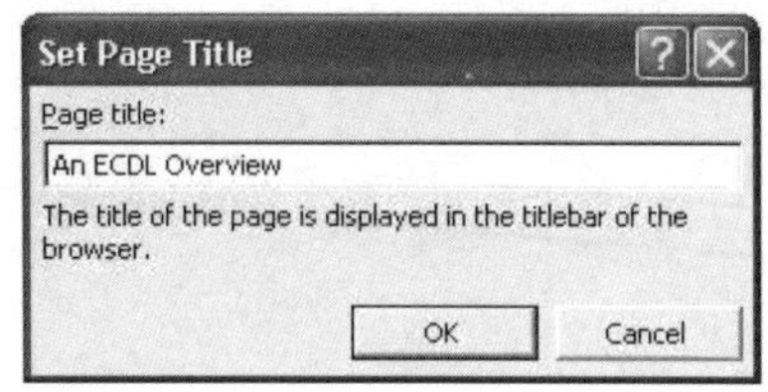

3) On the *Publish as Web Page* dialog box display, select the values as shown below.

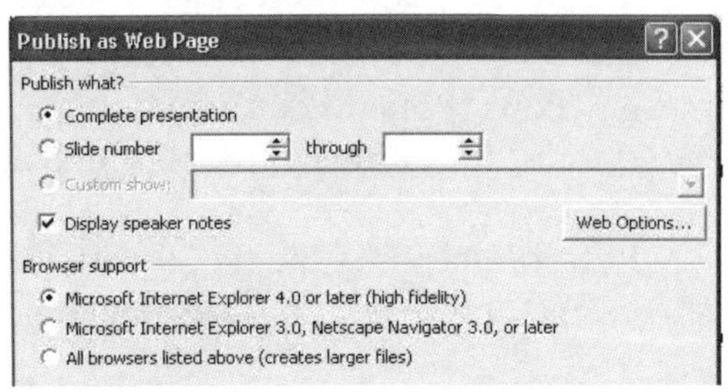

   To see how the web version of your presentation looks in a web browser, select the check box at the bottom of the dialog box.

   When finished, click **Publish**. .
4) After a few seconds, PowerPoint will perform the file conversion, and open the first page of your presentation in the web browser. You can close the file when finished.

HTML options

PowerPoint offers a range of options when converting a presentation to HTML. To view the choices available for an open presentation:

- Choose **File | Save as Web Page** and select the folder where you want to save the file.
- Click **Publish** to display the *Publish as Web Page* dialog box, and click **Web Options** to display a dialog box with four tabs.

Your main options are as follows:

- **Slide navigation controls:** In Exercise 42.2, you accepted the default of white text against a black background.
- **Location of files:** Where do you want the supporting files located? The default is in a separate subfolder.
- Screen size: The default is 800 x 600.

Saving slides as graphics

If you want to use your slides in other graphic programs, or within web pages, you can save them in one of the two common graphic formats: JPEG or GIF.

To save an open presentation as a graphic:

- Choose **File | Save As**.
- Select the folder where you want to save the file, and accept or amend the suggested file name.
- Click on the arrow to the right of the *Save as type* box.
- Select GIF Graphic Interchange Format (*.gif) or JPEG File Interchange Format (*.jpg), and click **Save**.
- PowerPoint asks if you want to convert the entire presentation or just the current slide. Respond as appropriate.

PowerPoint saves the file(s) with the extension .gif or .jpeg. Your original presentation file is unaffected.

Using PowerPoint slides in other applications

In general, you should not have to type information into one software application and then later type the same information into another application. For example, when you want to include in a Word document text that you have already entered to PowerPoint slides, you should not need to type it again.

To use text and/or graphics from a single slide, copy the item in PowerPoint (select it and press **Ctrl+c**) and paste it in Word (position the cursor and press **Ctrl+v**).

RTF format

To reuse an entire presentation in another application, the best option is to save the presentation in Rich Text Format (RTF). This is a format common to all Microsoft Office applications. The file name extension is .rtf.

To save an open presentation in RTF format:

- Choose **File | Save As**.

- Select the folder where you want to save the file, and accept or amend the suggested file name.
- Click the arrow to the right of the *Save as type* box.
- Select the *Outline/RTF (*.rft)* option, and click **Save**.

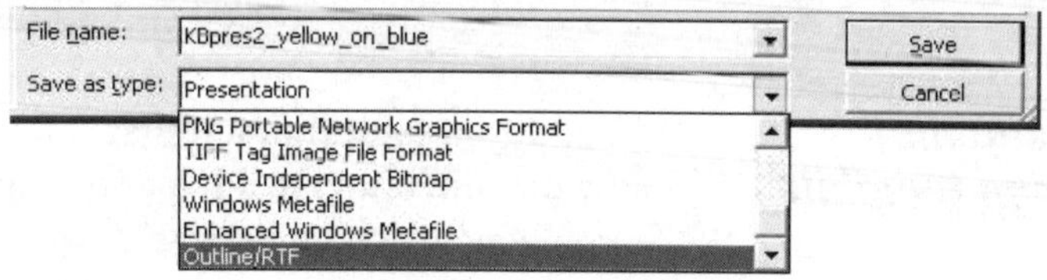

PowerPoint saves the file with the extension .rtf. Your original presentation file is unaffected.

Working with design templates

PowerPoint offers you the ability to save a presentation as a design template. You can then use the saved design template as a basis for quickly creating other, similar presentations.

To save an open presentation as a design template:

- Choose **File | Save As**.
- Select the folder where you want to save the file, and accept or amend the suggested file name.

Typically, PowerPoint suggests that you save your design templates in the following folder:

C:\Documents and Settings\Your Name\Application Data\Microsoft\Templates

- Click on the arrow to the right of the *Save as type* box.

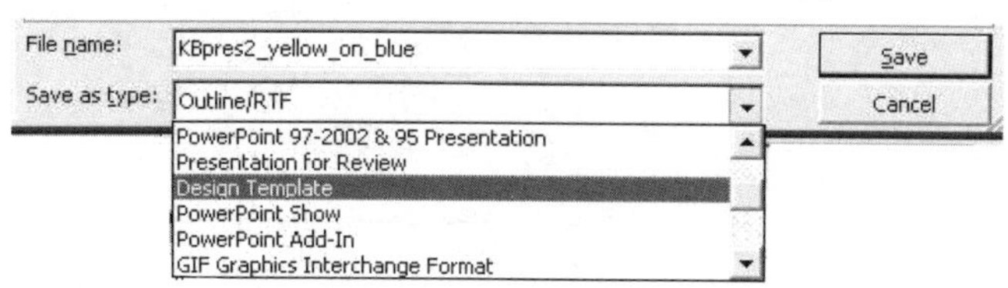

- Select the *Design Template (*.rtf)* option and click **Save**.

PowerPoint saves the design template with the extension .pot. Your original presentation file is unaffected. The next time you want to create a presentation, you can start with that saved design template and all the slides will take on its characteristics.

> **Design template**
>
> *A PowerPoint file containing a colour scheme and slide master with font settings, and possibly built-in graphics and text, which can be applied to a presentation. Design template file names end in .pot.*

Presupplied design templates

In addition to design templates that you may create yourself, PowerPoint comes with a wide range of professionally designed templates. You can use the design templates as supplied, and amend them according to your particular needs or taste, or to your company identity scheme, and save them for later reuse.

To view PowerPoint's presupplied design templates:

- Choose **File | New**.
- In the task pane, choose **New from template** and click **General Templates**.
- In the *Templates* dialog box, click once on the various templates listed to display a preview on the right of the dialog box.

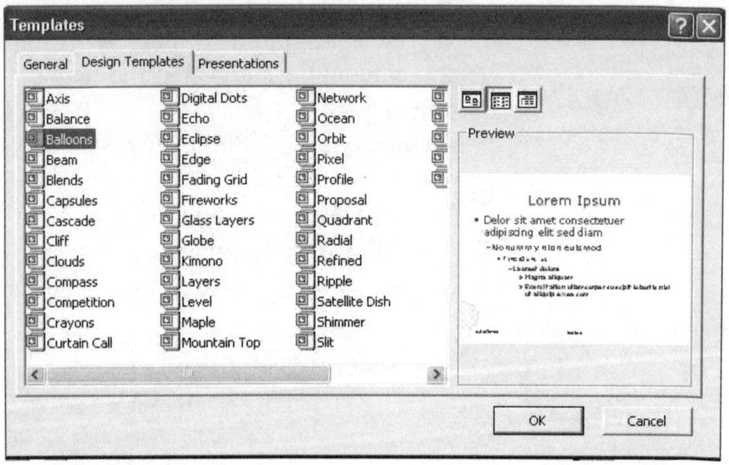

- When finished, click **Cancel**.

Design templates may contain colour schemes and slide masters with font formatting and, optionally, built-in text and graphics.

Applying a design template

You can apply a design template to a presentation in either of two ways:

- **New presentation:** Choose **File | New**, and select the required design template from the task pane.

- **Existing presentation:** Choose **Format | Slide Design**. In the task pane, click **Browse**. Select **Presentation Designs** in the *Apply Design Template* dialog box.
- Select the required design template from the list displayed.

When you apply a design template to an existing presentation, the slide master and colour scheme of the new template replace any slide master and colour scheme contained in the presentation.

Exercise 42.3: Applying a design template

1) Display the presentation that you worked on in Exercise 42.2.
2) In Normal view, choose **Format** | **Slide Design**. In the task pane, click **Browse**. Select **Presentation Designs** in the *Apply Design Template* dialog box.

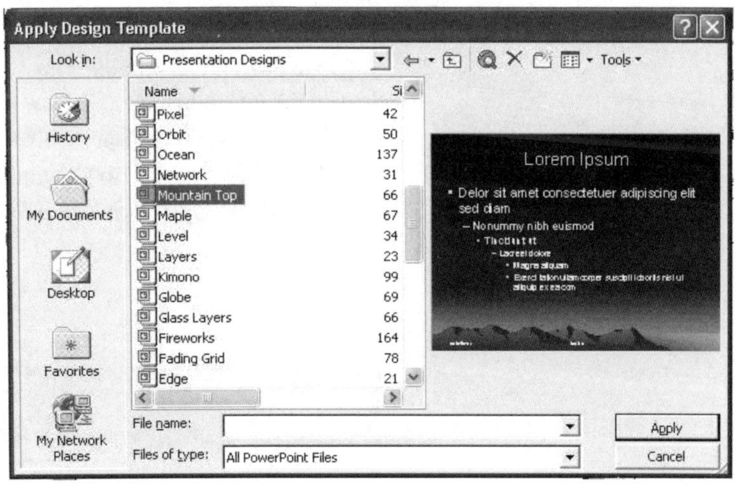

3) For this exercise, select the Mountain Top template, and click **Apply**.
4) Switch to Slide Show view to see the result. Pretty cool, eh?
5) Return to Normal view, and experiment with other design templates.
6) When finished, choose **File | Save As**, and save the presentation with a name that indicates its design template. If your initials are KB, for example, save it as KBpres2_factory.ppt. Close your presentation, but do not close PowerPoint.

At step 3 in Exercise 42.3 you applied the Factory.pot template. If you subsequently change your mind and want to use a different template, choose **Format | Apply Design Template**, and then select the template you want.

Importing spreadsheets and charts

In the previous sections of this module you learnt how to import pictures and sounds to your slides. PowerPoint also allows you to import numerical data and charts from spreadsheets.

In Exercise 42.4 you will create a new presentation and import data from an Excel worksheet to it. In Exercise 42.5 you will import an Excel chart to the presentation.

Exercise 42.4: Importing an Excel worksheet

1) Open Microsoft Excel. In a new workbook, enter the information shown on the right.

   Save the workbook with the file name rivers.xls.

	A	B	C
1	**River**	**Length**	**Location**
2	Nile	6693	North/East Africa
3	Amazon	6436	South America
4	Yangtze	6378	China
5	Huang He	5463	China
6	Ob-Irtysh	5410	Russia

2) Switch to PowerPoint, choose **File | New**. In the task pane, choose **New from template** and select **General Templates**. Select the design template called **Radial** and click **OK**.
3) In the task pane, choose **Text Layouts** and click the arrow to the right of the *Title Slide.* Click *Apply to Selected Slides*.
4) Type the following text as shown.

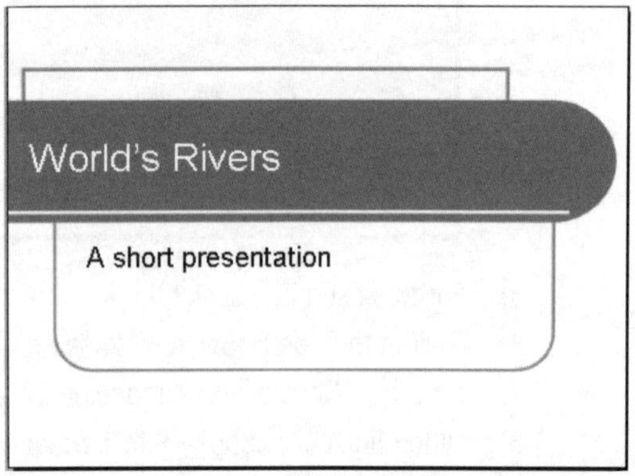

5) Insert a second slide by clicking **New Slide** on the *Formatting* toolbar. In the *Slide Layout* task pane, choose **Text Layouts** and click the arrow to the right of the *Title Slide.* Click *Apply to Selected Slides*.
6) In the top placeholder of your second slide, enter the following text:

   Longest Rivers

   Click anywhere outside the top placeholder to deselect it.

7) Choose **Insert | Object**. On the dialog box shown, select *Create from file*, and click **Browse.**

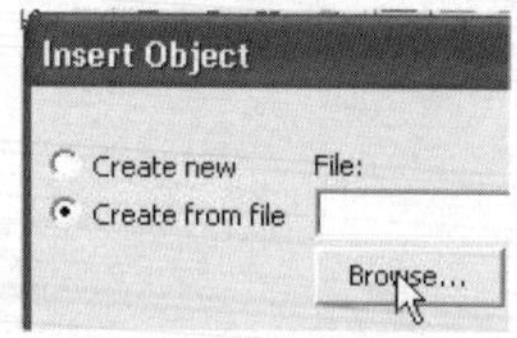

8) On the next dialog box, navigate to the folder where you saved the rivers.xls Excel file, select the file, and click **OK**. The Excel worksheet is inserted in your slide.
9) Reposition and resize the imported worksheet until your slide looks as shown.
10) Save your presentation with an appropriate name. If your initials are KB, for example, call it KB_rivers.ppt.

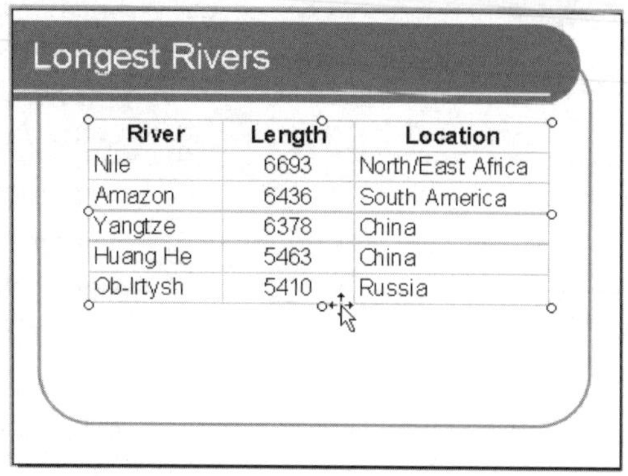

You can work with the imported worksheet as you would any imported picture. For example, you can place a border or shadow around it, and copy it to other slides or the slide master. A worksheet included on the slide master appears on every slide of the presentation.

To change the content or appearance of the worksheet, double-click it and use the Excel menus and toolbars displayed. To deselect the worksheet, click anywhere on the slide outside it.

Exercise 42.5: Importing an Excel chart

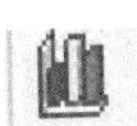

Chart Wizard button

1) Display the Excel worksheet you created and saved in Exercise 42.4.
2) Select the cell range A1:B6 and click **Chart Wizard** on the toolbar.

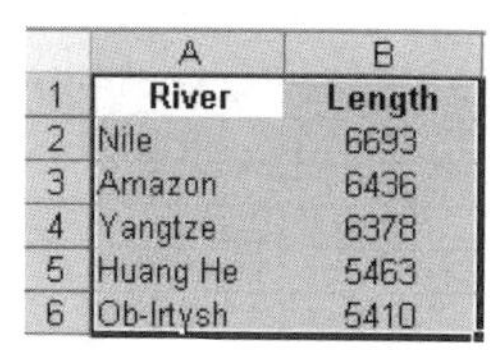

3) On the first *Chart Wizard* dialog box, select a chart type of bar chart, and click **Next**.
4) On the second and third *Chart Wizard* dialog boxes, accept the default values and click **Next**. On the fourth dialog box, click **Finish**. Excel creates the chart on your worksheet.

5) With the chart selected, copy it to the clipboard, click **New** on the *Standard* toolbar and paste the chart in the new workbook. Save the workbook as rivers_chart.xls. You can now close Excel.

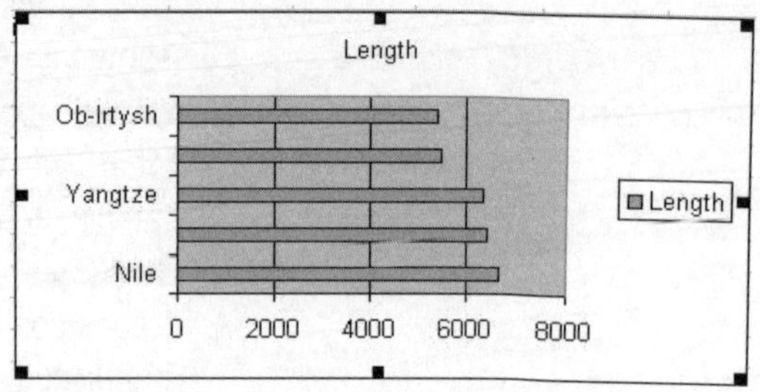

6) Switch to PowerPoint, and display the rivers presentation that you created in the previous exercise in Normal view.
7) Insert a third slide by clicking **New Slide** on the *Standard* toolbar. In the task pane choose **Content Layouts** and click the arrow to the right of *Blank.* Click *Apply to Selected Slides*.
8) Choose **Insert | Object**. In the dialog box shown, select **Create from file**, and click **Browse**.
9) In the next dialog box, navigate to the folder where you saved the rivers_chart.xls Excel file, select the file, and click **OK**. PowerPoint asks you if you want to update the linked information or not. Click **Yes**.

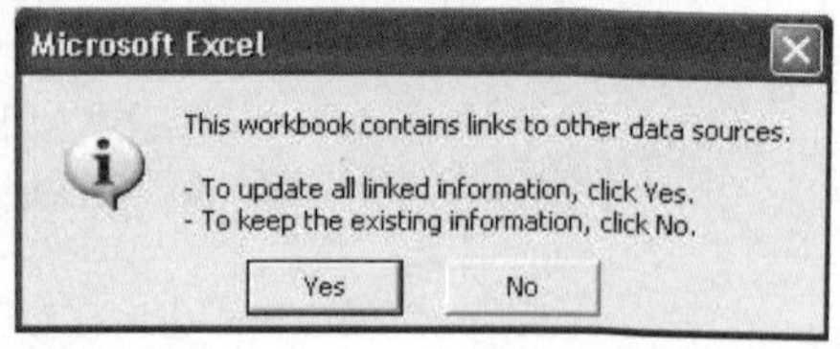

10) The Excel chart is inserted on your slide. Reposition and resize the imported chart until your slide looks as shown.

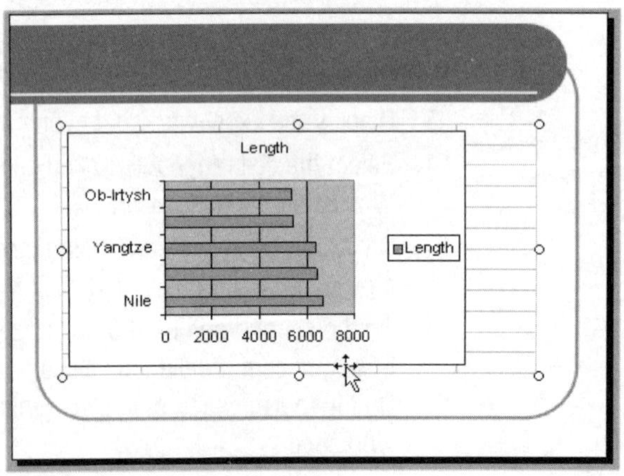

11) Save and close your presentation.

You may now save and close any open presentation, and close PowerPoint. You have completed the ECDL presentations module. Congratulations!

Chapter summary: so now you know

To help you share your files with others, PowerPoint 2002 allows you to save your presentations in a file format other than its own. The options include earlier versions of PowerPoint, HTML (the web page file format), graphic files (GIF and JPEG), and Rich Text Format (RTF).

You can also save a presentation as a *slide show*, so that it always opens as a ready-to-run slide show, whether you open it within PowerPoint or directly from the desktop. PowerPoint slide files end with the extension .pps. See Exercise 42.1.

Another option is to save the presentation as a *design template*, which you can then use as the basis for quickly creating other, similar presentations. Design templates may contain colour schemes and slide masters with font formatting and, optionally, built-in text and graphics. See Exercise 42.3.

In addition to design templates that you create yourself, PowerPoint comes with a wide range of professionally designed templates. You can use the design templates as supplied, or you can amend them according to your particular needs or taste, or to your company identity scheme, and save them for later reuse.

You can insert *spreadsheet* data, both numbers and charts, in a PowerPoint presentation. You can resize, reposition, place borders and shadows around, and copy-and-paste imported spreadsheet objects as you would imported pictures. See Exercises 42.4 and 42.5.

Quick quiz: presentation and file formats

Circle the correct answer to each of the following multiple-choice questions about presentations and file formats in PowerPoint.

Q1	How do you import a spreadsheet that you have used in Microsoft Excel into PowerPoint?
A.	Choose **Insert | Table**. In the *Insert Table* dialog box, select the number of columns and rows required, and click **OK**.
B.	Choose **Insert | Object**. In the dialog box shown, select *Create from file*, and click **Browse**. On the next dialog box, navigate to the folder where you saved the spreadsheet. Select the file and click **OK**.
C.	Choose **Format | Slide Layout**. In the *Slide Layout* task pane select the *Title, Text and Chart* slide layout found under *Other Layouts*. Click the arrow to the right of the slide layout and select **Apply to Selected Slides**.
D.	Choose **Insert | Object**. In the dialog box shown, select *Create new.* In the *Object type* box, select *Microsoft Excel Worksheet*, and click **OK**.

Q2	How do you save a presentation as a slide show?
A.	Choose **File | Save As**. In the *Save as type* box, select *Web Page*, and click **Save**.
B.	Choose **File | Save As**. In the *Save as type* box, select *Presentation*, and click **Save**.
C.	Choose **File | Save As**. In the *Save as type* box, select *PowerPoint Show*, and click **Save**.
D.	Choose **File | Save As**. In the *Save as type* box, select *Design Template*, and click **Save**.

Q3	To view a web version of a presentation, click ...
A.	Open published web page in browser.
B.	Display speaker notes.
C.	Show slide animation while browsing.
D.	Complete presentation.

Q4	How do you save a presentation in web format?
A.	Choose **File | Save as Web Page**, and select the folder where you want to save the file. In the *Publish as Web Page* dialog box, select the values required. When finished, click **Publish**.
B.	Choose **File | Save as**. In the *Save as type* box in the *Save As* dialog box, select *Presentation*. Click **Save**.
C.	Choose **File | Save as**. In the *Save as type* box in the *Save As* dialog box, select *Web Archive*. Click **Save**.
D.	Choose **File | Save as**. In the *Save as type* box in the *Save As* dialog box, select *Presentation for Review*. Click **Save**.

Q5	How do you apply a design template?
A.	Choose **Format | Slide Design**. In the *Slide Design* task pane, click **Animation Schemes**. Select *Elegant* found under *Moderate* in the *Apply to Selected Slides* box. Click **Apply to All Slides**.
B.	Choose **Format | Slide Design**. In the *Slide Design* task pane, click **Color Schemes**. Select the colour scheme slide with the dark green background found under *Apply a color scheme*. Click the arrow to the right of the colour scheme slide, and click **Apply to All Slides**.
C.	Choose **Format | Slide Design**. In the *Slide Design* task pane, click **Browse**. Double-click **Presentation Designs** in the *Apply Design Template* dialog box. Select the required template, and click **Apply**.
D.	Choose **Format | Slide Design**. In the *Slide Design* task pane, click **Browse**. Double-click **MseNewFileItems** in the *Apply Design Template* dialog box. Select the required template, and click **Apply**.

Answers

1: B, **2:** C, **3:** A, **4:** A, **5:** C.

7 Information and Communication

'The Internet is like a library.' You will hear this kind of statement a lot from people who know little about either.

If the Internet is a library, it's a strange one indeed. For starters, there is no indexing system. At any rate, the books are not arranged on numbered shelves but scattered on the floor. A lot of what is in the books is untrue, even in the non-fiction ones. There is no librarian and no information desk. Did we mention also that the lights are turned off?

What's more, you can make as much noise as you like when using the Internet, while at the same time collecting facts and figures (and fiction and music and video and sports results and stock prices and weather reports and recipes) from all around the world.

In fact, the principal use of the Internet is for e-mail – a way of sending messages from your computer to someone else's computer, whether they are in the next room or in the other hemisphere.

Think of this module as your chance to borrow knowledge and skills you'll never be asked to return, and to become part of an online electronic community. Welcome to the Internet Age!

Chapter 43: Exploring the web

In this chapter

Prepare to take your first steps in exploring the World Wide Web, or 'web' as it is popularly known. In this chapter you will visit and explore websites operated by national newspapers based in Australia, France, Germany and Italy, and by a Paris-based art gallery and an American music store, and you will download software from the ECDL site.

Also in this chapter you will learn the basics of operating Internet Explorer, the Microsoft software application for exploring – otherwise known as browsing or surfing – the web.

New skills

At the end of this chapter you should be able to:

- Start Internet Explorer and visit a website.
- Explore a website by scrolling down pages and clicking on hyperlinks.
- Move backwards and forwards through previously visited web pages.
- Open several windows at once in Internet Explorer.
- Print web pages, and use the main page setup and print options.
- Save text, images, audio and video, and complete pages from the web.
- Download software from the web.
- Access and use Internet Explorer's online help.

New words

At the end of this chapter you should be able to explain the following terms:

- Home page
- Website
- Web browser
- Address bar
- Web server
- Downloading

Basic concepts

In Chapter 5, we discussed the different kinds of computer network, and described the Internet as a worldwide network of interconnected networks. With a connection to the Internet, you can exchange e-mail with other users, and you can access information stored on computers all around the world.

The World Wide Web is a massive collection of documents in a particular format that can be accessed over the Internet and displayed using a browser. The documents can be linked together, and you use a program known as a browser to view the documents and to follow the links from one document to another. One such browser program is Microsoft Internet Explorer, which is described below.

It's not enough to have the software; you also need a modem to connect your computer to the telephone network (described in Chapter 3), and a subscription to an Internet service provider (ISP) (described in Chapter 5).

The ISP maintains a continuous connection to the Internet; you connect to the Internet by connecting your computer to the ISP's computer via the telephone network.

(If your computer is connected to a local area network (LAN), you will probably access the Internet via a server on that network rather than through a modem on your PC.)

Starting Internet Explorer

- Double-click the **Internet Explorer** icon.

  -or

- Choose **Start | All Programs | Internet Explorer**.

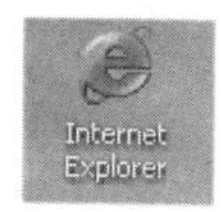

If your computer has a permanent Internet connection, you are ready to surf the web with Internet Explorer.

If you have a dial-up connection, you must first dial your Internet service provider (ISP). Internet Explorer may be set up to do this automatically. If not, you will need to dial your ISP separately.

Enter your user name and password (if Internet Explorer has not recorded them from the last time that you dialled your ISP), and click **Connect**.

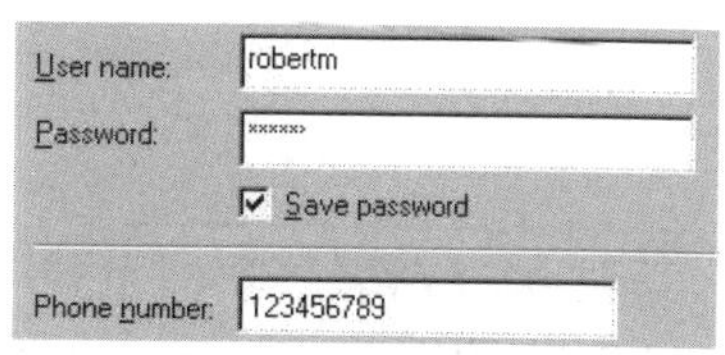

If your connection fails

If your connection to the Internet doesn't work, there are a number of things you should check:

- Have you entered the correct user name and password?
- Is your modem switched on?

Be aware that on occasions when demand is very heavy you may have difficulty accessing the Internet, particularly on a dial-up connection. Try again later.

Your browser's start page

Typically, Internet Explorer is set up so that it takes you to a particular web page whenever you start the application.

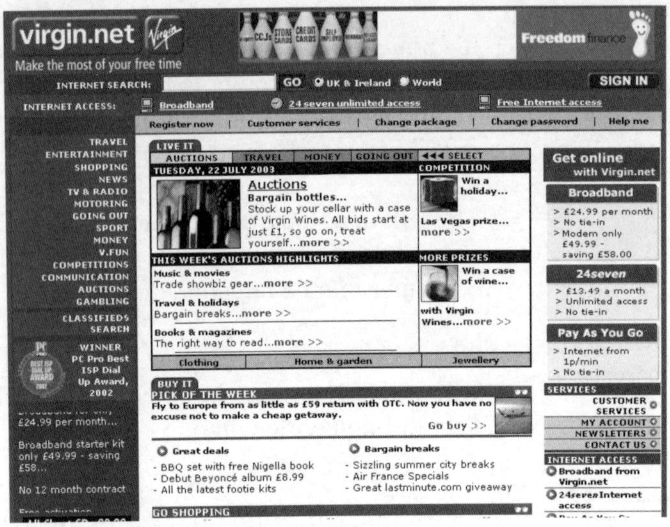

Home page of a typical Internet service provider (ISP)

If you obtained Internet Explorer from your ISP, this start page is probably the front page of the ISP's website. Such a front page is called a home page.

> ***Home page***
>
> *The first or front page of a website. Typically, it presents a series of links that you can follow to view the site's other pages.*

You will learn how to change Internet Explorer's start page in Chapter 46.

Visiting and exploring a website

In Exercise 43.1 you visit and explore the website of *The Age*, a newspaper published in Melbourne, Australia.

Exercise 43.1: Visiting and exploring a website

1) Choose **File | Open** or press **Ctrl+o**. (That is, hold down the **Ctrl** key and press the letter '**o**'.)
2) In the *Open* dialog box displayed, type www.theage.com.au, and click **OK**. Internet Explorer displays the home page of *The Age*'s website.

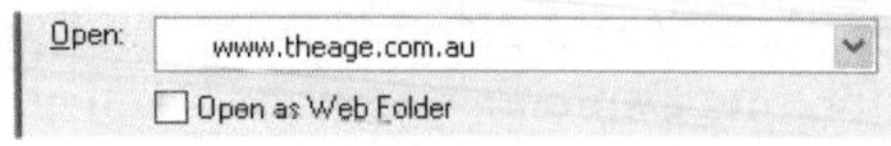

3) Along the left of *The Age*'s home page you can see a list of the newspaper's main sections – Breaking News, Classifieds, Extra, and so on.

   Scroll down the page to view the list in full.

   Each section name changes colour when you place your cursor on it, indicating that it is a hyperlink.

   A hyperlink is an item of text (or a graphic) on a web page that, if clicked, opens another web page or moves you to a different part of the page that you are on.

   Click on the *National* section.

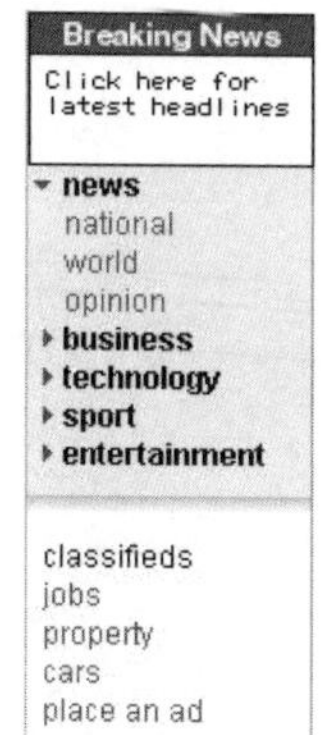

4) Internet Explorer now displays a new web page, the National News page.

   Here you can see summaries of the day's main news stories. Each summary ends with a hyperlink named *More*, and links to other related stories.
5) Click on any *More* hyperlink to display a web page containing an individual news story.

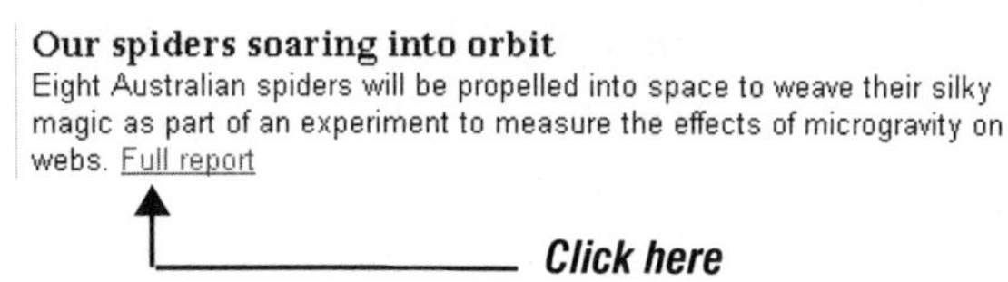

Leave the news story page open on your screen in preparation for Exercise 43.2.

You are now three pages deep inside *The Age* website.

- First, you visited the front or home page.
- Second, you visited the National News page, with its list of news summaries.
- Third, you visited a page containing a particular news story.

The Internet Explorer toolbar

As with Microsoft Office applications such as Word and Excel, Internet Explorer includes a *Standard* toolbar that offers fast, one-click access to commonly used actions. Rather than introduce all the toolbar buttons at once, we will explain each one as it becomes relevant.

In Exercise 43.2 you will use the **Back** and **Forward** buttons on Internet Explorer's *Standard* toolbar.

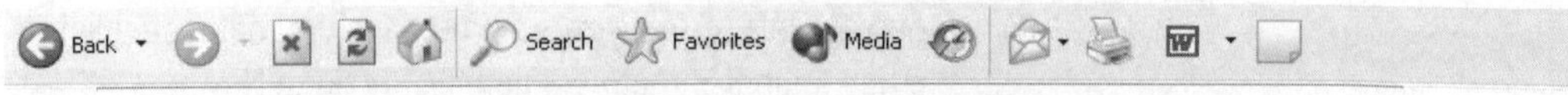

If the *Standard* toolbar is not currently shown on your screen, choose **View | Toolbars | Standard Buttons** to display it.

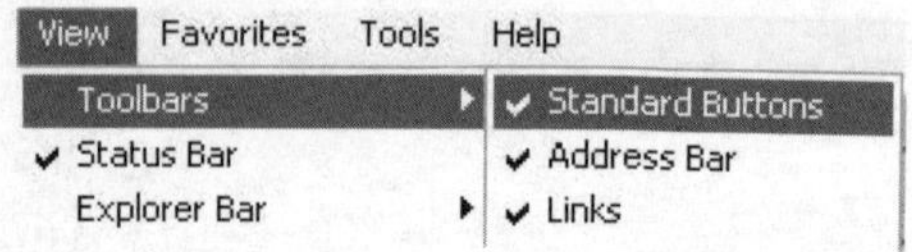

Moving through a series of web pages

In Exercise 43.2 you learn how to return to web pages that you visited earlier, and then move forward again to the ones you visited most recently.

Exercise 43.2: Moving backwards and forwards through web pages

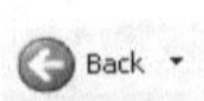

Back button

1) With a news story displayed from *The Age* newspaper, click once on the **Back** button, located on the left of Internet Explorer's *Standard* toolbar.

   This returns you to the web page you visited most recently – the National News page.

2) With the National News page displayed, click a second time on the **Back** button.

   This returns you to the second-last web page that you visited – the website's home page.

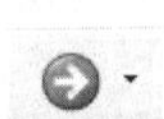

Forward button

3) With *The Age*'s home page displayed, click once on the **Forward** button. It is located just to the right of the **Back** button on the *Standard* toolbar.

   This button moves you forward, one page at a time, retracing your original movement through the website.

4) With the National News page displayed, click a second time on the **Forward** button.

   This brings you forward to the web page from which you originally began to move backwards – the individual news story page.

Browsing with the Address Bar

When you visit a web page, notice that its web address is displayed in the area immediately above Internet Explorer's main window. This is called the Address Bar.

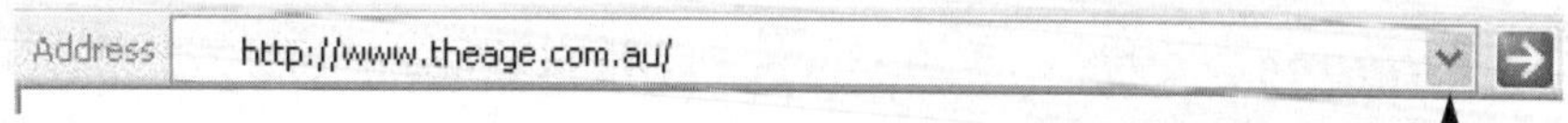

Click here to see the URLs of sites you have visited recently

You can also use the Address Bar to enter a web address. Although the Address Bar always displays 'http://' before a web address, you need not type 'http://' when entering an address.

Address Bar
An area above the main window that shows the address (preceded by 'http://') of the currently displayed web page. You can also use the Address Bar to enter a web address. (You need not type 'http://'.) *Http stands HyperText Transfer Protocol, the protocol that defines how messages are formatted and transmitted.*

If the Address Bar is not currently shown on your screen, choose **View | Toolbars | Address Bar** to display it.

Exercise 43.3: Entering an address in the Address Bar

1) Click anywhere in the Address Bar. This selects the currently displayed web address, which is then shown in reverse (white-on-black).
2) Use the **Backspace** or **Delete** key to remove the currently displayed web address. The Address Bar is now empty.

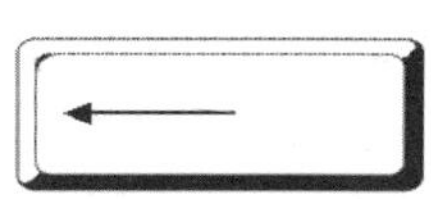

Removes the character to the left of the cursor

Removes the character to the right of the cursor

3) Type the following web address in the Address Bar, and click **Go** or press **Enter**:
   www.torontostar.ca
   Internet Explorer now displays the front page of Canada's *Toronto Star* newspaper.

Practise your web-browsing skills by clicking on hyperlinks to display pages within the Toronto newspaper, and by scrolling up and down each displayed web page.

Printing a web page

You can print out the currently displayed web page by choosing **File | Print**, selecting the *Current Page* option in the *Print* dialog box, and clicking **OK**.

Alternatively, you can specify that you want to print all or a range of pages, or just a part of a page that you have previously selected. You can also specify the number of copies you want to print, and whether you want multiple copies collated.

If the web page has a number of frames, click the **Options** tab in the *Print* dialog box. There you can specify whether you want a printout of the web page as it appears on the screen, of the individual frames separately, or of just the selected frame.

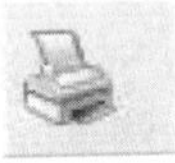

Prints current web page

If you simply want to print a single copy of the web page currently displayed, click the **Print** button on the Internet Explorer *Standard* toolbar. Clicking this **Print** button does not display the *Print* dialog box.

Choose **Print | Preview** to preview what the printed web page will look like.

Page setup options

Choose **File | Page Setup** to change the following page characteristics:

- **Paper size:** A4 is the European standard paper size.
- **Orientation:** Portrait ('standing up') or Landscape ('on its side').
- **Margins:** The distance of the page's printed content (text and graphics) from the edge of the paper. You can set each of the four margins (top, bottom, left and right) independently.
- **Header and footer:** You can include a number of automatically generated items in the header and footer areas of printed web pages. These are indicated in the *Page Setup* dialog box by codes, as follows:
  - &w: Page title
  - &u: Web page address.
  - &p: Page number in printout.
  - &P: Total number of pages in printout.

- &d or &D: Date of printing.
- &t or &T: Time of printing.

Saving from the web

If you see something on the web that you like – such as an image, some text, audio and video files, software, or even an entire web page – can you copy it from the website to your computer? Yes. This topic shows you how.

Saving an image

To save an image from the currently displayed web page, right-click on the image to display a pop-up menu. Next, choose **Save Picture As**, select the location on your computer that you want to save to, accept or change the current name of the image, and click **Save**.

You can also save pictures with the *Image* toolbar. This appears when you point to a picture on the web. You can:

- Save the image.
- Print the image.
- E-mail the image.
- Open the My Pictures folder.

Exercise 43.4 provides an example of saving an image from the web.

Exercise 43.4: Saving an image from a web page

1) Choose **File | Open** or press **Ctrl+o** and enter the following web address: www.pearson-books.com
2) Wait for the web page to load fully, and then right-click any book cover image.

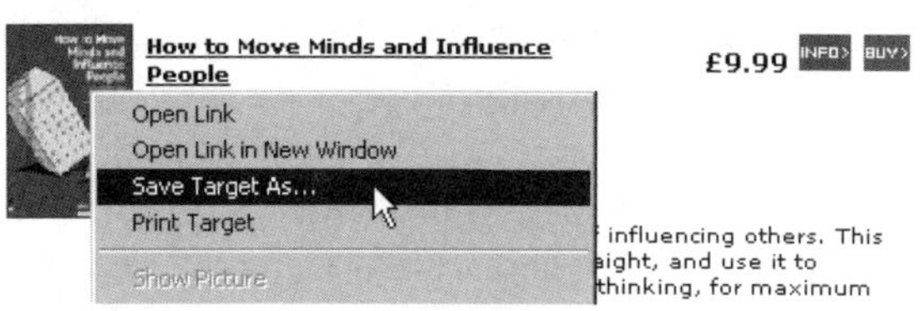

3) Choose **Save Picture As** from the pop-up menu displayed.
4) In the *Save Picture* dialog box then displayed, accept or change the image's file name, select the drive and folder you want to save the file to, and click **Save**.

(Alternatively, in Step 3 above, click **Copy**, and then paste the image into a currently open document.)

Image file formats

Most image files on the web are in either .gif (pronounced with a hard 'g', as in gift) or in .jpg (pronounced jay-peg) format.

Selecting and saving text

You can save and reuse all or a selected part of the text from the currently displayed web page. This is a two-step process:

- **Copy:** You select and then *copy* the text to the clipboard, a temporary holding area.
- **Paste:** You *paste* the text from the clipboard into another file, such as a Word document or an Excel spreadsheet.

Five points you should remember about the clipboard:

- The clipboard is temporary. Turn off your computer and the clipboard contents are deleted.
- You can view the contents of the clipboard by opening the *Clipboard* task pane (choose **Edit | Office Clipboard)**. This lists all items in the clipboard, with the newest item at the top of the list.

  Each item includes an icon representing the source application and a portion of copied text.
- Text stays in the clipboard after you paste from it, so you can paste the same piece of text into as many different files as you want.
- The clipboard can hold up to twenty-four items at a time. When you copy or cut a twenty-fifth item, the first item in the clipboard is deleted.
- Text copied from a web page and pasted into Word or other application may lose the formatting it had on the web.

Exercise 43.5 takes you through the steps of copying and pasting selected text from a web page. Exercise 43.6 shows how to copy a web address into a currently open document.

Exercise 43.5: Saving text from a web page

1) Choose **File | Open** or press **Ctrl+o**, enter the following web address, and press **Enter**:

   www.well.com/user/smalin/miller.html

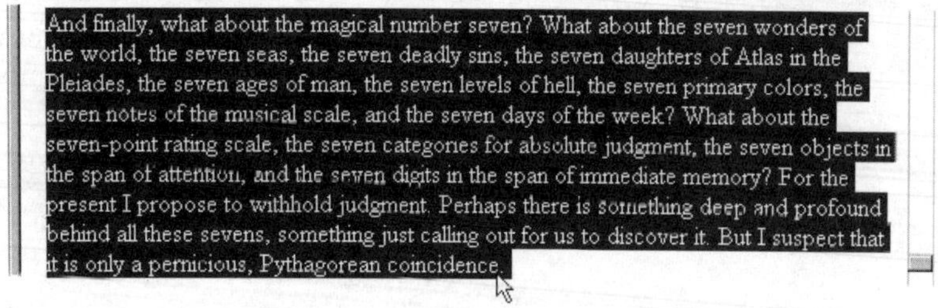
And finally, what about the magical number seven? What about the seven wonders of the world, the seven seas, the seven deadly sins, the seven daughters of Atlas in the Pleiades, the seven ages of man, the seven levels of hell, the seven primary colors, the seven notes of the musical scale, and the seven days of the week? What about the seven-point rating scale, the seven categories for absolute judgment, the seven objects in the span of attention, and the seven digits in the span of immediate memory? For the present I propose to withhold judgment. Perhaps there is something deep and profound behind all these sevens, something just calling out for us to discover it. But I suspect that it is only a pernicious, Pythagorean coincidence.

Here you will find a copy of George A. Miller's classic essay, *The Magical Number Seven, Plus or Minus Two: Some Limits on Our Capacity for Processing Information.*

2) When the web page has loaded fully, scroll down to the end of the page. (A quick way of moving to the bottom of a page is to press **Ctrl+End**.)

   Now, press **Page Up** two or three times until Internet Explorer displays the last paragraph of the essay, which begins with the words 'And finally'.

3) Click at the start of the paragraph and drag the mouse down and right until you have selected the entire paragraph. Your screen should look like that shown.

   When you select text, Internet Explorer displays that text in reverse (white text on black background), rather like the negative of a photograph.

4) Choose **Edit | Copy** or press **Ctrl+c** to copy the text to the clipboard.

5) Open Microsoft Word, open a new document, and choose **Edit | Paste** or press **Ctrl+v** to paste the selected text into Word.

When finished, you can close the Word document without saving it, and close Word.

Exercise 43.6: Copying a web address

1) Visit the Pearson Education website at the following web address: www.pearson-books.com

2) Right-click the *Computing* link at the left of the home page and choose **Copy Shortcut** to copy the web address to the clipboard.

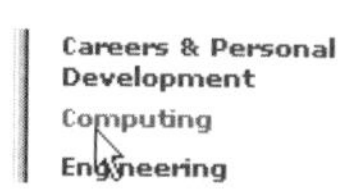

3) Maximize your Word document, right-click at the point where you want to insert the address, and choose **Paste**.

http://www.pearsoned.co.uk/Bookshop/subject.asp?item=2¶

Saving all text

When you want to save *all* the text from a web page, Internet Explorer offers you two options. You can:

- Choose **Edit | Select All**, and then copy the text to the clipboard.

  -or-

- Choose **File | Save As**, select the *Text File (.txt)* option, select the location on your computer that you want to save to, accept or change the default file name, and click **Save**.

Saving a web page

You can save an entire web page – including text, graphics and other components. Exercise 43.7 shows you how.

Exercise 43.7: Saving a web page

1) Visit the MP3 music website at www.mp3.com.
2) Choose **File | Save As**, select the *Web Page, complete (*.htm, *.html)* option, select the location on your computer to save to, accept or change the default file name, and click **Save**.

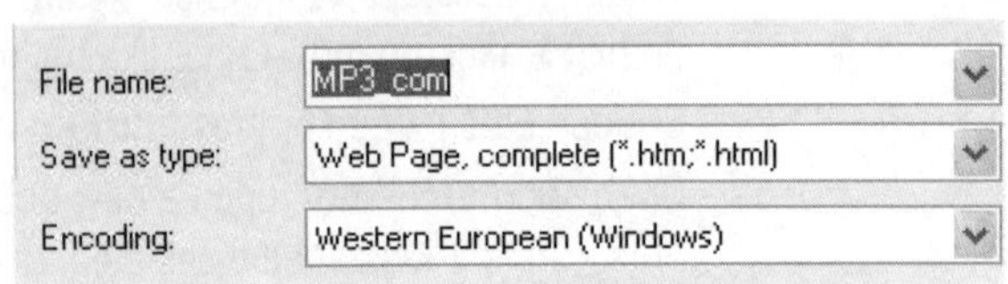

The web page is still on the website. You have saved only a copy of that page on your computer.

Downloading sound and vision

There are many websites that allow you to download music and videos. In most cases, these give you instructions on how to download.

Downloading software

Software companies now generally make their products available from the web for downloading. In many cases, you can download free or trial versions of a software application. Exercise 43.8 shows you how to download Winzip from the ECDL website. Winzip is a useful utility for zipping (compressing) and unzipping files.

Exercise 43.8: Downloading Winzip 8.0 from the ECDL website

1) Go to the ECDL Foundation website, www.ecdl.com, and navigate to the Download page.

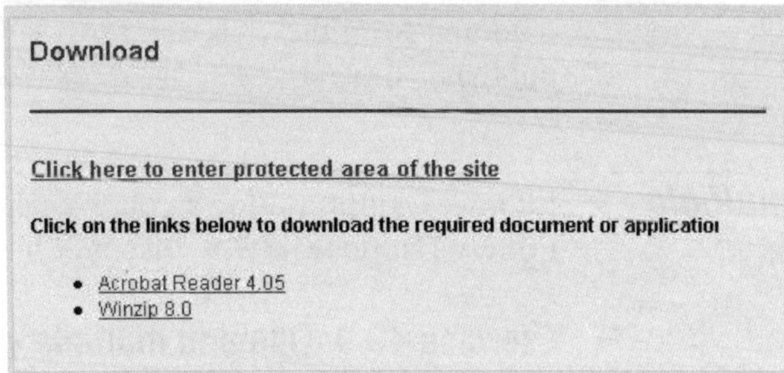

2) Click on the link to WinZip 8.0, and then click **Save** to specify where you want to save it on your PC.

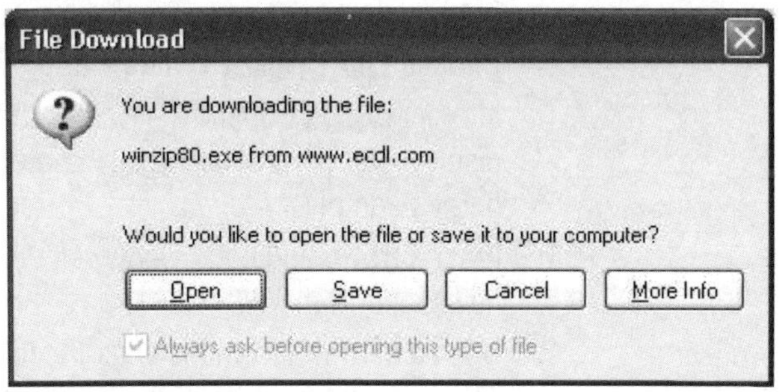

When you can't access a website

There will be times when you are frustrated! Perhaps the website you are looking for no longer exists. Perhaps it is a private website accessible only by authorized users within a company. Perhaps there is a technical problem with the server that hosts the website. Or, more commonly, perhaps you have entered an incorrect URL. In certain cases, you will be asked if you intended a similar web address, as in the example below, where the user mistyped railtrack as ralitrack.

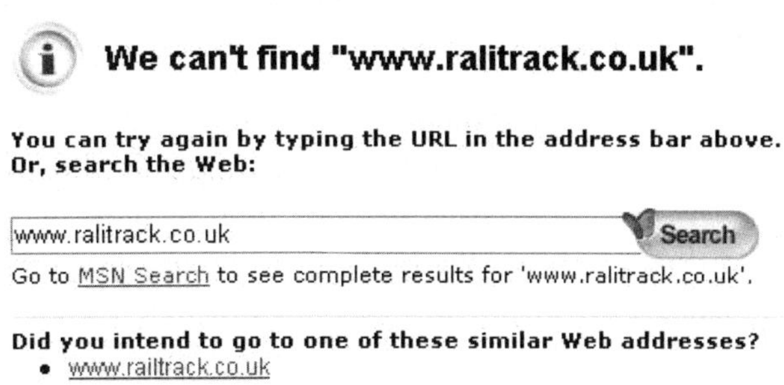

Copyright

As you have learnt, it's not difficult to copy text, images, audio and video and software from the web to your computer. But it may not always be legal. If you intend to reproduce copyright material that you obtained from the web, ask for permission from the author(s) and/or publisher first.

Opening multiple web pages

Internet Explorer allows you to open several web pages at one time. Follow Exercise 43.9 to discover how.

Exercise 43.9: Opening multiple web pages

1) Visit the following website: www.lemonde.fr

   Internet Explorer now displays the home page of the French newspaper *Le Monde.*
2) Choose **File | New | Window** or press **Ctrl+n**.

   Internet Explorer opens a new, second window. By default, the new window displays whatever web page is shown in the previous one – in this case, the home page of *Le Monde*.
3) Press **Ctrl+o** and enter www.welt.de, the web address of the German newspaper *Die Welt.*
4) Open a third window, and enter the following web address: www.lastampa.it. This is the home page of the Italian newspaper *La Stampa*.

   You can continue to open further windows in Internet Explorer – the only limit on the number of simultaneously open windows is the size of your computer's memory.
5) Close all windows except one. You close a window by clicking the **Close** button at the top-right of the Internet Explorer window or by choosing **File | Close**.

Designing your own web page

Once you've spent some time browsing the web, you might think it's time to develop your own website. And why not?

Websites are written in a language called HTML – which stands for HyperText Mark-up Language. If you want to see what HTML looks like, choose **View | Source** at any web page. The example below shows the HTML for the opening page of amazon.co.uk.

Choose **File | Exit** to close the HTML and return to the normal web view.

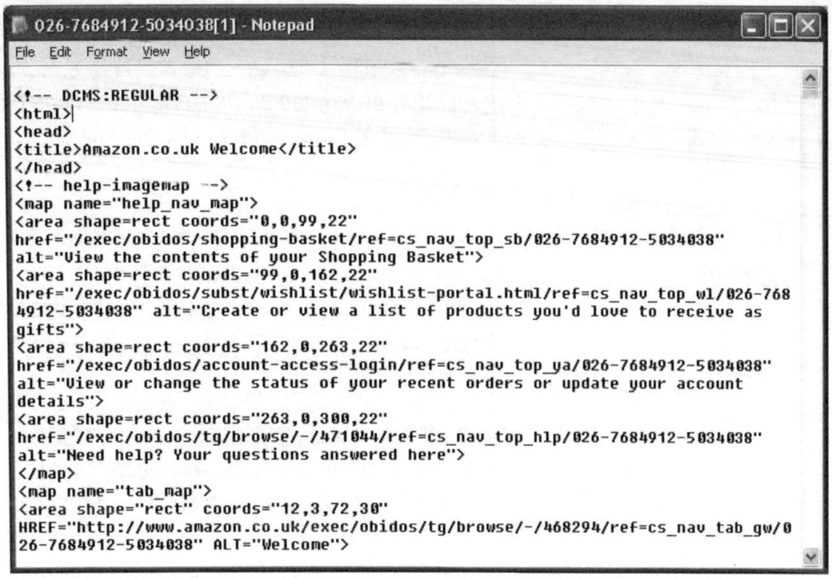


```
<!-- DCMS:REGULAR -->
<html>
<head>
<title>Amazon.co.uk Welcome</title>
</head>
<!-- help-imagemap -->
<map name="help_nav_map">
<area shape=rect coords="0,0,99,22"
href="/exec/obidos/shopping-basket/ref=cs_nav_top_sb/026-7684912-5034038"
alt="View the contents of your Shopping Basket">
<area shape=rect coords="99,0,162,22"
href="/exec/obidos/subst/wishlist/wishlist-portal.html/ref=cs_nav_top_wl/026-768
4912-5034038" alt="Create or view a list of products you'd love to receive as
gifts">
<area shape=rect coords="162,0,263,22"
href="/exec/obidos/account-access-login/ref=cs_nav_top_ya/026-7684912-5034038"
alt="View or change the status of your recent orders or update your account
details">
<area shape=rect coords="263,0,300,22"
href="/exec/obidos/tg/browse/-/471044/ref=cs_nav_top_hlp/026-7684912-5034038"
alt="Need help? Your questions answered here">
</map>
<map name="tab_map">
<area shape="rect" coords="12,3,72,30"
HREF="http://www.amazon.co.uk/exec/obidos/tg/browse/-/468294/ref=cs_nav_tab_gw/0
26-7684912-5034038" ALT="Welcome">
```

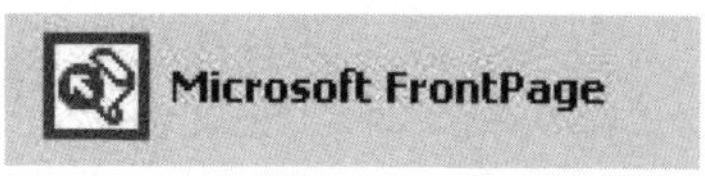

Writing directly in HTML is quite difficult, but fortunately, there are a number of editing and designing tools that you can use to make this easier, and that enable you to preview your design. The more popular tools include FrontPage and Dreamweaver.

The best web designs bring together a range of skills including writing and editing, graphic design and layout, information design, programming and technology skills. Perhaps the best way to start is to take inspiration from sites that you like or are impressed by.

Web words

In this chapter we have been using the word 'website'. Let's look at what this and related terms mean.

The Internet or 'Net' is an inter-network – a network of networks. On the Net, the word 'site' is used to describe a single network. If such a site includes a computer that acts as a web server, it becomes a website. The Net existed long before web servers, and today not every Net site includes a web server.

Website
An Internet-connected network that is owned and managed by an individual, company or organization, and that includes a web server.

Web servers and web browsers

What's a web server? It's a computer that stores files of a particular format, and makes them available ('serves them up') over the Internet to computer users who have a software application called a web browser.

Web server
A computer on an Internet-connected network that stores files and delivers them over the Internet in response to requests from web browsers.

What's a web browser? It's a software application that sends requests to a web server for files, and then displays the files on the user's screen. Microsoft Internet Explorer and Netscape Navigator are the two most popular web browser applications.

Web browser
An application such as Microsoft Internet Explorer that enables a user to request files from a web server over the Internet, and displays the requested files on the user's computer.

Online help

Like Excel, Access, PowerPoint and other Microsoft applications, Internet Explorer offers a searchable online help system:

- The 'help' in online help means that the information is there to assist you understand and use the application.
- The 'online' means that the material is presented on the computer screen rather than as a traditional printed manual.

You can search through and read online help in two ways: from dialog boxes, or from the **Help** menu.

Using help from dialog boxes

You can access online help directly from a dialog box, as Exercise 43.10 demonstrates.

Exercise 43.10: Using online help in a dialog box

1) Choose **File | Page Setup** to display the *Page Setup* dialog box.
2) Click the question-mark symbol near the top-right of the dialog box. Internet Explorer displays a question mark to the right of the cursor.

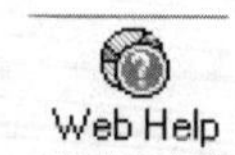

3) Click anywhere in the *Header* box.

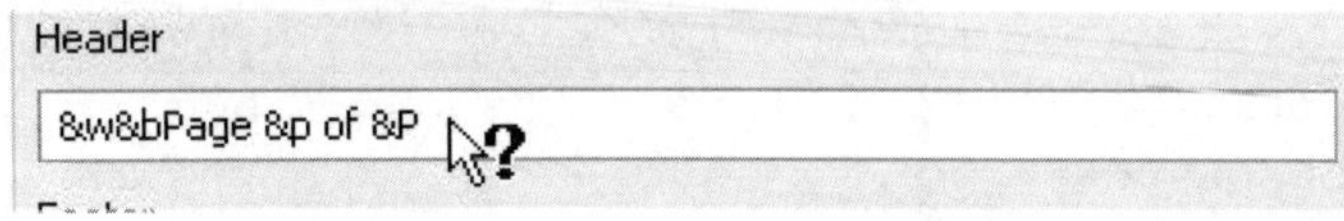

4) Internet Explorer now displays help text telling you about the various header codes.

Practise Exercise 43.10 with other dialog boxes in Internet Explorer.

Using Help menu options

You can also access online help from the **Help** menu. Choose **Help | Contents and Index** to display the four tabs of the *Help Topics* dialog box.

Contents tab

This offers short descriptions of Internet Explorer's main features.

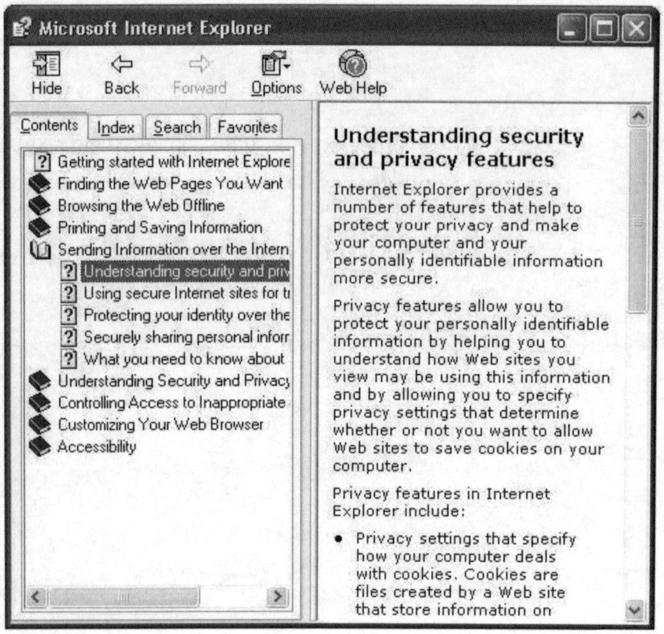

Where you see a heading with a book symbol, double-click to view the related subheadings.

Double-click a question-mark symbol to read the help text.

Index tab

Reading the material displayed on this tab is like looking through the index of a printed book. Just type the first letters of the word or phrase that you are interested in. Internet Explorer responds by displaying all the matches from the online help in the lower half of the dialog box. When you find the index entry that you are looking for, click the **Display** button.

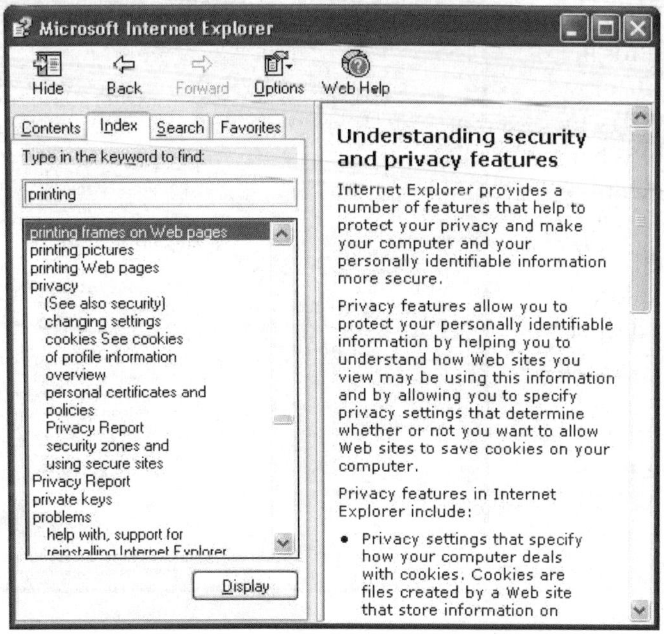

Search tab

Can't find what you are looking for in the **Contents** or **Index** tabs? Try the **Search** tab. When you type a word or phrase and click **List Topics**, Internet Explorer performs a deeper search of the online help. When you find the item you are looking for, double-click it to display it.

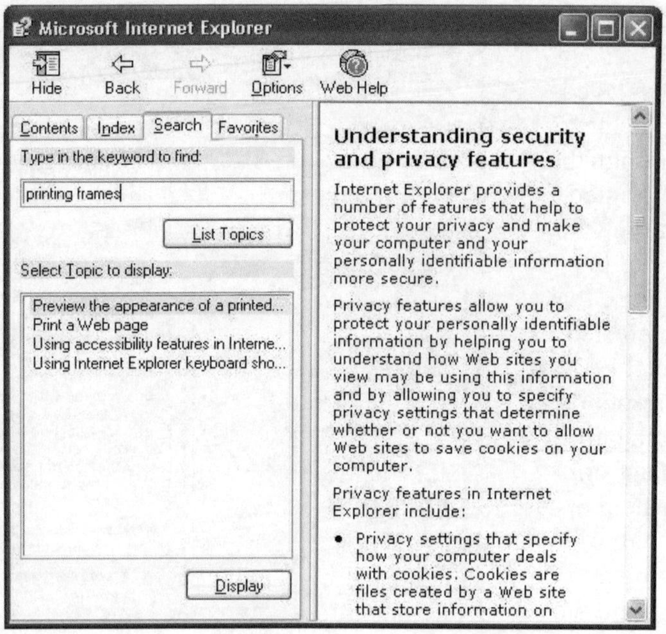

Favorites tab

You want to keep a list of help topics that you look up most frequently? Use the **Favorites** tab.

When you look up a help topic, you can add the topic to your favourites by clicking the **Add** button.

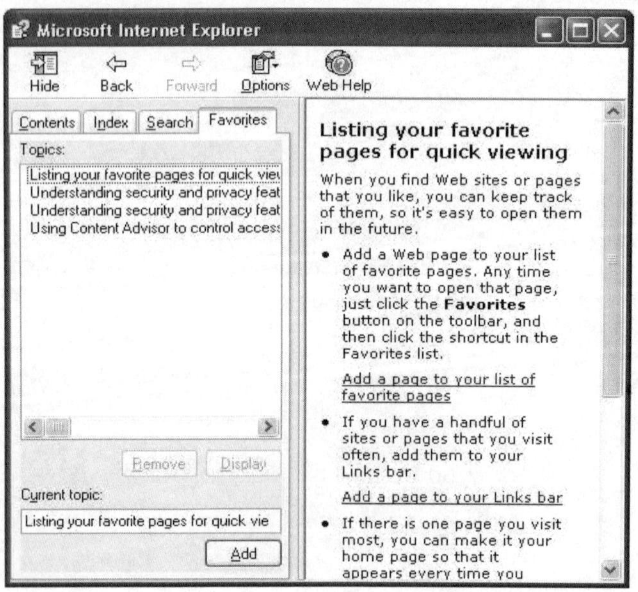

As you search through and read online help topics, you will see the following buttons at the top of the online help window:

- **Hide/Show:** Hides or displays the left-hand pane of the online *Help* dialog box.
- **Back/Forward:** Moves you backwards and forwards through previously visited help topics.

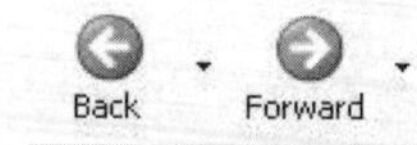

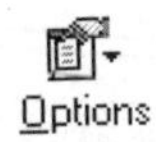

- **Options:** Offers a number of display choices, and enables you to print the currently displayed online help text.

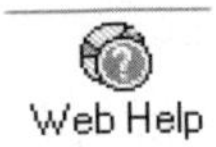

- **Web Help:** Takes you to Microsoft's web-based support site for Internet Explorer.

Take a few minutes to look through Internet Explorer's online help system.

Quitting Internet Explorer

You can close Internet Explorer by clicking the **Close** button or choosing **File | Close**.

You have now completed the first chapter of the ECDL information and communication module.

Chapter summary: so now you know

Internet Explorer is a *web browser* application that enables you to request information from *web servers* over the Internet.

Internet Explorer typically takes you to a particular web page – called the *start page* – whenever you start the application. If you obtained Internet Explorer from your ISP, the start page is probably the *home page* of your ISP's website.

A home page is the first or front page of a website. Typically, it presents a series of *hyperlinks* that you can follow to view the site's other pages.

You can enter a web address to Internet Explorer using the **File | Open** command, pressing **Ctrl+o**, or by typing it in the *Address Bar.* The Address Bar, located above the main window, always shows the address of the currently displayed web page. See Exercises 43.1 and 43.3 for examples of how to do these tasks.

Along the top of the Internet Explorer window is the *Standard* toolbar, which gives you one-click access to commonly used browsing actions such as moving back and forwards through previously visited web pages. See Exercise 43.2 for an example of how to do this.

You can open *multiple windows* in Internet Explorer at any one time, and display different web pages in each one. See Exercise 43.9 for an example of how to do this. The application also allows you to save web pages or selected images, text, audio and video from web pages on your computer. See Exercises 43.4, 43.5 and 43.7 for examples of how to do these tasks.

You can download software from the web – see Exercise 43.8.

Quick quiz: exploring the web

Circle the correct answer to each of the following multiple-choice questions about exploring the web.

Q1	How do you move backwards through web pages?
A.	Press the **Page Up** key.
B.	Press the **Forward** button.
C.	Press the **Backward** button.
D.	Press the **Go** button.

Q2	How do you browse with the Address Bar?
A.	Type a web address in the Address Bar and click **Go**.
B.	Type a search term in the Address Bar and click **Go**.
C.	Type a web address in the Address Bar and click **Search**.
D.	Type a web address in the Address Bar and click **Refresh.**

Q3	How do you save an image from the web?
A.	Right-click on the image, and choose **Properties** from the pop-up menu.
B.	Right-click on the image, and choose **Print Target** from the pop-up menu.
C.	Right-click on the image, and choose **Open Link** from the pop-up menu.
D.	Right-click on the image, and choose **Save Picture As** from the pop-up menu.

Q4	How do you save a web page?
A.	Choose **File | Save As** In the *Save as type* box, select **Text File** and click **Save**.
B.	Choose **File | Save As** In the *Save as type* box, select **Web page, complete** and click **Save**.
C.	Choose **File | Save As** In the *Save as type* box, select **Web Archive, single file** and click **Save**.
D.	Choose **File | Save As** In the *Save as type* box, select **Web page, complete**.

Q5	Which of the following keyboard shortcuts do you use to copy text from a web page?
A.	**Ctrl+b**
B.	**Ctrl+v**
C.	**Ctrl+c**
D.	**Ctrl+p**

Answers

1: C, **2:** A, **3:** D, **4:** B, **5:** C.

Chapter 44: Finding information within websites

In this chapter

Many websites contain hundreds – even thousands – of pages. The web-based edition of a daily newspaper, for example, typically consists of a hundred pages or more. If a newspaper offers an online archive of past issues over three years, the total number of pages on its website might exceed ten thousand.

Other examples of very large websites include those run by online retailers that stock tens of thousands of music CDs or several million books. Travel and holiday websites can also contain huge numbers of pages offering timetable and destination information.

How do you find particular items of information on such sites? This chapter shows you how. Also in this chapter you learn about web address standards and how different countries follow slightly different web addressing conventions.

New skills

At the end of this chapter you should be able to:

- Find a word or phrase on a web page.
- Use a site index to locate information within a website.
- Use a search engine to find information within a website.
- Use an interactive form to find information within a website.
- Describe the web address standards used in the USA, the UK, Italy, France, Germany, Australia and South Africa.
- Explain how folder and file names are incorporated within web addresses.

New words

At the end of this chapter you should be able to explain the following terms:

- Navigation bar
- Keyword
- Website search engine
- File transfer protocol (FTP)
- Interactive form
- Web address (URL)
- IP address

Finding text within a web page

To help you find a particular word or phrase on a web page, Internet Explorer provides the **Edit | Find (on this Page)** command. This command searches only:

- The currently *displayed* web page – not the entire website, and not the whole World Wide Web.
- The currently *loaded* part of the web page. Wait until a page is completely loaded (copied from the website to your computer's memory) before using the command.
- The *text* of the page. Words that are displayed within images are ignored.

Status bar indicates when web page has fully loaded

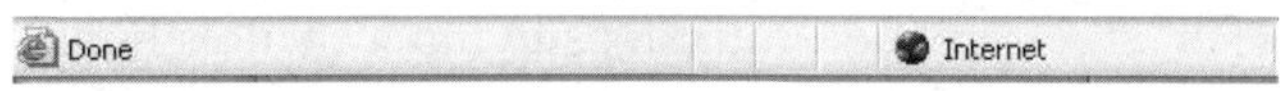

Exercise 44.1 shows you how to use this command on a lengthy, text-intensive web page.

Exercise 44.1: Finding information within a web page

1) Open Internet Explorer and visit the web page containing George A. Miller's essay, *The Magical Number Seven, Plus or Minus Two*. The address is: www.well.com/user/smalin/miller.html
2) Choose **Edit | Find (on this Page)** or press **Ctrl+f**, enter the word 'variance' in the *Find* dialog box, and click **Find Next**.

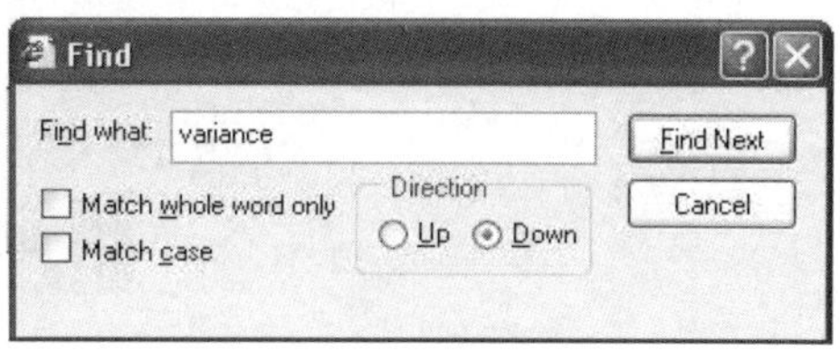

3) Internet Explorer takes you to the first occurrence of the word on the web page. The dialog box stays open on your screen.
4) To find further occurrences, click **Find Next** again. When finished, click **Cancel.**

Finding information within a website

Larger websites can contain many hundreds and even thousands of individual web pages. To help you locate particular information, such websites generally offer one or more of the following three features:

- **Site index:** Sometimes called a site map or site guide, this is a web page that lists the main contents of the website.
- **Search engine:** A program that searches for occurrences of text (words, numbers or other keyboard characters) that you enter, and

displays a list of all web pages that contain such text, together with a summary description of each listed page.

- **Interactive forms:** These enable you to request specific information. You will commonly find forms on travel and holiday websites, and on websites that sell highly configurable products (such as computers).

Website index pages

In the exercise below, you will display the index pages of three websites – that of a film database (IMDB), a media corporation (Pearson) and an Australian newspaper (*The Age*). In each case, you should navigate through the website by clicking on a number of links from the index page and, when finished, click the **Back** button to retrace your steps to the website's home page.

Exercise 44.2: Display the index page of three websites

1) Visit the website of the Internet Movie Database at www.imdb.com.
2) At the bottom of the home page click the hyperlink named *Index*.

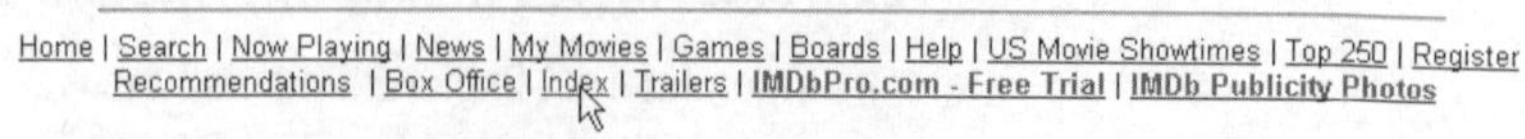

This brings you to the IMDB's index page, which lists of the website's contents. Use the index page to explore the website.

3) Visit the website of the Pearson media corporation at www.pearson.com.
4) At the bottom of the home page click the hyperlink named *Site Map* .

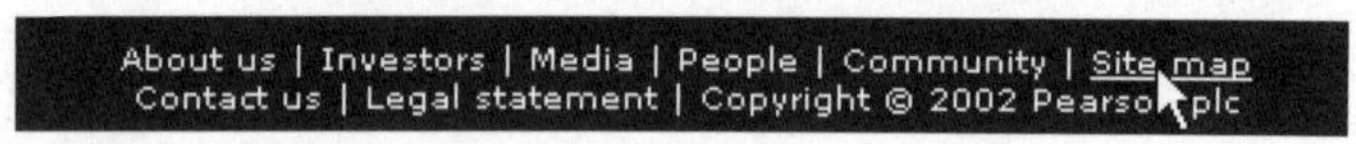

This brings you to the site map page of the website. Use this site map to explore the website.

5) Visit the website of *The Age*, a newspaper published in Melbourne, Australia, at www.theage.com.au. At the left of the home page you can see a link named *Site Guide*. (You may have to scroll down to see this.) Click it to display the contents of the *The Age*'s website. Use this to explore the website.

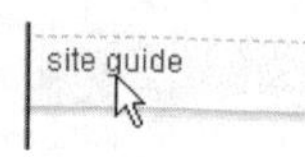

Some websites display their main links across the top of every front page; others list them down one side of the page. A list of the main website links is called a navigation bar or 'navbar'. A navbar may be made up of text or graphics.

Navigation bar
A horizontal or vertical list of hyperlinks to the main components of a website, such as Home (the front page), Site Index (or Site Map or Guide), Company Profile, Products, Services and Staff Contacts.

Site index
Also known as a site map or site guide, this is a web page that lists the main contents of a website.

Website search engines

Site indexes can help you to discover the range and depth of information available on a website. To find one or a few specific items, however, search engines are better.

Exercises 44.3, 44.4 and 44.5 provide examples of search engines on three websites – a film information site (Internet Movie Database), a magazine archive (*The Scout Report*), and an online dictionary of computer terminology (PC Webopedia).

Exercise 44.3: Searching a film database

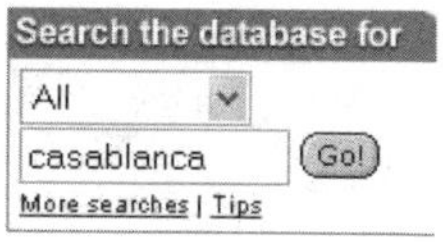

1) Visit the Internet Movie Database by entering the following address: www.imdb.com
2) In the *Search* box near the top left of the home page, enter a film title – for example 'Casablanca' – and click the **Go!** button.

The IMDB responds by listing pages from its database that relate to your selected film.

Exercise 44.4: Searching a magazine archive

1) Visit *The Scout Report* website. This weekly online publication identifies and reviews Internet resources of interest to researchers and educators. Its address is: www.scout.cs.wisc.edu
2) In the *Search* box near the middle of the home page, enter a subject in which you are interested – for example 'botany' – and click **Search**.

The Scout Report responds by listing articles from its archives that relate to your entered topic.

Exercise 44.5: Searching a computer dictionary

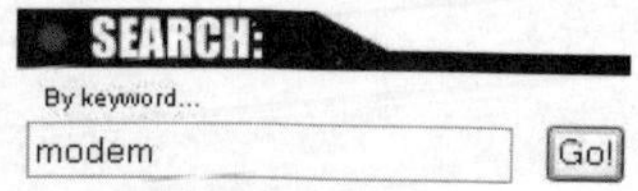

1) Visit the PC Webopedia website at www.pcwebopedia.com
2) In the *Search* box near the middle of the home page, enter a term you would like explained – for example 'modem' – and click **Go!**
   PC Webopedia responds by displaying a page containing an explanation of your entered word.

In Chapter 45 you will learn about search engines that enable you to search the web and not just an individual website. You will also learn how to perform searches with multiple keywords.

Now is a good time to define some of the terms related to searching a website, and to searching the web as a whole.

Keyword
Text or other keyboard characters entered into a search engine. The engine then displays or 'returns' a list of documents containing the entered text. Typically, the returned list provides links to the individual pages, and displays a summary description of each page.

Website search engine
A program that searches a website for keywords entered by the user. It displays or 'returns' a list of web pages on which it found occurrences of the entered word or words.

Interactive forms

On the web, an interactive form is a page containing blank boxes called fields into which you can enter information. Typically, you use forms to specify the particular type of product (for example, a music CD), service (for example, a legal service) or information (for example, train departure times) that you require.

You can also use forms to submit information to a website. When buying a book from an online book shop, for example, you will be presented with a form into which you enter your name and credit card details.

Interactive form
A series of fields on a web page that you use to request a specific item of information, or a product or service. You can also use a form to submit information, such as your name and credit card number.

Exercises 44.6 and 44.7 provide two examples of interactive forms on websites. The first enables you to request a map, the second to specify a PC configuration and view the corresponding price.

Exercise 44.6: Use an interactive form to request a map

1) Visit the Microsoft Mappoint website at www.mappoint.com.
2) On the home page, beneath the heading *Find a Map*, click the *Address In* option. (It should be selected by default.)
3) From the drop-down list box to the right of the *Address In* option button, select Portugal.

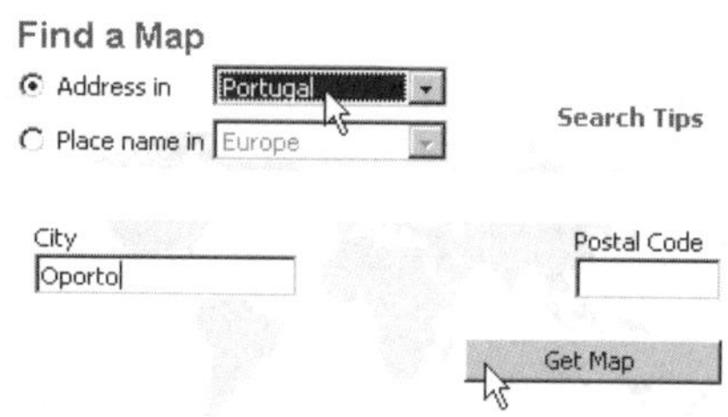

4) In the City box, type the name *Oporto*, and then click the **Get Map** button.
5) The website responds by displaying a map that matches your entered requirements.

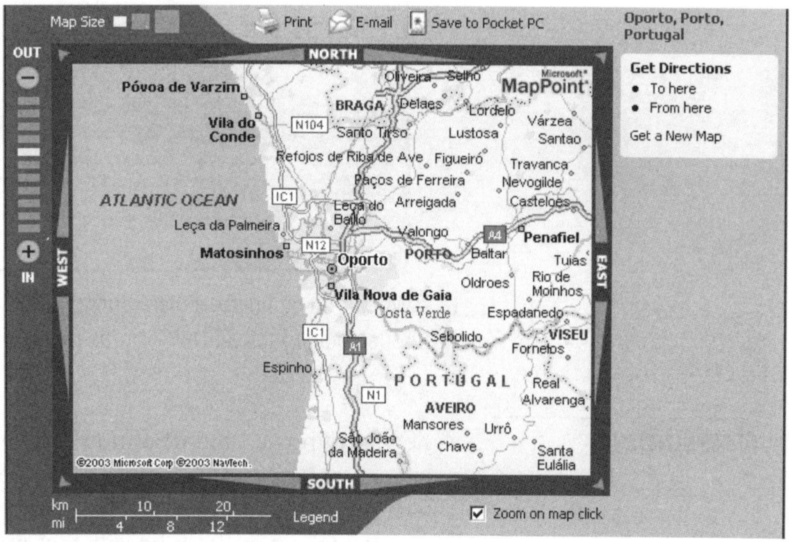

To practise, try some other locations.

Cars, sandwiches and personal computers are all examples of highly configurable products whose price varies with the combination of 'ingredients' chosen. In Exercise 44.7 you use a form to specify a PC's configuration and display the resulting price.

Almost all PC manufacturers now sell their products online. Note that the links and link names in the website chosen – Dell UK – may change slightly over time.

Exercise 44.7: Using a form to price a customized PC

1) Visit Dell's UK website at www.dell.co.uk.

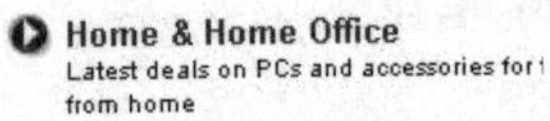

2) Click the link named *Home & Home Office*.
3) Click the *Desktops* link. You should now see a new page listing a number of PC models. Click any PC model series to see a new page that includes a link named *Configure & Buy*.

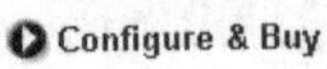

4) Click the link named *Configure & Buy*. You should now see a form that lists several components for such PC components as memory, monitor, hard drive, and so on.
5) Make and change a number of selections.

   Notice that as you do, the price of the PC displayed at the bottom of the web page changes accordingly.

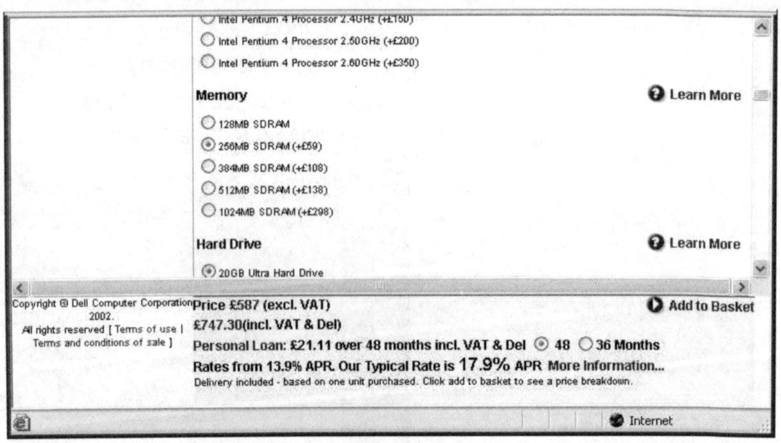

6) When you've finished experimenting with the form, click the **Back** button repeatedly to revisit Dell's home page.

Newsgroups

A newsgroup is a kind of online discussion group or forum, where users can gather and exchange views, opinions and information about a particular area of interest. The newsgroups of today have their origin in the electronic bulletin boards that many computer systems used to host, usually dealing with academic or scientific subjects.

Today, you can find newsgroups dealing with almost any subject you can think of, and the only tool you need to access them is your browser. One of the biggest and most popular newsgroup archives can be found on Google – go to www.google.com where you can view the high-level index or browse the complete list.

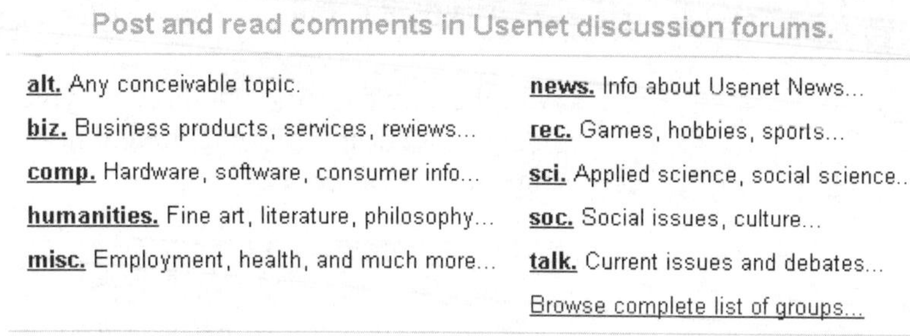

A typical series of messages (called a *thread*) begins with a question to the newsgroup seeking information, clarification or advice.

Contributors to the thread then add their own comments, and gradually the thread grows, often becoming quite large.

You can follow the complete thread of the discussion that follows by clicking on the links to the individual articles.

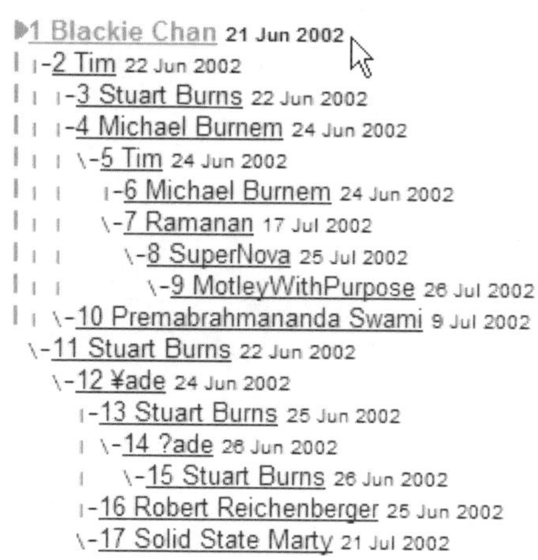

About web addresses

In this and the previous chapter you have been entering web addresses and visiting the associated web pages. A web page is just another type of computer file. Whereas Word files end in .doc, for example, and Excel files end in .xls, web pages end in .htm (or sometimes .html or .shtml). Let's look at web addresses in more detail.

To request a web page with Internet Explorer, you need to know two things:

- The name of the *web server* – the Internet-connected computer on which the particular web page is located.
- The name of the *web page* (that is, the file) on the web server.

Add these two items together and you get what is called a *web address*. Another, more technical, term for a web address is a URL (uniform resource locator).

URL (web address)
The unique address of a web page. It contains the name of the web server and includes (or implies) the name of the particular web page.

Sample URLs

The best way to learn about web addresses is to look at a few examples and discover why they are written the way they are. Here are the URLs of three American websites:

www.latimes.com	www.princeton.edu	www.cia.gov

In a US web address, the last part of the address – the so-called *suffix* – indicates the type of organization.

For a commercial business (such as the *Los Angeles Times* newspaper), the suffix is .com; for an educational institution (such as Princeton University), it's .edu; and for a government agency (such as the CIA), it's .gov.

Here are some Italian (.it), French (.fr) and German (.de) URLs:

www.google.it	www.smartweb.fr	www.lycos.de
www.ferrari.it	www.renault.fr	www.bmw.de
www.juventus.it	www.louvre.fr	www.bonn.de

In each case, the suffix indicates only the country. Addresses are not categorized by type.

British web addresses end in .uk, but they also include a component to identify the organization type: .co for commercial, .ac for the further and higher education sector, and .gov for government.

Here are a few examples:

www.ecdl.co.uk	www.mcc.ac.uk
www.landrover.co.uk	www.cam.ac.uk
www.thisislondon.co.uk	www.ox.ac.uk
www.itn.co.uk	www.bcs.org.uk
www.chelseafc.co.uk	www.amnesty.org.uk

A suffix for primary- and secondary-level schools, .sch.uk, is becoming increasingly popular.

Other countries that use two suffixes – one for organization type and one for the country itself – are Australia and South Africa. Here are some examples:

www.smh.com.au	www.southafrica.co.za
www.microsoft.com.au	www.icdl.co.za
www.ntu.edu.au	www.unisa.ac.za
www.uwa.edu.au	www.up.ac.za
www.ics.org.au	www.cssa.org.za
www.foe.org.au	www.sarl.org.za
www.deet.gov.au	www.finance.gov.za
www.thesource.gov.au	www.durban.gov.za

Practise your web surfing skills by visiting some of the URLs listed in this topic.

URLs and files

A URL specifies two things: the name of the web server and the name of a particular web page on that server. So, where is the web page name in this URL?

www.munnelly.com

Answer: when you enter just the web server name, the server displays the default web page. This is the front or main page of the website, and is usually called index.htm (it can also be called index.html or index.php).

The web address of www.munnelly.com, therefore, is really:

www.munnelly.com/index.php

Here are some other URLs with the name of the default web page included as part of the web address:

www.dfes.gov.uk/index.htm
www.nesta.org.uk/menu.html
www.birdsofbritain.co.uk/index.htm

Notice how a forward slash (/) separates the web page name from the web server name.

When you want to view a web page that is *not* the front or main page, enter a URL that includes the page name. For example:

www.bangor.ac.uk/depts.php
www.botany.com/narcissi.html
www.refdesk.com/paper.html
www.surfnetkids.com/pocahontas.htm

URLs and folders

On web servers, as on other computers, files are organized into folders. In the four examples given below, the web pages are in the main folders of the web servers. But web servers can also store pages in subfolders or sub-subfolders. Here are some examples of URLs that include subfolder names:

www.english-nature.org.uk/news/events.asp
www.lastampa.it/_WEB/_RUBRICHE/cinema/default_cineweb.asp
www.birdsofbritain.co.uk/british-mammals/big-cats.htm
www.nesta.org.uk/lowfat/news.html

A forward slash (/) separates folder names and page names.

Sometimes a URL contains just the web server and folder name, but not the name of the page within the folder. In such cases, your web browser displays the default web page within *that* folder. Again, this is typically called index.html (or index.htm). For example:

www.birdsofbritain.co.uk/accommodation

is really:

www.birdsofbritain.co.uk/accommodation/index.htm

Practise your web-surfing skills further by visiting some of the above URLs that contain folder and file names.

When finished, you can close Internet Explorer.

IP addresses

Do not confuse a web address with an IP address. IP addresses are numbers used to identify computers (including yours) on the Internet. An IP address consists of four sets of digits separated by full stops. Each set can be in the range 0–255.

Depending on how your Internet connection is set up, your IP address is either static (a permanent address that never changes) or dynamic (a temporary address that is allocated by your ISP each time you connect).

If your computer is on a local area network (LAN), it is probable that it has a different IP address that it uses to identify itself to other computers on the LAN.

If you need to find out what IP address your computer uses when it connects to the Internet, there are a number of websites you can contact – enter the search string "what is my IP address" (include the double quotation marks) at any search engine.

File transfer protocol (FTP)

File transfer protocol (FTP) is one of the foundations of the Internet. In order to allow the transfer of files across the Internet, through many different operating systems, computers and types of hardware, it was important to have everyone agree common rules (or protocols) that would govern the transfer, and that would guarantee its success. The file transfer protocol (FTP) was the result.

FTP works both ways. You use it frequently (often without realizing it) when you are downloading files via your browser. And if you have your own website, you probably use FTP to upload files to it.

To upload via FTP, you need an FTP client on your PC. Among the more popular FTP clients are BulletProof FTP (available from www.bpftp.com) and WS_FTP (available from www.ipswitch.com).

You can use an FTP client to connect to an FTP server, and many FTP servers allow you to log in anonymously.

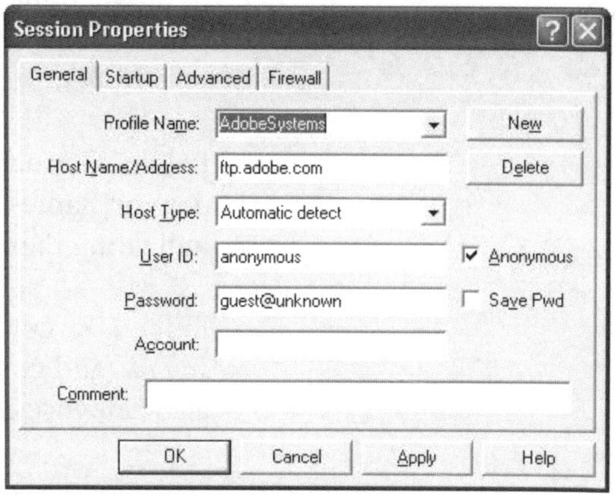

Using WS_FTP to log in anonymously to Adobe's FTP server

Well done! You have now completed the second chapter of the ECDL information and communication module.

Chapter summary: so now you know

Websites typically display a navigation bar or *navbar* – a horizontal or vertical list of hyperlinks to the main components of a website – along the top or down the left of each page.

Larger websites help users to navigate by providing one, two or all three of the following features:

- A *site index*, sometimes known as a site map or site guide, is a web page that lists the main contents of a website. It is similar in purpose to the contents page of a printed book. See Exercises 44.2, 44.3 and 44.4 for examples.
- A website *search engine* is a program that searches a website for *keywords* entered by the user. It displays or 'returns' a list of web pages on which it found occurrences of the entered word or words. See Exercises 44.3, 44.4 and 44.5 for examples.
- An *interactive form* is a series of fields on a web page that you use to request a specific item of information, or a product or service. You can also use a form to submit information, such as your name and credit card number. See Exercises 44.6 and 44.7 for examples.

A *newsgroup* is a kind of online discussion group or forum.

A *URL* is the unique web address that contains the name of the web server and includes (or implies) the name of the particular web page. Where no page is specified in an URL, the browser displays the default page, usually *index.htm* or *index.html*.

URLs have at least two parts, separated by a dot (.). In the USA, the first part is the organization's name; the second indicates its type. Commercial sites end in *.com*, educational sites in *.edu*, and government sites in *.gov*.

Italian, German and French sites are not categorized by type. Their domain names consist of just the organization name and a suffix indicating their nationality (*.it*, *.fr* and *.de*).

In the UK, commercial sites end in *.co.uk*, academic sites in *.ac.uk* or *sch.uk*, and government sites in *.gov.uk*. Australia and South Africa also categorize web addresses by organization type.

IP addresses are numbers used to identify computers (including yours) on the Internet.

FTP is a protocol for managing how files are transferred on the Internet.

Quick quiz: finding information within websites

Circle the correct answer to each of the following multiple-choice questions about finding information within websites.

Q1	Which key combination do you press to find information within a website?
A.	**Ctrl+x**
B.	**Ctrl+v**
C.	**Ctrl+c**
D.	**Ctrl+f**

Q2	What is a site index?
A.	A web page that lists the main contents of a website.
B.	A web page that lists the contents of the web page displayed.
C.	A web page that lists the web address of the website.
D.	A web page that lists keywords found in the website.

Q3	Another name for a web address is a ...
A.	GRL
B.	UFO
C.	RLU
D.	URL

Q4	A web address for a university in the UK ends in ...
A.	.co.uk
B.	.ac.uk
C.	.org.uk
D.	.gov.uk

Q5	A French web address ends in ...
A.	.uk
B.	.fr
C.	.de
D.	.za

Answers

1: D, **2:** A, **3:** D, **4:** B, **5:** B.

Chapter 45: Finding information and shopping on the web

In this chapter

A report published in early 2000 revealed that there were over one billion pages on the web, stored on almost five million websites. Some 85% of the pages were in English, and just over half (55%) of web addresses ended in .com. Faced with such a phenomenal amount of data, how can web surfers hope to locate individual items of information of interest to them?

It's not as difficult as it may sound – once you know how. In this chapter you will discover the techniques for searching and finding information on the web. You will also learn about shopping online – you can buy anything from CDs and books to software and hi-fi equipment on the web, and you can even do your weekly grocery shopping online.

New skills

At the end of this chapter you should be able to:

- Locate information on the web by navigating through the categories of a directory site.
- Locate information on the web by entering a keyword to search engines and meta search engines.
- Perform phrase searches using quotation symbols.
- Perform multiple keyword searches using the plus (+) and minus (-) logical operators.

New words

At the end of this chapter you should be able to explain the following terms:

- Web directory
- Web search engine
- Web meta search engine
- Logical search

Finding information on the web

If you are exploring the web for information on a particular topic, four types of website can help you find what you are looking for:

- **Directory sites:** These are websites that catalogue information on the web according to subject matter.
- **Search engines:** These are websites that search the web for keywords – occurrences of specified words or phrases.
- **Meta search engines:** These are websites that submit keywords to several search engines. In effect, they allow you to use multiple search engines at once.
- **Natural language search engines:** These are websites that accept queries in plain English – for example: 'Who is the Prime Minister of New Zealand?'

In this chapter you will learn about each type of website and discover how you can best use them to find the information you need.

Web directory sites

A directory website organizes information in an easy-to-follow, top-down structure. They tend to be selective, so that only the better sources of information are listed.

Unfortunately, the web changes so quickly that directory sites may not always be up to date.

The original and biggest directory site is Yahoo!, where you can browse information by category, sub-category and, more often than not, sub-sub-category. Exercise 45.1 provides an example.

Exercise 45.1: Finding information at Yahoo!

1) Open Internet Explorer and visit the Yahoo! website at www.yahoo.com.
2) Click the link named *Astronomy*, which is located in the *Science* category.

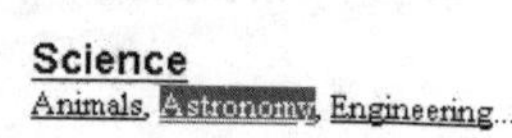

3) You are now shown a new web page. It lists astronomy sub-categories in alphabetic order. Click the link named *Planetaria*.

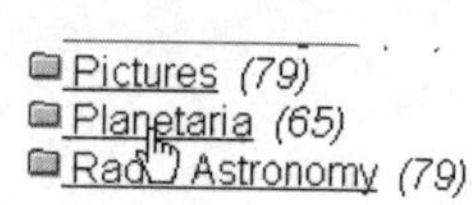

4) You are shown a third web page. This one lists the websites of some 50 planetaria, including Armagh (at www.armagh-planetarium.co.uk). Click on *Armagh Planetarium* to visit its web page.

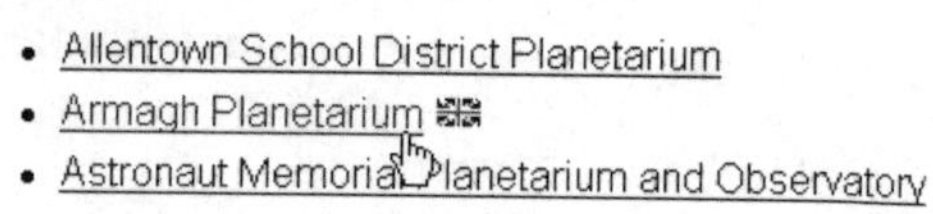

Exercise 45.1 demonstrates both the range and depth of information available on the web – and the usefulness of directory sites such as Yahoo!.

There are country-specific versions of Yahoo! available for a wide range of nations, including the UK, Ireland, France, Germany, Italy, Australia and New Zealand. You can link to them from the main site at www.yahoo.com. Other popular web directory sites include About.com and NetGuide.com.

Most directory sites also offer a search engine facility.

Web directory site
A website that lists and categorizes other sites on the web according to their subject matter. Typically, it offers several hierarchical layers, with a listing of website addresses at the lowest level.

Web search engines

A search engine allows you to enter a word or phrase, searches for instances of it, and then displays ('returns') a list of websites that match your entered word or phrase, with a summary of each. You can then click on the one that seems most appropriate to you.

Search engines do not search the entire web; they search their own smaller, regularly updated list of websites, which typically accounts for about 10–15% of the total number of sites on the web.

Web search engines work in a very similar way to the website search engines you met in Chapter 44. The main difference is that they search the web – and not just an individual website.

Search engines frequently find individual pages from websites that have nothing to do with what you are looking for. You can often discover unexpected gems of information this way, but be prepared to wade through a lot of irrelevant information too!

Exercises 45.2 and 45.3 provide examples of single keyword searches using search engines. In Exercise 45.2 you use Internet Explorer's default search engine.

Exercise 45.2: Searching with Internet Explorer's default search engine

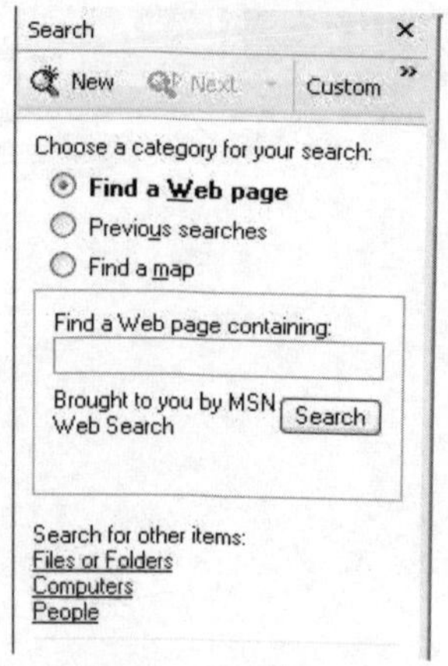

1) Click **Search** on Internet Explorer's *Standard* toolbar.
   This displays the *Search* bar to the left of the main window.
   (Your *Search* bar may look slightly different, depending on how Internet Explorer is set up.)
2) In the search box displayed, type the keyword 'ecdl'.
3) Click the **Search** button.
   You should now see a list of web pages that contain the word 'ecdl'.

You can change Internet Explorer's default search engine by clicking **Custom** at the top-right of the *Search* bar and selecting a different search engine.

The web offers dozens of search engines. You should explore the various options and choose the one that best suits your needs.

Here are some of the better search engine websites:

www.google.com	www.altavista.com
www.alltheweb.com	www.northernlight.com
www.excite.com	www.hotbot.lycos.com
www.webcrawler.com	www.lycos.com
www.go.com	www.ibound.com

In Exercise 45.3 you visit the Google search engine and use it to find information on ECDL.

Exercise 45.3: Searching the web with Google

1) Visit the Google search engine at www.google.com.

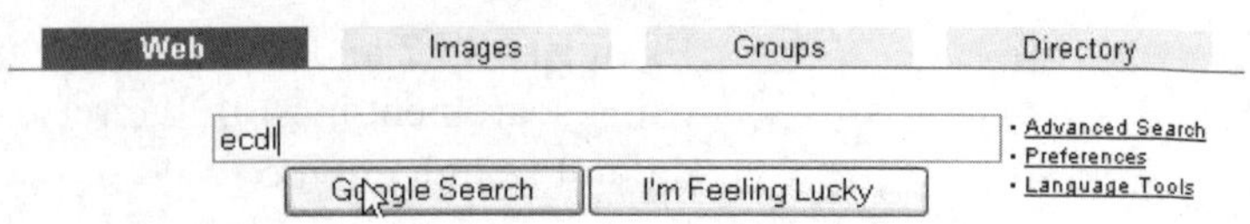

2) Enter the keyword 'ecdl' and click the **Google Search** button.
   Google responds by displaying a list of web pages that contain your entered keyword.

When your query returns more than a single page of results, search engines provide **Next** and **Previous** links at the bottom of each page to allow you to move forwards and backwards through the pages of results.

To print the result of a web search, simply print the results page(s) as you would any other web page.

Web search engine site
A website that enables you to search for material on the web by entering a word or phrase. The search engine returns a list of sites where the specified words were found.

Phrase searches

When searching for a phrase – a sequence of words in a particular order – enclose the phrase within double quotes. Phrase searches are commonly used to find information on people and organizations – even song lyrics. Here are some examples:

"Manchester United"
"Edgar Allan Poe"
"Ministry of Defence"
"Twist and Shout"

Why do you need to enclose phrases inside quotes? The answer is that if you search (say) for Manchester United rather than "Manchester United", your results may include pages that refer to Manchester Council or United Biscuits.

By placing quotes around a query, you ensure that you find only pages that:

- Contain *all* the words of your query.
- Contain the words in the *order* in which you type them.

Phrase search
A query to a search engine that is placed inside quotes. Only web pages containing all the entered words, in the order entered, are found.

Practise your phrase-searching skills by entering your full name, within quotes, to the Google search engine.

The plus operator

Often you want to search for multiple words that are not necessarily adjacent to one another. In such cases, phrase searches are inappropriate. Instead, use the plus (+) operator.

Suppose, for example, you want to find information about the rules of the card game Solitaire. You could enter:

solitaire +rules

Only web pages that contain both words should appear in your results. Note three points about the plus operator:

- You don't need to type the plus operator before the first word that you type in your query.
- Don't leave a blank space between the plus operator and the word following it.
- Leave a blank space after each word.

Here are some other examples:

Excel +XP +autosum
ECDL +Cyprus
Recipe +Thai
Shakespeare +Hamlet

You can combine the plus operator with phrases inside double quotes, as the following examples show:

algebra +"square roots"
"Excel XP" +"keyboard shortcuts"
Volkswagen +Golf +"metallic blue"
"Manchester United" +"David Beckham"
Shakespeare +"Shall I compare thee"
Bogart +Bacall +"The Big Sleep"

Exercises 45.4, 45.5 and 45.6 provide examples of web queries that contain the plus operator.

Exercise 45.4: Using the plus operator on NorthernLight

1) Visit the web search engine www.northernlight.com.
2) Type the following terms and click **Search**:

   Bizet +Carmen +Domingo

   Your results should include web pages that refer to performances of Bizet's opera *Carmen* that feature singer Placido Domingo.

Exercise 45.5: Using the plus operator on AltaVista

1) Visit the web search engine www.altavista.com.
2) Type the following terms and click **Search**: "James Bond" +"Sean Connery"

   Your results should include web pages about James Bond films that starred actor Sean Connery.

Exercise 45.6: Using the plus operator on Excite!

1) Visit the web search engine www.excite.com.
2) Type the following terms and click **Search**:

   London +restaurants +vegetarian

   Your results should include web pages listing restaurants in London that cater for vegetarians.

The plus operator is particularly useful when you find yourself overwhelmed with returns from a web search. By adding one or a few terms, each preceded by the plus operator, you can progressively refine your search so that you receive only the information you need.

The minus operator

Sometimes, you want a search engine to find pages that contain one word – but do *not* contain another word. You can do this using the minus (-) operator.

Suppose, for example, you want information about the solo career of singer Geri Halliwell, but don't want to be overwhelmed by pages relating to her former group, the Spice Girls. You could enter:

"Geri Halliwell" -"Spice Girls"

Similarly, to find information on the post-Beatles career of John Lennon, you could enter:

"John Lennon" -Beatles

If you are a fan of the original Star Trek series, but don't want pages relating to various follow-up series, you could enter:

"Star Trek" -Voyager -"Deep Space Nine" -"Next Generation"

In Exercise 45.7 you search the web for information on Windows XP, and exclude pages that mention the other versions of the Microsoft operating system, Windows 3.1, Windows 95, Windows 98, Windows NT, Windows 2000, Windows CE and Windows Me.

Exercise 45.7: Using the minus operator on Looksmart

1) Visit the web search engine www.looksmart.com.
2) Type the following and click **Search**:

   Windows -98 -95 -3.1 -NT -2000 -CE -ME

   Your search results should provide information only on Windows XP.

In Exercise 45.8 you will search the web for references to Waterloo that are not related to Waterloo, Belgium.

Exercise 45.8: Using the minus operator on Go

1) Visit the web search engine www.go.com.
2) Type the following and click **Search.**

   Waterloo -Belgium

   Your search results should list pages that refer to places named Waterloo in Canada, Australia, New Zealand, the UK and Sierra Leone, but only a few that refer to the Waterloo in Belgium. (Because not every page that refers to Waterloo in Belgium actually contains the word 'Belgium', some of the returned pages will relate to the Belgian town.)

In general, the minus operator helps you to get better results by allowing you to subtract terms that are not of interest. You can combine the plus and minus operators in a single search query.

Logical searches

A search of the web – or of a single website – that contains the plus and/or minus operators is called a logical search.

An alternative way of creating a logical search is to use the so-called Boolean operators instead of the plus and minus symbols. Named after their creator, 19th century mathematician George Boole, these operators include the words AND, OR and NOT, and are typically written in upper-case letters.

The following two logical searches, for example, produce the same results:

"James Bond" AND "Sean Connery"
"James Bond" +"Sean Connery"

Boolean searches have been used traditionally for database searches. On the web, however, the plus and minus operators are supported by more search engines, and are easier to remember and use.

Logical search

A web search that uses logical operators, such as the plus and/or minus symbols, to include and/or exclude specified words or phrases from the results.

Meta search engines

A meta search engine is a search engine that searches search engines. Just enter your word or phrase and the meta search engine submits it to a range of individual search engines, and returns the matching results.

Three popular meta search engines are:

www.dogpile.com
www.mamma.com
www.metacrawler.com

Exercise 45.9: Using the Dogpile meta search engine

1) Visit the meta search engine at www.dogpile.com.
2) Enter the following and click **Fetch**:

   "Access XP" +sort

   Your results will include web pages, found by a range of individual search engines, that describe sort operations in the Microsoft Access XP database application.

Natural language search engines

The Ask Jeeves website at www.ask.co.uk is an example of a search engine that accepts questions in plain English. Here are some sample queries that you could enter:

- Who is the Secretary-General of the UN?
- Who invented plastic?
- Who wrote *Catch 22*?
- What is the currency in Bali?
- What is the temperature in Florence?

A version of the search engine that returns web pages suitable for younger web surfers, Ask Jeeves for Kids, is at www.ajkids.com. You can find the US-based site at www.ask.com.

Exercise 45.10: Using the Ask Jeeves natural language search engine

1) Visit the Ask Jeeves website at www.ask.co.uk.
2) Type the following question and click **Ask:**
   How do I find an e-mail address?
   Ask Jeeves interprets your question and displays a screen with the answers at the top. In the lower half of the screen, it shows the results of entering the words in your question as keywords to various web search engines.

Shopping online

Online shopping websites want to spend your money, so they have generally made it very easy to shop. The interfaces are generally well designed – you select the items you want, place them in a shopping basket, and proceed to the checkout, where you pay by credit card.

One of the most popular online shopping sites is amazon.co.uk. Visit it to see what is on offer. You will see that, whenever you look at the details of a book or DVD, there is an icon close by offering you the opportunity to add the item to your shopping basket.

When you add one or more items to your shopping basket, a symbol appears offering you the opportunity to proceed to the checkout. From that point on, you are connected to a secure server where the communication is encrypted, and cannot be read by anyone else.

Once you get to the checkout, you are asked to fill out a form giving your name, address and credit card details. When you have finished, you can place your order. You can change your mind at any point until you place your order. You can also remove items from your basket.

If you are just window shopping, and don't want to buy anything, you can add items to your wish list, or even to a wedding registry. You can keep this private, or you can make it available to your family and friends, so that they know what presents to buy you.

Protected sites

A protected website is one to which access is restricted. Some companies make parts of their website available only to paying customers; others require users to identify themselves before allowing access to their site, so that they can better market their products and services.

To access a protected site, you typically provide your name and address, and sometimes other personal information. Some sites require your credit card details, so that you pay for the information they provide. You then choose a username (which is known to you and to the site owners) and a password (which is known only to you). The combination of username and password identifies you uniquely, so that the site owners are certain that it is you accessing the site, and so that nobody else can access the site in your name.

Chapter summary: so now you know

Directory websites such as Yahoo! catalogue information on the web according to subject matter. You can locate information on the web by navigating through the various category levels. See Exercise 45.1 for an example.

Web search engines trawl the web for keywords – occurrences of specified words or phrases – and return a list of websites where the specified words were found. See Exercises 45.2 and 45.3.

A *phrase search* is a query to a search engine that is placed inside quotes. Only web pages containing all the entered words, in the order entered, are found. Phrase searches are commonly used to find information on people and organizations.

A *logical search* is a web search that uses logical operators, such as the plus and/or minus symbols, to include and/or exclude specified words or phrases from the results. See Exercise 45.9 for an example.

If you are overwhelmed with irrelevant returns from a web search, add one or a few terms, preceded by the *plus operator*, to refine your search so that you receive only the information you need. See Exercises 45.4, 45.5 and 45.6 for examples.

The *minus operator* helps you get better web search results by allowing you to subtract terms that are not of interest. You can combine the plus and minus operators in a single search query. See Exercises 45.7 and 45.8 for examples.

A *meta search engine* is one that submits keywords to several other search engines, allowing you to use multiple search engines at once. See Exercise 45.9 for an example.

A *natural language search engine* such as Ask Jeeves accepts queries in plain English. See Exercise 45.10 for an example.

Online shopping sites are designed to make it easy for you to select goods and pay using a credit card through a secure server.

Quick quiz: finding information and shopping on the web

Circle the correct answer to each of the following multiple-choice questions about finding information and shopping on the web.

Q1	How do you search for information on PowerPoint 2002 in a search engine?
A.	In a search engine, type the following: PowerPoint +2002 and click **Search**.
B.	In a search engine, type the following: PowerPoint -2002 and click **Search**.

Q2	How do you search for information on PowerPoint that does not include PowerPoint 2002?
A.	In a search engine, type the following: PowerPoint +2002 and click **Search**.
B.	In a search engine, type the following: PowerPoint -2002 and click **Search**.

Q3	How do you search for the song 'Candle in the Wind'?
A.	In a search engine, type the following: "Candle in the Wind" and click **Search**.
B.	In a search engine, type the following: Candle + in + the + Wind and click **Search**.
C.	In a search engine, type the following: Candle -in -the -Wind and click **Search**.
D.	In a search engine, type the following: Candle in the Wind and click **Search**.

Q4	Which of the following is/are examples of logical searches?
A.	James Bond -Sean Connery
B.	James Bond +Sean Connery
C.	James Bond, Sean Connery
D.	"James Bond" +"Sean Connery"

Q5	Which of the following is an examples of a search query in a natural language search engine such as Ask Jeeves?
A.	Type the following and click **Ask**: James Bond -Sean Connery.
B.	Type the following and click **Ask**: James Bond +Sean Connery.
C.	Type the following and click **Ask**: How many times did Sean Connery play James Bond?
D.	Type the following and click **Ask**: James Bond and Sean Connery.

Answers

1: A, **2:** B, **3:** A, **4:** D, **5:** C.

Chapter 46: Taking control of the web

In this chapter

In this chapter you will discover how to adjust the appearance and operation of Internet Explorer to suit your working needs and personal taste. You will learn about Internet security such as hacking, viruses and fraud, and the security measures commonly used to try to defeat these – including firewalls, encryption and digital certificates and signatures.

You begin by learning how you can explore the web more quickly by switching off the display of images on web pages. If there is a particular web page that you visit very frequently, you will discover how to make it display automatically each time you start Internet Explorer.

Another convenient feature of Internet Explorer is its ability to save web addresses, and to group saved addresses into folders for easy reference.

You will learn how to control the display of Internet Explorer's toolbars and various other screen elements, and to specify how the application displays web page text.

New skills

At the end of this chapter you should be able to:

- Switch on and off the display of images on web pages.
- Save web addresses as favourites.
- Organize saved addresses into folders.
- Revisit saved web addresses.
- Change Internet Explorer's start page.
- Display and hide Internet Explorer's *Standard* toolbar and Address Bar.
- Display and hide Internet Explorer's four explorer bars: *Search*, *Favorites*, *Media* and *History*.
- Adjust the text size of displayed web pages.
- Understand some of the security issues you need to be aware of when you are using the Internet.

New words

At the end of this chapter you should be able to explain the following terms:

- Favorites
- Firewall
- Hackers
- Cookies
- Encryption and decryption
- Digital signatures and certificates
- Spam
- Internet cache files

Switching web page images off and on

Web pages with lots of images – or a few large ones – can take an unacceptably long time to display on your computer's screen. Often, these images will be advertisements, company logos and decorative elements that you may regard as inessential – especially if you are the one paying the telephone bill.

Internet Explorer icon indicating a non-displayed image on a web page

Internet Explorer allows you to switch off images, so that you can display web pages more quickly. When you switch off images, Internet Explorer displays only the text of visited web pages, together with a small icon indicating the location of each non-displayed image.

When you arrive at a web page that contains images that you want to display, you can then switch images back on again. Don't be afraid to try this feature – it will save you time and, as Exercise 46.1 shows, it's easy to use.

Exercise 46.1: Switching off images

1) Open Internet Explorer and choose **Tools | Internet Options**.
2) Click the **Advanced** tab, scroll down the list until you come to the **Multimedia** category, and then deselect *Show pictures*.
3) Click **OK**.

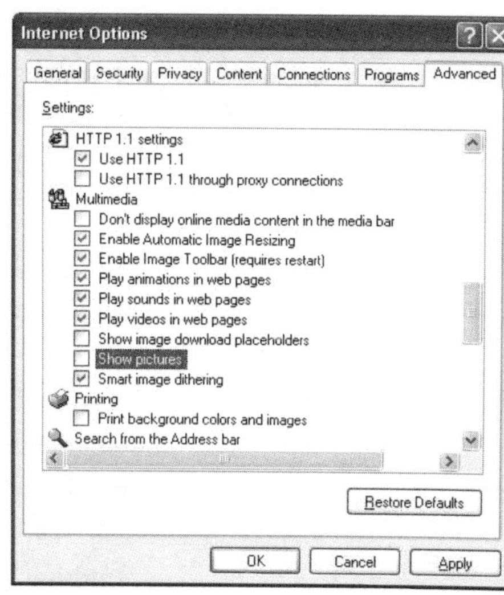

To display images on all web pages, simply reverse step 2 above.

When images are switched off, you can view an individual image by right-clicking its icon and then choosing **Show Picture**.

Favorites

As you browse the web, you will discover pages that you would like to return to at a later stage. You can tell Internet Explorer to store a web page's address by using the Favorites feature. Netscape uses a similar feature called Bookmarks.

Creating a favourite web page saves you needing to remember (or write down) that page's web address. To revisit such a page, you simply click its name from your list of saved Favorites – so much easier than retyping its address each time you want to visit it.

Favorites stores just web page addresses on your computer, not the actual pages themselves.

Exercises 46.2 to 46.4 take you through the steps of saving web addresses, organizing them into folders, and revisiting them.

Favorites
A list, stored in Internet Explorer, of website addresses. Favorites removes the need to remember or retype the URLs of frequently visited websites.

Exercise 46.2: Saving a web address

1) Visit the web page whose web address you want to save. For example: www.yahoo.com.

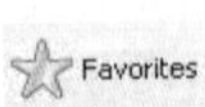

2) Is the *Favorites* area displayed to the left of Explorer's main window? If not, click **Favorites** on the *Standard* toolbar to display it.
3) At the top of the *Favorites* area, click the **Add** button.
4) You are now shown the *Add Favorite* dialog box. Accept or change the name of the web page whose address you are saving (in this case, Yahoo!).

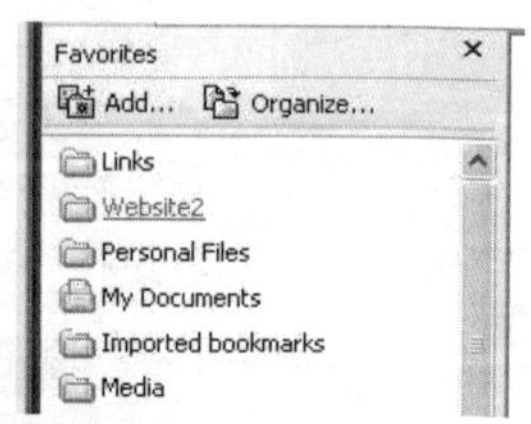

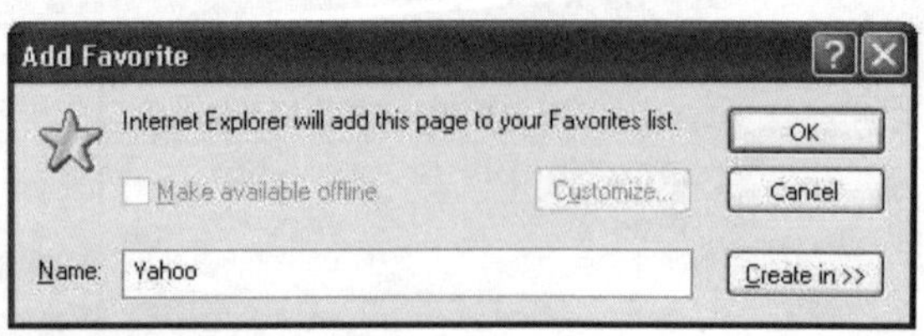

5) Click **OK**.

Internet Explorer adds the name of the currently displayed page as the last item in the Favorites list.

Organizing your Favorites

You can group Favorites in folders, so making them easier to find. In Exercise 46.3 you create a folder to store the addresses of search engine websites, and then add a number of web addresses to that folder.

Exercise 46.3: Managing Favorites in folders

1) Is the *Favorites* area displayed to the left of Internet Explorer's main window? If not, click **Favorites** on the *Standard* toolbar to display it.
2) At the top of the *Favorites* area, click the **Organize** button to display the *Organize Favorites* dialog box.

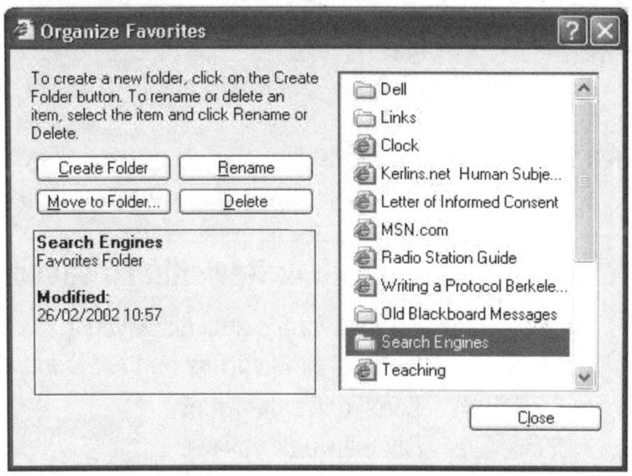

3) Select **Create Folder**, name the new folder *Search Engines*, and click **Close**.
4) Visit the following website:
www.altavista.com
5) At the top of the *Favorites* area, click the **Add** button.

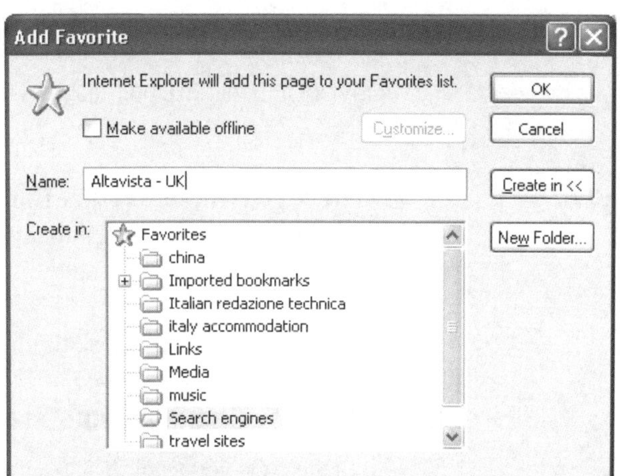

6) In the dialog box displayed, click **Create in <<**, select the *Search Engines* folder, and click **OK**.

7) Repeat steps 4, 5 and 6 for each of the following other search engine websites:

www.google.com
www.alltheweb.com
www.hotbot.com
www.excite.com
www.northernlight.com

Well done. You now have a folder of saved web addresses.

Deleting Favorites you no longer want

To delete a Favorite you no longer want, simply right-click it and choose **Delete**.

Revisiting a saved web address

Revisiting a saved web address is easy. In Exercise 46.4 you revisit a web address that you added as a Favorite in Exercise 46.3.

Exercise 46.4: Revisiting a saved web address

1) Is the *Favorites* area displayed to the left of Internet Explorer's main window? If not, click **Favorites** on the *Standard* toolbar.
2) Scroll down the list of Favorites until you see the *Search Engines* folder that you created in Exercise 46.3. Click on it.

3) Click a saved web address from the *Search Engines* folder – for example, AltaVista. Internet Explorer displays the associated web page.

Changing your start page

Your start page (which Internet Explorer calls the home page) is the web page that the program visits and displays when you open Internet Explorer.

Exercise 46.5 shows you how to change your start page.

Exercise 46.5: Changing your start page

1) Go to the page you want to display whenever you start Internet Explorer. For example, www.munnelly.com.

2) Choose **Tools | Internet Options** and select the **General** tab. In the *Home page* area of the dialog box, select **Use Current** and click **OK**.

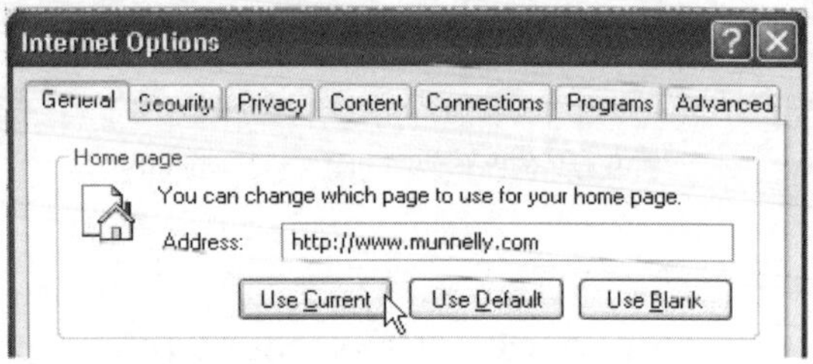

To display your preferred start page at any stage, click **Home** on Internet Explorer's *Standard* toolbar.

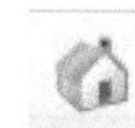

You can restore your original start page – the one set up when Internet Explorer was installed – by selecting the **Use Default** button.

To specify a blank start page – that is, no start page – select the **Use Blank** button.

Screen elements

Internet Explorer's main window is the area in which the application displays the web pages. Surrounding the main window are various screen elements designed to assist you explore and find information on the web:

- Across the top of the main window are the *Standard* toolbar and the Address Bar.
- The Search, Favorites, Media and History bars are displayed down the left when you choose their respective buttons on the *Standard* toolbar.

In this topic you will learn more about these screen elements.

Standard toolbar

You have already learnt the purpose of the following buttons on Internet Explorer's *Standard* toolbar: **Back, Forward, Home, Search, Favorites** and **Print**.

Two other important buttons are **Stop** and **Refresh**. Click the **Stop** button if the web page you are trying to view is taking too long to display. The **Refresh** button re-requests the current web page from the website. Click this button if a web page displays incorrectly or incompletely.

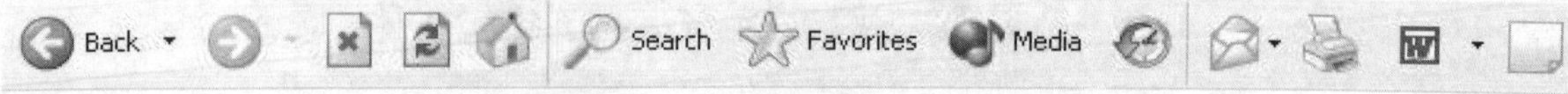

Standard toolbar

To hide the *Standard* toolbar, choose **View | Toolbars** and deselect the **Standard Buttons** option. To redisplay the *Standard* toolbar, choose **View | Toolbars** again and reselect **Standard Buttons**.

Address Bar

Beneath the *Standard* toolbar is the Address Bar. As you learnt in Chapter 43, this area shows the web address of the currently displayed web page. You can also use it to enter a web address: you type in the required address and then click the **Go** button or press the **Enter** key.

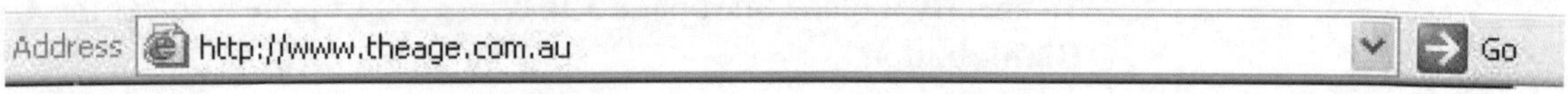

To hide the Address Bar, choose **View | Toolbars** and deselect the *Address Bar* option. To redisplay the Address Bar, choose **View | Toolbars** again and reselect *Address Bar*.

Explorer bars

This is the name that Internet Explorer gives to the four screen elements that you can display to the left of the main window. You can display only one at a time:

To view the Search bar, click **Search** on the *Standard* toolbar, or choose **View | Explorer Bar | Search**.

To view the Favorites bar, click **Favorites** on the *Standard* toolbar, or choose **View | Explorer Bar | Favorites**. You can then view your list of saved web addresses.

To view the Media bar, click **Media** on the *Standard* toolbar, or choose **View | Explorer Bar | Media**.

To view the History bar, click **History** on the *Standard* toolbar, or choose **View | Explorer Bar | History**.

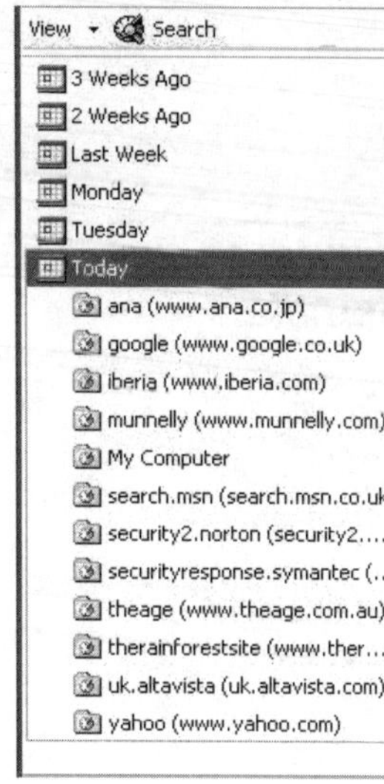

The History bar shows the web addresses that you visited in previous days and weeks. To revisit a web page in the History bar, click a week or day, click a website folder to display individual pages, and then click the page icon to display the web page.

You can sort or search the History bar by clicking the arrow to the right of the **View** button at the top of the History bar.

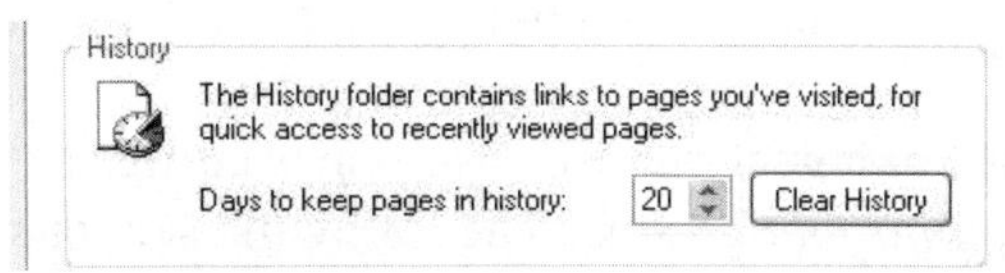

To change the number of days that Internet Explorer keeps track of your visited pages, or to delete the list completely, choose **Tools | Internet Options**, select the **General** tab, make the required change, and click **OK**.

Text size display

You can change the default size in which Internet Explorer displays text – a very useful feature if you have poor or limited vision.

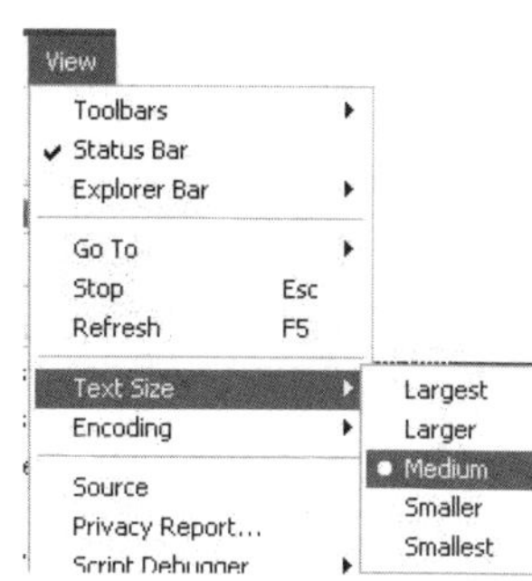

Choose **View | Text Size**, and select the size of text that you want.

You can revert to the default text size of Medium at any stage.

Finally, you can maximize the size of Internet Explorer's main window by choosing **View | Full Screen**.

To revert to normal display, click **Restore** at the top-right of the screen.

Some web pages – such as www.cnn.com – are designed with fixed-sized fonts, so that using the **View | Text Size** options does not change how they display.

Security on the Internet

While the Internet is a tremendous source of information and convenience (it's simple to book airline tickets or holidays from your computer), it is also a place where there is some fraud and some nuisance. On the fraud side, for instance, when you book your airline ticket over the Internet, you are usually required to pay by credit card, and you enter your credit card number into a web page directly connecting to the computer serving the airline.

Information is passing between your computer and the airline server, and it may be subject to eavesdropping along the way, whether close to you or very far away. Your credit card number, and a lot of other personal information, need to be protected. How are they protected?

For a general discussion on security, see *Chapter 8: Keeping your information safe*. The following sections describe some of the security issues that you need to be aware of when you use the Internet.

Encryption and decryption

The primary security against unauthorized eavesdropping on your Internet shopping and credit card details is provided by encryption of data. Encryption is a method of rearranging data so that it is unreadable on the Internet. So, even if unauthorized people get access to encrypted information, they cannot understand it or make any changes to it.

Encryption takes place on protected (secure) servers, which encrypt communication between you and them. For example, when you first surf to the Amazon.com website, the address bar of your browser shows http://www.amazon.com

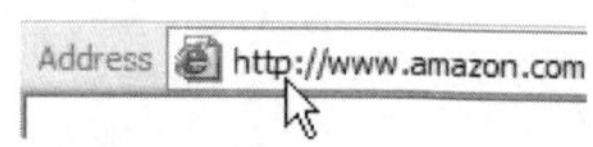

As soon as you sign in as a new or returning customer, the address bar shows https:// The new 's' indicates that you are now using a secure server that is encrypting your data.

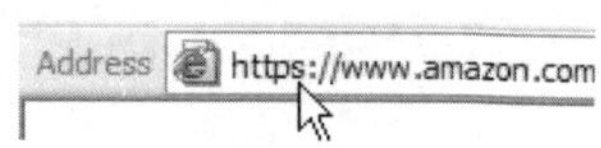

Once you are connected to a secure server, a lock symbol appears in your status bar as shown.

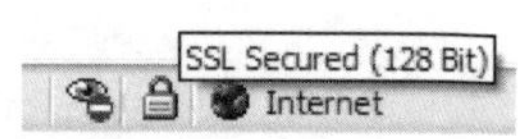

Digital certificates and signatures

As e-commerce becomes more popular, some websites require you to authenticate yourself before you can transact. One way to do this is with a digital certificate, which is like an electronic ID card. Digital certificates are issued within a legal policy and technical framework, known as Public Key Infrastructure (PKI).

A digital signature is an electronic signature to verify your identity as the signer or sender of a message, whether the message is encrypted or not. The message need not be encrypted, but it usually is.

Digital certificates and signatures are issued by *certification authorities*.

Protecting yourself against hackers

Hackers are people who break in to other people's computers, often (but not always) with the intention of causing damage. You need to take some precautions against being 'hacked' – see *Chapter 8: Keeping your information safe* for a general discussion on security.

One of the best ways to protect yourself against hackers is to install a firewall. A firewall is a set of software programs that guards your computer or network against uninvited visitors.

Beware of downloaded files

Files downloaded from the Internet are a common source of viruses. So, be very careful when you download files; in particular:

- Never open an e-mail attachment unless you know what it is. And just because it is from someone you know doesn't make it safe. Remember, you are more likely to receive viruses from people you know than from people you don't know.
- Never download a file from the Internet unless it is from a reputable organization.
- Always use the most recent virus-scanning software to check any downloaded files and e-mail attachments.

Protecting yourself against spam

Spam is the e-mail equivalent of junk mail: unsolicited e-mail, usually advertising products or services you don't want, or offering you untold wealth and the end to all your debts. From the spammer's point of view, there is one huge advantage over junk mail: it doesn't cost anything, not even the price of a postage stamp.

Organizations and individuals who send spam are often very ingenious in the ways that they build up their mailing lists. As a general rule, however, be careful about who you give your e-mail address to.

Most mail programs give you some defence against spam. For example, in Outlook you can add spammers' addresses to the Junk Senders' lists. This means that mail from these addresses is directed automatically into your *Deleted Items* folder.

To do this, choose **Actions | Junk E-mail | Add to Junk Senders List** while the spam mail is open.

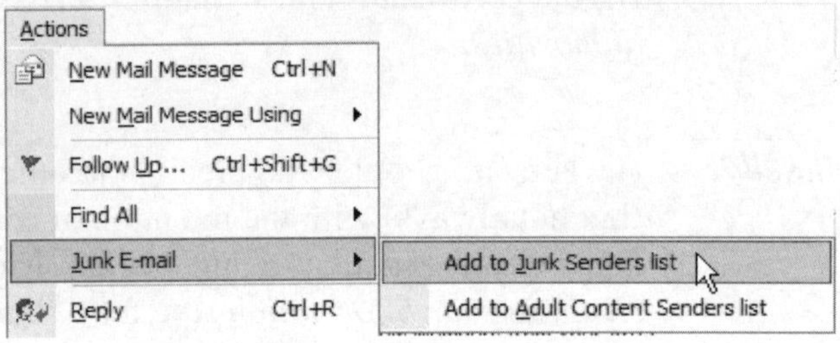

Cookies

A cookie is a small text file that is placed on your hard disk (in your Cookies folder) by a web server while you view a web page supplied by that server. In some cases the cookie just notes that you have been to the web page. In other cases, the cookie file contains information about your viewing habits, and about the kinds of products or information in which you have shown interest.

The next time you return to that web page, the new page served up to you by the web server is tailored to show the kinds of things which the cookie indicates as being of interest to you. As you click to view new items of interest, or as you search the Internet for pictures or sound files, the cookie is updated with the latest information gleaned about you.

Some online shopping sites use cookies so that they know who you are when you log on, and remember what you were interested in or bought the last time you logged on.

The great cookie debate argues either that cookies are a gross invasion of your privacy, or that cookies are of great use to web servers to better serve your Internet browsing.

Cookie
A small text file placed on your computer by a web server when you view a web page supplied by that server. A cookie works as a kind of ID card the next time you access that page. Only the web server that created the cookie can read it.

Enabling or disabling cookies

Internet Explorer includes a setting that you can use to set the level of cookies you are prepared to accept.

Open Internet Explorer and choose **Tools | Internet Options**, and then select the **Privacy** tab.

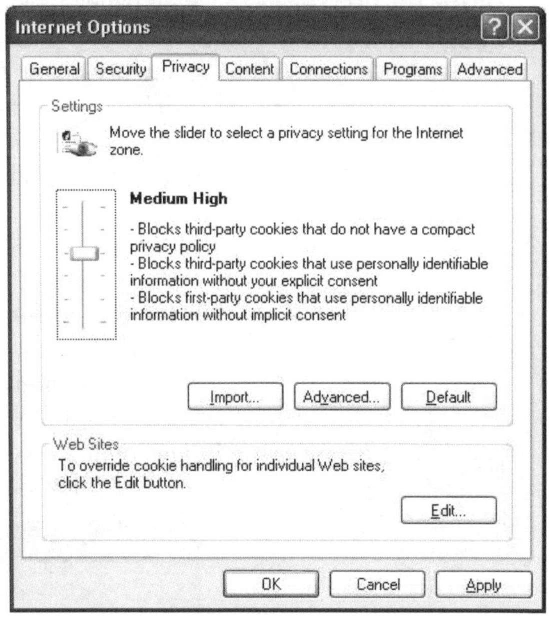

Move the slider to the bottom to accept all cookies, or to the top to refuse all cookies. Most people set the slider to *Medium High*.

Deleting cookies

You can delete all cookies stored on your PC.

In Internet Explorer, choose **Tools | Internet Options**, and in the *Temporary Internet files* section of the **General** tab, click **Delete Cookies**.

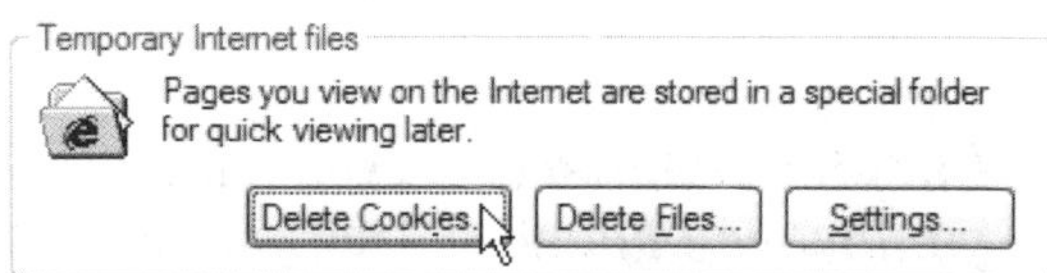

Deleting the History folder contents

The address of every website you view is recorded in the History folder of your PC.

If you wish, you can delete the contents of the History folder. In Internet Explorer, choose **Tools | Internet Options**, and in the *History* section of the **General** tab, click **Clear History** and click **Yes** to confirm.

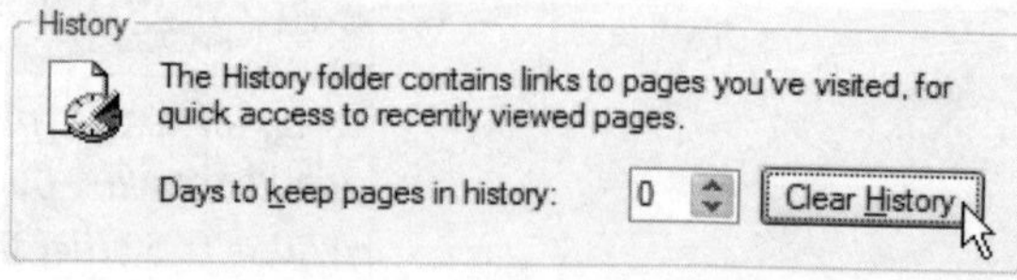

Deleting Internet cache files

Web pages that you view when surfing the Internet are saved in the Temporary Internet Files folder (sometimes called the cache). The main advantage of this is that data from those pages is retrieved quicker the next time you access the site the pages came from.

If you wish, you can delete Internet cache files.

In Internet Explorer, choose **Tools | Internet Options**, and in the *Temporary Internet files* section of the **General** tab, click **Delete Files**. When the *Delete Files* dialog box appears, check the *Delete all offline content* check box and click **OK**.

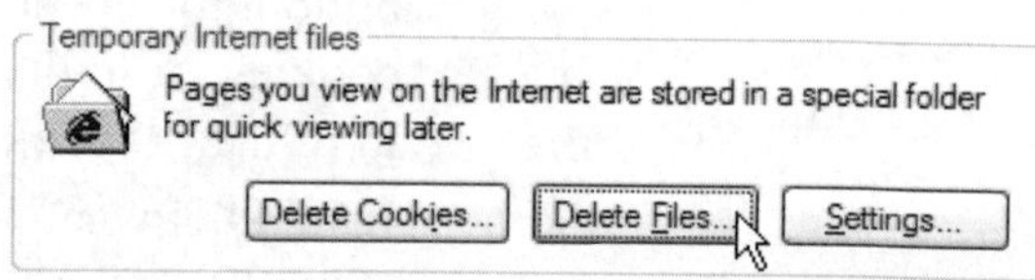

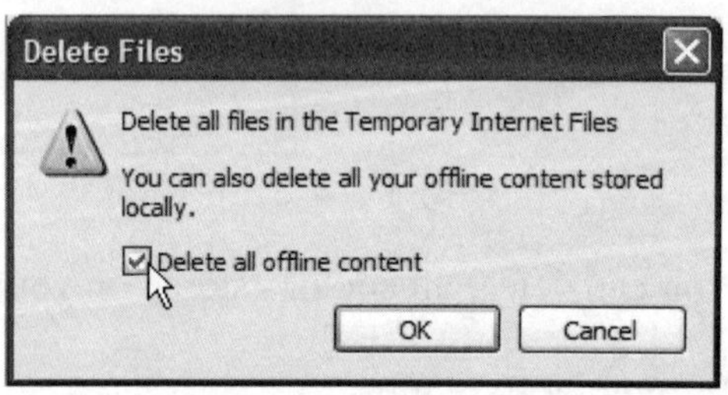

Chapter summary: so now you know

You can adjust the appearance and operation of Internet Explorer to suit your working needs and personal taste.

To display web pages more quickly, switch off the display of images. Internet Explorer displays only the text of visited web pages, together with a small icon indicating the location of each non-displayed image. See Exercise 46.1 for an example of how to do this task.

You can store web addresses, and organize them into folders for easy reference, using Internet Explorer *Favorites*. See Exercises 46.2, 46.3 and 46.4 for examples of how to do these tasks. If there is a particular web page you visit very frequently, you can make it your default *start page*. See Exercise 46.5 for an example of how to do this task.

Internet Explorer's *Standard* toolbar offers quick access to commonly used browsing actions. At the left of the main window you can display any of the following: the History bar, Search bar, Media bar or the Favorites bar.

Internet Explorer allows you to adjust the size in which text is displayed on-screen.

There are a number of security issues you need to be aware of when you use the Internet. When you are shopping on the Internet, your credit card details are *encrypted* so that they cannot be intercepted by unauthorized people. Some websites require you to identify yourself with a *digital signature* – these are issued by *certification authorities*.

Spam is the e-mail equivalent of junk mail. You can protect yourself against spam by blocking addresses from which you receive spam.

A *cookie* is a text file placed on your computer by a web page that you have visited. The next time you visit that page, the cookie acts as your ID card for that page. If you don't wish to receive cookies, you can disable them. You can delete the *history* of which web pages you have visited, and you can delete *temporary Internet cache files*.

Quick quiz: taking control of the web

Circle the correct answer to each of the following multiple-choice questions about taking control of the web.

Q1	How do you save a web address?
A.	Visit the web page whose address you want to save. Click the **Favorites** button. In the *Favorites* dialog box, click **Add**. Select the folder where you want to store the web page and click **OK**.
B.	Visit the web page whose address you want to save. Select the address that you want to save and press **Ctrl+c**. Open a Microsoft Word document and press **Ctrl+v**. Click **Save**.
C.	Visit the web page whose address you want to save. Click the **Search** button. In the *Search* dialog box, select *Find a web page*. Type the address of the web page and click **Search**.
D.	Visit the web page whose address you want to save. Click the **Favorites** button. In the *Favorites* dialog box, click **Add**. Select the folder where you want to store the web page and click **Cancel**.

Q2	What does the History bar display?
A.	Media options.
B.	Saved web addresses.
C.	Search items.
D.	Previously visited websites.

Q3	How do you change your start page?
A.	Select the web page that you want to display. Choose **Tools | Internet Options** and select the **General** tab. Under *Home Page* click the **Use Blank** button and click **OK**.
B.	Select the web page that you want to display. Choose **Tools | Internet Options** and select the **General** tab. Under *Home Page* click the **Use Default** button and click **OK**.
C.	Select the web page that you want to display. Choose **Tools | Internet Options** and select the **General** tab. Under *Home Page* click the **Use Current** button and click **OK**.
D.	Select the web page that you want to display. Choose **Tools | Internet Options** and select the **General** tab. Under *Home Page* click the **Use Current** button and click **Cancel**.

Q4	How do you change the size of the text in a web page?
A.	Choose **View | Text Size**, and select the size of the text that you want.
B.	Choose **View | Encoding**, and select the encoding that you want.
C.	Choose **View | Toolbars**, and select the toolbar that you want.
D.	Choose **View | Explorer Bar**, and select the Explorer Bar option that you want.

Answers

1: A, **2:** D, **3:** C, **4:** A.

Chapter 47: E-mail with Outlook

In this chapter

Question: what do most people use the Internet for? Answer: e-mail. It's fast becoming the preferred method of communication in business, and it is also used by friends and family as a way of staying in touch.

An e-mail travels from Europe to America in a matter of seconds, and can be read and replied to a minute later. This beats the humble stamped mail by days, and if you include the reply, by up to a week or more. It is also vastly cheaper to send fifty transatlantic e-mails than it is to send fifty letters to the same person, or to telephone the person even two or three times.

This chapter introduces you to Outlook, the Microsoft e-mail application. You will explore the application's main screen elements and discover how to arrange them to suit your personal taste.

You will also learn how to address, compose and send an e-mail over the Internet, and how to collect and read incoming e-mails addressed to you.

New skills

At the end of this chapter you should be able to:

- Start and quit Microsoft Outlook.
- Display the following four screen elements: Folder list, Message list, Preview pane and toolbar.
- Select an e-mail from a Message list and display it in the Preview pane.
- Select an e-mail from a Message list and display it in a separate window.
- Compose and send e-mails.
- Collect and read incoming e-mails.
- Print and delete an e-mail.

New words

At the end of this chapter you should be able to explain the following terms:

- Folder list
- Message list
- Preview pane
- E-mail collection

Starting Outlook

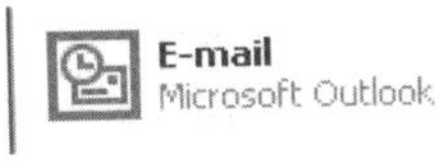

Double-click on the **Microsoft Outlook** icon or choose **Start | All Programs | Microsoft Outlook**.

If your computer has a permanent Internet connection, you are ready to send and receive e-mail messages with Outlook.

If you have a dial-up connection, you must dial your Internet service provider (ISP). Outlook may be set up to do this automatically. If not, you will need to dial your ISP separately.

Enter your user name and password (if Outlook has not recorded them from the last time you dialled your ISP), and click **Connect**.

Changing screen layout

You can change the layout of the Outlook screen so that the features you use most often are shown, and those you rarely use are hidden. This means that two people using Outlook might have screens that look very different. For the purpose of the exercises in this module, change the screen layout as directed in Exercise 47.1.

Exercise 47.1: Choosing the display elements

1) Choose **View** for Outlook to present a list of layout options.
2) Choose:

   View | Outline Pane

   View | Folder List

   View | Preview Pane

   View | Status Bar

3) Choose **View | Toolbars** and select the three toolbar options – *Standard*, *Advanced* and *Web*.
4) Choose **View | Current View | Messages**.

Your Outlook screen should have the same layout as shown below.

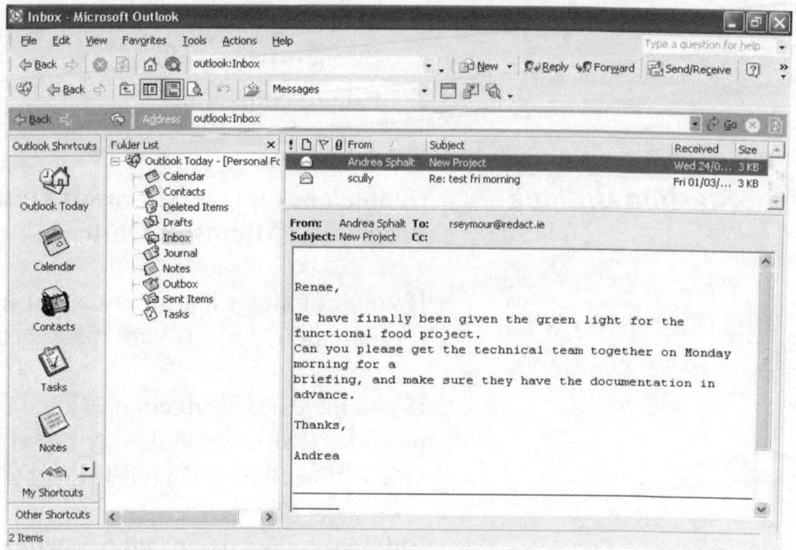

The four layout elements

Let's take a look at the four main screen elements of Outlook: Folder list, Message list, Preview pane and the toolbar.

Folder list

The Folder list shows five folders:

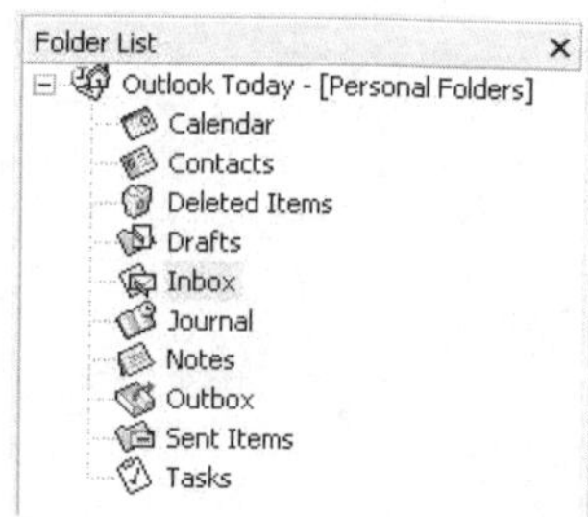

- **Inbox:** This is where all your incoming e-mails – those sent to you by other people – are held.
- **Outbox:** This can hold all your outgoing e-mails – those you have composed yourself – until you send them.
- **Sent Items:** This can hold copies of all the e-mails you have sent to other people.
- **Deleted Items:** This is where you put all e-mails – both incoming and outgoing – that you no longer want to keep.
- **Drafts:** This is where you store any e-mails that you have not finished composing.

When a folder contains an unread e-mail, Outlook displays the folder name in bold, and shows, in brackets, the number of unread e-mails in that folder.

In addition to the five e-mail folders provided with Outlook, you can create folders and subfolders of your own, and move e-mails in and out of them. You will learn how to do this in Chapter 49.

> **Folder list**
>
> *The part of Outlook where e-mails are stored and grouped according to type: received (Inbox), waiting to be sent (Outbox), already sent (Sent Items), marked for deletion (Deleted Items), and stored for later editing (Drafts). Users can create additional folders and subfolders for organizing their e-mails further.*

Message list

When you click any folder in the Folder list, Outlook displays the folder's contents in an area on the right of the screen called the Message list. This is known as 'opening the folder'.

Click on a folder to display its contents in the Message list

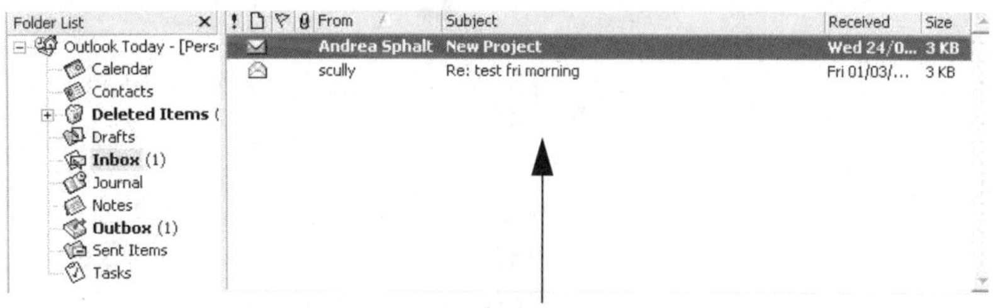

Message list

Outlook displays some basic details about each e-mail – the sender or recipient, the subject, and the date and time it was sent or received – and uses the following symbols to provide you with more information:

- A *read* e-mail, displayed in light type.

- An *unread* e-mail, displayed in bold type.

- An e-mail, whether read or unread, with one or more *files attached*. (You will learn about e-mail file attachments in Chapters 48 and 49.)

- An e-mail marked as *high priority*. (You will learn about e-mail priority in Chapter 48.)

> **Message list**
>
> *A list of the e-mails contained in the currently selected Outlook folder. Outlook displays a summary of information about each one.*

Preview pane

When you click on an e-mail in your Message list, Outlook displays the e-mail's contents in an area beneath the Message list called the Preview pane.

Click on an e-mail in the Message list to display its contents in the Preview pane

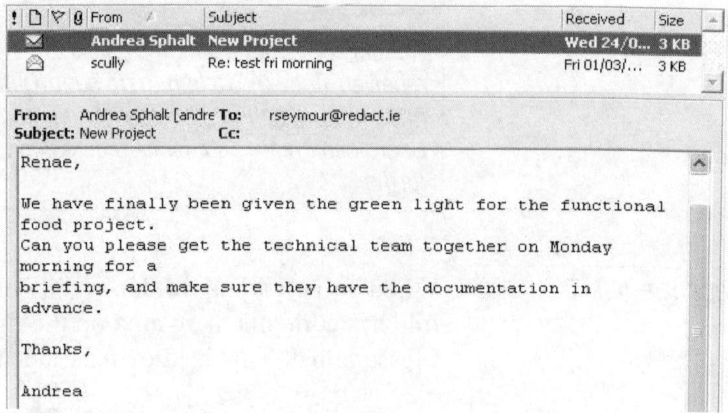

To display a different e-mail in the Preview pane, simply click on a different e-mail in the message list.

You can resize the Preview pane and the Message list by clicking on the border between them, holding down the mouse button, and dragging the border up or down.

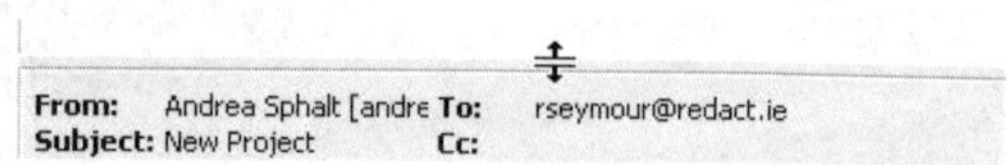

Preview pane
An area of the Outlook screen that shows the contents of the e-mail that is currently selected in the Message list.

If you receive a long e-mail, you may prefer to read it in a separate window. To do this, double-click the e-mail in the Message list.

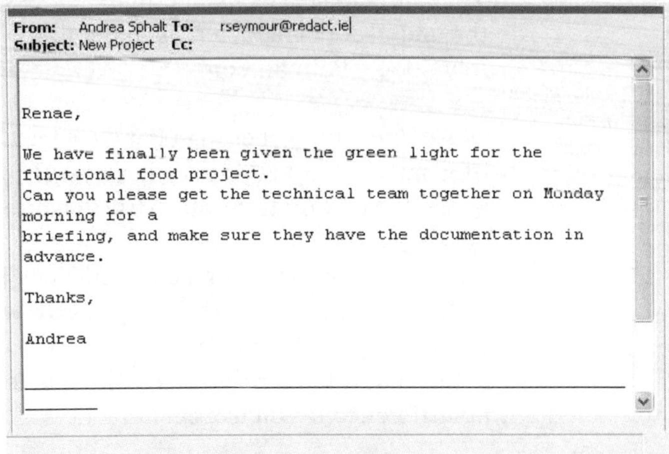

Close button

You can then minimize the e-mail's separate window (so that you can come back directly to it at any time), or maximize it (so that it fills the screen). When you are finished with it, close it by clicking the **Close** button at the top-right of the window. This closes only the e-mail's separate window – and not Outlook.

Outlook toolbar

The *Outlook* toolbar provides buttons that offer one-click access to the e-mail actions you will want to use most frequently. Different buttons are displayed according to which part of the Outlook screen you are working in.

Outlook toolbar

Rather than introduce all these buttons at once, we will explain each one as it becomes relevant in this module.

Composing and sending an e-mail

An e-mail address identifies a person at a location on the Internet. There are two parts to an e-mail address. The first part is the person's user name and the second part identifies the e-mail provider or domain where the mail is received and stored.

The parts are always joined (or divided) by the @ sign, so that e-mail addresses take the form of *username@domain.com.*

A typical example is johndoe@hotmail.com

There are no spaces in an e-mail address, but sometimes people use the underscore character, as in the following example: john_doe@hotmail.com

Most countries (other than the USA) use a national identifier instead of .com. So most addresses in Great Britain end in .co.uk, French addresses end in .fr, South African addresses end in .za, and so on.

See http://www.iana.org/cctld/cctld-whois.htm for a list of country codes.

E-mail addresses are usually written in lower-case letters, but it makes no difference if you use capital letters.

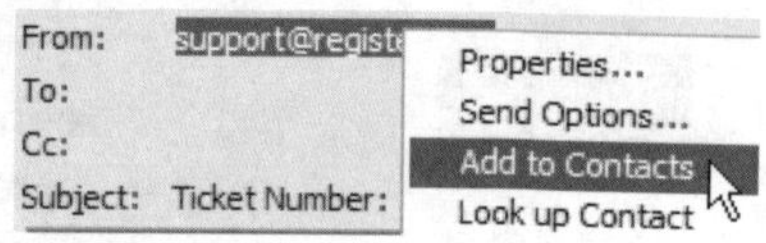

You don't have to type an e-mail address every time. When you receive an e-mail from someone, you can right-click the e-mail address and click **Add to Contacts**, so that in future you can click to add it to an e-mail, and avoid re-typing it.

Exercise 47.2 leads you through the steps of composing and sending an e-mail in Outlook.

Exercise 47.2: Composing and sending an e-mail

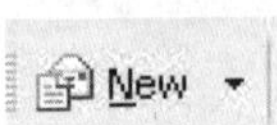

1) Choose **File | New | Mail Message** or click the arrow to the right of the **New** button on the toolbar. Select **Mail Message** from the drop-down list displayed.
2) Click in the *To* box, and type the address of the person to whom you are sending the e-mail.
   Notice that the address is underlined.
3) Click in the *Subject* box, and type a brief description of your e-mail.
4) Click in the main text box, and type the text of your e-mail.

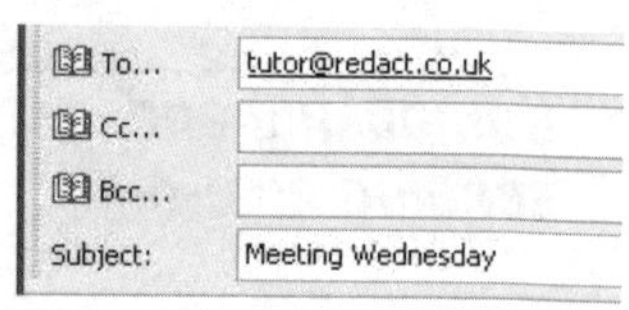

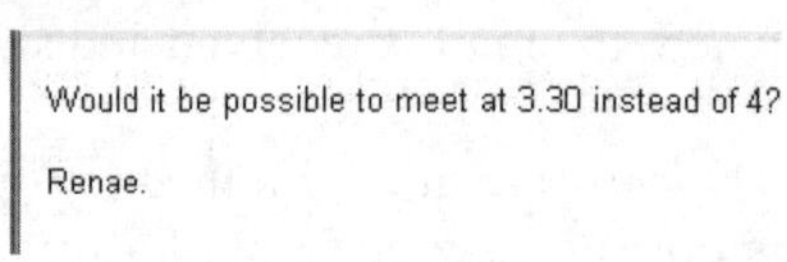

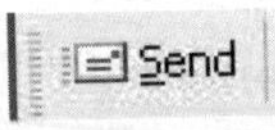

Sends current e-mail to Outbox or Internet

5) When you have finished typing, choose **File | Send Message**, or click the **Send** on the *New Message* toolbar.

Congratulations! You have now composed and sent your first e-mail.

What happens to your outgoing e-mail? The answer depends on:

- Your type of Internet connection – permanent or dial-up.
- Your selected e-mail sending option – immediate or in a group with other outgoing e-mails.

Outgoing e-mail: permanent Internet connection

When you send an e-mail, Outlook can transfer it directly to the Internet. To set up this option, choose **Tools | Options**, select the **Mail Setup** tab, select *Send immediately when connected*, and click **OK**.

If you do not select this option, your e-mail goes only as far as your **Outbox** folder. It remains there, along with any other outgoing e-mails, until you choose **Tools | Send and Receive | Send All** or click the **Send/Receive** on the *Outlook* toolbar.

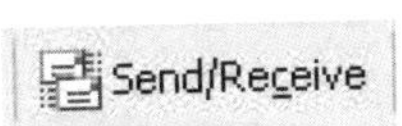

Sends all e-mails from Outbox to Internet, and fetches all incoming mail

Don't confuse the **Send** button on the *New Message* toolbar with the **Send/Receive** button on the *Outlook* toolbar.

- **Send button:** This sends the current e-mail to the Internet or to your Outbox folder, depending on how Outlook is set up.
- **Send/Receive button:** This sends all e-mails in your Outbox folder to the Internet.

Outgoing e-mail: dial-up connection

As with a permanent Internet connection, you can choose to send each e-mail immediately or to store them in your Outbox for sending later.

You would generally choose to hold all your outgoing messages in your Outbox until you were ready. That way, you can view and type e-mail messages without being connected to the Internet. You need only dial up your ISP when you are actually sending or receiving the mail, so that you can exchange all your messages (even hundreds of them, to all over the world) in a single local phone call.

Outgoing e-mail and the Sent Items folder

Outlook places a copy of all outgoing e-mails in your Sent Items folder, so that you have a copy of them for future reference.

Collecting and reading your e-mail

Just as you can send your outgoing e-mails one at a time or all together, you can collect your incoming e-mail as often as you like, either automatically or manually.

You can collect e-mail from the Internet in different ways:

- Automatically at specified time intervals. Choose **Tools | Options** and select the **Mail Setup** tab. Under *Send/Receive*, click *Send immediately when connected.* If you don't want to send mail immediately, click the **Send/Receive** button and change the timing to suit your needs.

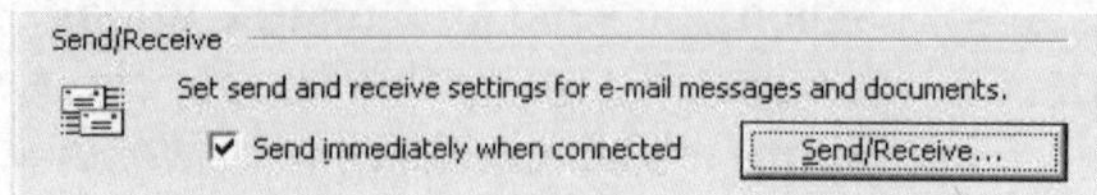

- Manually, by choosing **Tools | Send/Receive | Send and Receive All** or by clicking **Send/Receive** on the *Outlook* toolbar.

Even if you have set up automatic, timed e-mail collection, you can click **Send/Receive** at any stage to check whether any new e-mails have been sent to you.

E-mail collection: dial-up connection

If you are using a dial-up connection, you will generally use the same phone call to send your outgoing messages and collect any incoming messages. When you choose **Tools | Send and Receive | Send and Receive All** or click the **Send/Receive** button, that's what happens.

Don't confuse the action of collecting e-mail with the action of reading it. If you have a dial-up Internet connection, you can read your e-mail whether you are online or not. You need only go online to collect your e-mail from the Internet.

> **E-mail collection**
>
> *The action of transferring e-mails from the Internet to your computer. You must be connected to the Internet to collect e-mail, but you can read your collected messages whether you are online or not.*

E-mail collection at start-up

You can set up Outlook so that it collects your e-mails automatically from the Internet when you start the application. To do so, choose **Tools | Options**, select the **Mail Setup** tab, select *Send immediately when connected*, and click **OK**.

If you have a dial-up connection to the Internet, you may prefer not to select this option. Otherwise, Outlook will attempt to dial up your ISP every time you start the application.

Reading an e-mail

Outlook places incoming e-mails in your Inbox folder. When you click on your Inbox folder, your Message list shows all your received e-mails, with one e-mail highlighted. The text of that e-mail is shown in the Preview pane.

Click once on any other e-mail in the Message list to display its text in the Preview pane. Double-click on any e-mail in the *Message* list to display its text in a separate window.

The same technique applies irrespective of which folder the message is in: open the folder; select the message; read.

If you have more than one e-mail open in separate windows, you can switch between them by clicking their names on the Windows taskbar.

If you receive an e-mail from a source you don't recognize, be careful. Some e-mails carry viruses, either as attachments or as HTML code. If you have any doubts, do not open the e-mail or its attachment.

Changing Inbox display modes

Ensure that the Inbox is selected, and choose **View | Current View** to see a range of possible display options.

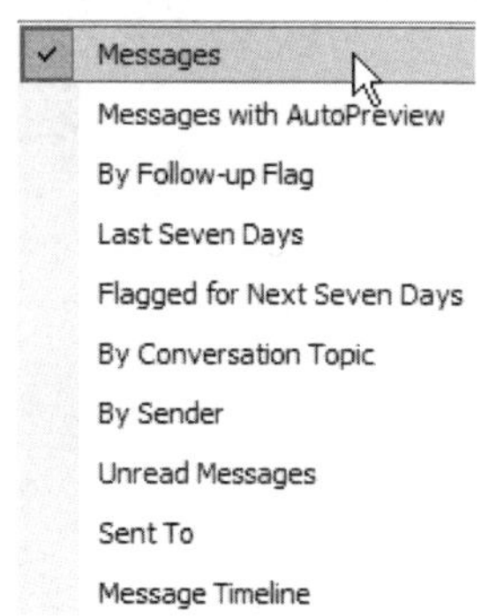

You can experiment with these.

It is possible to display or hide toolbars. To do this, choose **View | Toolbars** and click to display a toolbar, and then click to hide the same toolbar.

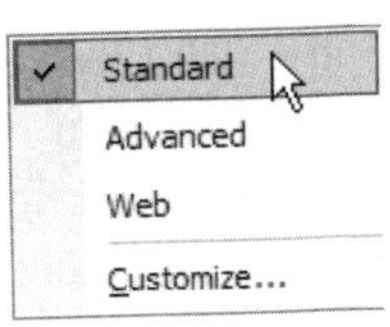

Toolbar options

Changing Inbox headings

If you wish, you can customize the headings that appear in your Inbox.

While the Inbox is open, choose **View | Current View | Customize Current View**, and click the **Fields** button.

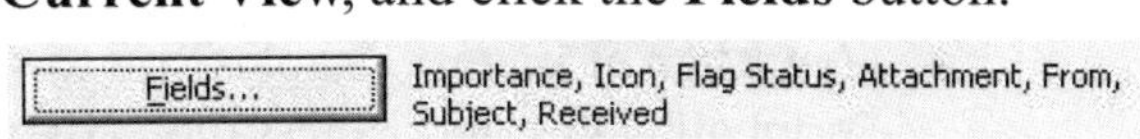

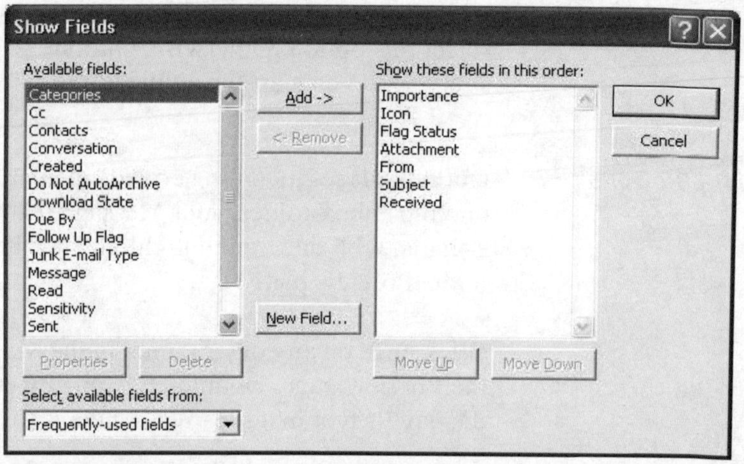

You then see the *Show Fields* dialog box, where you can specify the fields you want to include. The panel on the right shows the fields currently used; the panel on the left shows those that are available – that is, not used.

To add a field from the *Available fields* list, highlight it and click **Add**. To remove a field from the list of fields to be shown, highlight it and click **Remove**. When the list on the right shows the fields you want, click **OK**.

Inbox size limits

If you are using Outlook in the workplace, there is sometimes a limit on the size of your Inbox. Simple text e-mails are quite small and take up little space on a hard disk, but some people receive e-mails with music or video attachments some megabytes in size.

Although you usually receive a warning when you are close to exceeding your Inbox size limit, often your e-mail account is simply shut down until you contact your network administrator and ask for an increase in the size limit or else delete a number of e-mails. Such limits also apply to web mail services such as Hotmail and mail.com.

Printing an e-mail

To print an e-mail, open it and choose **File | Print** or click **Print** on the toolbar.

The *Print* dialog box gives you these options:

Print button

- **Number of pages:** Enables you to specify whether you want to print all pages of the message, only even pages, or only odd pages.

- **Number of copies:** Enables you to specify how many copies you want to print.
- **Print to a file:** Prints the message to a file instead of directly to the printer.

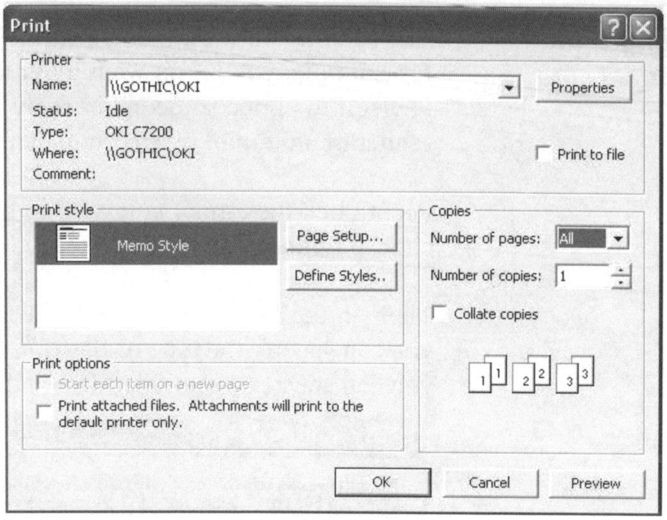

On the *Print* dialog box you can also specify whether you want multiple copies collated or whether you want to print attached files.

Deleting an e-mail

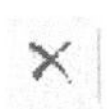

Deletes current e-mail

To delete an e-mail, irrespective of whether it is in your Inbox, Outbox, Sent Items or Drafts folder, just click on it in the Message list and choose **Edit | Delete**, or click **Delete** on the toolbar.

Is the e-mail really deleted? No. Outlook places it in the Deleted Items folder. To retrieve the e-mail:

- Click the Deleted Items folder in the Folder list. Your Message list now displays all deleted e-mails.
- Click the e-mail in the Message list and hold down the mouse button.
- Drag the e-mail from the Message list to the Inbox or other folder in the Folder list.

Manual e-mail deletion

You can permanently remove all deleted e-mails from Outlook by emptying the Deleted Items folder. To do so, select the Deleted Items folder in the Folder List, choose **Tools | Empty 'Deleted Items' Folder**, and click **Yes**.

Automatic e-mail deletion

If you don't want e-mails to be saved in the Deleted Items folder when you quit Outlook, choose **Tools | Options**, select the **Other** tab, select the *Empty the Deleted Items folder upon exiting* option, and click **OK**.

Flagging e-mail messages

You can *flag* your e-mails for further action – for example, you might want to remind yourself to phone someone or reply to the sender of an e-mail by a certain date.

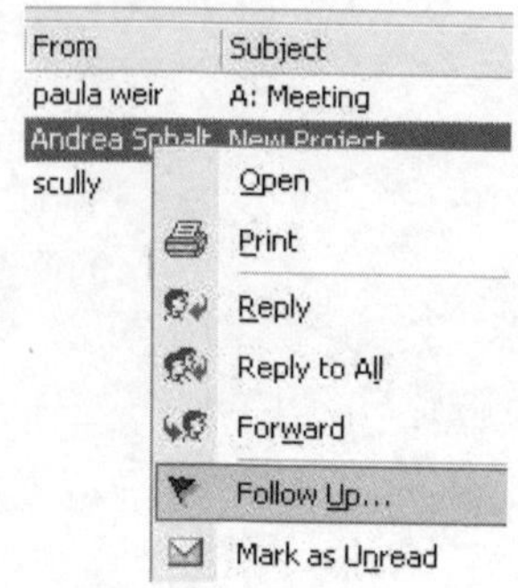

Right-click the e-mail you want to flag and choose **Follow Up**.

Then, in the *Flag for Follow Up* dialog box, you can specify the type of flag you want, and you can specify a reminder date and time.

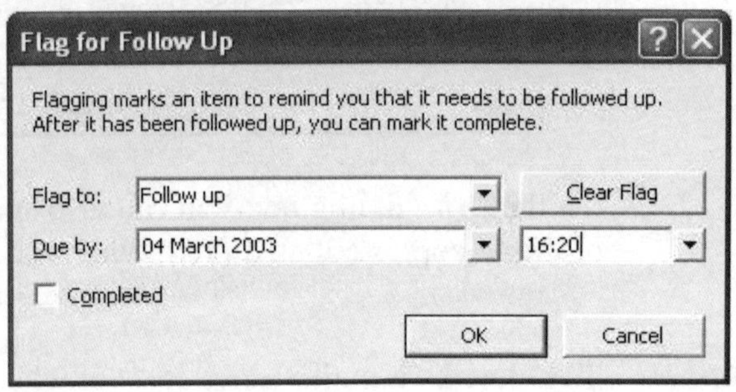

A reminder window pops up on your screen at the date/time you specified. At that stage, you can choose to open the item or dismiss it.

To clear a flag from an e-mail, right-click it and choose **Clear Flag**.

To mark an e-mail as read or unread (whether you have actually read it or not), right-click it and choose **Mark as Unread** or **Mark as Read** from the pop-up menu. (If you have previously opened the e-mail in question, you are offered the first of these options; if you haven't, you are offered the second.)

Quitting Outlook

To leave Outlook, choose **File | Exit**, or click the **Close** button at the top-right of the Outlook Window.

Using online help

Like Internet Explorer and other Microsoft applications, Outlook offers a searchable online help system. You can search through and read online help from dialog boxes, from the *Ask a question* box on the *Standard* toolbar, and from the **Help** menu.

Using help from dialog boxes

Exercise 47.3 provides an example of accessing online help from a dialog box.

Exercise 47.3: Accessing online help from a dialog box

1) Choose **Tools | Options**, and click the **Preferences** tab.

2) Click the question-mark symbol near the top-right of the dialog box. Outlook displays a question-mark to the right of the cursor.
3) Drag the mouse down to the option named *Tasks*.

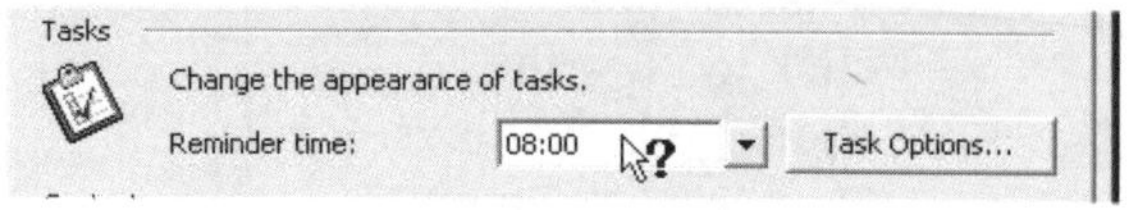

4) Click anywhere on the option check box or name.

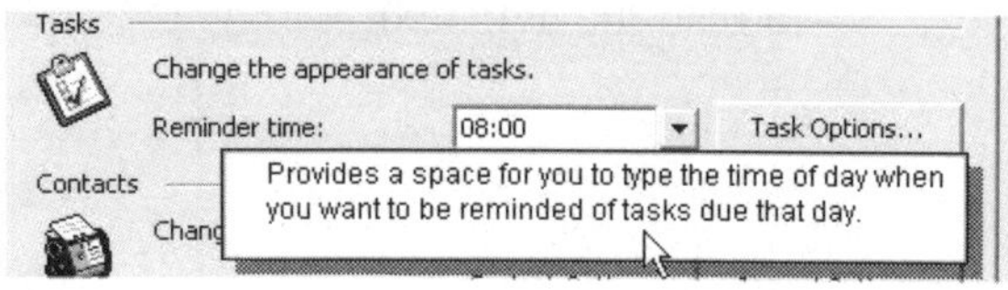

Outlook now displays help text telling you about the option.

Practise Exercise 47.3 with other dialog boxes in Outlook.

Using Help menu options

You can also access online help from the **Help** menu. Choose **Help | Microsoft Outlook Help** to display the three tabs of the *Help Topics* dialog box.

Contents tab

This offers short descriptions of Outlook's main features. Where you see a heading with a book symbol, double-click to view the related sub-headings. Double-click on a question-mark symbol to read the help text.

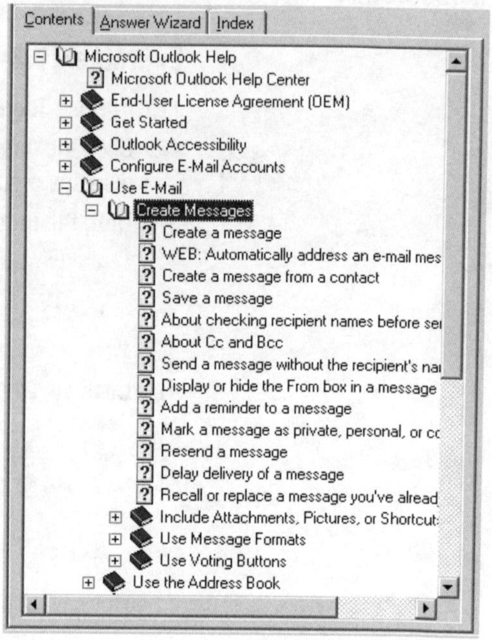

Answer Wizard tab

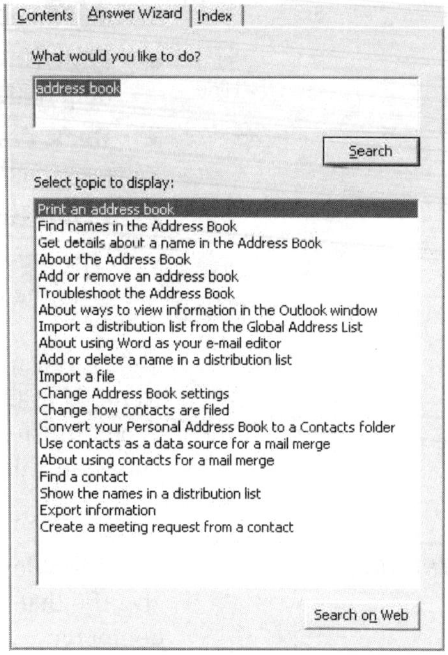

Can't find what you are looking for in the **Contents** or **Index** tabs? Try the **Answer Wizard** tab. When you type a word or phrase and click **Search**, Outlook performs a deeper search of the online help.

When you find the item you are looking for, double-click on it to display it.

Index tab

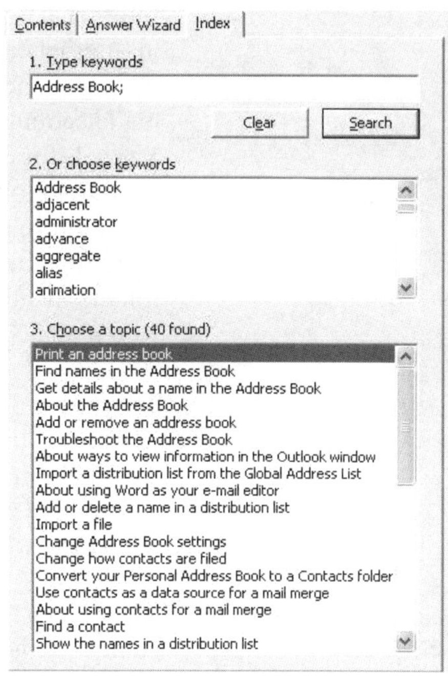

Reading the material displayed on this tab is like looking through the index of a printed book. Just type the first letters of the word or phrase you are interested in and click **Search**. Outlook responds by displaying all matches from the online help in the lower half of the dialog box. When you find the index entry that you are looking for, double-click it.

As you search through and read online help topics, you will see the following buttons at the top of the online help window:

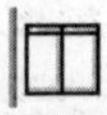

- **Auto Tile:** Enables you to view both the online help dialog box and the Outlook screen.

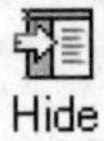

- **Hide/Show:** Hides or displays the left-hand pane of the online help dialog box.

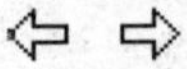

- **Back/Forward:** Moves you backwards and forwards through previously visited help topics.

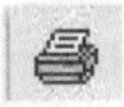

- **Print:** Enables you to print the help topic of your choice.

- **Options:** Offers a number of display choices, and enables you to print the currently displayed online help text.

Take a few minutes to look through the Outlook online help system. Remember that you are free to use online help during an ECDL test. When finished, you can close Outlook by clicking the **Close** button or choosing **File | Close**.

Web mail

It is possible to use e-mail without ever using Microsoft Outlook or a specific dial-up account or ISP, or without even owning a home computer.

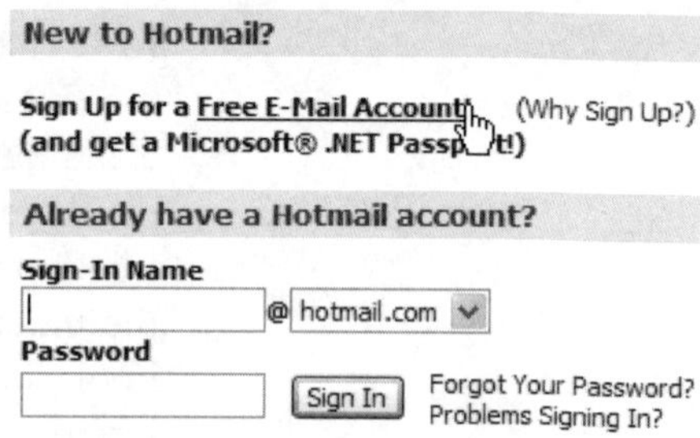

Many people access the Internet at work, in college and in Internet cafes. They use web browsers and can manage web mail accounts (with Hotmail or Yahoo!, for example) without ever downloading e-mails. Their entire e-mail program, including their inbox and other folders, resides on the Internet servers of those organizations offering web mail accounts.

They must only remember their sign-in name and password and they can access their e-mail and all related facilities from any browser anywhere in the world. This is a very flexible arrangement, as it enables the user to use any Internet-connected computer, anywhere in the world, to keep in touch with their work colleagues and friends.

Netiquette

Netiquette is a term that describes some very basic rules of online behaviour. There are various versions of these (check out www.onlinenetiquette.com), but some essentials have been widely accepted. Here are the basic rules you should try to practise:

- Use an anti-virus program to check your incoming e-mails, because some viruses use your address book to send themselves to everyone you know.
- Use a spelling checker to correct your outgoing e-mails. Nobdoy wnats ot raed rbbuish.
- Never send very large file attachments to people without first asking their permission. A large file could take a long time to download, depending on the connection speed of the recipient's computer.
- Be careful about sending certain file types to friends at their work e-mail addresses. You might get them fired from their jobs.
- Never use ALL CAPITALS when replying to an e-mail. This is regarded as SHOUTING and should be avoided. Avoid using all lower-case too – this is lazy and gives a bad impression of you and your ability to use a keyboard properly.
- Help your e-mail recipients to know what your e-mail is about by accurately indicating the subject matter in the Subject field. They should not have to read your e-mail to discover its contents.
- Never include contact or personal details of others in your e-mails without their permission.
- Try to achieve a balance between being too brief in your e-mails (which can cause offence in certain cultures) and being too long-winded. People only have limited time to deal with their e-mail inbox. Consider also that extreme informality does not suit all recipients.
- Some people could be very hurt if you copy their content and use it in your e-mails without permission, whether you copy text, images or other material.
- Beware e-mail virus warnings that demand you send them to everyone you know. Many of these are hoaxes. Instead, get anti-virus software updates regularly. Don't worry less knowledgeable users unnecessarily.

Chapter summary: so now you know

Microsoft Outlook is an *e-mail application* that enables you to *compose* (address, write and edit) new e-mails, *send* e-mails (from your computer to the Internet), *collect* incoming e-mails (from the Internet to your computer), and *read* collected e-mails.

To help you organize your e-mails, Outlook contains a built-in *Folder list* in which messages are stored and grouped by type: received (*Inbox*), waiting to be sent (*Outbox*), already sent (*Sent Items*), marked for deletion (*Deleted Items*), and held for later editing (*Drafts*). Users can create additional folders to further organize their e-mails.

You can collect your incoming e-mails *manually* from the Internet, or you can set up Outlook to collect them *automatically* each time you start the application and/or at preset time intervals.

You can also tell the application to send each outgoing e-mail as soon as you have finished composing it – or to store outgoing e-mails in your Outbox folder for sending in a group later.

If you have a dial-up Internet connection, you can read and compose e-mails whether you are online or not. You need go online only to send and collect your e-mail. You can keep copies of all outgoing e-mail in your Sent Items folder.

When you open a folder, Outlook displays the e-mails that it contains in a *Message list*, together with a summary of information about each one.

Clicking once on an e-mail in a Message list displays that e-mail's contents in a *Preview pane* under the Message list. Clicking twice displays the e-mail in a separate window.

When you delete an e-mail, Outlook places it in the Deleted Items folder. You can empty the Deleted Items folder manually or set up Outlook to empty it automatically each time you close the application.

You know the basic rules of *netiquette*.

Quick quiz: e-mail with Outlook

Circle the correct answers to each of the following multiple-choice questions about e-mail with Outlook.

Q1	The Send button sends your mail to...
A.	the recipient.
B.	the Outbox folder.
C.	Sent Items.
D.	Drafts.

Q2	Incoming mails are found in the Outbox.
A.	True.
B.	False.

Q3	Copies of all the e-mails you send are stored in which folder?
A.	Inbox.
B.	Drafts.
C.	Outbox.
D.	Sent Items.

Q4	How do you delete an e-mail?
A.	Select the e-mail and choose **Edit | Cut**.
B.	Select the e-mail and choose **File | Close All Items**.
C.	Select the e-mail and choose **Tools | Empty 'Deleted Items' folder**.
D.	Select the e-mail and click the **Delete** button or choose **Edit | Delete**.

Q5	How do you remove e-mails from the Deleted Items folder?
A.	Select the Deleted Items folder. Choose **Tools | Mailbox Cleanup** and click **OK**.
B.	Select the Deleted Items folder. Choose **Actions | Junk E-mail | Add to Junk Senders List** and click **OK**.
C.	Select the Deleted Items folder. Choose **Tools | Empty 'Deleted Items' Folder**, and click **OK**.
D.	Select the Inbox. Choose **Edit | Delete** and click **OK**.

Answers

1: B, **2:** B, **3:** D, **4:** D, **5:** C.

Chapter 48: More about outgoing e-mail

In this chapter

In this chapter you will discover some of the options available for composing and sending e-mails.

You will learn how to copy text into an e-mail from another application, how to check the spelling in your e-mails, how to mark an e-mail as high priority, and how to send the same e-mail to several people (there are several ways of doing this).

You will also learn how to create a signature and to append it to your outgoing e-mails, and how to attach files to outgoing e-mails – such as word-processed documents, spreadsheets, or photographs of your dog.

New skills

At the end of this chapter you should be able to:

- Copy text into an e-mail.
- Check the spelling in an e-mail.
- Send the same e-mail to several recipients.
- Send a blind copy of an e-mail.
- Set the priority of an outgoing e-mail.
- Add a signature to outgoing e-mails.
- Attach a file to an outgoing e-mail.
- Explain why an e-mail may 'bounce', and know what to do about it.
- Manage your outgoing e-mail queue.

New words

At the end of this chapter you should be able to explain the following terms:

- Cc (Carbon copy)
- E-mail file attachment
- Message priority
- Drafts folder
- Blind copy (Bcc)
- Signature (sig) file
- Bounced e-mail

Copying text into e-mails

Typing text directly into Outlook is just one way of composing an e-mail. Another is to reuse previously typed text by copying it from another e-mail (whether received or sent), and then pasting it into the new one.

As Exercise 48.1 shows, you can also copy text into an outgoing e-mail from another application such as a Microsoft Word document. (You have to be familiar with Microsoft Word and have a Word document ready to use before attempting Exercise 48.1. Otherwise, you'll just have to take our word for it!)

Exercise 48.1: Copying text from Word to Outlook

1) Open Microsoft Word and open the document that contains the text you want to copy into your e-mail.
2) Select the text for copying by clicking at the start and dragging the cursor to the end.

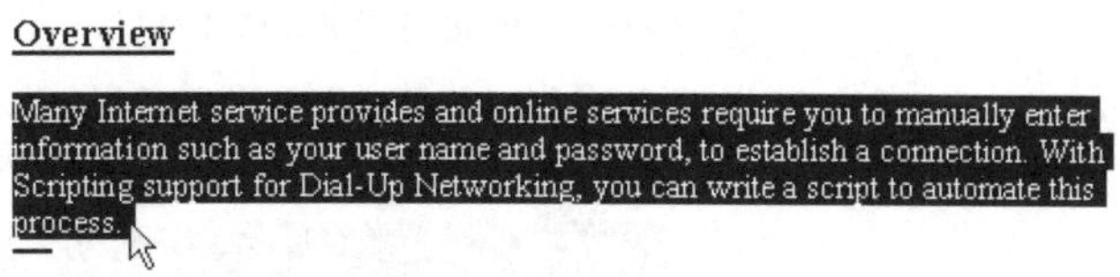

(To select all the text in a Word document, hold down the **Ctrl** key and click anywhere in the left margin.)

3) Choose **Edit | Copy** or press **Ctrl+c** to copy the selected text to the clipboard.
4) Open Outlook and either open the e-mail you want to paste the text into or compose a new e-mail.

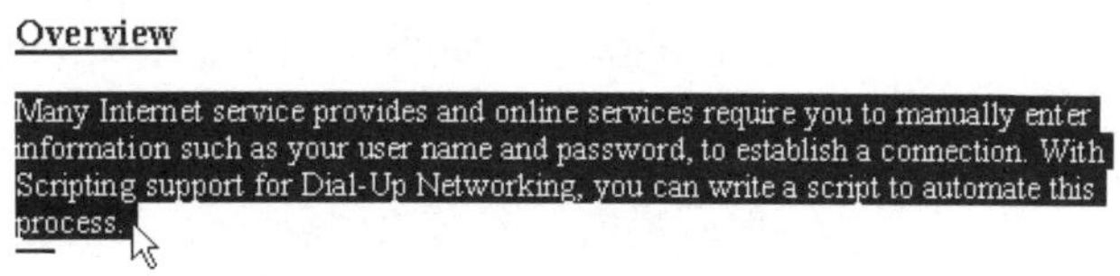

5) Position the cursor where you want the copied text to appear in your e-mail, and choose **Edit | Paste** or press **Ctrl+v**.

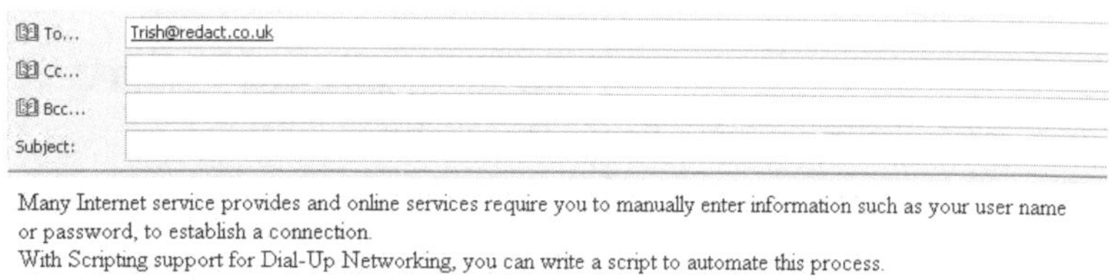

Checking your spelling

How's your spelling? Outlook can check your spelling and suggest corrections to errors in two ways:

- When you send the e-mail (the automatic option).
- When you choose the **Tools | Options | Spelling** command or click **Spelling** on the *New Message* toolbar (the on-request option).

You can set up Outlook to check your e-mail after you click **Send** on the *New Message* toolbar.

It uses the same spelling dictionary as Word and other Microsoft Office applications. If you do not have any of these installed on your computer, spellchecking in Outlook is not available.

Exercise 48.2: Switching on the spelling checker

1) **Choose Tools | Options** and click the **Spelling** tab.
2) Select the following two options, and click **OK:** *Always suggest replacements for misspelled words*, and *Always check spelling before sending.*

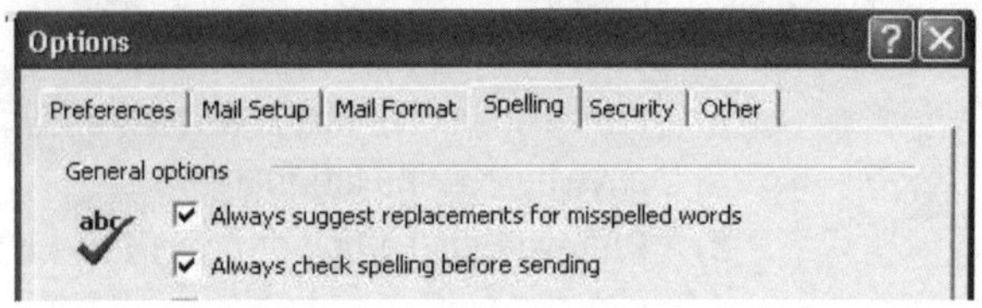

Subsequently, when you send an e-mail, you will be alerted to any word in your e-mail that Outlook does not recognize and offered some alternatives. (Not all unusual spellings are wrong, however, and not all usual spellings are right.)

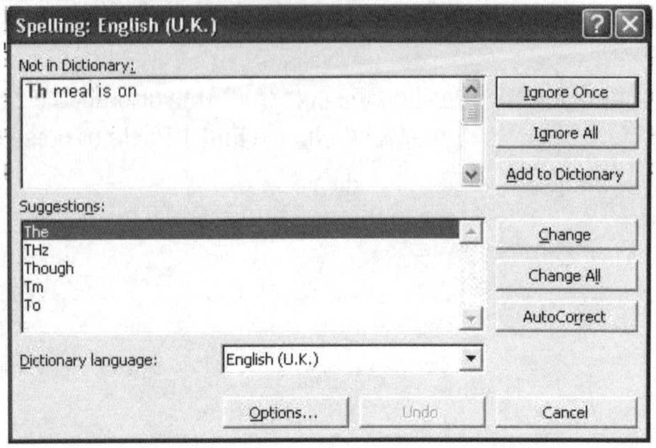

You can **Ignore** the alert, **Change** the problem word to the alternative highlighted, or **Add** the word that caused the problem to the dictionary so that it does not cause any further alerts.

Finding an e-mail address

You've seen that sending an e-mail is easy, provided you know the e-mail address of the person you are writing to. Where do you find these addresses? There are five main sources: business cards, incoming e-mails, websites, the Find People option, and the Outlook Address Book:

- **Business cards:** Most people in business today include their e-mail address on the business cards. (Some include *only* their e-mail address – they don't want to be contacted any other way!)
- **Incoming e-mails:** Many of the people you want to send e-mails to have already been in contact with you. Simply go to your Inbox, find an e-mail from the right person, copy their address to the clipboard and paste it into your e-mail.
- **Websites:** If you know the organization to which the person belongs, find its website. Many of them (particularly colleges and government agencies) include e-mail directories.
- **Find People option:** Outlook provides an option that lets you quickly locate e-mail addresses from web-based directories.

  Choose **Tools | Address Book** and select the **Edit | Find People** button.

  From the *Look in* drop-down list, select a directory service.

  Type the name of the person you are looking for, and click **Find Now**.

  This feature works only when you are connected to the Internet. (And it's not guaranteed to find the person you want.)
- **Address book:** An Outlook feature that enables you to record e-mail addresses for easy reference. (You will learn about the Address Book in Chapter 50.)

E-mailing multiple recipients

You can send an e-mail to more than one person. There are three ways of doing this: several equal recipients, one main recipient with copies to others, and blind carbon copy. You use each for different purposes.

Several equal recipients

If you want to send the e-mail to several people, enter each of their e-mail addresses in the *To* box, separated by a comma or semi-colon.

To make a string of multiple addresses easier to read, include a space after each comma or semi-colon.

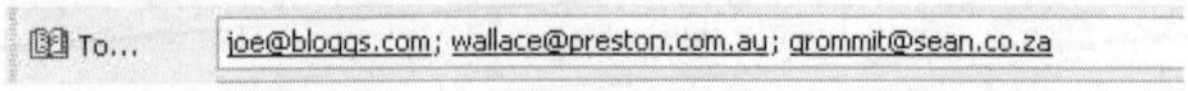

One main recipient, with copy to another

To send a copy of the e-mail to another person, enter their e-mail address in the *Cc* (Carbon copy) box. Generally, you use the *Cc* box to enter the e-mail address of other recipients you think should see this e-mail as a matter of courtesy or organizational procedure.

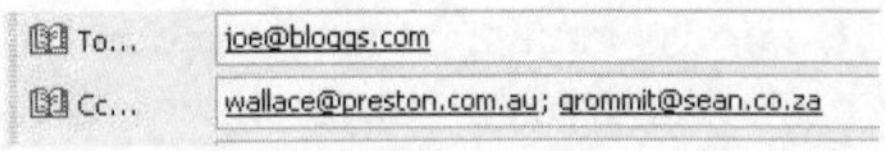

Cc is like that: it conveys those kinds of subtle but powerful messages that make office life exciting. You can enter as many e-mail addresses as you want in the *To* box and in the *Cc* box.

Cc (e-mail carbon copy)
A field in an e-mail header where you can enter the addresses of people to whom you want to send a copy of the e-mail.

Blind carbon copying

With blind copying, you send a copy of the e-mail to the second person without the main recipient knowing about it. If Word is your e-mail editor you reveal the *Bcc* box by clicking the arrow to the right of the **Options** button, and then clicking **Bcc**. If you are using the Outlook e-mail editor in a new message, choose the **View** menu and click the **Bcc** field.

You simply enter in the *Bcc* box the e-mail addresses of anyone you want to blind-copy the e-mail to. Note that:

- Bcc recipients know the names of the To and Cc recipients.
- The To and Cc recipients do not know the names of the Bcc recipients.
- The Bcc recipients do not know each other's names.

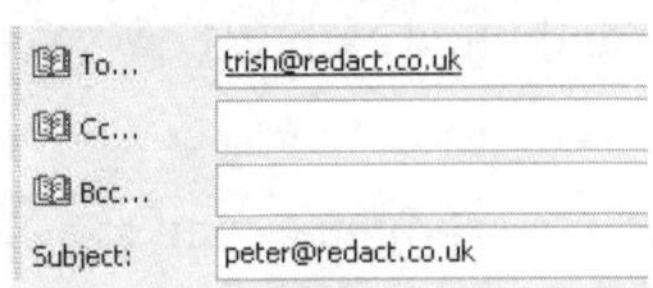

Bcc sends even more subtle messages than Cc. Let's say you send an e-mail to Trish and Bcc Peter. This has the following effects:

- Trish (To recipient) gets the e-mail.
- Peter (Bcc recipient) learns that Trish got the e-mail (and sees what the e-mail was).
- Trish is not aware that Peter knows that she got the e-mail, or what was in it.
- Peter knows that Trish doesn't know that he knows.
- Peter knows that you don't want Trish to know that he knows.

Fun, isn't it? Again, you can enter as many e-mail addresses as you wish in the *To* box and in the *Bcc* box, and you can include both Cc and Bcc recipients in the same e-mail.

Bcc (e-mail blind carbon copy)
A field in an e-mail header that enables you to copy an e-mail to other recipients. Bcc recipients can view addresses in the To and Cc fields, but not addresses in the Bcc field. To and Cc recipients cannot view any addresses in the Bcc field.

Mass e-mail and blind carbon copying

A common use (or abuse) of the *Bcc* field is for the sending of mass e-mails that advertise products or services.

The sender places *all* the recipients' addresses in the *Bcc* field, so that no one recipient knows who else also received the e-mail. Should the e-mail fall into the hands of a competing company, they are unable to view the sender's list of clients and prospects. In the *To* field, the sender types their own e-mail address.

Every e-mail you send must have at least one address in the *To* box, otherwise it will 'bounce' back to you. (Bounced e-mails are explained later in this chapter.)

Attaching files to e-mails

E-mails are generally short text messages. But suppose you want to send a family photograph to your uncle, a spreadsheet to your accountant, a PowerPoint presentation to head office, or a beautifully formatted word-processed document to your tutor? Easy. You send it as an *attachment* to your e-mail message.

To attach a file to an e-mail, follow the steps in Exercise 48.3.

Exercise 48.3: Sending an attachment

Attaches file to current e-mail

1) Compose your e-mail in the normal way.
2) Choose **Insert | File** or click **Insert File** on the *New Message* toolbar.
3) In the *Insert File* dialog box, locate the file you want to attach to your e-mail, and click **Insert.**

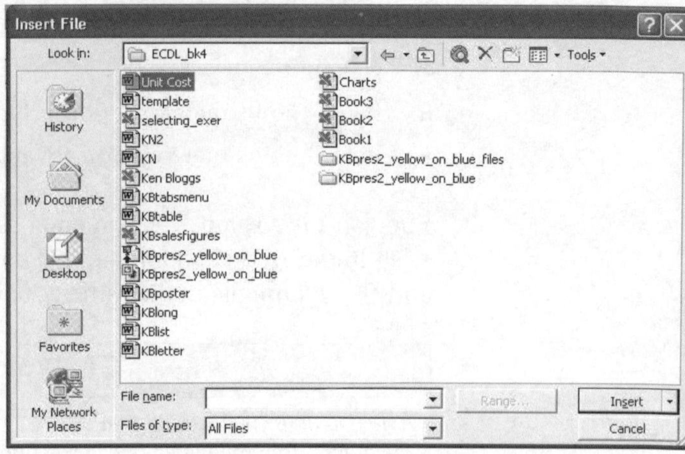

Outlook adds a line in the e-mail header to show the attachment file name and file size. To attach multiple files, repeat steps 2 and 3 above.

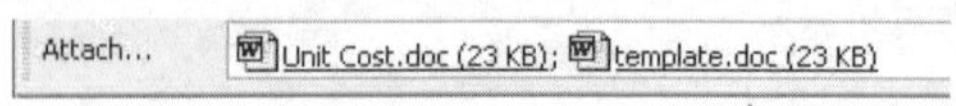

4) Click **Send** to send the e-mail with its attachment.

Remember that the person who receives your attached file can work with it only if they have the appropriate software application.

E-mail file attachment
A file, typically a formatted file such as a Word document, that is appended to and sent with an e-mail.

Deleting an attachment

If you decide against sending the attachment, right-click it and click **Remove**. It is immediately removed from the e-mail.

E-mail priority

All the e-mail you send is important, right? But some of it is more important than others, and you want to make sure that the recipient knows it. Exercise 48.4 shows you how to mark an outgoing e-mail as high priority.

Exercise 48.4: Sending a high priority e-mail

1) Compose the e-mail in the usual way.
2) Click **Importance: High** on the *New Message* toolbar.

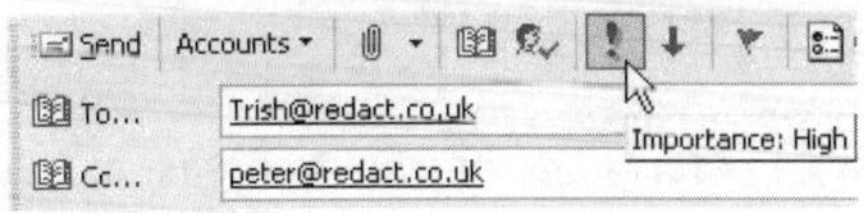

3) Click **Send** on the *New Message* toolbar.

High-priority e-mails (incoming or outgoing) are identified by a red exclamation mark. Use the high-priority setting sparingly. If every e-mail you send is high priority, then they will all be treated in the same way.

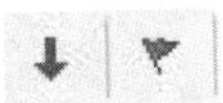

You can also send e-mails with a low priority setting in exactly the same way. But who wants to do that? (Low priority e-mails are identified by a blue down arrow.)

The priority of an e-mail does *not* affect the speed with which it is transmitted over the Internet or an internal e-mail network.

You can also change the priority status of e-mails you have received. This is a useful way of highlighting e-mails that you want to come back to at a later stage.

E-mail message priority
An indication to an e-mail recipient of a message's urgency, typically represented by a coloured symbol, such as a red exclamation mark. The priority of an e-mail has no impact on the speed with which it travels over the Internet or private network.

Bounced messages

If you send an e-mail to someone and, for whatever reason, it cannot be delivered, you usually receive a message to that effect. Such e-mails are said to 'bounce' – you send them out; they bounce right back.

The most likely reason for an e-mail bouncing is that you have typed an incorrect address: did you spell it right? Did you put in all the right punctuation? Did you put in a hyphen (-) instead of an underscore (_)?

Bounced e-mail
An e-mail that, for whatever reason, fails to reach its recipient, and is returned to its sender with a message to that effect.

Occasionally, your e-mail fails to get through and you don't get any message to that effect. While this is rare, it does happen. Don't assume that just because you sent the e-mail, the recipient definitely received it. If it's that important, ask them to acknowledge receipt, either in your e-mail or automatically. Exercise 48.5 shows you how.

Exercise 48.5: Requesting a receipt

1) Compose a new e-mail in the normal way.
2) Click **Options** on the *New Message* toolbar. Under *Voting and Tracking options*, select *Request a delivery receipt for this message* or *Request a read receipt for this message.*

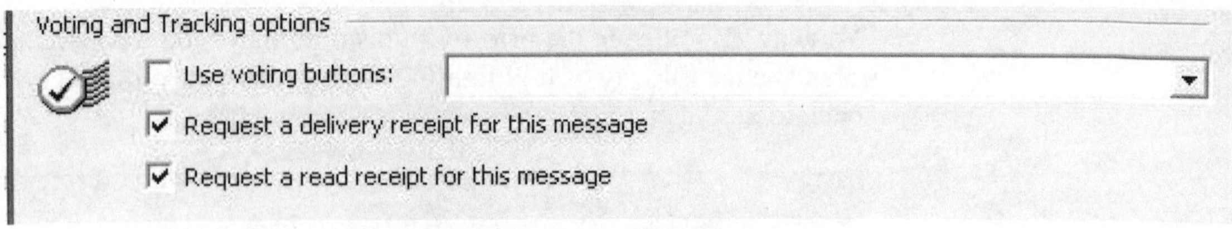

3) Send the e-mail as normal.

When the e-mail is received and opened by its recipients, they are informed that you have requested confirmation. They can choose whether to send the confirmation, but they don't have to do any work – they just click **Yes** or **No**.

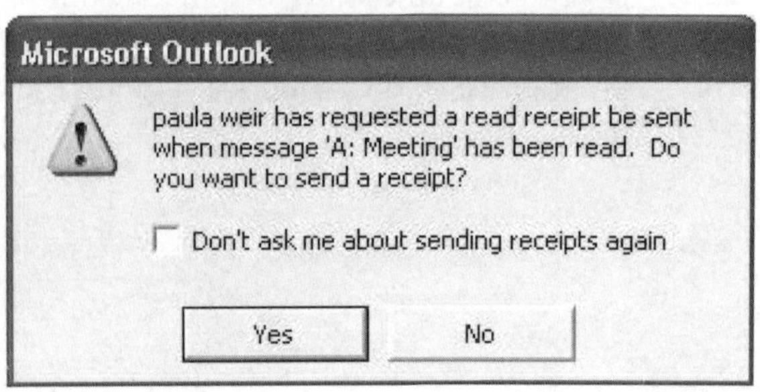

E-mail signatures

When you compose an e-mail, you may want to finish it off with a small block of text as a signature. The easiest and most efficient way to do this is to create a *signature* (sometimes known as a signature file or a sig file). Outlook will append this to your outgoing e-mails – either automatically to all e-mails or only to ones that you select.

Most people include their name and contact details. Some add an advertising slogan, a short message, or a link to their website. You can also create different signature files for different purposes.

Creating a signature

Follow Exercise 48.6 to learn how to create an e-mail signature file.

Exercise 48.6: Creating your signature

1) Compose a new e-mail in the normal way.
2) Choose **Tools | Options**, select the **General** tab and click the **E-mail Options** button.
3) Click the **E-mail Signature** tab. In the *Type the title of your e-mail signature or choose from the list* box, type a name for your signature.
4) Under *Create your e-mail signature*, enter your name, address, telephone number and other contact details. Click **Add**.

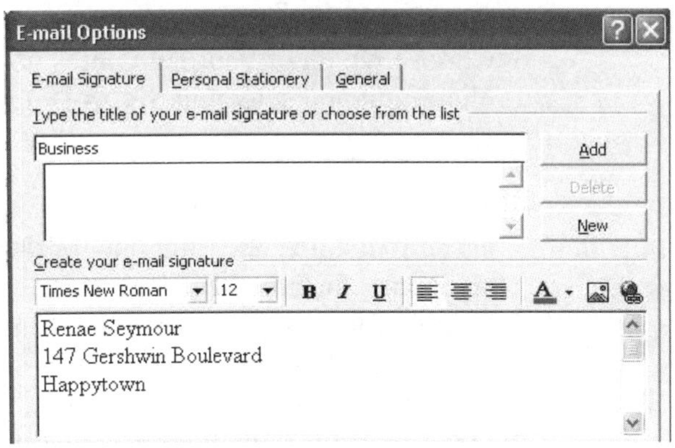

5) Select the default e-mail signature in the *Signature for new messages* and in the *Signature for replies and forwards* box. Click **OK**.

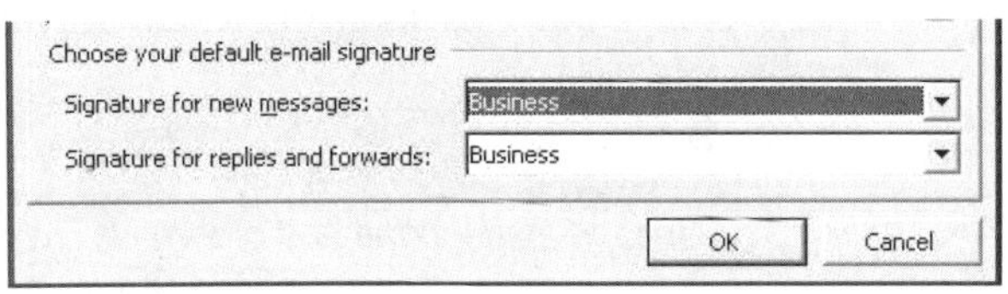

Outlook automatically appends your signature to all subsequent e-mails you compose and send. If you want to be more selective, do not select a default e-mail signature in the *Signature for replies and forwards* box.

Alternative signature files

To create a second (or a third ...) signature file, choose **Tools | Options**, and select the **General** tab. Click the **E-mail Options** button, select the **E-mail Signature** tab and click the **New** button.

Proceed exactly as when you created your first signature file.

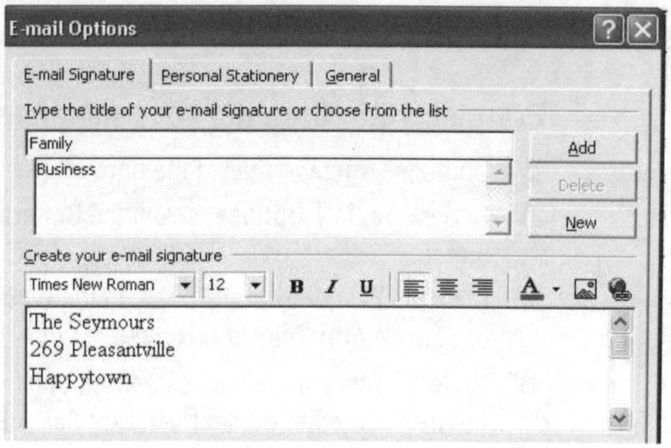

Choose which of your signatures you want to be the default by clicking it and selecting **Set as Default**. Finally, click **OK**.

Changing the appearance of your signature files

You can change the appearance of your signature files, so that it is easier to identify the right one for the circumstances. You might have a signature file called Business, one called Personal, and one called Family, for example. Or one for your team and another for head office.

To do this, choose **Tools | Options**, and select the **General** tab. Click the **E-mail Options** button, select the **E-mail Signature** tab. Under *Type the title of your e-mail signature or choose from the list*, click the signature you want to change. Make the desired changes in the *Create your e-mail signature* box. Click **Replace**.

Signature (sig) file
An appendage at the end of e-mails. Typical contents include full name, occupation or position, phone and fax numbers, and e-mail and website addresses. Some people also include a favourite quote, company slogan or short personal statement.

The Drafts folder

If your e-mails are held in your Outbox folder until you click the **Send/Receive** button, you have the luxury of being able to change your mind.

You can delete an e-mail in the Outbox in the same way as any other e-mail. You select it in the Message list, and do any of the following: click **Delete** on the toolbar, choose **Edit | Delete**, or press the **Delete** key.

Alternatively, you might want to move the e-mail into the Drafts folder while you think about it some more.

Saving e-mail to the Drafts folder

The Drafts folder is where you keep your half-finished thoughts, your letters of resignation, your job applications, until you are sure that they are right and you want to send them.

To put a new e-mail into the Drafts folder, compose the e-mail as normal and choose **File | Save**. To revisit an e-mail in the Drafts folder, open the folder, select the e-mail in the Message list, and double-click it to open it. You can then make any changes or additions, and either save it again to the Drafts folder or send it.

You can also move an e-mail directly from the Drafts folder to the Outbox by dragging it from the Message list to the Outbox in the Folder list.

Drafts folder
An area within Outlook where you can store e-mails that you are not yet ready to send. You can open and edit e-mails in the Drafts folder, as required.

Text size display

You can change the default size in which Outlook displays text – a very useful feature if you have poor or limited vision.

Choose **View | Current View | Customize Current View**. Click the **Other Settings** button. Under *Column headings* click the **Font** button.

Select the required font and click **OK**. Do the same for the other headings – *Rows* and *Autopreview*. Finally, click **OK**.

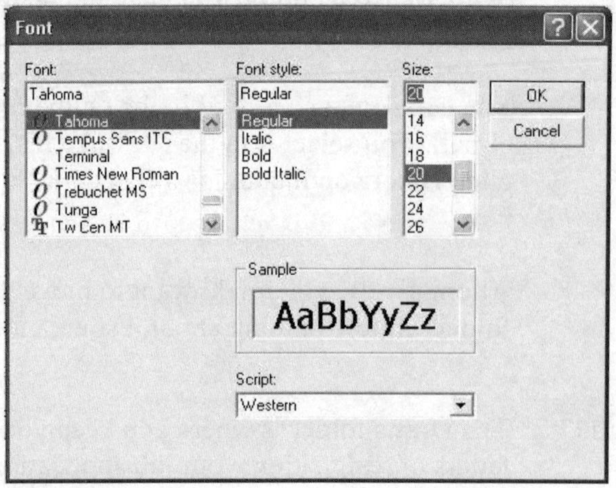

When finished, you can close Outlook. You have now completed the sixth chapter of the ECDL Information and Communication module.

Chapter summary: so now you know

You can *copy text* from a word processor or other application to an e-mail in Outlook, and you can *spellcheck* your e-mail messages as you would a document in Microsoft Word. See Exercises 48.1 and 48.2 for examples of how to do these tasks.

You can address an outgoing e-mail to *multiple recipients* – as equal addressees (To), as *carbon-copied* addressees (Cc), or as *blind carbon-copied* addressees (Bcc). Bcc recipients can view addresses in the *To* and *Cc* fields but not addresses in the *Bcc* field. To and Cc recipients cannot view the addresses in the *Bcc* field.

When sending an e-mail to several people, separate each e-mail address by a comma or semi-colon. You can optionally include a space after each comma or semi-colon to make the addresses easier to read.

You can flag your messages as *high* or *low priority.* This indicates the message's urgency to the recipient, but has no impact on the speed with which it is sent over the Internet or private network. See Exercise 48.4 for an example of how to do this.

You can append a *signature file* to your outgoing messages, and choose a different signature file for different audiences. Typical signature contents include full name, occupation or position, phone and fax numbers, and e-mail and website addresses. Some people also include a favourite quote, company slogan or short personal statement. See Exercise 48.6 for an example of how to do this.

You can *attach* formatted *files* – such as pictures, spreadsheets and word-processor documents – to your e-mails. See Exercise 48.3 for an example of how to do this.

A *bounced e-mail* is an e-mail that, for whatever reason, fails to reach its recipient and is returned to its sender with a message to that effect.

The *Drafts folder* of Outlook is where you can store messages that you are not yet ready to send.

Quick quiz: more about outgoing e-mail

Circle the correct answer to each of the following multiple-choice questions about outgoing e-mail in Outlook.

Q1	How do you switch on the spelling checker in Outlook?
A.	Select **Tools | Options**, and click the **Spelling** tab. Select the options required.
B.	Select **Tools | Options**, and click the **Mail Format** tab. Select the options required and click **OK**.
C.	Select **Tools | Options**, and click the **Mail Setup** tab. Select the options required and click **OK**.
D.	Select **Tools | Options**, and click the **Spelling** tab. Select the options required and click **OK**.

Q2	How do you send an e-mail to one person and copy others in on it?
A.	Enter the e-mail address of the main recipient in the *To* box, and enter the e-mail addresses of other recipients in the *Bcc* box. Click **Send**.
B.	Enter the e-mail address of the main recipient in the *To* box, and enter the e-mail addresses of other recipients in the *Cc* box. Click **Send**.
C.	Enter the e-mail address of the main recipient in the *To* box, and leave the *Ccc* box and *Bcc* box blank. Click **Send**.
D.	Enter the e-mail address of the main recipient in the *To* box, and enter the e-mail addresses of other recipients in the *Cc* box.

Q3	How do you send an e-mail to one recipient without the other recipients knowing?
A.	Enter the e-mail address of the main recipient in the *To* box and the *Cc* box. Enter the e-mail addresses of other recipients in the *Bcc* box. Click **Send.**
B.	Enter the e-mail address of the main recipient in the *Cc* box and the *Bcc* box. Click **Send.**
C.	Enter the e-mail address of the main recipient in the *To* box, and enter the e-mail addresses of other recipients in the *Cc* box. Click **Send**.
D.	Enter the e-mail address of the main recipient in the *To* box and the *Cc* box. Enter the e-mail addresses of other recipients in the *Bcc* box.

Q4	How do you send an attachment?
A.	Choose **Insert | File** or click the **Insert File** button. Locate the file you need in the *Insert File* dialog box and click **Insert**.
B.	Choose **Insert | File** or click the **Insert File** button. Locate the file you need in the *Insert File* dialog box and click **Cancel**.
C.	Choose **Insert | File** or click the **Insert File** button. Locate the file you need in the *Insert File* dialog box and click **Insert**. Click **Send**.
D.	Choose **Insert | Symbol**. Locate the symbol you need in the *Symbol* dialog box and click **Insert**. Click **Send**.

Q5	Where do you find the options for e-mail signatures?
A.	Choose **Tool | Options**, select the **Spelling and Grammar** tab, and click **Check Document**.
B.	Choose **Tool | Options**, select the **User Information** tab, and click **OK**.
C.	Choose **Tool | Options**, select the **Edit** tab, and click **Settings**.
D.	Choose **Tool | Options**, select the **General** tab, and click **E-mail Options**.

Answers

1: D, **2:** B, **3:** A, **4:** C, **5:** D.

Chapter 49: More about incoming e-mail

In this chapter

In this chapter you will explore some of the options available with incoming mail.

You will learn how to forward received e-mails to other people, how to send replies to the sender or to everyone who received the original e-mail, and how to copy text between e-mails or from an e-mail to a word processor or other application.

You will also discover how to open any file attachments that you receive, and how to save or delete them.

Another topic covered is mail folders – how to create new ones of your own, how to sort the e-mails they contain in different ways, and how to search through your mail folders for specific e-mails.

New skills

At the end of this chapter you should be able to:

- Forward a received e-mail to another person.
- Reply only to the sender of an e-mail.
- Reply to all the recipients of the original e-mail.
- Copy text between e-mails and from an e-mail to another application.
- Open, save and delete file attachments.
- Create and delete mail folders.
- Transfer e-mails between mail folders.
- Search in your mail folders for a particular e-mail.

New words

At the end of this chapter you should be able to explain the following terms:

- E-mail forwarding
- E-mail reply to sender only
- E-mail reply all

Actions with your incoming e-mail

In Chapter 47 you learnt how to display a received e-mail from your Message list by clicking on it once (to view it in the Preview pane) or twice (to view it in a separate window). In this chapter you will discover the various actions that you can perform on a received e-mail. In summary, these are:

- Forward it to someone else.
- Reply only to the person who sent it.
- Reply to the sender and to any other people who also received the message.
- Copy text from it to an outgoing e-mail or to Microsoft Word or to another application.
- Open, save or delete any files it may have attached to it.

Forwarding an e-mail

If you receive an e-mail that you want to pass on to someone else, the simplest way is to forward it. Follow Exercise 49.1 to discover how.

Exercise 49.1: Forwarding an e-mail

1) Select the e-mail you want to forward from your Message list by clicking on it once or twice.

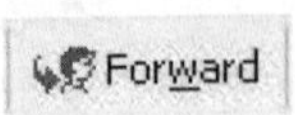

Forwards current e-mail

2) Choose **Action | Forward** or click **Forward** on the toolbar.

   Outlook opens a window that looks like a window for creating a new e-mail, with two differences:

   - The *Subject* box shows the subject of the original e-mail, preceded by the abbreviation FW:.
   - The original e-mail is shown and identified.

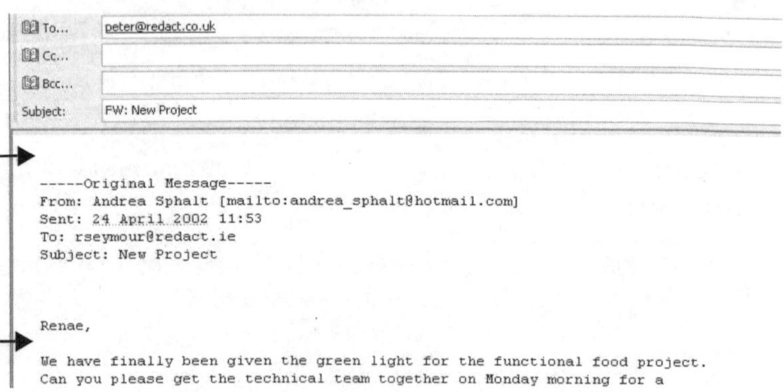

Area for entering your comments with forwarded e-mail

Text of e-mail for forwarding

3) In the *To* box, type the address of the person to whom you want to forward the e-mail.

4) In the message area, add text of your own. (It is helpful to the recipient if you clearly distinguish your own comments from the original message.)
5) Click **Send.**

E-mail forwarding
The act of passing to another person an e-mail that you have received. You typically include some comments of your own in the forwarded e-mail.

Replying to sender only

When you receive an e-mail message, you can send a reply either to the person who sent it to you (only), or to all the people who received the original e-mail.

Most often, you will want to reply to the person who sent you the e-mail. Exercise 49.2 shows you how.

Exercise 49.2: Replying to the e-mail sender only

1) Select the e-mail you want to reply to from your Message list by clicking on it once or twice.

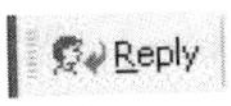

Replies only to the sender of the current e-mail

2) Chose **Actions | Reply** or click **Reply** on the toolbar. The window that opens up looks like the window for creating a new e-mail, with two differences:
   - The *To* box and the *Subject* box are already completed.
   - The original e-mail message is shown and identified.

Area for entering reply

Text of e-mail you are replying to

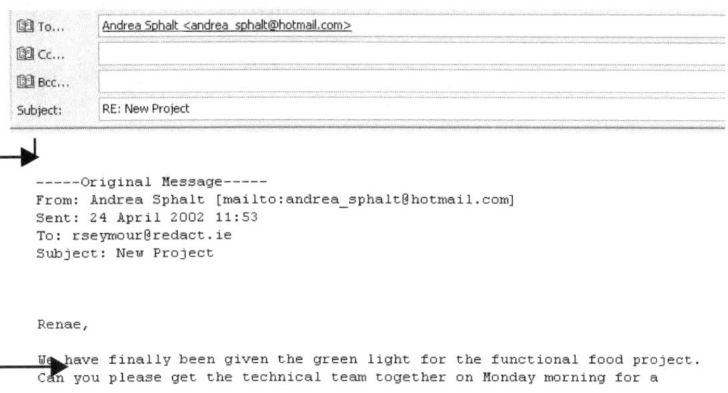

You can edit the *Subject* box if you wish. You can also remove all or part of the original e-mail to which you are replying.

3) Enter the text of your reply in the message box, above the words 'Original Message'.
4) Click **Send**.

Remember, it's not very helpful to get a single word reply to an e-mail ('yes' or '4.30'). The person who reads it could have sent hundreds of e-mails, and could be reading your reply several days later. That's why including the original message with your reply is a good idea.

However, if the original message is very long, and your answer is 'yes', it is helpful to cut out those parts of the original message that do not require a response, so that it becomes very obvious what you are agreeing to.

E-mail reply to sender only
The act of replying to a received e-mail. Only the person who sent you the e-mail gets your reply. The reply typically includes the text of the original e-mail.

Replying to all recipients

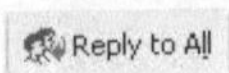

Replies to the sender and all other recipents of the current e-mail

The Reply to All option enables you to reply to an e-mail, with your reply going to everyone who received the original message. You use it in exactly the same way as the Reply (to sender only) function.

You will find this feature particularly useful when working with a number of people on a project (drawing up a contract, for example) or discussing something that requires unanimous agreement (to schedule a meeting, for example)

To use this option with a received e-mail, choose **Actions | Reply to All** or click **Reply to All** on the toolbar.

E-mail reply to all
The act of replying to a received e-mail. Everyone who received the original e-mail also gets your reply. The reply typically includes the text of the original e-mail.

Copying and moving the text of a message

You can reuse the text of one e-mail in another e-mail, or in another application such as Microsoft Word. And you can move text around within the same message. Practise your text-moving skills with Exercises 49.3 and 49.4.

Exercise 49.3: Copying e-mail text within Outlook

1) Open an e-mail or compose a new one.
2) Select the text you want to copy by clicking at the start of the text and dragging the cursor to the end.
3) Choose **Edit | Copy** or press **Ctrl+c**.

4) Go to where you want to insert the copied text, either within the same e-mail or in another e-mail.
5) Choose **Edit | Paste**, or press **Ctrl+v**.

Exercise 49.4: Copying e-mail text into another application

1) As in Exercise 49.3, select the text you want to copy and press **Ctrl+c**.
2) Open the second application (such as Microsoft Word), position the cursor where you want the copied text to appear, and press **Ctrl+v**.

In each case, you can move the text in question (that is, delete it in its original location and insert it in its new location) by choosing **Edit | Cut** instead of **Edit | Copy**, or pressing **Ctrl+x** instead of **Ctrl+c**.

Deleting text

To delete text, select the text you want to delete, and then do any of the following: choose **Edit | Cut**, press **Ctrl+x**, or press the **Delete** key.

Receiving file attachments

Most e-mails are simple, self-contained text messages. Some, however, come with files attached – spreadsheets, formatted documents, presentations, graphics or audio files, for example. You can identify an e-mail with a file attachment as follows:

- In the Message list, it is shown with a paper-clip icon.

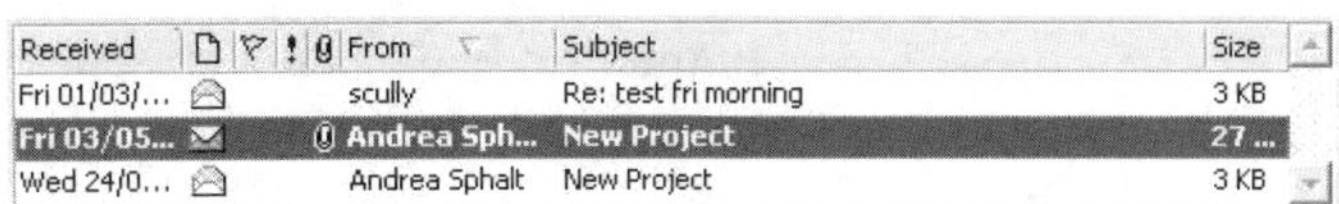

- In the Preview pane, the e-mail header shows the attachment type.

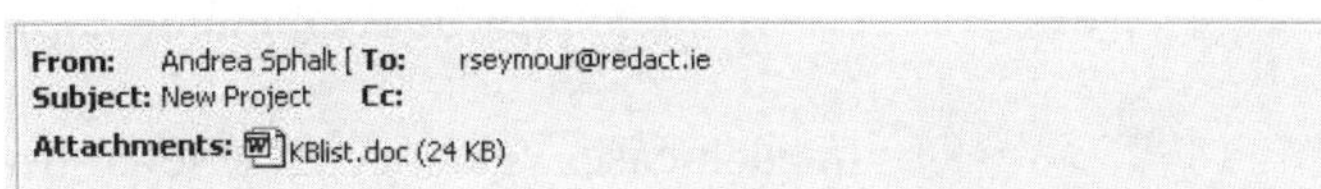

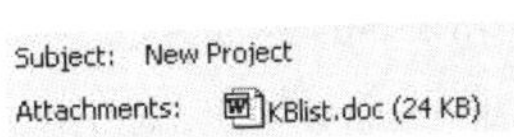

- If displayed in a separate window, the e-mail header shows an *Attachments* box, with the name and size of the file.

Opening attachments

You can open a file attachment only if you have an application that is capable of opening it. If someone sends you an attachment that was created in an application that is not installed on your computer (or even a different version of a program that is installed), you may not be able to open it.

You can open an attached file in either of two ways:

- If viewing the e-mail in the Preview pane, click the attachment icon in the e-mail header. Outlook prompts you to save the attachment to disk or to open it. Make your selection and click **OK**.
- If viewing the e-mail in a separate window, double-click the file in the *Attachments* field. Outlook prompts you to save the attachment to disk or to open it. Make your selection and click **OK**.

Saving attachments

You can save an attached file in any of the following ways:

- Choose **File | Save Attachments**. (This command is available regardless of whether you are viewing the e-mail in the Preview pane or in a separate window.)
  -or-
- In the Preview pane, right-click the attachment icon in the e-mail header and choose **Save As** from the pop-up menu.
  -or-
- In a separate e-mail window, right-click the file name in the *Attachments* box, and choose **Save As** from the pop-up window.

In each case, you specify where on your computer you want to save the file, accept or change the file name, and click **Save**.

If you open an attachment and do not save it, you can subsequently open it only from within Outlook. If you save it, you can subsequently open it from within Outlook and from the relevant application.

If you save an attachment and subsequently delete it, you will not be able to open it *either* from within Outlook or from within the application. And if you delete the e-mail without first saving the attachment, the attachment is also deleted.

Careful: attachments can be dangerous

Files attached to e-mail messages are among the most common ways of spreading computer viruses. For this reason, you should install a virus protection application on your computer that scans incoming e-mail attachments.

Using e-mail folders

Once you start using e-mail, you'll probably get a lot of it. Some of it is important at the time but has a short shelf-life ('Meet you for lunch' – 'OK'). Some of it you need to keep for reference (the minutes of the project meetings). Some of it is simply junk mail. How do you keep it organized so that you can find what you want, when you want it? You create *mail folders*, that's how.

Exercise 49.5: Creating a new folder

1) Choose **File | New | Folder**.
2) Type the name you want to give the new folder.
3) Click on the name of the folder in which you want your new folder to be located.
   - If you want it to be on the same level as the Inbox, Outbox and other main folders in Outlook, click Outlook Today – Personal Folders.
   - If you want it to be a subfolder of an existing folder such as your Inbox, click that folder.

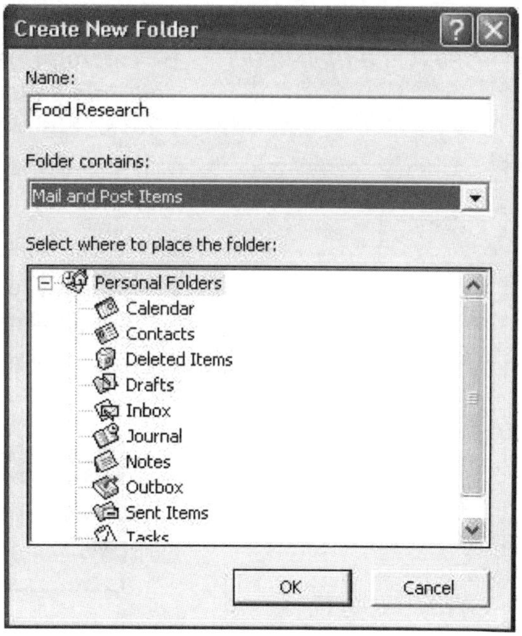

4) Click the arrow to the right of the *Folder contains* box to select the type of items that you want to put into the folder.
5) Click **OK**.

Transferring e-mails between folders

As Exercise 49.6 demonstrates, you can transfer an e-mail from one folder to another.

Exercise 49.6: Moving an e-mail from your Inbox to another folder

1) Open your Inbox folder and, in the Message list, select the e-mail you want to move.
2) Choose **Edit | Move to Folder**.
3) Click the folder into which you want to move the message. Click **OK.**

Alternatively, click the e-mail in the Message list, and drag it to the folder in the Folder list on the left of the screen. What folder do you use for junk mail and last week's invitations to lunch? Deleted Items, of course!

If you choose **Edit | Copy to Folder** in Exercise 49.6 above, the e-mail will be copied to the second folder – it will appear in both folders.

Deleting a mail folder

Be careful. It is possible to delete a mail folder, but you can't change your mind afterwards. The folder and all its contents will disappear forever. Follow the steps in Exercise 49.7 to discover how.

Exercise 49.7: Deleting a folder

1) In the Folders list, click to select the folder you want to delete.
2) Choose **File | Folder | Delete "folder name"** or right-click the folder and select **Delete "folder name"** from the pop-up list displayed.
3) You are asked to confirm that you really do want to delete it.
4) Click **Yes.**

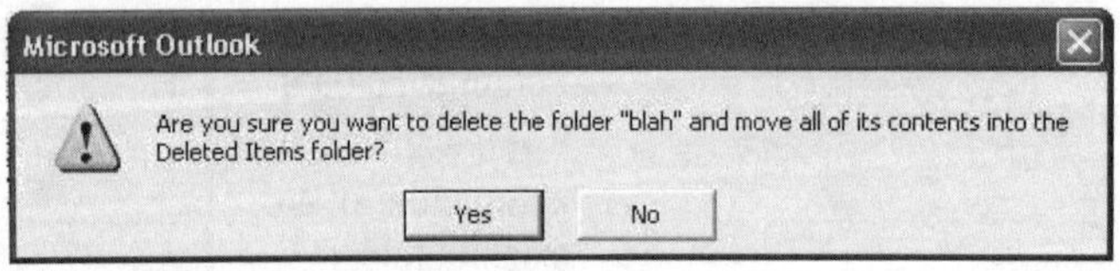

Searching for specific e-mails

You know that someone – you can't remember who – sent you details of the new MP3 music player. Your friend in Australia sent you a message sometime around Christmas. You need to see all the replies you received to your mail on the subject of tomorrow's meeting. How do you find what you want?

The quickest way of finding these needles in your e-mail haystack is to use the *Find Message* function. Exercise 49.8 provides an example.

Finds a specific e-mail

Exercise 49.8: Finding a particular e-mail

1) Choose **Tools | Find** or click **Find** on the toolbar.
2) In the *Look for* box, fill in whatever you know about the message – who it was from (or, if you sent it, who it was to), the subject, or some word or phrase in the text of the message. You don't have to use full words: even a single letter is enough. You can also specify a range of dates.
3) Specify the folders that you want to search.

4) Click **Find Now**. Outlook displays a list of messages that satisfy your criteria. When you see the one you want, double-click it to open it.

Sorting messages in a folder

An alternative way of finding a particular message is to sort the items in the folder. If you sort your Inbox alphabetically by the name of the sender (the *From* field), you can find all the messages from a particular person, for example. Or you can find your most recently received messages by sorting it on the *Received* field.

Exercise 49.9: Sorting the contents of a mail folder

1) Click your Inbox in the Folders list.
2) In the Message list, click the word *From* in the header. Outlook sorts your messages alphabetically by the name of the sender.

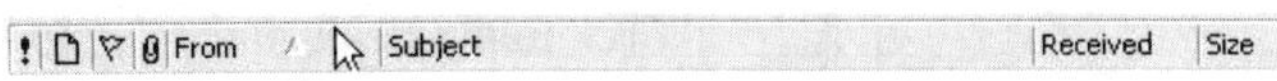

3) Click on the word *From* again. Outlook re-sorts the messages into reverse alphabetic order.
4) Click the *Received* field in the header. Outlook sorts your messages into the order in which they were received. As before, you can reverse the order by clicking *Received* again.

When finished, you can close Outlook. You have now completed the seventh chapter of the ECDL information and communication module.

Chapter summary: so now you know

Outlook allows you to perform various actions on e-mails that you receive from others.

You can *forward* an e-mail to someone else, typically accompanied by some comments of your own, which you enter in the text area above the original e-mail. See Exercise 49.1 for an example of how to do this. You can *reply to the sender only*, so that only the originator of the e-mail sees your reply, or you can *reply to all recipients* of the original e-mail. See Exercise 49.2 for an example of how to do this.

Another option you have is, by using *copy and paste*, to insert the text of a received e-mail into an outgoing e-mail or in another application such as Microsoft Word. See Exercises 49.3 and 49.4 for examples of how to do this.

Outlook indicates whether an incoming e-mail has a *file attachment*. You can open, save and delete attachments. File attachments may contain viruses, and you should use a reliable virus protection application to scan them.

You can create *mail folders* to keep your e-mails organized; see Exercise 49.5 for an example of how to do this. You can sort the e-mails in any folder, and you can use the *Find* function to search for a particular e-mail by sender, receiver, subject or date. See Exercises 49.8 and 49.9 for examples of how to do this.

Quick quiz: more about incoming e-mail

Circle the correct answer to each of the following multiple-choice questions about incoming e-mail in Outlook.

Q1	How do you forward an e-mail?
A.	Click **Reply to All**, and in the *To* box type the name of the person you want to send the e-mail to. Click **Send**.
B.	Click **Reply**, and in the *To* box type the name of the person you want to send the e-mail to. Click **Send**.
C.	Click **Forward**, and in the *To* box type the name of the person you want to send the e-mail to.
D.	Click **Forward**, and in the *To* box type the name of the person you want to send the e-mail to. Click **Send**.

Q2	How do you reply to the e-mail sender only?
A.	Click **Reply to All**, and type the message that you want to send. Click **Send**.
B.	Click **Reply**, and type the message that you want to send. Click **Send**.
C.	Click **Forward**, and type the message that you want to send. Click **Send**.
D.	Click **Reply**, and type the message that you want to send.

Q3	How do you reply to all recipients of an e-mail?
A.	Click **Reply**, and type the message that you want to send. Click **Send**.
B.	Click **Forward**, and type the message that you want to send. Click **Send**.
C.	Click **Reply to All**, and type the message that you want to send. Click **Send**.
D.	Click **Reply to All**, and type the message that you want to send.

Q4	How do you move an e-mail from your Inbox to another folder?
A.	Select the e-mail that you want to move. Choose **Edit | Move to Folder**. Click the folder into which you want to move the e-mail. Click **OK**.
B.	Select the e-mail that you want to move. Choose **Edit | Copy to Folder**. Click the folder into which you want to move the e-mail. Click **OK**.
C.	Select the e-mail that you want to move. Choose **File | New | Folder**. Type the name of the folder and select where you want to locate your folder. Click **OK**.
D.	Select the e-mail that you want to move. Choose **File | Folder | Copy "Inbox"**. Select where you want to locate your folder. Click **OK**.

Q5	How do you save an attachment?
A.	Choose **File | Save Attachments**. Specify where you want to save the file, and click **Save**.
B.	Choose **Save**. Specify where you want to save the file and the file name. Click **Save**.
C.	Choose **Save**. Specify where you want to save the file and the file name.
D.	Choose **Edit | Move to Folder**. Specify where you want to save the file and the file name. Click **OK**.

Answers

1: D, **2:** B, **3:** C, **4:** A, **5:** A.

Chapter 50: Address Book and contact groups

In this chapter

By now, you have probably noticed that e-mail addresses can be difficult to remember. Some are cryptic (bill@xyz.com); others are complex (bs_p.sales@xy.pqrcorp.co.uk). Even within the one organization, different people use different conventions (billsmith, bsmith, bill.smith, bill_smith, bsmth...). How do you remember all these addresses?

You don't – you keep them in your *Address Book.*

In this chapter you will learn how to organize your contacts in your Address Book, so that you don't have to remember their e-mail addresses and enter them each time you want to send them a message.

You will also discover how to set up contact groups (also called mailing lists), so that you can send the same message to large groups of people in a single operation.

New skills

At the end of this chapter you should be able to:

- Add, change and delete contacts in your Address Book.
- Create contact groups that can be e-mailed all at once.

New words

At the end of this chapter you should be able to explain the following terms:

- E-mail contact
- Address Book
- Display name (alias)
- Distribution list

Your Address Book

Outlook contains an area called an *Address Book* where you can keep information about the people you communicate with.

You can record all sorts of details about your contacts – obvious things like their name, address and phone number (and e-mail address), and less obvious things, like their birthday and the names of their children.

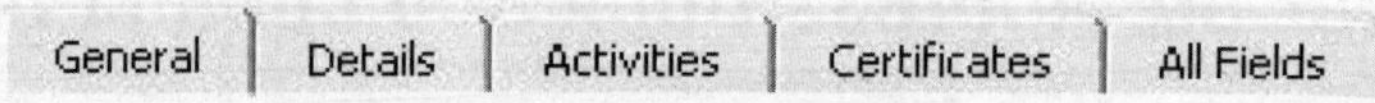

E-mail contact
A person or organization whose details (such as name and e-mail address) you have recorded in the Address Book of your e-mail application.

Address book
A feature of an e-mail application that enables you to record details about your e-mail contacts for easy reference.

Entering contacts

In Exercise 50.1 you will practise entering a new contact in your Outlook Address Book.

Exercise 50.1: Adding a contact to your Address Book

1) Open your Outlook Address Book by choosing **Tools | Address Book**.
2) Click the **New** button. In the *New Entry* dialog box select **New**, put the entry in the *Contacts* folder and click **OK**.
3) In the **General** tab, type the full name and e-mail address of one of your contacts.
4) Type the e-mail address of your contact in the *E-mail* box. If you wish, type a short, easy-to-remember version of their name (even a single letter) in the *Display as* box. This is the display name that will be displayed in your Address Book.
5) Click **Save and Close**.

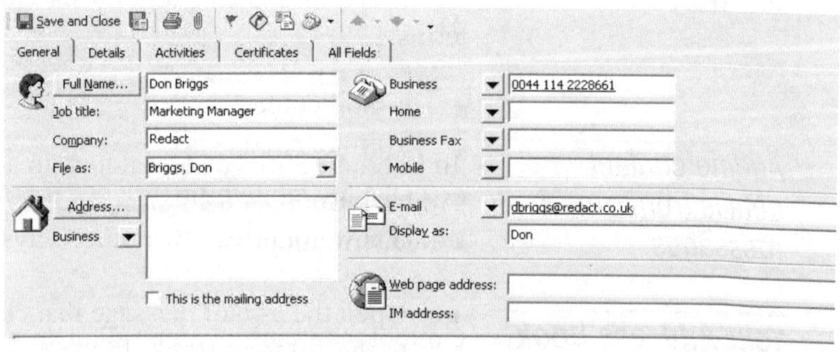

To create several new contacts in one operation, choose **File | New | Contact**.

Display name

A shortened form of an e-mail address that you can enter in the Display as *field of a message as an alternative to typing the contact's e-mail address in full.*

Contacts: the minimum details

At a minimum, each contact in your Address Book must contain a first name, a last name and a display name. All other contact details are optional. The first two you enter; the third is supplied, by default, by Outlook.

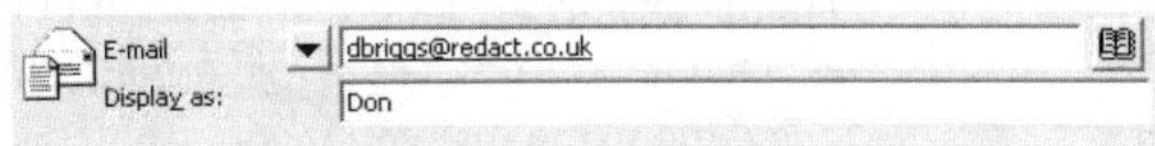

The display name is the name that appears in the *To* field of e-mails that you send to that contact, and in the *From* field of e-mails you receive from that contact. You can change the default display name by typing in a different name.

Editing contacts

At any time, you can change the details of a contact or add further details, simply by:

- Choosing **Tools | Address Book** to open your Address Book.
- Double-clicking to select the relevant contact.
- Overtyping, deleting or adding the new information.

To delete a contact, open your Address Book, select the relevant contact, and do any of the following: click the **Delete** button, press the **Delete** key, or choose **File | Delete.**

Adding contact details from e-mail messages

In Exercise 50.1 you learnt how to add a new contact by opening your Address Book, and entering and saving the relevant details. You can add a new contact in two other ways:

- Open the e-mail message that contains the name you want to add to the Address Book. In the *From* field, right-click the name, and then click **Add to Contacts** from the pop-up menu.
- When replying to an e-mail, right-click on the name in the *To* field, and choose **Add to Contacts** from the pop-up menu.

Sorting your contacts

You remember her first name but not her last name? You know the telephone number but not the name of the company? With a normal telephone directory, you'd have a problem. With Outlook – no problem. Exercises 50.2 and 50.3 take you through the steps.

Exercise 50.2: Sorting by first name (method 1)

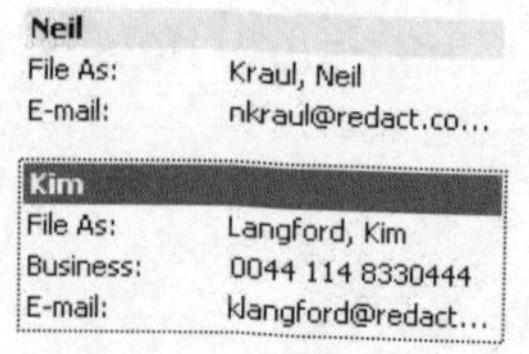

1) Click the *Contacts* folder.
2) Choose **View | Current View | Address Cards**.
3) Outlook displays a list of contacts with their display names. You can scroll through the list to find the name that you recognize.

   You can then easily find a person by their first name by scrolling through the list.

Exercise 50.3: Sorting by telephone number (method 2)

1) Click on the *Contacts* folder.
2) Choose **View | Current View | Phone List**.
3) Click the words **Business Phone** in the header row. Click the same words a second time.

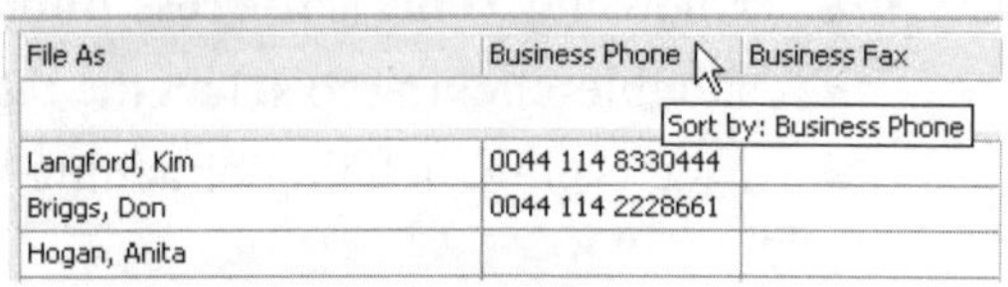

4) Note that the order changes with each click, from ascending to descending to ascending again.

   You can now find the name of the person you want by scrolling to the telephone number you recognize.

Distribution lists

If you use e-mail regularly to stay in touch with your football team, your research group or your extended family, you already know that you can send the same message to them by including all their names in the *To* or *Cc* box. (Remember to separate them with semi-colons, and to have at least one name in the *To* box.)

However, after a while, all that typing can get a bit tedious. What do you do? You set up what is known as a distribution list. Exercise 50.4 shows you how to create a distribution list and add members to it. Exercise 50.5 shows you how to send a message to a distribution list.

Exercise 50.4: Setting up a distribution list

1) Choose **File | New | Distribution List**.
2) Give the distribution list a name by typing in the *Group Name* box.

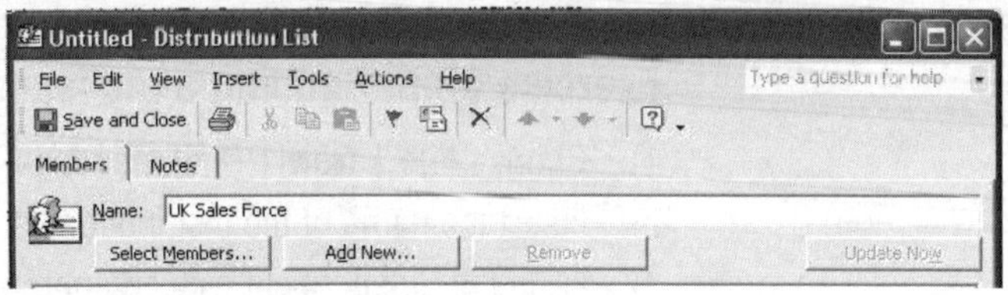

3) Two situations are now possible:
   - The people you want to include in your new distribution list are in your Address Book.
   - The people you want to include in your new distribution list are not in your Address Book.
4) If a person is already in your Address Book, click **Select Members** to view a new dialog box that contains your Address Books. Click the Address Book with the e-mail addresses you want in the *Show Names from the* box. Type the name that you want to include in the *Type Name or Select from List* box. In the list below, click the contact name and then click **Members**.

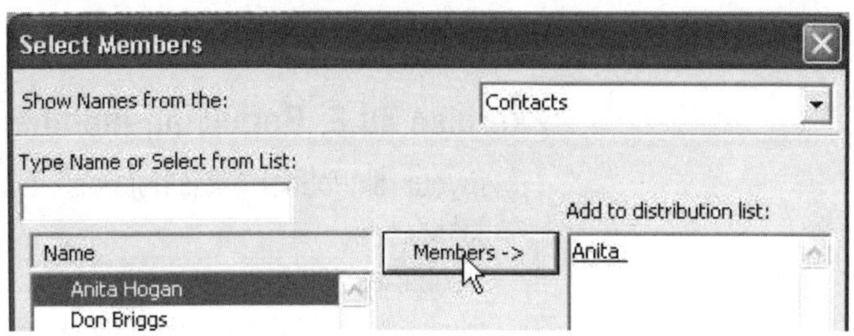

   When finished, click **OK** to return to the *Distribution List* dialog box. Now go to step 6.
5) If the people you want to include are not in your Address Book, and you don't want them to be (because you never want to address them as individuals), click **Add New**. In the *Add New Member* dialog box type their display name and e-mail address. Select *Add to Contacts* if required, and then click **OK**.

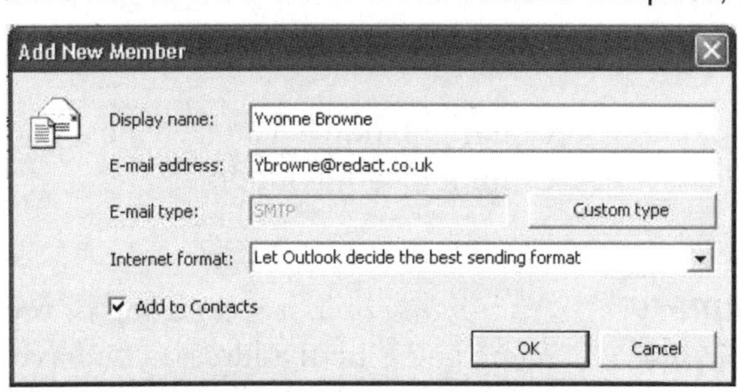

6) When you have finished, click **Save and Close**.

Distribution list
A list of e-mail addresses to which you can send a message in a single operation by entering the list's name in the To *field of the message.*

Exercise 50.5: Sending a message using a distribution list

1) Choose **File | New | Mail Message.**
2) Insert the name of the distribution list in the *To* field of the message.
3) Fill in the *Subject* field with an appropriate content, and type your message.
4) Click the **Send** button. Outlook sends the message to everyone in the group.

Lists within lists

A distribution list may contain the names of other distribution lists. For example, your Global Sales list might consist of three distribution lists – the Europe sales team, the US sales team and the Rest of World sales team.

An individual may be a member of more than one distribution list. At any time you can change the composition of your distribution list by adding new members (as in Exercise 50.4) or removing members (as in Exercise 50.6).

Exercise 50.6: Removing members from the distribution list

1) If your distribution list is not open, open it in the **Contacts** folder in the **Folder List**.
2) Double-click the name of the contact group.
3) Click the name of the person you want to remove, and click **Remove**.
4) Click **Save and Close**.

If you remove a name from a distribution list, they still remain in your Address Book and in any other distribution list of which they are a member. However, if you delete (or change) a name in your Address Book, it is deleted (or changed) in every distribution list of which it is a member.

Congratulations! You have now completed the ECDL Information and Communication module.

Chapter summary: so now you know

An *e-mail contact* is a person or organization whose details (such as name and e-mail address) you have recorded on e-mail application software. Outlook allows you to record a wide variety of information about your contacts, spread over eight tabs of a dialog box.

At a minimum, each contact must contain a first name, a last name and a *display name*. The first two you enter; the third is supplied, by default, by Outlook. You can change the display name to a shortened form of an e-mail address as an alternative to typing the contact's e-mail address in full.

An *Address Book* is that part of your e-mail application where your contacts are stored for easy reference. You can type contact information directly into your Address Book, or you can add contact details to the Address Book from outgoing or incoming messages.

Outlook allows you to edit contact details, and to sort contacts according to such headings as last name and phone number.

A *distribution list* is a list of e-mail addresses to which you can send a message in a single operation by entering the list's name in the *To* field of the message. A distribution list may contain the names of other mailing lists. You can change the composition of a distribution list by adding or removing members. An individual may be a member of more than one distribution list.

Quick quiz: Address Book and contact groups

Circle the correct answer to each of the following multiple-choice questions about the Address Book and contact groups in Outlook.

Q1	How do you add a contact to your Address Book?
A.	Choose **Tools | Address Book**. Click **New Entry** and click **OK**. Select the entry type and the location and click **OK**. In the **General** tab type the name and details that you want to include. Click **Save and Close**.
B.	Choose **Tools | Address Book**. Click **New Entry** and click **OK**. Select the entry type and the location and click **OK**. In the **General** tab type the name and details that you want to include.
C.	Choose **Tools | Address Book**. Click **New Entry** and click **OK**. In the **General** tab type the name and details that you want to include. Click **Save and Close**.
D.	Choose **Tools | Address Book**. Click **New Entry** and click **OK**. In the **General** tab type the name and details that you want to include.

Q2	To set up a distribution list you choose ...
A.	**File | New | Folder**.
B.	**File | New | Contact**.
C.	**File | New | Distribution List**.
D.	**File | New | Office Document**.

Q3	How do you remove a person from a distribution list?
A.	Open the *Contacts* folder. Select the distribution list and click the name of the person you want to remove. Click **Update Now**, and then click **Save and Close**.
B.	Open the *Contacts* folder. Select the distribution list and click the name of the person you want to remove. Click **Add New**, and then click **Save and Close**.
C.	Open the *Contacts* folder. Select the distribution list and click the name of the person you want to remove. Click **Select Members**, and then click **Save and Close**.
D.	Open the *Contacts* folder. Select the distribution list and click the name of the person you want to remove. Click **Remove**, and then click **Save and Close**.

Q4	A display name is a shortened form of a person's e-mail address.
A.	True.
B.	False.

Q5	To sort a list of contacts by telephone number you choose ...
A.	**View | Current View | Address Cards.**
B.	**View | Current View | Phone List.**
C.	**View | Current View | By Company.**
D.	**View | Current View | By Location.**

Answers

1: A, **2:** C, **3:** D, **4:** A, **5:** B.

INDEX